Microsoft® Exchange Server 2013 Inside Out: Connectivity, Clients, and UM

Paul Robichaux

PUBLISHED BY
Microsoft Press
A Division of Microsoft Corporation
One Microsoft Way
Redmond, Washington 98052-6399

Copyright © 2013 by Paul Robichaux

Library of Congress Control Number: 2013948709
ISBN: 978-0-7356-7837-8

Printed and bound in the United States of America.

First Printing

Microsoft Press books are available through booksellers and distributors worldwide. If you need support related to this book, email Microsoft Press Book Support at mspinput@microsoft.com. Please tell us what you think of this book at http://www.microsoft.com/learning/booksurvey.

Microsoft and the trademarks listed at http://www.microsoft.com/about/legal/en/us/IntellectualProperty /Trademarks/EN-US.aspx are trademarks of the Microsoft group of companies. All other marks are property of their respective owners.

The example companies, organizations, products, domain names, email addresses, logos, people, places, and events depicted herein are fictitious. No association with any real company, organization, product, domain name, email address, logo, person, place, or event is intended or should be inferred.

This book expresses the author's views and opinions. The information contained in this book is provided without any express, statutory, or implied warranties. Neither the authors, Microsoft Corporation, nor its resellers, or distributors will be held liable for any damages caused or alleged to be caused either directly or indirectly by this book.

Acquisitions Editor: Anne Hamilton
Developmental Editor: Karen Szall
Project Editor: Karen Szall
Editorial Production: nSight, Inc.
Technical Reviewer: Tony Redmond; Technical Review services provided by Content Master, a member of CM Group, Ltd.
Copyeditor: Kerin Forsyth
Indexer: Lucie Haskins
Cover: Twist Creative • Seattle

Contents at a Glance

Table of Contents

What do you think of this book? We want to hear from you!

Microsoft is interested in hearing your feedback so we can continually improve our books and learning resources for you. To participate in a brief online survey, please visit:

microsoft.com/learning/booksurvey

Foreword for Exchange 2013 Inside Out books

Those seeking an in-depth tour of Exchange Server 2013 couldn't ask for better guides than Tony Redmond and Paul Robichaux. Tony and Paul have a relationship with the Exchange team that goes back two decades, to the days of Exchange 4.0. Few people have as much practical knowledge about Exchange, and even fewer have the teaching skills to match. You are in good hands.

Over the past few years, we have seen significant changes in the way people communicate; a growing number of devices, an explosion of information, increasingly complex compliance requirements, and a multigenerational workforce. This world of communication challenges has been accompanied by a shift toward cloud services. As we designed Exchange 2013, the Exchange team worked hard to build a product and service that address these challenges. As you read these books, you'll get an up-close look at the outcome of our efforts.

Microsoft Exchange Server 2013 Inside Out: Mailbox and High Availability covers foundational topics such as the Exchange Store, role-based access control (RBAC), our simplified approach to high availability, and the new public folder architecture. It also covers our investments in eDiscovery and in-place hold. As you read, you'll see how Exchange 2013 helps you achieve world-class reliability and provides a way to comply with internal and regulatory compliance requirements without the need for third-party products.

Microsoft Exchange Server 2013 Inside Out: Connectivity, Clients, and UM explores the technologies that give users anywhere access to their email, calendar, and contacts across multiple devices. It also explains how to protect your email environment from spam, viruses, and other threats and describes how Exchange 2013 can connect with Office 365 so you can take advantage of the power of the cloud.

From our new building-block architecture to data loss prevention, there's a lot to explore in the newest version of Exchange. I hope that as you deploy and use Exchange 2013, you'll agree that this is an exciting and innovative release.

Enjoy!

Rajesh Jha
Corporate Vice President - Exchange
Microsoft Corporation

Introduction

This book is for experienced Exchange administrators who want to gain a thorough understanding of how client access, transport, unified messaging, and Office 365 integration work in Exchange Server 2013, the latest version of the Microsoft enterprise messaging server first released in October 2012 and updated on a frequent basis since. It isn't intended to be a reference, and it isn't suitable for novices.

In 2011, when Tony Redmond and I were working together to present the Exchange 2010 Maestro workshops in cities throughout the United States, we spent a lot of time talking about the nature of an ideal Exchange book. It should be comprehensive enough to cover all the important parts of Exchange, with enough detail to be valuable to even very experienced administrators but without just parroting Microsoft documentation and guidance. As far as possible, it should draw on real-world experience with the product, which of course takes time to produce. Out of those talks came Tony's idea to write not one but two books on Exchange 2013. A single book would either be unmanageably large, both for author and reader, or would omit too much important material to be useful.

Although Tony's *Exchange 2013 Inside Out: Mailbox and High Availability* (Microsoft Press, 2013) draws on his long and broad experience with the nuances of the Exchange mailbox role and how to put it to work, this book covers all the other things Exchange does, including client access, transport, unified messaging, and the increasingly important topic of Office 365 integration. Because Exchange 2013 is an evolution of Exchange 2010, we decided to use *Microsoft Exchange Server 2010 Inside Out* (Microsoft Press, 2010) as the base for the new book. For the topics in this book, so much has changed since Exchange 2010 that only a small amount of the original material remains. The rest is new and was written to take into account the many changes and updates that Exchange 2013 has undergone since its original release.

I have had the good fortune to work with and around Exchange for nearly 20 years. During this time, I've seen the Exchange community, product team, and product evolve and grow in ways that might not have been predictable back in 1996. If you went back to, say, 2000 and told the Exchange product group, "Hey, in 2013, your product will be deployed to hundreds of millions of users worldwide, many with tiny handheld computers that are more powerful than your desktop, and a whole bunch of them running as a Microsoft-hosted service," you'd be bound to get some skeptical looks, and yet here we are.

I hope that you enjoy this book and that you'll read it alongside Tony's *Microsoft Exchange Server 2013 Inside Out: Mailbox and High Availability*. The two books really do go together. Tony and I exchanged technical editing duties for our respective books, so we share responsibility for any errors you might find.

Acknowledgments

I was incredibly fortunate to receive a great deal of help with this book from a variety of sources. A large group of Exchange experts from the Microsoft Most Valuable Professional (MVP) and Microsoft Certified Systems Master (MCSM) communities volunteered their time to read early drafts of the chapters as they were produced; their mission was to identify shortcomings or errors and to suggest, based on their own experience, ways in which the book could be improved. This book is much better thanks to their efforts, which I very much appreciate. My thanks to Kamal Abburi, Thierry Demorre, Devin Ganger, Steve Goodman, Todd Hawkins, Georg Hinterhofer, Miha Pihler, Maarten Piederiet, Simon Poirier, Brian Reid, Brian R. Ricks, Jeffrey Rosen, Mitch Roberson, Kay Sellenrode, Bhargav Shukla, Thomas Stensitzki, Richard Timmering, Steven van Houttum, Elias VarVarezis, Johan Veldhuis, and Jerrid Williams. My thanks also go to the broader MCM and MVP communities, particularly Paul Cunningham, Brian Desmond, and Pat Richard, for discussing topics or sharing scripts that informed the material I wrote.

In addition to these volunteers, I benefited greatly from the efforts of many people from the product team, including Diego Carlomagno, Bulent Egilmez, David Espinoza, Kern Hardman, Pavani Haridasyam, Tom Kaupe, Roy Kuntz, Lou Mandich, Jon Orton, Tony Smith, Greg Taylor, and Mini Varkey. Extra thanks to Rajesh Jha for taking the time to write the foreword for both books—no easy task considering how often Tony and I have hassled him about various matters.

Finally, you wouldn't have this book at all if it weren't for the stalwart efforts of Karen Szall, Valerie Woolley, and a cast of dozens at Microsoft Press. Karen never lost her temper despite the many vigorous discussions we had about my failure to meet deadlines or my obstinacy toward some of the requirements imposed by the Microsoft crack legal department. Thanks to them all for producing such a good-looking finished product.

Errata & book support

We've made every effort to ensure the accuracy of this book and its companion content. Any errors that have been reported since this book was published are listed on our Microsoft Press site at oreilly.com:

http://aka.ms/EXIOv2/errata

If you find an error that is not already listed, you can report it to us through the same page.

If you need additional support, email Microsoft Press Book Support at *mspinput@microsoft.com*.

Please note that product support for Microsoft software is not offered through the addresses above.

We want to hear from you

At Microsoft Press, your satisfaction is our top priority, and your feedback our most valuable asset. Please tell us what you think of this book at:

http://www.microsoft.com/learning/booksurvey

The survey is short, and we read every one of your comments and ideas. Thanks in advance for your input!

Stay in touch

Let's keep the conversation going! We're on Twitter: *http://twitter.com/MicrosoftPress*.

Client access servers

The Exchange Client Access Server (CAS) role in Exchange 2013 is a critical part of delivering the features and functionality that users depend on.

In Exchange Server 4.0, Exchange Server 5.0, and Exchange Server 5.5, client access was provided by the single server role that then existed. Exchange 2000 introduced the notion of a *front-end* server—a server that didn't necessarily have any mailbox data but to which clients could connect to reach a server that *did* have mailbox data. Exchange 2007 gave us the first iteration of the CAS role, and that role was enhanced in Exchange 2010.

Since its introduction in Exchange 2007, the CAS role has been responsible for three types of traffic:

- External connections from Internet clients running any of the supported protocols offered by Exchange.

- Internal connections from intranet clients, again using any supported protocol.

- Connections that were proxied or redirected from other CAS servers. These connections might come from CAS servers running the same version of Exchange, earlier versions, or later versions.

However, the way in which the CAS role handles this traffic, the nature of the protocols supported, and the implementation behind this support have changed significantly in Exchange 2013. The Exchange 2013 CAS role now has two primary tasks: to authenticate user requests and locate the correct server to handle the user's request.

Take a look.

CAS architecture demystified

In Exchange 2013, the CAS has evolved further into what appears on the surface to be a simple proxy that handles client connections. However, a great deal is going on below the apparently simple surface, and you explore it in this chapter. How did the CAS role reach this point? As Exchange has changed over time, Microsoft has steadily worked to separate three related parts of Exchange that began life as a set of closely coupled subsystems:

- The code that handles mailbox storage, transport, and processing. The Information Store service is the best-known part of this code, but lots of other components contribute to moving messages between sender and recipient and then storing them for future use.

- The code that handles interactions with clients, including retrieving messages from the Store; formatting messages for a particular client (such as Outlook Web App); or providing client services for synchronization, message addressing, and so on.

- The business logic that Exchange uses to determine whether a request or data item is valid. For example, the Exchange business logic is supposed to catch whenever an application requests creating a corrupt item, such as a calendar item whose ending time is before its start time.

Figure 1-1 shows the results of this architectural approach in Exchange 2010. Protocol components on the server on the left communicate with both the protocol and storage layers on the right. The business logic layers on a server communicate with the protocols and storage layers on the same server *and* the same layers on other servers. This causes all sorts of actual and potential problems. For example, an older client access server might not know how to proxy specific types of traffic or protocol requests that should be sent to a newer-version CAS. This architecture also has so many dependencies among layers (both on the same server and across servers) that deploying Exchange in anything but the simplest topology required extra redundancy, such as guaranteeing that both a Hub Transport and CAS server would be in each site that had a Mailbox server.

The design goals for Exchange 2013 included a sweeping redesign of all three layers and the way they interoperate and communicate. The phrase "every server is an island" has been tossed around by various Microsoft engineers, and it neatly captures one of the main goals: eliminating linkages between disparate layers across servers so that the protocol layer on one server will only communicate with the protocol layer on other servers, never the storage or business logic layers. In this model, there should be no contact from the storage or business logic layers on one server with any layer on another server. Another goal was to eliminate the need for the CAS to maintain information about the clients with which it was communicating or the contents or *state* of their sessions.

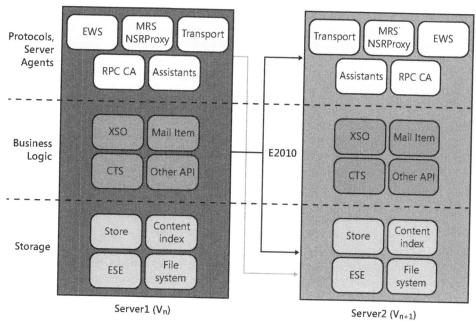

Figure 1-1 The Exchange 2010 architecture

These changes result in the architecture shown in Figure 1-2. Note that all the communications between protocol handlers now take place directly with the corresponding protocol handlers on another server. This essentially turns the CAS role into a stateless proxy that does not render or process client data (although it does publish some data of interest to clients). The CAS authenticates the user connection, determines where the correct target for the requested protocol or services is, and either redirects or proxies the client to that target. That's it. To be more precise, the CAS offers the following services:

- Client protocol access for IMAP, POP, Outlook Web App, the Exchange Administration Center (EAC), Exchange ActiveSync, and Exchange Web Services (EWS). The CAS proxies or redirects traffic for these protocols to the appropriate Mailbox server.

- Proxying requests for the Offline Address Book (OAB) to an available Mailbox server so that compatible clients can download OAB updates as they become available.

- Autodiscover, the client-oriented service that enables a compatible mobile or desktop client to find service endpoints for mailbox access, Outlook Web App, mobile device sync, and unified messaging.

- Front End Transport (FET), which accepts inbound SMTP traffic and proxies it to an Exchange 2013 Mailbox server or an Exchange 2007/2010 hub transport server. FET doesn't store or queue any messages.

- The Unified Messaging Call Router service (UMCR), which redirects incoming uni-fied messaging requests to the appropriate Mailbox server. (For more on UMCR, see Chapter 6, "Unified messaging.")

- Proxied connections to the Availability service, which provides free/busy information for users in the organization.

- A proxy engine for the Mailbox Replication service (MRS); the MRS proxy accepts requests from outside the organization for cross-forest mailbox moves, imports, and exports and then redirects them to the appropriate Mailbox server. (For more on MRS and the role of the proxy component, see *Microsoft Exchange Server 2013 Inside Out: Mailbox and High Availability* (Microsoft Press, 2013) by Tony Redmond.)

- Initial authentication for all the services it supports; for example, the CAS would authenticate an inbound EWS request before sending it elsewhere.

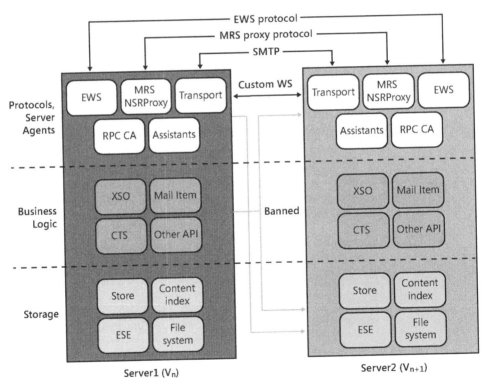

Figure 1-2 The Exchange 2013 architecture

It is also interesting to note what the Exchange 2013 CAS role does *not* do. In particu-lar, it does not provide direct access for Messaging Application Programming Interface

(MAPI) clients using remote procedure calls (RPC) directly over TCP. This change essentially means that the RPC client access (RCA) layer is no longer present on the Exchange 2013 CAS (it now lives on the Mailbox role), so the CAS role now only has to deal with Outlook Anywhere instead of with direct connections.

Why did Microsoft make this change? It turns out that two primary factors drive the change: the Microsoft desire to improve the robustness of client connections to the Mailbox server and the ongoing need to simplify the code underlying the product. Both of these factors, in turn, are driven by the emergence of Office 365.

INSIDE OUT Oh no! Microsoft TMG is gone! What am I going to do now?

When Microsoft announced in September 2012 that it would retire its Threat Management Gateway (TMG) product, there was quite an uproar in the Exchange community. That's because TMG is the best-known reverse proxy solution that supports Exchange. With TMG out of the picture, many customers worried that they would no longer be able to secure their Exchange deployments adequately. This turns out to be a needless worry. Here's why.

First, if you currently have TMG, it will be supported until 2022 or so. At Microsoft, Greg Taylor uses the analogy of a pickup truck: if you have a truck now, it doesn't stop working and become useless because the manufacturer stops making new models. Of course, sometime before 2022, Microsoft likely will release a version of Windows Server that TMG doesn't support, but that isn't a problem you have to solve right now.

Second, Microsoft still sells the Forefront Unified Access Gateway (UAG) product, which works perfectly well with Exchange. It is harder to understand and configure, and it's more expensive than TMG, but it's still supported.

In addition, other vendors have stepped in to fill the void left by the absence of TMG. In particular, Kemp Technologies has shipped its Exchange Security Pack (ESP), which functions as a capable reverse proxy for Exchange that provides preauthentication, supports Windows PowerShell, and includes a number of other nifty features. Competitors such as F5 Networks and Cisco also have reverse proxy solutions that work well with Exchange.

A number of companies are still selling appliances that run TMG, so if you really must have TMG, this might be an option for you.

Most important, you should question whether you actually need a reverse proxy at all. When Exchange 2003 and Internet Security and Acceleration (ISA) Server 2003 shipped, the security of both Exchange and Windows was shaky. Since then, Microsoft has made great strides in hardening both products, and it's reasonable to ask whether you need a separate reverse proxy at all. After all, when you think about what a load balancer does, it is essentially a packet filter; it only allows traffic on TCP port 443 to Exchange, and it might even do preauthentication. As the time approaches for sunsetting your existing TMG deployment, you should consider whether you need *any* reverse proxy. The Exchange team blog has an interesting post by the aforementioned Greg Taylor at *http://blogs.technet.com/b/exchange/archive/2013/07/17/life-in-a-post-tmg-world-is -it-as-scary-as-you-think.aspx* that outlines some arguments for and against a reverse proxy.

Remember that in the 2013 CAS architecture, connections asking for mailbox data will always be made only to the active copy of the mailbox database that contains the requested data. That means that 2013 CAS needs a way to identify which mailbox database it needs to talk to, not merely the server that contains (or used to contain) it. In Exchange 2007, clients connected to the RPC endpoint; in Exchange 2010, clients connected to an FQDN that represents the RPC endpoint (for instance, HSV-MBX14.contoso.com). This FQDN could point to a CAS array object or directly to an individual CAS. If the mailbox databases hosting the user's mailbox were moved due to a failover or switchover, the client had to update its local MAPI connection profile to reflect the change, and this requires the client to be restarted. In Exchange 2013, by contrast, Outlook profiles now use a globally unique identifier (GUID) representing the mailbox as the endpoint name to connect to. This GUID, which is just a property on the mailbox, remains the same no matter which server has the active mailbox database copy; the CAS can resolve the GUID to the particular server that has the active copy of the mailbox database. This approach means that the 2013 CAS can seamlessly connect to the new active copy of a database without interrupting its connection to the client, so the client will never even be aware that a different copy has become active.

Because each Exchange 2013 CAS and Mailbox server can independently determine which Mailbox server should receive traffic for a particular mailbox, the RpcClientAccessServer property on the mailbox database is no longer necessary; it's still present, but Exchange 2013 ignores it.

Another equally important side effect of this change is that the need for the RPC client access array object has vanished. You might recall that the point of this object, often just called a CAS array, was to provide a single name (and thus a single connection point) for your CAS servers (whether you had one or many) so that clients could address any CAS in the array. Now that any Exchange 2013 CAS can authenticate an incoming request and proxy it to the correct Mailbox server, it no longer matters to the client which CAS it

communicates with, so having a logical object for clients to connect to is no longer necessary. Note that CAS servers are still treated as though they're in a logical array when you
put them behind a load balancer; there's no longer a need for an Exchange-specific object.

INSIDE OUT   Don't put firewalls between CAS and Mailbox servers

Like its ancestors, Exchange 2013 does not support the deployment of firewalls
between the CAS and Mailbox roles. It is not possible to deploy CAS servers in the
perimeter network with a firewall protecting the Mailbox servers because Exchange
uses too many open ports to make most security professionals happy. You can have
Windows Firewall configured on servers because Exchange will configure it to allow
communications automatically, but not on a hardware firewall.

See *http://technet.microsoft.com/en-us/library/bb331973.aspx* for a list of ports
Exchange 2010 uses; Microsoft has not yet released an updated list for 2013, but there
are few significant changes.

CAS authentication methods

Many Exchange administrators never tangle with the issues surrounding client authentication because the default settings that Exchange uses for a single-version installation just
work. However, as the topology becomes more complex, or when you begin mixing versions, the type of authentication enabled becomes of great importance.

The authentication method matters because the Exchange 2013 CAS role will always send
the requests it receives to other servers, and those servers will expect authentication information about the user who is connecting. If the user's mailbox is on an Exchange 2013
Mailbox server, the CAS can proxy directly to the HTTP proxy endpoint. If, however, the
user's mailbox is on an Exchange 2007 or Exchange 2010 server, the CAS proxies to the
Outlook Anywhere endpoint defined on that server. More properly, the 2013 CAS proxies
Outlook Anywhere requests to a virtual directory named /rpc on the older server. The settings on this virtual directory govern which authentication methods the downlevel server
will accept. This is why you have to enable Outlook Anywhere on all older CASs running on
internal-facing sites.

There are actually three areas where you can specify authentication on the CAS, and they
are independent of one another. You may configure authentication settings for internal clients (that is, those that connect to an internal URL, as described in the "External and internal URLs" section later in this chapter), external clients, and the RPC virtual directory itself.

The Exchange 2013 CAS supports several types of authentication, not all of which are available to on-premises customers; for example, Office 365 allows the use of Microsoft accounts (formerly known as Windows Live IDs and now more properly called Microsoft Online Services IDs) for authentication, but you can't use them in your own deployment. For the purposes of this book, the interesting types of authentication are as follows:

- Basic authentication passes user credentials in cleartext, so it must be used in combination with Secure Sockets Layer/Transport Layer Security (SSL/TLS).

- Kerberos authentication is the type Windows uses natively for client–server authentication. After a user logs on to a domain controller, he receives a Kerberos credential that can be passed to other servers and services to authenticate the user without requiring re-entry of the user's credentials. Kerberos was designed at MIT expressly to allow secure network authentication on untrusted networks, so it doesn't expose usernames or passwords in cleartext. However, it requires clients to be able to connect to a Kerberos key distribution center (KDC), which in Windows means they need to be able to reach a domain controller—something that often won't be possible for Exchange clients that are outside the firewall, not joined to an Active Directory domain, or not running Windows.

- NTLM authentication is the Windows predecessor protocol to Kerberos. Rather than depending on a centralized KDC, NTLM depends on an exchange of an encrypted challenge and response sequence. Unlike Kerberos credentials, an NTLM authentication token is only valid for the server that originally issued it.

- Integrated Windows Authentication (IWA) is what Microsoft calls the Internet Information Services (IIS) setting that enables native Kerberos and NTLM logon. This is the native method IIS uses for client and server authentication. With IWA enabled, servers request and accept Kerberos authentication, but they also accept NTLM authentication from clients that can't use Kerberos.

- Form-based authentication (FBA) is the familiar authentication method Outlook Web App uses; users see a form the Outlook Web App code generates. When they enter their credentials in the form, their browser performs an HTTP POST to an HTTPS URL on the Exchange server, so the credentials are encrypted in transit. The server then uses the credentials to authenticate the user against Active Directory; if authentication succeeds, the server generates an encrypted cookie that it returns to the client, and the client submits that cookie with each subsequent request to prove that it's previously authenticated. Some reverse proxy solutions (notably TMG) can put up their own FBA authentication page to allow preauthenticating Exchange users before they actually are allowed to connect to Exchange.

The distinctions among these authentication types can be confusing, in part because of where they can be applied. For example, to set authentication on the Outlook Anywhere virtual directory with the Set-OutlookAnywhere cmdlet, you have four choices:

● The –ExternalClientAuthenticationMethod parameter enables you to set the authentication method Exchange accepts from clients that connect to the external URL.

● The –InternalClientAuthenticationMethod parameter enables you to set the authentication method that Exchange accepts from clients that connect to the internal URL.

  Note that for both of these parameters, you only get to pick one authentication method for each client type.

● The –IISAuthenticationMethods parameter enables you to set multiple authentication methods that IIS will use. This might seem unnecessary—after all, you can set internal and external client authentication methods, so why would you need a separate way to set the methods that IIS itself will accept? The answer is that if you have a firewall between your external clients and your CAS servers, the firewall might be translating authentication methods. For example, TMG might accept basic authentication from the client and then reauthenticate to the CAS, using IWA, so IIS needs to be configured to accept IWA.

● The –DefaultAuthenticationMethod parameter applies the authentication type you specify to the ExternalClientAuthenticationMethod, InternalClientAuthenticationMethod, and IISAuthenticationMethods parameters—so you can use this switch alone to set all the authentication properties in one go.

If you configure basic authentication for Outlook Anywhere on a server, IIS only enables basic authentication on the /rpc virtual directory. To accept proxy requests from Exchange 2013, the /rpc virtual directory needs to accept Integrated Windows Authentication (IWA, previously known as NTLM) connections; otherwise, Kerberos won't work. However, if you just modify this setting directly in IIS, Exchange will overwrite it. Instead of changing the IIS settings directly, you need to use Set-OutlookAnywhere to change the settings on all your earlier CAS servers so that internal (between CAS) connections are authenticated with Kerberos while external (client) connections continue to use basic authentication. To do this, use Set-OutlookAnywhere like this:

```
Set-OutlookAnywhere –Server HSVCAS02 –ClientAuthenticationMethod Basic
-IISAuthenticationMethods Basic, NTLM
```

Not only do you have to pick the right authentication type, you must also choose wisely where you apply the authentication type you want to use! An Exchange 2013 CAS role has separate settings for external and internal authentication.

External vs. internal

When you consider what the CAS role does, it makes perfect sense to distinguish between two sources of client connections: internal clients on the organization's network and external clients that connect through a firewall by using one of the supported and enabled client protocols. Some organizations want to allow both internal and external clients to connect without restriction, whereas others limit external connections. Most organizations that deploy Exchange also want the flexibility to configure CAS behavior independently for internal and external connections.

The primary objects of interest for the external-versus-internal split are the URLs to which clients connect and the authentication methods that clients may use. To see the settings in effect on a CAS, you have to use a variety of cmdlets because each protocol has its own settings for these objects. For example, to see the external and internal configuration settings for Outlook Anywhere on a CAS named PAO-EX01, you could do the following:

```
Get-OutlookAnywhere -Server PAO-EX02 | fl -property *ternal*
```

```
ExternalHostname                   :
InternalHostname                   : pao-ex02.betabasement.com
ExternalClientAuthenticationMethod : Negotiate
InternalClientAuthenticationMethod : Ntlm
ExternalClientsRequireSsl          : False
InternalClientsRequireSsl          : False
```

These settings, which are unchanged from the installation defaults, show that external and internal clients use different authentication methods and that the external hostname isn't set. Compare those results to the output of Get-WebServicesVirtualDirectory, which has been edited to remove extraneous items:

```
Get-WebServicesVirtualDirectory -Server PAO-EX01 | fl -property *ternal*
```

```
InternalNLBBypassUrl         :
InternalAuthenticationMethods : {Ntlm, WindowsIntegrated, WSSecurity, OAuth}
ExternalAuthenticationMethods : {Ntlm, WindowsIntegrated, WSSecurity, OAuth}
InternalUrl                  : https://pao-ex01.betabasement.com/EWS/Exchange.asmx
ExternalUrl                    https://mail.betabasement.com/EWS/Exchange.asmx
```

Here the external and internal URLs have different values, and the virtual directory object has a set of authentication methods defined instead of a single authentication method. Why the differences?

External and internal URLs

Autodiscover publishes the external and internal URLs in the Outlook Anywhere settings, and on the Outlook Web App, EWS, EAS, and other virtual directories, to clients. It's up to the client to decide which of those two URLs to use. Of course, if one of them is blank, that makes the client's decision very easy. Presuming that both URLs are set, and their values are different, the client must decide based on its own knowledge of its network location or just by trying first the internal URL and then the external URL if the first attempt fails.

Exchange 2013 sets the internal URL for these services by default to the name of the server plus the path to the virtual directory (for instance, *https://pao-ex01.betabasement.com /EWS/Exchange.asmx* for EWS). The external URL is blank by default; you must set it yourself for each of the services you want to be externally accessible.

TROUBLESHOOTING

EWS clients report that they can't communicate with Exchange

Service Pack 2 of Outlook 2011 for Mac OS X seems to have an odd bug. Suppose that you have Outlook 2011 configured on an Apple laptop to talk to an Exchange 2013 server. You use the client while connected to the internal network, so when Autodiscover provides URLs, Outlook correctly detects and uses the internal URL. You shut down the laptop and take it to the local coffee shop, open it, and connect to that network. Outlook detects the change in network configuration, performs a new Autodiscover operation, and then ignores the external URL, so you don't reconnect to the Exchange server and don't get any new mail. This doesn't happen consistently, but it is a longstanding bug.

The problem is that this behavior is identical to what you'd see if the external URL were blank or set incorrectly: the client performs an Autodiscover, tries the internal URL, and then tries the external URL when the internal URL is unreachable. If the external URL is unreachable too, the client can't connect. The same thing can happen with the Lync desktop client for Windows or Mac OS X; it depends on EWS access to read free/busy, calendar, and contact data, so if your external URL is set incorrectly, Lync might report that it's having problems connecting to Exchange.

A default installation of Exchange 2013 leaves the ExternalUrl property of the EWS virtual directory blank. You need to set it to the correct value for external client access on all your Internet-facing CAS servers, or you'll experience these problems. The "Designing namespaces" section later in the chapter covers this topic in more depth.

External and internal authentication

Along with the URL connection points that you specify for internal and external client access, Exchange maintains separate settings for which authentication methods each client endpoint supports. In general, you should leave the default authentication settings for the CAS virtual directories alone; changing them without a good reason is a great way to break your Exchange deployment in interesting and subtle ways. One common symptom of incorrect authentication settings is a stream of repeated authentication prompts in Outlook or Outlook Web App.

> **Note**
>
> In Exchange 2013 RTM and Exchange 2013 CU1, it is possible for users to see multiple authentication prompts when their connections are redirected from one Internet-facing CAS to another, but in Exchange 2013 CU2 and later, the authentication credentials for Outlook Web App connections are re-sent, too, so that users only have to sign in once.

There are a few exceptions to this guideline, most of which involve coexistence with older versions of Exchange. For example, when you deploy an Exchange 2013 CAS into an existing Exchange 2007 or Exchange 2010 organization, you should configure things so that all CAS traffic goes to the Exchange 2013 CAS first because it can proxy or redirect traffic to earlier versions as necessary. For this to work, you must ensure that all your CAS servers, of any version, are configured to use basic authentication for the client and NTLM authentication on the virtual directory. Basic authentication is the lingua franca of all the HTTP-based protocols, so it will always need to be enabled for EWS, EAS, and Autodiscover.

> **Note**
>
> Microsoft has prepared a master list of all the default permissions and URLs on virtual directories for the Exchange 2013 CAS role. This list is extremely useful as a reference in case you accidentally change something and end up with undesirable side effects. It's available at *http://technet.microsoft.com/en-us/library/gg247612(v=exchg.150).aspx*.

Managing virtual directory settings

A default installation of a multirole Exchange 2013 server leaves you with seven virtual directories: Autodiscover, ECP, EWS, EAS, OAB, Outlook Web App, and Windows PowerShell. You can see and change the authentication and URL settings on these virtual directories in two ways. First, you can use the appropriate Set cmdlet (for example,

Set-EcpVirtualDirectory, Set-OabVirtualDirectory); second, you can use EAC. To use EAC, switch to the Servers tab and then choose the Virtual Directories tab, as shown in Figure 1-3. Opening the properties of a virtual directory by double-clicking it, or selecting it and clicking the pencil icon, produces a dialog box like the one shown in Figure 1-4.

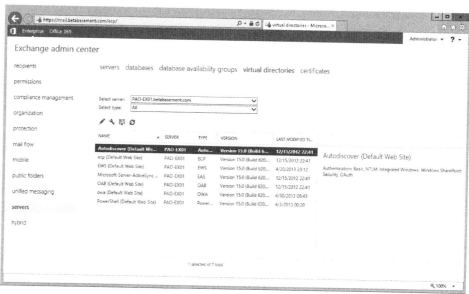

Figure 1-3 Editing virtual directory settings in EAC

Each virtual directory might have its own specific settings; for example, the EWS virtual directory has a check box for controlling whether the MRS proxy endpoint is enabled, as shown in Figure 1-4, whereas the Exchange Control Panel (ECP) virtual directory allows you to enable FBA, a setting not present on other virtual directories except /owa.

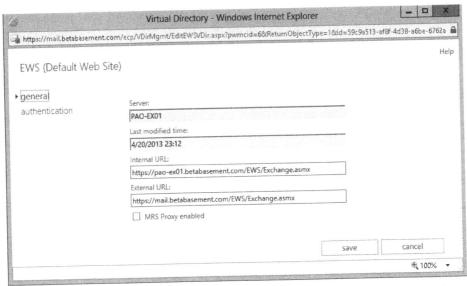

Figure 1-4 The settings for the default EWS virtual directory, which include an internal and external URL

The death of affinity

Another very important side effect of the decoupling of the CAS and Mailbox roles is a sharp reduction in the need for *client affinity*. Affinity means that a session for a given client remains with the same CAS for the duration of the connection. In other words, after a client connects to a particular CAS, the same CAS would continue to service the connection until the connection is terminated. To do this, the CAS must maintain session state so that any load balancers in the path know which CAS handles which connection. Sessions or protocols in which client affinity is maintained are said to be sticky. If a load balancer or reverse proxy solution doesn't support affinity, it will break some Exchange 2007 and Exchange 2010 Exchange services or reduce the performance of others by forcing users to reauthenticate each time the session moves to a different CAS, so this is clearly an area that you need to get right when deploying those versions of Exchange.

Exchange 2013 does away with the requirement for session affinity at the load balancer level; the load balancer doesn't have to maintain client affinity because any client can connect to any CAS and be proxied to the Mailbox server with the active copy of the mailbox database. This holds true for every protocol, so the protocols (such as Outlook Web App) that required sticky affinity in prior versions no longer have that restriction.

I mentioned that a failure of affinity would result in the client being asked to reauthenticate. Exchange 2013 does away with this circumstance by changing the way it uses cookies to cache authentication. In Exchange 2010, whatever CAS a client connects to provides an encrypted cookie after the client is authenticated. Passing that cookie to a different CAS means that the receiving CAS can't read it, so it has to ask the client to authenticate again. In Exchange 2013, the CAS authentication cookie is encrypted with the public key of the certificate assigned to the CAS, so any server that has the corresponding private key can decrypt the cookie. If you follow the Microsoft recommendation of putting the same cer- tificate on all your CAS servers (more on that in the "Certificate management" section later in this chapter), then any CAS can decrypt the cookie.

Load balancing made simpler

If you've ever had to pass any Microsoft certification exams involving networking, you probably remember the Open Systems Interconnect (OSI) model, with its seven layers (physical, data link, network, transport, session, presentation, and application, more easily remembered with the mnemonic, Please Do Not Throw Sausage Pizza Away). The TCP/IP internetworking model doesn't correspond exactly to the OSI model, but at least for the first four layers, it's fairly close. For discussing CAS load balancing, you're most interested in layers 4 and 7.

Layer 4 load balancing

At layer 4 (L4), the network layer, a load balancing device only has information about the Internet provider (IP) address and port to which the client is connecting. All the other potentially useful information, such as the URL it has requested or any cookies or query parameters associated with its request, is encoded in IP or User Datagram Protocol (UDP) datagrams and has been encapsulated. L4 devices don't de-encapsulate those datagrams to read the payload, so an L4 load balancer has to make decisions about where to route traffic based solely on the requested destination. L4 load balancers are therefore less com- plex to design, maintain, and support—they don't know or care what's happening at the application layer.

Layer 7 load balancing

Layer 7 (L7) load balancers are often labeled application-aware or smart because they can see the application-layer traffic, including the specific URLs clients request and any cookie or session information the client passes as part of its request. Consider the case when a load balancer sees a request from a mobile device for a URL such as *https://nacltl14se01 .contoso.com/Microsoft-Server-ActiveSync?jQAJBBCz0DFoa3Zf/Y1CsFFhMg2bBErZMzwCV1A =HTTP/1.1*. An L4 load balancer sees only two pieces of information: the name of the requested server (nacltl14se01.contoso.com) and the requested protocol (HTTPS, meaning TCP port 443). After the connection passes through the load balancer, the CAS sorts out the connection and gets it to the right place, but that's too late to have any notion of protocol awareness. By contrast, an L7 load balancer sees the same information, but it also knows the specific URL being requested, and it can see the synchronization key. In fact, the L7 load balancer can terminate the incoming SSL connection and then inspect the packets and discover the protocol to which the connection is directed.

Exchange offers a rich set of protocols and services, including Exchange Web Services (EWS), Outlook Web App, Exchange ActiveSync (EAS), the Offline Address Book (OAB), and the Exchange Administration Center (EAC), each of whose endpoint is represented as an IIS virtual directory. The problem is that a target CAS might be inoperative—or, worse, only one of its supported protocols might have failed. The new Managed Availability capability built into Exchange 2013 attempts to resolve problems, such as a failed protocol, automatically after it detects an issue by noting that client connections are failing. In this instance, the resolution might be to recycle an application pool or even to restart a server. However, an L4 load balancer sees a CAS in the whole rather than distinguishing among the different protocols the CAS might be able to handle, some of which are healthy and some of which might not be. With L7, the load balancer would be aware that Outlook Web App is up, but EAS is down on a specific target CAS, and be able to take action to redirect traffic as individual protocols changed their status.

Given that a load balancer's job is to distribute traffic among all the servers in its array, you might wonder whether the extra knowledge an L7 load balancer has available makes a difference. The answer is an unequivocal yes. An L4 load balancer can determine whether the target IP address is up or down by pinging it—and that's about all it can do. Some L4 load balancers can perform HTTP health checks too, but the checks are limited to a single virtual IP address. A server that is turned on, plugged in to the network, and not running Exchange services at all will give the same response to a basic L4 load balancer as one that has the Exchange 2013 CAS role on it. When a service or protocol handler fails or slows down, an L4 load balancer can't tell. This leads to the possibility that the load balancer will continue to direct incoming traffic to a machine that cannot properly handle it; of course, you could argue that Managed Availability (covered in depth in *Microsoft Exchange Server 2013 Inside Out: Mailbox and High Availability*) will restore service automatically so that the load balancer won't run into this situation. However, an L7 load balancer can tell not only whether the network layer of the server is responsive but also whether the actual protocol or service the client is asking for—Outlook Web App, EAS, Outlook Anywhere, and so on—is performing properly, and it can route traffic accordingly. In addition, many L7 load balancers, such as those sold by F5 and Kemp Technologies, can perform health checks on individual services and applications so they know when an EAS endpoint, IMAP server, or whatever becomes unavailable or returns to normal service. The Managed Availability service includes a health check URL for each monitored service that any load balancer (or other monitoring tool) can use; querying the service virtual directory with /healthcheck.htm appended (for example, /owa/healthcheck.htm) will return an HTTP 200 response if the service is healthy.

DNS round robin

Strictly speaking, DNS round robin is a load balancing technology, too, although it probably doesn't seem that way at first glance. When you configure multiple IP addresses for a single Domain Name System (DNS) name, the DNS server returns all those addresses to any client that requests them, changing the order in which they appear each time. Two clients that ask a DNS server to resolve the same DNS name will get the same addresses but in a different order. Because most clients just use the first IP address the DNS server returns, this provides a simplistic means of spreading client load across multiple machines. Microsoft makes a point of saying that what it calls modern HTTP clients (including Outlook 2010 and Outlook 2013 and some compliant Exchange ActiveSync implementations) are smart enough to try each of the IP addresses they receive when they get a round robin response. It doesn't matter whether any particular client gets different CAS servers when it makes two sequential requests because the Exchange 2013 CAS is now stateless. Unfortunately, they don't tell you which clients are considered modern. For example, Safari 6.x for Mac OS X implements this behavior, whereas Safari for Windows doesn't. Although Microsoft officially supports this address resolution behavior, I don't recommend that you rely on it unless you can ensure that all your clients support it.

Even without this implementation-dependent behavior, round robin DNS has a critical flaw: it has absolutely no awareness of the state of the machines or services whose IP addresses it is handing out. If the DNS server is configured to resolve mail.contoso.com to 192.168.0.200, 192.168.0.201, and 192.168.0.202, and the machine at 192.168.0.201 is down, the DNS server will continue handing out that address as the first entry to one-third of the clients that contact it. In addition, because clients or intermediate servers might cache DNS results, changes you make manually might not be immediately visible to clients. The counterbalance for these flaws is that every modern DNS server implementation supports round robin DNS, so implementing it is easy and inexpensive. It is most often used to provide load balancing for SMTP because SMTP is stateless by nature and, thus, it doesn't matter which server two sequential clients connect to.

Windows Network Load Balancing

Microsoft began offering Windows Network Load Balancing (WNLB) in Windows 2000. Since then, it has steadily upgraded WNLB functionality, and yet relatively few Exchange sites use it, even though it's included with Windows. There are two reasons for this. First is that WNLB is unintelligent; that is, it lacks service awareness because it does not check ports and services on a server before considering it a suitable candidate for load balancing. Essentially, if a server has a pulse, NLB thinks it is good. In addition, there is no communication between Exchange and NLB, and Exchange does not attempt to balance client connections across all the CAS servers in the array.

More significantly, you cannot use WNLB with servers that are members of a Database Availability Group (DAG). Windows Failover Clustering (WFC) is incompatible with WNLB. If you separate the CAS and Mailbox roles, you could use WNLB to load balance traffic across your CAS servers, but if you want to use multirole servers, as Microsoft recommends, those servers can *either* be load balanced with WNLB *or* be DAG members. Because DAGs offer such a powerful solution for high availability, WNLB just isn't widely deployed with Exchange. Round robin DNS gives you essentially the same load balancing capability with Exchange 2013 without having to worry about separating the CAS and Mailbox roles.

Choosing a load balancing solution

Given the choice among WNLB, DNS round robin, an L4 load balancer, and an L7 load balancer, which should you choose? First, it's important to understand that no matter which solution you choose, the basic behavior will be the same:

- If you're using a load balancer or Windows NLB, clients see a single virtual IP address and FQDN for the entire set of load balanced servers. If you're using round robin DNS, each server in the array needs to have its own resolvable IP address to which clients can connect.

- The number of servers in the load balancing array is determined by the load balancer. For example, WNLB arrays are limited to 32 servers (in Windows Server 2012); other manufacturers have different limits.

- Incoming client connections arrive at the load balancer, and it determines where to send them. However, L4 and L7 load balancers make this decision using different information. L4 looks only at the destination IP and port, whereas L7 needs to look at the connection contents. This necessarily implies that an L7 load balancer must be able to terminate SSL connections so it can inspect the contents and refer connections to the appropriate server.

With those factors in mind, your next decision is the balance between functionality and cost. L4 load balancers are quite inexpensive, but they offer limited functionality compared to L7 solutions. However, one way to work around this difference in functionality is to use one namespace per protocol as described in the "Designing namespaces" section later in this chapter. By doing so, the L4 load balancer can distinguish among requests for different services because each service or protocol has a unique FQDN and virtual IP. However, L7 load balancers offer a much wider range of functionality, most significantly the ability to monitor the health and performance of individual services. Those additional capabilities demand a price premium, which many customers are willing to pay. Exchange itself is agnostic on the question because it is not integrated with or aware of either L4 or L7 load balancing.

A related question is whether to deploy physical or virtualized load balancing appliances. As software-defined networking (SDN) becomes more common, this will become a question of increasing interest; at least for now, very few organizations have deployed virtualized switches or routers, with the exception of switches integrated with hypervisors. Virtualizing your load balancers offers the same benefits, and drawbacks, as virtualizing any other part of your Exchange infrastructure. I tend to prefer physical load balancers because they don't impose the additional overhead and complexity of a virtual machine (VM) host; however, for organizations with smaller networks, or in which VM host space is abundant and well managed, virtualized load balancers offer no essential differences in functionality from their physical counterparts and might be an appropriate choice.

The role of Outlook Anywhere

It's important to understand that Outlook Anywhere is now *the* protocol by which Outlook connects to Exchange 2013. Whereas earlier versions would allow RPC connections directly to the Mailbox server, using plain TCP, Exchange 2013 uses RPC over HTTPS everywhere all the time. That means that one of the first things you should do now, before you even consider adding Exchange 2013 to your existing Exchange 2007 or Exchange 2010 deployment, is enable Outlook Anywhere on all your servers and verify that it works. This requirement holds true for *every* CAS server, even those that are not Internet-facing.

Although this requirement might seem odd, there's a good reason for it. The Exchange 2013 CAS role server includes a new proxy engine, httpproxy.dll. This replaces the role of the old rpcproxy.dll, and Exchange 2013 CAS thus cannot proxy RPC traffic directly. When it receives HTTPS encapsulated RPC traffic, it cannot de-encapsulate it directly; instead, it must proxy it to another CAS server that still has rpcproxy.dll. For this proxy operation to succeed, the Exchange 2013 mailbox server or the downlevel CAS servers must have rpcproxy.dll installed (it's installed by default on the Exchange 2013 mailbox role), and they must be enabled for Outlook Anywhere. Luckily, enabling Outlook Anywhere is simple; on an Exchange 2007 or Exchange 2010 CAS, you can use the Enable-OutlookAnywhere cmdlet, like this:

```
Enable-OutlookAnywhere -Server 'PAO-EX03' -ExternalHostname 'pao.contoso.com'
-ClientAuthenticationMethod Basic -SSLOffloading $false -IISAuthenticationMethods
Basic, NTLM
```

When you specify the –ClientAuthenticationMethod switch but not –IISAuthenticationMethods, the IIS authentication methods are set to NTLM plus basic. This is exactly what you want for a mixed organization—remember, you need every CAS in the organization to accept Outlook Anywhere traffic.

If you prefer, you can use the Exchange 2010 wizard for configuring Outlook Anywhere on your Exchange 2010 servers, the wizard will lead you through specifying external and internal URLs and authentication methods (see Figure 1-5).

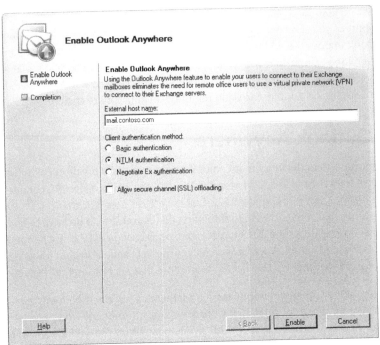

Figure 1-5 The Exchange 2010 Enable Outlook Anywhere Wizard, available from Exchange Management Console (EMC)

By default, Exchange 2013 is already configured to use Outlook Anywhere; the only task required on your part is to install a valid certificate for Outlook Anywhere to use on the CAS. The Outlook client will complain if it receives a self-signed certificate from the server unless you manually add it to the trusted certificate authority (CA) store on the client computer, which is a hassle. Instead, you should plan to install a certificate from either an internal CA in your organization or a trusted external CA on your CAS. (Certificate configuration is discussed later in the chapter, in the "Certificate management" section.) Interestingly, the Mailbox server can use a self-signed certificate for Outlook Anywhere communications because the CAS ignores those certificates. (More precisely, it knows the connection has been authenticated with Kerberos, so it only cares whether the certificate can be used for encryption.)

Designing namespaces

You will often hear the term "namespace" bandied about when discussions turn toward the CAS role. In this context, "namespace" is essentially a fancy way of saying "URL" or "FQDN." The namespace used for a particular protocol is whatever URL or FQDN clients running that protocol connect to. ("Namespace" has different and much more complex connotations when used to refer to XML documents, C# or C++ programs, and other fields.) For example, an Exchange 2010 RPC client access array might have a namespace of *mail.contoso .com*, but the namespace for Outlook Web App in the same environment might be *owa .contoso.com*. The process of designing namespaces for Exchange 2007 and Exchange 2010 is complex and error-prone, and Microsoft has greatly simplified it for Exchange 2013, but it is still not exactly what I'd call simple.

Using a single namespace

The simplest possible design is to use a single namespace (such as mail.contoso.com) for all services except Autodiscover. This might require you to use split DNS or other methods of DNS manipulation to ensure that internal and external clients get the correct address for this namespace, but it is difficult to argue against the resulting simplicity.

One name per service?

One way of achieving selective control is to publish specific connectivity points for each protocol as part of your external namespace. Therefore, instead of having the catch-all *mail. contoso.com*, you'd have a set of endpoints such as eas.contoso.com, ecp.contoso.com, owa. contoso.com, and so on. The advantage is that the L4 load balancer now sees protocol-specific inbound connections that it can handle with separate virtual IPs (VIPs). The load balancer can also monitor the health of the different services that it attaches to the VIPs and make sure that each protocol is handled as effectively as possible. The disadvantage is that you have more complexity in the namespace, particularly in terms of communication to users, and you have to either ensure that the different endpoints all feature as alternate names on the SSL certificates that are used to secure connections or buy a more expensive wildcard certificate. None of this is difficult, but it's different from before. What you gain from the transition from L7 to L4 you lose (a little) on extra work.

To accomplish this, you need to use either EAC to set the external URL for each virtual directory on each server or the appropriate Set-*VirtualDirectory cmdlet on the appropriate servers. The simplest way to do this is something like the following:

```
Get-ActiveSyncVirtualDirectory | Set-ActiveSyncVirtualDirectory -ExternalURL
activesync.contoso.com
```

Of course, this will require you to ensure that you have correctly registered your servers in DNS and that the certificates on the servers are configured with the correct subject and subjectAlternativeName fields.

Using a single internal name for Outlook Anywhere

Every Exchange server has its own unique Windows computer account name, but Exchange is perfectly happy to ignore that name in favor of a name you assign. This can be a source of both great utility and great aggravation, depending on whether you configure it properly. Note that the server name Exchange presents isn't the same as the internal or external URL. On a default Exchange installation, if you check the external hostnames defined for Outlook Anywhere, they'll be blank, like this:

```
Get-ClientAccessServer | Get-OutlookAnywhere | select identity, *hostname
```

Identity	ExternalHostname	InternalHostname
PAO-EX01\Rpc	(Default Web Site)	pao-ex01.betabasement.com
PAO-EX02\Rpc	(Default Web Site)	pao-ex02.betabasement.com

This obviously makes it hard for external clients to use Outlook Anywhere, which is addressed in the next section. However, note that each of the two servers has its server FQDNs listed in the InternalHostname field. It would simplify both load balancing and failover operation if both those servers had the same internal hostname; in that case, the load balancer *or* a client could just resolve the internal hostname (in this case, mail.betabasement.com) and carry on with its work.

```
Get-OutlookAnywhere | Set-OutlookAnywhere -InternalHostname mail.betabasement.com
-InternalClientsRequireSsl $true
```

The −InternalClientsRequireSsl flag is required; you don't have to set it to $true, but if you do not, your internal clients won't attempt to encrypt their Outlook Anywhere traffic, including credentials, so this is pretty much a mandatory setting.

External names for Outlook Anywhere

Choosing an external name for Outlook Anywhere is slightly trickier. The name you choose has to be externally resolvable; for that reason, the consensus seems to be that you should choose a name different from the internal hostname. A common design pattern is to use "outlook" as the internal hostname and "mail" as the external hostname, so you'd see something like this when performing a Get-OutlookAnywhere:

```
Get-OutlookAnywhere | select identity, *hostname
```

```
Identity                          ExternalHostname         InternalHostname
--------                          ----------------         ----------------
PAO-EX01\Rpc (Default Web Site)   mail.betabasement.com    outlook.betabasement.com
PAO-EX02\Rpc (Default Web Site)   mail.betabasement.com    outlook.betabasement.com
```

In Exchange 2010, if the internal and external hostnames are both externally resolvable, but the internal hostname isn't actually reachable from the Internet, Outlook clients can try to connect to the internal hostname first. They'll fail, of course, but this adds an unwanted startup delay. Exchange 2013 doesn't have that problem, but many still consider it a best practice to have the internal hostname both unreachable and unresolvable from the external world. However, you cannot do this if you're using a single namespace with split DNS as described in the "Using a single namespace" section earlier in this chapter.

The Front End Transport service

The Front End Transport (FET) service is discussed in much more depth in Chapter 2, "The Exchange transport system." However, it can be explained very simply. FET is a service that accepts SMTP connections and redirects them to Mailbox servers. It doesn't queue mail for delivery, meaning that it doesn't have to keep a queue database, participate in the Exchange 2013 shadow redundancy or Safety Net features, or do anything other than authenticate recipients (if configured to do so) and pass SMTP traffic to other servers. Because FET doesn't queue anything, if it cannot immediately reach a proxy target, the FET service will return a transient SMTP error to the sender, forcing it to try again later. This is a neat trick because it shifts the burden of ensuring reliable message delivery away from the CAS and back to the sending server, whatever SMTP software it's running.

One consequence of the new FET behavior becomes evident when you have a single server on which both the Mailbox and CAS roles are installed. The transport services that belong to the Mailbox role don't receive the message directly—instead, inbound messages on that machine arrive at the FET service, which then proxies them to the Mailbox Transport service. If you look at the headers for an inbound message, you'll see more hops than you might otherwise expect. Figure 1-6 shows the output from the free Message Header Analyzer app installed on an Exchange 2013 server. (This free app and other Office apps for Outlook and Outlook Web App are described in more detail in Chapter 3, "Client management.") Note that three hops are shown for the message: it is received by the FET service on PAO-EX01, sent to the Mailbox Transport service on PAO-EX01, and then sent to the Mailbox Submission service on PAO-EX01.

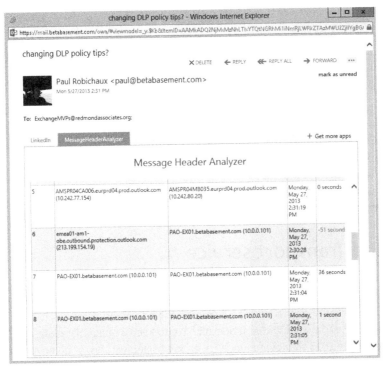

Figure 1-6 The Message Header Analyzer app running in Outlook Web App, showing the message headers for a message that a multirole Exchange 2013 server received

Autodiscover

Microsoft introduced the Autodiscover service in Exchange 2007 as a solution for the perennial problem of how to help users configure Outlook and Exchange ActiveSync with the name of their mailbox and the server that hosts the mailbox the first time they connect to Exchange. Information about the mailbox's location is subsequently held in the Outlook profile. A profile can still be configured manually, but it's a lot easier to let Autodiscover do the work for you, especially because Outlook overwrites manually configured settings that conflict with settings it gets from Autodiscover. This all works very nicely unless the mailbox for which you are attempting to configure access is hidden from Exchange address lists, in which case, Autodiscover won't be able to find the mailbox, and you'll have to configure the profile manually. Outlook can also requery Autodiscover if it loses connection to the mailbox.

Outlook 2007, Outlook 2010, Outlook 2011 for Mac OS X, and Outlook 2013 support Autodiscover, as do Outlook RT for Windows RT and the built-in mail clients for Windows Phone and Apple iOS. Each of these clients performs an Autodiscover request at start-up,

as a result of which they receive an Autodiscover manifest that contains a wealth of useful information. The Exchange ActiveSync and regular Autodiscover manifests are different; the regular XML manifest is several hundred lines long, but you can see an excerpt in
Figure 1-7, which shows the output from the Outlook 2013 Test E-Mail AutoConfiguration
dialog box. To access this dialog box yourself, hold down the Ctrl key and right-click the
Outlook icon in the system tray; you'll see the Test E-mail AutoConfiguration command in
the context menu. After filling in the username and password fields, a successful test shows
results like those in the figure. In this case, you can see that Autodiscover has returned URLs
for the Availability service, the out of office (OOF) service, the OAB download endpoint, the
Unified Messaging service, and various parts of the Exchange Administration Center (EAC)
that are used within Outlook (although they are still labeled Exchange Control Panel in
Outlook 2013).

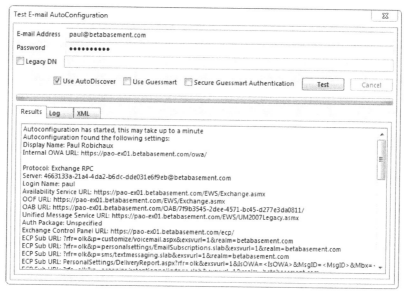

Figure 1-7 The Test E-mail AutoConfiguration dialog box in Outlook 2013, showing a portion of
the data returned from a successful Autodiscover request

One of the most important pieces of information Autodiscover returns is which server
contains the user's mailbox. In Figure 1-7, because Autodiscover was run against a mailbox
on an Exchange 2013 server, the returned endpoint is actually a GUID; the Server line
in the returned results is 4663133a-21a4-4da2-b6dc-dde031e6f9eb@betabasement
.com rather than a more conventional FQDN. The mailbox might move without warning
because of a failover, a switchover, or a mailbox move; thanks to the mechanism described
earlier, Outlook doesn't have to start a new connection because it only communicates with
the CAS. However, Outlook for Windows will repeat Autodiscover every 60 minutes or
after losing connectivity to the mailbox. Other Autodiscover clients generally have similar

behavior, although the intervals might vary. Besides information about the primary mail-box, Autodiscover also returns configuration data about public folder mailboxes, shared mailboxes, and site mailboxes if they're in use.

The Autodiscover process

Autodiscover clients follow a predictable process to make requests. Understanding this process is valuable because knowing the steps in the process eliminates any mystery from discussions of why a particular client got the results it did.

The basic Autodiscover process works like this:

1. The client provides credentials, normally in the form of an SMTP email address and a password.

2. If the client is domain joined, it queries Active Directory for a list of service connection point (SCP) objects, the nature and use of which are described in the "Accessing Autodiscover through SCPs" section later in this chapter. If that query succeeds, the client will have a URL against which to try Autodiscover.

3. If the SCP query fails, the client tries to perform HTTPS POST operations against a sequence of well-known URLs. This often happens because the client either isn't domain joined or cannot reach a global catalog server to look for SCPs. Examples include mobile devices, Outlook for Windows running on home PCs, and Outlook for Mac OS X. The process for constructing these well-known URLs requires the client to treat the right side of the email address that the user provided in step 1 as a server name to which other items are added. For example, if the user enters carrie@ contoso.com as her email address, her client first uses *https://contoso.com /autodiscover/autodiscover.svc* and then tries *https://autodiscover.contoso.com /autodiscover/autodiscover.xml*.

4. If the initial connection attempt to the well-known URLs fails, the client makes an unencrypted HTTP GET request against *https://autodiscover.contoso.com /autodiscover/autodiscover.xml*, expecting to receive an HTTP 302 redirect result that points to the correct Autodiscover URL. This mechanism is useful when you have a public website that uses split-brain DNS to remain separate from your internal network. Outlook will, and other clients might, generate a warning to tell the user that the server is redirecting the client to another address.

5. If the client still can't get a valid Autodiscover URL, it can query for a DNS SRV record named _autodiscover.tcp.domain. The underscore at the beginning of the record is mandatory. This record should return the FQDN of the real Autodiscover endpoint. If the query succeeds, the client can use the returned name to create a URL by appending /autodiscover/autodiscover.xml to it and attempting an HTTPS POST.

6. As a last-ditch effort, the client will look for a local XML configuration file if you've set HKEY_CURRENT_USER\Software\Microsoft\Office*X.0*\Outlook\Autodiscover to point to the path of a properly formatted Autodiscover manifest. (In this case, the *X* in the registry key refers to the Office version: 14 is Office 2010, and 15 is Office 2013.)

The Autodiscover client might receive a number of responses. In the best case, it receives an actual Autodiscover manifest. It might also receive an HTTP redirect, using the 302 result code. The server might also require the client to authenticate by returning an HTTP 401 or 403 error code, and, of course, the client might receive an HTTP error 404 if it tries to request Autodiscover data from a server that isn't an Autodiscover endpoint.

If you want to see what URLs will be returned to an Autodiscover client, you can use Get-ClientAccessServer –AutoDiscoverServiceInternalURL.

Accessing Autodiscover through SCPs

When you install a new CAS server, it registers an object known as a *service connection point* (SCP) in Active Directory. The SCP is a pointer that associates one or more service endpoints (in the form of a URL or FQDN) with a particular service and server. SCPs are used for a variety of other objects, and application developers can even register their own services by using SCPs. By querying Active Directory, software can get a list of all the end-points that offer a particular service. Figure 1-8 shows some of the properties associated with the SCP registered when the Exchange 2013 CAS named PAO-EX01 was installed. The serviceBindingInformation attribute for an Exchange SCP contains a URL based on the FQDN of the server, and the related keywords attribute on the object lists the site to which the CAS server belongs. When a domain-joined client can reach a global catlog (GC), it will bind to the GC by using the user-provided credentials and query for SCPs.

An SCP can act as a referral from one forest to another to help clients to find Autodiscover information when Exchange is deployed in a multi-forest scenario. The URLs returned from the SCPs essentially act as pointers to CASs to which clients can connect to be redirected to whatever Mailbox server currently hosts their mailbox.

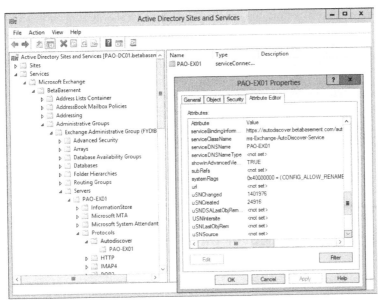

Figure 1-8 An example SCP object shown in the Active Directory Sites and Services snap-in

Accessing Autodiscover through well-known URLs

There's nothing magic about the URLs that Autodiscover uses, but the Autodiscover protocol specification calls out how they should be formed, and Exchange servers automatically
create the necessary virtual directories to handle Autodiscover queries. You don't need to
modify the internal and external URLs manually for the Autodiscover virtual directory; leave
them blank so that Exchange correctly constructs the well-known URLs described earlier in
this chapter.

The role of Exchange providers

Autodiscover manifests contain a list of Exchange *providers*, XML elements that specify
the services available and the methods required to connect to them. They're sometimes
called Outlook providers, too. These components of the manifest get their name from the
actual providers—code that runs on the Exchange server to look up the appropriate settings and return them. Here's an example provider block (that I have shortened for print)
returned by an Autodiscover query from an Exchange 2013 multirole server; it's wrapped in
a *<Protocol>* XML element:

```
<Protocol>
    <Type>EXCH</Type>
    <Server>4663133a-21a4-4da2-b6dc-dde031e6f9eb@betabasement.com</Server>
        <ServerDN>/o=BetaBasement/ou=Exchange Administrative Group
```

```
(FYDIBOHF23SPDLT)/cn=Configuration/cn=Servers/cn=4663133a-21a4-4da2-b6dc
-dde031e6f9eb@betabasement.com</ServerDN>
        <ServerVersion>73C0826C</ServerVersion>
        <MdbDN>/o=BetaBasement/ou=Exchange Administrative Group
(FYDIBOHF23SPDLT)/cn=Configuration/cn=Servers/cn=4663133a-21a4-4da2-b6dc
-dde031e6f9eb@betabasement.com/cn=Microsoft Private MDB</MdbDN>
        <PublicFolderServer>mail.betabasement.com</PublicFolderServer>
        <AD>PAO-DC01.betabasement.com</AD>
        <ASUrl>https://pao-ex01.betabasement.com/EWS/Exchange.asmx</ASUrl>
        <EwsUrl>https://pao-ex01.betabasement.com/EWS/Exchange.asmx</EwsUrl>
        <EmwsUrl>https://pao-ex01.betabasement.com/EWS/Exchange.asmx</EmwsUrl>
        <EcpUrl>https://pao-ex01.betabasement.com/ecp/</EcpUrl>
        <EcpUrl-um>?rfr=olk&amp;p=customize/voicemail.aspx&amp;exsvurl
=1&amp;realm=betabasement.com</EcpUrl-um>
        <EcpUrl-ret>?rfr=olk&amp;p=organize/retentionpolicytags.slab&amp
;exsvurl=1&amp;realm=betabasement.com</EcpUrl-ret>
        <EcpUrl-sms>?rfr=olk&amp;p=sms/textmessaging.slab&amp;exsvurl
=1&amp;realm=betabasement.com</EcpUrl-sms>
        <EcpUrl-tm>?rfr=olk&amp;ftr=TeamMailbox&amp;exsvurl=1&amp;realm
=betabasement.com</EcpUrl-tm>
        <OOFUrl>https://pao-ex01.betabasement.com/EWS/Exchange.asmx</OOFUrl>
        <UMUrl>https://pao-ex01.betabasement.com/EWS/UM2007Legacy.asmx</UMUrl>
        <OABUrl>https://pao-ex01.betabasement.com/OAB/7f9b3545-2dee-4571-bc45
-d277e3da0811/</OABUrl>
        <ServerExclusiveConnect>off</ServerExclusiveConnect>
    </Protocol>
```

As you can see, this provider includes the distinguished name (DN) of the server, the DN of the mailbox database, and, most important, the GUID of the user's mailbox (in the Server element). It also contains a set of URLs for various services. If you look at a complete Autodiscover manifest, though, you'll see several of these *<Protocol>* elements. They serve different purposes:

- The EXCH provider block is used for internal connections for Exchange 2007 and Exchange 2010 services. This data includes port settings and the internal URLs for the Exchange services that you have enabled.

- The EXPR block serves data for external Outlook Anywhere connections for Exchange 2007 and Exchange 2010 services. This setting includes the external URLs for the Exchange services that you have enabled.

- The WEB setting contains the best URL for this particular user to reach Outlook Web Access for the user to use.

- The EXHTTP block is new for Exchange 2013. It's intended to supersede the EXCH and EXPR blocks for modern clients (meaning Outlook 2010 SP1 with the latest roll-ups and later versions). EXHTTP is generated by the Exchange 2013 CAS from the provider data supplied by the internal and external providers, and the data it returns provide a roadmap for the client to know which CAS to connect to, whether it's internal or external. There will be two EXHTTP blocks; the client will try the first one it encounters, which provides the internal settings, and then fall back to the second one, which provides the external settings.

Retrieving configuration information with Autodiscover

After the client successfully connects to an Exchange 2013 Mailbox server by using Autodiscover, it receives a manifest that contains a number of useful data items. The client is supposed to cache these data items. For example, Outlook stores several of them in the user's Outlook profile; a mobile device client might store them in whatever manner makes sense. Perhaps the most important piece of this data is the location of the user's mailbox, but there are a number of other important items.

After the client connects to a Mailbox server, it attempts to retrieve the configuration information for its mailbox and the location of the various Exchange services. This step ensures that the profile is kept updated with the latest mailbox settings and that Outlook knows how to find the following:

- Out of office information

- Availability information from the calendars of other users

- Locations to download the Offline Address Book (OAB) files

- UM information (if used)

- Information about the location and availability of shared or site mailboxes

- Information about the location and availability of public folder servers

Another important update the client receives is the name of the server to which it should connect for future queries. This server becomes the endpoint that replaces the name of the original Mailbox server that is used in the profile for previous versions of Exchange. Keep in mind that if an Autodiscover client that connects from the Internet cannot connect to the Autodiscover service, client functions that depend on retrieving Autodiscover manifest information probably won't work. For example, if Autodiscover access is misconfigured, a user who takes his work laptop home and tries to connect using Outlook Anywhere might find that Outlook appears to connect normally but that he can't change his out of office message because Outlook doesn't know where the OOF service is.

INSIDE OUT Who is the client talking to?

The XML data returned by an Autodiscover request is generated by a CAS in the same site as the Mailbox server that holds the requested mailbox. This means that in mixed environments, you might see Exchange 2010–style Autodiscover data returned for users whose mailboxes are still on Exchange 2010 even though the initial Autodiscover request will go to an Exchange 2013 CAS. When the Exchange 2013 CAS proxies the Autodiscover request to the Exchange 2010 CAS on the same site as the Exchange 2010 Mailbox server holding the user's mailbox, that Exchange 2010 CAS generates the Autodiscover data, and the Exchange 2013 CAS returns it to the client.

INSIDE OUT Updating Autodiscover

Outlook—and other clients—don't just perform Autodiscover once; mailboxes can move, server assignments can change, networks might have service interruptions, and clients can physically move between sites. For these reasons, clients usually perform periodic rediscoveries to keep their knowledge of which endpoints they should be talking to up to date. Outlook requests Autodiscover data at start-up and every 60 minutes thereafter. It might also query Autodiscover if it cannot connect to the Mailbox server, in which case it will retry its request every five minutes until it succeeds or until Outlook shuts down.

Although there are rarely good reasons to do so, you can modify the interval at which Outlook performs this query by running the Set-OutlookProvider cmdlet to set a new cache lifetime in hours. For example, to set the lifetime to be three hours:

```
Set-OutlookProvider -id 'msExchAutoDiscoverConfig' -TTL 3
```

Understanding CAS proxying and redirection

The Exchange 2013 CAS role doesn't directly serve any data to clients; instead, it provides two ways for clients to connect to the correct server: *proxying* and *redirection*. In a proxied connection, the CAS accepts data from the client and forwards it to the correct server; in a redirected connection, the CAS responds to the client request with the FQDN of the server it should ideally be talking to.

In Exchange 2013, the CAS only redirects connections in a very limited number of cases. That is by design because redirections shift work from the server to the client by forcing it to reconnect, and not all clients properly handle redirections.

Proxying

CAS proxying was fairly complicated in Exchange 2007 and Exchange 2010. It is considerably simpler in Exchange 2013, but there are still several edge cases that lurk, somewhat confusingly, to cover situations when traffic must be proxied to downlevel Exchange servers or across complex Active Directory site topologies.

First, you need to stipulate that two things must take place before the CAS can proxy anything at all. The CAS that initially accepts the connection (here referred to as the original CAS) must authenticate the client to see whether it should have access, and it must determine which Mailbox server is currently hosting the active copy of the mailbox database.

After these steps have been completed, the CAS can proxy traffic. The simplest case of proxying involves IMAP and POP, which the CAS will always proxy without regard to the version of Exchange on the target Mailbox server.

Several Exchange protocols, including Outlook Anywhere, Autodiscover, Outlook Web App, Exchange ActiveSync (EAS), the Availability service, and Exchange Web Services (EWS), can be carried over HTTP or HTTPS. The good news is that the CAS role doesn't have to care about the contents of the traffic for most of these protocols, just about the destination endpoint. For example, a client with a mailbox homed on Exchange 2010 that makes an Autodiscover request will receive Autodiscover data from an Exchange 2010 CAS because the Exchange 2013 CAS role will proxy that Autodiscover request to an Exchange 2010 CAS, ideally on the same site as the Exchange 2010 Mailbox server that hosts the target mailbox.

There are a few exceptions to this general rule, all of which involve coexistence with downlevel versions of Exchange. For example, suppose an Exchange 2013 CAS named PAOCAS02 receives an Autodiscover request for a user whose mailbox is hosted on an Exchange 2007 server named AUSMBX03. The Exchange 2013 CAS will detect that the user's mailbox is on Exchange 2007 and proxy the connection to an Exchange 2013 Mailbox server, which will return an Autodiscover manifest itself instead of proxying that request to AUSMBX03. That is possible because the Exchange 2013 Mailbox role includes special code for handling Autodiscover requests on behalf of Exchange 2007 mailboxes. (Outlook Anywhere proxying is a special case because of the differences in Outlook Anywhere among Exchange 2007, Exchange 2010, and Exchange 2013, so it's discussed in the "The role of Outlook Anywhere" section earlier in the chapter.)

In topologies that have multiple Exchange 2010 CAS servers that could be proxy targets, the Exchange 2013 CAS role has to know which downlevel servers can accept traffic. This is implemented using a simple mechanism: at start-up, the Exchange 2013 CAS queries Active Directory to get a list of all the Exchange 2007 or Exchange 2010 CAS servers. It then sends an HTTP HEAD request to each protocol virtual directory of those servers every 60 seconds. The HEAD request just asks for the page header of an endpoint, as distinguished from the more common HTTP GET request, so it's a lightweight way to see whether the protocol virtual directory is actually available. If the downlevel server responds with a 300-series or 400-series HTTP result, the Exchange 2013 CAS considers that particular virtual directory on the target server available. If the request times out or produces a 500-series HTTP result, the HEAD request is immediately retried; if the second attempt fails, that virtual directory is considered down, and no traffic will be proxied to it.

INSIDE OUT   Exempting an Exchange 2010 CAS as a proxy target

If you want a particular Exchange 2010 CAS to be exempted from proxying traffic, you can do so provided you have at least Service Pack 3 on it. You might want to do this, for example, if you know the CAS will be down for maintenance or if you plan to decommission it. The trick is to use the –IsOutOfService parameter to Set-ClientAccessServer, like this:

```
Set-ClientAccessServer –identity HSV-CAS06 –IsOutOfService $true
```

After you run that command, HSV-CAS06 won't receive any more proxy traffic from Exchange 2013 CAS servers until you reset IsOutOfService.

Redirection

Exchange 2013 redirects CAS connections in the following cases:

- When an inbound unified messaging call arrives. The Session Initiation Protocol (SIP), discussed in more detail in Chapter 6, is built around the idea of redirects for call routing, and the Unified Messaging Call Router service on the CAS takes full advantage of this.

- When a client requests Outlook Web App and the target mailbox is on Exchange 2007. CAS 2013 redirects the client to an Exchange 2007 CAS. This is mandatory because Exchange 2007 can't accept a proxied Outlook Web App connection from Exchange 2013.

- When a client requests an Outlook Web App connection and the target mailbox is on Exchange 2013 in another Active Directory site, but only if the ExternalURL property is set on the foreign-site CAS. For example, suppose that a client connects to an

Internet-facing CAS named HSV-CAS04 on an Active Directory site named Huntsville, but the active copy of the mailbox is actually on a Mailbox server named PNS-MBX02 in the Pensacola Active Directory site. If ExternalURL is set on PNS-MBX02, then HSV-CAS04 will return that URL to the client so it can connect directly. If ExternalURL is not set on the Pensacola server, or if it is set to the same value as is set on HSV-CAS04, then HSV-CAS04 will proxy the connection instead.

There's another case when the 2013 CAS role should redirect. When a user types the FQDN of the CAS without including /owa on the end, a new redirection module provided by Exchange and loaded into IIS automatically redirects the user to Outlook Web App. This is a labor saver for users; although it was possible to do the same thing in Exchange 2007 and Exchange 2010, it required manual configuration.

CAS coexistence and migration

From a coexistence perspective, it is critical to update your Exchange organization so that all incoming CAS traffic flows first to an Exchange 2013 CAS. This is probably the biggest required change you'll face from a CAS perspective, although if you are using load balancing and want to take advantage of the end of the requirement for affinity, those changes will run a close second.

Routing inbound traffic to the 2013 CAS role

Making this change is mostly a matter of configuring systems other than Exchange. In most environments, you'll have to do some or all of the following to get traffic flowing to the right place:

- Evaluate your Active Directory site topology to decide whether there are any aspects of it you want to change.

- Obtain and install certificates that match the appropriate server names (see the "Certificate management" section later in the chapter for more on this).

- Be ready to update your reverse proxy, firewall, and/or load balancer to send inbound connections to the new CAS servers. (However, don't actually make the updates until the new servers are installed!)

- Review your internal and external DNS configuration and make any necessary updates.

After you have completed these prerequisite steps, you can install a single Exchange 2013 CAS and verify that traffic is flowing as you would expect. Where should you install that CAS? Microsoft recommends putting it on whichever Internet-facing site currently handles

Autodiscover requests, because that will allow the 2013 CAS to handle Autodiscover requests correctly for mailboxes on Exchange 2013 servers and whatever earlier versions you have around.

After installing that first CAS, you need to verify that it is reachable from the Internet, using whatever external URLs you want it to use. This will probably involve using Set-OutlookAnywhere and the Set-*VirtualDirectory cmdlets. At that point, you can add more Exchange 2013 servers, either as individual or multirole servers.

Removing ambiguous URLs

In Exchange 2010, Microsoft recommended that the CAS array objects should not be directly resolvable by external clients. One way to achieve this was to implement split-brain DNS, which is what many sites did. Microsoft also recommended assigning separate names for the CAS array object (to which ordinary MAPI RPC clients connect) and the Outlook Anywhere hostname. However, if you assigned the same name to those services, everything would still work fine. That led many administrators to take a shortcut that seemed perfectly reasonable at the time: they set the internal HTTP namespace to the same name as the RPC client access array and then depended on split-brain DNS to keep internal clients from connecting to the external IP address for the array and vice versa. Because that seemed to work well, many of them went ahead and assigned the same externally resolvable FQDN for other services such as Exchange ActiveSync or Outlook Web App.

The problem with this approach is that after you install an Exchange 2013 CAS, your MAPI clients will stop working! Why? They'll eventually try to connect to the single FQDN you have defined, which now points at an Exchange 2013 CAS. The Exchange 2013 CAS won't accept MAPI RPC connections, so those clients won't be able to connect unless they can successfully fall back to Outlook Anywhere; their ability to do so will depend on how the individual client is configured.

The recommended Microsoft way to fix this is to change the name on the CAS array object to a unique value and then update the *RpcClientAccessServer* value on your Exchange 2010 mailbox databases to point to that FQDN. That covers the case of newly created or manu-ally updated Outlook profiles; for the other profiles, enable Outlook Anywhere for all clients and servers *before* you deploy Exchange 2013. By doing so, you ensure that your Outlook clients can successfully connect to the Exchange 2013 CAS even if they are unable to make a MAPI RPC connection. Brian Day at Microsoft has a long post on the Exchange team blog that goes into greater depth on how to resolve this situation, and I encourage you to read it before proceeding with your upgrade from Exchange 2010 to Exchange 2013: *http:// blogs.technet.com/b/exchange/archive/2013/05/23/ambiguous-urls-and-their-effect-on -exchange-2010-to-exchange-2013-migrations.aspx*.

Certificate management

Although both the CAS and Mailbox roles use certificates, the CAS role depends on them much more heavily, which is why I'm talking about them so early in the book. Although Exchange 2013 (like the two preceding versions) installs self-signed certificates on each server as you install it, most organizations find that self-signed certificates don't meet their needs.

How Exchange uses certificates

Choosing the right set of certificates begins with understanding how Exchange uses certificates. The Mailbox and CAS roles each use certificates in a variety of ways:

- To give clients a way to authenticate the identity of a server. This is the most common use, and it's the one that generates the most work for Exchange administrators due to certificate name mismatches or other trust issues that cause user complaints.

- To authenticate a client or device to the server. This use, known as *client certificate authentication*, is interesting because a device that authenticates with a user's certificate doesn't have to send or even have the user's Windows credentials, so a compromised device can't be exploited to gain access to other services.

- To secure SMTP mail in transit by encrypting the SMTP connection with Transport Layer Security (TLS). TLS protection is automatically applied when Exchange servers in the same organization exchange mail; it can also be enabled for communications with external servers. This use is covered in more detail in Chapter 2.

- To give servers a way to authenticate the identity of other servers. This use, known as *mutual TLS*, is primarily of interest when integrating with Lync Server because Lync depends on mutual TLS. See Chapter 8, "Office 365: A whirlwind tour," for more on this use.

Windows, and applications that use it, can also use certificates for other purposes such as IPsec encryption or digitally signing executable code or Windows PowerShell scripts. I won't consider those purposes in the context of Exchange, although I will point out that Exchange does not, and cannot, use the IIS 8.0 centralized certificate store, a nifty feature in Windows Server 2012 that would be of great use if Exchange supported it.

If you only run Exchange for an internal network and never want to allow access from the Internet, the set of self-signed certificates installed as part of the Exchange 2013 setup program is sufficient for your purposes as long as you're willing to put up with a few shortcomings. Outlook Web App and Exchange ActiveSync users will have to install the self-signed certificates or face nagging browser warnings. For domain-joined computers running Windows, you can install the self-signed certificate from your Exchange CAS servers the trusted root certification authorities store on the PC (or use a Group Policy Object to distribute the certificate to multiple PCs around the organization). Afterward, the PCs that have installed the certificate—but only those PCs—will then trust that Exchange CAS server for future connections. Of course, if you want to add or change CAS servers in the future, you'll have to add those certificates, too. Multiply the need to install the self-signed certificates for every CAS server you deploy on every computer and mobile device used to access Outlook Web App, EAS, or EAC, and you can see just how much work you might be setting up for yourself to make the self-signed certificates usable in a production environment. On the upside, the self-signed certificates generated by Exchange 2013 CAS servers when they are installed last for five years, so at least your work will last a reasonable amount of time. Of course, this isn't an acceptable approach for most organizations. Self-signed certificates don't work well for providing services to external clients across the Internet; unless you can persuade other companies to install your self-signed certificates in the trusted root store of their servers, the self-signed certificates created for CAS servers by the Exchange setup program will never be trusted outside your network. The upshot is that these certificates cannot be used to secure client communications from the Internet.

Where to get certificates

If you will not rely on self-signed certificates, that leaves you with two choices: you can plan and deploy a proper installation of the Windows Certificate Services feature on one of your servers and build your own internal public key infrastructure (PKI), or you can buy certificates from a trusted third party. Each approach has its pros and cons.

Buying a third-party certificate costs money. That's the biggest problem with it; each certificate can cost US$300 or more for a one-year validity period. For that money, however, as long as you buy from a trusted company such as Verisign or DigiCert, you get a certificate that will be universally accepted by other organizations and a broad assortment of computers and mobile devices. Be forewarned that some companies charge per certificate, per server; in this case, if you buy a single certificate and install it on three servers, you have to pay for it three times. For example, both Verisign and Thawte license certificates are based on the number of servers that will use them—a cost you should know up front.

Setting up your own PKI doesn't cost anything, and it gives you total control over what certificates are issued and what they're used for. Mistakes are easy to fix because you can always just issue a replacement certificate. If you want to deploy Windows features such as the Encrypting File System (EFS) or support for smart card–based logon, being able to issue your own certificates to users without paying a third party is valuable. However, no one in the outside world will trust your internal CAs, so you'll have to add your CA certificates to the trust list of every remote device or server that should trust it—the same problem you have with self-signed certificates. Of course, you can finesse this problem by paying a third-party CA to issue a certificate to *your* CA, at which point, your certificates are considered trustworthy by anyone who trusts the external CA. This can become expensive quickly, however.

Certificate contents

No matter who issues it, each SSL certificate contains a public and private key that encrypt data exchanged between a server and clients. The CAS provides a copy of its public key to clients that connect to it. The clients can encrypt communications with the public key, and the CAS can decrypt the communications using its private key, so anything sent between client and server is secure. A shared key generated by the client secures data sent from the CAS to the client (see *http://support.microsoft.com/kb/257591* for details on how this connection occurs). The client encrypts the shared key by using the CAS's public key and then transmits this data to the CAS. The CAS can then decrypt the shared key to know how it should encrypt communications so that even if someone were to intercept data packets flowing between client and server, she would not be able to break into the data because she doesn't have the shared key.

In addition to the key material, certificates have a number of embedded attributes, including a validity period, a subject name, and one or more optional subject alternative names (SANs). When you request a certificate for a server, the CA that issues the certificate digitally signs the embedded attributes so they cannot be changed after issuance. If you request a certificate with the wrong name or make some other error in the request, you'll have to have the certificate reissued because you can't just edit it in place. When it's reissued, you still have to install the newly issued certificate on all the servers it was on before. After a reissue, the issuing CA normally revokes the original certificates within 24 hours, meaning that if you don't get the new certificate in place quickly enough, you'll start hearing complaints from users who receive certificate expiration warnings.

What certificates do you need?

The business of deciding what certificates and how many certificates should be deployed can be complex. Here are a number of suggestions to guide the process:

- **Minimize the number of certificates in use**   The more certificates you use, the more it will cost for their purchase and the more complex the environment becomes.

- **Use SAN certificates**   Normal certificates contain a single name, but SAN certificates have multiple SANs, each of which is a hostname. These are simpler to deploy and reduce the number of certificates that are required. For example, a single SAN certificate could contain enough names for a two-node Exchange 2013 deployment: autodiscover.contoso.com, mail.contoso.com, hq-ex01.contoso.com, and hq-ex02 .contoso.com, thus making that single certificate useful for a variety of purposes.

- **Don't use individual computer hostnames as the primary distinguished name for certificates**   Whenever possible, use the names of arrays for Internet and intranet access to services (such as ActiveSync) because these are flexible and expandable.

- **Remember that you can assign different certificates to different purposes**   For example, if you're using unified messaging (UM; see Chapter 6), you'll want the computer name in each certificate, but instead of requesting a public CA SAN certificate for each Mailbox server, you can get a single public certificate with the HTTPS namespaces you're using and then use an internal CA to issue certificates for UM that you can then enable with Enable-ExchangeCertificate.

Requesting and applying certificates

Microsoft recommends using the certificate management tools built into EAC to request and apply certificates, mainly because the wizard interviews you to ask what services the certificate will be used for. Unlike in Exchange 2010, when you finish the wizard, you don't get to see the Exchange Management Shell (EMS) command that the wizard is actually executing, which is too bad. However, the wizard itself is simple to use. It's available in EAC on the Certificates slab of the Servers tab. Pick the server you want from the drop-down menu and then click the plus (+) icon to open the first page of the wizard, where you select whether you're creating a self-signed certificate or a request for a CA-issued certificate (whether private or external). You'll be asked to specify a friendly name for the certificate, whether you want to request a wildcard certificate, and where you want to store the generated certificate request when it's done. Then comes the most important part of the wizard: the page, shown in Figure 1-9, that enables you to specify which services should be included in the certificate. EAC fills in these values according to the external and internal URLs you have set for the virtual directories on the target server. If you don't want a particular service name included as a SAN for the certificate, just leave its value blank.

The next step in the wizard is shown in Figure 1-10. The wizard shows you the list of SANs it will include in the certificate request. This list is drawn directly from the list of services you specified in the preceding step; add or remove a service, and you'll see the list of SANs change.

After you're happy with the list of SANs, you still have a couple of wizard pages to fill out. You have to specify some information about the organization requesting the certificate, and you have to provide a name and path where the request should be stored. At that point, EAC will generate the actual certificate request and store it; you'll need to refer to the instructions provided by your certificate issuer to submit the request and retrieve the completed certificate.

Figure 1-9 Selecting services for a new certificate in EAC

Figure 1-10 Reviewing the list of SANs for a new certificate in EAC

Of course, if you prefer, you can use the New-ExchangeCertificate cmdlet to create a request for a certificate that you can send to your preferred certificate vendor. For example, this command creates a request for a SAN certificate that covers three hostnames:

```
New-ExchangeCertificate –GenerateRequest –Path 'C:\Temp\Cert.req' –SubjectName
'c=US;O=Contoso ;CN=Mail.contoso.com' –DomainName 'mail.contoso.com,
autodiscover.contoso.com, legacy.contoso.com' –PrivateKeyExportable $True
```

After you have the certificate in hand, you add it to the certificate store on the target machine. The private key is generated when the request is made. This key remains on the server that generates the request and is not provided to the CA. However, the PrivateKeyExportable flag indicates that you want to allow the private key to be exported and moved to another machine; this allows the single SAN certificate to be used on multiple hosts if mail.contoso.com, autodiscover.contoso.com, and legacy.contoso.com are actually separate machines. When you receive the SSL certificate, you can import it into Exchange with the Import-ExchangeCertificate cmdlet or by clicking the ellipsis (...) icon in the certificate toolbar in EAC. At that point, you can assign the certificate for use by the services you identified earlier, using either the Enable-ExchangeCertificate cmdlet or EAC.

INSIDE OUT   Minimizing the number of hostnames

In addition, it's a good idea to minimize the number of hostnames that clients have to deal with by using split DNS to provide different addresses for the same name for Internet and intranet access. This enables you to have the same name (such as mail.contoso.com) no matter from where a client accesses the service.

Moving mail

The CAS role is a critical part of the Exchange feature set, but you could certainly argue that the transport system is just as important—without transport, there's no way to transfer mail between servers, and we'd be back in the days of Microsoft Mail and Lotus cc:Mail, when individual servers were disconnected islands of email use. In the next chapter, you'll dig into the guts of the Exchange 2013 transport system and see how Exchange implements this important functionality.

The Exchange transport system

Over time, Exchange Server has evolved significantly. Early versions combined directory, message transport, and message storage services on a single server (for instance, Exchange 5.5). Later versions split those functions into separate roles that could be collocated or placed on separate servers, as with the five server roles included in Exchange 2007 and Exchange 2010. As you learned in Chapter 1, "Client access servers," though, Exchange 2013 consolidates the number of server roles back down to two: client access servers and Mailbox servers. This consolidation means that some functions, such as mail transport, are actually handled by both roles, at least in part.

A quick introduction to Exchange transport

Exchange 2007 transformed message transport by introducing the Hub Transport role as a central nexus for all messages. Every message sent or received in an Exchange 2007 or Exchange 2010 organization is guaranteed to pass through at least one hub transport server, and every message in an Exchange 2013 server is likewise guaranteed to pass through the transport components on at least one Mailbox server. This guarantee means that Exchange can ensure that several valuable actions take place:

- All messages are consistently processed according to whatever policies are currently in place. These policies can include both inbound and outbound filtering, the application of data loss prevention policies, or the application of rules that redirect, modify, or block messages.

- The transport path for all messages is logged on every Mailbox server a message touches. This enables tracing the path of a message from origin to destination, a very useful ability when people start asking why they aren't getting mail.

- Mailbox servers can keep temporary copies of messages until they receive confirmation that the message has been delivered to a downstream server. If a temporary failure keeps the message from being delivered immediately, the temporary copy can be used to send messages along a different route.

- Messages for a given mailbox are delivered only to the active copy of the mailbox database that hosts that mailbox.

- Message flow within the organization and between the organization and the outside world can be monitored and managed.

In terms of the Exchange transport system, the focus for a messaging administrator is to make sure of the following:

- The default connectors that Exchange creates during setup are configured to meet the needs of the organization.

- The messaging system can handle outages of any duration gracefully.

- Any safeguards necessary to meet regulatory or legal requirements are in place.

- Any custom connectors required to connect Exchange 2013 to clients, applications, devices such as copiers or scanners, or other messaging systems are in place and operational.

- Out-of-the-ordinary situations are handled effectively.

- Data required for monitoring and reporting are gathered and available.

With these points in mind, consider how things work inside the Exchange transport system.

The transport pipeline: An overview

Microsoft refers to the *transport pipeline* throughout the Exchange developer and administrative documentation. This term can be a bit confusing because it can refer to two separate but related concepts. At a high level, the pipeline consists of the components illustrated in Figure 2-1, which shows the Client Access and Mailbox roles as logically separate even though they can be, and often are, on the same Exchange 2013 server. Here's how inbound message flow works at this level of abstraction:

1. Inbound messages arrive on a receive connector. These messages can originate from the Internet, other Exchange organizations, or other servers within the same organization, or they may be placed in the drop directory.

2. The Front End Transport (FET) service (MSExchangeFrontendTransport.exe) proxies the message to the Transport service on a Mailbox server.

3. The Transport service (MSExchangeTransport.exe) accepts the proxied connection. Microsoft describes the Transport service as "virtually identical to the Hub Transport server role in previous versions of Exchange," meaning that it's responsible for categorizing messages, performing message routing, applying transport rules, and inspecting or modifying message headers and contents.

4. The Transport service establishes an SMTP connection to the Mailbox Transport Delivery service (MSExchangeDelivery.exe). This service accepts incoming messages and delivers them to the information store, using a remote procedure call (RPC). Think of it as an adapter between the RPC-based store and the wide world of SMTP; the Transport and FET services don't communicate directly with the store service. In fact, the only place RPCs are used in Exchange 2013 transport is when the Mailbox Transport Delivery and Mailbox Transport Submission services are communicating with the store. All interserver communications for transport purposes are performed using SMTP.

Outbound message traffic follows a roughly similar path. When a user sends a new message, the client first stores the message in a folder: the Sent Items folder for users running Microsoft Outlook in cached mode, the Outbox for users running Outlook in online mode (or Outlook 2011 for Mac OS X), or the Drafts folder for Outlook Web App. The Mailbox Transport Submission service picks up the message from the originating folder with RPC. The submission service then sends it to the Transport service, either on the same server or on another, at which point it is treated like any other incoming message.

There are a few exceptions to these processes. For example, applications or administrators might inject messages directly into the Mailbox server by putting them into the pickup or replay directories. In general, though, this basic workflow describes how messages move through the transport system.

Chapter 2

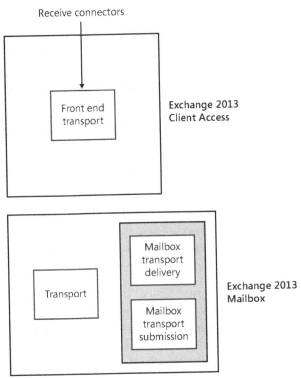

Figure 2-1 A high-level view of the Exchange 2013 message transport pipeline

Message routing: An overview

The message routing implementation of Exchange 2013 differs in some important ways from that of its predecessors. In Exchange 2010, the Active Directory site was the primary boundary for message routing; that is, Exchange 2010 servers within a single site assume that they can communicate without restriction to route messages. This is very similar to the way message routing worked in Exchange 5.5; the Exchange 2000 and Exchange 2003 concepts of routing groups and routing group connectors are thankfully gone. Exchange 2013 continues to use the Active Directory site as a unit of message routing scope, but it also adds a new scope: that of the database availability group (DAG). Standalone Mailbox servers (those that are not DAG members) use site membership as a routing boundary, whereas DAG members use DAG membership instead. This is an interesting change, but it makes sense in light of the other architectural changes in Exchange 2013. In addition, DAG members are assumed to have robust connectivity to each other, even for a DAG which spans multiple Active Directory sites.

On standalone servers, it seems obvious that an incoming message for a mailbox should be delivered only to the database that hosts that mailbox. However, in DAGs, incoming messages for a mailbox should only be delivered to the active copy of the database that contains that mailbox. The Mailbox Transport Delivery service is the only component that can deliver messages to a mailbox database, so the routing architecture needs to provide a way for a sending server to identify which server's Mailbox Transport Delivery service should eventually receive the message. This need is filled by the Active Manager component, thanks to its knowledge of which servers host active copies of each database.

Another major side effect of the use of DAGs as a message routing boundary is that the DAG itself provides resilience for the Transport service. If you stretch a DAG across multiple physical sites, any DAG member server can handle message transport, essentially giving you stretched transport without any additional deployment or configuration work.

The Transport service is responsible for message routing; the component known as the categorizer determines the next hop for a message and then delivers it to the appropriate queue for the selected destination. This queue might result in SMTP sending the message to another server or to the Mailbox Transport Delivery service for delivery to a local mailbox database. In fact, three types of destinations are known to Exchange 2013: mailbox databases, mail connectors, and distribution group expansion servers. Every message that leaves the Transport service on an Exchange 2013 Mailbox server will be bound for one of those three destinations; of course, any of them can end up forwarding mail to a further destination.

Each of these destination types has a set of servers known as a *delivery group* that can accept mail for that destination. For example, the delivery group for a mailbox database contains all the servers of the same Exchange version as the server that holds the target mailbox database in the same Active Directory site. The delivery group for a connector contains all the Exchange 2013 Mailbox servers and Exchange 2010 or Exchange 2007 hub transport servers that could deliver messages to that destination. Delivery groups are discussed in more depth in the "Delivery groups" section later in this chapter.

Exchange 2013 transport architecture in depth

Figure 2-3, adapted from Microsoft documentation, shows a more detailed representation of the Exchange transport architecture. The basic design discussed in the preceding introductory sections is still there, but many additional components are worth discussing. First, here are some new vocabulary words:

- *Agents* are logically separate pieces of code that transform or process messages in some way. They implement the business logic that tells Exchange how to categorize, route, and deliver messages under various conditions. For example, the anti-spam and anti-malware filtering components of Exchange (described in Chapter 5, "Message hygiene and security") are implemented as protocol agents. Routing agents, delivery agents, and submission agents are all used at various points in the transport life cycle. Except for the message hygiene–related agents, in general, you can't directly add, remove, or configure the agents that ship as part of Exchange. However, Microsoft provides a set of application programming interfaces (APIs) that enable you (or anyone) to write special-purpose transport agents, and you can add them to or remove them from the pipeline.

- *Queues* are familiar to experienced Exchange administrators; they provide a logi-cal structure for predictable processing of messages by imposing a first-in, first-out (FIFO) order with a twist. Each destination can have 20 messages queued per connec-tion. If you have 80 messages in a queue for contoso.com, Exchange will open four connections and try to send messages 1, 21, 41, and 61. Depending on the size of the messages, it's possible that messages 21–40 might be delivered before message 1 arrives if that message is large. The queues you see in Exchange 2013 are different in some important ways from previous versions, as you'll see later in the chapter.

- *Events* are occurrences that trigger action by an agent or service. For example, an internal transport event known as OnMessageSend is fired when a message is queued for sending. Transport agents take action on messages when these events occur.

With that vocabulary in mind, take a look at Figure 2-2, which shows the out-put of the Get-TransportPipeline cmdlet on a multirole Exchange 2013 CU2 server. Get-TransportPipeline gives you an overview of the current arrangement of the pipeline on a server as long as at least one message has passed through the transport system on that server since its services were started. The left-side column shows each of the transport events available in the pipeline, and the TransportAgents column indicates which transport agents are activated when each event is triggered. Notice that most of the transport agent action happens with the events associated with receiving messages: OnSubmittedMessage, OnResolvedMessage, OnRoutedMessage, and OnCategorizedMessage.

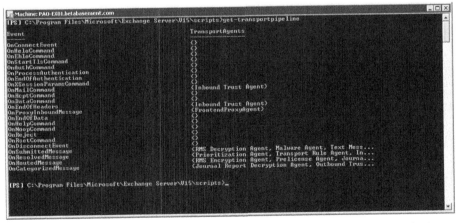

Figure 2-2 Get-TransportPipeline, showing the currently registered transport agents in the pipeline

Microsoft identifies four primary tasks of the Transport service on Mailbox servers. You can think of these tasks as parts of the Transport service; each part has its own subcomponents, some of which are configurable and visible and others of which function more or less invisibly:

- **SMTP receive**   This part of the Transport service receives inbound messages, performs the anti-malware and anti-spam scanning discussed in Chapter 5, and applies transport rules. If the message makes it through this process without being rejected or generating a nondelivery report (NDR), it goes to the message submission queue.

- **Message submission queue**   This component accepts messages from the SMTP receive component and holds them for categorization. It also picks up messages from the Pickup and Replay directories, which provide a means for your own applications and other components of Exchange to submit messages to Exchange for processing without using SMTP.

- **The categorizer**   This component processes messages from the submission queue in FIFO order. It then has to decide where to send them. To make this decision, the categorizer resolves recipient names, including expanding distribution groups, resolves message destinations, and applies any mail flow restrictions set at the organization level. After those tasks have been completed, the categorizer queues the message for delivery to the next hop, which can be a DAG, a mailbox database, a server in another Active Directory site or forest, or an external SMTP domain.

- **SMTP send**   This is sort of a generic task because the actual process of sending the message to the defined next hop might involve submitting it to a local mailbox database through the Mailbox Transport Delivery service, moving it to the Transport service on another server or to the Front End Transport service on a CAS for delivery to a remote domain on the Internet.

The diagram shown in Figure 2-3 makes this arrangement more explicit; it shows the FET, Transport, Mailbox Transport Submission, and Mailbox Transport Delivery services in context, including links between them.

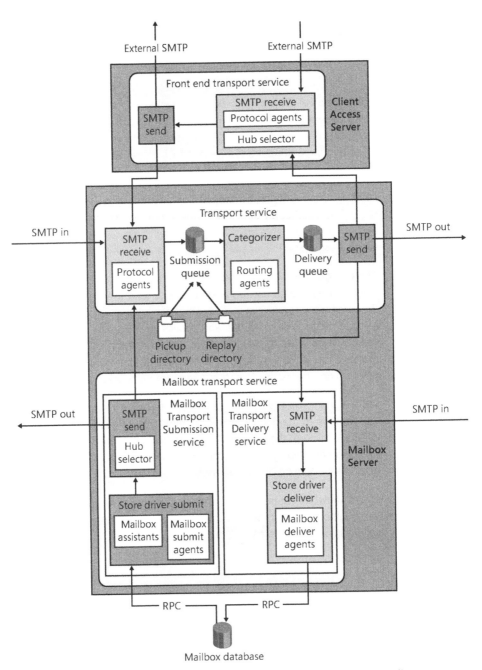

Figure 2-3 A more detailed view of the Exchange 2013 message transport pipeline

Gwinnett Tech Library

The arrangement of mail flow between these services has some interesting consequences.

- If multiple Mailbox servers are available in the target delivery group, the Mailbox Transport Submission service selects one on a load-balancing basis. (There are some additional nuances to this process, which is described in more detail in the "Exchange 2013 and Active Directory" section later in this chapter.)

- Outgoing messages leave by SMTP to other Mailbox servers or through connectors as defined by the administrator. Older versions of Exchange supported a variety of gateways and services for interoperation with fax systems, Lotus Notes, and so on, but the interfaces these services used are no longer supported in Exchange 2013. If you have a business requirement to remain connected to earlier systems, you must keep at least one older Exchange server around to provide that connectivity, or move to using SMTP as the transport mechanism for those systems—a better idea overall.

- The Transport service applies message policies when the categorizer has expanded the set of addresses for messages. The policies are applied through transport rules that can perform processing from the mundane (apply disclaimer text to outgoing messages) to complex (block messages from traveling between different groups of users). The Transport service also invokes any journal rules you define to capture message traffic at this stage.

- All the Mailbox servers in the organization share a common transport configuration that dictates settings such as the maximum message size Exchange can transport, the maximum number of recipients on an incoming message, and the connectors that are available to Exchange (including connectors hosted by Exchange 2010 or Exchange 2013 edge servers). Active Directory holds the configuration settings, including details of transport and journal rules; many of these settings can be manipulated with the Set-TransportConfig cmdlet.

- Individual Exchange 2010 Edge Transport servers receive their configuration with Active Directory by means of a push subscription process.

- For Exchange organizations that contain both Exchange 2007 and later versions, transport rules are stored in version-specific containers in Active Directory. Installing Exchange 2013 copies any existing transport or journal rules from the earlier version to the new one, but after that point, the rules are not synchronized. As Exchange 2013 creates new rules, they are stamped with the version number of Exchange (that is, 15.0.516.32 for Exchange 2013 RTM), and Exchange 2010 ignores the rule with a newer version so there's no conflict. This process is necessary because new versions of Exchange may introduce new predicates and actions that shouldn't be exposed to older versions because they cannot be interpreted. Because of this version-based separation, you should move as much transport processing as possible to the newest version of Exchange that you have deployed in your environment as soon as feasible.

The actual implementation of the transport function in Exchange 2013 depends on four services: Front End Transport, Transport, Mailbox Transport Submission, and Mailbox Transport Delivery.

The Front End Transport service

The Front End Transport (FET) service seems to do very little; it handles all inbound and outbound SMTP traffic for clients (including IMAP or POP clients, devices such as scanners, and line-of-business applications) and outside systems. In this role, FET is the first point on your network that SMTP traffic touches after it passes through the firewall or whatever other perimeter network solution you have in place. As with the other services that run on the CAS role, the FET service doesn't store any data; it maintains no queues and is essentially stateless (meaning that it doesn't maintain state information for client communications). In fact, the only real persistent data the FET service generates are the SMTP protocol logs it can optionally generate. It proxies connections only.

Installing the CAS role causes Exchange to generate a set of default receive connectors for the FET to use. (See the "Receive connectors" section later in this chapter for more details.) FET also provides an outbound SMTP service, an often-overlooked aspect of its design. (Most Exchange administrators are more concerned with how inbound mail gets in than how outbound mail gets out!) Mailbox servers send their outbound messages through the FET so that all SMTP traffic leaving an Exchange organization originates only from its CAS servers.

INSIDE OUT   Outbound mail behaves differently

Exchange 2013 won't send any outbound mail from your organization to the Internet until you configure a send connector to do so. As previously noted, the default receive connectors will accept inbound Internet mail. This is the opposite of the behavior in Exchange 2010, which would happily send outbound mail but wouldn't receive it until you granted anonymous users permission to use a receive connector.

The Transport service

The Transport service handles most of the functionality of the Hub Transport service from Exchange 2007 and Exchange 2010, plus new features introduced in Exchange 2013. That means that this service is responsible for processing transport, journal, and data loss prevention rules among its other duties.

The Transport service maintains one queue for each internal Exchange mailbox database. The nature of DAGs means that the Transport service doesn't need to know or care which server is hosting the database, just what the target database is. The Mailbox Transport Delivery service takes care of finding the correct database, as you will see in the following section.

The Mailbox Transport Delivery service

When the Mailbox Transport Delivery service wants to deliver a message addressed to an internal recipient, it first has to determine what database the recipient's mailbox is in. This is a straightforward Active Directory lookup the FET or the Transport service can perform; in either case, the properties are delivered with the new SMTP MESSAGECONTEXT verb that Exchange 2013 supports. Armed with that information, the service's next step is to figure out which server currently holds the active copy of that mailbox database. If the service is running on a DAG member and the recipient is in a database within the same DAG, this requires the Mailbox Transport Delivery service to query Active Manager, which returns the necessary information; the service then uses SMTP to deliver the message to the Transport service if the target server is remote or to the Mailbox Transport Submission service if the current server holds the active copy of the mailbox database.

The Mailbox Transport Submission service

The Mailbox Transport Submission service has only one job: it retrieves messages from mailboxes by using RPC and then submits them to the Transport service by using SMTP. To do this, it must take advantage of the fact that messages when submitted are stored in a predictable place in the user's mailbox, as described earlier; the client puts the message in a well-known location so that it can be received and submitted.

The role of connectors

Connectors in Exchange 2013 function in a very similar fashion to their Exchange 2007 and Exchange 2010 counterparts. Connectors are still logical objects that are stored in Active Directory and read by the Transport services, so they know what logical connections are intended to exist, and certain connector types might still cause third-party software to be loaded and executed by the transport system. In fact, the primary difference is that most of the options for connectors now must be set in Exchange Management Shell (EMS) because Exchange Administration Center (EAC) doesn't include all the options that were accessible in past versions of Exchange Management Console (EMC). As EAC evolves, hopefully some of these options will return.

You manage connectors in the Mail Flow section of EAC; there are separate tabs for managing send and receive connectors (Figure 2-4). When you select a connector, EAC helpfully shows a summary of the connector's options on the right side of the EAC window.

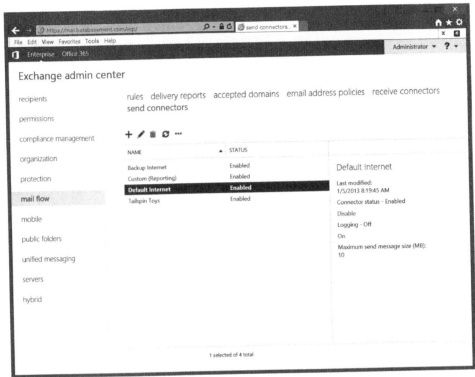

Figure 2-4 Manage send and receive connectors through the Mail Flow section of EAC

There are a few differences in the way send connectors work compared to previous versions. Probably the biggest is that linked connectors, the feature that allowed you to manage send and receive connectors to the same domain as a single unit, have been deprecated. Instead, now you must manage send and receive connectors as independent entities. In addition, the maximum message size on send connectors now defaults to 35 MB instead of 10 MB, a reflection of the growing prevalence of large email attachments. Why 35 MB? If you MIME-encode a message with a 25 MB attachment, it turns out to be about 35 MB. (Keep in mind that there may be separate size limits, larger or smaller than the ones on your send connectors, for mailboxes, organizations, and other connectors.)

Another difference is that the interface you use in EAC to create connectors asks you to specify the purpose of the connector; EAC enables you to create only SMTP send and receive connectors, so the purpose has to involve exchanging mail by using SMTP with servers on the Internet, with internal applications, with trusted partners, or with non-Outlook clients. The options you see during the connector creation process might change according to the intended usage you specify for the connector. For example, when you create a partner connector, you must use MX delivery; the smart host options are disabled, presumably because all mail on that connector will be going directly to the partner.

Send connectors

Send connectors are logical conduits through which outbound mail flows. When you create a send connector, its definition is stored in Active Directory, and that connector may be used by any Mailbox server in the organization. Unlike prior versions of Exchange, you won't see an event log warning if your connector has multiple source servers from different Active Directory sites. The most obvious use for a send connector is to send mail out to the Internet; this requires you to create a new connector specifically for Internet delivery. However, you can create send connectors that route to any specific SMTP domain (or set of domains).

Basic send connector options

The basic process of creating a new send connector requires four steps:

1. Give the connector a name and choose a type (Figure 2-5). You can choose to create a connector to be used for custom applications, to send mail to servers within your organization, to send mail to the Internet, or to send mail to trusted external domains such as business partners.

2. Specify whether you want it to pass mail through a single smart host or to deliver mail by performing Domain Name System (DNS) MX record lookups. Depending on the connector type you chose in the first step, you might not be able to enable smart host delivery. If you enable smart host delivery, you'll be asked to specify what kind of authentication mechanism to use when Exchange connects to the smart host. It could be that you have an SMTP server that's set up as an open relay for general use within the company, in which case, you won't have to use authentication, or you might have to provide a username and password for basic authentication. The smart host can be another Exchange server; if so, you'd use Exchange Server Authentication, or it might support IPsec for encrypted communication between the two servers.

   Along with the choice of whether to use smart host or direct MX delivery is a new option, Use The External DNS Lookup Settings On Servers With Transport Roles, which appears on the second page of the New Send Connector process (see Figure 2-6). This check box controls whether Exchange uses the specific DNS settings associated with its source servers (as described later in this section) or the Windows-provided DNS servers configured on the server's network interface cards (NICs).

3. Specify the address spaces you want this connector to handle. The simplest address space is "*", indicating that the connector can match any SMTP domain; whichever address spaces you specify for the connector will be used to define which messages the connector may accept. The Scoped Send Connector check box that appears on the address space page controls whether the connector is available for routing by any hub transport or Mailbox server in the organization. The default is to leave the check box cleared. However, if you select the check box, Exchange constrains the connector so that only Mailbox servers on the same site as the source server can use it for routing. Servers outside the site will not evaluate the connector as a possible target. Exchange 2010 would automatically choose a source server for you, but EAC requires you to pick one when you create the connector; you can always change the scoping setting or the list of source servers with Set-SendConnector or EAC later.

INSIDE OUT The cost value assigned to an address space

Each address space is given a value for the cost of the connection. One (1) represents the best possible connection value, and the range goes up to one hundred (100). The cost enables Exchange to differentiate between two routes. For example, two smart host relays might be available within an organization: one defined for the America site and one for the Europe site. Servers on the Europe site will have a natural affinity with the smart host relay defined on that site and will ignore the one defined in America even if the address cost is equal. This is logical because of the rule that a connector on the local site is always used whenever possible and because the additional site link cost of routing to America always makes that connector more expensive than the one available on the Europe site.

4. Specify which servers can send messages over this connector; the servers you define are considered source servers for the connector, so other servers can pass messages to them for onward routing.

When you've completed these steps, the connector will be added to Active Directory and become immediately available (pending Active Directory replication delays) for use by all the servers that are allowed to use it.

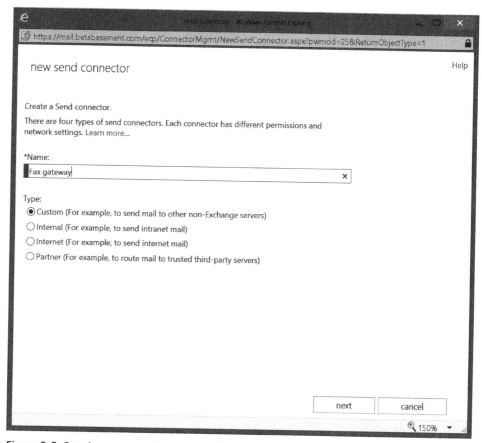

Figure 2-5 Creating a new send connector gives you four choices for the connector's intended use

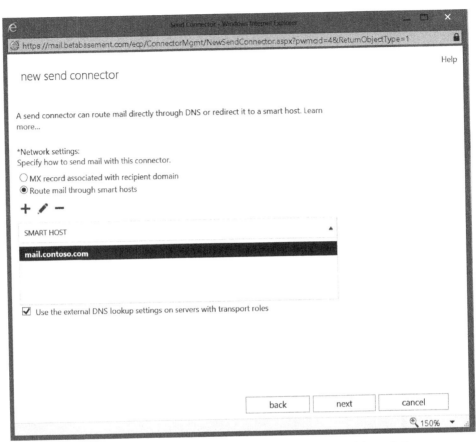

Figure 2-6 Creating a new send connector that specifies routing all mail through the mail.contoso.com smart host

INSIDE OUT   Centralizing outbound mail flow

When you create a send connector, you're giving implicit permission to the servers defined as connector sources to send mail directly to the destination. This might not be what you want. For example, consider a large network that has Exchange 2013 Mailbox servers on five physical sites, with multiple send connectors defined on each site for efficiency and redundancy. By default, that means messages leaving the network can appear to originate from the IP addresses of any of the Mailbox servers associated with the connectors. In such a situation, you might want to force the Mailbox servers to pass their messages through a proxy beforehand. You can tell Exchange to do this by selecting the Proxy Through Client Access Server check box on the connector properties page or by using the Set-SendConnector –FrontEndProxyEnabled cmdlet; when this option is set, servers using the connector proxy their messages through FET on a CAS on the same Active Directory site. That mail will appear to the outside as though it originated with the CAS. This may turn out to be a significant issue when you define SRV records (as described in Chapter 5), or when other servers attempt to perform DNS checks to verify the identity of your servers—make sure that you have correct external DNS data registered for whichever servers originate your outbound mail.

Send connectors have a large number of other options that are not currently displayed or accessible through EAC. The output of Get-SendConnector shows them, like this:

```
Get-SendConnector -id "Default Internet" | fl
```

```
AddressSpaces                      : {SMTP:*;1}
AuthenticationCredential           :
CloudServicesMailEnabled           : False
Comment                            :
ConnectedDomains                   : {}
ConnectionInactivityTimeOut        : 00:10:00
DNSRoutingEnabled                  : True
DomainSecureEnabled                : False
Enabled                            : True
ErrorPolicies                      : Default
ForceHELO                          : False
Fqdn                               :
FrontendProxyEnabled               : False
HomeMTA                            : Microsoft MTA
HomeMtaServerId                    : PAO-EX01
Identity                           : Default Internet
IgnoreSTARTTLS                     : False
IsScopedConnector                  : False
IsSmtpConnector                    : True
MaxMessageSize                     : 10 MB (10,485,760 bytes)
Name                               : Default Internet
Port                               : 25
ProtocolLoggingLevel               : None
RequireOorg                        : False
RequireTLS                         : False
SmartHostAuthMechanism             : None
SmartHosts                         : {}
SmartHostsString                   :
SmtpMaxMessagesPerConnection       : 20
SourceIPAddress                    : 0.0.0.0
SourceRoutingGroup                 : Exchange Routing Group (DWBGZMFD01QNBJR)
SourceTransportServers             : {PAO-EX02, PAO-EX01}
TlsAuthLevel                       :
```

```
TlsCertificateName              :
TlsDomain                       :
UseExternalDNSServersEnabled    : False
```

Most of these properties have self-evident results; for example, MaxMessageSize and ConnectionInactivityTimeOut are descriptive names, and it's easy to imagine what they control. If you need to change any settings, you can do it with the Set-SendConnector command. Assume that you want to change the maximum message size that flows across the connector to 25 MB and change the time period after which a connection is dropped for inactivity to five minutes. The command is:

```
Set-SendConnector –Identity 'Default Internet' –MaxMessageSize 25MB
-ConnectionInactivityTimeOut 00:05
```

Receive connectors

Receive connectors are conceptually much simpler than send connectors. Each receive connector listens on the specific IP address and port you assign it, determines whether an incoming connection is from the range of IP addresses with which it's allowed to communicate, and carries out SMTP conversations when such connections are established. Receive connectors use *permission groups* to determine whether the sender is permitted to use the connector. A permission group is a predefined set of permissions granted on an object (in this case, the connector) to a class of security principals, such as "anyone who has an Exchange mailbox" (Exchange users) or "any other Exchange server in this organization" (Exchange servers). This model is familiar because it's how you assign permissions on NTFS objects: put users into groups, nest groups as appropriate, and then assign permissions to the groups. You can find details of all the permission groups, and the permissions each includes, in TechNet at *http://technet.microsoft.com/en-us/library/jj673053(v=exchg.150) .aspx*. As an example, Table 2-1 describes the permissions included in the AnonymousUsers and ExchangeUsers permission groups.

TABLE 2-1 Example permission groups

Permission Group	Security Principal	Included Permissions
AnonymousUsers	Anonymous User Account	Ms-Exch-SMTP-Submit Ms-Exch-SMTP-Accept-Any-Sender MS-Exch-SMTP-Accept-Authoritative-Domain-Sender Ms-Exch-Accept-Headers-Routing
ExchangeUsers	Authenticated User Accounts	Ms-Exch-SMTP-Submit Ms-Exch-SMTP-Accept-Any-Recipient Ms-Exch-Bypass-Anti-Spam Ms-Exch-Accept-Headers-Routing

When you install the CAS role, you get three connectors. The first, named Default Frontend serverName, uses the Internet-standard TCP port 25 for SMTP traffic. In a welcome change from Exchange 2007 and Exchange 2010, the standard SMTP connector accepts anonymous inbound mail by default; you therefore don't have to do anything to enable your CAS servers to receive email from the Internet. The Client Frontend serverName connector is intended for use by clients; it listens on TCP port 587 and only accepts Transport Layer Security (TLS)–protected or Secure Sockets Layer (SSL)–protected traffic. A third connector, named Outbound Proxy Frontend serverName, is intended to receive messages from send connectors on Mailbox servers.

Exchange 2013 automatically creates receive connectors for you as part of setup. Which connectors you get depends on which server roles you install. On a Mailbox server, two connectors are created:

- The Default *serverName* connector accepts SMTP traffic from servers inside the organization. On a multirole server, it listens on TCP port 2525; on a Mailbox-only server, it listens on TCP port 25.

- The Client Proxy *serverName* connector accepts connections on TCP port 465 from messages received by the Client serverName Receive Connector on CAS servers only.

Both of these connector types use nonstandard ports, and both have authentication settings that allow them to accept only messages from Exchange servers and authenticated users in the local Active Directory forest. However, they have no IP address restrictions. Clients shouldn't connect to them directly; instead, clients should be configured to connect to the client connector that listens on TCP 587, and that connector will proxy connections as necessary to the Client Proxy connector.

If you run Get-ReceiveConnector on an unmodified server, the result shows all five default receive connectors, like this:

```
Get-ReceiveConnector -server pao-ex02
```

Identity	Bindings	Enabled
PAO-EX02\Default PAO-EX02	{0.0.0.0:2525, [::]:2525}	True
PAO-EX02\Client Proxy PAO-EX02	{[::]:465, 0.0.0.0:465}	True
PAO-EX02\Default Frontend PAO-EX02	{[::]:25, 0.0.0.0:25}	True
PAO-EX02\Outbound Proxy Frontend PAO...	{[::]:717, 0.0.0.0:717}	True
PAO-EX02\Client Frontend PAO-EX02	{[::]:587, 0.0.0.0:587}	True

Each receive connector also has an attribute known as TransportRole; this attribute can take on one of two values, HubTransport or FrontEndTransport, that indicate how the connector is to be used. You can't change this value for the default connectors, though you have to specify it if you create your own (and after specifying it, you can't change it there either).

Speaking of which, Microsoft mentions several times in its documentation that a "typical installation" won't need any additional receive connectors; as you can see from the listings, the Default Frontend PAO-EX02 connector is ready to receive TCP port 25 traffic from all IPv4 and IPv6 addresses. However, you might want to create new connectors to enforce specific permissions or handle traffic from certain servers or ports in a particular way. Before you consider creating a new receive connector, you should ask yourself the following questions:

1. What server will host the new connector?

2. What transport role will the target server fulfill? If you have a multirole server, a transport listener already is on TCP port 2525, but if you create a new receive connector for transport bound to port 25, both FET and Transport will listen on port 25 at the same time. This cannot happen, so you get unpredictable results. (The service that starts first listens on the port; the other one does not.) To fix this, you must avoid creating additional connectors using the default ports on a multirole server.

3. What function does the new connector serve? Will it connect two internal Exchange organizations, handle other internal SMTP traffic, connect Exchange 2013 to Exchange 2003, or have another use?

4. What special settings such as the maximum size of inbound messages apply to the connector?

5. What permissions are necessary for clients that will use the receive connector?

After you've done so, you can create a new receive connector with EAC or EMS. The process for doing so in EAC is straightforward as long as you understand what it's actually asking you; when you open the new Receive Connector page in EAC (Figure 2-7), you have to specify the connector name, whether it's a hub or FET connector, and its type. The type you pick determines the permissions Exchange applies to the connector as well as the default settings. The New Receive Connector process offers the following types:

- **Custom**   Allows the greatest flexibility over the use of the connector. A connector of this type can be used for many purposes, including cross-forest connections and connections to other SMTP-based mail systems that operate within the firewall.

- **Internal**   Used for connections between this Exchange organization and other Exchange organizations that operate within the firewall. When you create an internal connector using EAC, you can't define the port on which it listens.

- **Internet**   Used to allow unencumbered connections from external SMTP servers.

- **Partner**   Used for TLS-secured connections with specified partner domains. (See the discussion in the "TLS security" section later in this chapter.)

- **Client**   Used to support POP3 and IMAP4 client connections or, perhaps, devices such as scanners or copiers that can send mail by using SMTP.

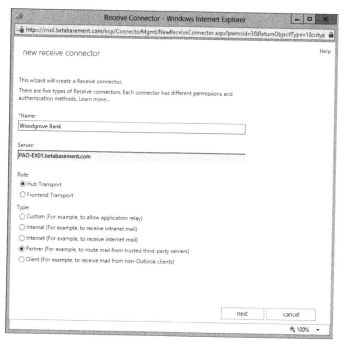

Figure 2-7 Creating a new receive connector for partner traffic from Woodgrove Bank

The type that you choose is reflected in the settings visible on the Security page of the connector properties in EAC or in the output of Get-ReceiveConnector; each type of connector has its own characteristic combination of assigned permission groups and authentication methods. Receive connectors support seven authentication mechanisms, as shown in Table 2-2. The Default *serverName*, Client Proxy *serverName*, Default Frontend *serverName*, and Outbound Proxy Frontend *serverName* connectors all support the TLS, Integrated, BasicAuth, and BasicAuthRequireTLS methods. All except the Client Frontend connector also support ExchangeServer authentication.

TABLE 2-2 Authentication mechanisms for receive connectors

Authentication Mechanism	Description
None	No authentication.
TLS	The connector advertises that it supports TLS and will accept TLS requests; this mode requires you to configure the connector with a specific certificate, which will be offered to the remote end.
Integrated	NTLM and Kerberos (Integrated Windows) authentication. Only useful with other servers in the same forest.
BasicAuth	Basic authentication. Requires an authenticated logon, which is evaluated like any other domain logon.
BasicAuthRequireTLS	Basic authentication over a connection that has been secured with TLS. Requires a server certificate.
ExchangeServer	Exchange Server authentication (Generic Security Services application programming interface [GSSAPI] and Mutual GSSAPI).
ExternalAuthoritative	Causes Exchange to treat messages arriving on this connector as though they originated from an internal server; normally, this connector type is used in conjunction with IPsec or other types of network transport encryption.

Suppose you needed to create a receive connector to accept mail from a remote system running Linux qmail. You could easily create it with EMS, using a command similar to this:

```
New-ReceiveConnector -Name "Receive From Tailspin Toys" -Usage Custom -Bindings
'0.0.0.0:9925' -RemoteIPRanges '192.168.70.71' -Server PAO-EX02
```

After the connector has been created, you can see its properties with the Get-ReceiveConnector cmdlet:

```
Get-ReceiveConnector -id "PAO-EX01\Default Frontend PAO-EX01" | fl
```

```
        RunspaceId                              : 3d9854bc-c9bc-494d-a641-39f1d5186336
        AuthMechanism                           : Tls, Integrated, BasicAuth,
        BasicAuthRequireTLS, ExchangeServer
        Banner                                  :
        BinaryMimeEnabled                       : True
        Bindings                                : {[::]:25, 0.0.0.0:25}
        ChunkingEnabled                         : True
        DefaultDomain                           :
        DeliveryStatusNotificationEnabled       : True
        EightBitMimeEnabled                     : True
        BareLinefeedRejectionEnabled            : False
        DomainSecureEnabled                     : True
        EnhancedStatusCodesEnabled              : True
        LongAddressesEnabled                    : False
        OrarEnabled                             : False
```

```
SuppressXAnonymousTls                        : False
ProxyEnabled                                 : False
AdvertiseClientSettings                      : False
Fqdn                                         : PAO-EX01.betabasement.com
ServiceDiscoveryFqdn                         :
TlsCertificateName                           : <I>CN=betabasement-PAO-DC01-CA,
DC=betabasement, DC=com<S>CN=pao-ex01.betabasement.com


Enabled                                      : True
ConnectionTimeout                            : 00:10:00
ConnectionInactivityTimeout                  : 00:05:00
MessageRateLimit                             : Unlimited
MessageRateSource                            : IPAddress
MaxInboundConnection                         : 5000
MaxInboundConnectionPerSource                : 20
MaxInboundConnectionPercentagePerSource : 2
MaxHeaderSize                                : 128 KB (131,072 bytes)
MaxHopCount                                  : 60
MaxLocalHopCount                             : 8
MaxLogonFailures                             : 3
MaxMessageSize                               : 36 MB (37,748,736 bytes)
MaxProtocolErrors                            : 5
MaxRecipientsPerMessage                      : 200
PermissionGroups                             : AnonymousUsers, ExchangeServers,
ExchangeLegacyServers
PipeliningEnabled                            : True
ProtocolLoggingLevel                         : Verbose
RemoteIPRanges                               : {::-ffff:ffff:ffff:ffff:ffff:ffff
:ffff:ffff, 0.0.0.0-255.255.255.255}
RequireEHLODomain                            : False
RequireTLS                                   : False
EnableAuthGSSAPI                             : False
ExtendedProtectionPolicy                     : None
LiveCredentialEnabled                        : False
TlsDomainCapabilities                        : {<I>CN=MSIT Machine Auth CA 2,
DC=redmond, DC=corp, DC=microsoft, DC=com<S>CN=mail.protection.outlook.com,
OU=Forefront Online Protection for Exchange, O=Microsoft, L=Redmond, S=WA,
C=US:AcceptCloudServicesMail}


Server                                       : PAO-EX01
TransportRole                                : FrontendTransport
SizeEnabled                                  : Enabled
TarpitInterval                               : 00:00:05
MaxAcknowledgementDelay                      : 00:00:30
AdminDisplayName                             :
ExchangeVersion                              : 0.1 (8.0.535.0)
Name                                         : Default Frontend PAO-EX01
```

Chapter 2

Note that when you create a new receive connector its TransportRole setting is set to HubTransport. I'm not sure why; this is not the role you want your inbound connectors to use because incoming mail should be processed by FET first so FET can route the message to the correct delivery group. When inbound mail is received by a connector whose TransportRole setting is HubTransport, the mail won't be passed to the Hub Selector agent until it reaches a FET service somewhere along its transport path.

INSIDE OUT Foreign server transport delays

When your Exchange servers are receiving mail from non-Exchange servers, you might find that the default connection timeout value of 10 seconds creates excessive delays, leading to queue growth and possibly user complaints. This added delay is often an issue when configuring SMTP coexistence between Exchange and Lotus Domino, for example. If you notice slow throughput or long queues on the sending side in such a configuration, consider shortening the value of the ConnectionTimeout property on the connector object to reduce the delay.

When you create a new connector, Exchange applies basic default settings. You might consider making some changes, including:

- Adding some permission groups to the connector. When you create a custom connector, Exchange assigns permission groups based on the type of the connector, but it can't know the exact purpose the connector will serve, so you might need to make changes. In this case, you need Anonymous Users to allow the qmail systems to send messages through the connector. Because you created the connector with a –Usage flag of Custom, Exchange 2013 adds this permission group automatically.

- Changing the authentication method the connector advertises and supports. A custom purpose connector should certainly be configured to support TLS to protect email in transit from eavesdropping.

- Changing the banner issued in a 220 SMTP command when a connection is made by a remote server. If not set, Exchange 2013 issues Microsoft ESMTP MAIL Service with the current date and time. Some administrators consider this a security risk because it tells potential hackers that they have connected to Exchange. A replacement banner must start with 220 and contain only 7-bit ASCII characters. You can change the banner with EMS.

- Changing the other settings such as maximum message size, the number of recipients in a message header, and so on. These changes can be done only through EMS.

Because the majority of the settings you might want to change can be accessed only through EMS, it's convenient to update everything through the shell. Here's a command to update your new connector to allow basic authentication, display an updated banner, reduce the maximum message size to 3 MB, and add an administrative comment to indicate what you have done. A comment can be up to 256 characters, and if you add one, it is best practice to incorporate your name so that everyone knows who made the changes.

```
Set-ReceiveConnector -Identity 'PAO-EX02\Receive From Tailspin Toys'
-AuthMechanism 'tls, basicauth'  -Banner '220 Drop the bass' -MaxMessageSize 3MB
-Comment 'PaulR 20 May 2013: Configured for TLS'
```

Your connector will now transmit mail from the remote server to Exchange, but one final step is required to enable the connector to support relaying of messages to any destination domain, which is what you might want to do if Exchange acts as the point of external email connectivity to the Internet. To allow relaying, grant a specific permission to anonymous connections before Exchange accepts these connections. Here's how:

```
Get-ReceiveConnector -Identity 'PAO-EX02\Receive From Tailspin Toys' |
Add-ADPermission -User 'NT AUTHORITY\ANONYMOUS LOGON' -ExtendedRights
'ms-Exch-SMTP-Accept-Any-Recipient'
```

This step also forces any messages coming through the connector to pass through anti-spam checking or to resolve P2 addresses in the message header. (The SMTP address of the sender will be left intact.)

Routing group connectors

If you have an earlier Exchange 2003 infrastructure that depends on routing groups, you'll be interested to know that Exchange 2013 can still communicate with it as long as it's in a separate organization. Microsoft doesn't support direct upgrades from Exchange 2003 to Exchange 2013, a reasonable stance given the difference in the products' ages. In fact, you can't install Exchange 2013 in an organization that contains Exchange 2003 servers. However, you might have a mixed organization that contains Exchange 2003 or Exchange 2007 that you want to upgrade. If so, a routing group connector (RGC) might be useful. If you have a multirole box, transport listens on port 2525, but if you create a new receive connector for transport bound to port 25, both FET and Transport listen on port 25 at the same time. This cannot happen, so you get unpredictable results. (The service that starts first listens on the port; the other one does not.)

The only way to create and manage RGCs is in EMS. You can use the New/Get/Set-RoutingGroupConnector cmdlets to manage these connectors; Microsoft documentation describes their use. However, you will probably be better served by moving away from RGCs and using SMTP connectors wherever possible; the SMTP connectors will continue to be supported in the future.

Delivery agent and foreign connectors

Sometimes, you might need your Exchange system to communicate with a remote system that doesn't support SMTP. Very few such systems remain, luckily for all of us, because SMTP is a much more interoperable and robust protocol than almost all the ancient protocols it has outlasted. However, if you have fax gateways or services that communicate with things such as industrial control or inventory processing systems, you might need a way to integrate them with Exchange. In previous versions of Exchange, Microsoft supported a set of interfaces for creating a *foreign connector*, which was merely a connector that depended on externally provided code to tie Exchange to the remote system. The foreign connector was registered in Exchange as a message routing destination and then implemented either as a set of custom dynamic link libraries (DLLs) or by dropping messages into the Pickup directory on an Exchange SMTP server. The new delivery agent architecture replaces this system with a combination of executable code that runs on an Exchange transport server (the delivery agent itself) and a delivery agent connector, which integrates the delivery agent into the Exchange transport mechanism by providing services such as queuing, message tracking, and monitoring. It's unlikely that you will create your own delivery agents, but I mention them here for completeness.

Securing mail with Transport Layer Security (TLS)

By default, SMTP traffic is unencrypted, which leads to the common analogy that sending SMTP messages across the Internet is like sending postcards—anyone who sees them in transit can easily read the contents. Many organizations have sensitive material they want to send in email; one way to facilitate this is to use Transport Layer Security (TLS) to provide transport encryption for SMTP sessions. TLS-protected SMTP ensures that an eavesdropper cannot read traffic from the SMTP session, although it does nothing to protect the email while it's stored on the sender's or recipient's server.

There are actually two ways Exchange can use TLS. The first, and simplest, is opportunistic TLS. This just means that Exchange accepts a TLS request if the remote server requests it. Exchange 2013 enables TLS by default, and it includes a self-signed certificate, so opportunistic TLS is always available unless you disable it. Second is mutual TLS. Although TLS is normally intended to be used as a transport encryption mechanism between two servers, if each server verifies the identity of the other's certificate, it can also be used as an authentication method. Lync depends heavily on mutual TLS, and you can configure Exchange to use it as well. Microsoft says that Domain Security, which I'll talk about in a minute, is ". . . the set of features, such as certificate management, connector functionality, and Outlook client behavior that enables mutual TLS as a manageable and useful technology."

Opportunistic TLS doesn't perform any kind of certificate validation other than checking to see that a certificate is presented. Self-signed certificates are accepted, and even expired certificates are tolerated. The requirements for mutual TLS are considerably stricter because

Exchange performs a full certificate check, including checking the validity dates of the certificate and looking at the certificate revocation list for the issuer to verify that the certificate remains valid.

It's worth pointing out that there are multiple versions of the TLS protocol. Version 1.2 is the latest, and it's the version Exchange prefers. Other mail servers might not support version 1.2, so the TLS negotiation process includes a way for each end of the conversation to indicate the versions it supports. On the Exchange side, the version of TLS offered and accepted—and the cryptographic algorithms used in the TLS conversation—is controlled by the settings on the Windows secure channel (schannel) subsystem. The "TLS/SSL Technical Reference" article on TechNet (*http://technet.microsoft.com/en-us/library /cc784149(v=ws.10).aspx*) explains how to check or modify which algorithms Windows enables; even though the article is for Windows 2003, the same controls apply equally to later versions of Windows.

Chapter 2

INSIDE OUT Do the sites you're talking to support TLS?

If you're wondering whether it is worth the effort to configure TLS for your servers, it's natural to wonder whether the servers with which you're exchanging mail support TLS. It turns out that there's an easy way to find out: visit the CheckTLS.com website, which offers a variety of tests you can run to see whether a given SMTP domain is capable of accepting or sending mail by using TLS-protected SMTP. The test includes a sender test (in which the site sends you an email showing the results of its attempt to use TLS when sending the message) and a recipient test, in which you specify a recipient address and plug in the name of the domain in which you're interested. You'll see a live transcript of the SMTP conversation showing the entire TLS negotiation and a grid showing the results for each of the MX records associated with the target domain (Figure 2-8). This is a valuable and quick way to determine both whether your own TLS implementation is correct and whether the domains to which you want to connect are capable of handling TLS traffic.

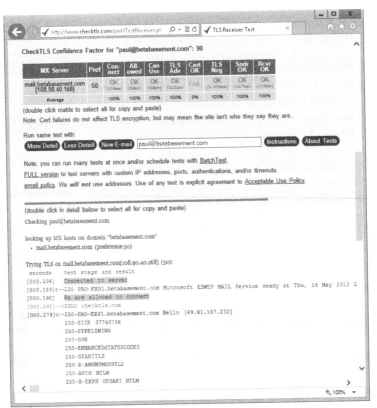

Figure 2-8 Results of the CheckTLS.com site when run against the Betabasement.com test domain used for this book

Using basic TLS

TLS is always used (in fact, TechNet describes it as mandatory) between all instances of the Transport service on Mailbox servers. When TLS is enabled on an Exchange transport server, the list of commands returned in response to an SMTP EHLO includes the STARTTLS command. When an SMTP server sees that verb returned in the EHLO response, it knows that it can send the STARTTLS verb to begin TLS negotiation. The presence of this verb provides a quick way to check whether a remote server might be capable of accepting TLS traffic from your servers. Use Telnet to connect to its SMTP listening port, send EHLO, and see whether you get STARTTLS back.

Configuring a send or receive connector to use TLS is straightforward. First, you run Set-SendConnector or Set-ReceiveConnector with –RequireTls set to $True. The

TlsCertificateName parameter, which also applies to both Set-SendConnector and Set-ReceiveConnector, enables you to specify which certificate the connector should present to the remote end of the connection. If you don't set this parameter, the server uses whatever certificate is configured for the SMTP service. You can check this with Get-ExchangeCertificate:

```
Get-ExchangeCertificate | where {$_.Services -like "SMTP"}
```

```
Thumbprint                                    Services  Subject
----------                                    --------  -------
345CBFDB600B15A6DBC32282C64AD52CED009EDB      ....S..   CN=pao-ex01.betabasement.com
6D7F7149D6DB7E4BDDAE592FE5F38B9CFE3EF323      ....S..   CN=*.betabasement.com,
O=Black Dot LLC, L=Mountain View, S=CA, ...
F8DB6FE019548C945D01FAF7C0447DD172CA9899      ....S..   CN=Microsoft Exchange Server
Auth Certificate
```

If multiple certificates are assigned for SMTP use, Exchange chooses the best one by first identifying which certificates, if any, have fully qualified domain names (FQDNs) that match the FQDN of the local server. If only one is found, it is used. If more than one matches, Exchange sorts the certificates in order of their Valid From date and uses the most recent one.

However, if you want to prevent a send connector from using TLS, you can just run Set-SendConnector with the –IgnoreSTARTTLS flag. With this flag set, send connectors will not advertise that they support TLS, and send connectors will not send the STARTTLS verb to remote servers that do advertise it. If you want a specific receive connector not to advertise or accept TLS, you must specify the SuppressXAnonymousTls flag. Be forewarned that if you do this to the default receive connectors, you might break mail flow inside your organization—Exchange 2013 expects to be able to use TLS within the organization.

INSIDE OUT   WAN optimization controllers and TLS

Large organizations often have large, complex, multisite networks connected by relatively expensive wide area network (WAN) links. Companies such as Riverbed, Cisco, and Blue Coat make devices generically known as *WAN optimization controllers* that watch and optimize site-to-site traffic by compressing or shaping it. Many of these devices can handle Messaging Application Programming Interface (MAPI) and SMTP traffic, but they have to be able to decrypt that traffic to do their magic. Because Exchange transport uses TLS by default, however, you can't just drop one of these devices in the network path between Exchange 2013 transport servers and expect everything to work. Microsoft has a complete guide to configuring Exchange transport to support these devices at *http://technet.microsoft.com/en-us/library /ee633456(v=exchg.150).aspx*, and most individual vendors have similar documents. Briefly, the process requires you to create dedicated connectors, which are configured *not* to use TLS, and then to configure Exchange routing to use these connectors to channel SMTP traffic through the appliances.

You can also specify the level of TLS protection the connector applies. The default for both send and receive connectors is to use TLS for transport encryption only. If you want a send connector to use TLS only with remote servers whose certificates can pass a full certificate validation, use the TlsAuthLevel parameter, which can be set to three values:

- **EncryptionOnly**   The default. Means that the connector should use TLS for transport encryption without attempting to verify the certificate.

- **CertificateValidation**   Enables both transport encryption and basic certificate validity checking. The certificate chain and validity dates are checked, and the issuer's certificate revocation list is searched to ensure that the presented certificate hasn't been revoked.

- **DomainValidation**   The most secure level. Enables transport encryption and certificate validation, but also checks to ensure that the FQDN of the presented certificate is valid. In this case, "valid" means that it matches the value you set with the TlsDomain parameter to Set-SendConnector, if one exists, or the sender's SMTP domain if you didn't explicitly set one.

Suppose you wanted to make sure that you were using TLS whenever exchanging mail with users of the Microsoft Outlook.com service. You could do the following to enable TLS with the appropriate settings:

```
Set-SendConnector -id "PAO-EX01\Outlook.com" -TlsAuthLevel DomainValidation
-TlsDomain protection.microsoft.com
```

For a receive connector, you use the TlsDomainCapabilities flag to indicate the level of TLS support on the connector.

Using domain security

A server that's configured to use TLS can actually perform mutual TLS authentication in one of two ways. The normal way is to examine the certificate the remote end presents and attempt to validate it through the normal X.509 certificate verification mechanism. Another, perhaps more interesting way is for Exchange to check Active Directory for the existence of a certificate associated with the server. If this check (known by Microsoft as Direct Trust) succeeds, the certificate isn't validated, on the assumption that the local administrators' decision to add the certificate to Active Directory supersedes the opinion of the issuing certificate authority (CA).

Exchange servers use Direct Trust internally automatically to support the X-ANONYMOUSTLS verb and the associated authentication. However, Domain Security doesn't automatically do this because Domain Security doesn't currently work on the Front End Transport service. Very few organizations are willing to enable direct SMTP connectivity between their Mailbox servers and the Internet, so it appears that this feature is of little use as presently built in Exchange 2013.

Queues in Exchange 2013

If you look at the set of queues for an Exchange 2013 server (which you can see with a quick run of the Get-Queue cmdlet), you'll see that the queues break down into a few well-defined groupings. Each mailbox database has its own destination queue, as does each DAG and Active Directory site. Somewhat surprisingly, Active Directory forests have their own queues, as do external SMTP domains; these two groups could be combined because delivery to a remote forest uses SMTP, but Microsoft evidently sees some advantage in keeping them separate.

When the Transport service processes messages in a queue, it attempts to deliver the first message in the queue; if the message delivery succeeds, it updates the transport high availability (HA) system (described in more detail later in this chapter) to indicate that delivery was successful. If not, the message remains queued and is retried at a later time. After a preset number of retry attempts, or after the retry interval expires, the message is considered undeliverable and returned to the sender with a nondelivery report (NDR).

As mentioned earlier in this chapter, there are some important differences between queues in Exchange 2013 and those in previous versions. The basic behavior of queues remains the same: messages enter a queue and remain there until they are retrieved and processed by some other component.

Queue types

Different queues are used for different purposes, so it should come as no surprise that Exchange supports multiple types of queues, each with its own purpose.

The *submission queue* holds and organizes messages that are awaiting processing by the categorizer. All arriving messages on a server are delivered to this queue, and the categorizer processes each of them, redirecting them to other queues as appropriate.

Chapter 2

Delivery queues are the most familiar type; they contain messages that are being sent using SMTP. The destination can be remote or local. There will be one delivery queue for each destination. For example, if you have messages concurrently flowing to 17 remote SMTP domains through the Internet, you'll have at least 17 delivery queues.

Messages that can't be delivered might end up in two additional, delivery-related queues. The *Unreachable queue* contains messages for destinations that cannot be routed to. For example, if Amy addresses a message to an SMTP domain that has no MX record, that message will eventually end up in the Unreachable queue. Messages with invalid recipients can end up here, too. Exchange periodically retries messages from this queue, so each message eventually is either returned with an NDR or delivered. Interestingly, this queue is hidden in both EMS and EAC unless messages are in it. Likewise, the *poison message* queue is normally invisible and empty. It receives and holds any message that makes a Transport service crash; the idea is that such messages can be stuffed into this queue and kept out of the way before they cause further harm. Poison messages are not automatically resubmitted, and the poison queue is never automatically cleared.

There are also two sets of queues used for redundancy in the transport system: shadow redundancy queues and the hidden Safety Net queue. They're discussed in the "High availability and Exchange transport" section later in this chapter.

Queue databases

As in Exchange 2010, all queued messages are stored in an Extensible Storage Engine (ESE) database, which by default is located at %ExchangeInstallPath%\TransportRoles\data \Queue. The use of ESE for queuing means that you manage the queue as a database rather than as a collection of files. The queue database itself (Mail.que) has associated ESE transaction log files (Trn*.log), a checkpoint file (Trn.chk), and reserved log files (Tnres00001. jrs and Tnres00002.jrs), just as any other ESE database would have.

One important difference in Exchange 2013 queuing behavior has to do with how messages are stored in the queue database. Exchange 2007 and Exchange 2010 added and removed individual messages. High message volumes therefore meant high volumes of table adds and drops in the database. Exchange 2013 aggregates all messages that arrive each hour into a single table. For example, messages arriving between 9 A.M. and 10 A.M. local time go into a single table; at 10 A.M., the server opens a new table and puts messages in it, deleting the 9 A.M. table after it has verified that all messages therein have been delivered.

The location of the mail queue database files is set in the EdgeTransport.exe.config configuration file, and you can move it to a more suitable location if required. Here's an excerpt from that file showing the default settings:

```
<add key="QueueDatabaseMaxConnections" value="4" />
<add key="QueueDatabaseLoggingFileSize" value="5MB" />
<add key="QueueDatabaseLoggingBufferSize" value="5MB" />
<add key="QueueDatabaseMaxBackgroundCleanupTasks" value="32" />
<add key="QueueDatabaseOnlineDefragSchedule" value="1:00:00" />
<add key="QueueDatabaseOnlineDefragTimeToRun" value="3:00:00" />
<add key="QueueDatabasePath" value="C:\Program Files\Microsoft\Exchange
Server\V15\TransportRoles\data\Queue" />
<add key="QueueDatabaseLoggingPath" value="C:\Program Files\Microsoft\
Exchange Server\V15\TransportRoles\data\Queue" />
<add key="IPFilterDatabasePath" value="C:\Program Files\Microsoft\Exchange
Server\V15\TransportRoles\data\IpFilter" />
```

Table 2-3 lists other important parameters relating to the mail queue database that are held in EdgeTransport.exe.config.

INSIDE OUT   Consider moving the mail queue database to a nondefault location

It is a good idea to consider moving the mail queue database away from the default location under the drive used to hold the Exchange binaries on Mailbox servers that handle a large volume of messages. Microsoft recommends keeping the transport queue for Exchange 2013 on the system disk, which should be protected with RAID-1. If you decide to move it, the simplest way is probably to use the Move-TransportDatabase.ps1 script from the Exchange scripts folder. For example, this command moves the database and its log files to the F:\Exchange\Queues folder. The script requires the target volume to have 2 GB of space in addition to the size of the current queue database.

```
C:> .\Move-TransportDatabase -QueueDatabasePath F:\Exchange\Queues
-QueueDatabaseLoggingPath F:\Exchange\Queues
```

TABLE 2-3 EdgeTransport.exe.config parameters influencing mail queue database operation

Parameter	Meaning
QueueDatabasePath	Defines the location of the mail queue database. You have to create the directory, stop the Transport service, copy the database files, and then restart the Transport service.
QueueDatabaseLoggingPath	Defines the location of the transaction log files for the mail queue database. This does not have to be the same location as for the mail queue database.

Parameter	Meaning
QueueDatabaseLoggingBufferSize	Defines the memory in bytes used to cache records before they are committed to a transaction log. The default is 5,242,880 bytes (5 MB).
QueueDatabaseLoggingFileSize	Defines the maximum size of a transaction log. The default is 5,242,880 bytes.
QueueDatabaseOnlineDefragEnabled	Defines whether Exchange performs online defragmentation to maintain internal database structures. The default is $True.
QueueDatabaseOnlineDefragSchedule	Defines the time Exchange starts online maintenance. The default is 1:00:00 (1 A.M.).
QueueDatabaseOnlineDefragTimeToRun	Defines how long Exchange is allowed to run online maintenance. The default is 3:00:00 (three hours).

Queue velocity

One of the early lessons new administrators learn about Windows performance is that the number of items in a queue (such as the disk I/O queues the Windows I/O manager maintains) can be a valuable reflection of the health of a system or component. Exchange 2013 calculates three properties on queues that help indicate how the queue is performing. The IncomingRate and OutgoingRate properties indicate the rate at which messages are arriving and departing, and the Velocity property is calculated by subtracting the IncomingRate value from the OutgoingRate value. Combine these with the MessageCount value, which tells you how many messages are actually in the queue, and you can get a good sense of what's going on with a particular queue.

The incoming and outgoing rate properties are calculated by tracking the number of messages that arrive in 12 five-second windows and then averaging that amount. An example might help make the calculations more understandable. Suppose that for the past 60 seconds, the message flows for each five-second period are as shown in Table 2-4. Taking the average of the inbound messages yields an average over the one-minute period; it gives an IncomingRate value of 6 (72 messages/12 5-second periods) and an OutgoingRate value of 4.9 (59 messages/12 5-second periods). The queue velocity is thus 1.1. The fact that the value of Velocity is positive means that messages are arriving faster than they are leaving; if that trend continues, the queue will never be fully emptied. However, you can't evaluate the OutgoingRate and IncomingRate values in isolation; you need to consider the number of queued messages, too. A high count of messages in the queue and a Velocity value that's close to zero means the queue is busy but efficiently processing messages. A low message count with a high or low velocity, or a high message count with a negative Velocity value, might indicate a problem with message flow, either with delivering messages to this particular queue (which would account for a low IncomingRate and message count) or delivering them from the queue to anyplace else (a low OutgoingRate). Ultimately, though, the most important measurement of queue health is whether your queues clear consistently and in a reasonable time; any time messages back up in a queue, you should pay careful attention to ensure that the backup isn't a sign of a more serious problem.

TABLE 2-4 Sample message timings

Time	5	10	15	20	25	30	35	40	45	50	55	60	Total
Messages in	12	3	5	7	14	4	1	3	2	7	9	5	72
Messages out	4	8	1	2	6	10	5	7	8	3	4	1	59

Viewing queues

Messages move quickly through Exchange—in general, the existence of more than a few messages in a queue indicates that the server is under load or that network conditions are unable to carry the current level of traffic. You can view the current contents of the queues with the Queue Viewer (described in its own section later in the chapter), the Get-Queue cmdlet, or the Get-QueueDigest cmdlet. The difference between the latter two cmdlets is that Get-Queue shows queues on a single server, whereas Get-QueueDigest summarizes the queue status on multiple servers.

Using Get-Queue

The following sample shows the output from the Get-Queue cmdlet on an Exchange 2013 server with the Mailbox and Client Access roles installed. If you execute this cmdlet without passing a server name, Exchange displays details of the queues on the current server.

```
Get-Queue –Server PAO-EX01 –SortOrder: –MessageCount
```

```
Identity       DeliveryType Status MessageCount Velocity RiskLevel OutboundIPPool NextHopDomain
--------       ------------ ------ ------------ -------- --------- -------------- -------------
PAO-EX01
\Submission    Undefined    Ready  5            0        Normal    0              Submission
PAO-EX01\15    SmtpDeliv... Retry  1            0        Normal    0              pao-ex02
PAO-EX01\16    DnsConnec... Active 1            0        Normal    0              robichaux.net
PAO-EX01\17    DnsConnec... Active 1            0        Normal    0              microsoft.com
PAO-EX01\18    DnsConnec... Con... 1            0        Normal    0              acuitus.com
PAO-EX01\3     SmtpDeliv... Ready  0            0        Normal    0              pao-ex01
PAO-EX01\19    DnsConnec... Ready  0            0        Normal    0              gmail.com
```

In this instance, you sort the output by the number of messages on the queue. The minus sign in front of the *MessageCount* parameter means that you want to sort in descending order. Put a plus sign (+) in front of the parameter to sort in ascending order. For example, to sort the queues by status, you can use a command like this:

```
Get-Queue –Server PAO-EX01 –SortOrder: +Status
```

The –Filter parameter is also available to select queues from the full set. For example, here's how to select the queues that hold more than 20 messages:

```
Get-Queue –Server ExServer1 –Filter {MessageCount –gt 20} –SortOrder:
–MessageCount
```

Queue status

A queue status of Ready indicates that the queue is capable of accepting messages for onward processing. You might see a Connecting status indicating that Exchange is connecting to a remote server to be able to pass queued messages. An Active status indicates that Exchange is transferring messages from the queue; a status of Retry indicates that the queue is waiting for the retry interval on the queue to elapse so it can attempt redelivery.

The overall appearance of the output looks very much like Exchange 2010, but a number of important differences exist. By default, the queue velocity is shown, although in this case it's zero, which doesn't tell you much. The message bound for the next hop domain of pao-ex02 is going to another Exchange server in the same organization; rather than showing the identity of the target mailbox database, the destination is shown as the target server because that server is responsible for deciding which database the message should be delivered to.

Queues are visible on a transient basis. In other words, the Transport service creates queues as necessary and tears them down when no messages are queued. If you look at a server during a period of heavy demand, you might see queues for every database in the local site (assuming that a message has recently been sent to a recipient in each database) and queues for servers in all the other Active Directory sites within the organization. If you look at the queues on the same server at a time of low demand, all the queues might have disappeared except for the submission queue that submits messages to the categorizer. Unlike mail delivery and remote delivery queues, the submission queue is persistent, and you will find one submission queue per server. Exchange also clears queues when messages expire, which occurs by default after a message is more than two days old. The logic here is that a two-day-old message is not very useful to the recipient, so it is better to return it to the sender so that she can contact the intended recipient by using another mechanism.

In addition to the Submission queue and any domain-specific or database-specific queues, you might also see the Poison and Unreachable queues, as previously described. If you don't see these queues, that's actually a good sign; it means the server doesn't have any undeliverable or suspect messages.

To ensure uniqueness, the transport system builds queue names from the server name plus a number that it increments over time. The number is reset when the Transport service restarts.

Using Get-QueueDigest

The Get-QueueDigest cmdlet is a notable improvement in queue management for Exchange 2013. It presents a summarized view of all active queues on multiple servers; you can use it to get an overview of queue activity for all servers in the forest, all members of a DAG or Active Directory site, or all servers on a specified list. Get-QueueDigest supports the –Filter flag so that you can perform server-side filtering. It's very simple to use:

- The –Forest flag shows queues for all servers in the current forest.

- The –Dag option accepts a comma-separated list of one or more DAG names. For example, Get-Queue –DAG "Palo Alto,Huntsville" shows all active queues on all servers that are members of either of those DAGs.

- Use –Server to specify a comma-separated list of server names and show their queues.

- The –Site option takes a comma-separated list of Active Directory site names.

These options are mutually exclusive, so you can only specify one at a time. The output of Get-QueueDigest shows all the queues that are currently active within the specified scope:

```
Get-QueueDigest -Server PAO-EX01,PAO-EX02
```

GroupByValue	MessageCount	DeferredMessageCount	LockedMessageCount	StaleMessageCount	Details
------------	------------	------------	------------	------------	-------
mail.yourmomshouse.com					
	2	0	0	0	{PAO-EX01\34}

Using the Exchange Queue Viewer

Although Exchange 2013 is based on the EAC instead of the older-style management tools based on the Microsoft Management Console, it turns out that not everything an administrator might want to do can be done in EAC. One example is viewing the contents of queues; the current release of EAC doesn't include any way to see them. You can also use the Exchange Queue Viewer to examine the contents of the transport queues (Figure 2-9). The Queue Viewer is a Microsoft Management Console (MMC) that was part of the

Exchange 2010 EMC toolbox collection and is now a standalone tool. The major advantage of the Queue Viewer is that it provides an easy-to-use method to see what's happening on queues and to examine the properties of messages that are currently in a queue. The Transport service is capable of processing even large messages very quickly, so the Queue Viewer refreshes its display every five seconds or so to provide an up-to-date picture of what's happening on a hub transport server.

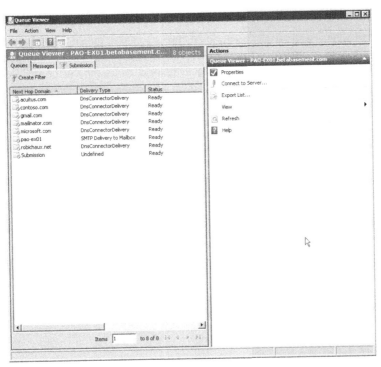

Figure 2-9 The Exchange Queue Viewer

INSIDE OUT Where the messages are being processed

Remember that if you are operating within a DAG, messages might be submitted to a remote Mailbox server if one is available in the site rather than being processed locally, as is the case for standalone servers. Because Exchange can deliver to any transport server in the primary delivery group (based on least cost), the messages might not appear where you expect. A few administrators have made the mistake of looking at queues on the local server and seeing no activity when all the messages they were trying to monitor were being processed elsewhere.

All the actions reviewed here in the cmdlets that work with queue contents are supported by the Queue Viewer. Most experienced administrators prefer to use EMS to interrogate message queues because EMS responds faster to queries; it doesn't have to allow for the overhead imposed by the Queue Viewer graphical user interface (GUI). However, it is nice to have the choice.

Enabling prioritized message delivery

Users often imagine things that aren't true about the systems they use. This is true in the case of mail priorities; I've seen many otherwise knowledgeable users (and administrators) who think that marking a message high priority in the client causes it to be delivered faster or more reliably. Sadly, that is not the normal case; although there are messaging systems that evaluate the user-specified message priority when making routing and transport decisions, Exchange has not always been one of them. In Exchange 2013, Microsoft supports a feature known as *priority queuing* that does exactly this. When you enable it, messages that are marked high priority are sent before normal priority messages, and low-priority messages are sent after normal messages. When priority queuing is enabled, the categorization and routing mechanisms described earlier, in the "Exchange 2013 transport architecture in depth" section, remain unchanged; the primary difference is that the Transport services arrange messages in each delivery queue according to their priority.

Table 2-5 lists the settings in EdgeTransport.exe.config that affect priority queuing. To enable or disable it, adjust the value of the PriorityQueuingEnabled key and then stop and restart the Transport service. (Restart-Service MSExchangeTransport in EMS will do the trick.)

TABLE 2-5 Priority queuing settings in EdgeTransport.exe.config

Parameter	Meaning
PriorityQueuingEnabled	When set to *true*, enables the use of priority queuing. The default value is *false*.
MaxHighPriorityMessageSize	Specifies the maximum size of a high-priority message. Messages that exceed this size are treated as normal priority messages.
LowPriorityDelayNotificationTimeout NormalPriorityDelayNotificationTimeout HighPriorityDelayNotificationTimeout	Timeout values for notifying the sender that message delivery is delayed. Normally, you'll set the HighPriorityDelayNotificationTimeout to a much shorter value than the other two on the theory that people who send high-priority messages would appreciate early notification of delivery delays. The default values for these settings are 8 hours for low, 4 hours for medium, and 30 minutes for high- priority messages.

Parameter	Meaning
LowPriorityMessageExpirationTimeout NormalPriorityMessageExpirationTimeout HighPriorityMessageExpirationTimeout	Interval during which the Transport service keeps trying to send a message; after this interval expires, the message is returned with an NDR. Low and normal messages default to a 2-day timeout; high-priority messages default to an 8-hour timeout.
MaxPerDomainLowPriorityConnections MaxPerDomainNormalPriorityConnections MaxPerDomainHighPriorityConnections	Values that control how many total outbound connections the Transport service can make to an individual domain. The sum of these numbers must be equal to or less than the value set for the *MaxPerDomainOutboundConnections* parameter of Set-TransportConfig.

You should be aware of how the priority queuing settings interact with the settings imposed by the Set-TransportService cmdlet. Both the priority queuing mechanism and Set-TransportService allow you to define delay notification and expiration timeouts. If the value of one of the NormalPriorityDelayNotificationTimeout or NormalPriorityMessageExpirationTimeout values in EdgeTransport.exe.config conflicts with the corresponding Set-TransportService values, the priority queuing version wins. Because Set-TransportService doesn't have separate values for low-priority or high-priority messages, this conflict only affects the timeout values for normal priority messages.

Managing queues

In normal operation, Exchange will fill and drain queues with no need for administrators' intervention. Sometimes, however, you might need to intervene manually and manage queues or messages. Apart from the tools available in the Exchange Queue Viewer, EMS offers several cmdlets that you can use to manage various aspects of queue behavior. For the most part, you probably won't need them, but if and when you do, you'll find that there's no real substitute.

Viewing and managing messages in a queue

Sometimes, you'll see that messages start to accumulate on queues and the count does not decrease even when the server is lightly loaded and there are no apparent problems that would cause you to think that messages should fail to be transferred. At this point, you might want to investigate further by looking at the messages that are in the queue. For example, this command fetches full details of the current condition of a queue:

```
Get-Queue -id PAO-EX01\33 | fl
```

```
    RunspaceId        : db46566a-e5df-46ac-8510-647ee397f666
    DeliveryType      : SmartHostConnectorDelivery
```

```
NextHopDomain          : pao-ex45.contoso.com
TlsDomain              :
NextHopConnector       : 334b5e19-564a-4659-a3a2-a9e2d4a16e16
Status                 : Retry
MessageCount           : 1
LastError              : 451 4.4.0 DNS query failed. The error was: DNS query
failed with error ServerFailure
RetryCount             : 0
LastRetryTime          : 5/18/2013 7:14:15 PM
NextRetryTime          : 5/18/2013 7:15:23 PM
DeferredMessageCount   : 0
LockedMessageCount     : 0
RiskLevel              : Normal
OutboundIPPool         : 0
NextHopCategory        : Internal
IncomingRate           : 0
OutgoingRate           : 0
Velocity               : 0
QueueIdentity          : PAO-EX01\33
Identity               : PAO-EX01\33
```

You can see immediately that the queue is building because DNS has reported that it cannot resolve the name of the smart host that is configured to service the send connector. The ServerFailure message is a catch-all error that covers any problem resolving a name through DNS. The solution is to validate the name of the smart host and make sure that DNS can resolve it; when you do so, mail automatically resumes flowing through the queue when it reaches the next retry interval.

Sometimes, a remote server does not respond to a request to connect to exchange messages. In this case, you see this error:

```
"421 4.2.1 Unable to connect. Attempted failover to alternate host, but that did not
succeed. Either there are no alternate hosts, or delivery failed to all alternate
hosts."
```

The *NextHopDomain* property indicates where Exchange is trying to send the message; it might reflect the name of an internal server, the name of an SMTP server such as a smart host, or the name of the Active Directory site to which Exchange is trying to transfer the message. In the last case, if there is only one Mailbox server in the target site, it's a fair chance the problem is with this server. However, if more than one Mailbox server operates within the site, the problem could be with any of them. Hub transport servers reject connections if they begin to exhaust resources using a feature called back pressure (see the "Back pressure" section later in this chapter), so this is another item for your checklist. You should verify that the Store is running on the server; the database that hosts the recipient's mailbox might be dismounted or inoperative for some reason.

The Get-Message cmdlet reveals details of the messages in the stuck queues. For example:

```
Get-Message
```

```
Identity              FromAddress              Status  Queue         Subject
----------            -----------              ------  ------        --------
PAO-EX01\34\15234248...
                      paul@betabasement.com    Ready   PAO-EX01\34   Travel plans for
TechEd Europe
PAO-EX01\34\15234248...
                      paul@betabasement.com    Ready   PAO-EX01\34   Re: deadline for
chapter 2
```

If more than a few messages are queued, it might be more convenient to pipe this output to a text file and review the data using the file. If necessary, you can see the details of an individual message by using its identifier to select the message. In this example, the first message in the preceding list is specified by its ID:

```
Get-Message -Identity 'PAO-EX01\34\15234248998925' | Format-List
```

```
RunspaceId                      : db46566a-e5df-46ac-8510-647ee397f666

Subject                         : Travel plans for TechEd Europe
InternetMessageId               : CDBD9FBE.5499C%paul@betabasement.com
FromAddress                     : paul@betabasement.com
Status                          : Ready
Size                            : 3.479 KB (3,562 bytes)
MessageSourceName               : SMTP:Default PAO-EX01
SourceIP                        : 10.0.0.101
SCL                             : -1
DateReceived                    : 5/18/2013 7:14:15 PM
ExpirationTime                  : 5/20/2013 7:14:15 PM
LastError                       :
RetryCount                      : 0
Recipients                      :
ComponentLatency                :
MessageLatency                  : 00:08:59.0205734
DeferReason                     : None
LockReason                      :
IsProbeMessage                  : False
Priority                        : Normal
OutboundIPPool                  : 0
ExternalDirectoryOrganizationId : 00000000-0000-0000-0000-000000000000
Directionality                  : Undefined
MessageIdentity                 : PAO-EX01\34\15234248998925
Queue                           : PAO-EX01\34
Identity                        : PAO-EX01\34\15234248998925
IsValid                         : True
ObjectState                     : New
```

Note that, unlike Exchange 2010, Exchange 2013 uses longer numbers to identify messages in queues. The ID number of a message in a queue has nothing to do with the Message-ID property of that message, which will be persisted as the message is moved around SMTP servers on the Internet.

Suppose you identify an individual message, or group of messages, that you don't want to be delivered. You can suspend a message with the Suspend-Message cmdlet by passing the message identifier. In this case, Exchange keeps the message on the queue but does not attempt to process it until an administrator releases the message:

```
Suspend-Message -Identity 'PAO-EX01\34\15234248998925'
```

To release the message, use the Resume-Message cmdlet:

```
Resume-Message -Identity 'PAO-EX01\34\15234248998925'
```

The Remove-Message cmdlet deletes a message from a queue. In this example, you send an NDR back to the sender to tell him what's happened. If you set the *–WithNDR* parameter to $False, Exchange deletes the message without sending an NDR:

```
Remove-Message -Identity 'PAO-EX01\34\15234248998925'-WithNDR $True
```

You do not have to suspend a message before you can delete it.

Exchange 2013 has another useful operation that you can perform on messages. With the Export-Message and Assemble-Message cmdlets, you can easily select messages and export them, including their component parts, to a text file. Exporting a message doesn't remove it from a queue. You can only export a message when it has been suspended with Suspend-Message or when the queue that contains it has been suspended with Suspend-Queue. The exported messages can be inspected or edited and then dropped back into the Pickup or Replay directories. This gives you a quick way to move messages stuck in a queue on a server to another server where they could be sent to their destination.

Chapter 2

INSIDE OUT Exporting messages: not a particularly large risk

Administrators can use Export-Message to copy messages while in transit—and those messages will probably be unencrypted unless the sender used Active Directory Rights Management Service (AD RMS), Pretty Good Privacy, S/MIME, or a similar solution to protect them when they were originally sent. By default, the Export-Message cmdlet is available to users who hold the Transport Queues role-based access control (RBAC) management role assignment, which means that not every admin will have access to the cmdlet in the first place. Although a malicious insider could just grab every message and then inspect it, that would be time-consuming; for this to be a useful attack, he would have to wait until he knew that an interesting message was about to be sent and grab it from the queue (possibly freezing the queue to make it easier). There are many other easier ways for an attacker to get message contents, so the risk of this cmdlet as an information disclosure vehicle seems pretty low.

Export-Message takes as its argument the ID of the message you want to export. If you're exporting a single message, it's easy to pipe the output of Export-Message to the AssembleMessage.ps1 script, which will turn the binary object Export-Message returns into a readable .eml-format file. Something like this will work:

```
Get-Message -Identity 'PAO-EX01\34\15234248998925' | Export-Message | AssembleMessage
-Path c:\temp
```

Things get a bit more complicated if you want to export multiple messages. Getting the messages is easy; Get-Message (with or without the –Filter parameter) enables you to select the messages quickly that you want to export, and then you can pipe them to Export-Message. However, the AssembleMessage.ps1 script is fairly stupid and expects to be called once per message, with a unique pathname each time. One way to solve this is by using code such as this:

```
$theMessages = @(Get-Message -queue PAO-EX01\34)
$theMessages | foreach {$i++; Export-Message $_.Identity | AssembleMessage -path
("c:\temp"+$i+ ".eml")}
```

The first line retrieves all the messages from the target queue and stores them in an array; the second pipes the contents of the array to ForEach-Object, passing each message in turn to Export-Message and thence to AssembleMessage.ps1 for processing.

Suspending and resuming queues

Earlier in the chapter, I mentioned the states a queue can be in: suspended, active, retrying, ready, and so on. It is sometimes useful to put queues explicitly into one of these states without regard to what state Exchange thinks it should be in. For example, you might want to stop mail delivery temporarily to a particular remote domain, or you might want to force a connection so that Exchange attempts immediate redelivery of messages that have been stalled waiting for a remote server.

The Resume-Queue and Suspend-Queue cmdlets are very useful for this purpose. For example, if you suspend the submission queue on a server, no further messages flow into or out of that server until you resume it. Because this includes messages used for Managed Availability, suspending the submission queue is a rather drastic measure to take, but sometimes stopping mail flow *right now* is precisely what you want. You suspend and resume queues by specifying their name, like this:

```
Suspend-Queue PAO-EX01\34
```

Although you could enumerate the queues and then pick one targeted at a specific destination, it would probably be faster just to run Suspend-Queue contoso.com if you wanted to block all mail flow to a specific destination. When you suspend a queue, EMS prompts you to confirm that you really want to suspend it; you can override this by adding the –Force parameter. Resuming or retrying a queue doesn't require confirmation. Both the Resume-Queue and Retry-Queue cmdlets support the –Filter parameter so that you can easily do things such as forcing an immediate reconnection attempt for any queue on a server that is currently in the retry state:

```
Retry-Queue -Filter {Status -eq "retry"}
```

Submitting messages through the pickup directory

The pickup directory typically is used to introduce messages created by applications into the Transport service. For example, a monitoring agent might detect an application failure and generate a message like the one shown in the following example.

```
To: SystemAdmins@betabasement.com
From: AppWarning@contoso.com
Date: 14 November 2013 01:42AM
Subject: Warning - BetaBox Application failure
MIME-Version: 1.0
Content-Type: text/html; charset="iso-8859-1"
Content-Transfer-Encoding: 7bit
<HTML><BODY>
</TABLE>
<h3>
The BetaBox application has experienced a failure on server BBOX188.
Please check!
</h3>
<TABLE>
<TR><TD>Application</TD><TD>Problem Details</TD></TR>
<TR><TD>BBOX Version 2.010</TD><TD>The application is not responding to prompts
</TD></TR>
</BODY></HTML>
```

By default, the pickup directory is located in \TransportRoles\Pickup. You can modify this location with the Set-TransportServer cmdlet. For example:

```
Set-TransportServer -Identity ExServer2 -PickupDirectoryPath 'C:\Exchange
\PickupDirectory'
```

The basic idea is for an application to create a text file with an .eml extension that complies with the basic SMTP message format and places the file in the pickup directory. Every five seconds (this interval cannot be altered), Exchange checks the pickup directory and attempts to process any file with an .eml extension that it finds there.

INSIDE OUT   Processing a large volume of messages

Files with any extension other than .eml are ignored. Exchange will process up to 12 messages from the pickup directory every 5 seconds and will leave any remainder to be processed the next time around if more than this number of .eml files is present. You can instruct Exchange to process more files at one time with the Set-TransportServer cmdlet if you need to accommodate a larger volume of messages generated by applications. For example:

```
Set-TransportServer -PickupDirectoryMaxMessagesPerMinute 250
```

The file is first renamed with a .tmp extension and then examined by Exchange to see whether it contains the necessary structure to allow the file to be converted into a message. If all is well, the message is placed in the submission queue, and the .tmp file is removed from the pickup directory. If the file is not properly formatted, Exchange changes the extension to .bad and leaves the file in the pickup directory where, hopefully, an administrator deals with it. For example, if you use a mailbox alias rather than the full SMTP address of the mailbox in the From field, Exchange will reject the file. It's possible for a failure to occur that causes the Transport service or the server to cease running when messages are being processed from the pickup directory. In this case, the .tmp files will remain in the directory, and Exchange will process them again the next time it scans for new messages. A slight potential exists for duplicate messages to be delivered as a result. Administrators won't be aware that duplicates have been delivered, but this is unlikely to be of much concern because users can detect and eliminate duplicates when these messages arrive in their Inboxes.

A message file consists of header fields and text. The basic requirements are as follows:

- Only text files with an .eml extension are processed.

- At least one email address must exist in the To, Cc, or Bcc fields. All addresses must be in SMTP format.

- Only one email address must be in the From or Sender field. If a single address is in both fields, Exchange uses the address in the From field as the message originator. It is possible to provide multiple addresses in the From field (separate each address with a comma), but in this instance, you must also provide a single address in the Sender field that Exchange then uses as the message originator. Outlook displays these messages as if the address specified as the Sender sent the message on behalf of the first address in the From list. In all cases, the email address for the message originator should be valid; otherwise the message might be dropped by an anti-spam agent somewhere along its route.

- For plaintext messages, a blank line must be between the header fields and the text that forms the message body. A blank line is not required for Multipurpose Internet Mail Extensions (MIME)–format messages.

- The maximum header size is 64 KB, and no more than 100 recipients can be specified in the header.

If present, Exchange removes the Received and Resent header fields because these header fields aren't supported when submitted through the pickup directory. Bcc recipients are also removed to preserve their anonymity. If only Bcc recipients are present, Exchange replaces them with Undisclosed Recipients in the header. If the date field is missing, Exchange will use the date and time the file was taken from the pickup directory. Finally, to help identify messages that come in through the pickup directory, Exchange adds a Received header indicating that the message came from the pickup directory.

The role of the Replay directory

The replay directory resubmits exported Exchange messages and receives messages from foreign gateway servers. Like the pickup directory, Exchange checks the replay directory every five seconds and processes any messages it finds there. The messages that are introduced into the replay directory are formatted by the foreign gateway to comply with Exchange requirements; the gateway performs whatever conversion is required to transform message contents from the format.

> **Tip**
> You shouldn't attempt to introduce new messages through the replay directory because messages placed there aren't filtered to remove possibly incorrect headers. Use the pickup directory when you need to submit a new message to Exchange.

Message throttling

Email servers that act as the gateways to large companies can be overwhelmed or swamped by large volumes of incoming messages. The servers can either attempt to deal with the volume the best they can and eventually work through the backlog that inevitably accumulates, or the software can monitor, recognize, and take action to manage the condition to maintain an orderly processing regime. *Message throttling* is the mechanism Exchange 2013 uses to manage peaks in incoming message traffic. Unlike other Exchange 2013 throttling mechanisms, which aim to prevent ill-behaved clients from consuming large quantities of system resources without good reason, message throttling applies only to SMTP message flow through the Exchange 2013 transport system.

Message throttling in Exchange 2013 is surprisingly complex; it is based on the quality of service (QoS) mechanisms introduced in Exchange 2010 SP1. In brief, Exchange 2013 transport servers calculate an average delivery cost for the message. This cost takes into account the size of the message, the number of recipients, and how often that user has sent messages. High values for any or all these metrics raise the average delivery cost. In this case, "high values" means more than 500 recipients or a message size greater than 1 MB. The Microsoft Exchange Throttling service monitors this cost and creates a budget for each user; when a user exceeds his budget, his messages are lowered in priority so that they take longer to transfer. (Note that that the priority imposed by the throttling service supersedes any priority set by the user when she sends a message.) In addition to budget calculations, the Microsoft Exchange Throttling service tabulates the Average RPC Latency and Requests/Second counters on the mailbox database to derive a numeric health value, indicating how much load is being placed on the database. This health value is used to bias the amount of budget available to users on that mailbox database.

You can apply throttling parameters to the following:

- **On the Transport service**   This is done with the Set-TransportService and Set-MailboxTransportService cmdlets. (Some parameters can also be set through EAC.) Typically, you only need to apply throttling to servers that deal with external traffic, although you might have to apply throttling on transport servers positioned on a busy hub site.

- **A receive connector**   This is done with the Set-ReceiveConnector cmdlet. Again, you usually only need to pay attention to the receive connectors that handle incoming traffic from outside the organization.

- **A send connector**   This is done with the Set-SendConnector cmdlet.

The default values Exchange sets are usually sufficient for most purposes and need to be changed only if monitoring reveals that hub transport, or edge servers are struggling to cope with incoming traffic. For example, the situation deserves investigation if you see large queues accumulating at peak times that do not reduce when peak times pass. This might be caused by a simple lack of processing capacity, or it could be caused by other conditions that you can address by tweaking the throttling parameters. Table 2-6 summarizes the different parameters you can use to control transport throttling.

TABLE 2-6 Available parameters for transport throttling

Set value with	Parameter	Effect
Set-TransportService or Set-MailboxTransport-Service	MaxConcurrent-MailboxDeliveries	Sets the maximum number of threads used for concurrent delivery to mailboxes through the Store driver across the entire organization. The default is 20.
Set-TransportService or Set-MailboxTransport-Service	MaxConcurrent-MailboxSubmissions	Sets the maximum number of delivery threads a server can use to accept messages from databases through the Store driver across the organization. The default is 20.
Set-TransportService	MaxConnectionRate-PerMinute	Sets the maximum rate at which new inbound connections can be created to receive connectors by the transport server. The default is 1,200 connections per minute.
Set-TransportService or server properties in EAC	MaxOutbound-Connections	Sets the maximum number of concurrent outbound connections a transport can open through send connectors. The default value is 1,000. You can set this value to Unlimited to allow the server to create as many connections as resources allow.
Set-TransportService or server properties in EAC	MaxPerDomain-OutboundConnections	Sets the maximum number of connections that can be opened to a single domain through send connectors. The default value is 20. You can set this value to be Unlimited.
Set-TransportService	PickupDirectoryMax-MessagesPerMinute	Sets the maximum number of messages the Transport service attempts to load from the pickup and replay directory per minute. The default value is 100 messages per minute per directory. Exchange polls these directories every five seconds, so the value you set should be divisible by 12 to arrive at the number Exchange processes each time it polls.
Set-ReceiveConnector	ConnectionInactivity-TimeOut	Sets the maximum idle time that the receive connector maintains an open SMTP connection with another server. The connection is closed when the period elapses. Defaults to five minutes on the Transport service on Mailbox servers, five minutes on the FET, and one minute on edge transport servers.

Chapter 2

Chapter 2

Set value with	Parameter	Effect
Set-ReceiveConnector	ConnectionTimeOut	Sets the maximum time an SMTP connection can remain open even if the other server continues to transmit data. The default value is 10 minutes for the Transport service on Mailbox servers, 10 minutes on FET, and 5 minutes for an edge server. Logically, this value must be higher than the value of the *ConnectionInactivityTimeOut* parameter.
Set-ReceiveConnector	MaxInboundConnection	Sets the maximum number of concurrent inbound connections a receive connector can support. The default value is 5,000.
Set-ReceiveConnector	MaxInbound-ConnectionPercentage-PerSource	Sets the maximum number of inbound connections a receive connector permits from a single source. The value is expressed as the percentage of available remaining connections. The default value is 100 percent on the default receive connector on the Transport service of a Mailbox server and 2 percent for all other receive connectors in the Transport or FET services.
Set-ReceiveConnector	MaxInbound-ConnectionPerSource	Sets the maximum number of inbound connections a receive connector allows from a single server. The default value is Unlimited on the Default Receive connector on the Transport service for a Mailbox server and 20 for other receive connectors on the Transport and FET services.
Set-ReceiveConnector	MaxProtocolErrors	Sets the maximum number of SMTP errors a receive connector tolerates before it closes a connection with another server. The default value is 5.
Set-ReceiveConnector	TarpitInterval	Sets the delay parameter Exchange uses when it suspects that another server is attempting a directory harvest attack. The default value is 5 seconds.
Set-SendConnector	ConnectionInactivity-TimeOut	Specifies the maximum time a send connector maintains an open SMTP connection with another server. The default value is 10 minutes.

Back pressure

The Exchange transport engine is designed to process extremely large volumes of messages, but sometimes a server might not have the physical capability to handle incoming or outgoing messages. For instance, a Mailbox server might come under load from another source that consumes much of the available memory, or the disk space on some drives might come close to being exhausted. In these circumstances, the back pressure feature enables the Transport service to continue running normally and process queued messages while it temporarily rejects incoming messages to stop new messages from being queued. In this scenario, the sending SMTP servers have to queue the messages until the situation that caused pressure on Exchange is relieved. As load on the server reduces to free memory, or disk space becomes available because some files are deleted, Exchange starts to accept incoming connections and process new messages.

A variety of factors influence when the service starts indicating that back pressure is in effect; the Exchange 2013 documentation goes into great detail about these factors (see *http://technet.microsoft.com/en-us/library/bb201658(v=exchg.150).aspx*), but the short explanation is that available disk space, the number of uncommitted message queue transactions, the number of messages in the Submission queue, and the amount of RAM are all factors.

It's important to know that back pressure doesn't stop Exchange from accepting incoming SMTP connections, but when a connection has been accepted, the server might reject the MAIL FROM command from the sending server with an error such as 452 4.3.1 Insufficient system Resources. The Transport service will log events 15004, 15006, and 15007 with source MSExchangeTransport in the application event log to indicate that back pressure is in effect; event ID 15005 indicates that a previously scarce resource is less scarce. These events tell you which resource triggered.

> **Note**
>
> Back pressure only applies to the Transport service on Mailbox and edge transport servers because the FET service doesn't queue messages.

Table 2-7 shows how Mailbox servers react to medium and high back pressure conditions. As you can see, under medium load, basic message flow is preserved because Mailbox servers can connect to send mail to each other and are willing to accept messages from Mailbox servers. However, they will not accept incoming traffic from other SMTP servers. As pressure builds, the Mailbox server will eventually stop accepting connections and wait until pressure decreases. A number of other actions might be triggered to reduce back pressure without stopping message flow altogether. For example, if the Submission queue is under pressure, the Transport service will start slowing message flow by increasing the tarpit interval to 10 seconds; if that doesn't reduce the pressure, the tarpit delay is gradually increased in 5-second increments (up to a maximum of 55 seconds/message). If *that* doesn't solve the problem, the Transport service will start rejecting incoming messages as a last resort.

TABLE 2-7 The effect of back pressure settings on Mailbox servers

Resource Usage	Connections from legacy Transport servers	Connections from other SMTP servers	Store driver connections from mailbox servers	Pickup and Replay submissions	Internal mail flow
Medium	Allowed	Rejected	Allowed	Rejected	Working
High	Rejected	Rejected	Rejected	Rejected	No flow

INSIDE OUT   Settings are being tuned based on real-world experience

Microsoft has tuned the back pressure settings, which are stored in the EdgeTransport. exe.config file, to reflect real-life experience in production. Although you can adjust these settings, Microsoft strongly recommends against it. It has set the values in the default configuration based on field testing inside Microsoft IT and by Technology Adoption Program (TAP) partner deployments. You can expect tuning to continue in this space as Microsoft and administrators learn how to control back pressure situations better.

Message routing in depth

Message routing in Exchange 2013 is a combination of familiar concepts (such as least-cost routing) from previous versions and brand-new concepts such as delivery groups. The goal of message routing remains to deliver each message to its recipients in as little time as possible, but the means by which Exchange 2013 achieves this goal are somewhat different from previous versions.

Delivery groups

Exchange 2013 has five types of delivery groups:

- **Routable DAG**   This type of delivery group type represents an entire DAG. As far as Exchange routing is concerned, delivering a message to any server in the DAG is good enough. Delivery to the delivery group is considered complete when the message arrives at any server in the DAG, at which point, it goes to the Mailbox Transport service on the server that holds the active copy of the target mailbox database.

- **Mailbox delivery group**   This type of delivery group contains all the Exchange servers of a particular version in a single Active Directory site. For example, all the standalone Exchange 2013 Mailbox servers in the HQ-PAO site are treated as part of the same mailbox delivery group, with the Exchange 2010 servers in the same site grouped into a separate mailbox delivery group. When the message is delivered to any server in a mailbox delivery group, that server uses its version's delivery method; an Exchange 2013 server uses SMTP to pass the message to the Mailbox Transport service on the target server, which sends it to the Mailbox Transport Delivery service. Exchange 2007 and Exchange 2010 servers submit the message by using RPC directly to the target mailbox database.

- **Mailbox server list**   This delivery group type represents a server that is configured to expand distribution groups.

- **Active Directory sites**   As in Exchange 2007 and Exchange 2010, message routing can use Active Directory site membership to determine the best way to reach a server. Messages delivered to an Active Directory site delivery group can go to any Exchange 2010 hub transport or Exchange 2013 Mailbox server in the site; that server is expected to identify the correct target server within the site and pass the message on.

- **Connector source servers**   This delivery group type contains down-level Exchange hub transport servers and Exchange 2013 Mailbox servers that are scoped as hosting send connectors or foreign connectors. The reason this group type exists is to enable Exchange to identify and route messages efficiently to a connector serving a particular destination when all it knows is which servers have access to the connector.

Table 2-8 shows the way hub transport, Mailbox, and edge transport servers map into these delivery group types. It's important to note that a single server can be part of multiple destination groups. For example, an Exchange 2013 Mailbox server that is a DAG member will be part of a routable DAG delivery group but might also simultaneously be a member of a connector source delivery group if it hosts a connector.

TABLE 2-8 Destination types and delivery groups

	Exchange 2013 Mailbox	Exchange 2007/2010 hub transport	Exchange 2007/2010 edge transport
Mailbox database in a DAG	Routable DAG	Mailbox delivery group	N/A
Mailbox database on standalone server	Mailbox delivery group	Mailbox delivery group	N/A
Connector	Connector source server	Connector source server	AD site
Distribution group expansion server	Server list	Server list	N/A

Interestingly, even though the FET role would seem like a logical object to use as part of a delivery group, it is never used as such. Keeping the FET out of delivery groups forces the FET on all servers to communicate with the mailbox role, which is necessary to guarantee that transport rules and other transport-related processing take place.

Exchange 2013 and Active Directory

Microsoft describes Exchange 2013 as a "site-aware application," meaning that it can use site information stored in Active Directory to make decisions about which Active Directory resources (such as domain controllers and global catalog servers) to use. Exchange goes beyond the traditional behavior of site-aware applications by using Active Directory site membership as an input to the message routing process. The TechNet documentation page that describes Active Directory-based routing in Exchange 2013 says that "[a]n efficient Active Directory topology doesn't require any changes to support Exchange 2013," but that statement ignores the question of how Active Directory is used by the transport system in particular and Exchange in general.

At the highest level of abstraction, an Active Directory site is just a collection of IP subnets that you've defined as being near each other. By registering a site definition in Active Directory, every computer running Windows on the network becomes able to determine what site it's on by calling the DsGetSiteName function, which takes an IP address as input. Any Active Directory client, whether an Exchange server or a workstation, can thus efficiently figure out its site membership as long as it knows its IP address. Changing the IP address of a machine or changing the list of subnets associated with a particular site will both result in changing the site membership for that computer.

In Exchange 2013, topology discovery actually takes place in two ways. The Active Directory Topology Service runs on every CAS or Mailbox server. At startup, the service performs DNS queries to locate every global catalog (GC) and domain controller (DC) in the forest, chooses a single GC to use as its source of information from the forest

configuration-naming context, and ranks the remaining DCs according to their site connectivity. Exchange components that need to retrieve information from Active Directory
do it by querying the Active Directory Topology Service, which caches the results of those
queries. Each server Active Directory Topology Service instance also tracks which Active
Directory site the server is in (using the Netlogon service on a nearby domain controller)
and then stamps the result in the msExchServerSite attribute on its own server object in
Active Directory. The Active Directory Topology Service updates the server's site membership every 15 minutes, and netlogon updates every 5 minutes, so a delay of up to 20 minutes can occur before a change in site membership is reflected in message routing. Keeping
this attribute on the server object enables servers to decide quickly what Active Directory
site they're in without having to perform DNS lookups.

The Transport service also has its own separate, routing-specific, topology module whose
purpose is to discover all the routing-related objects. This service retrieves a list of all Active
Directory sites, IP site links, and Exchange servers in the forest and then uses it to build a
routing map. The msExchServerSite attribute on the retrieved server objects matches servers to sites, and then the server's local routing table is updated every 15 minutes thereafter.

Designing Active Directory to support Exchange

In times of old, administrators charged with designing Exchange 5.5 systems would draw
maps of their networks to identify regions of what Microsoft called high-bandwidth connections. At the time, they were talking about 64 Kbps connectivity! The idea was to identify boundaries within which high-speed connectivity was possible and then use those
boundaries as the basis for designing Exchange 5.5 sites. Although the Exchange-specific
site object is long gone, it has counterparts in the modern implementation of Active
Directory. The Active Directory site and its related site link and site link bridge objects give
you a way to segment a large network into smaller pieces.

Microsoft recommends preparing for your Exchange 2013 deployment by document-
ing your existing Active Directory topology. This documentation, which can be prepared
manually or with an automated tool such as the Microsoft Active Directory Topology
Diagrammer (*http://www.microsoft.com/en-us/download/details.aspx?id=13380*). The point
of making such a diagram is that it helps you identify where your existing Active Directory
sites are physically located, how they're configured, and how they're linked. All these
are important factors when deciding where to put your Exchange 2013 servers because
Active Directory site membership might affect how you design your DAGs (as described in
Chapter 9, "The Database Availability Group," in *Microsoft Exchange Server 2013 Inside Out:
Mailbox and High Availability*), message routing, and general use of Active Directory.

Microsoft's general recommendations for the placement of Exchange 2013 servers remain
unchanged from previous versions; because Exchange Mailbox and Client Access servers
need access to Active Directory global catalog servers, you should plan to have a GC on

any site that contains an Exchange 2013 server. Any site that contains a Mailbox server must also contain a Client Access server, and Microsoft recommends that any site you think should contain Mailbox servers should have at least two Mailbox servers to provide redundancy. There are other placement considerations, too, such as the relationship between which Active Directory sites you have and where your DAG member servers are placed. IP site links between Active Directory sites are important enough that they're discussed in the next section.

Most of the time, we don't have the luxury of designing a completely new Active Directory infrastructure that perfectly supports both business requirements and the needs of Exchange. However, in many cases, minor adjustments to the Active Directory topology can benefit you by ensuring that your Exchange servers have uninterrupted access to global catalog servers, and each other, when needed.

How Exchange uses Active Directory for message routing

Because the Active Directory site is one of the primary items Exchange uses when deciding how messages will be routed, a thorough understanding of the routing process depends on knowing how Active Directory sites factor in.

The most important thing you should know about message routing in Exchange 2013 is that an Exchange 2013 server always tries to connect to the target delivery group directly unless you have established a hub site for concentrating message flow. Establishing a hub site causes all mail to flow through servers on that Active Directory site if it's on the least cost path. If the source server cannot, or is not allowed to, establish a direct connection to the target delivery group, it will attempt to route the message using least-cost routing. Finding the least-cost route seems like a simple enough task, but a number of nuances in the process make it more complex, especially if the Active Directory administrators haven't paid much attention to site link costs. After all, if replication works, who cares what value the site link costs are?

The algorithm by Exchange used is:

1. Determine the lowest-cost route to the destination by adding up the IP site link costs along each possible path. If the ExchangeCost value is set for an IP site link object, that cost is used; otherwise, the normal IP site link cost value is used.

2. Rank the possible paths based on their cost.

3. The lowest overall path cost is the preferred route.

4. If there are multiple paths with the same cost, the one with the fewest number of hops is the preferred route.

5. If there are multiple paths with the same cost and the same number of hops, the path is chosen according to which site comes first in alphabetical order.

6. Determine whether a hub site exists. If so, mark it as the next hop for the message. If not, set the next hop to be the target delivery group.

7. If there are multiple recipients on the message, repeat steps 1 through 3 for each additional recipient. Compare the set of possible paths to see whether there is a site in common; if so, mark that site as the next hop.

8. Attempt to deliver the message directly to the next hop.

If a direct connection to the next hop fails, and the message is not being delivered to a DAG, Exchange performs an operation known as *queuing at the point of failure*. It reverses the least-cost routing path to discover the server that is closest to the destination. If no servers outside the home site can be contacted (normally due to a network outage), the message is queued on the server that currently has it and will be retried every minute until it is delivered or it expires from the queue after two days. You can configure these settings with the Set-TransportServer cmdlet. For instance, this command sets the retry interval to five minutes and the timeout interval to three days:

```
Set-TransportServer –Identity ExServer1 –MessageRetryInterval 00:05:00
–MessageExpirationTimeOut 3.00:00:00
```

> **Tip**
> You shouldn't change these intervals unless you have good reason to do so. If you do change them, make sure that the same values are applied on all Mailbox servers across the organization to have consistent behavior.

For delivery to a server in a DAG, of course, Exchange tries to deliver the message to any DAG member on any Active Directory site that isn't the least-cost site; if those attempts all fail, it performs queuing to the point of failure.

It's important to understand that least-cost routing determination is not a one-time process that only happens on the originating server. The same process occurs on each hub transport server the message passes through to allow further optimization of the route. How connector scoping can influence routing is discussed in the "Selecting a send connector" section later in this chapter.

Overriding Active Directory site link costs

Because Active Directory site membership is such an important part of routing, you might find that you want to adjust the Active Directory topology in your organization to control how messages flow. This process usually begins by capturing the existing Active Directory topology, using the previously mentioned Active Directory Topology Mapping tool; you can gain another valuable piece of information by mapping Exchange servers to sites. You can extract a list of servers and their sites with:

```
Get-ExchangeServer | Select Name, Site
```

With that information in hand, you can identify whether you'd like to change anything about the topology. One possible area of improvement is that the IP site link costs that are configured for Active Directory might not represent the best cost for message routing. There are many reasons this could be the case. Active Directory might be in production for a long time, and the original IP site link costs have never been updated to reflect the current underlying network connections—and, after all, if Active Directory replication works, why worry about revising or updating the site link costs? It's also true that companies might have different teams in charge of Active Directory and Exchange, and the two teams might not see eye to eye when it comes to assigning the most efficient costs for routing. Such is life. Exchange offers a way around the problem by substituting an Exchange routing cost for a link to replace the Active Directory IP site link cost. This is done with the Set-ADSiteLink cmdlet. For example, to assign an Exchange cost of 10 to the Palo Alto–Pensacola site link, you'd use a command like this:

```
Set-ADSiteLink -Identity 'Palo Alto-Pensacola' -ExchangeCost 10
```

The Get-ADSite cmdlet reveals all the sites currently defined in Active Directory, and the Get-ADSiteLink cmdlet returns a list of current site links. The Transport service begins to use the new cost in its least-cost routing calculations immediately when you configure an Exchange-specific cost for a link. Adding an Exchange-specific cost for a site link does not affect or influence Active Directory replication in any way. Exchange uses the cost only to calculate the optimum routing path for messages.

You can also use the Set-ADSiteLink cmdlet to set a maximum message size for the link. This can be useful if you have a site that sits at the end of an extended link and can't afford to have large messages transmitted across the connection. This might be the case when you have a hub-and-spoke network that connects large data centers with branch offices or, indeed, when connections such as satellite links are used to communicate with ships and other locations in hard-to-reach places. The Transport service generates an NDR or any attempt to send a larger message across the link. Here's an example of how to set a maximum message size:

```
Set-ADSiteLink -Identity 'Pensacola-Corry Station' -MaxMessageSize 1MB
```

INSIDE OUT Do you need another layer of complexity?

Assigning an Exchange-specific routing cost should be done only when absolutely necessary. It might improve the efficiency of routing when first introduced, but moving away from the basic IP site link costs Active Directory maintains introduces another layer of complexity to manage.

The question of hub sites

Many messaging deployments were designed around hub-and-spoke networks in the days when wide-area networking was expensive and unreliable. This is a less popular design option today now that bandwidth is much more plentiful and much less expensive. Many companies are exploiting cheap bandwidth to centralize the delivery of IT services and applications in very large data centers. Some of these projects need to reintroduce elements of hub and spoke routing when the data center is the hub that hosts the vast majority of computing resources and the spokes go down to a small set of branches that support users who cannot connect to the center to use IT services for one reason or another. Other instances occur when a firewall separates two parts of a company, each of which has its own Active Directory site, and all communications have to be channeled through a hub site between them.

The Set-ADSite cmdlet is used to mark an Active Directory site as a hub site. For example:

```
Set-ADSite -Identity 'Central Hub Site' -HubSiteEnabled $True
```

You can use the Get-ADSite cmdlet to reveal whether any of the current sites are configured as hub sites.

When a Mailbox server calculates the least-cost path for an outbound message, it sees whether any of the sites in the path are marked as hub sites. If none of the sites is considered a hub, the server attempts to connect to a server in the target site to deliver the message. If a hub site is found, the mailbox server attempts to connect to a Mailbox server (or a legacy hub transport server) in that site to deliver the message to it for subsequent onward routing to its destination.

Chapter 2

Selecting a send connector

A single organization can contain multiple send connectors, so Exchange has to decide which one to use when sending an outbound message. Here's what Exchange does to select a send connector:

1. Gathers a list of all available send connectors.

2. Discards any disabled connectors or any connectors that are down.

3. Discards all connectors that have a maximum message size less than the size of the message.

4. Selects connectors that are available (in scope) for the originating server and whose address space accommodates the recipient's domain. (An address space of * matches all domains.)

5. Selects the connector that has the closest address space match. For example, if one connector has an address space of * and another has an address space of fabrikam. com, any messages addressed to the fabrikam.com domain will be routed to the second connector.

6. If more than one available connector exists, determines the best choice by the following:

    a. Least routing cost based on aggregated site costs. A connector in the local site will always be preferred over a connector hosted in a remote site.

    b. Whether the connector is hosted by the same Mailbox server that is making the routing decision. A connector on the same server is always preferred over a connector on another hub transport server on the same site.

    c. Alphanumerically, meaning that the connector name that comes first in alphanumeric order is used.

Hopefully, your messaging environment is organized in such a way that Exchange never has to resort to alphanumeric selection from a range of connectors hosted by servers in the local site!

The impact of scoping

Scoped send connectors (those with their *IsScopedConnector* property set to $True) are not visible to servers outside their home Active Directory site. Therefore, servers on other sites cannot include the connector in their routing tables and thus will not route messages across the connector when they calculate the least-cost route for delivery to external recipients.

Routing calculation happens at every hub transport server that a message passes through, so that a message follows the least-cost path at all times. Therefore, if a message passes through a site that contains a connector that offers a lower cost path, the hub transport server on that site recomputes the route and redirects the message. Any connector hosted on the site is considered when the optimum path is determined, including scoped connectors that were invisible to the hub transport server on the site where the message was originally dispatched. This aspect of Exchange routing might mean that messages pass through a connector when you don't anticipate this happening.

For example, assume that a user in the fabrikam.com domain sends a message to two Internet recipients at contoso.com. The fabrikam.com user doesn't have a connector in her Mailbox server's home site. Fabrikam's network is configured to use a hub site for message routing. The hub site has two send connectors. One is not scoped and has an address space of SMTP:*. This connector is known throughout the organization, and it's the destination connector selected by the originating server. However, the second connector is scoped and has an address space of SMTP:*.contoso.com. The Mailbox server on the hub site examines the recipient addresses and determines that the scoped connector, which is included in the hub site's routing table, is a better match and therefore puts the message in the queue for the scoped connector. This is all extremely logical to Exchange but might puzzle administrators if they monitor queues and observe a lack of expected traffic across the general-purpose send connector or an increase in traffic across the scoped connector. It's really not all that important if the two connectors use the same Internet connection, but it could be an issue if you have connection paths with different configurations (such as the maximum message size) and need to force messages along a specific path with scoped connectors.

Because Exchange routing is recalculated on each site a message passes through, the only way you can prevent unwanted traffic from going across scoped connectors is to place these connectors on separate sites that don't host other send connectors. If you place scoped connectors on sites that support a lot of traffic going to and from other destinations, the potential for rerouting will always exist for messages because they are handled by Exchange servers on the site.

Exchange 2013 and DNS MX lookups

Exchange is completely dependent on Active Directory and DNS. A misconfigured DNS server—or, worse still, a mistake in configuring the DNS settings on an Exchange server—can lead to all sorts of ill behavior. One common problem involves getting the right DNS client configuration for servers that need to resolve both internal and external DNS names. This so-called split-brain DNS scenario is common when servers are multihomed to both an internal network and the Internet, as transport servers often are. To help resolve this problem, Microsoft enables users to customize DNS lookup settings, for Exchange only, on individual servers. To see these settings, open EAC, navigate to the Servers tab, and double-click a server to open its properties dialog box. Switch to the DNS Lookups tab (Figure 2-10). This part of the server properties window contains two sets of controls: one for external DNS lookups (which are performed for MX record resolution) and one for internal DNS lookups. For each of these control sets, you can specify whether a particular adapter's settings should be used for resolution, or you can provide the IP addresses (not an FQDN, although you may use an IPv4 or IPv6 address) of DNS servers you want Exchange to use. When these settings are in place, Exchange performs DNS queries only against the servers you set, ignoring the normal settings on NICs. This feature is a mixed blessing; it is very convenient to be able to tell Exchange exactly which DNS servers to use, but if you make a mistake here, or if another administrator makes a change without your knowledge, it can be tricky to troubleshoot.

The Set/Get-TransportService cmdlets give you access to these settings from within EMS, which is quite useful for ensuring that all your servers have consistent settings. For example, this cmdlet will set each of the Exchange 2013 servers in your organization to use the popular OpenDNS service for external DNS resolution:

```
Get-TransportService | Set-TransportService -ExternalDNSAdapterEnabled $false
-ExternalDNSProtocolOption Any -ExternalDNSServers 208.67.222.222
```

In addition to changing these settings on the Transport service, you can make the same changes to the Front End Transport service by substituting Set-FrontEndTransport in the preceding command. Both services also accept parameters for choosing which NIC the settings apply to and whether you want to use UDP, TCP, or both for DNS queries.

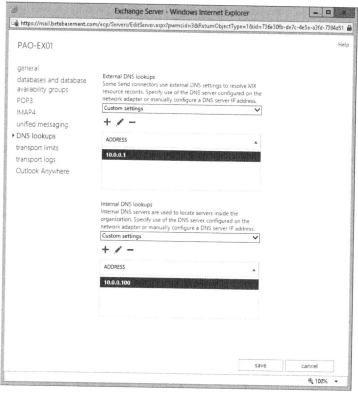

Figure 2-10 DNS settings now specified for individual Exchange servers

Delayed fan-out

Exchange uses a technique called delayed fan-out to optimize the use of network band-width to transport messages. After a message goes through the categorizer, Exchange knows the full recipient list and can then calculate the routing path for the message. After you have a message with multiple recipients, it's likely that different routing paths are necessary to get the message to the destination servers. Typically, email systems fan out and create as many copies of the message as required to travel the different routes. This technique works, but it means that all the copies are created on the originating server, and each copy must be processed separately. If some of the recipient mailboxes are in the same database, multiple copies of the same message travel across the same connector to the same destination.

To avoid this problem, Exchange examines the routing path for each recipient of a message to determine how it can transfer the fewest copies of the message across common routing paths before it needs to fan out into separate copies. Some copies will have to be gener-ated immediately, but in many instances, a single copy can be routed across a common link to another Mailbox server in another site, which can then create multiple copies for local delivery. The determination of the most efficient delayed fan-out for a message is arrived at by identifying the hub transport servers that will create multiple copies. Each of these Mailbox servers is referred to as a fork in the routing path.

INSIDE OUT   The advantages of delayed fan-out

Delayed fan-out might seem like an esoteric tweak to a well-known routing technique. However, its application can result in substantial savings when messages with large attachments travel across common paths. Consider a message sent by a user on site A with a 10 MB attachment that's sent to 100 users, 80 of whom are on site B. With normal fan-out, the Mailbox server on site A creates 80 copies of the message and sends them to a server on site B, so a total of 800 MB travels across the network between the two sites. With delayed fan-out, just one copy travels between sites A and B, and a server on site B fans that one copy out to the 80 recipients. This saves 790 MB of bandwidth *on a single message!* This might not be important if you enjoy unlimited cheap bandwidth, but it can be a critical factor in achieving speedy message transmission across low-bandwidth site connections.

High availability and Exchange transport

High availability has long been an important focus for the Exchange product group. An email system that can't store and retrieve mail reliably isn't much use to anyone. This focus has led to the release of several generations of high availability (HA) and disaster recovery (DR) features, beginning with transaction logging and continuing through storage groups, local and cluster continuous replication, and the DAG architecture. In Exchange 2007, the Exchange team broadened its definition of what HA means by adding a system for protecting messages against data loss in transit. Consider when server A is sending a message through SMTP to server B. If server A fails before the message is completely delivered, or if server B fails after the message has been accepted but before it has been delivered to the next hop, the original message might never be delivered. Exchange 2007 addressed this potential data loss by introducing the *transport dumpster*, an unfortunately named caching system that retained copies of messages sent between Exchange 2007 servers until their safe arrival could be verified. The point of the transport dumpster was to preserve copies of messages so they could be replayed if a cluster failure occurred during message transport.

In Exchange 2010, Microsoft added a complementary feature known as shadow redundancy. Microsoft designed it to increase the resilience of Exchange to outages in the transport system and to complement its investment in HA for other areas of the product. The transport dumpster provides redundancy for messages following a failover, and shadow redundancy provides the same capability for messages while they are in transit elsewhere inside the organization. Unlike the transport dumpster, Exchange 2010 shadow redundancy didn't depend on clustered servers and worked even if you only deployed standard Mailbox servers and didn't use DAGs. The net effect is that the Exchange 2010 transport system gained a form of near-stateless operation in terms of its ability to recover messages after a failure.

Exchange 2013 makes some significant changes to both of these features.

- Shadow redundancy caches a copy of every message sent or received within the delivery group until the other server has signaled acceptance of the message transfer. This covers communications with Exchange servers and any other SMTP server.

- Shadow redundancy uses DAGs and Active Directory sites as HA boundaries; this boundary system helps the shadow redundancy system keep the minimum possible number of redundant messages while still ensuring transport integrity. Within a DAG that spans multiple Active Directory sites, shadow redundancy prefers to shadow messages in remote sites to provide a higher degree of site resiliency.

- The transport dumpster feature now has a catchy new name, Safety Net. After the Transport service accepts a message on a server, it goes into that server's Safety Net queue until the Safety Net timeout period has expired.

- Each Mailbox server has its own Safety Net queue, but Safety Net itself is now redundant so that each server maintains a secondary Safety Net queue on another server. This provides additional protection against failure of the primary Safety Net server.

The shadow redundancy and Safety Net features work together with the DAG architecture (and all the other HA and data safety features in the store) to provide comprehensive protection for messages from the time they are submitted by a client until they are either delivered or leave the Exchange organization. Microsoft succinctly sums up the difference between Safety Net and shadow redundancy by saying, "Safety Net begins where shadow redundancy ends." That's because shadow redundancy maintains redundant copies of messages in transit, whereas Safety Net keeps redundant copies of messages after they've been delivered. Think of shadow redundancy as a mechanism that helps make sure that messages are delivered, whereas Safety Net is used to ensure that previously delivered messages that were lost during a failover can be replayed.

Figure 2-11 shows a high-level view of the transport HA flow. The process works like this:

1. A message arrives on HSVEX01, an Exchange 2013 Mailbox server, from outside the transport HA boundary. Say that it arrives from outside the organization.

Chapter 2

2. Before accepting delivery of the message and sending a 220 status code back to the originating server, HSVEX01 opens an outbound SMTP connection to HSVEX03 and sends a copy of the message to it. HSVEX03 stores this message in its shadow redundancy queue. After it has done so, it acknowledges receipt of the message back to HSVEX01. Now a safe copy of the message can be redelivered in case HSVEX01 fails.

3. HSVEX01 delivers the message. It accepts the message delivery by sending a 220 result back to the sending server. It then routes the message to the Mailbox Transport Delivery service for delivery to the local recipient.

4. HSVEX01 moves a copy of the message to its local primary Safety Net database. It also generates a *discard status message* for HSVEX03 that is locally stored in a queue for HSVEX03. This status message says, "I delivered the message, and you don't need to keep a copy any longer."

5. HSVEX03 polls HSVEX01 for the discard status message every two minutes.

6. When the discard status message becomes available, HSVEX03 knows that it is safe to move its copy of the message to its shadow Safety Net queue. (More on the distinction between the primary and shadow Safety Net queues in the "Safety Net" section later in this chapter.)

7. The message remains in both the primary and shadow Safety Net stores until the message expires. If a mailbox database failover occurs, any unexpired messages in the primary Safety Net database will be resubmitted to the new active database copy, which will accept only messages it doesn't already have. If the primary Safety Net isn't available, the shadow Safety Net will resubmit the messages instead.

INSIDE OUT   Trading performance for safety

The fact that Exchange is keeping extra copies of messages in the shadow redundancy and Safety Net subsystems might lead you to wonder whether there's a performance impact. Of course there is: every message is stored at least twice, meaning that the I/O impact of transport operations is at least doubled. However, the real impact of this additional overhead is small. The messages are kept for a relatively short time, and the additional load is distributed across multiple servers. The extra redundancy is well worth the slight performance penalty.

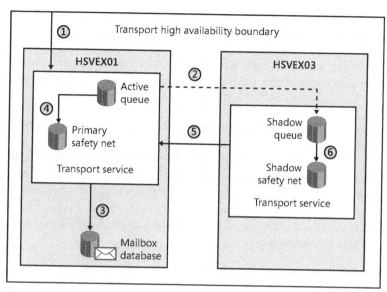

Figure 2-11 The stages of the Exchange HA transport process

Shadow redundancy

Shadow redundancy complements the other Exchange features that contribute to high availability, such as database replication, which concentrate on removing databases, disks, and servers as potential single points of failure. The major goal for shadow redundancy is to eliminate transport servers as a single point of failure as SMTP messages come into and flow out of the messaging infrastructure. As long as multiple servers exist within the delivery group, shadow redundancy makes it possible to remove an edge or Mailbox server (or lose a transport server through an outage) without losing any messages. This also means that you can take a transport server offline to apply a software upgrade or perform other maintenance without worrying about any messages that might exist in its queues. Of course, all this is true as long as you have shadow redundancy enabled (it is enabled by default) and your topology meets the minimum requirements; you need at least two Mailbox servers to use shadow redundancy.

Shadow redundancy depends on three fundamental principles:

- Whenever a user sends a message from an Exchange 2013 Mailbox server, the Mailbox Transport Submission service retains a hashed copy of the message in the Sent Items folder of the user's mailbox. The message remains in the Sent Items folder until the transport server has accepted ownership for the message and placed it in its transport database. The hub transport server that is currently processing a message is known as the primary server. If the message is ever lost through an outage somewhere along its route, Exchange can resubmit the copy from the transport database on the primary server and route it to its destination.

- Each hop queues a discard status after it delivers the message to the next hop. The previous hop queries for that discard status every two minutes. All Exchange checks for at a given hop is whether the next hop acknowledges delivery.

- When the primary server is sure that a message has been successfully delivered, discard events are generated to inform servers that they can remove any copies they have of the message. Transport servers generate heartbeats between each other in their SMTP communications to indicate that they are available. If a primary server cannot be contacted based on missing a number of heartbeats over a predetermined interval, Exchange can transfer the primary server role to another transport server (that has a copy of the message), which can then resubmit the message, using the copy in its shadow queue.

Shadow redundancy operates on edge and Mailbox transport servers to keep copies of messages (called shadow copies) in a special queue until they have been successfully delivered to all the next hops in the message paths. After a server has received discard notifications for all the hops in the path of a message, it knows that it can remove the shadow copy of the message from its transport database. If any of the hops fail to generate a discard notification, the Transport service queues the message for redelivery.

INSIDE OUT   Discard notifications

The discard notifications have a low impact on bandwidth because they are very basic SMTP transactions between servers. Think of something like, "Server X: I've received message ID 136146." Exchange 2013 servers exchange data about discard notifications during special-purpose connections, a change from previous versions, which did so during regular SMTP connections. A server can also establish a separate connection to another server to retrieve data about messages that it had previously sent to allow it to decide whether to discard its copy.

Shadow redundancy is configured on an organization-wide basis by setting the ShadowRedundancy property with the Set-TransportConfig cmdlet. For example:

```
Set-TransportConfig –ShadowRedundancy $True
```

When shadow redundancy is enabled, Exchange 2013 servers still send messages normally if a shadow copy cannot be persisted for some reason. You might prefer to reject messages

if they can't be protected; you can then use the Set-TransportConfig
–RejectMessageOnShadowFailure command to force rejection of any message for which a
shadow copy cannot be created. Messages rejected for this reason generate an SMTP error:
"The SMTP response code is 451 4.4.0 Message failed to be made redundant." However, if
you don't have at least two Mailbox servers in each Active Directory site (or multiple DAG
members in multiple Active Directory sites), enabling RejectMessageOnShadowFailure
might lead to unexpected mail rejections if Exchange can't create a shadow copy.

When shadow redundancy is enabled, Exchange servers insert an XSHADOWREQUEST
ESMTP command into the interaction they conduct with other SMTP servers to establish
whether those servers support shadow redundancy and to provide the heartbeat that indicates server availability. Exchange 2010 used the XSHADOW verb; the Exchange 2013 verb
is different so that Exchange 2010 won't attempt to store its shadow copies on Exchange
2013 servers.

Discard notifications are also implemented through an SMTP extension called XQDISCARD.
Exchange refers to primary and shadow copies of messages and primary and shadow servers. The primary message is the copy that is in transit between an originating server and
the other transport servers that should receive copies; the shadow is the copy maintained
until the Transport service is certain that the primary message has been successfully transferred to everywhere it should go. The primary server is the one that is currently processing
the message along its path to eventual delivery. Shadow servers have already processed the
message and are waiting to be notified that they can discard their shadow copy.

> **Note**
>
> The obvious sign that messages are waiting for notifications to come back is their pres-
> ence on the shadow redundancy queue on a Mailbox server. Messages stay on this
> queue until Exchange is sure that they have been transmitted successfully.

Two other transport configuration settings are used to control how shadow redundancy
works:

```
Set-TransportConfig –ShadowResubmitTimeSpan 4.00:00:00
–ShadowMessageAutoDiscardInterval 3.00:00:00
```

The first parameter in this command sets the interval during which shadow retries
will be performed to four days (the value of ShadowResubmitTimeSpan is specified as
dd.hh:mm:ss), meaning that Mailbox servers will try to contact each other for up to four
days before concluding that a server is unavailable. If a server is deemed unavailable, it can
no longer function as a primary server. The next parameter specifies the period after which
discard notifications are discarded; in this case, discard notifications are removed after
three days.

Chapter 2

Shadow Redundancy Manager: The answer for servers that don't support shadow redundancy

A component within the Transport service called Shadow Redundancy Manager (SRM) monitors the flow of messages, their current delivery status, and the reconciliation of discard notifications that come back from other transport servers to indicate that messages have arrived there. SRM can manage transmission to servers that don't support the concept of shadow redundancy and therefore don't issue confirmations back to Exchange when they accept messages. In these instances, a successful SMTP connection and transfer is deemed sufficient confirmation that the message has been moved to the next hop, and SRM will mark it as if a confirmation message had been received from the other mail server. When the remote server has accepted the message, it is moved to the sending Exchange server's Safety Net system.

For messages sent within a transport HA boundary, the normal behavior of shadow redundancy takes advantage of the way Exchange 2013 message routing works. When a Mailbox server on an Active Directory site or DAG receives an inbound message, it tries to deliver that message directly to the target server. If there is no shadow copy, the Transport service chooses a Mailbox server on the site or DAG and uses it as a shadow redundancy partner.

Exchange also attempts to apply the principle of shadow redundancy to incoming messages even if they originate on servers that don't support the feature. In this case, Exchange accepts the message, makes a shadow copy, and then attempts to deliver it onward. Figure 2-12 illustrates this process. An Internet SMTP server contacts HSVEX01 to deliver a message to it. The standard SMTP conversation process takes place with a twist; normally, an SMTP server acknowledges receipt of the message and delivers it onward after the sender signals the end of the message. In this case, HSVEX01 immediately opens an outbound SMTP connection to a randomly selected shadow redundancy partner on another site (if available) or the same site. The default is to connect up to four servers in remote sites, falling back to two local servers if necessary. Each failed connection causes Exchange to wait 30 seconds before trying again; after Exchange decides that it can't connect to a shadow partner, it continues processing the message.

Assume that HSVEX01 chooses HSVEX03 as its shadow redundancy partner. That connection is used to deliver a shadow copy of the message to HSVEX03, which stores it in the shadow queue. After HSVEX01 has delivered the message, HSVEX03 acknowledges receipt. Only then does HSVEX01 return an acknowledgement to the Internet sender. If for some reason HSVEX03 cannot or does not acknowledge receipt of the shadow copy, HSVEX01 can attempt shadow redundancy delivery to another server, or it can refuse delivery of the message so that the other server has to resend it later.

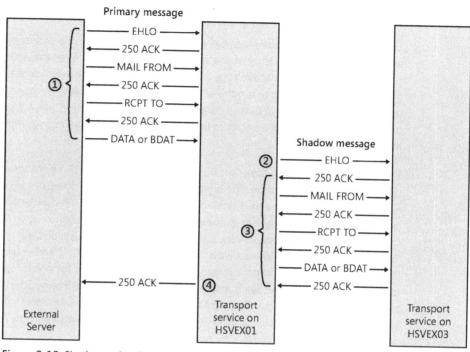

Figure 2-12 Shadow redundancy flow for an external message

When a message arrives from the outside world, the process of picking the shadow redundancy partner is a little different. If the receiving server (HSVEX01 in this example) is a member of a DAG, it will choose another Mailbox server in the same DAG. If the DAG has member servers in multiple Active Directory sites, HSVEX01 first tries to connect to a DAG member on a different site. (You can control this by using Set-TransportService –ShadowMessagePreference.) If the receiving server is not a DAG member, the Transport service will always connect to a Mailbox server on the same Active Directory site.

In an organization that has a complex routing topology or when some connections are not immediately available, it might take some time before a message is delivered to all hops. You do not want the SMTP connection with the other Mail server to time out because this would cause it to resend the message. To get around the problem, Exchange sets a value for the maximum time (in seconds) that it will wait for the message to be processed. In Exchange 2013, this time is 600 seconds, a value that currently cannot be changed. If the time delay elapses, Exchange issues an acknowledgment to the originating server. This system could result in some messages being lost if a Mailbox server fails and loses its transport database. However, in practical terms, the risk is not high.

Safety Net

The Exchange transport dumpster was intended to maintain a cache of successfully delivered messages as a last-ditch, just-in-case recovery mechanism. After a message was successfully submitted to the active copy of a mailbox database, the message was persisted in the transport dumpster so that if the active mailbox database failed, the message could be resubmitted to the newly activated database. This protected against when a message had been delivered to the active database but the active database had not yet replicated to all its passive copies.

Safety Net is based on the transport dumpster architecture, but there are some important differences in implementation. The biggest is that the transport dumpster in Exchange 2007 and Exchange 2010 was a single point of failure, but Safety Net is redundant; there are primary and shadow Safety Net queues. These queues are still maintained in the transport queue database on Mailbox servers, just as they were in earlier versions, although they are logically separate. Safety Net is always enabled; you can't turn it off, and you can't explicitly control how much disk space it uses. You *can* adjust the time for which messages are kept in Safety Net with the Set-TransportConfig –SafetyNetHoldTime, which defaults to two days; the longer you set the hold time, the more disk space Safety Net will consume, although its ultimate consumption is tied to the rate at which messages pass through your organization.

The Transport service on the Mailbox server sends a message to Safety Net after it has been delivered. There are actually two Safety Nets. The primary Safety Net for a given message is on the Mailbox server that last held the message before its successful delivery, and the shadow Safety Net is on whichever server has the shadow redundancy copy of the message—so two messages might have different primary *and* shadow Safety Net locations.

> **Note**
> If you turn off shadow redundancy, you are implicitly turning off the shadow Safety Net feature because it depends on shadow redundancy. This makes Safety Net a single point of failure again, as the transport dumpster in previous versions was; the risk of doing so is low, but you should be aware of it before disabling shadow redundancy.

In normal operation, messages go into Safety Net, stay there until the period defined by SafetyNetHoldTime is reached, and then expire. It's more interesting to talk about what happens when Safety Net needs to redeliver messages, though! Redelivery begins when the Active Manager component initiates a failover. (Switchovers don't activate Safety Net.) After the failover is complete, Active Manager on the target server initiates message resubmission, and messages from the primary Safety Net (if it's still up) begin flowing into the Transport service, which accepts any previously unseen messages.

If the primary Safety Net doesn't respond to this request, Active Manager continues requesting resubmission from the primary for 12 hours. At the end of that interval, Active Manager sends a broadcast message to all the Mailbox servers within the transport HA boundary (which, you'll recall, is either a DAG or an Active Directory site) asking for shadow Safety Net messages from the time period of the original failure. The shadow Safety Net instances on the Mailbox servers inside the transport HA boundary resubmit their local message copies.

Transport rules

Exchange 2007 was the first version to include transport rules, which enable administrators to create conditional processing for messages as they pass through the Transport service. Rules can be applied to messages that remain within the organization or those that enter or leave the organization. Many rules are designed to ensure that users comply with company or legal regulations. The same kind of intervention and examination of en route messages was possible with earlier versions of Exchange, but only at the expense of developing expensive, installation-specific event sinks that could only be written by developers with substantial knowledge of Exchange internals. Event sinks were not for the fainthearted, but as the complexity of the tasks that messaging systems were called on to perform increased, it became more obvious that a simple method to introduce conditional processing was required. Exchange 2007 therefore provides a set of cmdlets and EMC wizards to enable administrators to create and deploy transport rules across an organization. Exchange 2010 and Exchange 2013 improved on this foundation by adding more actions, predicates, conditions, and exceptions in rules. This expanded functionality does not mean that you will never be forced to write your own code for message handling; conditions exist that cannot be handled by transport rules. For example, you cannot call your own code from a transport rule to access directories other than Active Directory. To help illustrate the comprehensive range of predicates available to Exchange 2013 transport rules, Table 2-9 lists some of the most common predicates you'll encounter. Details about the full set can be found in the Exchange documentation in TechNet.

TABLE 2-9 Examples of transport rule predicates

Predicate type	Predicates
Identify the sender	From a specific person From a member of a distribution list From users inside or outside the organization From a sender with a specific value in an Active Directory property From a sender in a specified range of IP addresses

Chapter 2

Predicate type	Predicates
Identify the recipient	When a recipient is a specific person (To, Cc, or Bcc) When any of the recipients is a member of a distribution list (To, Cc, or Bcc) When the recipient is inside or outside the organization or in a partner domain When a message is sent from one distribution list to another When a recipient has a specific value in an Active Directory property
Message characteristic	When the message has an attachment with a size greater than or equal to a limit When the message is marked with a specific importance When the message is a specific type When the message has a spam confidence level (SCL) that is greater than or equal to a limit When the message is marked with a specific classification When the message subject contains specific words When a message's attachment contains specific words When a message has an attachment that contains executable content

Transport rules you've developed for Exchange 2007 and Exchange 2010 will continue to work with Exchange 2013. More precisely, your existing rules will be cloned and Exchange 2013 will use the clones, meaning that changes you make to the original rules won't be honored by Exchange 2013. However, these older transport rules are very much a subset of the enhanced rules you can deploy with Exchange 2013. Upgrades such as the ability to make decisions about email processing based on Active Directory attributes for both senders and recipients make transport rules more powerful and flexible.

The new data loss prevention (DLP) feature in Exchange 2013 is based on the transport rule engine. In fact, when you create a DLP policy (a topic covered in the "Data loss prevention" section later in this chapter), you see new transport rules appear. Although you can modify these rules, keep in mind that by doing so you might accidentally disable some aspect of scanning required for compliance with a particular DLP policy, so be careful.

You can create your own rules in EAC or EMS. EMS gives you a great deal of control, but it's a little harder to figure out (and then type in) the exact syntax required for complex rules. EAC includes 10 predefined rule templates that you can use to set up common rules quickly, such as a rule to filter messages based on size or to apply disclaimers (see Figure 2-13). You access the EAC rule creation interface through the Mail Flow section of EAC. If these predefined rule templates don't do what you want, you can use the Create A New Rule option to create a new blank rule that you can customize, or you can use the New-TransportRule and Set-TransportRule cmdlets in EMS to build the rules.

INSIDE OUT Script it once, keep it forever

I'm a big fan of using EMS whenever possible to automate repetitive operations. Creating transport rules might not seem to be repetitive, but writing an EMS script to create the rules you need makes sense; you can write and test the script in your test environment, and, after the rules are working exactly as you want them, you can run the script in your production environment to create the rules. Using a script has the benefit of enabling you to update or adjust rules easily when needed, and the script itself documents which rules you've defined in your environment and how they're configured. Scripting your rules is particularly helpful in hybrid or mixed environments because rules are stored separately for each version of Exchange that you have deployed.

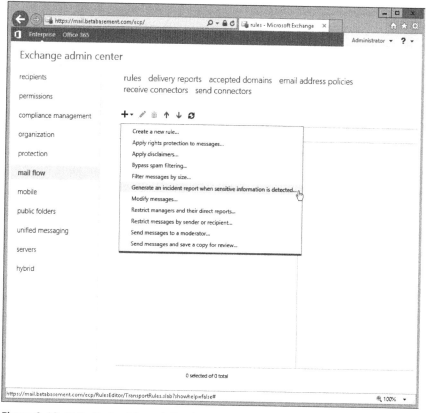

Figure 2-13 EAC offering 10 predefined templates for quickly creating basic rules

Transport rule structure

All transport rules share a basic structure. A rule is composed of three parts: conditions, actions, and exceptions. The EAC rule creation wizard leads you to the specification of each part when you create or modify a transport rule.

- The *conditions* of a rule tell the Transport service what criteria to use when deciding whether a message matches the rule; for example, Apply This Rule To All Outgoing Messages or Apply This Rule To Members Of A Specific Distribution Group. Each condition contains one or more *predicates*; think of predicates as similar to search terms. (See *http://technet.microsoft.com/en-US/library/dd638183(v=exchg.150).aspx* for a complete list of predicates and conditions available in Exchange 2013.)

- The *actions* of the rule specify what the rule does when it's triggered by a message that matches its conditions. Actions can modify the message or its properties, or they can take some action such as forwarding the message for moderation or dropping it and returning an NDR to the sender. (See *http://technet.microsoft.com/en-US/library/aa998315(v=exchg.150).aspx* for the current list of actions available in Exchange 2013 transport rules.)

- *Exceptions* override conditions. For example, don't apply the rule if the sender is in a specified distribution group.

Apart from naming the rule and providing some comments so that other administrators know the purpose of the rule and perhaps who created it and when it was implemented, all you need to do is answer three simple questions to create a rule: When should the rule be triggered (conditions)? When should it *not* be triggered (exceptions)? What should it do when triggered (actions)? However, Exchange 2013 transport rules have some additional optional properties that might be useful to you when defining a rule (see Figure 2-14). The mode of the rule controls whether it is enforced or merely advisory, the activation and deactivation dates enable you to make a rule effective only during a defined period, and the new Generate An Incident Report And Send It To action enables you to trigger an email notification to specified recipients when a rule is triggered.

You can specify that when the rule is triggered, it can be associated with an audit severity level. This level is normally used for data loss prevention rules so that you can maintain a log of instances when a rule was triggered—a serious violation should receive different attention than a minor accidental disclosure.

After you create a rule, it is stored in the configuration-naming context of your Active Directory forest, and all Mailbox servers in the organization have access to it. Any change to the set of rules (including adding or deleting rules or changing the conditions, exceptions, or actions of an existing rule) is replicated to all domain controllers in the organization; this replication triggers each Mailbox server to reload the rule set from its preferred domain controller. Rules are stored in a version-specific container, so if you have existing Exchange 2007 transport rules, they will be imported into the Exchange 2013 version container. At that point, if you make changes to the transport rules in any version of Exchange, you'll have to make the same changes manually in the Exchange 2007 version. For example, suppose you install Exchange 2013 in an existing Exchange 2007 organization and then modify an existing transport rule using EAC. You'll have to make a corresponding change to the Exchange 2007 version of the rule. The same restriction applies to hybrid organizations; Office 365 stores transport rules separately, so after the initial synchronization, changes you make on one side have to be repeated on the other.

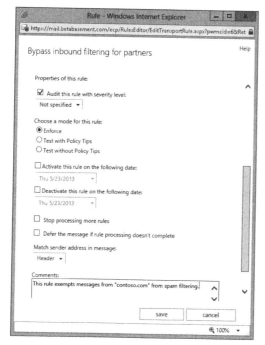

Figure 2-14 Setting some of the Exchange 2013–specific properties on a transport rule

How transport rules are applied

Transport rules are applied to messages by the transport rules agent after the full recipient list is determined by the categorizer. In Exchange 2013, the transport rules agent activates when the OnResolvedMessage transport event fires; this is a change from previous versions that allows a wider range of actions to be applied because the rule isn't triggered until the message has been accepted. The specific actions enabled by this feature provide conditional overrides of routing decisions, but these actions are not currently enabled in on-premises versions of Exchange 2013.

The transport rules agent applies rules to every message from an anonymous sender, meaning that rules always apply to email received from the Internet. Rules apply to messages originated by authenticated senders, too, of course, but depending on the type of message, the actual behavior of the agent might vary. For example, rules that require inspecting the content of a message or attachment can't be applied to messages encrypted with S/MIME, although messages protected with Active Directory Rights Management Services (AD RMS) may still be processed normally by the same rules.

The process of rule application works as follows:

1. The message is passed to the transport rule agent. The agent checks the message type to see whether transport rules can be applied to the message; if not, the message is ignored.

2. The rule with the lowest priority is retrieved and evaluated. If the rule is active (meaning that if activation and deactivation dates are set on the rule that the current date falls between them), evaluation continues.

3. If the rule has no conditions or exceptions, it is immediately applied. Otherwise:

4. If the rule has one or more conditions, the conditions are evaluated to see whether the message matches. If there are multiple conditions, the message must match all of them. If a condition contains multiple values, any match of the condition will apply. For example, a rule with a condition of The Recipient Is and values of Paul Robichaux or Tony Redmond will match any message when the recipient is either of those values.

5. If the rule has a matching condition, and one or more exceptions are defined, the exceptions are evaluated. If *any* part of *any* exception matches, the rule will not be applied to the message.

6. If the result of step 2 indicates that the message should be processed by the rule, all the rule's actions are applied in the order in which they appear in the rule. Note that some actions might cause rule processing to stop—for example, if you delete the message, no further rules can process it!

7. The priority is incremented, and the process returns to step 2. When there are no more rules, processing stops.

Setting transport rule priority

Because rules are processed in priority order, you might need to adjust the priority of individual rules to get them in the proper order. Each rule has a priority, ranging from 0 (zero, the highest) to the number of rules in the system minus 1—if you have 10 rules, the last rule's priority will be 9.

When you open EAC and open the rules section of the Mail Flow tab, EAC lists the current set of transport rules in priority order. You can adjust the priority up or down by using the icons in the toolbar. The new priority becomes effective immediately.

The same effect can be gained with EMS by first retrieving a list of rules with Get-TransportRule and then setting the required priority. For example:

```
Get-TransportRule
```

```
Name                             State     Priority   Comments
----                             -----     --------   --------
Ethical Wall: Traders-Analysts   Enabled   0    Ethical wall to prevent users in the Traders
Contractor email access to
  outside                        Enabled   1    This rule blocks contractors from sending email
Confidential material scanning   Enabled   2    Rule to scan for confidential material and
External access control          Enabled   3    This rule checks for the presence of
Stop Top Secret Mail Leaving     Enabled   4    This rule stops any message marked with the Top
Company disclaimer               Enabled   5    This transport rule applies the approved company
Purchasing Approvals             Enabled   6    First stage in the purchasing approvals workflow
Purchasing Sanctions             Enabled   7    Second stage in the purchasing approvals workflow
Users in Dublin                  Enabled   8    This rule prepends some text to users who are
Test rule                        Disabled  9
```

```
Set-TransportRule -Identity 'Contractor email access to outside domains'
-Priority 2
```

Apart from establishing a clear order of precedence for rule execution, priority can some-times provide a workaround to a limitation that exists in transport rules. Some rule con-ditions evaluate a property of a message against multiple values (such as The Sender Contains 'contoso.com' Or 'tailspintoys.com'), but others can examine that property for only one value. For example, a rule can check for an SCL value determined for a message but only look for one value because the predicate applies that restriction. Thus, if you want to check for two SCL values (say, 5 or 6), you need multiple rules. You could have one rule to check for an SCL value of 5, another to check for an SCL value of 6, and have both apply an update action to write a value into the message header. A third rule that follows the other rules could then check for the value in the message header and take whatever action is required. It's an imperfect but effective way of extending transport rule functionality to work around a small limitation.

See *http://technet.microsoft.com/en-us/library/dd638183(v=exchg.150)* **for more information on transport rule predicates.**

It is critically important that you test new rules before you start to rely on them. In particular, rule priority can act in ways that might surprise you because DLP rules, described in the next section, are added at the bottom of the priority list. If you create a rule that applies a disclaimer and stops further rule processing, no lower-priority rules will be executed when that rule is executed. Therefore, your DLP rules might not be run when you expect them to be.

Active Directory Rights Management Services and transport rules

Some Exchange features combine a high degree of potential usefulness with a high risk that a misconfiguration will cause lots of unpleasantness. The combination of Active Directory Rights Management Services (AD RMS) and transport rules is a great example. AD RMS is intended to provide content protection for messages and Office documents by encrypting them and embedding a template that compatible clients use to control what the user can do with the message or document. For example, a CEO who sends a message out to her employees can tag the message with the AD RMS Do Not Forward template and compatible clients (including Outlook 2007/2010/2011/2013 and Outlook Web App 2010/2013) will allow the recipients to read the message but not forward it. AD RMS differs from other encryption solutions, such as S/MIME, in that it isn't primarily intended to provide protection against eavesdropping or information disclosure; instead, it is meant to give the creator of a message or document a reasonably robust tool to control further dissemination of the protected item.

The utility of AD RMS comes about because it puts decisions about information distribution and control in the hands of the people who create content, and it allows administrators to apply organization-wide rules that automatically apply protection at the transport layer. The risk comes about because it is easy to create a rule that applies protection to messages so that legitimate recipients can't read the things they need.

Exchange 2013 offers two new AD RMS integration features that are worth mentioning in this context. First, you can create a transport rule that applies AD RMS protection templates based on the source IP of the client that sends the message. For example, you could create a rule such that all users on the IP subnet belonging to the legal department would automatically have their messages tagged as Do Not Forward. Second, you can create a transport rule that applies AD RMS protection based on the data loss prevention (DLP) engine's evaluation of the sensitivity of a message. For example, you could create a transport rule that would apply an AD RMS template if DLP detects a credit card number in a message.

There are a few key things to remember when considering or planning an AD RMS deployment for use with Exchange:

- Rule priority matters. Once AD RMS has protected a message, other transport rules may not be able to modify the message, so it's important to make sure you get the rules in the correct order.

- Client access isn't universal. The Outlook client included in Windows Phone 8, for example, can handle RMS-protected messages, but the client included in Apple iOS devices cannot. Outlook Web App 2013 allows messages to be deprotected on the server side and displayed to the client, but the availability of offline mode means that recipients may end up with unprotected cached copies of sensitive messages on their local PCs.

- AD RMS must be internally and externally accessible if you want external Outlook or mobile clients to be able to read AD RMS messages.

- User frustration is likely. The Exchange transport system attempts to prelicense AD RMS–protected messages when it can so that recipients don't have to reach back to the on-premises AD RMS server and authenticate before opening a message, but this isn't always possible. It is incredibly aggravating to see a message in your Inbox and then not be able to read it because you can't contact the AD RMS server.

As it previously did with Active Directory, Microsoft has ported AD RMS to the Azure cloud service, which makes it much more attractive. AD RMS service configuration and deployment is non-trivial, so being able to use a hosted cloud service is likely to entice more companies to take advantage of the protection. Azure RMS addresses the issue of service availability and thus reduces the likelihood of user frustration. However you deploy AD RMS, be prepared to devote extra testing and training time to make it as painless as possible for your users.

Data loss prevention

Microsoft has made much of the data loss prevention (DLP) features in Exchange 2013, and not without reason. Inadvertent data breaches, when an authorized user accidentally divulges sensitive data by sending it to someone who isn't supposed to have it, are an increasingly common and severe problem. In most jurisdictions, such breaches open up the organization to civil and regulatory liability, and in some, a breach of medical, financial, or personal information can even lead to criminal sanctions. Exchange 2013 DLP attempts to prevent these breaches by allowing you to define and apply DLP policies. These policies act in two ways. They include rules that block certain patterns of data (such as credit card numbers or social insurance numbers, such as U.S. Social Security numbers (SSNs) or UK National Insurance numbers), and you can create Policy Tips that appear when users compose messages or add attachments that might violate whatever DLP policies are in effect. Both of these mechanisms piggyback on existing Exchange infrastructure components. DLP policy rules are based on the transport rule system, and Policy Tips are similar in behavior and implementation to the MailTips feature described in Chapter 5, "Mailbox management," of *Microsoft Exchange Server 2013 Inside Out: Mailbox and High Availability*.

A *DLP policy* is a package of settings that specifies what specific types and items of data the policy is supposed to look for. The policy's XML file defines how to match two types of items: *entities* and *affinities*. An entity definition specifies a set of patterns that identify some kind of data item that a policy might match, such as a credit card number. An affinity definition tells the DLP engine about a set of related items that might appear in proximity within a particular type of document or message, such as a medical records document or a corporate financial statement. The existing DLP policies don't define any affinities; third-party developers can do so, but there is no current user interface that allows administrators or users to define affinities. The current implementation of DLP is based entirely on entities.

When you activate a DLP policy, that policy creates new transport rules (and related settings) that look for the kinds of entities and affinities the policy is supposed to monitor.

Matching is handled by a component of the Transport service that performs what Microsoft calls deep content analysis. This process applies several analytical methods, including keyword matches, matching of terms against dictionaries, pattern matches, and specific tests for individual data item types. Microsoft gives the example of calculating a checksum on certain number patterns to see whether they match the checksum rules for credit card numbers. This analysis is performed on message bodies and attachments; if a match is found, the action associated with that particular rule is triggered.

DLP policies

There are three ways for you to define a policy. You can use one of the 40 templates that ship with Exchange 2013, you can import a policy from an external source, or you can define your own policy from scratch. Microsoft has detailed documentation on how to construct your own policies (see *http://technet.microsoft.com/en-us/library /jj674310(v=exchg.150).aspx*), and the EAC dialog box in which you select a template to apply has a Learn More link that claims to point to a page of DLP templates supplied by third parties. (There's nothing there as of this writing.) The most likely means of applying DLP in your organization is to use one of the built-in templates. If you create your own policy from scratch, you have to define all the individual rules to recognize items you wish to match, with the attendant risk of missing something, so most organizations will probably stick with the Microsoft-defined template set to start with.

When you define a policy, you set it to operate in one of three modes:

- Test Without Policy Tips is the default for a newly applied policy. In this mode, the policy's rules operate normally, detecting entities or affinities defined by the policy. Whatever action the rule would have taken is reflected by an entry in the server's message tracking log. However, the actions specified by the policy won't be applied. This is similar to what happens when you run an EMS command with the –WhatIf flag.

- Test With Policy Tips runs the content analysis process against messages as they are processed, and it scans messages in compatible clients (Outlook 2013 only at present) to see whether any of the defined Policy Tips should be displayed. However, actions associated with the rules or with Policy Tips (such as preventing a user from sending a message without overriding the Policy Tip) aren't applied.

- Enforce activates the rules and Policy Tips associated with the policy. Depending on the policy settings, this might cause noncompliant messages to be blocked, although you can define exceptions that allow users to override the policy and send suspect messages anyway.

> **Note**
>
> You can also set these modes on individual rules; that allows you to have a policy with rules that are either enforced or in test mode as the policy evolves or as you modify the rules to meet your business requirements.

In addition to setting the mode, you can also specify what Microsoft calls an incident management mailbox. This is an internal recipient that receives reports any time a user triggers a DLP rule. The idea behind this mailbox is that you can use it to maintain an audit log of potential or actual breaches; with that in mind, you'll want to think carefully about which mailbox to use and who should have access to it.

Data loss prevention rules

DLP rules are transport rules, and you can see them in the Rules section of the Mail Flow tab in EAC. You also see them if you edit a DLP policy. The difference in viewing rules through these two locations is that the DLP policy only shows the rules associated with it, whereas all the rules defined in the organization show up in the Rules section.

DLP rules use a newly introduced predicate in their conditions: If The Message Contains . . . Sensitive Information. This is a shorthand way to say, "if the message contains any data item that looks like it matches any of the data items I care about for this particular policy." There's a list of sensitive data item types at *http://technet.microsoft.com/en-us /library/jj150541(v=exchg.150).aspx*, including various types of bank routing numbers, passport numbers, and so on. When you use this predicate in a rule, the rule will be triggered any time it detects a potential match to any of the sensitive item types the policy uses. For example, if you apply the U.S. Financial Data DLP template, you'll get a set of rules that show up along with any other transport rules you have defined. If you open the U.S. Financial: Scan Email Sent Outside – Low Count rule, you'll see a dialog box similar to the one in Figure 2-15. The rule has two conditions: the recipient is external to the organization, and the message contains specific sensitive items (a credit card number, a U.S.-format bank account number, or an American Banking Association bank routing number). If these conditions both match, the rule fires, and the user sees a Policy Tip that warns her but doesn't prevent her from sending the message.

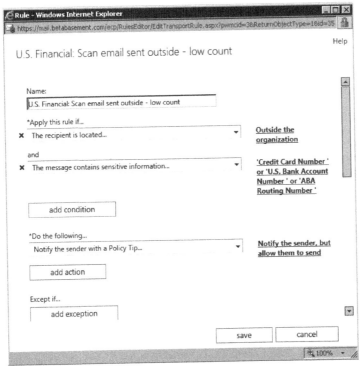

Figure 2-15 The U.S. Financial: Scan Email Sent Outside – Low Count rule triggered by the presence of credit card, bank account, or bank routing numbers

Because of the way this rule is written, it should be clear what it *won't* do: warn users about other types of potentially sensitive data (such as U.S. SSNs or German driver's license numbers), warn users when they're sending sensitive data inside the company, or prevent users from sending a message with sensitive information. If you want any of these behaviors, you must either customize this particular rule or add new ones.

Exchange 2013 features a number of new parameters for transport rules the DLP system uses. Walk through the five new rules that are created when you apply the U.S. Financial

Data DLP policy to see how these rules differ from ordinary transport rules and how they work together:

- U.S. Financial: Allow Override has a single condition. It looks for the word "override" in the message subject; if the condition matches, it sets the X-Ms-Exchange -Organization-Dlp-SenderOverrideJustification header to the *TransportRule override* value. An exception applies if the user overrides the displayed Policy Tip for this rule.

- U.S. Financial: Scan Email Sent Outside – Low Count triggers when a user includes sensitive information in the form of a credit card number, U.S. bank account number, or ABA number. The reason the rule name has "low count" in it is that the rule triggers when there are nine or fewer sensitive items in the message. The message will be audited with a severity level of Medium, and the user will receive a Policy Tip, but the message won't be blocked. No exceptions are defined.

- U.S. Financial: Scan Email Sent Outside – High Count checks for 10 or more pieces of sensitive information in a single message. The condition is the same as the low-count rule, but the actions are different. The user gets a Policy Tip, but the message is blocked unless the user overrides it by providing a business justification. The message is audited with a severity of High, too, so you can see the attempt to send it.

- U.S. Financial: Scan Text Limit Exceeded has a condition of The Message Didn't Complete Scanning, so it triggers when a message couldn't be completely checked for any reason. The only result of this rule is to set the audit level to *High*; the message will still be sent.

- U.S. Financial: Attachment Not Supported triggers when a message contains an attachment type that cannot be inspected; it uses the Any Attachment's Content Can't Be Inspected condition, the intention being that a message that can't be scanned (perhaps because it has an encrypted attachment) will generate a medium-severity audit event because it might warrant further investigation.

> **Note**
>
> Matt Green's blog at *http://www.greenconsultingonline.com/2012/09/office-365 -preview-data-loss-prevention-templates/* offers a useful summary of which conditions and actions are present in each of the Exchange 2013 CU1 DLP templates that are intended for use in the United States.

This might not seem like a very comprehensive set of rules, but it is enough to meet the scope of this particular DLP policy. If a user tries to send a message with sensitive data, unless he overrides, it will generate an auditing entry, and messages with large numbers of sensitive data items will be blocked. Other policies might vary the type of sensitive items checked for or the actions applied when a sensitive message is sent, but they all share the same basic patterns. It is important to understand an essential point about DLP policies: they invariably require several rules to build a policy. Unlike transport rules, which react to specific conditions, DLP rules are usually designed to work in tandem with other rules that allow for different behavior for different conditions. For instance, a user is warned when a low count of sensitive information is detected (one rule) but will be blocked if a threshold is exceeded (another rule).

Policy Tips

Policy Tips give users a visual indication when they compose or attempt to send a message that might violate one of the DLP policies then in effect. In this way, Policy Tips are just like MailTips: when the tip appears, it's supposed to provide a timely warning, suggesting that the user might want to reconsider whatever she's doing. Figure 2-16 shows a Policy Tip triggered by the U.S. Financial DLP policy discussed earlier in the chapter; in this case, the message includes credit card information that shouldn't be sent outside the organization.

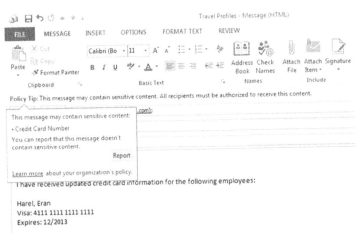

Figure 2-16 Policy Tip warning the user that the message contains potentially sensitive data

Exchange ships with Policy Tips for all its supported languages. Although you cannot modify them, seeing which tips exist might be interesting. These tips aren't displayed or accessible in EAC, but you can see them in EMS with the Get-PolicyTipConfig cmdlet. You must specify the –Original parameter to see the Microsoft-supplied tips. You can also include a –Language parameter to see only tips in a particular language, like this:

```
Get-PolicyTipConfig -Original -Locale en
```

```
Identity                    Value
--------                    -----
BuiltIn\en\NotifyOnly       This message may contain sensitive information. All reci...
BuiltIn\en\RejectOverride   This message may contain sensitive information. Your org...
BuiltIn\en\Reject           This message may contain sensitive information. Your orga...
```

You can't modify built-in Policy Tips, although you might create your own custom tips by using the New/Set-PolicyTipConfig cmdlets or EAC. For example, to create a custom Policy Tip to be used when a user sends a message containing an employee ID number, you could do the following:

```
New-PolicyTipConfig -name en\NotifyOnly -Value "This message contains an internal
employee ID number. Disclosing these numbers externally is against company policy."

New-PolicyTipConfig -name fr\NotifyOnly -Value "Ce message contient un numéro
d'identification interne des employés. La divulgation de ces numéros à l'extérieur
est contre la politique de l'entreprise."

New-PolicyTipConfig Url -value "http://intranet.betabasement.com/DisclosurePolicy
.htm"
```

These cmdlets create notification Policy Tips for English and French; the third cmdlet sets the URL displayed in the Policy Tip. (Interestingly, "Url" must be capitalized precisely or the cmdlet will fail.) You can create one Policy Tip per language per type. That is, you only get one NotifyOnly for English, but you can add a NotifyOnly for any other language, too. When you create your own Policy Tip messages, you can use one of four notification actions. NotifyOnly displays a notification without taking any action, Reject blocks the message from being sent, RejectOverride rejects the message unless the user puts "Override" in the subject line, and Url specifies that the Policy Tip should show the compliance URL you set with *New-PolicyTipConfig Url*.

If you prefer to use EAC, you might be puzzled at first because there's no obvious way to change Policy Tips settings. The solution lies in the DLP Policy Tips settings icon, which looks like a document with check marks and a superimposed gear. It's the next-to-last icon in the EAC toolbar in the Data Loss Prevention section of the Compliance Management tab.

Microsoft claims that you can change which built-in Policy Tip is triggered in a DLP rule, but this doesn't seem to be working as of Exchange 2013 CU2.

Journaling

The first journaling features built into Exchange were rudimentary and focused on the simple capture of messages delivered to target mailboxes or databases so that they could be examined later if deemed necessary. This kind of journaling is known as *message-only journaling*. Exchange 2007 introduced a more comprehensive kind of journaling known as *envelope journaling*, which captures all the information contained in message envelopes along with the message body. Envelope journaling data includes details of all recipients, including Bcc recipients and members of distribution groups.

Exchange journaling is simple to understand. When you enable it, the journaling agent (which runs on every Mailbox server in the organization) copies all messages sent to or received by a set of targets. The goal of this feature is to provide a simple way for a recipient to get copies of all messages, including their metadata, so that the messages can be archived, scanned, or otherwise processed.

> **Note**
>
> In this case, "all messages" means exactly that. Journaling captures messages that are protected with AD RMS, S/MIME, or other types of message encryption. See the TechNet help topic, "Journal report decryption," at *http://technet.microsoft.com/en-us /library/dd876936(v=exchg.150).aspx* if you want to allow AD RMS–protected messages to be decrypted as part of the journaling process.

Since Exchange 2007, there have been two types of supported target: a mailbox database or targets defined by a *journal rule*. If you have Exchange standard Client Access Licenses (CALs), you can only use standard journaling, in which all messages sent or received on a specified mailbox database are journaled. If you upgrade to Exchange enterprise CALs, you gain permission to enable what Microsoft calls premium journaling, which uses journal rules to specify which senders' or recipients' messages should be journaled.

If you're familiar with journaling in Exchange 2007 or Exchange 2010, you won't be surprised to know that Microsoft says, "There is little difference between journaling functionality in Exchange 2013, Exchange 2010, and Exchange 2007." In either case, the steps required to set up journaling are quite simple:

1. Identify the target of the journaling operation. This will be a mailbox database if you're using standard journaling or a user or distribution group if you're using premium journaling. All the target's messages will be captured and sent to the journaling recipient.

2. Identify the journaling recipient. This can be any mail-enabled object inside or outside the organization. As long as the recipient can receive SMTP messages, it will work fine, with one exception: you cannot use an Office 365 mailbox as the journaling recipient for on-premises mailboxes, although the reverse is not true. In hybrid deployments, Microsoft requires you to use an on-premises mailbox for

journaling both on-premises and cloud-based mailboxes. Third-party journaling products depend on this behavior to work—Exchange sends journaled messages to the appliance, software, or device that's responsible for the actual journaling, and then the recipient does all the work.

Journal reports

Journal reports contain the envelope journaling information, presented in such a way that these data can be used as the basis for forensic investigation of email communications. Journal reports meet legal evidentiary requirements and enable investigators to understand the full life cycle of a message.

The body of a journal report includes data such as sender information, message identifier, addressee list (including Bcc), the content, group membership, and so on. All of the recipient metadata for the message are recorded in the journal report, including the complete recipient set from the SMTP envelope (defined as the P1 recipient list in RFC 2821) as well as how each recipient was added to the message. Some recipients are explicitly added to a message by the sender, whereas others might be added by the transport system when a distribution group is expanded or when a transport rule adds a recipient, as when a message is Bcc'd to a sender's manager. The journal report also captures whether the message was forwarded and, if so, who received copies. In addition to the message header information, the original message is attached to the journal report. Attaching a copy of the original message ensures that all the original message headers and properties are fully retained.

> **Note**
>
> This is an important difference with transport rules that forward copies of messages to recipients because these copies are not intended to be faithful replicas of the original message and can have some information removed from the header.

Exchange 2007, Exchange 2010, and Exchange 2013 journal reports are in Summary Transport Neutral Encapsulation Format (S/TNEF). S/TNEF is a richer form of the simpler TNEF format that allows more information (for instance, Outlook voting buttons) to be transported with messages. S/TNEF parts can be carried within a Multipurpose Internet Mail Extensions (MIME) message. Technically, journal reports are MIME-encoded with their content-transfer-encoding field set to binary. Exchange has used S/TNEF format to transport messages between servers since Exchange 2000 and converts this format to standard MIME when messages are transferred across an SMTP connector to an external email system. If you use an external archive system through SMTP, you can configure its domain to accept messages in MIME or S/TNEF.

The data written into journal reports is structured so that data items are written in pairs of fields and values separated by colons. The data captured include the following:

- **Sender**   The SMTP address of the message sender.

- **Subject**   The subject of the message being journaled.

- **Message-id**   The internal message identifier Exchange creates when the message is first submitted to the Transport service. The message identifier is unique and remains with the message for its entire life cycle.

- **Recipient list**   Each recipient is listed as a To, Cc, Bcc, or Recipient (undetermined type) together with the SMTP address. Extra information is given if the recipient is included in the message as the result of an action such as group message, address rewriting, or transport rule intervention.

The journal reports generated for messages internal to an Exchange organization differ from those created for messages that come into Exchange from SMTP connectors. Internal messages have access to a much richer set of information about message recipients (referred to as extended fields). For internal messages, Exchange can verify that the message came from the mailbox shown as the sender. Because the message has been categorized by the transport system, a lot of data about the recipients is available, so you know that most recipients were added as a result of group expansion. Journal reports for messages coming in from an external SMTP domain contain less information because Exchange doesn't know who the sender really is and can only report that a mailbox received the message but can't say whether it was a To, Cc, or Bcc recipient. Finally, the attached message for an external sender is in MIME format, whereas messages attached to journal reports for internal messages are in S/TNEF.

When it's generated, the journaling agent submits the journal reports for delivery through SMTP to the journal destination. Exchange treats journal reports differently from other messages in that they do not generate NDR reports and do not expire on message queues. Not expiring on queues means that journal reports will not be dropped due to messaging outages and will be delivered to the journal destination when the outage is resolved. This is important because the ability to track communications forensically depends on the availability of all reports and would be compromised if some reports expired.

When multiple journal reports are generated

A single journal report is normally generated per message. However, there are circumstances when Exchange is forced to generate multiple reports. In large organizations, messages might be addressed to a very large number of recipients to exceed the chipping size defined for the hub transport server. The chipping size is defined in the value ExpansionSizeLimit setting in the EdgeTransport.Exe.xml configuration file. The default

is 1,000, so if Exchange processes a message that has more than 1,000 recipients, it splits the message into multiple copies so that no copy of the message has more than 1,000 recipients. When this happens, a separate journal report is created for each copy.

Multiple journal reports are also created any time that Exchange has to bifurcate a message. Assume that you send a message addressed to a distribution group that is set to be expanded on a Mailbox or hub transport server in a remote site. The message is also addressed to a set of individual Cc recipients. Exchange creates one journal report for the Cc recipients because the message can be routed to these addresses by the first hub transport server. Another journal report is generated by the second hub transport server after it has expanded the membership of the distribution group and routed the message to those recipients. The second journal report contains information about the members of the distribution group. Both journal reports contain a copy of the original message, and the two can be reconciled because both contain the message identifier of the original message.

Even encrypted messages protected by information rights management (IRM) can be intercepted and copied by journaling. However, you need to enable journal report decryption to allow this to happen. Messages copied by transport rules remain encrypted. You can enable journal report decryption (or disable it, for that matter) using the Set-IrmConfiguration cmdlet. Enabling decryption means that the Journal Report Decryption agent runs against AD RMS–protected messages and decrypts messages that were protected by the user using Outlook or Outlook Web App, plus messages that were automatically protected either by Outlook protection rules or by Exchange transport rules. Once decrypted, these messages are journaled just like unencrypted messages, so bear in mind that they will be visible to anyone who has access to the journaling system.

Alternate journal recipients

If Exchange encounters a problem when it attempts to deliver a journal report to the journal destination, its default behavior is to re-queue the message to be attempted again. This is sufficient to handle transient issues such as a temporary network outage. However, it can become an issue if a fundamental problem occurs, such as a catastrophic failure of the server that hosts the mailbox serving as the journal recipient. Depending on the kind of journaling being performed, these outages can result in large queues, and you might prefer to redirect journal reports while the problem exists. You can configure an alternate journal recipient for this purpose, to which Exchange redirects journal reports if it detects an NDR condition for the primary journal recipient. You configure the alternate journal recipient with the Set-TransportConfig cmdlet by setting the –JournalingReportNdrTo parameter to the SMTP address of the alternate. For example:

```
Set-TransportConfig –JournalingReportNdrTo 'AlternateComplianceMailbox@fabrikam.com'
```

When an NDR condition occurs for a journal report, Exchange checks whether an alternate recipient is available. If not, the journal reports are required, but if an alternate is available, Exchange sends the NDR containing the journal report to the alternate recipient and removes the journal report from its queue. The advantage here is that removing items from message queues reduces the load on hub transport servers by avoiding the need to retry messages continually that cannot get through. The NDRs arrive in the alternate mailbox and can be accessed there to be re-sent when the problem is addressed and the normal journal recipient becomes available again.

INSIDE OUT Potential issues with alternate recipients

Although an alternate recipient provides an immediate fix for a problem that enables Exchange to continue to process journal reports during an outage, there are a few issues that need to be thought through before you can implement an alternate recipient.

First, if the alternate recipient is unavailable for any reason, Exchange deletes the NDRs, and some journal reports will be lost. For example, if the alternate recipient is a mailbox and its quota is exceeded due to a flood of incoming NDRs, it will reject further messages and cause them to be dropped. Therefore, the alternate recipient has to be able to cope with the load generated by journaling during the outage.

Second, a considerable amount of effort might be required to process the NDRs after the outage is over. You will have to open the mailbox, select each NDR, and re-send the journal report to have Exchange redeliver the reports to the journal recipient. This is fine for 10 or 20 NDRs, but opening and resending NDRs rapidly becomes boring.

Last, your legal team has to be satisfied that routing to an alternate recipient does not compromise any requirements that your company has to satisfy. They might be concerned that potential exists for interference with journal reports during the recovery operation and want to know who will recover journal reports from NDRs, how the recovery will proceed, and how to be sure that no journal reports are missed.

Even if an alternate recipient is a viable option for your company, if you use a mailbox as the journal recipient, it might be a better approach to minimize the possibility that an outage will interfere with processing by locating the mailbox on a database that is protected by multiple database copies within a DAG. In the event of a database failure, the Transport service will reroute journal reports to the mailbox in the newly activated copy and continue processing. This approach avoids any of the potential problems discussed previously.

first step is to restrict the number of users who can open the mailbox to the bare minimum of authorized users.

After securing basic access, you should consider three steps to help lock down the journal recipient mailbox:

1. Prevent unwanted messages from cluttering up the mailbox by restricting access to authenticated users. Senders outside the organization are blocked.

2. Prevent internal users from inadvertently attempting to send messages to the mailbox by not listing it in the Global Address List (GAL). People can still send messages to the mailbox by using its SMTP address, but this would be a deliberate action, so take the following step.

3. Prevent anyone but the journal agent from sending messages to the mailbox by restricting acceptable senders to the special Microsoft Exchange address.

You can enforce these restrictions as follows:

```
Set-Mailbox 'Compliance Monitoring Mailbox' -HiddenFromAddressBookEnabled $True
-RequireSenderAuthenticationEnabled $True -AcceptMessagesOnlyFromSendersOrMembers
'Microsoft Exchange'
```

If you open a mailbox that's used as a journal recipient, you'll see that all the journal reports are waiting in the Inbox. A busy journal recipient rapidly accumulates items and could easily amass tens or hundreds of thousands of items in the Inbox if left alone. Some mechanism is therefore required to clean out the journal recipient on a regular basis. Unless the mailbox database contains just a few mailboxes that generate a relatively light load, having someone review and clean out the contents of the journal recipient's mailbox is probably unworkable if thousands of new items arrive daily. A more automated approach is usually required, which accounts for the popularity of using a mail contact pointing to the SMTP address of an archiving product that processes new journal items as they arrive.

Changing organization-level transport settings

In Exchange 2000 and Exchange 2003, the Global Message settings define properties such as the maximum message size. Exchange 2007 omitted a global way to set these parameters through EMC, but Exchange 2010 brought this feature back under the Organization Configuration object. Exchange 2013 has a similar feature, but it's a little buried; you must navigate to the Mail Flow section of EAC, select the Receive Connectors tab, and click the ellipses icon in the toolbar so you can choose the Organization Transport Settings command. That displays the dialog box shown in Figure 2-17, which admittedly doesn't offer many options. You can use the Limits tab to change the maximum send and receive message sizes for the organization (although these are overridden by the limits you set on individual servers or connectors; user limits are applied first, then connector limits, then server limits, and finally organizational limits). You can use the Safety Net tab to change the hold time and retention time discussed earlier in the section on Safety Net, and the Delivery tab provides a way to copy the postmaster email address for the delivery status notification (DSN) error codes you specify. The most valuable control across all these tabs is on the bottom of the Delivery tab, with which you set the postmaster address that external senders see when they receive a DSN. If you don't set it, postmaster@*yourDomain* is used.

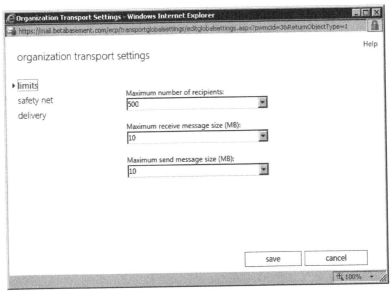

Figure 2-17 The Limits section of the organization transport settings dialog box to control the default sizes for send and receive message limits

Just because EAC doesn't show many options doesn't mean there isn't more to see. The Get-TransportConfig and Set-TransportConfig cmdlets give you access to all the supported settings (although, as with many other aspects of Exchange 2013, some of the parameters you can see and set, such as *HygieneSuite* and *OpenDomainRoutingEnabled*, are officially undocumented because they are reserved for Microsoft use in the Office 365 service). For example, the settings reported by the Get-TransportConfig cmdlet for an organization might look like the following output:

```
Get-TransportConfig
```

```
AddressBookPolicyRoutingEnabled           : False
AnonymousSenderToRecipientRatePerHour      : 1800
ClearCategories                            : True
ConvertDisclaimerWrapperToEml              : False
DSNConversionMode                          : UseExchangeDSNs
```

```
ExternalDelayDsnEnabled                                            : True
ExternalDsnDefaultLanguage                                         :
ExternalDsnLanguageDetectionEnabled                                : True
ExternalDsnMaxMessageAttachSize                                    : 10 MB
(10,485,760 bytes)
ExternalDsnReportingAuthority                                      :
ExternalDsnSendHtml                                                :
ExternalPostmasterAddress                                          : True
GenerateCopyOfDSNFor                                               :
HygieneSuite                                                       : {}
InternalDelayDsnEnabled                                            : Standard
InternalDsnDefaultLanguage                                         : True
InternalDsnLanguageDetectionEnabled                                :
InternalDsnMaxMessageAttachSize                                    : True
(10,485,760 bytes)                                                 : 10 MB
InternalDsnReportingAuthority                                      :
InternalDsnSendHtml                                                : True
InternalSMTPServers                                                : {10.0.0.10,
10.0.0.101, 10.0.0.102}
JournalingReportNdrTo                                              : <>
LegacyJournalingMigrationEnabled                                   : False
LegacyArchiveJournalingEnabled                                     : False
LegacyArchiveLiveJournalingEnabled                                 : False
RedirectUnprovisionedUserMessagesForLegacyArchiveJournaling        : False
RedirectDLMessagesForLegacyArchiveJournaling                       : False
MaxDumpsterSizePerDatabase                                         : 18 MB
(18,874,368 bytes)
MaxDumpsterTime                                                    : 7.00:00:00
MaxReceiveSize                                                     : 10 MB
(10,485,760 bytes)
MaxRecipientEnvelopeLimit                                          : 500
MaxRetriesForLocalSiteShadow                                       : 2
MaxRetriesForRemoteSiteShadow                                      : 4
MaxSendSize                                                        : 10 MB
(10,485,760 bytes)
MigrationEnabled                                                   : False
OpenDomainRoutingEnabled                                           : False
RejectMessageOnShadowFailure                                       : False
Rfc2231EncodingEnabled                                             : False
SafetyNetHoldTime                                                  : 2.00:00:00
ShadowHeartbeatFrequency                                           : 00:02:00
ShadowMessageAutoDiscardInterval                                   : 2.00:00:00
ShadowMessagePreferenceSetting                                     : PreferRemote
ShadowRedundancyEnabled                                            : True
ShadowResubmitTimeSpan                                             : 03:00:00
SupervisionTags                                                    : {Reject, Allow}
TLSReceiveDomainSecureList                                         : {}
TLSSendDomainSecureList                                            : {}
VerifySecureSubmitEnabled                                          : False
VoicemailJournalingEnabled                                         : True
HeaderPromotionModeSetting                                         : NoCreate
Xexch50Enabled                                                     : True
```

Chapter 2

Setting a new value in the transport configuration is easy:

```
Set-TransportConfig –MaxSendSize 50MB
```

Table 2-10 lists the most important properties you can set with the Set-TransportConfig cmdlet and their meaning. See TechNet or the Exchange help file for more information.

Table 2-10 Global transport settings that can be set through the Set-TransportConfig cmdlet

Parameters	Meaning
ClearCategories	Controls whether the transport engine clears Outlook categories during content conversion. The default is $True.
DSNConversionMode	Controls how Exchange handles delivery status notifications (DSNs) that are created by earlier versions of Exchange or non-Exchange messaging systems. The default value is UseExchangeDSNs, which forces a conversion to the DSN format Exchange 2010 uses. An alternate is PreserveDSNBody, which converts DSNs to Exchange 2010 format but preserves any customized text they might contain. You can also specify DoNotConvert, which does exactly what it says.
ExternalDelayDSNEnabled	Specifies whether Exchange should create a DSN if messages from external recipients cannot be delivered immediately. The default is $True.
ExternalDSNLanguage-DetectionEnabled	Controls whether Exchange attempts to send a DSN in the same language as the original message. The default is $True.
ExternalDSNMaxMessage-AttachSize	Defines the maximum size of the attachments sent with a DSN. The default is 10 MB. If the attachments exceed this value, Exchange sends a DSN that includes the original headers but no attachments.
ExternalPostmasterAddress	This property specifies the email address that Exchange inserts into the From header field of a DSN sent to an external recipient. The default is $Null, meaning that Exchange uses the default postmaster address from the hub transport or edge server that generates the DSN (postmaster@ defaultaccepteddomain.com, where defaultaccepteddomain.com is the default accepted domain for the organization). If a value is entered in this property, Exchange uses it instead.
GenerateCopyOfDSNFor	Defines whether any DSN messages are copied to the Postmaster mailbox (as defined by Set-TransportServer). The desired DSNs are defined by their code (for example, 5.1.1). By default, no messages are copied.

Parameters	Meaning
HeaderPromotionMode-Setting	Controls whether Exchange creates named properties for values contained in custom X-headers on incoming messages. The default is NoCreate, so Exchange does not. You can also set this property to MustCreate to force creation or MayCreate to allow creation for messages received from authenticated senders.
InternalDelayDSNEnabled	Determines whether Exchange creates DSNs for messages from internal senders that cannot be delivered immediately. The default is $True.
InternalDSNMaxMessage-AttachSize	Serves a similar purpose to ExternalDSNMaxMessageAttachSize and has the same default value of 10 MB.
InternalSMTPServers	A list of IP addresses of SMTP servers that the anti-spam agents consider internal and therefore ignore as a potential source of spam.
JournalingReportNdrTo	The mailbox the journaling agent will send journal reports to if the journal mailbox is unavailable.
MaxReceiveSize	The maximum size of message the organization can receive.
MaxRecipientEnvelopeLimit	The maximum number of recipients that can be in the header of an incoming message (including the results of group expansion; groups are counted as one even if many recipients are in the group).
MaxRetriesForLocalSite-Shadow and MaxRetriesFor-RemoteSiteShadow	Controls the number of attempts an Exchange Mailbox server makes when submitting a shadow copy of a message in the same site (default is 2) or a remote site (default is 4).
MaxSendSize	Sets the maximum size of message that can be sent within the organization.
OrganizationFederated-Mailbox	Specifies the SMTP address of the federated mailbox used for federated delivery with other organizations.
RejectMessageOnShadow-Failure	Indicates whether failure to submit a shadow copy of a message should cause Exchange to reject the original message. Defaults to $True. When this parameter is set to $True, messages are rejected with the SMTP code 450 4.5.1. When this parameter is set to $False, the message is accepted without making a shadow copy.
Rfc2231EncodingEnabled	Specifies whether RFC 2231 MIME encoding is enabled within the organization. The default is $False.
SafetyNetHoldtime	Controls how long messages are stored in Safety Net after being successfully delivered. The actual time is the sum of the time you specify here and the time set with Set-TransportService –MessageExpirationTimeout.

Parameters	Meaning
ShadowMessageAuto-DiscardInterval	Specifies how long a primary server maintains discard events for shadow messages. If the shadow server doesn't query the events within this interval, the primary server discards them. The default value is 2.00:00:00 (two days).
ShadowMessagePreference-Setting	Controls where you want shadow copies of messages to be submitted. The default, PreferRemote, attempts to deliver shadow copies to a remote site if one is reachable; other permissible values are LocalOnly and RemoteOnly.
ShadowRedundancyEnabled	Specifies whether the shadow redundancy feature is enabled within the organization. The default is $True.
ShadowResubmitTimeSpan	Indicates how long a server waits before deciding that a primary server has failed and takes over processing shadow messages in the shadow queue for the unavailable server. The default value is 03:00:00 or three hours. This replaces the ShadowHeartbeatRetryCount parameter, which is still available for Exchange 2010 backward compatibility.
TLSReceiveDomainSecureList	Contains a list of domains that are configured for mutual TLS authentication through receive connectors.
TLSSendDomainSecureList	Contains a list of domains that are configured for mutual TLS authentication through send connectors.
TransportRuleAttachment-TextScanLimit	Sets the limit for the amount of text that is extracted and scanned for transport rule and DLP rule checks. The default is 150 KB. If the message contains attachments that have more than this amount of text, only the specified amount is checked.
VerifySecureSubmitEnabled	Set to $True to force MAPI clients to submit messages over a secure channel (encrypted RPCs). The default is $False. By default, Outlook 2007 and Outlook 2010 use a secure channel, but previous versions do not.
VoicemailJournalingEnabled	Defines whether voicemail messages can be journaled by the journal agent. The default is $True.

It is possible for a message size to fluctuate as it makes its way from initial entry through an edge or hub transport server to final delivery. Format conversion, encoding, and agent processing are reasons message size can change. It is undesirable to reject a message just because its original size has swelled due to en route processing. The first time a message passes through a hub transport server, Exchange stamps a message with an X-header called *X-MS-Exchange-Organization-OriginalSize* and uses this field to store the original message size. Downstream checks performed by hub transport servers on other sites use this data instead of the current message size when they decide whether to block a message. Note that some messages bypass checking, including system messages, agent-generated messages, and anything to do with journaling and message quarantining.

Setting server-level behavior

In addition to the settings that govern transport behavior at the organizational level, you can modify transport settings on individual servers. Exchange 2013 actually has three cmdlets for managing server-level settings. Set-FrontEndTransportService controls settings used by FET on the CAS, Set-TransportService controls the behavior of the Transport service, and Set-MailboxTransportService controls the behavior of the Mailbox Transport Submission and Mailbox Transport Delivery services. Because these services often are collocated on the same server, it's useful to know which settings are available through which cmdlet. (For compatibility reasons, the Set-TransportServer cmdlet is still present and supported, but it is deprecated, so don't get in the habit of using it; it will disappear in a future version.)

Logging

Exchange 2013 supports a rather bewildering array of logging capabilities. The three Transport services can each log information about a variety of activities, over and above the normal status, warning, and error messages they might register in the system's Windows application event log. Some of these activities are common to all three services, whereas other logs are maintained by specific services. Why keep these logs at all? Their contents can be invaluable when you're trying to understand why a message didn't arrive when and where it was supposed to; although you probably won't use these logs on a daily basis, they are useful whenever you need to understand why messages are not being transported as you expect.

There are three types of logs that all three of the Transport services can independently maintain:

- **Connectivity logs** capture the date, time, source, destination, and direction of all connections to a server. Connectivity logging is on by default; if you look at the server connectivity logs in their default path of C:\Program Files\Microsoft\Exchange Server\V15\TransportRoles\Logs\Hub\Connectivity, you'll see entries for shadow redundancy submissions, ordinary SMTP delivery, and every other significant server-to-server connectivity event. Other components might log different data in the connectivity logs, too, although connectivity logs don't show the details of protocol-level conversations.

- **Receive protocol and send protocol logs** show the details of conversations: which party to the conversation said what and what the response was. These logs are off by default; you normally enable them only if you identify or suspect problems with a specific protocol's connectivity because the logs are quite verbose.

In addition to these shared log types, individual services maintain a number of logs. Table 2-11 summarizes the log types by component.

Table 2-11 Logs kept by the Transport services

Service	Log type	Notes
Front End Transport	Agent log	Logs actions and configurations taken by agents.
Mailbox Transport	Mailbox delivery agent	Records actions taken by the Mailbox delivery agent only.
	Mailbox submission agent	Records actions taken by the submission agent.
Transport	Active user statistics	This log records user activity, including the number of messages and bytes sent or received. You can't disable this log type.
	Agent	Logs agent actions for the Transport service.
	Information Rights Management	This log shows activity related to transport decryption of information rights management (IRM) messages.
	Message tracking	These logs are used to power Get-MessageTrackingLog and the rest of the message tracking functionality in EMS and EAC.
	Queue	These logs record queue actions, such as freezing or resuming queues. You can't turn queue logging off.
	Routing table	The routing table logs are a set of XML files that outline the routing topology Exchange uses; the logs are updated periodically. They used to be viewable with the Routing Log Viewer in Exchange 2010, but that tool was dropped in Exchange 2013.
	Server statistics	The server statistics log contains detailed information about the server's activity, including the number and size of messages sent and received, the number of DSNs generated, and the calculated end-to-end latency for message transport.

Controlling logging

EAC has a very limited set of controls for logging behavior, as shown in Figure 2-18. Use the Transport Logs tab of the server properties dialog box to enable message tracking and connectivity logging and to change the paths for those logs and the send and receive protocol logs.

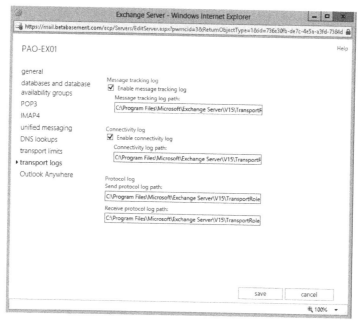

Figure 2-18 The Transport Logs section of the Organization Transport Settings dialog box allows you to control message tracking and connectivity logging.

Much more extensive control is possible if you use EMS. Each of the services' logging behavior for a service can be changed with the appropriate Set- cmdlet for the target service. For example, if you want to change how FET logs things, you'd use Set-FrontEndTransportService with the parameters to specify the options you want. Each of the logs supports parameters that control whether logging is enabled, how big log files may grow before a new log is created, and how long logs are kept. Each of these parameters has a name that begins with the type of log (AgentLog, ConnectivityLog, IRMLog, et cetera), followed by the parameter name (MaxAge, Path, and so on). When you know this, it is fairly easy to construct commands to do what you want done. For example, you might customize the connectivity logging behavior as follows:

```
Get-TransportService | Set-TransportService –ConnectivityLogEnabled $true
–ConnectivityLogPath c:\logs\Connectivity –IrmLogEnabled $true –IrmLogPath
c:\logs\ADRMS
```

Logs are named with a prefix (CONNECT, RECV, and ACTVUSRSTAT are examples) plus the date; some logging subsystems also include other items. The first log created on a day is named using a convention of *YYYYMMDD-1.log* where *YYYYMMDD* represents the year, month, and day. For example, the first active user statistics log created on March 2, 2014 is named ACTVUSRSTAT1.020140302-1.log. By default, Exchange creates a new log after it captures 10 MB of data in that log file. (You can adjust this with the LogMaxSize parameter.)

The second log created on March 2, 2014 would be named ACTVUSRSTAT1.020140302-2. log, the third ACTVUSRSTAT1.020140302-3.log, and so on.

Each log type has a maximum amount of data that is kept, which defaults to 250 MB. A circular logging scheme keeps the logs in the directory under this size by removing the oldest logs to free up space for new logs. You can increase the amount of storage assigned to connectivity logs by setting the value like this:

```
Set-TransportService -Identity HSV-EX02 -ConnectivityLogMaxDirectorySize 500MB
```

Assuming the directory storage threshold is not exceeded, logs are normally retained for 30 days. Because only the most recent logs are typically used to debug connectivity problems, you might decide to reduce this period. For example, here's how you would set the retention period for the connectivity logs on a server to 15 days:

```
Set-TransportService -Identity HSV-EX02 -IRMLogMaxAge 15.00:00:00
```

TROUBLESHOOTING

How did I get two connectivity logs with the same name?
Exchange creates the directory if the specified path doesn't exist. It does move the current or any other connectivity logs that already exist to the new location. However, it begins to use the new location to capture connectivity data immediately after the change is made, so you might end up with two logs with the same name if you copy the logs from the original logging directory to the new one. A quick rename of the old log sorts the problem out.

Interpreting protocol log files

Protocol logging tracks the steps that occur in SMTP conversations to transfer messages between Exchange and other servers. The logging is at a lower level than tracking the connections because it captures details such as the authentication between servers and the SMTP verbs used in the conversations. Protocol logging is disabled by default, so you have to enable logging on a per-connector basis before Exchange will generate logs. All the logs for a given server go into the protocol logging directory whose location you specify with the –ReceiveProtocolLogPath and –SendProtocolLogPath parameters to Set-TransportService, Set-MailboxTransportService, and Set-FrontEndTransportService. That's right—each of these services maintains its own set of protocol logs. In fact, there are eight total sets of protocol logs: SMTP send and receive on the Front End Transport service, SMTP send and receive on the Transport service, and separate SMTPReceive and SMTPSend logs for both the delivery and submission portions of the Mailbox Transport services. (Note that no logs actually are generated for the Mailbox Transport submission for SMTP receive because the submission service never actually receives SMTP email.) This might seem confusing, but having so many logs gives you a great deal of flexibility in troubleshooting because you can enable logging and review data from only the parts of the transport process that are giving you trouble.

Like the other log types, protocol log output is in comma-separated value (CSV) format. Figure 2-19 illustrates typical content from an SMTP receive log (some steps have been removed from this extract for the sake of clarity). The example shows how two Exchange transport servers set up an SMTP connection between each other to exchange messages. After the normal SMTP interchange of supported verbs, the connection is encrypted with TLS, and then the sending server begins to transmit the message header fields, beginning with the sender information (MAIL FROM). The receiving server validates that the recipient is OK by checking that the sender is not blocked. (The recipient might be a restricted address that only accepts messages from a defined set of senders.) You can also see the new XSHADOW ESMTP (extended SMTP) verb that sends information for the shadow redundancy feature of the transport dumpster. The message content was actually transmitted with a binary transfer (BDAT). The final step disconnects the link between the two servers.

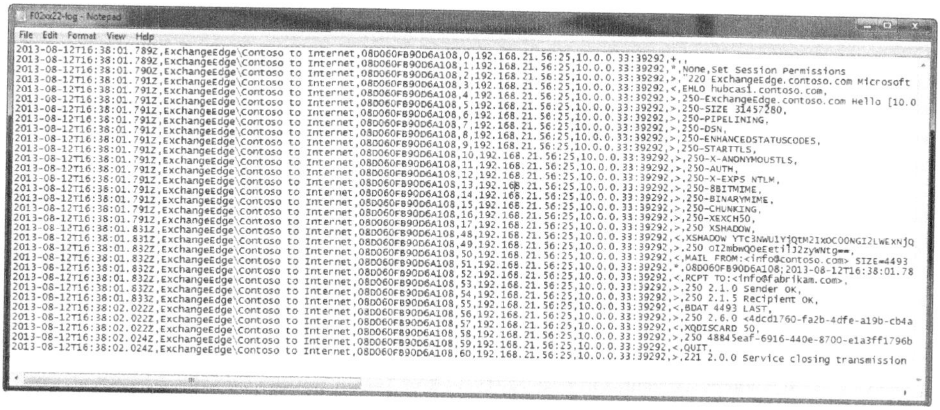

Figure 2-19 Excerpts from a protocol log displayed in CSV form

The content of a send protocol log is very similar. For example, if you look at the transactions generated to send a message through an external SMTP relay, you see Exchange identifying itself with EHLO, creating a TLS-secured connection if this is supported by the relay server, sending the message, and closing the link.

INSIDE OUT Use LogParser

Combing through protocol logs (or, actually, most kinds of logs) is tedious. It's easy to miss fine details, and the process of correlating log entries across multiple servers is painful unless you can automate it, which might be easier than you think. Microsoft has developed a tool called LogParser (available from *http://www.microsoft.com/en-us /download/details.aspx?id=24659*) that essentially gives you a query engine that works against several flavors of log file. You construct queries using an SQL-like syntax, and LogParser runs them against the log sets you specify. For example, when this query is run from your IIS log directory, it will parse your IIS logs (which, as you'll recall from Chapter 1, record a great deal of CAS-related activity) and give you a sorted list show- ing the most active Exchange ActiveSync users:

```
logparser "SELECT cs-username, Count(*) AS EASHits from ex*.log WHERE
cs-uri-stem LIKE '%Microsoft-Server-ActiveSync%' AND cs-username IS NOT NULL
GROUP BY cs-username ORDER BY EASHits Desc" -rtp:-1
```

If you're familiar with SQL, then LogParser will be easy to understand. If you're not, there are many examples of various queries and reports of use for Exchange on the Internet, and a few web searches will quickly find samples that you can adapt to get the data you want.

The first question you must resolve when you decide how to configure protocol logging is which connectors or services should have logging enabled. Earlier in the chapter, I dis- cussed which connectors are created on CAS and Mailbox servers; a combined server has a total of five receive connectors. The two connectors in which you're most interested are the Default Frontend *Servername* and Client Frontend *Servername* connectors, which listen on TCP ports 25 and 587, respectively. The following commands enable protocol logging on these two receive connectors on a server named PAO-EX02:

```
Set-ReceiveConnector -Identity 'PAO-EX02\Default Frontend PAO-EX02'
-ProtocolLoggingLevel Verbose
```

```
Set-ReceiveConnector -Identity 'PAO-EX02\Client Frontend PAO-EX02'
-ProtocolLoggingLevel Verbose
```

The same steps work for enabling logging on send connectors. There are two types of send connectors. Explicit, or normal, send connectors are defined to handle traffic to specified SMTP domains; Exchange also creates a special intra-organization send connector on every hub transport server to send messages within the organization. You can enable protocol logging for a normal connector as follows:

```
Set-SendConnector -Identity 'Smart Relay via contoso.com' -ProtocolLoggingLevel
Verbose
```

Because you don't have an identifier to pass to identify the intra-organization send connec-tor, you can't configure protocol logging for it using Set-SendConnector. Instead, you use the Set-TransportService cmdlet as follows:

```
Set-TransportService -Identity ExServer1 -IntraOrgConnectorProtocolLoggingLevel
Verbose
```

The Set-TransportService cmdlet also specifies the location of the send and receive logs, the maximum size of each log (default 10 MB), the overall size of the log directory, and the age limit for the logs. The location for the protocol log directory is the only setting you can configure with EAC. Just as with connectivity logs, Exchange uses a circular logging mecha-nism to keep the protocol logs under these thresholds. The following command shows how to configure the various settings:

```
Set-TransportService -Identity ExServer2 -ReceiveProtocolLogPath 'C:\Logs
\SMTPReceive' -SendProtocolLogPath 'C:\Logs\SMTPSend'
-ReceiveProtocolLogMaxFileSize 20MB -SendProtocolLogMaxFileSize 20MB
-ReceiveProtocolLogMaxDirectorySize 500MB  -SendProtocolLogMaxDirectorySize 500MB
-ReceiveProtocolLogMaxAge 15.00:00:00 -SendProtocolLogMaxAge 15.00:00:00
```

As with connectivity logging, it is best practice to use the same settings for all transport servers in the organization. This is easily accomplished as described in the previous section to configure the connectivity log settings by using Get-TransportService to fetch a list of all hub transport servers and using that list as input to Set-TransportService to implement the settings.

Customizing transport system messages

Exchange 2013 enables you to customize two kinds of system-generated transport mes-sages: delivery status notifications (DSNs) and quota warning messages. In all versions prior to Exchange 2007, if you wanted to use customized text in system-generated messages, you had to ask Microsoft to supply a custom-built replacement DLL that contained the customized text. Apart from the cost to build the new DLL, you took on two additional problems. First, the customized DLL might compromise support. In practice, if Microsoft supplied the customization, you probably received support for the work. This didn't apply if someone other than Microsoft did the work. Second, the customization had to be tested and deployed to every hub transport server in the organization after Microsoft released a roll-up update or service pack. Later versions of Exchange solved this problem by enabling you to customize and localize the text used in NDRs and quota warning messages by using the New-SystemMessage cmdlet.

Exchange DSNs

Over time, it is inevitable for Exchange to be unable to deliver some of the messages that arrive to a hub transport server for processing. The destination mailbox might be full, the mailbox might have been disabled or deleted, the recipient address might be invalid, and so on. Failed messages cause Exchange to generate nondelivery messages, a form of DSN message, to inform the sender that something unexpected has occurred with her message. DSN messages fall into five categories:

- **Relayed** DSNs generated when a user requests a delivery receipt for a message that passes out of the Exchange organization to a remote SMTP server. Tracking the delivery is no longer possible, so Exchange notifies the user that his message has been relayed to the point at which it has left the organization. The delivery status for messages sent to another Exchange organization can be tracked successfully, so a relayed DSN is not generated in this case.

- **Delayed** These DSNs are generated by a hub transport server when queued messages exceed the threshold set for the generation of delay notifications. The default value is four hours. You can change the delay threshold with the Set-TransportService cmdlet. For example, to reduce the delay threshold to two hours, you'd use a command similar to the following. Note that this setting is server-specific, and you therefore have to apply it to all hub transport and edge servers if you want to impose consistent processing across an organization.

  ```
  Set-TransportService -Identity ExServer2 -DelayNotificationTimeOut 02:00:00
  ```

- **Success** These DSNs are generated when a user requests a delivery receipt for an outgoing message. The DSN is an indication that Exchange has definitely delivered the message to the destination mailbox.

- **Failed** These are NDRs stating that delivery failed for some reason, such as quota exhausted for the destination mailbox or lack of authorization to send to a recipient. The Transport service automatically generates these messages and includes the original message for the user to deal with, including the ability to use client-specific features to resend the message after correcting the fault that caused the NDR.

- **Expansion** A group is expanded and a message is delivered to multiple recipients.

NDRs are usually fairly easy to interpret. Sometimes, you might need to modify the text to satisfy organizational requirements or to include some information that is more meaningful to your users. To facilitate this need, Exchange splits the text that it inserts in an NDR into two parts: a brief explanation of the problem in plain language to tell the user why her message failed and a more comprehensive and technical section that contains troubleshooting information for administrators.

The layout of an NDR places the user text first so that it is immediately obvious and can be read even on mobile devices that download only partial messages. The troubleshooting section contains these important pieces of information:

- The FQDN of the hub transport server that generated the NDR.

- The name and email address of the recipient that caused the problem.

- The FQDN for any remote server involved in the message.

- The enhanced DSN status code. These are codes such as 5.1.1 (unknown addressee) or 5.7.1 (unauthorized to send to addressee) defined in RFC 3463 that are generated by SMTP servers to indicate why a message failed.

- Message headers. SMTP message headers for the failed message are included to provide further diagnostic data.

FQDN and the remote server

NDRs might not always contain details about a remote server because the message could be rejected by the server to which the Mailbox server first submitted the message. When a transport server has a message rejected by a remote SMTP server (for example, the destination address is invalid), the FQDN of that server and the response (such as RESOLVER.RST.NotAuthorized; not authorized) received from the remote server are recorded so that the administrator knows what happened when Exchange attempted to transfer the message.

Given the complexities of modern messaging systems, there are numerous reasons Exchange might not be able to deliver a message to an internal or external recipient. Table 2-12 lists the DSNs for the most common error conditions you'll meet.

Table 2-12 Common causes for message delivery to fail

DSN code	Problem
4.4.7 – Message expired	Exchange was not able to deliver the message within two days (the default), so the message expired and has been removed from the delivery queue. Alternatively, an administrator deleted the message from a queue for some reason. The user should resend.
5.1.1 – Wrong email address	The intended recipient cannot be found in the directory of the receiving system, so the message cannot be delivered. The user might have mistyped the address or even used an outdated message from the Outlook nickname cache. In either case, he will have to fix the address and resend the message.
5.1.3 – Incorrect address format	Exchange believes that the format for the address is incorrect, so it can't be delivered. The user has to fix the address and resend.

DSN code	Problem
5.1.4 – Duplicate address	The receiving email system has detected a duplicate address. The user can't do much about this problem because the remote administrator has to resolve the duplicates before anyone can send to this address.
5.1.8 – Bad sender address	For some reason, a remote server cannot accept mail from the sender. The only thing anyone can do is read the diagnostic information and figure out what happened.
5.2.0 – Generic failure to deliver	All sorts of problems with mailboxes can cause this to occur, including a missing SMTP address, an invalid SMTP address, or an invalid forwarding address. The administrator has to check the recipient's mailbox to verify that everything is correct.
5.2.2 – Mailbox quota exceeded	The recipient's mailbox is full and can't accept incoming messages. She has to reduce the mailbox under quota or have the quota increased to accept new messages.
5.2.3 – Message too large	Either the recipient or the sender is not allowed such a large message.
5.2.4 – Dynamic distribution group query is wrong	Exchange cannot resolve the query to populate the recipients in a dynamic distribution group. The administrator has to fix this problem by verifying the query used for the group.
5.3.4 – Message too large to route	Some component along the message path was unable to route the message because of a size restriction. The restriction could be on a connector, imposed by the organization configuration, or imposed by a remote server.
5.4.4 – Unable to route	Normally, this is because a user attempts to send a message to a domain that doesn't exist anymore, so Exchange cannot route the message.
5.5.3 – Too many recipients	There are too many recipients in the message header. The only solution is to reduce the number of recipients and resend the message. Remember that distribution groups count as one recipient no matter how many recipients they include, so use distribution groups whenever possible.
5.7.1 – Lack of authorization	The sender doesn't have the necessary authorization to send to a recipient.

Customizing NDRs

You can customize the text presented to users in an NDR or create system messages to associate with new DSN codes that are used with transport rules. As an example, assume that you think the text Exchange 2013 uses in DSNs for error code 5.1.1 can be improved. This code is used when Exchange cannot deliver a message because the recipient is unknown. In other words, Exchange cannot find a mail-enabled group, contact, mailbox, or public folder with the address in the message header. The uncustomized text is, "The email address you entered couldn't be found. Check the address and try resending the message. If the problem continues, please contact your help desk."

You use the New-SystemMessage cmdlet to assign customized code to a DSN code. In this case, you want to assign new text to DSN 5.1.1 for English language messages that come from internal senders. Here's what the command looks like. Note that the Internal parameter is set to $False; this instructs Exchange that the message is intended for use outside the organization. If the message was purely for internal use, as in the case of a customized message used with a transport rule, you'd set the Internal parameter to $True.

```
New-SystemMessage –Language en –DsnCode 5.1.1 –Text "Unfortunately our email system
was unable to find your correspondent in our directory so we couldn't deliver the
message. Please check your little black book to validate the email address that you
used or contact the recipient by phone or fax." –Internal $False
```

For messages intended for internal recipients, you could customize the text further to add a URL that users can click to get more detailed guidance. You can amend the text for an existing customized message with the Set-SystemMessage cmdlet. Here's an example:

```
Set-SystemMessage –Identity en\Internal\5.1.1 –Text "We couldn't deliver your message
because the email address that you provided was not found in the corporate directory.
Please check <a href='http://contoso.com/directory.html'>Corporate Directory</a> to
find the correct email address to use"
```

Note the way the identity for the customized message is composed from the language code (en = English), whether it is intended for internal or external use, and the DSN code. Of course, to complete the job, you have to provide customized text for every language in use within the organization and decide whether you need to customize the text external recipients see.

Testing the customized text

When you've finished composing the text to use, you can use the Get-SystemMessage cmdlet to check that the customized message is in place and all its properties are as expected:

```
Get-SystemMessage –Identity en\Internal\5.1.1 | Format-List
```

The output is:

```
Text             : We couldn't deliver your message because the email address
that you provided was not found in the corporate directory. Please check
<a href='http://contoso.com/directory.html'>Corporate Directory</a> to find the
correct email address to use
Internal         : True
Language         : en
DsnCode          : 5.1.1
QuotaMessageType :
```

```
AdminDisplayName   :
ExchangeVersion    : 0.1 (8.0.535.0)
Name               : 5.1.1
DistinguishedName  : CN=5.1.1,CN=Internal,CN=9,CN=DSN Customization,CN=Transport
Settings,CN=contoso,CN=Microsoft Exchange,CN=Services,CN=Configuration,
DC=contoso,DC=com
Identity           : en\Internal\5.1.1
```

Customized system messages are stored in the Exchange configuration data in Active
Directory and are replicated throughout the organization to be available to all transport
servers. You can maintain different sets of customized DSNs for hub transport and edge
servers. You might want to do this to provide additional information in the internal DSNs
that you don't want to reveal to external recipients. If you want to use customized DSNs for
messages that edge servers process, you have to customize the DSNs on each of your edge
servers by using the same technique explained here.

CHAPTER 3

Client management

Although administrators think of Exchange Server as a complex, server-based system, the reality is that many of the millions of Exchange users worldwide think of their email system as Microsoft Outlook. This is a testament to the Microsoft Office team's branding efforts, but it also reflects a simplistic view of the Exchange client landscape. The truth is that there are six categories of Exchange clients:

- Outlook remains the Microsoft premium fat or rich client. Microsoft long ago made a conscious decision to tie client-side and server-side features together in Exchange and Outlook so that key features in each new release require you to deploy the client and server together for maximum benefit. Outlook 2013 still uses Messaging Application Programming Interface (MAPI) (although it's now tunneled over HTTPS), and Outlook 2007 and Outlook 2010 are still fully supported.

- Outlook Web App has come a long way since Microsoft introduced the first versions in Exchange 5.5. The modern Outlook Web App client looks and behaves very much like Outlook 2013, and it supports a broad array of browsers on both conventional computers and mobile devices. The addition of a special touch mode for tablets, coupled with an offline mode for selected modern browsers, shows some tantalizing indications that Microsoft intends the web-based Outlook Web App experience to match or surpass native mobile-device clients in both flexibility and capability.

- On the other hand, the fact that Microsoft is now shipping Outlook Web App clients as native applications for the Apple iPad and iPhone is an indication that there's a place for purpose-built mobile clients. These clients, collectively known as Outlook Web App for Devices (perhaps indicating a future release for other platforms), don't use Exchange ActiveSync; instead, they are based on a combination of Exchange Web Services (EWS) and HTML5. The current iOS versions provide full calendar and mailbox access, including push notification support, offline capability, and a wealth of other features formerly reserved for Apple's native device clients.

- Speaking of native clients, another category of Exchange client includes Exchange ActiveSync (EAS) clients such as Apple Mail for iOS and the Windows Phone 8 version of Outlook. These clients, the EAS protocol itself, and the management thereof are described fully in Chapter 4, "Mobile device management."

- EWS is the protocol that Outlook 2011 for Mac OS X (hereafter just called Outlook 2011) uses exclusively. Many other applications, including Outlook 2010 and Outlook 2013 and the Lync client, use EWS because it provides a straightforward, non-MAPI way to access and modify pretty much every type of Exchange data object, including messages, contacts, rules, and folders. Another example: SharePoint uses EWS to access and store data in site mailboxes. EWS is also portable across platforms; Linux, Mac OS X, iOS, Windows Phone, and Android clients also use EWS.

- A last category comprises clients using POP3 and IMAPv4. Although these protocols are mature and remain popular on Linux clients, they offer limited features and poor performance compared to newer protocols such as EAS and EWS. Microsoft has invested little to no engineering resources in updating Exchange 2013 POP/IMAP support compared to previous versions, and these protocols are discussed only briefly in this chapter.

In Exchange 2013, Microsoft has made dramatic changes to the client experience in several ways. It's added new features, such as site mailboxes, that use and require the latest version of Outlook. It's made many changes intended to improve the built-in Outlook Web App client and extended and improved the EWS and EAS application programming interfaces (APIs) of which other clients take advantage.

Choosing a client

The first question many organizations have when they consider deploying a new version of Exchange is, "What client should we use?"

Outlook

Over the years, the strength of the relationship between the Exchange and Outlook product teams has waxed and waned. Like most other large enterprises, organizational changes and political maneuvering have influenced the degree to which these teams work together. The most noticeable area of collision between the two teams' plans has been the release schedule of their respective flagship products. In the past, some versions of Office have shipped before the corresponding Exchange release, whereas others have shipped after Exchange. In either case, this poses a conundrum for companies that want the better-together experience that Microsoft always promises. Deploying Exchange or a new version of Office is a challenge, and doing them both concurrently is even more challenging. For example, Exchange 2010 was released before Outlook 2010, limiting the ability of early Exchange adopters to realize full value from their deployment. Office 2013 didn't ship until after Exchange 2013, but the delay in getting Exchange 2013 Cumulative Update 1 (CU1) out the door provided a handy opportunity to plan and execute Office deployments while waiting for the ability to deploy Exchange 2013 into existing Exchange 2007 or Exchange 2010 environments.

What version of Outlook should you deploy? Answering this question is easier for small companies than it is for large ones. The law of numbers conspires to create much greater complexity when a new application must be distributed to tens of thousands of desktops and issues such as user training, preparing the help desk to support the rollout, and the cost of new software licenses and potential hardware upgrades are considered. For example, the introduction of the Office fluent interface (featuring the ribbon) in Outlook 2007 caused a lot of controversy because it was unfamiliar to users. Office 2013 makes a number of large changes to the user interface and application features, and these changes have not been universally welcomed by users so far. This is why so many companies continue to run older versions of Outlook; they see little value in going forward with an upgrade that promises great cost for new licenses and deployment while offering little obvious return in the form of user productivity, lower support costs, or anything else. The fact that the Exchange server Client Access Licenses (CALs) no longer include a license for Outlook also makes it harder for companies to justify an early upgrade.

Table 3-1 briefly summarizes major features in each Outlook version and how they work with Exchange 2013.

TABLE 3-1 Comparing different versions of Outlook

Outlook Version	Major Features
Outlook 2003	Introduction of cached Exchange mode and smarter networking to enable faster and more efficient synchronization between server folders and local replicas. Exchange 2010 requires Outlook 2003 SP2. Not supported by Exchange 2013.
Outlook 2007	Introduction of Autodiscover functionality to enable automatic configuration of user profiles. Movement away from public folders as the repository for shared data such as free/busy and Offline Address Book (OAB) to use web-based distribution instead. First implementation for managed mail and retention policies.

Chapter 3

Outlook Version	Major Features
Outlook 2010	The first 64-bit version of Outlook (also available for 32-bit platforms). Supports features such as MailTips and message tracking from within Outlook. Far more developed and feature-complete version of messaging record management (document retention) policies. Supports cross-organization calendar sharing to help customers deploy in mixed on-premise/hosted deployments. Supports conversation view of email threads (also works with earlier versions of Exchange) and the ability to ignore threads in which you're not interested in email. Outlook 2010 also supports personal archives located on Exchange 2010 servers and can open up to three Exchange mailboxes in addition to the primary mailbox.
Outlook 2013	Revamped user interface, including touch mode for Windows tablets and touchscreen devices. Support for site mailboxes and modern public folders. Changes sync behavior in cached Exchange mode. Supports EAS connections to Outlook.com. Various user interface additions, including inline replies and the Weather Bar, a subwindow that displays weather in the calendar view.

Outlook 2013

Outlook 2013 brings some interesting new functionality to the equation. Whether the new features are worthwhile enough to consider an upgrade is different for every company.

Since Microsoft introduced cached Exchange mode in Outlook and Exchange 2003, it has continually worked to make sync faster and more bandwidth-efficient. However, one area it hasn't previously addressed much is the question of what should be synced in the first place. Outlook 2013 offers two new features to improve the user's experience: Exchange Fast Access and the new sync slider.

As Exchange and Outlook have evolved together, the way synchronization works has changed, too. Exchange Fast Access is the latest stage in this evolution; the basic idea is that a sync operation that takes long enough for the user to notice should continue in the background. Exchange Fast Access immediately syncs the user's most recent email and all his calendar data whereas older mail items are synced in the background. For example, a user who returns from a long vacation will see her most recent messages right away. You can turn off this feature by setting the HKEY_CURRENT_USER\software\policies\microsoft \office\15.0\outlook\hybrid\localcaching DWORD to 0, but you can't configure any other aspect of Fast Access.

The sync slider is intended to handle a different problem. The traditional approach to sync control has been to allow (or force) the user to choose which folders to synchronize. This is great if you're a power user, but it falls far short for users who don't necessarily know which folders they actually use because they file and find items through Outlook search tools. The new Outlook sync interface (shown in Figure 3-1) instead asks users to choose how much mail they want to sync based on time. The idea here is that even nontechnical users can decide whether they need a month, a year, or all their email synced, so the slider enables the user to make that choice. Outlook is supposed to handle the rest.

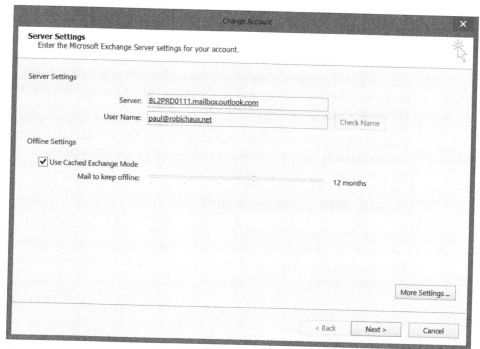

Figure 3-1 The Outlook account settings dialog box, which now includes a slider that controls synchronization behavior

If the slider is set to anything other than All (the rightmost value), you see a subset of your mail while in cached mode. If you scroll to the bottom of a list or perform a search, you'll see that Outlook provides a link telling you that more results are available on the Exchange server; clicking that link loads additional messages from the server. Interestingly, the slider doesn't affect sync for calendar items, contacts, tasks, or notes; all those items are always synchronized.

By default, Outlook 2013 syncs 12 months of mail, which is plenty for many users. However, you might want to apply a consistent value for this setting to avoid confusing users (and the resulting help desk calls) who don't see mail they expected. The SyncWindowSetting registry value (a DWORD under HKEY_CURRENT_USER\Software\Policies\Microsoft \Office\15.0\Outlook\Cached Mode) enables you to set the slider value through a Group Policy object (GPO). Set the value to the number of months of mail data you want to sync; legal values are 0 (meaning the entire mailbox), 1, 3, 6, 12, or 24. The sync mechanism deposits mail in a compressed OST file; more precisely, some data items in the file are compressed, and others are not. Microsoft claims up to a 40 percent space savings compared to older versions of Outlook.

Another change is that Outlook 2013 can open up to 9,999 Exchange mailboxes concurrently, not all of which have to belong to the same Exchange organization. This is a significant increase over the Outlook 2010 limit of 10 mailboxes! By default, Outlook imposes a limit of four mailboxes. This is deliberately set to prevent Outlook from taking up huge amounts of system resources on a client PC, which would occur if someone attempted to open 10 or 20 mailboxes. However, you can increase the limit for concurrent open mailboxes up to the maximum by updating the value held in the registry at HKCU\Software \Microsoft\Exchange\MaxNumExchange.

Outlook 2013 also includes some miscellaneous new features, such as a weather display and the ability to warn you when you use phrases such as "see attached" or "I've attached" but then don't include an actual attachment.

Outlook 2010 and Outlook 2007

Microsoft fully supports Outlook 2007 and Outlook 2010 with Exchange 2013, provided that they are updated to the required versions. Outlook 2010 requires SP1 with the November 2012 cumulative update (CU), and Outlook 2007 requires SP3 and the November 2012 CU.

If you use either of these versions, you'll miss out on some key Exchange 2013 features:

- You can't access site mailboxes from Outlook, although they are still available from within Microsoft SharePoint.

- Your users won't see data loss prevention (DLP) Policy Tips warnings in Outlook 2013.

- Your users can't install or run apps from the Office Store.

Outlook 2007 users will miss out on some additional features that were first introduced in Exchange 2010:

- No user interface is available to display the MailTips the server provides.

- Outlook 2007 doesn't understand the internal identifiers Exchange uses to connect related items in a conversation, so none of the conversation-related features (including conversation views, the ability to clean up a conversation, and the Ignore button) are supported.

- Integration with the settings slabs in Outlook Web App to allow managing group information, editing unified messaging (UM) settings (such as call answering rules), and so on are missing. However, users can still open Outlook Web App options slabs directly to access these options.

- Personal archives are accessible only if you deploy the update for Outlook 2007 released by Microsoft in late 2010.

- Outlook 2007 can render voice mail previews as plain HTML in the message body but lacks the control necessary to play the voice content if you click part of the voice mail preview. Also, it cannot process protected voice mail.

- You cannot send Short Message Service (SMS) messages from Outlook 2007.

- There is no support for retention tags and policies.

Earlier versions of Outlook

Outlook 2003 and earlier versions are no longer supported. Apart from the countless improvements and bug fixes in newer versions, there are two important technical reasons the earlier versions aren't supported. First, Exchange 2013 requires clients to use Autodiscover, and Outlook 2007 was the first Outlook client to support it. Second, Exchange 2013 allows clients to connect only through RPC-over-HTTPS (or Outlook Anywhere), which was first supported in Outlook 2003.

Outlook Web App

As Outlook Web App and Outlook have matured, Microsoft has made Outlook Web App look and behave more like Outlook with each successive release. That raises the question of what the company's long-term intentions are. I think it's safe to say that the Office team will keep making new versions of Outlook as long as there is an Office team and, likewise, that the Exchange team will keep improving Outlook Web App. The enhancements in Outlook Web App 2013, though, seem to point to something else: Microsoft is laying the groundwork to obviate the need for third-party Exchange ActiveSync clients on smart phones and tablets in two ways:

- By improving the browser-based experience as evidenced by the combination of a touch mode in Outlook Web App, designed to make Outlook Web App friendlier on devices that lack a mouse or trackpad, and the availability of offline storage

- By shipping native apps for Apple iOS (and possibly for other platforms in the future) that can replace the built-in Mail and Calendar applications

In late 2012 and early 2013, a pair of serious bugs in Apple's iOS caused problems for Exchange administrators who suddenly found their servers flooded with transaction logs. Since then, Microsoft and Apple have begun working much more closely to ensure that iOS

Chapter 3

and Exchange get along well, and the Exchange team has added both bug fixes and new features to help prevent a misbehaving client from causing server-side problems. Even with these changes, though, it probably makes sense for Microsoft to enable Exchange 2013 customers to ditch the built-in clients for many use cases (although some actions, such as sending a message from a built-in photo app, for example, might still require use of the built-in client).

New features in Outlook Web App 2013

The biggest new feature in Outlook Web App 2013 is its new interface, which was explicitly designed to look like Outlook 2013. The interface features much more white space, and most icons have been either removed or replaced by text labels. For instance, there are no icons in the folder list on the left side of the window, and the icon-based toolbar of previous versions is largely gone (see Figure 3-2). Opinions are divided over this visual style; some people really like it, whereas others say that it uses screen space inefficiently and that there's too much white.

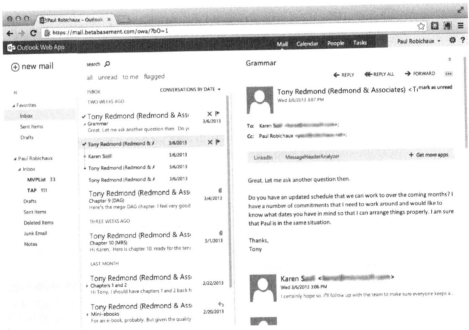

Figure 3-2 The Outlook Web App 2013 mail interface in Chrome on Mac OS X

Whether or not you like it, though, it's safe to say that this design will be with us for a while, given that the same design elements are used in Xbox, Windows 8, and the other components of the Office 2013 family.

Extending Outlook Web App with apps

Almost every significant desktop and mobile operating system platform has its own store in which third parties can sell applications for the platform. Apple started it, but Microsoft, Google, BlackBerry, Nokia, and other vendors have all followed suit. The expansion of the store model has now expanded further with the introduction of the Office Store in Office 2013. Microsoft now provides a centralized place where companies of all sizes can sell add-ins for Office, such as executable add-ins for Microsoft Excel or Outlook, document templates for Office Word, or applications that plug in to Outlook 2013 and Outlook Web App 2013. This last category, of course, is what this chapter focuses on the most.

Microsoft refers to this new application development model as the *cloud app model*; it is predicated on the idea that a lightweight app that connects to web service APIs is a useful way to add new functionality to desktop Office applications, SharePoint sites, and Outlook Web App. Applications built using this model are essentially containers of HTML and JavaScript that connect to websites to offer actions based on the context and content of the document or page on which they are triggered. If you remember Microsoft Smart Tags for Office 2007, this model should sound familiar; the cloud app model shares with it the notions that the document or page is the center of activity for the user and that the app should offer services that make sense in context.

The Outlook client itself has long had a number of extensibility models that enable developers to create software that integrates with Outlook on the client. The new model supplements but does not replace the existing extension capabilities. For example, cloud apps for Outlook Web App (and SharePoint) are installed on the server, either for individual users or the server, but not on individual users' computers. The apps are constrained in the types of data they can access because they run in the security context of the user's browser. However, because these apps can integrate with third-party web services, they can offer a surprising degree of utility. The Office Store catalog at *http://office.microsoft.com/en-us /store/apps-for-outlook-FX102804983.aspx* lists several dozen apps that are intended to plug in to Outlook 2013 and Outlook Web App 2013, including extensions that integrate consumer services such as Twitter, LegalBox, and LinkedIn, plus utilities of various sorts. You can also deploy apps by publishing them in an internal app catalog, which gives you a straightforward way to publish apps for enterprise users. This app catalog can be stored on an Exchange server, a SharePoint site, or in a file.

Administrators can block individual apps, turn off apps for the organization, or turn off apps for an individual user. The last feature enables you to prevent an individual user from installing apps that run in her local instance of Outlook 2013 because the Outlook Web App app model requires the apps to be stored in the user's mailbox on the server. In addition, separate Outlook 2013–specific features enable you to control app behavior within Outlook. For more information on configuring and managing these apps, see the "Managing Office Store apps for Outlook Web App" section later in this chapter.

Chapter 3

Browser and operating system support

The best way to summarize the state of browser and operating system support for Outlook Web App 2013 is to say it's broad. Microsoft characterizes Outlook Web App support in three ways:

- Light refers to a fairly limited set of features. In Light mode, there's no drag-and-drop, and the user experience looks essentially just like Outlook Web App Light mode in Outlook 2007 (with a few minor stylistic changes). Figure 3-3 shows the Outlook Web App Light mode in Microsoft Internet Explorer 10 on Windows 8.

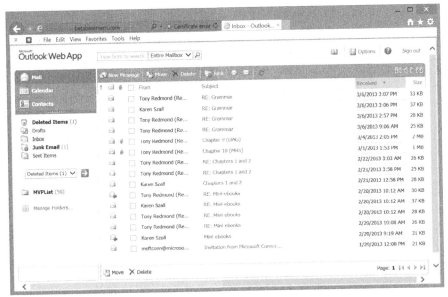

Figure 3-3 The Outlook Web App 2013 mail interface in Light mode on Internet Explorer 10 on Windows 8

- Good is better than Light; it adds some additional features to the Light experience.

- Best gives users the full Outlook Web App 2013 experience, including automatic refresh of message lists, autocompletion of address fields, drag-and-drop, and more. Some browsers also get touch mode and offline support.

Table 3-2 summarizes the support levels for various combinations of operating systems and browsers. Internet Explorer versions 9 and 10, Safari version 6 on Mac OS X, Firefox version 17, and Chrome version 24 are the minimum versions for the Best mode experience across platforms. Chrome, Safari, and Internet Explorer 10 offer offline access in addition to the Best experience.

There is currently no way to force downgrades for a client; for example, if you want to force your Firefox users to get the Good or Light experience, you can't. You can append "?layout=light" to the Outlook Web App URL to force it into Light mode for a particular client, although this is not officially documented anywhere. In addition, you can use Set-OWAVirtualDirectory –LogonPageLightSelectionEnabled to control whether users can choose Light mode themselves or Set-OWAVirtualDirectory –OWALightEnabled to control whether Light mode is available at all.

TABLE 3-2 Browser and operating system support for Outlook Web App 2013

Operating System	Browser	Support level
Windows XP, Windows Server 2003	Internet Explorer 7	Light
	Internet Explorer 8	Good
	Firefox 17+	Good
	Chrome 24+	Good plus offline access
Windows Vista, Windows Server 2008	Internet Explorer 8	Good
	Internet Explorer 9	Best
	Firefox 17+	Good
	Chrome 24+	Good plus offline access
Windows 7	Internet Explorer 8	Good
	Internet Explorer 9	Best
	Internet Explorer 10	Best
	Firefox 17+	Best
	Chrome 24+	Best plus offline access
Windows 8	Internet Explorer 10	Best plus offline access
	Firefox 17+	Best
	Chrome 24+	Best plus offline access
Mac OS X 10.5+	Chrome 24+	Best plus offline access
	Firefox 17+	Best
	Safari 6+	Best plus offline access
Linux	Firefox 17+	Best
	Chrome 24+	Best plus offline access

Notice that Table 3-2 doesn't mention mobile browsers; that's on purpose. Microsoft only supports touch mode for Outlook Web App on a smaller set of browsers: Safari for the Apple iPad and Internet Explorer 10 for Windows RT and Windows 8.

Chapter 3

Deprecated features from Outlook Web App 2010

Microsoft giveth, and Microsoft taketh away. In every new release of Exchange, along with the new features we get, some old ones are removed, and Outlook Web App 2013 is no exception. The deprecated feature that's garnered the most commentary is spell checking; Outlook Web App 2013 depends on the browser to do it rather than including it as a feature. This is an eminently reasonable decision, given the capabilities of modern browsers. Some other features were cut from the RTM version of Exchange 2013 that you might or might not miss:

- Attachment previews are now generated by an Office Web Apps server instead of by the WebReady feature included in Exchange 2010. See the "The role of Office Web Apps Server" section later in this chapter for more details.

- Concerning distribution list moderation, you can't moderate messages sent to distribution lists in Outlook Web App 2013.

- S/MIME encryption and signatures aren't supported in Exchange 2013, although Microsoft documentation says they will be supported in a future version.

- You can only have the reading pane on the right side of the window; there's currently no option to move it to the bottom.

- You can't reply to email messages that are embedded as attachments to other messages.

Mac OS X

If you have Mac OS X users, you essentially have four client choices. Which one you choose will depend in large measure on the number of Mac users you have, how vocal they are, and their tolerance for (or appetite for) aggravation.

- You can deploy Outlook 2011, part of Mac Office 2011. Although it shares a name with Windows Outlook, Mac Outlook is a very different beast, with a completely different user interface and many differences in functionality compared to the Windows version. Because it is a Mac-native application, and because the entire Office suite is familiar to most Mac users, this is a fairly safe choice. Having said that, Outlook 2011 has a reputation for being buggy and slow, though many of the supposed bugs are actually design choices that some Mac users don't like.

- You can use Apple's Mail and iCal applications, which come bundled with the operating system. They support EWS, and they are generally stable and performant. However, they are not very good as email and calendar clients compared to Outlook Web App or Outlook, with many missing features and some annoying behaviors (such as sometimes failing to hide deleted messages) that stem from their legacy as IMAP/POP clients. Apple has gradually been improving the degree of Exchange support in each Mac OS X release, and die-hard Mac users will probably prefer this option to having to learn to use Outlook.

- You can let your Mac users have Outlook Web App, which requires little to no effort on your part and gives them a pretty good experience overall. However, because Outlook Web App is a browser-based application, it requires the use of a supported browser, and it doesn't offer all the features the native desktop clients do.

- You can run Outlook 2007, Outlook 2010, or Outlook 2013 in a Windows virtual machine. This gives users a true cross-platform experience because they are literally running the same code your Windows users do. Many organizations already provide virtualized Windows desktops for their Mac users; if not, setting up and deploying this option on a wide scale can be a challenge (and an expensive one at that).

Outlook Web App for Devices

Despite the rather clumsy name, Outlook Web App for Devices is a very cool addition to the field of Exchange clients. Released as an almost complete surprise in July 2013, the Outlook Web App for Devices clients run on most models of iPad (iPad 2 and later) and iPhone (iPhone 4S and later). The visual appearance of the client is very faithful to the browser-based version of Outlook Web App running on modern desktop browsers; the icons, typography, spacing, color scheme, and so on are nearly identical to what you see when loading Outlook Web App in Internet Explorer 10 or a recent version of Chrome or Firefox. Perhaps more importantly, the app offers a number of features that aren't available in the built-in apps shipped by Apple, including the ability to send and read messages protected with Active Directory Rights Management Services (AD RMS), access to personal archive mailboxes, the ability to display MailTips, and full integration of Office apps.

The app includes modules for email, calendar, and contact access. The calendar portion of the app (see Figure 3-4) is a huge improvement over the native iOS calendar app; it maintains a very close visual resemblance to the desktop Outlook 2013 client and provides full access to shared calendars. The biggest feature of interest in the contacts module is that contacts from your Exchange accounts can be synchronized with the local contact store, meaning that name resolution for phone calls will work properly.

The implementation of the app is interesting. Rather than using Exchange ActiveSync, as the native clients on iOS and Windows Phone do, Outlook Web App for Devices uses EWS for mail synchronization. The app itself includes a middleware layer that Microsoft calls PAL (for "platform abstraction layer") that ties the JavaScript implementation of Outlook Web App together with native functionality on the device. Local storage is provided by the SQLite database engine included with iOS. From the server's perspective, the traffic

Chapter 3

generated by the mobile app looks like a mix of browser Outlook Web App operations and EWS traffic.

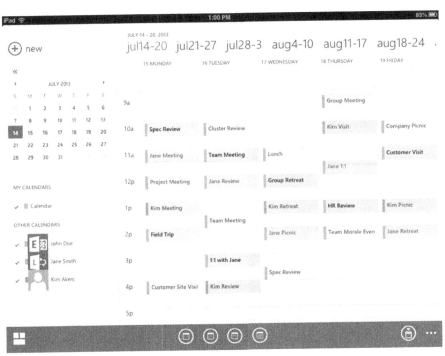

Figure 3-4 Outlook Web App for Devices can display shared calendars, and the result is visually nearly identical to the desktop Outlook 2013 client

The app maintains its own separate data store, so if it receives a remote wipe request, it erases all the application data and settings but doesn't affect any other data on the device. Likewise, security policies that you apply with mailbox or Outlook Web App policies on the server will be honored and enforced by the app, without any impact on the device operating system or on other applications. This is a welcome change for bring-your-own-device (BYOD) organizations because it means that issuing a remote wipe to a user won't remove the user's photos, music, or other personal data from a device that he owns.

As with the Office productivity apps for iOS, Outlook Web App for Devices was released first for Office 365 users. It is currently only supported for Office 365 tenants; Microsoft has said that it will enable it for use with on-premises Exchange 2013 deployments, but as of late 2013 it has not yet done so. As a means of giving customers incentives to move to Office 365, this isn't a bad strategy, but it seems to leave a bad taste in the mouths of many on-premises customers who feel like second-class citizens.

Managing Outlook for Windows

You can do much of what you need to do to manage Outlook clients on Windows by changing settings on the Client Access Server (CAS) itself, as described in Chapter 1, "Client access servers." This section talks specifically about actions you might need or want to perform to ensure the smooth functioning of your organization's Outlook clients.

Managing Outlook Anywhere

Outlook Anywhere was first introduced in Exchange 2003, and it has evolved quite a bit since then. The benefits of allowing clients to get their email without requiring a virtual private network (VPN) connection are significant, but previous versions of Outlook and Exchange have sometimes made Outlook Anywhere configuration somewhat complicated. Exchange 2013 simplifies the Outlook Anywhere world by making it the only protocol Outlook can use to access Exchange mailboxes. This eliminates much of the confusion inherent in trying to figure out which protocol the client would use under different circumstances. Exchange 2013 greatly streamlines the Outlook Anywhere deployment experience, too, because all you need to do is install a valid Secure Socket Layer (SSL) certificate on your client access servers and then make a few minor configuration tweaks. In this case, "valid" means that the certificate is issued by a certification authority (CA) the clients can trust—either a public CA or an internal CA whose certificate chain is on the trust list for the clients. Although you may install a public CA certificate on your Mailbox servers, this is not necessary.

Right out of the box, if you don't do anything, Outlook Anywhere works fine for internal clients. It might or might not work for external clients, depending on how you've set up your Internet-facing and internal-facing CAS servers. When you first install a plain Exchange 2013 Mailbox server, the Outlook Anywhere virtual directory is configured with an internal hostname that matches the machine FQDN, but the external hostname is blank, and SSL is not required to connect. For all your Internet-facing CAS servers, you should set an external hostname and enable the use of SSL for both internal and external clients. For example, suppose you wanted to configure an Internet-facing server named PAO-EX01; that's easily done with the following command:

```
Set-OutlookAnywhere -id 'PAO-EX01\rpc (Default Web Site)' -ExternalClientRequiresSSL
$true -InternalClientRequiresSSL $true -externalHostname 'mail.betabasement.com'
```

The "CAS authentication methods" section in Chapter 1 outlines the authentication methods Exchange can use in various scenarios, including Outlook Anywhere. An unmodified Exchange 2013 installation will have negotiate authentication set up for external clients and NTLM/Kerberos set for internal clients; this is generally optimal as is, so don't change it unless you have a very good reason.

Chapter 3

Coexistence among Exchange 2007, Exchange 2010, and Exchange 2013 Outlook Anywhere is fairly simple to set up. The key is to point all incoming Outlook Anywhere traffic at an Exchange 2013 CAS. However, the Exchange 2013 CAS role doesn't have the remote procedure call (RPC) proxy code contained in RPCproxy.dll because it's not an RPC proxy! That means the Exchange 2013 CAS uses HTTP proxying to send the encapsulated RPC-over-HTTP packets to an Exchange 2007 or Exchange 2010 CAS, which does have RPCproxy.dll and thus can de-encapsulate the Outlook Anywhere packets. This design has a couple of side effects: you must have the RPCproxy.dll installed on your Exchange 2007 or Exchange 2010 CAS servers, and you must have those servers configured for Outlook Anywhere. You must enable Outlook Anywhere on every Exchange 2007 and Exchange 2010 CAS, even if it's not Internet-facing, because Exchange 2013 can proxy traffic to internal servers as part of its proxy process. Coexistence proxying also requires an authentication change; you must configure your Exchange 2007 and Exchange 2010 CAS servers to allow integrated Windows authentication on the /rpc virtual directory.

INSIDE OUT Everything is internal

One consequence of the Outlook Anywhere changes in Exchange 2013 is that Outlook always displays the internal hostname in the Exchange Proxy Settings dialog box, even if Outlook is connecting to the external hostname because it's on an external network. Microsoft claims in KB article 2754898 that this is by design, but it's not clear why the company would design it this way; keep this in mind in case your users complain that their Outlook clients are connecting to the "wrong" server.

Managing Autodiscover

The "Autodiscover" section in Chapter 1 describes what the Autodiscover protocol is and how it works. The key thing to remember with respect to the use of Autodiscover in Outlook is that the Autodiscover XML manifest typically gives you all the clues you need to understand the cause of any problems you encounter. The Exchange 2013 implementation of Autodiscover is different in a few respects from that of earlier versions. First, remember that Exchange 2013 emits two EXHTTP nodes as part of its Autodiscover response: one for the internal Outlook Anywhere configuration and one for the external version, in that order. Outlook clients are supposed to try these two configurations in order, ignoring any older EXPR elements. The new EXHTTP nodes are part of why you have to update Outlook 2007 and Outlook 2010 with the November 2012 (or later) CU before they work properly with Exchange 2013. In addition, Autodiscover itself doesn't require any configuration because it merely publishes the URLs and service names that are configured on other objects, such as the Exchange ActiveSync virtual directory and the endpoints for Outlook Anywhere.

Using the Exchange Remote Connectivity Analyzer

One of the coolest things about the Exchange team is its habit of innovating in ways that other product groups later copy. For example, Exchange was the first Microsoft product to use what we now think of as AJAX; the team was the first to produce a best-practices analyzer to help customers ensure that their deployments were optimized; and it was the first to include support for Microsoft Windows PowerShell. Another first that deserves mention in the context of client management is the Exchange Remote Connectivity Analyzer, or ExRCA. ExRCA is a tool originally championed by the Exchange product support team, which was seeking a better way to help customers troubleshoot connectivity problems. The tool analyzes many aspects of the connection between an Outlook or mobile client and your Exchange server, including the certificates used, the CAS configuration, and how Autodiscover is configured, and it tells you when it finds problems in a clear, easy-to-read report that makes it easy to resolve problems. Figure 3-5 shows a sample ExRCA report.

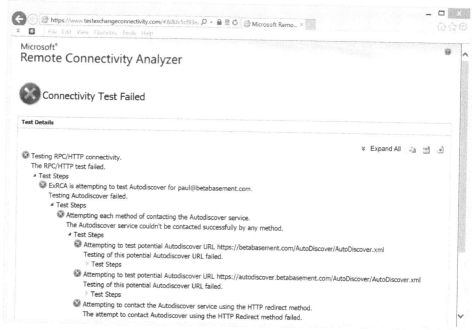

Figure 3-5 An example, intentionally bad: an ExRCA report showing multiple failures

The ExRCA tool itself is available in two versions. The online version, hosted at *http://www.testexchangeconnectivity.com*, performs tests for Outlook Anywhere, Autodiscover, EWS, and EAS connectivity. These tests can be performed against your own on-premises Exchange installation or against an Office 365 tenant. The online ExRCA also performs Lync Autodiscover and connectivity tests. There is a second, client-based version that you download from the Clients tab of the ExRCA website and run on a local client. The local version, properly known as the Microsoft Connectivity Analyzer, is useful when you want to see why a particular client (or a client in a particular location or network) is having trouble.

Using the online version of ExRCA

The biggest thing to remember when using ExRCA online is that it requires you to provide credentials for an account in your Exchange organization. Although Microsoft is trustworthy, it is of course a bad idea to use an administrative account for this; instead, you should use an ordinary user account, ideally one that you use only for testing and that is normally disabled in Active Directory except when you're actually testing.

The first page of the ExRCA website asks you to choose a test (Figure 3-6). The Autodiscover and Outlook Anywhere tests are probably of greatest interest to most administrators, although there are other tests for various aspects of Exchange, Lync, and Office 365 connectivity.

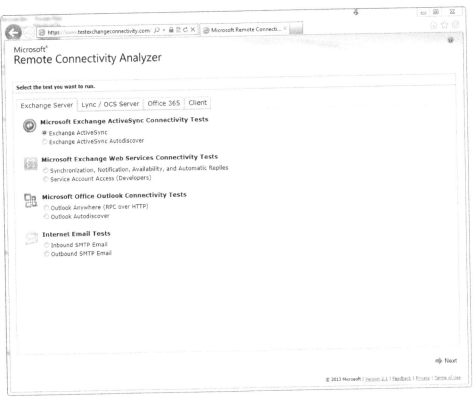

Figure 3-6 The opening page of ExRCA, requiring you to choose a test to run

When you've chosen a test type, you see a page similar to that shown in Figure 3-7. You must supply credentials for the test account you're using, and you must select a check box that indicates that you understand and accept that the working account you specify might be compromised and that you accept responsibility for it. You also have to fill out a CAPTCHA verification field; when you've done so, you can start the test by clicking the Perform Test button.

Figure 3-7 ExRCA requires logon credentials, which you must carefully safeguard

ExRCA then performs the requested test. When it's done, you get a neatly formatted report page. The report makes clear which operations succeeded or failed; failed operations usu-ally include a link labeled "Tell me more about this issue and how to resolve it" that takes you to a page with more information on the specific failure. This is where ExRCA really shines; it's simple to run ExRCA against a new Exchange deployment (or one for which you have newly assumed responsibility) and get clear prescriptive guidance on how to fix the issues ExRCA finds. You can save ExRCA results as XML or HTML reports if you want to, which can be handy when tracking the progress of issues over time.

Using the Microsoft Connectivity Analyzer

The Microsoft Connectivity Analyzer (MCA) is relatively new; released in early 2013, it complements ExRCA by providing a downloadable tool you can run directly from a client machine. MCA is packaged using the Microsoft ClickOnce technology, so it can easily be installed directly from a web browser even by users who don't have local administrative privileges on their computers.

To download MCA, open the Client tab on the ExRCA website and click the Microsoft Connectivity Analyzer link; the MCA installation process walks you through the actual installation. Be aware that you will need version 4.5 of the .NET Framework installed on the client PC and that (depending on your browser) you might also need to configure the browser to allow ClickOnce deployments. When you have the tool running, you see the start page shown in Figure 3-8. Note that this is providing essentially the same options as the ExRCA page, but it's formatted and worded in a much more approachable way for users who aren't Exchange administrators. Clicking any of the links on this page prompts the user for whatever other information MCA needs, including logon credentials. When you've plugged in the requested information, clicking Next starts the test.

After the test completes, you see a summary page; if any problems were found, the page typically says "Administrator Assistance May Be Required." Separate buttons enable the user to save the test results (presumably to give to the administrator) or review them himself. When you review an MCA report, you'll notice the same basic format as you see in ExRCA; each test is labeled with an icon indicating whether it passed or failed, and most tests have a disclosure triangle by which you can expand the results to see more details. MCA reports also have the Tell Me More link, which is handy when you're asked to review test results MCA has gathered but is probably less useful for end users.

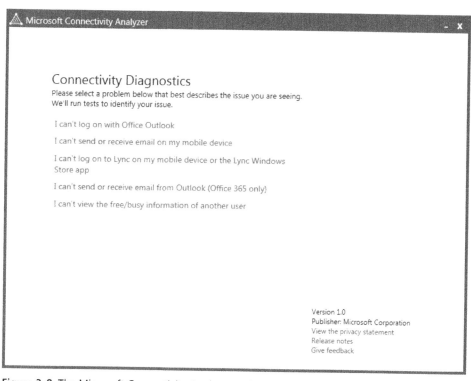

Figure 3-8 The Microsoft Connectivity Analyzer main page, a simplified rendition of the options available in ExRCA

Outlook settings and group policies

Outlook has long offered a set of Group Policy–based controls to simplify administration in large environments. You can apply these customizations by using the traditional method of attaching the Office-specific administrative templates (available from *http://technet .microsoft.com/en-us/library/cc178992.aspx*) or by using the Office Customization Tool (OCT), a topic that deserves a book of its own due to its complexity. The mechanics of applying Group Policy object (GPO) customizations to Outlook are outside the scope of this book, but it's worth mentioning some of the most interesting settings; a full list is available from *http://technet.microsoft.com/en-us/library/ff631135.aspx*.

- You can prevent Outlook from using PST files in two ways. First, you can prevent it from using PST files at all. Second, you can allow it to open existing PST files but prevent it from allowing them to grow. Both of these Group Policy settings are described more fully later in the chapter in the "Controlling PST files" section.

Chapter 3

- You can disable Exchange Fast Access by using the HKEY_CURRENT_USER\software \policies\microsoft\office\15.0\outlook\hybrid!localcaching value, although this doesn't expose a user interface in either OCT or the GPO template file.

- You can control how many months of cached email data are synchronized with the HKEY_CURRENT_USER\software\policies\microsoft\office\15.0\outlook \hybrid!syncwindowsetting value, as described earlier in the chapter.

- By default, Outlook searches both locally cached email and email on the server; Microsoft calls this hybrid searching. If you want to restrict Outlook to performing searches on only local messages, you can set the User Configuration\Administrative Templates\Microsoft Outlook 2013\Outlook Options\Preferences\Search Options GPO option.

- Normally, Outlook helpfully tries to turn Internet URLs and Universal Naming Convention (UNC) paths into clickable hyperlinks. Some organizations try to discourage users from clicking links in email and might want to turn this feature off; to control this, use the Internet and network path into the hyperlinks setting under the User Configuration\Administrative Templates\Microsoft Outlook 2013\Outlook Options GPO.

- You can disable the display of MailTips by using the User Configuration \Administrative Templates\Microsoft Outlook 2013\Outlook Options\Preferences \Email Options GPO setting or the HKEY_CURRENT_USER\software\policies \microsoft\office\15.0\outlook\options\mail!disablemailtips value. Setting this doesn't have any effect on the display of Policy Tips for data loss prevention.

The new Office app extensibility model gets its own set of controls. All of them live in the GPO template under User Configuration\Administrative Templates\Microsoft Office 2013 \Security Settings\Trust Center node:

- If you don't want your Office users using apps for Office, you can block them using the Block Apps for Office setting; there's no way to block apps only within Outlook. You either block apps from all desktop Office programs or none.

- If you want to let users run apps for Office but not install them from the Microsoft Office Store, set the Block The Office Store setting.

- There are multiple settings for controlling the activation behavior of apps; these are intended to give you a way to throttle or block apps that use too much CPU or RAM when run from within Outlook. These controls are mentioned at *http://technet .microsoft.com/en-us/library/jj219429.aspx#BKMK_Managing*. However, as of this writing, Microsoft hasn't documented specific values that might make sense for these GPO settings, so I recommend leaving them alone.

Pre-staging OST files for Outlook 2013 deployment

When a user synchronizes her mailbox with Outlook for the first time using cached Exchange mode, Outlook downloads every item in every folder in her primary mailbox and stores it in a local OST file—that's the cache to which "cached Exchange mode" refers. This can be a slow process, depending on the speed of the user's network connection and the amount of email to be downloaded; for large deployments, the network burden of having many users downloading their email at the same time can be an issue, too. To simplify the process of deploying Outlook, and to reduce the amount of network traffic, Microsoft supports a process of creating an initial OST file. You can think of this much like preseeding a DAG replica; the idea is to create a copy of the OST file over a high-speed network, save it, and then provide it to the user offline. The basic process works like this:

1. Log on to a machine running Outlook 2013, using an account that has permission to log on to the user's mailbox. This can be the user's mailbox or a separate administrative account that has the Send As and Receive As permissions on the target user.

2. Delete any existing OST files or Outlook profiles. Although this step is not strictly necessary, it reduces the chances that you'll accidentally copy the wrong OST file.

3. Create a new Outlook profile for the target user, making sure that cached Exchange mode is enabled. Set the sync slider described earlier to the appropriate value for the amount of mail you want the OST to contain.

4. Launch Outlook and wait for the OST to synchronize.

5. Quit Outlook and then move the OST file from %userdata%\Local Settings \Application Data\Microsoft\Outlook to where it is reachable from the user's computer. You could also burn it to a DVD, put it on a USB stick, and so on.

Repeat this process for each of the users for whose mailboxes you want OST files. With a bit of work, you could probably automate this process if you have a large number of mailboxes to deploy.

To stage the OST file, do the following:

1. Log on to the user's machine as the user.

2. Copy the OST file back to its home; if you accept the Outlook defaults when creating the profile, this will be %userdata%\Local Settings\Application Data\Microsoft \Outlook.

3. Create a new Outlook profile for the user, specifying the OST location you used in step 2.

4. Log on to Outlook.

Chapter 3

When Outlook starts, it will download any changes that were made to the original mailbox contents on the Exchange server to bring the OST up to date. However, because you allowed the OST to synchronize initially, the volume of changes that have to be synced should be much smaller than that required for a full download.

Controlling PST files

PST files are an unwelcome part of many Exchange deployments. In the early days of Exchange, it made sense to let clients keep their own stores of email to help relieve the storage burden placed on the server; a typical email server might only have been able to support a few hundred 25 MB mailboxes, so letting users keep their own local stashes of mail made sense. However, the messaging world has changed in several important ways. Exchange efficiently supports mailboxes of 10 GB or even larger, and storage is cheap enough that having terabytes of space on a server is no longer uncommon. Compliance and records retention are increasingly important for many organizations, too. Given these factors, it makes sense to examine whether PST files are still useful and relevant. There are many good reasons to banish PST files from your organization, including the fact that mail stored in local workstation PSTs is essentially invisible from any compliance, security, or backup tools you have in place for your Exchange data.

If you want more information about compliance issues, see Chapter 11, "Compliance management," in *Microsoft Exchange Server 2013 Inside Out: Mailbox and High Availability* by Tony Redmond (Microsoft Press, 2013).

Assuming that you want to limit or eliminate the use of PST files in your organization, you have three choices: configure Outlook to restrict them, use the Microsoft PST Capture tool to find and ingest PST files on your network, or use a third-party tool.

Restricting use of PST files in Outlook

The Outlook Group Policy settings give you control over two aspects of how Outlook uses PST files. First, you can prevent Outlook from opening PST files at all with the *DisablePST* value (HKEY_CURRENT_USER\Software\Policies\Microsoft\Office\X.0\Outlook\DisablePST, where X is the version of Outlook—for instance, 15.0 for Outlook 2013). When this value is present and set to 1, Outlook will not open any PST files that might be present in the user's Outlook profile, nor will it allow users to create new PST files or add existing PST files to a profile.

Your second option is to allow users to open their existing PSTs but not to allow those PST files to grow in size. The *PSTDisableGrow* value (HKEY_CURRENT_USER\Software\Policies\Microsoft\Office\X.0\Outlook\PST\PSTDisableGrow) prevents Outlook from allowing the PST file to grow in size; users can open their existing files and remove items from them, but users cannot add new items.

Although you can deploy these settings on individual machines, it is much more productive to use Windows Group Policy objects (GPOs) to do the work for you. Microsoft provides GPO templates for each version of Office that already incorporate the settings; you add the appropriate administrative template to the GPO that targets the desired users, enforce the settings you want, and allow the GPO mechanism to replicate the settings to target computers.

Using the Exchange PST Capture tool

After years of ceding the world of PST management to third parties, Microsoft introduced its own PST management tool, PST Capture. The function of the tool is simple: You install an agent on each of your workstations and then you install the PST Capture service itself on a server. The agents scan individual machines, looking for PST files, and then send information about the files they find to the central server.

PST Capture really involves a two-step process: discovering the PST files according to search criteria you plug in and then importing the resulting files to users' mailboxes. If the target mailboxes are within your Exchange organization, the PST Capture service sends the mail through CAS servers; if you're importing PSTs to mailboxes hosted on Office 365, the capture tool sends mail data directly to the cloud.

To use the tool, first you install the PST Capture service and console; Microsoft recommends installing them on a dedicated computer. The service requires a service account with permission to read and modify mailboxes on the Exchange servers you're using. To be more precise, the account under which you run the service needs the Exchange Organization Management role-based access control (RBAC) role.

Install the agent on computers you want to be able to scan. The agent is packaged as an MSI file that supports silent installation, so you can push it using Group Policy or other automated installation methods. The agent normally requires you to specify the PST Capture server to which you want it to talk, but you can do this from the command line like so:

```
msiexec /i PSTCaptureAgent_x86.msi /q CENTRALSERVICEHOST=deathToPSTs.contoso.com
SERVICEPORT=6674
```

The more interesting question is really where you install the agent. Obviously, you want it on machines that are likely to have PST files. That might include desktop or laptop computers the organization owns, file servers, or network-attached storage (NAS) devices. (Although NAS devices can be scanned with the console, they can't normally run the agent.) You have to trade off the work required to install (and, later, remove) the agent on the computers in your organization versus the benefit of identifying and getting rid of PST files, bearing in mind that users with non-domain-joined machines running Outlook Anywhere might still have PST files stashed away on laptops or desktops at home.

Chapter 3

After you install agents, you can perform a search. You can control which computers are included in the search and specific folders you want included or excluded in the search. For example, you can exclude the Windows system directory with a single check box. You can schedule the search or perform it immediately.

When you've completed a search or supplied your own manual import list containing the names and paths of the PSTs you want to import, you can start an import operation. You can import PSTs to a specific folder in the target user's mailbox, or you can dump the contents in the Inbox. For example, say the PST has a top-level folder named Old Mail with subfolders named 2011 and 2012. If you select the Inbox option, the user sees a new folder named Old Mail as a subfolder of the Inbox. If you select a specific target folder, the Old Mail folder will be created as a child of that folder. You can also specify that you want PST items imported into the user's archive mailbox, presuming that he has one. In either case, you must use the PST Capture console to link each PST file with the mailbox to which it should be imported. Because the console shows you the computer name and local path of each PST it finds, it should be simple to identify which PSTs belong to which users, but specifying that in the console can be a time-consuming operation.

For more details on the care and feeding of the PST Capture tool, see the Microsoft documentation at *http://technet.microsoft.com/en-us/library/hh781033(v=exchg.141).aspx*.

Exploring third-party solutions

When Microsoft delivered the initial version of the PST Capture tool, it entered a market that already contained a number of solutions for identifying and importing PST files, including PST Attender from Sherpa Software, the Migrator product from TransVault, and others. As with many other Microsoft add-ons, the PST Capture tool does much but not all the work third-party tools do. You have to decide whether the additional features (which might include better reporting, more flexible scheduling, or a wider range of configuration options) justify the expense of buying a tool you might not need to run on an ongoing basis.

Blocking client connections to a mailbox

Exchange enables you to disable any or all client connection protocols, including MAPI, on a per-user basis. You might need to do this if you want to prevent users from running earlier versions of Outlook that don't support features you need (such as messaging records management features like managed folders) or because the users in question are required to use Outlook Web App.

Whereas Exchange 2007 and Exchange 2010 required you to make this change through the Mailbox Features tab of the user's account properties, in Exchange 2013, you can do it either through Exchange Management Shell (EMS) (by using Set-CASMailbox) or the mailbox features tab of the user's mailbox properties dialog box in Exchange Administration Center (EAC) (Figure 3-9). If you disable MAPI for a user, that user cannot use Outlook to connect to her mailbox.

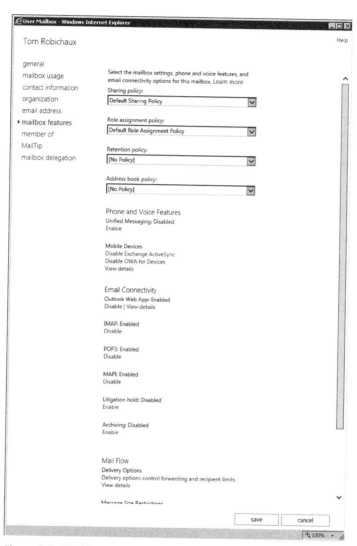

Figure 3-9 Disabling MAPI access for a user

The Set-CASMailbox cmdlet supports a number of parameters to control how an individual mailbox can use MAPI to connect to a mailbox on an Exchange server:

- **MAPIBlockOutlookRpcHTTP** Enables you to determine whether you allow Outlook clients to connect over RPC over HTTP through Outlook Anywhere. Set the parameter to $True to block RPC over HTTP access and $False to allow access.

- **MAPIBlockOutlookVersions** Enables you to control which versions of Outlook can connect to Exchange. You might use this setting to force users to upgrade to a more modern version of Outlook by blocking Outlook 2007. If a user attempts to use a blocked version of Outlook, he will see the error message shown in Figure 3-10. Outlook clients configured for cached Exchange mode continue to work offline, but they cannot connect to the server until an administrator lifts the block.

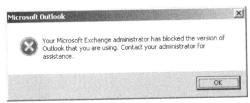

Figure 3-10 A user discovers that he can't use this version of Outlook to connect to Exchange

- **MAPIBlockOutlookNonCachedMode** Enables you to determine whether you allow Outlook clients to connect in online mode to the server. Set this parameter to $True to allow online access or to $False to force clients to connect in cached Exchange mode. Somewhat confusingly, users blocked from online access see the same message shown in Figure 3-10, followed by another error message to tell them that Outlook is unable to open their default email folders. Pointing to the version of Outlook rather than the need to use cached Exchange mode might confuse the help desk when users report their problem.

Microsoft identifies Outlook builds using a scheme of major release, minor release, build number. The major release number is shared across all the Office applications. The Office 14 suite includes Outlook 2010, Office 15 includes Outlook 2013, and so on. (Microsoft did not produce an Office 13 suite.) The minor release indicates whether the build is in the original RTM build, a service pack, or a cumulative update, and the build number is incremented daily to include code and fixes checked in by engineers. Here are the build numbers for some example Outlook versions:

- Outlook 2007: 12.4518.1014

- Outlook 2007 SP1: 12.6425.1000

- Outlook 2010: 14.0.4760.1000

- Outlook 2013 RTM: 15.0.4481.1003

To discover the client version to specify in the MAPIBlockOutlookVersions parameter, you can look at the properties of Outlook.exe itself, use the Programs control panel, or check with the useful list of client versions that Microsoft maintains at *http://technet.microsoft.com/en-us /library/aa996848.aspx.*

Before you start blocking any particular version of Outlook on Exchange 2013, you might want to know which users are currently using which versions to connect to your existing Exchange infrastructure. On Exchange 2007 and Exchange 2013, this command will give you a CSV file listing each user who's running Outlook along with the version of Outlook she's using. This helps simplify decisions about which versions to block on which mailboxes:

```
Get-MailboxServer | Get-LogonStatistics | Select
UserName,ClientName,ClientVersion,LogonTime | 'Export-Csv
-Path ExchangeClientVersions.csv
```

When you know which versions you want to block, the next step is to construct a version string that does the trick when passed to Set-CASMailbox. A single version by itself blocks only that version. A range of two versions blocks those versions and any in between. Specifying a single version blocks all versions either before or after that version, depending on where you put it. You can combine multiple version strings by separating them with semicolons. A few examples might help make this clearer:

- Set-CASMailbox –MAPIBlockOutlookVersions "12.0.6504.5000" blocks Outlook 2007 SP2 only. Any other version can connect.

- Set-CASMailbox –MAPIBlockOutlookVersions "12.0.4518.1014-14.0.6023.1000" blocks Outlook 2007 SP2 only and all versions up to and including Outlook 2010 SP1. Any earlier or later version can connect.

- Set-CASMailbox –MAPIBlockOutlookVersions "-15.0.4128.1014" blocks any version earlier than the public beta of Outlook 2013, including the public beta itself. Any later version can connect.

- Set-CASMailbox –MAPIBlockOutlookVersions "-15.0.4481.1003" blocks any client version later than Outlook 2013 RTM. Any earlier version can connect.

When you're blocking, you should always include an explicit allow for version 6.0.0 to support Exchange server-side MAPI connections (server connections always use MAPI version 6.0), like this:

```
Set-CASMailbox –Identity 'Simpson, Katherine' –MAPIBlockOutlookVersions '-6.0.0;
-15.0.4128.1014'
```

Chapter 3

You have to wait up to 120 minutes for the cached information about the mailbox to expire from the Store's cache. Alternatively, you can restart the Information Store service, but apart from test situations, this is definitely not the best approach because it will affect all the mailboxes connected to the server.

You can check whether any restrictions are in place for any protocols on a server by using the Get-Mailbox cmdlet to examine the ProtocolSettings property of each mailbox. If a restriction is in place for a specific client version, you see that version number listed. If an administrator has completely disabled MAPI access for the mailbox, you see "MAPI" and no version number. For example:

```
Get-Mailbox –Server PAO-EX01 | Where {$_.ProtocolSettings -ne $Null} | Select Name,
ProtocolSettings
```

```
Name                      ProtocolSettings
--------                  ----------------
Cannon, Paul              {MAPI§§§§-6.0.0;10.0.0-11.5603.0§§§§}
Kol, Ayla                 {MAPI§0§§§§§§§}
Simpson, Katherine        {OWA§1, IMAP4§0§§§§§§§§, POP3§0§§§§§...
```

You can also use the Get-CASMailbox cmdlet to check for MAPI blocks. Get-CASMailbox is more interesting because it also allows you to return the value of the MAPIEnabled property (False if the user is completely blocked from using MAPI) and to see the details of all the protocol settings you can set on a mailbox. However, you cannot specify a server name to check against, so Get-CASMailbox is less efficient because it will scan the entire organization unless you restrict its scope by using a server-side filter to focus on one server:

```
Get-CASMailbox –Filter {ServerName -eq'ExchServer1'} | Where {$_.ProtocolSettings
-ne $Null} | Select Name, ProtocolSettings, MapiEnabled
```

```
Name                      ProtocolSettings            MAPIEnabled
--------                  ----------------            -----------
Cannon, Paul              {MAPI§§§§-6.0.0;10.0.0-...   True
Kol, Ayla                 {MAPI§0§§§§§§§}              False
Simpson, Katherine        {OWA§1, IMAP4§0§§§§§§§§...   True
```

In addition to imposing blocks on MAPI connections, you can use the Set-CASMailbox cmdlet to disable client access to other protocols. For example:

- **To disable access to POP3**   Set-CASMailbox –Identity Bond –PopEnabled $False

- **To disable access to IMAP**   Set-CASMailbox –Identity Bond –ImapEnabled $False

- **To disable access to Outlook Web Access**   Set-CASMailbox –Identity Bond –OWAEnabled $False

- **To disable user access using Outlook Web App for Devices**   Set-CASMailbox –Identity Bond –OWAforDevicesEnabled $False. Note that this setting might not do anything useful when run against an on-premises mailbox because Outlook Web App for Devices is only officially supported against Office 365 mailboxes.

- **To disable access to ActiveSync**   Set-CASMailbox –Identity Bond –ActiveSyncEnabled $False

Blocking client access to a Mailbox server

Implementing blocks on a mailbox basis is useful, but sometimes you want to block all access to a Mailbox server. For example, you might want to update the server with some software or apply and update without having users impose load on the server or potentially interfere with the upgrade. One of the many advantages to the Exchange Database Availability Group (DAG) architecture is the way it simplifies maintenance; you can put a DAG member into maintenance mode, work on it, and then bring it online again. This process, which is described fully in Chapter 9, "The Database Availability Group," in *Microsoft Exchange Server 2013 Inside Out: Mailbox and High Availability*, means that you'll probably never have to block client access to a DAG member server explicitly. What if you have a standalone server, though?

You could apply such a block with EMS by searching for all mailboxes hosted in active databases on the server and using the Set-CASMailbox cmdlet to disable MAPI access, but it is more convenient to be able to apply the block centrally. For all versions from Exchange 2000 to Exchange 2007, you could block MAPI clients from connecting to a Mailbox server by configuring the Disable MAPI Clients key in the registry. This key is intended to enable administrators to require the deployment of a base-level version of Outlook. Put another way, it stops users from attempting to connect with earlier versions that might not meet your company's security requirements because the earlier software doesn't include recent anti-spam and antivirus features such as beacon blocking.

This registry key doesn't work on Exchange 2010 or Exchange 2013. For those versions, if you want to block MAPI connections on a particular CAS, you must take another tack. Choose from two approaches if you need to block connections to a Mailbox server.

- Use the Set-RPCClientAccess cmdlet. This cmdlet allows you to block all MAPI connections coming from specific versions. For example, this command blocks access to any version of Outlook prior to Outlook 2007 (major release 12).

    ```
    Set-RPCClientAccess -Server ExCAS01 -BlockedClientVersions
    "0.0.0-5.65535.65535; 7.0.0-11.99999.99999"
    ```

The problem is that all connections to all Mailbox servers supported by the CAS server will be blocked. This might be an effective method to use on small sites that have just one CAS server and one Mailbox server.

- On larger sites that support multiple CAS and Mailbox servers, you can set a per-mailbox block with the Set-CASMailbox cmdlet for every mailbox on the server that you want to maintain. For example:

```
Get-Mailbox -Server PAO-EX01 | Set-CASMailbox -MAPIBlockOutlookVersions
'-6.0.0;10.0.0-12.4406.0'
```

Both mechanisms are equally effective as a block. The choice between the two therefore comes down to whether you can block all connections flowing through a CAS server no matter what Mailbox server they are destined for, or you need to block connections to just one specific Mailbox server.

Using the Office Configuration Analyzer Tool

Outlook for Windows is a complex program that's evolved over a long period of time. Despite the fact that parts of it have been completely rewritten over time, there are still occasions when a particular machine (or group of machines, depending on whether you use imaging or cloning) might not behave the way you expect. Microsoft used to provide a free tool known as the Outlook Configuration Analyzer Tool, or OCAT, to help diagnose problems with Outlook installations. For Office 2013, Microsoft replaced OCAT with OffCAT, the Office Configuration Analyzer Tool. The purpose of OffCAT is to analyze the configuration and installation of the Office applications on a given machine and report back on any problems, real or potential, that exist. OffCAT is similar in spirit to the Exchange Best Practices Analyzer (ExBPA) and other tools that look at a static configuration and check it against a set of best practices defined by one of Microsoft's product teams.

OffCAT is available from Microsoft's website at *http://www.microsoft.com/en-us/download /details.aspx?id=36852*. It's packaged in a number of ways, including as a ZIP file containing the application and its support files or as a Windows Installer file that actually installs the application for you. No matter how you get it onto the target system, once you launch it, you'll be in familiar territory because it works very similarly to ExBPA. When you launch OffCAT, it asks you if you want it to check for updates to its rule base, which is packaged as a separate downloadable XML file so that updates to the rules don't require updates to the application itself. After you've installed updates, you see a page that lists all of the Office programs from Access to Word; each program's name is a link that takes you to a page like that shown in Figure 3-11.

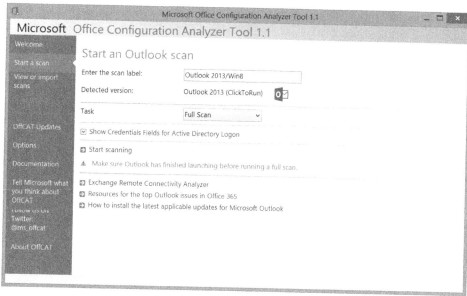

Figure 3-11 Starting an Outlook scan

Once you start the scan, the OffCAT display changes to reflect which specific scan tasks are being executed. In Figure 3-12, the tasks include a check of the current Outlook profile (helpfully named "Outlook") for consistency and possible corruption and checks of the folders in both the primary mailbox and personal archive mailbox for the user who is currently logged on. OffCAT performs several dozen checks of various configuration and data items, including some related to the Outlook configuration on the local machine for the current user; some related to the Outlook installation and configuration; and some related to folders, items, and other structures inside the current user's mailbox. For this reason, you must have Outlook running to perform an OffCAT scan, and if you quit Outlook (or it crashes) during the scan, the results you get might be incomplete or even unusable.

Chapter 3

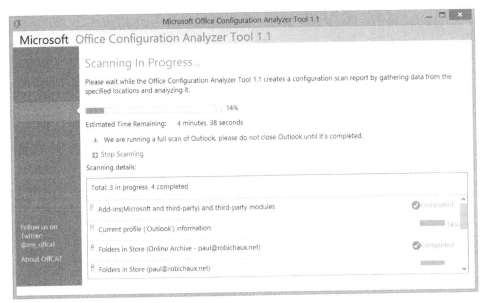

Figure 3-12 An OffCAT scan of Outlook 2013 in progress

The amount of time required to run the scan varies according to the speed of the computer being scanned, the amount of data in the user's mailbox, and a number of other factors. Having said that, a typical scan of Outlook alone will normally take less than five minutes. At the end of the scan, you'll see a results report (Figure 3-13) that is reminiscent of the results shown by various other Microsoft configuration analysis tools. In this case, the scan results include a note that there were items found in the Sync Issues folder, that mysterious synchronization problem report repository that often fills with items for no apparent reason. Other errors found by the scan, but not visible in the figure, include several problems related to a corrupt calendar item from 2008. Each problem reported includes links to Microsoft documentation or Microsoft Knowledge Base articles that propose corrective action for the reported problem.

You can also run OffCAT from the command line, meaning that you can push it to client systems and run it with a logon script or as part of a GPO. Although it might not be necessary to periodically scan all your client systems for problems related to Office configuration, it would certainly be a good idea to scan machines on which users have reported problems, and it might be worthwhile to scan your clients as part of your preparations for upgrading to a new release of Office.

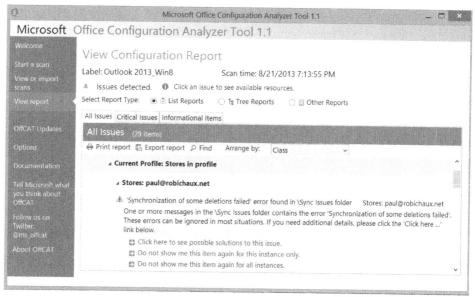

Figure 3-13 The results of an OffCAT scan showing problems with data in the scanned mailbox

Managing Outlook Web App

Users don't typically think of Outlook Web App as an application on its own; they think, "Oh, it's the webpage I use to get email." Exchange administrators, however, know quite well that Outlook Web App is a separate application that runs under Internet Information Server (IIS); its role is to retrieve user mail data, display it, and interact with the user. In Exchange 2013, Outlook Web App only runs on Mailbox servers, so some of the ways we interact with and manage it as administrators have changed from previous versions. The primary vehicle for changing Outlook Web App settings is the Outlook Web App virtual directory created during installation of the Mailbox role; you will become quite adept at using Set-OWAVirtualDirectory and Set-OWAMailboxPolicy to control the various options in Outlook Web App.

Outlook Web App mailbox policies

Exchange 2013 supports the ability to allocate different levels of functionality to Outlook Web App users through policies. As with the other types of policies Exchange supports, Outlook Web App policies are intended to enable you to create a group of settings and then apply those settings to mailboxes without having to modify the individual mailboxes. Microsoft added Outlook Web App policies in Exchange 2010 to give administrators a more granular way to control access to Outlook Web App features. All the features Outlook

Web App policies can control can also be controlled by changing settings on an individual Mailbox server, and many of them can be modified by changing settings on user mailboxes.

Exchange includes a default Outlook Web App policy, but that default isn't applied to any mailboxes unless you manually do so. You can create as many Outlook Web App mailbox policies as you like and then apply a maximum of one Outlook Web App policy to each mailbox. If you don't apply any policies to a mailbox, a user's access to Outlook Web App features is controlled by the segmentation properties defined for the Outlook Web App virtual directory on each CAS server. Figure 3-14 shows the EAC view for Outlook Web App mailbox policies, which you use to create and modify policies. EAC helpfully shows you a summary of the currently selected policy's settings on the right side of the window.

Figure 3-14 Viewing the list of Outlook Web App policies in EAC

The easiest way to apply any mailbox Outlook Web App policy, including the default policy, to a set of mailboxes is with the Set-CASMailbox cmdlet. For example, this command fetches all the mailboxes that belong to the North America organizational unit (OU) and pipes them to Set-CASMailbox to apply the default Outlook Web App mailbox policy:

```
Get-Mailbox –OrganizationalUnit 'North America'| Set-CASMailbox
-OwaMailboxPolicy 'Default'
```

What should you put in the default Outlook Web App policy? It depends. The default Outlook Web App policy included with Exchange basically duplicates the default out-of-the-box segmentation properties of the Outlook Web App virtual directory as it's installed on a Mailbox server. It permits access to all Outlook Web App features, including the premium client.

To create a new Outlook Web App mailbox policy, open the Permissions section of EAC, select the Outlook Web App policies tab, and click the plus (+) icon. A wizard then enables you to select which features you want users to access (Figure 3-15). You can choose any or all of the available features in the policy, several of which were added in Exchange 2013 CU2.

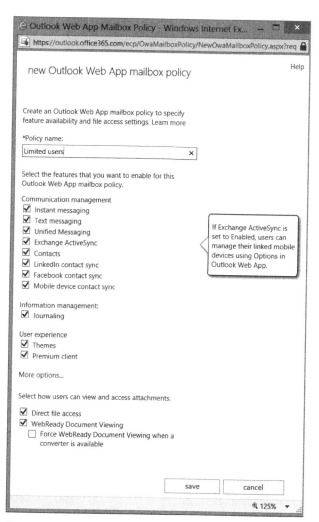

Figure 3-15 Creating a new Outlook Web App mailbox policy

Table 3-3 lists the features shown on the Features tab of the EAC dialog box for an Outlook Web App mailbox policy. Some of these features depend on other components (text messaging, public folders, and instant messaging, for example), and others require a very good reason before you disable them. For example, it usually doesn't make much sense to disable the Change Password feature because handling user requests to change passwords creates extra work for help desks.

TABLE 3-3 Outlook Web App features controllable through Outlook Web App policies

Feature	Meaning	Available through
Instant messaging	If enabled, and if you've configured Lync properly, users can access IM functionality from within Outlook Web App, including the ability to view presence information. If disabled, these features are unavailable.	Outlook Web App
Text messaging	If enabled, users can create and send text (SMS) messages from Outlook Web App. If disabled, this feature is removed.	Outlook Web App
Unified messaging	If this feature is enabled and the mailbox is enabled for UM, users can access and manage their UM settings through Exchange Control Panel (ECP). If disabled, the option is removed.	ECP
Exchange ActiveSync	If enabled, users can access details of the mobile devices they have synchronized, including the ability to wipe devices if they are lost and retrieve logs containing details of synchronization operations. If disabled, the option is removed from ECP.	ECP
Contacts	If enabled, users can access their Contacts folder in Outlook Web App. If disabled, the icon is removed from Outlook Web App.	Outlook Web App
LinkedIn contact sync	Controls whether Office 365 users are allowed to synchronize their LinkedIn contacts with their Exchange contacts folder.	Outlook Web App
Facebook contact sync	Controls whether Office 365 users are allowed to synchronize their Facebook contacts with their Exchange contacts folder.	Outlook Web App
Mobile device contact sync	Controls whether users running Outlook Web App for Devices are allowed to sync their Exchange contacts to the device using the app.	Outlook Web App for Devices
All Address Lists	If enabled, users can see all defined address lists in the directory. If disabled, they can see the Global Address List (GAL) only.	Outlook Web App

Feature	Meaning	Available through
Public Folders	If enabled, users can access and work with public folders. If disabled, the icon is removed from Outlook Web App.	Outlook Web App
Journaling	If enabled, users can see the Journal folder in their folder list. If disabled, Outlook Web App hides the folder.	Outlook Web App
Notes	If enabled, users can see and modify note items in Outlook Web App. If disabled, Outlook Web App hides the Notes icon.	Outlook Web App
Search Folders	If enabled, users can access search folders created by Outlook. If disabled, these folders are suppressed.	Outlook Web App
Inbox rules	If enabled, users can create and modify rules through ECP. If disabled, the option is suppressed. However, Exchange continues to respect any rules created with Outlook.	ECP
Recover Deleted Items	If enabled, users can recover deleted items. If disabled, users cannot recover deleted items with Outlook Web App, but Exchange will continue to preserve these items in the Recoverable Items folder.	Outlook Web App
Change password	If this feature is enabled, users can change their account password from Outlook Web App. If disabled, Outlook Web App will not prompt users when their password is approaching its expiry date (prompts start 14 days in advance), and they cannot see the option to change their password in ECP.	Outlook Web App /ECP
Junk email filtering	If enabled, users can access the options to control junk mail processing such as blocked and safe user lists. If disabled, the option is removed from ECP.	ECP
Themes	If enabled, users can select a theme other than the default and apply it to Outlook Web App and ECP. If disabled, the option is suppressed.	Outlook Web App /ECP
Premium client	If enabled, users can use the premium client with a browser that supports this client. If disabled, users are forced to use the standard client no matter what browser they use.	Outlook Web App
Email signature	If enabled, users can access the option to create or modify email signatures and apply them to outgoing messages. If disabled, the option is removed from ECP.	ECP

Chapter 3

Feature	Meaning	Available through
Calendar	If enabled, users can access the Calendar application. If disabled, the icon is removed from Outlook Web App.	Outlook Web App
Tasks	If enabled, users can create and manage tasks in Outlook Web App. If disabled, the option is suppressed.	Outlook Web App
Reminders and notifications	If enabled, Outlook Web App provides users with notifications of new messages, meeting reminders, and so on. If disabled, these notifications are suppressed.	Outlook Web App

Managing Outlook Web App mailbox policies in EMS

A new policy can also be created with EMS. For some odd reason, this is a two-step process. First, you create the new policy with the New-OWAMailboxPolicy cmdlet, and then you use the Set-OWAMailboxPolicy cmdlet to define which features are enabled or disabled by the policy. For example, here's a policy that allows users to use the premium client while removing some of the more esoteric features:

```
New-OWAMailboxPolicy -Name 'Limited OWA features'
Set-OWAMailboxPolicy -Identity 'Limited OWA features'
-ActiveSyncIntegrationEnabled $True -AllAddressListsEnabled $True
-CalendarEnabled $True -ContactsEnabled $True -JournalEnabled $True
-JunkEmailEnabled $True -RemindersAndNotificationsEnabled $True
-NotesEnabled $True -PremiumClientEnabled $True -SearchFoldersEnabled $False
-SignaturesEnabled $True -SpellCheckerEnabled $True -TasksEnabled $True
-ThemeSelectionEnabled $False -UMIntegrationEnabled $False
-ChangePasswordEnabled $True -RulesEnabled $True -PublicFoldersEnabled $False
-SMimeEnabled $True -RecoverDeletedItemsEnabled $True
-InstantMessagingEnabled $False -TextMessagingEnabled $False
```

There are a number of Outlook Web App mailbox policy settings that are only available through EMS, too:

- DefaultTheme enables you to specify the name of an Outlook Web App theme that users receive by default, for instance, Set-OWAMailboxPolicy –DefaultTheme "Orange". The only way I've found to get a list of theme names is to look at the version-specific folder under V15\ClientAccess\OWA; for example, on an RTM Exchange 2013 server, the theme folders will be in V15\ClientAccess\OWA\15.0.516.30\Owa2 \resources\themes.

- DelegateAccessEnabled controls whether users who have delegate access to another mailbox can open the other mailbox in Outlook Web App. Users who are delegates can still open whatever mailboxes they have access to from Outlook. In a similar vein,

ExplicitLogonEnabled controls whether a user is allowed to open another user's mailbox from within Outlook Web App without logging out and logging back in as the target user.

● DisplayPhotosEnabled, SetPhotoEnabled, and SetPhotoURL affect whether and how sender photos are displayed within Outlook Web App; SetPhotoEnabled governs whether users can set their own photo from within Outlook Web App. If they cannot, Outlook Web App attempts to use photos from Active Directory if they are present and DisplayPhotosEnabled is set to $True. SetPhotoURL is the URL users are sent to when they attempt to change their photo from within Outlook Web App; it is often set to a SharePoint page.

● IRMEnabled controls whether Outlook Web App allows users to read or send messages that have been protected with Active Directory Rights Management Services (AD RMS).

● PredictedActionsEnabled enables an Outlook Web App feature that is supposed to customize the commands and icons the user sees according to what they're doing. This is an intriguing idea (much like adaptive menus in Office 2003), but it's not widely used in Outlook Web App, and it's not clear yet whether users are even aware that it exists.

● OrganizationEnabled turns off some organization-level settings. For example, when this is set to $False, users don't see separate options for internal and external out of office (OOF) messages, and the Resources tab on calendar items is hidden.

Applying an Outlook Web App mailbox policy

After you have created an Outlook Web App mailbox policy, you can use either EAC or EMS to apply the new policy. EMS is simple; you use Set-CASMailbox with the –OWAMailboxPolicy switch. For example, to apply the policy defined earlier, you could do the following:

```
Set-CASMailbox –Identity 'Andrews, Ben (IT)' –OWAMailboxPolicy 'Limited OWA Features'
```

If you'd rather use EAC, you can apply the policy by selecting the user on the Recipients page of EAC, opening its properties dialog box, and clicking the View Details link beneath the Outlook Web App label. That displays the dialog box shown in Figure 3-16; use the Browse button to select the policy you want to apply.

Exchange enforces the new policy the next time the user logs on to her mailbox.

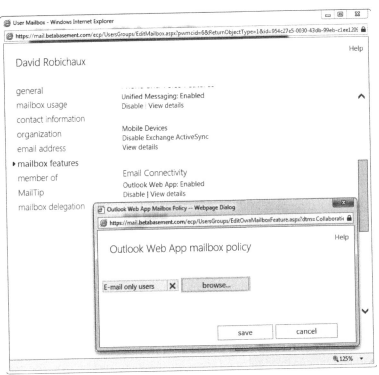

Figure 3-16 Selecting an Outlook Web App mailbox policy for a user

Controlling offline Outlook Web App use

Both EAC and EMS enable you to control whether users may use Outlook Web App in offline mode. This isn't a simple on/off toggle, though. By default, any user who has an offline-compatible browser is allowed to turn offline mode on. That's because the default value of the AllowOfflineOn setting in the default policy is AllComputers. Outlook Web App 2010 and earlier versions allowed users to specify whether the computer from which they were logging on should be treated as a public or private computer. Outlook Web App 2013 doesn't give users this choice by default. If you want to restrict offline use to private computers, you can, but it's a two-step process. First, you use Set-OWAMailboxPolicy –AllowOfflineOn PrivateComputersOnly and then you enable the private/public computer choice by running Set-OWAVirtualDirectory –LogonPagePublicPrivateSelectionEnabled.

If you want to prevent offline access for some reason such as the fear that users will accidentally leave important or sensitive data on a public computer, set the value of AllowOfflineOn for the target policy to NoComputers and then apply the policy as desired. Remember, the policy won't be applied until the next time each user logs on.

Of course, there's another aspect to controlling offline use of Outlook Web App: the client browser itself has to be configured to allow offline access. In Internet Explorer, this takes the form of the Allow Website Caches And Databases setting (Figure 3-17), which must be enabled for the browser to actually cache any data. Although this setting is enabled by default in Internet Explorer 10 on Windows 8, you might find that it's disabled on other versions, or your users might accidentally turn it off, not realizing what it does. To check or change the setting, do the following:

1. Open the Internet Explorer settings dialog box with the Tools | Options menu command.

2. On the General tab, click the Settings button in the Browsing history command group.

3. When the Website Data Settings dialog box appears, switch to the Caches And Databases tab and verify that the Allow Caches And Databases check box is selected.

4. Click OK to dismiss the Website Data Settings and Internet Options dialog boxes.

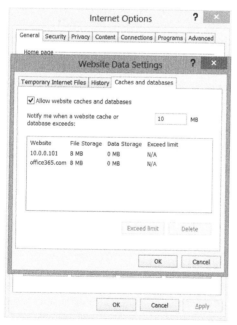

Figure 3-17 Make sure that Internet Explorer is configured to allow web apps to store data locally if you want OWA offline mode to work

Controlling attachment access and rendering

Although feature segmentation is the most obvious use of Outlook Web App policies and receives the most attention, you can also control other aspects of how users work with Outlook Web App through these policies. In particular, you have a fair amount of flexibility in specifying how users may work with attachments in Outlook Web App.

When a user receives a message with an attachment, administrators can control:

- Whether the user sees the attachment at all; if the attachment file type is blocked, the user cannot access it through Outlook Web App.

- Whether the attachment type is allowed and whether the user must use the rendering tools available within Outlook Web App to see a web-based rendering of the attachment data (a feature known as WebReady Document Viewing). This feature displays only HTML text, graphics, and XML-formatted files.

- Whether a rendered attachment should be displayed using the Office Web Apps component (WAC) if it's available. WAC supports Microsoft PowerPoint, Word, and Excel files.

- If rendering is available, whether a user must see a web rendering first before downloading or opening the file.

- Whether the user can open the attachment file directly or whether it must first be saved to disk (which allows local anti-malware scanners to scan it before opening).

This sounds like a fairly complex set of options, and it is. It is challenging to balance users' need to work with documents sent as attachments and the potential security risks that come along with allowing access to complex document formats. The broad scope of Outlook Web App controls for attachment access gives you the tools to adjust what your users can do based on their needs and your organization's security policy.

Attachment access

Outlook Web App categorizes files into four groups:

- *Allowed* files are deemed innocuous and safe to open on the client computer. The list includes types such as Word documents (.doc and .docx extensions) and Windows bitmaps (.bmp extension) that you can be reasonably sure will not contain malicious code.

- *Blocked* file types pose a significant risk to a computer when a user opens them because they can contain executable code. These files include types such as Windows batch files (.bat extension) and Windows command files (.cmd extension).

- *Force save* files are those that a user cannot open directly; instead, she must save them to disk before they can be opened. These types include Adobe Shockwave (.swf) and Director (.dcr) files.

- *Unknown* files are those that are not included in the other lists. The Outlook Web App mailbox policy or Outlook Web App virtual directory setting specifies what should be done with these files; the default is to require them to be saved to disk before opening.

Outlook Web App performs special processing for attachments marked as Force To Save. This means that the user has to save the attachment to his local disk before he can view its contents. As Outlook Web App downloads the attachment from the server, it checks whether it is XML or HTML. In this case, Outlook Web App runs some code called Safe HTML to strip out any malicious XML or HTML code. If the attachment is another type, Outlook Web App examines the content to see whether it actually contains XML or HTML code. This check is performed to ensure that no attachment is ever downloaded that could contain malicious code that could introduce a virus or another dangerous program onto the PC. If hidden XML or HTML code is detected, Outlook Web App strips the attachment and replaces it with a text file to tell the user that the attachment was removed.

The list of file types that are allowed, blocked, and Force To Save can be managed through EAC only. There are actually separate lists for the file types and MIME types you want to allow; you can add items to the allowed, blocked, or forced-save list by either file type or MIME type, using the appropriate value: AllowedFileTypes, AllowedMimeTypes, BlockedFileTypes, BlockedMimeTypes, ForceSaveFileTypes, and ForceSaveMimeTypes. There are separate copies of these lists for each Outlook Web App mailbox policy and each Outlook Web App virtual directory; as a best practice, you should use Outlook Web App mailbox policies to control file access so that the settings you want are consistently applied to users no matter what server they communicate with.

The role of Office Web Apps Server

In Exchange 2007 and Exchange 2010, Microsoft licensed a set of third-party libraries for WebReady Document Viewing. This was a sensible move given that the third-party supplier had already solved the problem of how to render many file types efficiently in a web browser, but it also meant that Microsoft was at the mercy of the vendor for updates to handle new file formats or fix security problems. As part of the Office 2013 release, the Office team built Office Web Apps Server, a separate, standalone server application that, among its other capabilities, Exchange 2013 can use to render PowerPoint, Excel, and Word documents. The Office Web Apps feature is also known as Web Apps component (WAC).

Setting up Office Web Apps is outside the scope of this book, but the TechNet documentation at *http://technet.microsoft.com/en-us/library/jj219458(v=office.15* describes the process well.

Assuming that you have Office Web Apps configured, integrating it with Exchange is simple because there are essentially only two tasks you need to perform. First, you must tell your Exchange servers where the Office Web Apps farm is. You do this with the Set-OrganizationConfig cmdlet and its WACDiscoveryEndPoint parameter, which accepts the URL of the WAC farm. After doing so, the second step is to configure the Outlook Web App virtual directory or (preferably) Outlook Web App mailbox policy to enable the use of WAC for rendering content on public and/or private computers, which you do with the WacViewingOnPrivateComputersEnabled and WacViewingOnPublicComputersEnabled parameters to Set-OWAMailboxPolicy or Set-OWAVirtualDirectory (both of which are true by default).

Optionally, you can force users to view documents using WAC before saving them to disk. This is annoying to end users, but it helps reduce the risk that they'll leave copies of sensitive documents lying around. If you want to enable this feature, the ForceWacViewingFirstOnPrivateComputers and ForceWacViewingFirstOnPublicComputers parameters to Set-OWAMailboxPolicy or Set-OWAVirtualDirectory enables it.

Managing Outlook Web App virtual directory settings

Many of the settings available to control Outlook Web App behavior are duplicated on the Outlook Web App mailbox policy and the Outlook Web App virtual directory objects. This gives administrators some flexibility; in small organizations with only a handful of servers, it's easy to apply settings directly to the Outlook Web App virtual directories, and larger organizations can use Outlook Web App mailbox policies to ensure that the right users get the right settings no matter what servers they use. A fair number of settings are unique to the Outlook Web App virtual directory, though. The Outlook Web App virtual directory settings that pertain to proxying, redirection, and client authentication were discussed in Chapter 1. The integration settings used with Lync are described in Chapter 7, "Integrating Exchange 2013 with Lync Server." That leaves us with a fairly eclectic group of settings available for Set-OWAVirtualDirectory, some of which are nonetheless quite useful.

The Outlook Web App 2013 logon page has intentionally been designed to have a very clean, spare look. The default version includes text fields for the user's logon credentials and a big Outlook Web App logo, and that's all. This is a sharp contrast to the cluttered look and tiny print of the Exchange 2007 and Exchange 2010 Outlook Web App logon pages. However, the new design also takes away some options that were formerly right on the logon page; users can't tell Exchange whether they are on a public or private computer, nor can they voluntarily use the Light mode when they have a slow or unreliable connection. You can fix these two issues by using the LogonPageLightSelectionEnabled and LogonPagePublicPrivateSelectionEnabled parameters to Set-OWAVirtualDirectory; setting them to true enables the corresponding option on the Outlook Web App logon page. You might have to run iisreset to force the changes to appear, though. In addition to these changes, the logon page is commonly used to display an informational message, such as a warning telling users that unauthorized access is prohibited. You can add these types of messages by editing the logon page, but any such edits will be overwritten when you deploy an Exchange cumulative update or service pack.

You can set the default language users will see when they log on. Outlook Web App uses the language set for a user's mailbox to render the user interface, but it can't do that until the user has logged on. If the user has set a preferred language in his browser, Outlook Web App renders the logon page in that language. However, Set-OWAVirtualDirectory –LogonAndErrorLangauge enables you to set the default language users see when they haven't specified one themselves; you must supply the language code (LCID) of the language you want to use. (Language selection for mailboxes is covered in more detail in Chapter 5, "Mailbox management," in *Microsoft Exchange Server 2013 Inside Out: Mailbox and High Availability*.

You can also change the way Outlook Web App interprets what the user types into the user name field of the logon page. By default, Outlook Web App accepts credentials in three formats. A user named Erik Rucker could thus choose to enter his credentials as domain\ username (contoso\ruckere; Microsoft refers to this format as full domain), or he could use his Universal Principal Name (UPN) of ruckere@contoso.com. A third option is to use just the user name, but for this to work Outlook Web App has to know what default domain to use—if Erik just types in ruckere, Outlook Web App has no way to know which of the available Active Directory domains it should sign in to. To solve this, set the default domain by using the DefaultDomain switch. If you want to require users to use a particular format, you can set it with the LogonFormat switch: –LogonFormat FullDomain requires domain\user-name, –LogonFormat UserName accepts the user name if (and only if) the default domain is also set, and –LogonFormat PrincipalName enables UPN sign-in, but only for users whose UPN is the same as their email address.

Managing Outlook Web App timeouts

You're probably familiar with the timeout values Outlook Web App 2003 and later support; the idea behind these timeouts is that, after a certain period of inactivity, Outlook Web App automatically logs the user out so that a nosy or malicious person can't piggyback on a legitimate user's session. By default, Outlook Web App sessions time out after six hours. This behavior is controlled by two parameters to the Set-OrganizationConfig cmdlet:

- ActivityBasedAuthenticationTimeoutEnabled controls whether timeouts are applied. (The default is $True.)

- ActivityBasedAuthenticationTimeoutInterval specifies the time after which a session is considered idle and thus closes.

Managing Office Store apps for Outlook Web App

In the mobile device world, we have the "bring your own device" (BYOD) model, which democratizes mobility by putting the choice of which device to use, and which apps to run on it, in the hands of individual users. Microsoft is now extending a similar level of choice to end users by allowing them to install and run Office Store apps that run inside Outlook Web App. These apps are hosted on the Mailbox server; by default, individual users can install and run apps, as can administrators. Many organizations will want to retain a degree of control over app installation, so fortunately Exchange 2013 includes some controls. The apps themselves are bundles that can contain HTML, CSS, and JavaScript, along with a manifest file that specifies the app's capabilities (such as whether it can run in Outlook, Outlook Web App, or both) and the level of privilege required to install. An application developer can mark an application as installable by users or administrators. The develop-ment model for Outlook-based apps (described at *http://msdn.microsoft.com/en-us/library /fp161135.aspx*) is quite flexible. You can write applications that work on specific types of messages, your apps can modify their appearance or behavior depending on the device where they run, and apps that can run within Outlook 2013 can take advantage of extra services by calling Exchange Web Services routines.

Exchange 2013 CU2 ships with four built-in apps:

- Action Items analyzes the text of your email messages and suggests action items (in the form of Exchange tasks) that are related to the message content.

- Bing Maps scans messages and calendar items for addresses and offers you maps and directions by adding a tab of map data to the window.

- Suggested Meetings reviews the text of messages and suggests appointments that might be added to your calendar.

- Unsubscribe provides a simplified interface for unsubscribing from newsletters, sales email, or other possibly unwanted messages.

Because these apps are built in, you cannot remove them, although you can disable them.

Who can install and configure apps?

Thanks to the RBAC infrastructure that underlies Exchange, when Microsoft adds new features, it often provides a separate management role to control the use of those fea-tures. Outlook apps are no exception; Exchange 2013 adds four new RBAC roles. The Org Marketplace Apps role grants permission to install and configure apps that come from the Microsoft Office Store; the Org Custom Apps role grants the ability to install and man-age apps that come from internal enterprise distribution points. In the same vein, the My

Marketplace Apps and My Custom Apps user roles grant users the ability to install and manage their own apps.

Enabling or disabling apps at the organization level

By default, the app integration feature is enabled. You can change this with Set-OrganizationConfig –AppsForOfficeEnabled; when it is set to $false, no new apps can be activated for or by any user in the organization. However, changing this setting doesn't remove any existing apps, nor does it prevent users from accessing them. If you want to disable user access to apps completely, you must remove any apps you've added and then disable the built-in apps as described in the next section.

Installing, removing, and configuring apps

Figure 3-18 shows the Apps tab of the Organization slab in EAC. The installed apps are listed; for each app, you can see who provides the app, whether it's available to users, and which users can access the app. When you select an app, the details pane on the right side of the window changes to show the app version, what permissions it requires, and a description provided by the app vendor.

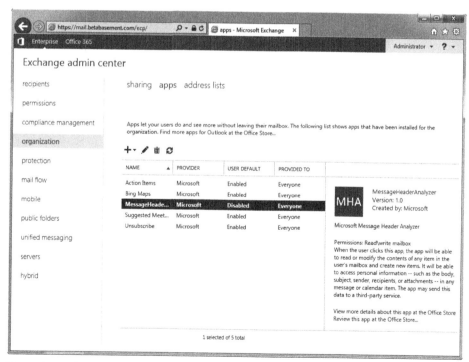

Figure 3-18 The Apps tab of the Organization slab in EAC, showing the installed apps available to users throughout the organization

To add or remove an app, just use the appropriate icons in the toolbar. You can add apps from the Office Store itself or from a URL you specify; the latter option enables you to add apps from a SharePoint app catalog or a local or shared folder. When you install an app, you'll see a confirmation dialog box similar to the one in Figure 3-19; in this case, the LinkedIn app is only asking for permission to read mailbox items, and the summary text reflects that.

INSIDE OUT Apps outside the United States

The Office Store is not yet available in every market that Microsoft serves. In many countries, when you visit the store page, you'll see a message stating that "there are no apps available for Office or SharePoint available for your country/region at this time." This mirrors what's happened with other vendors' app stores; the Apple App Store, Amazon's app store, Google Play, and the Microsoft Xbox Music and Xbox Video have all rolled out to additional countries over time after first being introduced in the United States, and it appears that Microsoft is doing the same in this case. Music, video content, and books are usually licensed separately in each region or territory; downloadable apps can be too, although the Office Store license agreement doesn't seem to place any restriction on transnational app sales. Microsoft has made no public statements about its plans to take the Office Store worldwide, though, so you might have to keep checking for its availability if you're in an area that can't use it currently.

You can also add or remove apps by using EMS; the New-App and Remove-App cmdlets correspond to the toolbar icons. However, using New-App means that you don't get any of the additional data shown in the Office Store.

When you install a new app, it shows up as disabled, and users have no access to it. To change the app's availability, click the pencil icon to open the settings dialog box shown in Figure 3-20. The app can be made available to users by selecting the Make This App Available To Users In Your Organization check box, but just making it available doesn't mean that users will necessarily be able to use it. The group of three option buttons in this dialog box lists the states an individual app can take on: optional and enabled by default, optional and disabled by default, or mandatory. The "by default" in the first two options is there because users can enable or disable optional apps themselves, whereas apps marked as mandatory are always enabled. Users won't see any explicit notification of new apps, and the apps themselves don't appear until the next time a user launches Outlook 2013 or opens Outlook Web App. If you're deploying a new app, you'll need to tell your users about it yourself.

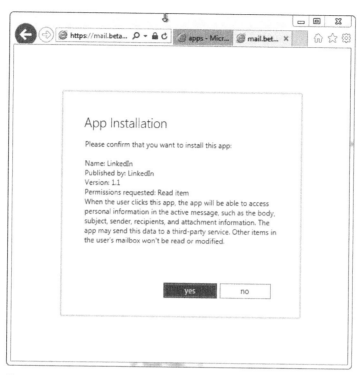

Figure 3-19 The app installation confirmation dialog box

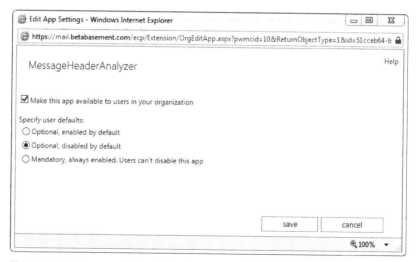

Figure 3-20 The app settings dialog box

Removing apps is easy; select the app, click the Delete icon (it looks like a trashcan), and answer the confirmation dialog box by clicking Yes. The app is removed immediately, and users can no longer access it.

Managing apps from EMS

There are several new cmdlets used for managing apps for individual users. Microsoft classes these as recipient cmdlets because they enable, disable, add, remove, or configure apps for one or more specific users. Each app has a unique identity, represented as a globally unique identifier (GUID), but most of the time you'll use the app's friendly name to keep track of which apps are present.

The Get-App cmdlet returns a wealth of data about individual apps, but to get it, you'll need the application ID. To get the ID for an individual app, you can do something like this:

```
get-app -OrganizationApp | ft DisplayName, AppID
```

```
DisplayName                    AppId
-----------                    -----
LinkedIn                       333bf46d-7dad-4f2b-8cf4-c19ddc78b723
MessageHeaderAnalyzer          62916641-fc48-44ae-a2a3-163811f1c945
Bing Maps                      7a774f0c-7a6f-11e0-85ad-07fb4824019b
Suggested Meetings             bc13b9d0-5ba2-446a-956b-c583bdc94d5e
Unsubscribe                    d39dee0e-fdc3-4015-af8d-94d4d49294b3
Action Items                   f60b8ac7-c3e3-4e42-8dad-e4e1fea59ff7
```

The OrganizationApp parameter specifies that you just want to see applications that are scoped to the organization. These might be apps from the Office Store or custom enterprise apps; the distinction between organization apps and user apps is that the organization apps are stored at the organization level and are potentially available to all users in the organization.

There are several other interesting properties on the individual applications, including the XML for the application manifests (stored in the ManifestXml property) and the application's scope and permissions.

If you run the Get-App cmdlet by itself, you get a summary of the apps installed in your organization:

```
Get-App
```

```
DisplayName                    Enabled            AppVersion
-----------                    -------            ----------
LinkedIn                       False              1.1
MessageHeaderAnalyzer          False              1.0
```

```
Bing Maps                     True                      1.0
Suggested Meetings            True                      1.0
Unsubscribe                   True                      1.0
Action Items                  True                      1.0
```

Each app's display name and version are shown. The value in the Enabled column reflects whether the app is enabled or disabled by default, not whether it's available to any particular user. To see the state of applications for a particular user, you specify that user with the –mailbox switch to Get-App, like so:

```
get-app -mailbox paul
```

```
DisplayName                       Enabled                AppVersion
-----------                       -------                ----------
LinkedIn                          True                   1.1
MessageHeaderAnalyzer             True                   1.0
Bing Maps                         True                   1.0
Suggested Meetings                True                   1.0
Unsubscribe                       True                   1.0
Action Items                      True                   1.0
```

Notice that this summary shows the LinkedIn and MessageHeaderAnalyzer apps as enabled for my mailbox, even though their default state in the previous output was disabled. That's because I enabled those apps directly for my mailbox.

You can change the enabled state of apps with the Enable-App and Disable-App cmdlets. These change the default state of the app for all users unless you pass the –Mailbox parameter. For example, if you install a new app and then use Disable-App on it, the app will be disabled by default for new users, but they can still enable it themselves.

If you want to change the enabled or disabled state of an app for users directly, you do that with the Set-App cmdlet. For example, to prevent users from seeing or using the MessageHeaderAnalyzer app, you could use a command like the following to turn it off:

```
Get-App | where {$_.DisplayName –like "MessageHeaderAnalyzer"} | Set-App
–OrganizationApp –Enabled:$false
```

The Enabled property controls whether the app is enabled for (and thus visible to) users. You can use the –DefaultStateForUser switch to control whether an enabled app is turned on for users by giving it a value of Enabled or Disabled; if you use –DefaultStateForUser AlwaysEnabled, that forces the app on.

Which users see these changes depends on two other parameters to Set-App. The –ProvidedTo switch can be set to Everyone or to SpecificUsers; in the latter case, you can either pipe in a set of mailboxes or use the –UserList switch. For example, to make the app named ScreenShotChecker available to all users in the Legal group, you could do the following:

```
$a = Get-DistributionGroupMember Legal
Get-App | where {$_.DisplayName -like "ScreenShotChecker"} | Set-App -OrganizationApp
-ProvidedTo SpecificUsers -UserList $a -DefaultStateForUser AlwaysEnabled
```

Self-service app management for users

After an app is installed, either by you or a user, an individual user might be able to enable or disable optional applications from within Outlook Web App 2013 or Outlook 2013 (which actually uses the EAC options component, as shown in Figure 3-21). Their ability to do this depends on their having the appropriate RBAC roles, as described earlier in the chapter (which they will have by default). Users can manage apps from Outlook Web App by clicking the Options icon (the gear in the upper-right corner of the window) and choosing Manage Apps, or from Outlook 2013 by opening the backstage view and choosing the Manage Apps link. In either case, the view similar to that shown in Figure 3-21 will appear; one important difference between this view and the one shown in Figure 3-18 is that this view includes a user-installed app (as indicated by the value of *User* in the Installed By column).

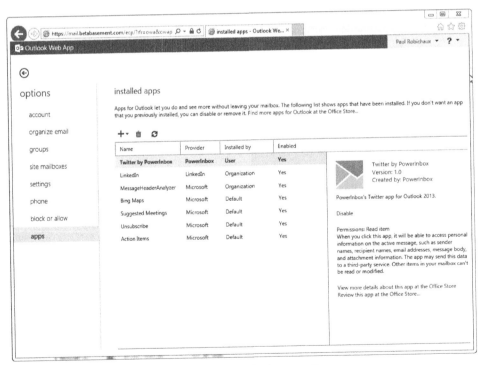

Figure 3-21 The list of installed apps for an individual user mailbox

From this screen, users can add and remove their own apps. They can't disable or enable user apps; the presumption is that if you don't want access to an app, you can just remove it instead of disabling it. Individual users also cannot change the enablement state for organization apps; only administrators can do that.

Customizing Outlook Web App

Themes define the color scheme and graphic elements used for Outlook Web App. Exchange 2007 introduced support for customizable Outlook Web App themes; Exchange 2013 continues this support by including a set of 22 themes that users can apply to customize their Outlook Web App session's appearance. Administrators don't have control over user choice and cannot impose a theme on users, although they can set a default theme that users will have unless they change it.

You can also create your own theme and include corporate logos, color schemes, and so on. Creating a complete theme is a very extensive customization of the Outlook Web App user interface (UI). The simplest way to do this is to copy one of the existing themes (located in \Program Files\Microsoft\Exchange Server\V15\ClientAccess\owa\Current\ themes) and then edit the files you find there, being careful to preserve exact dimensions.

Many companies liked the idea of incorporating some aspect of their corporate identity in Outlook Web App without doing the work to create a theme. The complete source code of the Outlook Web App application is distributed with Exchange, and the classic solution to the problem is to customize some of the files used for the default theme. Microsoft published customization guides for Exchange 2007 and Exchange 2010, but as of this writing has not yet done so for Exchange 2013. However, the most common customizations—color scheme and logo changes on the logon page—are fairly simple to apply.

Figure 3-22 shows the logon page with callouts showing the parts of the logon page. You can use this information to develop the necessary customizations to comply with corporate branding. The graphic files and style sheets used to render the logon page are stored in Program Files\Microsoft\Exchange Server\V15\FrontEnd\HttpProxy\Owa\ Auth\Current \themes\Resources. You are free to edit any of these, although the items shown in Figure 3-22 are the most common ones that administrators want to customize.

Chapter 3

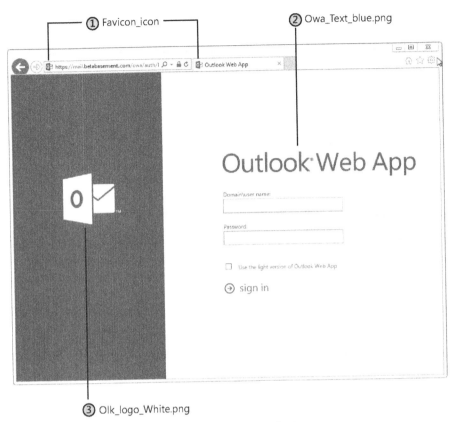

Figure 3-22 Components of Outlook Web App customization

Another common request is to add text or graphics to the logon page, either instead of or in addition to changing the existing graphics. This is much more challenging now that the Outlook Web App logon page includes touch support; rather than a largely static page, as in previous versions, the Outlook Web App 2013 logon page is full of scripts that dynamically determine what kind of device the user is connecting from. However, you can make simple customization by doing the following.

To customize the logon page with some new text, do the following:

1. Make a copy of the \Program Files\Microsoft\Exchange Server\V15\FrontEnd \HttpProxy\owa\auth\Logon.aspx file. This file tells IIS how to render the logon page when a user connects to Outlook Web App.

2. Create a file that contains the HTML you want displayed on the page and then save it in the same directory as Logon.aspx. Give it an easily remembered name.

3. Open the Logon.aspx file with a text editor and search for the <div class="signInError" string. This is where Outlook Web App displays an error message if logon fails. Right above this line, insert an #include directive to instruct Outlook Web App to read and display the text contained in the file you created in step 2; wrap the line in a <div> tag, using class "signInExpl". The code in Logon.aspx will then look something like this:

```
<div class="myCustomText" class="signInExpl">
<!-- #include file="contoso-disclaimer.inc" -->
</div>
<div class="signInError…
```

4. Save Logon.aspx and restart an Outlook Web App session. (You don't have to restart Microsoft Internet Information Services [IIS] or any of the Exchange services.)

5. You can take the same approach to update Logoff.aspx if you want users to see a customized message when they sign out of Outlook Web App.

6. When you are happy with the customization, you can apply it on all CAS servers by copying your modified files. There is no automatic mechanism to apply this kind of customization on every CAS server in an organization.

INSIDE OUT Customizations will be overwritten by future product updates

The other thing to remember is that any customization of one of the Outlook Web App components will almost certainly be overwritten by cumulative updates and service packs. CU1 overwrites Outlook Web App customizations, and there is no reason to doubt that future updates will be any different. That's why you should keep careful documentation about any customization you apply to Outlook Web App to make it easier to apply it after you upgrade Exchange. You should also keep a copy of both the original and customized versions of any file you change so you can review them in the future. It's also fair to say that there is no guarantee that Microsoft will not change the way Outlook Web App works in a future version and render this method of customization—or any method of customization—invalid, so be prepared to build some time to test and perhaps do a little recoding for Outlook Web App customizations into every deployment plan.

Managing Outlook for Mac

Although it shares the Outlook name with its Windows sibling, the Mac version of Outlook is a very different beast. It doesn't use MAPI, relying exclusively on EWS instead. It lacks some features of the Windows version (such as support for MailTips, Policy Tips, personal archives, data leak prevention policy tips, site mailboxes, modern public folders, and retention policies), but in exchange it adds some Mac-specific features such as the ability to insert pictures easily from an iPhoto library and full integration with Apple's Spotlight desktop search tool. As an Exchange administrator, virtually none of what you know about administering Outlook for Windows will be useful when administering and managing Mac Outlook, with some notable exceptions.

- First is Autodiscover. The Mac version of Outlook fully supports Autodiscover. If your Exchange environment passes the ExRCA Autodiscover tests, then Outlook 2011 should connect to it just fine. Keep in mind that Mac Outlook doesn't perform service connection point (SCP) lookups, as Windows Outlook does. From that standpoint, just treat Mac Outlook like a Windows Outlook client that's trying to connect from outside the corporate network.

  However, you might notice an issue when a roaming client (such as a Mac laptop) connects from the corporate network and then roams to outside the corporate network. If Autodiscover finds an internal-facing URL, Outlook 2011 will happily keep trying to use it even after the laptop roams back to the Internet or another network where it should be using an external-facing URL. The fix for this is to edit the account settings of the affected account and put the correct external URL back in.

- Second is that, unlike Windows Outlook, the Mac version doesn't have any way to see the current connection status or to force a reconnection, meaning there's no easy way to force a new Autodiscover request. The fastest way to do this is to quit and re-launch the client. To force a reconnection, you can also use the Work Offline menu item under the Outlook menu; use it to switch to offline mode and then switch back to online mode.

- Third is that the Mac client can import PST files from Outlook 2003, Outlook 2007, Outlook 2010, and Outlook 2013. Mac Outlook doesn't use OST files. It also cannot export email to PST.

- Fourth is that Set-CASMailbox has separate parameters that enable you to block the EWS edition of Entourage and Mac Outlook—EwsAllowEntourage and EwsAllowMacOutlook.

Mac Outlook has a useful logging feature that is in a somewhat unusual location. If you enable connection logging, it will give you details on Autodiscover requests, folder and item synchronization through EWS, and Lightweight Directory Access Protocol (LDAP) access to domain controllers (DCs) and global catalogs (GCs). To turn on logging, you must do the following:

1. Launch Outlook 2011.

2. Choose the Error Log command in the Windows menu.

3. When the Errors window appears, click the large gear icon in the upper-right corner of the window.

4. In the resulting dialog box, make sure the Turn On Logging For Troubleshooting check box is selected and then click OK.

Outlook immediately creates a new file named Microsoft Outlook_Troubleshooting_0.log on the Mac OS X desktop. As long as Outlook is running, it will continue to append entries to this log until you repeat the preceding steps and clear the logging check box.

Managing Outlook Web App for Devices

Managing Outlook Web App for Devices is a weird combination of managing Outlook Web App and managing Exchange ActiveSync devices. If you disable EAS access to a server or a mailbox, clients using that mailbox or server won't be able to connect with Outlook Web App for Devices. You have finer-grained control, though, because there are several settings in the Outlook Web Access mailbox policy object that let you control what users of the mobile app may do. As of Exchange 2013 CU2, the only Outlook Web App for Devices–specific argument to Set-OWAMailboxPolicy is AllowCopyContactsToDeviceAddressBook, which controls whether the device is allowed to cache the user's contacts in the device's address book. If this setting is false, the user can still see her contacts in the app, but they're not visible to the built-in phone app or other apps that depend on the system address book for name or number resolution. However, a number of other parameters (such as –IRMEnabled) are of interest because they control features that are available through Outlook Web App for Devices. If you create an Outlook Web App access policy that disables one of these features (say, integration with Office apps), the feature will be disabled for any user who is subject to the policy, whether the user accesses Outlook Web App through the browser or through the mobile app.

POP3 and IMAP4

POP3 and IMAP4 are Internet email protocols that a wide variety of clients and servers support. Fans of these protocols love the lightweight nature of their connections, which is one of the reasons they have long been the protocols of choice for free email services such as Outlook.com and Gmail (Hotmail-supported POP3; Gmail supports both protocols). POP3 is the older and less functional protocol. IMAP4 is more functional than POP3 but less functional than MAPI.

Nevertheless, modern IMAP4 clients, including Outlook, can build a rich range of features around the rudimentary but superefficient communications to download messages from a server. Of course, unlike MAPI, POP3 and IMAP4 are both protocols that clients use to retrieve messages from a server. Both of these protocols transfer mail to the client. IMAP and POP clients must use SMTP to send outbound mail.

Apart from age, the fundamental differences between the two protocols are as follows:

- POP3 downloads messages to a client and removes them from the server.

- POP3 supports a very limited set of folders on the server (essentially, the Inbox).

- IMAP4 can leave copies of downloaded messages on the server.

- IMAP4 can access any folder a server exposes and download messages from the folders to client-side replicas.

- IMAP4 allows a live-sync mode in which the client holds open a connection to the server; this provides a more Outlook-like sync experience in which messages trickle in to the Inbox as they arrive instead of arriving in batches when a POP3 connection is made.

The majority of clients that connect to Exchange 2013 through POP3 and IMAP4 belong to four categories:

- Users in an educational establishment such as a university, where the priority is on providing basic email services at the lowest possible cost.

- Users who access an Exchange mailbox with IMAP to avoid having to buy Outlook licenses. (Of course, now that the Windows 8 and Windows RT Mail clients support using EAS, users on those platforms can get the benefits of faster and more robust synchronization from EAS, using their existing Exchange mailbox client access licenses [CALs]).

- Users who don't like Outlook. Often, these people have used a client such as Eudora or Thunderbird for many years and don't see a reason to change.

- Users who run an operating system that doesn't support the premium version of Outlook Web App or who simply prefer to use IMAP. Many Linux and UNIX users are in this category. In fact, so are users of Surface RT devices, given that no native version of Outlook is available in Windows RT currently.

The attraction of using free POP3 or IMAP4 clients is the avoidance of Outlook license fees. This is less of an issue in large corporations that negotiate enterprise licensing agreements with Microsoft that include the entire Office application suite. For this reason, relatively few users in large corporate deployments use POP3 or IMAP4 clients. Outlook Web App is available if they don't want to use Outlook, and it's easier for the help desk if a limited number of clients are in use. Another reason is that POP3 and IMAP4 clients are purposely designed to work across any server that supports these protocols. They therefore do not support features that are specific to Exchange, such as MailTips, unified messaging integration, and so on.

For the remainder of this discussion, I focus on setting up the Exchange 2013 IMAP4 server and configuring clients to connect to the IMAP4 server. The steps to set up and configure POP3 access are conceptually similar, but because very few Exchange sites actually use POP, it's not covered here.

Configuring the IMAP4 server

When you install Exchange 2013, the setup program creates the Microsoft Exchange POP3 and Microsoft Exchange IMAP4 services to support client connections through these protocols but does not start the services. There are actually two services for each protocol. The Microsoft Exchange IMAP service runs on the CAS, whereas the Microsoft Exchange IMAP Backend service runs on the Mailbox role, with corresponding services for POP. If you have a multirole server, you'll see both services.

The services aren't started or enabled by default as part of the Microsoft overall strategy of reducing the attack surface of computers by disabling unneeded services; its thinking is that because most sites won't use IMAP or POP, the services should remain off. Therefore, the first step to support POP3 or IMAP4 clients is to start these services. In addition, you should change the startup state for the services from Manual to Automatic so that Windows starts them every time the server is booted:

```
Set-Service msExchangeImap4 –StartupType Automatic
Set-Service msExchangeImap4Backend –StartupType Automatic
Start-Service –Service msExchangeImap4Backend
Start-Service –Service msExchangeImap4
```

After starting the IMAP services, they will listen on two ports: TCP 993 for connections using SSL and TCP 143 for connections using either Transport Layer Security (TLS) or no security at all. You usually don't have to make any configuration changes after the service is started. However, clients won't know where to connect. Outlook Web App includes the ability to show users what IMAP, POP, and SMTP settings they should plug in to their clients, but this advertisement is turned off by default. To make these settings visible in Outlook Web App for users who are IMAP-enabled or POP-enabled, you need to do the following:

- To advertise IMAP or POP settings, use Set-IMAPSettings or Set-POPSettings with the –ExternalConnectionSettings parameter, which should include the FQDN of the machine and the port number and encryption scheme.

- To advertise SMTP settings, use Set-ReceiveConnector –AdvertiseClientSettings:$true –FQDN fqdn.

Therefore, to publish mail.betabasement.com as the server name for a server named pao-ex01.betabasement.com, you could do the following:

```
Set-IMAPSettings –ExternalConnectionSettings mail.betabasement.com:995:SSL
Set-ReceiveConnector "Client Frontend PAO-EX01" –AdvertiseClientSettings:$true
–FQDN mail.betabasement.com
```

After this change, you must run iisreset before Outlook Web App will update. After you've done so, users will see a new link labeled Settings For POP or IMAP Access on the Account tab of their Outlook Web App settings page. Clicking that link displays a window similar to the one shown in Figure 3-23. Keep in mind that Exchange will show whatever FQDN you specify; if it's wrong, clients will see the wrong information.

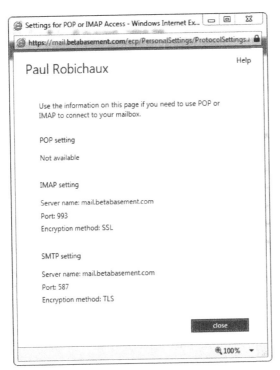

Figure 3-23 Displaying client configuration information for an IMAP user

Figure 3-24 shows the properties that are usually of most interest to administrators when they configure IMAP connectivity for Exchange 2013. The default configuration is for the IMAP service to listen on all available IPv4 and IPv6 addresses using TCP ports 143 and 993; you can change these bindings by using the two lists of IP addresses in the settings dialog box.

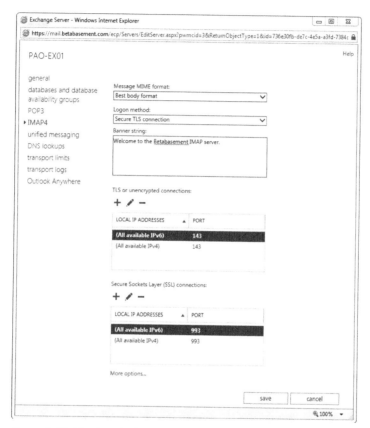

Figure 3-24 Viewing the basic properties of the Exchange IMAP4 server

The More Options link below the SSL bindings list expands the settings list to include time-out values and connection limits.

See TechNet for detailed information on these settings.

The Get-IMAPSettings and Set-IMAPSettings cmdlets retrieve and set configuration settings for the IMAP4 server. The equivalent cmdlets for POP3 are Get-POPSettings and Set-POPSettings. For example, to retrieve the current configuration for a multirole server named PAO-EX01, use the following command:

```
Get-IMAPSettings –Server PAO-EX01
```

```
ProtocolName                         : IMAP4
Name                                 : 1
MaxCommandSize                       : 10240
ShowHiddenFoldersEnabled             : False
UnencryptedOrTLSBindings             : {[::]:143, 0.0.0.0:143}
SSLBindings                          : {[::]:993, 0.0.0.0:993}
InternalConnectionSettings           : {PAO-EX01.betabasement.com:993:SSL,
PAO-EX01.betabasement.com:143:TLS}
ExternalConnectionSettings           : {mail.betabasement.com:993:SSL}
X509CertificateName                  : PAO-EX01
Banner                               : The Microsoft Exchange IMAP4 service is
ready.
LoginType                            : SecureLogin
AuthenticatedConnectionTimeout       : 00:30:00
PreAuthenticatedConnectionTimeout    : 00:01:00
MaxConnections                       : 2147483647
MaxConnectionFromSingleIP            : 2147483647
MaxConnectionsPerUser                : 16
MessageRetrievalMimeFormat           : BestBodyFormat
ProxyTargetPort                      : 9933
CalendarItemRetrievalOption          : iCalendar
OwaServerUrl                         :
EnableExactRFC822Size                : False
LiveIdBasicAuthReplacement           : False
SuppressReadReceipt                  : False
ProtocolLogEnabled                   : False
EnforceCertificateErrors             : False
LogFileLocation                      : C:\Program Files\Microsoft\Exchange Server
\V15\Logging\Imap4
LogFileRollOverSettings              : Daily
LogPerFileSizeQuota                  : 0 B (0 bytes)
ExtendedProtectionPolicy             : None
EnableGSSAPIAndNTLMAuth              : True
Server                               : PAO-EX01
Identity                             : PAO-EX01\1
```

If you change any of the configuration settings for the IMAP4 server, you have to restart the Microsoft Exchange IMAP4 service. It's common to find that you want to turn on protocol logging to help debug connections from a particular client. To enable protocol logging for IMAP4 clients, you need to enable logging and tell Exchange where it should create the log. Enabling logging in Exchange 2007 requires you to edit a configuration file, but in Exchange 2010 and 2013, you can enable logging with the Set-IMAPSettings cmdlet. For example:

```
Set-IMAPSettings –Server PAO-EX01-ProtocolLogEnabled $True –LogFileLocation
'C:\Logs\'
```

Logging generates a mass of data on the server, some of which is fairly obtuse if you are not familiar with debugging IMAP connections. Clients can also generate logs, and if you need to provide data to help a support representative solve a problem, you should generate server and client logs to ensure that they have full knowledge of what the client is sending and how the server is responding.

Configuring IMAP4 client access

From a user perspective, it is easy to configure a POP3 or IMAP4 client to connect to Exchange 2013. For my example, I chose the Thunderbird free IMAP4 client that you can download from *http://www.mozillamessaging.com/en-US/thunderbird/*. Two connections must be configured before an IMAP4 client can download and send messages.

- An IMAP4 server hosted by an Exchange 2013 CAS or multirole server must be ready to accept client connections so that IMAP4 clients can access mailboxes and download folders and items.

- An SMTP receive connector must be available to accept client connections to allow IMAP4 clients to relay outgoing messages through SMTP.

The steps required to configure the client to connect to Exchange 2013 are as follows:

1. Set the authentication setting to Basic for the IMAP4 server on the CAS to which you want to connect the client. This is sufficient for testing purposes because it ensures that just about any IMAP4 client can connect. When you have established that connections work freely, you can increase the level of security by moving to Integrated Windows Authentication or Secure Logon, depending on which authentication mechanisms the client supports.

2. Restart the IMAP4 server to effect the change in the authentication setting.

3. Configure the client with the name of the CAS server and the user name in domain name\account name format. In the case of the Mac OS X version of Thunderbird, this requires filling out the dialog box shown in Figure 3-25.

Chapter 3

Figure 3-25 Configuring basic IMAP account settings in Thunderbird

4. Connect the client to prove that messages can be downloaded.

5. Check that the Permission Groups assigned to the default client receive connector on the server that you want to use for sending outbound messages allows anonymous connections. Again, this is the easiest setting to use to test outgoing message connectivity and should ensure that all types of client can connect to send messages. When you know that messages are flowing, you can increase the security. Thunderbird (and most other IMAP clients) supports STARTTLS security with user name and password credentials, so the receive connector doesn't need to allow anonymous connections because these authenticated connections will be regarded as Exchange users.

After messages are being downloaded and sent freely, the next step is to configure LDAP access to Active Directory so that you can use Active Directory as an address book. The details of how to configure a connection to Active Directory vary from client to client, as does the ability of the client to use the data fetched from Active Directory. Some clients can only browse Active Directory, whereas others, such as Thunderbird, can validate email addresses against Active Directory as they are entered into message headers.

You can use the following process to configure Thunderbird or a similar client:

1. Set the name of the connection to Active Directory or whatever else you like as an illustrative name.

2. Set the directory server hostname to the FQDN of a global catalog server that is reachable from the client. Ideally, this should be a global catalog server in the same site as the CAS server.

3. The base distinguished name (DN) provides a starting point for LDAP searches in the directory. You will probably want to use the root of the directory tree for your domain.

4. The port number is set to 3268 rather than the standard port (389) LDAP uses.

5. The bind DN should be set to the user's SMTP address.

To test the connection, open the client address book and search for some mailboxes that you know exist. You should be able to see mailboxes, contacts, and distribution groups.

INSIDE OUT   Only minor issues

Two small issues are the following:

- The LDAP searches executed by a client might ignore Exchange-specific filters. For example, if you select the Hide From Exchange Address Lists check box for an object, it stops Outlook and Outlook Web App users from seeing that object through the GAL. However, this block means nothing to other clients, and the hidden objects will probably be revealed to users.

- Along the same lines, an LDAP search against Active Directory doesn't impose any filters to eliminate objects that are not mail-enabled, so you'll probably be able to see security groups such as Enterprise Admins. However, you won't be able to send email to these objects because they don't have email addresses.

These are small hiccups along the road, and because users have read-only access to directory information that reveals some objects that other clients don't show isn't really very serious.

Client throttling

Clients can occasionally create an excessive load on an Exchange server. The reasons this happens are many and varied but usually involve some form of software bug that causes the client to communicate in an unpredictable manner and so create an out-of-the-ordinary load. The usual corrective action taken in previous versions is first to identify the errant client with the Exchange User Monitor (ExMon) utility and then terminate its connection to relieve the strain on the server and restore normal levels of responsiveness to other clients. You can then figure out what action the client was taking to cause the problem and resolve the situation. However, this can be a labor-intensive process, and it doesn't scale well. To help protect against misbehaving clients in Office 365, Microsoft introduced a feature in

Exchange 2010 known as client throttling, which enables administrators to set limits pro-actively on what clients can do; more precisely, it enables them to establish policies that control what resources, and how many of them, clients may consume for various kinds of connections. When a client exceeds the limit for resource usage, it's not usually blocked altogether; instead, its requests are delayed. The net effect is that clients who are using more than their fair share of any particular resource will have their access to that resource reduced, with a gradual reduction in the amount of slowdown that allows the client to recharge.

Exchange 2013 client throttling policies can be applied to several distinct applications and protocols:

- Exchange ActiveSync (EAS)

- Outlook Web App

- POP3 and IMAP4

- Exchange Web Services (EWS; this category includes unified messaging users and users running Entourage or Outlook for Mac OS X)

- Discovery searches

- Cross-forest access (including hybrid access between on-premises and Office 365 tenants)

- Message sending using SMTP

- Windows PowerShell and PowerShell Web Services

A default policy is automatically created and enforced within the organization when you install Exchange 2013. This policy, named GlobalThrottlingPolicy_GUID, is intended to be the baseline policy for any user who doesn't have a more specific policy applied. Although you can change the limits enforced by the default policy, Microsoft doesn't recommend doing so (and you may not remove or rename the default policy). That's because you can create additional policies that provide more granular control over resource usage and then assign those policies to users. Any throttling setting not explicitly specified in a policy is inherited from the global policy, so you can quickly build policies that control exactly the resources you want while allowing other resources' usage to be governed by the global policy.

The policy comes into effect when the percentage of CPU usage by Exchange exceeds the threshold defined in the CPUStartPercent property of the default policy. This setting is applied on a per-service basis. The default value for CPUStartPercent is 75, so when one of the Exchange services monitored for client throttling reaches this threshold, Exchange begins to apply any throttling restrictions that are defined in the default policy or on a per-mailbox basis to ensure that the server can continue to provide a reasonably smooth service to all clients.

In general, four common parameters are associated with each type of resource usage:

- CutoffBalance controls the level at which Exchange starts denying access to a resource. Think of this as a hard maximum limit for using the resource; after the client hits it, it will be blocked from that resource until it recharges.

- RechargeRate is the speed at which the user's resource budget recharges or refills. For example, a client that sends a large number of messages and hits the recipient rate limit will fall below the limit and regain full access as time passes.

- MaxBurst controls how far above the standard resource limit a client may go in short bursts.

- MaxConcurrency sets the limit for how many concurrent connections or actions a single client may take.

Individual protocols or applications might have additional settings, too; see the TechNet documentation for the New-ThrottlingPolicy cmdlet for a complete list.

Throttling policies can be managed only through EMS. You can view details of the default policy with this command:

```
Get-ThrottlingPolicy | Where {$_.IsDefault -eq $True} | Format-Table
```

A lot of data is output when you examine the attributes of a throttling policy. However, you can break them down into the categories listed earlier. Thus, you can retrieve the settings that govern EWS clients with:

```
Get-ThrottlingPolicy | Select Ews* | Format-List
```

```
EwsMaxConcurrency              : 27
EwsMaxBurst                    : 300000
EwsRechargeRate                : 900000
EwsCutoffBalance               : 3000000
EwsMaxSubscriptions            : 5000
```

The output for the EWS parameters indicates that multiple thresholds are currently in place to control user workload: the maximum concurrency for any user is set to 27 (the range is from 0 to 100), meaning that a user can have up to 20 active EWS sessions. A connection is maintained from the time a request is made to establish it until the connection is closed or otherwise disconnected by a user action (logging off). If a user attempts to establish more than the allowed maximum, that connection attempt will fail. The EwsMaxBurst, EwsRechargeRate, and EwsCutoffBalance limits are set, too, indicating that limits for specific resource usage are in place. The max burst and recharge rate are both expressed in milliseconds; the user can have a burst of up to five minutes of heavy EWS activity before being blocked.

Similar groups of settings are available for the other client categories. For example, you can find those applying to Outlook Web App with:

```
Get-ThrottlingPolicy | Select OWA* | Format-List
```

TROUBLESHOOTING

Exchange is throttling BlackBerry Enterprise Server activities

Introducing client throttling had an unfortunate side effect on some applications that impose heavy demands on Exchange. The BlackBerry Enterprise Server (BES) provided the best example because the account it uses essentially mimics a hyperactive user who accesses multiple mailboxes to fetch and send messages to mobile devices. The usual problem was that Exchange throttled BES activities because it exceeded the RCA maximum concurrency threshold. The solution was to create a new throttling policy that set the value of the RCAMaxConcurrency parameter to $Null and then assigned the new policy to the BES account. This is a step the administrator can perform after installing BES.

A number of specific parameters are available to control workload generated through Windows PowerShell:

- **PowerShellMaxConcurrency (default value 18)**   This constraint is applied in two ways. It defines the maximum number of remote Windows PowerShell sessions a user can have open on a server at one time. It also defines the maximum number of cmdlets EMS can execute concurrently.

- **PowerShellMaxCmdlets (default no limit)**   Sets the number of cmdlets a user can execute within the time period specified by PowerShellMaxCmdletsTimePeriod. After the value is exceeded, no future cmdlets can be run until the period expires.

- **PowerShellMaxCmdletsTimePeriod (default no limit)**   The period in seconds Exchange uses to determine whether the maximum number of cmdlets constraint has been exceeded.

- **ExchangeMaxCmdlets (default no limit)**   Specifies the number of cmdlets a user can execute within the time period set by PowerShellMaxCmdletsTimePeriod. After the constraint is exceeded, Exchange slows down the execution of other cmdlets.

- **PowerShellMaxCmdletQueueDepth (default no limit)**   Specifies the number of operations Exchange allows a user to execute. Operations are consumed by cmdlets as they run. They are also consumed by internal operations. (For example, the PowerShellMaxCurrency operation uses two operations.) Microsoft recommends that, if set, the value of PowerShellMaxCmdletQueueDepth should be set to three times the value of PowerShellMaxConcurrency. Exchange does not apply this constraint to the code run by ECP or EWS.

Three additional settings can constrain the consumption of general resources:

- **MessageRateLimit (default no limit)**   Governs the number of messages per minute that a user can submit to the transport system for processing. Messages over the limit are placed in the user's Outbox until the server can accept them. The exception is for clients such as POP3 and IMAP4 that submit directly to the transport system using SMTP. If these clients attempt to submit too many messages, their request is declined, and they are forced to reattempt later.

- **RecipientRateLimit (default no limit)**   Specifies the number of recipients that can be addressed in a 24-hour period. For example, if this value is set to 1,000, the user may address messages to up to 1,000 recipients daily. Messages that exceed this limit are rejected.

- **ForwardeeLimit (default no limit)**   Specifies a limit for the number of recipients that can be configured in Inbox Rules for the forward or redirect action.

INSIDE OUT   Storing the default throttling identifier in a variable

You'll note that the default throttling policy is given a value such as DefaultThrottlingPolicy_dade6c60-e9cc-4692-bc6a-71771158a82f as its name and identifier. I suspect that this is a joke played on us by the Microsoft engineers because no sensible human being could think that such a name is understandable. If you plan to work with a policy, you might want to store the identifier in a variable so you can use it to refer to the policy with which you want to work. For example:

```
$TP = (Get-ThrottlingPolicy).Identifier
Set-ThrottlingPolicy –Identity $TP –DiscoveryMaxKeywords 15
```

If you create a new policy with the New-ThrottlingPolicy cmdlet, the values from the default policy are inherited. All you have to do is state values for the settings you want to change. Thus, you can do:

```
New-ThrottlingPolicy -Name 'Restricted CAS Access' -RCAMaxConcurrency 10
```

To apply the new policy, you can either make it the default:

```
Set-ThrottlingPolicy -Identity 'Restricted CAS Access' -IsDefault $True
```

or apply it selectively to users:

```
Set-Mailbox -Identity 'David Jones' -ThrottlingPolicy 'Restricted CAS Access'
```

Mobile device management

Perhaps no other area of the messaging and collaboration world has changed more, or more rapidly, than mobility. To put this in perspective, when Exchange Server 2007 shipped, no one had yet heard of the iPhone; BlackBerry (the company formerly known as Research in Motion, or RIM) ruled the mobile email space with its BlackBerry device line, and the smartest of smart phones had nowhere near the capability of a desktop PC. In addition, relatively few users had smart mobile devices. Fast forward to the release of Exchange 2013, and the mobility landscape looks completely different: Apple's iOS and Google's Android are the top two mobile platforms, BlackBerry is making a play for continued relevance with version 10 of the BlackBerry operating system, and Microsoft continues to put its weight behind the Windows Phone family. Meanwhile, smart phones have taken just over 50 percent of the total phone market in the United States, and market trends indicate that within five years, as much as 70 percent of all mobile phones worldwide will be smart phones. Factor in the increasing ubiquity of tablet computers, such as Apple's iPad, the Microsoft Surface RT and Surface Pro, and various Android-based tablets, and the need for mobile device synchronization becomes even clearer.

Against this background, the relentless march toward personalization of business IT accustoms end users to choosing and using whichever devices they personally prefer; the "bring your own device" (BYOD) trend is here to stay, despite the difficulties it poses for IT decision makers, risk managers, and administrators. (For that reason, BYOD is also sometimes said to mean "bring your own disaster!") To cite one example, when an employee syncs her smart phone with the company Exchange server and then loses the phone, and you have to erase it, she loses all her personal data too. No currently shipping smart phone operating system can distinguish between locally stored data and data that's synced to an Exchange server, so Exchange-initiated remote wipes erase everything on the phone. However, if you did just erase data associated with a synchronized Exchange account, sensitive items (such as attachments originating in that account) could still be in the extant portions of the device. Numerous other security, capability, and control issues make BYOD difficult to deal with, so a number of vendors have tried to solve various aspects of the situation with mobile-device management solutions that offer a greater degree of visibility and control over how mobile devices interact with corporate networks.

It's important to point out that Exchange itself is not a mobile device management (MDM) solution. Exchange does have a way to define policies that are, in theory, capable of limiting what a connected device may do, and it has some ability to allow, block, or quarantine devices. In practice, however, if you really want to manage how devices connect to your network and what they can do when connected, you probably need a third-party MDM solution.

All about Exchange ActiveSync

Before delving into the details of how to manage mobile device interaction with Exchange, you need a solid understanding of the Exchange ActiveSync (EAS) protocol. Microsoft licenses this protocol to a huge array of third parties, ranging from major smart phone manufacturers such as Apple and Samsung to competitors such as IBM Lotus, Google, and Kerio. Because Microsoft has licensed EAS so aggressively, the Exchange team is in the somewhat unusual position of profiting directly from the success of products such as Google Android and Apple iOS that compete directly with other Microsoft products such as Windows Phone. Having said that, the decision to license EAS to all who would pay for it has proven to be a wise one; EAS is now the de facto standard for mobile device email synchronization. The licensing terms don't require licensees to implement any particular version or feature set, which can occasionally be a problem, as you will shortly see, and there's no requirement to use the license; Google dropped support for EAS in its free Gmail edition in mid-2013.

A quick tour of EAS history

Microsoft originally connected mobile devices to Exchange data through the Mobile Information Server (MIS) product. Codenamed Airstream and first released for Exchange 2000, MIS was essentially a proxy that converted between the Wireless Application Protocol (WAP) clients on circa 1998 feature phones and WebDAV, which MIS used to communicate with Exchange itself. This protocol was known as AirSync.

In Exchange 2003, Microsoft released the first implementation of what we know today as Exchange ActiveSync (EAS). Rather than using WAP directly, EAS depended on having a client on the mobile device that could speak EAS natively to the server. The EAS versions provided in Exchange 2003 RTM and Exchange 2003 SP1 were written by the Windows Mobile team and were the only platforms for which compatible clients were available. In Exchange 2003 SP2, the Exchange team took over the protocol and added true push support (which Microsoft still calls DirectPush), Global Address List (GAL) searching, and the ability to create policies to control what the device was allowed to do.

In Exchange 2007, EAS got a new version number (12.0) and a widely expanded set of features, including the ability to flag messages and support for Autodiscover. It was also noteworthy for its introduction of server-side search, which solved the ongoing problem of finding old messages in mailboxes too large to sync to the device in their entirety.

Exchange 2007 SP1 produced EAS 12.1; this version of the protocol was revised to use what is now called a hanging sync operation. This type of sync takes advantage of HTTP connections, which can be left open indefinitely without requiring any action from the requesting device or the server. (The exact mechanics of the hanging sync operation are discussed in the "Device synchronization" section later in the chapter.) Moving to the use of hanging sync operations sped up mail delivery to EAS devices quite a bit with little effect on device battery life, although it sometimes required firewall reconfiguration. Mobile devices generally can let their radios go into an idle state while waiting for data to be returned from an open connection, so keeping the hanging sync open didn't chew through the device battery, and EAS includes provision for adjusting the length of the hanging connection to accommodate network timeouts imposed by device manufacturers or mobile carriers.

Exchange 2010 introduced version 14.0 of EAS. It added a few new policies, but most of the changes in this version had to do with new capabilities made available to the client such as passing the data required for the device to display threaded conversations, enabling synchronization of note items in the user's Notes folder, and adding the ability to look up a user's free/busy state from the device. Exchange 2010 SP1 brought EAS 14.1, which added only one new policy—whether a device is allowed to use information rights management (IRM) over EAS—and a few minor features such as the ability to fetch and display GAL photos in the client. Exchange 2010 SP2 added Outlook Web App Mini, a lightweight version of Outlook Web App that was intended for feature phones but little else. (Outlook Web App Mini is gone in Exchange 2013.)

Exchange 2013 doesn't make any major changes to the EAS protocol. The version remains at 14.1, although Microsoft might update the protocol version in a service pack or cumulative update. As you've seen by now, Exchange 2013 does make some significant changes to mobile device capability in the form of a touch-enabled, tablet-friendly, and smart phone–friendly version of Outlook Web App that even includes offline access for some browsers.

Chapter 4

> **Note**
>
> In Exchange 2013, Microsoft changed some, but not all, of the Exchange Management Shell (EMS) cmdlets used to manage mobile devices. Annoyingly, it kept both the old and new names for these cmdlets; amusingly, the Exchange Administration Center (EAC) itself will sometimes display warnings telling you that a particular cmdlet has been deprecated and replaced with a new one! The Clear-ActiveSyncDevice, Get-ActiveSyncDevice, Get-ActiveSyncDeviceStatistics, Get-ActiveSyncMailboxPolicy, New-ActiveSyncMailboxPolicy, Remove-ActiveSyncMailboxPolicy, and Set-ActiveSyncMailboxPolicy cmdlets are now officially deprecated, and you should use the *-MobileDevice and *-MobileDeviceMailboxPolicy cmdlets in their stead.

What it means to "support EAS"

If you look at a comprehensive list of the features in each EAS version (such as the one Microsoft maintains on the TechNet wiki at *http://social.technet.microsoft.com/wiki /contents/articles/1150.exchange-activesync-client-comparison-table.aspx*), you'll notice that your device doesn't support most of them. This is true whether your mobile device operating system comes from Microsoft, Apple, Google, Palm, Nokia, or anyone else. To understand why this is, it's necessary to know that EAS depends on three separate but interrelated components:

- The EAS protocol specifications, which Microsoft publishes on the web at *http:// msdn.microsoft.com/en-us/library/cc425499(v=exchg.80).aspx*, set out how the protocol works and how compliant servers and clients are supposed to work. The specification sets out what commands are available, how client and server communicate, how errors are handled, and so on. Throughout the rest of the chapter, I'll refer to the protocol specifications by the abbreviated names Microsoft gives them. For example, MS-OXDISCO is the Autodiscover specification; MS-ASPROV is the EAS device setup protocol, and so on.

- Exchange Server implements EAS on the server side (as do a handful of competing messaging products from companies that have licensed the Microsoft EAS patents). The Exchange implementation is composed of a web application that interacts with the client through the Microsoft-Server-ActiveSync virtual directory and code to handle user interaction through Outlook Web App for remote device management, logging for administrators, and policy management.

- Mail clients on a particular device act as EAS clients; they send commands to the Exchange server by using the EAS protocol and then act on the responses they get. This is a rather vague description because one client's functionality can differ dramatically from other clients'. Outlook 2013 can use EAS to synchronize with the Microsoft consumer service, Outlook.com, for example, and its feature set is considerably different from that of the built-in Windows 8 and Windows RT Mail clients, both of which also use EAS. The iOS mail client behaves differently from the Windows Phone mail client, and so on.

With this understanding, you can probably see how two devices might provide dramatically different client experiences, even when used against the same Exchange mailbox. For example, versions 14.0 and later of the EAS protocol support an interface that enables devices to download and read IRM-protected messages. Exchange 2010 and later implement that support on the server side. Windows Phone 7.x and Windows Phone 8 mail clients include IRM support, but Apple's clients do not because Apple largely ignores the requirements of enterprises in favor of designing consumer-friendly products. In practice, that means a user who has, say, an iPad and a Nokia Lumia both synced to his mailbox will find that some things work on one device but not on the other, even though both devices claim to support EAS.

INSIDE OUT Clients are free to lie about what they support

Because the server and client components of EAS are independent, the client is free to ignore specific parts of a policy or lie about whether it supports them. The EAS spec makes a clear differentiation among fully compliant devices, partially compliant devices, and noncompliant devices. A fully compliant device is one that implements all the settings specified by a policy. A partially compliant device applies some but not all the settings in a policy, probably because the necessary code to apply one or more settings is not implemented in the operating system. A noncompliant device can synchronize with Exchange but essentially ignores policy settings because it does not recognize or accept a policy provided to it by the server. Sometimes the distinction between partially compliant and noncompliant is a thin one. For example, there is no system-wide setting in iOS to disable use of Bluetooth, so the iOS EAS client doesn't attempt to implement that specific policy restriction. If you create a policy that turns off Bluetooth and an iOS user tries to sync, she can. Because iOS accepts the policy and honors the other settings, it's considered to be partially compliant, even though it doesn't implement part of the policy you defined. Apple caused quite an uproar when it was discovered that at least one version of iOS falsely claimed to honor the EAS policy setting requiring device encryption when the device was actually unencrypted; the takeaway here is that you should not assume the client software is being honest about which policy features it implements. Every EAS client at least appears to handle the policy basics, such as requiring and enforcing passwords, but you should test any features you find especially important to ensure that they really work.

In 2011, Microsoft introduced a logo certification program (*http://technet.microsoft.com /en-us/exchange/gg187968.aspx*), the intent of which was to give client developers a minimum standard of EAS functionality. In exchange for implementing that standard, third parties could label their products as "Designed for Exchange ActiveSync." However, as of this writing, none of the major third-party vendors has bothered to have its products certified, so this program seems effectively dead.

> **Note**
> Microsoft maintains a page showing known EAS issues with different clients at *http://support.microsoft.com/kb/2563324*. It's not necessarily a comprehensive list because it only reflects issues that Microsoft is tracking through its own processes. It must verify that the problem exists, and will generally work with the EAS client implementer to do so, before acknowledging the problem on this list. When new bugs emerge (as when a third party ships a new revision of its mobile operating system that contains new EAS client bugs), it takes a while for the issue to be reported to Microsoft, analyzed, reproduced, and added to this list.

How Exchange ActiveSync works

The goal of Exchange ActiveSync (EAS) is to synchronize a user's mailbox data (or at least a subset of it) efficiently to a mobile device that has limited bandwidth, battery power, and CPU. This sync might take place over a cellular data network, in which case, the network might or might not suffer high latency and frequent interruptions. It's important to keep these constraints in mind as you see how the protocol works.

Device synchronization begins when a client contacts an Exchange Client Access Server (CAS) to request synchronization. The synchronization process requires the device to reach TCP port 443 on the Exchange CAS so it can make HTTPS requests to the Microsoft-Server-ActiveSync virtual directory, so assume that no port or connectivity problems might prevent the device from making contact. Finally, assume that the device is properly configured to accept whatever Secure Socket Layer (SSL) certificates the CAS presents to it. (What happens when it's not configured is discussed later in the chapter in the "Certificate management" section.)

The client's initial request doesn't have anything to do with synchronization—first it has to know which version of EAS the server speaks. Typical mobile device clients can work with EAS 12.0 or later, but there are some implementation changes from 12.x to 14.0, so the device needs to know how to interpret server responses. The client can discover the server version in one of two ways. It begins by sending the HTTP OPTIONS command to the server; if the client gets no response or a response that doesn't include the server's version data, it instead attempts a synchronization request with a synchronization key of 0. This key has a special meaning, as you see shortly. This fallback method normally happens when a firewall or reverse proxy server blocks the HTTP OPTIONS command or responses to it. In either case, the server responds with two headers. MS-ASProtocolCommands contains a comma-delimited list of the EAS commands the server accepts, and MS-ASProtocolVersions is a comma-delimited list of version numbers the server speaks. For Exchange 2013 servers, the header reads, "MS-ASProtocolVersions: 12.1, 14.0, 14.1."

WBXML

The Microsoft EAS protocol documentation typically shows neatly formatted XML data being passed between client and server. However, if you use a network monitoring tool to sniff the actual device–server traffic, you see what looks like garbage. The protocol actually encodes much of its data by using WBXML, the Wireless Application Protocol (WAP) Binary XML format. WBXML dates back to the late 1990s, making it ancient by mobile protocol standards; it was developed to provide an industry-standard compressed format for effi- ciently transmitting XML over limited-bandwidth cellular links. Some network monitoring software, including Wireshark and Microsoft NetMon, include parsers that can turn WBXML into easily readable XML. Microsoft built EAS on top of the WBXML encoding standard, so that each of the 20 or so EAS commands and the command's parameters and options can be represented compactly. However, manually reading WBXML is tiring and error-prone, so humans normally use regular XML formatting for writing about EAS, and that's the conven- tion this book uses.

Autodiscover

EAS devices may use Autodiscover, just as desktop clients do. However, the rules for Autodiscover when used in conjunction with EAS are slightly different. Autodiscover actu- ally has two schemas. The full version is intended for desktop clients and includes endpoint data for a variety of services, as described in Chapter 1, "Client access servers." The mobile version, which uses the mobilesync schema, is much lighter; it specifies a small subset of responses compared to the full protocol.

There's another difference that has to do with the discovery process. For a domain-joined desktop client, Autodiscover can use service connection points (SCPs) to find the possible endpoints for a new connection efficiently. The typical first step for such a client would be to query for SCPs. However, mobile devices typically can't be domain joined and, even if they could be, probably wouldn't have access to a Lightweight Directory Access Protocol (LDAP) server to query for SCPs unless they were using a virtual private network (VPN). Accordingly, mobile EAS devices don't attempt SCP discovery. Instead, they follow the rest of the Autodiscover workflow. The exact sequence of operations can vary from client to cli- ent; section 3.1.5 of the Autodiscover HTTP protocol spec (MS-OXDISCO) recommends the following sequence, but client developers are free to reorder these steps:

1. The device performs an HTTP POST to *http://domain/Autodiscover/Autodiscover.xml*. In this case, domain is the SMTP domain the user specified when she provided an email address to the device. If that doesn't work, the process continues.

Chapter 4

2. The device performs an HTTP POST to *https://autodiscover.domain/Autodiscover /Autodiscover.xml*.

   In either of these cases, the CAS can return an Autodiscover manifest or an HTTP 302 redirect. (Earlier versions of Exchange could also return an HTTP 451 redirect, but very few clients handled this properly, so Microsoft dropped that feature.) If the CAS provides a redirect, the client is supposed to honor it and try again with the new URL. The spec calls for the client to warn the user that the server has issued a redirection, but not all clients honor this suggestion.

3. Both of the HTTP POST requests were authenticated; that is, they contained credentials the CAS could use to determine whether the user should be given access. If neither of those requests succeeded, the next client step is to try an unauthenticated HTTP GET for *http://autodiscover.domain/Autodiscover /Autodiscover.xml*. The only legitimate responses from the server are to return an HTTP 302 redirection or an error. This step is important because it enables a single organization to support many SMTP domains; Office 365 uses this mechanism to provide Autodiscover support for hundreds of thousands of tenants.

4. If the direct URL queries didn't return an Autodiscover endpoint, the client may perform a DNS SRV record query for _autodiscover._tcp.*domain*. If the query is successful, it should return a hostname, in which case, the client is expected to try an HTTP POST to the *https://host/Autodiscover/Autodiscover.xml* URL.

If any of the preceding steps result in a connection to an actual Exchange CAS, the client is supposed to interpret the Autodiscover manifest discussed in Chapter 1 and use the MobileSync element returned as part of that manifest as the EAS endpoint. If none of these steps result in a connection, most mobile device clients give users the option to enter the server name manually, in which case, they'll attempt a direct HTTPS connection to *https:// serverName/Microsoft-Server-ActiveSync*. No mechanism is provided for changing the name of this virtual directory; clients always use it no matter what server FQDN they get back from Autodiscover.

EAS policies

As with other parts of Exchange, the primary means of controlling what individual users can do with EAS is the EAS mailbox policy. When you install Exchange, it creates a default EAS policy, which is applied to each mailbox at the time it's enabled for EAS (which also happens by default when you enable the mailbox). The basic policy is quite permissive; it allows all devices to synchronize all types of items and imposes only the minimum require- ments for PIN security; a four-digit PIN is all that's required. The MS-ASPROV specification calls out the individual policy elements and their permissible values; more of the specifics of what policies you can configure are discussed later in the chapter in the "Mobile device mailbox policies" section. For now, it's enough to know that the client is supposed to apply any policy it receives from the server, and the server decides which policy to pass to the client based on which EAS policy is defined for the user mailbox.

EAS mailbox policies aren't applied by distribution group membership, organizational unit (OU) membership, or any other similar construct; you must assign policies to every mailbox yourself, although you can use something such as Get-DistributionGroupMember to get a list of mailboxes and then pass it to Set-CASMailbox to set policies en masse.

Licensing for EAS policies can be confusing; some policies require you to have an enterprise client access license (ECAL) for each mailbox that uses them. These policies are not all implemented on all devices, though; *http://technet.microsoft.com/en-us/library/bb123484(v =EXCHG.80).aspx* has a list of which policies require the ECAL, and you might find that you either aren't using them or don't have device support for them. (Nevertheless, the ECAL is often a bargain when you factor in the other features it licenses.)

Device provisioning

A newly configured device must first be provisioned, or loaded with an initial policy that tells it which security settings are required to talk to the server. After initial provisioning, the device might still need to be provisioned when the server's security policies change. The EAS protocol handles this by requiring the client to include a policy key with each request it makes. Any time the client sends a sync or update request, the server can look at the policy key header it receives; if the key indicates that the client has an out-of-date policy, the server returns a status code that tells the client to request an updated policy. The server can also return an HTTP status code of 449, which the device interprets as a command to request provisioning from the server.

In addition, after the device receives a remote wipe request, it is expected to send an acknowledgment back to the server, which is done through a provisioning request. Because the wipe request can be issued at any time, the server signals to the device that it should execute the wipe operation by returning a flag that signals the client to provision again.

> **Note**
>
> The provisioning process depends on the client's honesty; there is no enforcement mechanism that enables the server to verify that the client really did apply the provided policy. Keep that in mind as the discussion about how the provisioning process works proceeds.

Chapter 4

Provisioning is a two-step process, as shown in Figure 4-1: the client sends a Provision command to the server, which responds with an acknowledgement. The client then sends a second Provision command acknowledging the server acknowledgement and requesting the actual policy; the server's response to this second command contains the policy settings the device is expected to apply. The client is then supposed to return an acknowledgement indicating that it applied the policy. Notice that the client doesn't ask for, and cannot select, a specific policy; the server is responsible for knowing which policy to assign based on the assigned EAS mailbox policy for that mailbox.

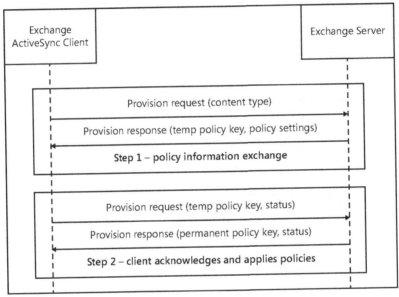

Figure 4-1 The provisioning process, which requires two steps to complete

A walk through the provisioning process for a device that doesn't have a policy will help clarify how the provisioning mechanism is supposed to work.

1. The device connects to the CAS and makes some kind of EAS request, usually with the FolderSync command. As part of this request, it sends a policy key. The EAS spec requires a synchronized device with no policy (such as a newly configured device that's never synced before) to pass a policy key of 0. Because a single device might have a client that supports multiple EAS accounts, you're really referring to a single account on the device not having a policy.

2. The server sees the policy key of 0, indicating that the client has no valid policy. It returns a status code, which signals the client that it must apply a policy before being allowed to synchronize.

3. The client sends the Provision command, along with a block of device information that includes the device type, information about its operating system, its phone number, and other useful information. This information is sent as part of every Provision command, not just when the client has no existing policy. In EAS 14.1 and later, this information is required, although the server doesn't cross-check the client's answers.

4. The server responds with a policy, including a temporary policy key. The exact contents of the policy will vary depending on the version of Exchange and EAS in use.

> **Note**
>
> Almost every EAS response from the server will contain a <Status> element; the client can interpret this to tell whether the request was successful. A status of 1 means that the request was successful; other values indicate various types of errors.

5. The client sends the second Provision request, this time using the temporary policy key received from the server in step 4. It must also include a <Status> element that indicates whether the policy was completely applied, partially applied, not applied due to a failure, or not applied because the device is managed by a third-party mobile device management system. This status indication is important because one element of the EAS mailbox policy is whether you choose to allow nonprovisionable devices.

6. The server checks the policy key it received and sees that it matches the temporary value it originally provided. This signals that the client received the policy the server sent and applied it, so the server returns a second, permanent, policy key, which actually reflects the current policy in use.

Now that the client has a permanent policy key, it can synchronize folders or do whatever else it originally wanted to do. When it sends an EAS command, it includes the new policy key, and the server accepts it until the server policy changes. When the policy changes, any subsequent commands sent by a client with an out-of-date policy key will cause the server to return a Status element indicating that the client must provision again, at which point it repeats the provisioning process starting at step 3.

When the provisioning process is complete, the server applies any device access rules that might be pertinent.

Chapter 4

Device synchronization

EAS 12.1 and later clients make sync requests to the server by issuing the FolderSync, Ping, or Sync EAS commands, depending on whether they want to synchronize the folder hierarchy or the items within a selected folder. Each of these commands must include a sync key that tells the server the specific folder in which the client is interested. A sync key of 0 is issued by the device to indicate that it doesn't know which version of EAS the server is running and triggers a version discovery as described earlier in this chapter. However, a SyncKey element of 0 in a FolderSync command also has another meaning: it tells the server to send back the folder hierarchy so the client can choose which folders to sync. One sync key is used for folder hierarchy synchronization, and then each individual folder from the hierarchy that is selected for synchronization has its own unique sync key. This allows the client to sync only the folders that the user selects; the client is responsible for keeping track of these sync keys and sending the appropriate one with each sync request.

Both the FolderSync and Sync commands basically tell the server, "Please send any new items since the last sync." The Ping command asks the server to send a response when new data become available, at which point the client sends a Sync or FolderSync command. As described earlier in this chapter, this is a hanging sync request (which Microsoft, somewhat confusingly, calls a Ping in the EAS documentation). Here's what happens:

1. The device issues a request with a default lifetime of 15 minutes. This lifetime is known as the heartbeat interval. The point of the request is to notify the server that the client wants notification of any item that changes in any folder that's tagged for synchronization. The list of folders to synchronize is established during the initial device synchronization and updated any time the device user changes the folder list.

2. During that interval, the client is expecting no response (indicating that no new items have arrived), a network timeout, an HTTP 200 OK response from the server, or an update notification from the server.

   - If the server doesn't send back any response, the device can idle its radios and wait for a network activity signal from the mobile operator to wake them up again.

   - If the network connection times out, the client makes a new request with a shorter heartbeat interval. If the network connection fails during this time, it might be because an intermediate firewall has terminated it due to inactivity; if it happens often, you might need to adjust the timeout interval on your firewalls.

   - If the client sees a 200 OK response with no data, it indicates that nothing has changed on the server side, so the client goes back to step 1.

3. If the client receives a 200 OK response with data, the contents of received data vary according to whether the client originally sent a Ping or a Sync command. If the client sent a Ping, the response indicates that the client must now send a Sync. However, the response to a Sync command contains a set of Add, Change, or Delete entries. Each of these entries indicates a change that must be synchronized; the response also contains the contents of the new or changed item. The client modifies its local copy of the folder accordingly. Because Ping commands require an additional round trip to the server, EAS clients that use them are at a disadvantage in terms of sync performance and battery efficiency, so I expect to see the Ping method die out over time.

Whenever a new item arrives or an existing item is changed in a synchronized folder, the server delivers a response to the sync request. This response does not contain the new items; rather, it's a signal to the client that it should request a new sync, and the new items are delivered in response. If no new item arrives during the sync window, the client repeats its request.

Capturing device-side changes

What about new items generated on the client? If you send a mail message, reply to a meeting invitation, add a contact, or make some other kind of change that creates or removes an item in a synchronized folder, the client immediately initiates a sync instead of waiting for the heartbeat interval to expire. The preferred method for doing this is to use specific EAS commands that are appropriate to the change being made. For example, the SmartReply command is intended for clients to use to indicate that they're replying to a given message, whereas MoveItems signals that an item is being moved from one folder to another, and MeetingResponse is for accepting or rejecting meeting invitations.

The reason for having separate commands is that they make the conversation more efficient. For SmartReply, for example, the client can send a SmartReply command with the text of the reply; then the server takes care of assembling the recipient list and previous message contents and updating the reply/forward status of the original message. Not every EAS client uses these commands; for example, iOS versions before 5.0 didn't. A decent EAS client can also batch changes so that you can read, flag, delete, reply to, and move messages while the device radios are off and then sync all those changes in a batch when the radios are turned back on. This behavior is purely a client requirement, however; neither the protocol nor the server require, or even expect, that the client will work properly offline, but users do!

Some details to consider

Mobile device synchronization is a complex process; there are lots of edge cases to consider. For example, what should the server do if there are multiple devices synchronized to

Chapter 4

the same mailbox and they try to post conflicting changes? How should the server behave when the client sends part of an update (say, the first half of an attachment to an outgoing message) and then vanishes from the network? The MS-ASCMD protocol specification describes in great detail how the various EAS commands are supposed to work, and you'll see that there are many exceptions and special cases designed to deal with these sorts of issues. If you want that level of detail, reading the EAS protocol specifications is the only way to get it, although it can be a long, dry process. Having said that, remember that developers have a fair amount of latitude in how they choose to implement the client side of EAS, and the decisions they make affect how well EAS works on various devices.

Remote device wipes

The ability to erase a lost or stolen device remotely to ensure that sensitive data is protected from disclosure is an important part of EAS. When a remote wipe is initiated by an administrator or user, ActiveSync sends a wipe command to the device, which then executes the appropriate command locally. The client then acknowledges the wipe command back to the server, with an indication of success or failure. The following steps happen in an EAS 14.x client. (The steps are slightly different for EAS 12.x; see the protocol documentation for details.)

1. The administrator or user requests the device to be erased. This sets a flag on the mailbox that indicates that the device should receive a wipe request.

2. The client connects to the Exchange CAS by using EAS.

3. The client sends a sync request.

4. The Exchange server responds with a status code of 140, indicating that the device must provision itself again.

5. The device sends the Provision command.

6. The server returns a flag commanding the device to erase itself: <RemoteWipe/>.

7. The device returns an acknowledgement that it received the wipe command.

8. The device completes the wipe process. The details of what exactly is erased varies across devices; the standard behavior is to erase everything, but some devices might not erase removable storage cards, or they might erase only data that came from the EAS account that requested the wipe. (This is what BlackBerry devices using the BlackBerry Balance feature do. A remote wipe issued by the BlackBerry server administrator can either completely erase the device or just remove all data synchronized with that server while leaving personal data alone.) The MS-ASPROV specification says, "The client SHOULD then destroy all data that it has ever received

from the server and erase any stored credentials used to access the server. The client SHOULD NOT wait for or rely on any specific response from the server before proceeding with the remote wipe."

Note that if you send a remote wipe request to a device that doesn't support the wipe function, the device will not be able to execute the request, and the data will remain. However, synchronization of future data will fail, so you can at least prevent any more sensitive data from going to the device. The different degrees of support offered by various device types for remote wipe functionality are a good reason for you to test this feature before approving a device type for deployment. The Exchange CAS sends a confirmation email when a device acknowledges a wipe request. If a user issues the command through Outlook Web App, he receives the confirmation message, and if an administrator issues the request, the administrator and the user associated with the device both receive confirmation messages.

CAUTION

It's important to realize that a remote wipe command is a best-effort attempt to erase the device. The server cannot guarantee that the device is erased; a crafty attacker might be able to prevent the device from connecting (and thus receiving the wipe command) by putting an unlocked device into airplane mode, removing the device battery, keeping the device in a foil pouch that blocks radio signals, or taking other measures to prevent the connection. Therefore, there's no way to ensure that a wipe attempt is successful unless the thief attempts to connect to Exchange to download new mail. This is one reason strong passwords and maybe even encryption should be used to protect sensitive corporate information that's stored on mobile devices.

INSIDE OUT   Handling remote wipes for departing employees

The fact that a device must authenticate before any EAS communication concerning policies (including device wipe commands) is possible introduces the issue of how to deal with people who leave the company. Most companies have well-developed procedures the IT department uses when it is notified that someone is leaving; the usual first step IT takes is to disable the employee's account or change her password so that she can no longer log on to any corporate system. This is a good way to protect confidential information that's held in corporate systems, but it does nothing to remove the information the employee has on her mobile device.

The departure process might require the employee to hand in her mobile device on the day her employment finishes, but what happens if the employee owns the device? The obvious answer is that you should issue a wipe command to remove at least all the email from the device, but this step is impossible if you disable the account because the device won't be able to authenticate. The lesson here is, therefore, that you need to issue the wipe command and make sure that it is acknowledged before the employee's account is disabled. A savvy employee can just turn off the device radios in advance if she knows or expects that they are to be terminated, or she can even restore the phone from its last backup after the device has erased itself. In either case, the employee would then have access to stored data already on the phone despite the wipe request.

Another serious issue related to remote device erasure that you need to be aware of is that in some countries, such as Germany, employers aren't legally allowed to erase employee-owned devices. It is therefore a good idea to design and implement a written company policy that covers BYOD devices; the policy should set out conditions under which a wipe may be issued, what liability (if any) the employee faces for a lost or stolen device, and so on.

INSIDE OUT   Delegating remote wipes

In many organizations, a group such as the end user support help desk will normally handle support requests for problems with device synchronization. Thanks to the flexibility of role-based access control (RBAC; described fully in Chapter 5, "Mailbox management," of *Microsoft Exchange Server 2013 Inside Out: Mailbox and High Availability* in Exchange 2013, you can easily create a role group that gives a help desk team (or any other group you select) permission to send remote wipe commands to EAS devices. The Exchange team blog post at *http://blogs.technet.com/b/exchange/archive/2012/09/12 /rbac-walkthrough-of-creating-a-role-that-can-wipe-activesync-devices.aspx* contains full instructions, but the basic process is simple: create a new management role based on the Mail Recipients role, create a role group for the people who should be able to exercise the Remote Wipe role, and then remove all of the unneeded EMS cmdlets.

Device access rules

Exchange 2010 introduced the ability to allow or block specific devices, either blocking them for individual users or by type of device. It also provides the ability to quarantine new devices, blocking them from synchronization until an administrator approves them. This feature is implemented by device access rules administrators define to control what devices are allowed to synchronize with the Exchange server.

It's important to understand that device access rules control whether a given device is allowed to talk to the server at all; if there is a device access rule to allow, block, or quarantine a given device explicitly, that rule controls whether the client can establish an EAS sync partnership. After the partnership is established, mobile device mailbox policies are applied to control the settings and behavior required or banned on the device, but first it has to go through the allow/block/quarantine (ABQ) process.

Device access rules give administrators a straightforward way to prevent classes of devices from connecting to Exchange servers. Many organizations have wholeheartedly embraced the BYOD model; those that have not will find ABQ a useful way to apply some restrictions on EAS connections, especially when bugs in a particular client cause problems for Exchange itself.

ABQ depends on the fact that each device that connects has a unique ID known as a DeviceID. Some devices might also provide other unique identifiers such as a phone number or International Mobile Equipment Identifier (IMEI); you can see these other identifiers in the sync logs, but the DeviceID is the primary key that makes decisions about which devices may connect. Apart from device-unique identifiers, there are other ways to identify devices, such as the device operating system, friendly name, or model. The Get-MobileDevice cmdlet shows these identifiers as provided by the device:

```
FriendlyName            : Black iPhone 4
DeviceId                : ApplQR24426SA4T
DeviceImei              :
DeviceMobileOperator    :
DeviceOS                : iOS 6.1 10B144
DeviceOSLanguage        : en
DeviceTelephoneNumber   :
DeviceType              : iPhone
DeviceUserAgent         : Apple-iPhone3C1/1002.144
DeviceModel             : iPhone3C1
FirstSyncTime           : 1/26/2013 3:37:07 PM
UserDisplayName         : betabasement.com/Users/Paul Robichaux
DeviceAccessState       : Allowed
DeviceAccessStateReason : DeviceRule
DeviceAccessControlRule : iPhone (DeviceType)
ClientVersion           : 14.1
ClientType              : EAS
AdminDisplayName        :
ExchangeVersion         : 0.20 (15.0.0.0)
Name                    : iPhone§ApplQR24426SA4T
```

When a device attempts to connect, it must first authenticate. Exchange then uses the process shown in Figure 4-2 to decide whether it should be allowed to connect. There are three places at which restrictions can be applied:

- A device or device family can be allowed, blocked, or quarantined for an individual user. This is often used to allow certain individuals to use unsupported devices (perhaps for testing) in organizations that normally block nonstandard devices. User-level blocks or allows take precedence over device access rules and the generic rule. Unfortunately, there's no good way to allow a single user to sync with an entire device family; you have to specify the devices individually.

- A device class or device family can be allowed, blocked, or quarantined. For example, you might put a block rule in place to keep old versions of Apple iOS devices from connecting because those versions have bugs that can lead to corrupt or missing calendar appointments. You could also use this feature to block beta versions of a given operating system to keep your early adopters in check until the device operating system has been tested.

- Devices or families for which no specific rule exists can be allowed, blocked, or quarantined.

This last point is worthy of a bit more discussion because it is where most organizations will define their device connection policy. The default is that any device not specifically blocked elsewhere will be allowed to connect; this is perfect for organizations that are committed to BYOD. However, you can choose to configure that default rule to block all devices that are not specifically approved elsewhere, which gives you a simple way to control which users and devices are permitted to use EAS. You can also have the default rule quarantine devices that don't have a specific match, which is useful if you want to be flexible about allowing devices while retaining some control over new devices. By using this approach, you can allow any device to sync after you have approved it.

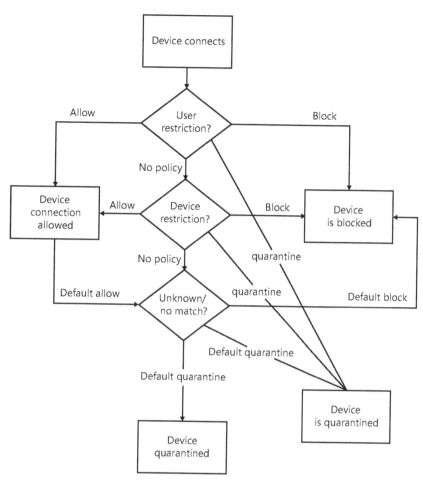

Figure 4-2 The device access rule evaluation process enabling you to allow or block devices by user device family or default

How quarantine works

The quarantine mechanism starts when Exchange has decided that the device should be quarantined according to the workflow shown in Figure 4-2. After this determination has been made, the device is allowed to establish a provisional sync partnership; that's sufficient to allow the device to receive a single quarantine message from the server, but that's all. This message is supposed to explain to the device owner why the device isn't synchronizing. You can customize the text of the message by adding your own explanation to the system-generated quarantine message.

CAUTION

If you set the default behavior to quarantine all devices that are not specifically permitted by an access rule, Exchange merrily quarantines the synthetic devices the Managed Availability subsystem uses for testing whether EAS is up. This results in frequent messages to the administrator, telling you that a device belonging to HealthMailbox<GUID> has been quarantined. To avoid this, you could add a device access rule that allows all members of the EASProbeDeviceType family to synchronize, but Microsoft has not publicly commented on the possible security or operational side effects of doing this.

If Exchange decides that a given device should be quarantined, it sends a notification to the end user (see Figure 4-3). This notification appears on the quarantined mobile device because of a one-time sync operation permitted by the quarantine process. It also appears on the user's other devices; it's a regular email message. If you've specified any email addresses to notify when a device is quarantined, Exchange sends a notification message to those email addresses. At that point, the device isn't allowed to sync until an administrator releases it from quarantine. Unfortunately, the notification mail that administrators receive doesn't include a link to do this; you must manually open the Mobile Device Access tab in EAC to free or permanently block a quarantined device.

One important aspect of quarantine to know is that if you create a device access rule or set the global default setting to quarantine new devices, existing devices that were already syncing properly might suddenly become quarantined. To prevent this problem, you can preemptively exempt existing devices from quarantine by running a script such as the following, written by Exchange MVP Steve Goodman. This script uses Get-CASMailbox to retrieve all mailboxes that have at least one EAS partnership and then iterates over each of those mailboxes, adding the list of all known devices for each mailbox to the mailbox's list of allowed devices.

```
# Retrieve mailboxes of users who have a connected ActiveSync Device
$CASMailboxes = Get-CASMailbox -Filter {hasactivesyncdevicepartnership -eq
$true
   -and -not displayname -like "CAS_{*"} -ResultSize Unlimited;

# Approve each device
foreach ($CASMailbox in $CASMailboxes)
{
  # Array to store devices
  $DeviceIDs = @();
```

```
# Retrieve the ActiveSync Device Statistics for the associated user mailbox
[array]$ActiveSyncDeviceStatistics = Get-ActiveSyncDeviceStatistics -Mailbox
  $CASMailbox.Identity;
# Use the information retrieved above to store information one by one about
each ActiveSync Device
foreach ($Device in $ActiveSyncDeviceStatistics)
{
  $DeviceIDs += $Device.DeviceID
}
Set-CasMailbox $CASMailbox -ActiveSyncAllowedDeviceIDs $DeviceIDs

# Display Useful Output that can be piped to Export-CSV or just shown as the
script runs
$Output = New-Object Object
$Output | Add-Member NoteProperty DisplayName $Mailbox.DisplayName
$Output | Add-Member NoteProperty AllowedDeviceIDs $DeviceIDs $Output
}
```

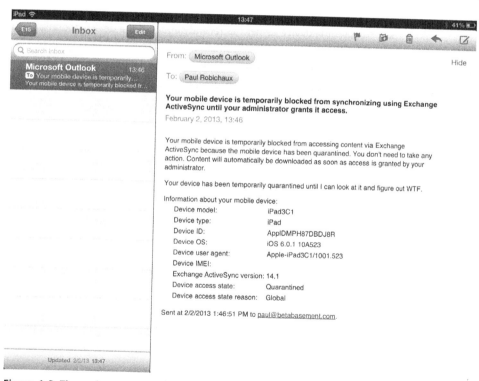

Figure 4-3 The end-user quarantine message clearly identifying the device being quarantined

INSIDE OUT Mobile operating system upgrades

For a given device, neither the device ID nor the IMEI will change. (In fact, the IMEI assumed immutability is a key part of the worldwide mobile phone network.) However, when you update your mobile device to a new version of the vendor's operating system, that will change the device's self-reported operating system identifier, and that might cause Exchange to treat the device differently. For example, consider when you have a default quarantine rule and device access rules that allow Windows Phone 7.5 and Windows Phone 8 devices to connect. A user who updates his phone to Windows Phone 7.8 will find that his newly updated phone is quarantined, even though it was previously allowed. Unless a personal exemption is on his mailbox for the device ID, the device can't sync because its operating system identifier no longer matches either of the device access rules. In the same vein, a device that is quarantined and has generated a quarantine message will trigger a new quarantine message the first time it tries to sync after an operating system update. If you see unexpected behavior related to sudden quarantines or device sync failures, it is probably worth checking to see whether the device owner has recently updated the device operating system. An example of this occurred in early 2013 when Apple shipped iOS 6.1 with a bug that caused it to retry to sync calendar items endlessly, causing Exchange servers to fill up their transaction log volumes; until Apple shipped a fix, the best available workaround was to block devices running iOS 6.1.

In general, it is best to not create a global allow rule for a specific device model or class because then any user enabled for EAS can sync any devices that match that class. If you want to restrict which devices a specific user can use to sync, just leave the default policy setting as quarantine and then selectively unblock the specific device by using the ActiveSyncAllowedDeviceIDs parameter with Set-CASMailbox.

Managing Exchange ActiveSync

In keeping with the Microsoft general philosophy of enabling reasonable default behavior for most aspects of Exchange, you can do absolutely nothing to a stock installation of Exchange, and users will be able to synchronize their mailboxes with mobile devices by using EAS. This might or might not be what you want, so knowing how to manage EAS and EAS devices is very useful.

Organization-level settings

At the organizational level, your only options relate to the default behavior that should be applied to new devices that are not specifically managed by a device access rule or personal exemption. When such a device connects to Exchange, you can choose to allow it to connect, to block it, or to put it in quarantine. You can specify one or more email addresses that should receive quarantine notifications; the user who syncs the quarantined device will always get one. Finally, you can specify some text that will be included in the quarantine message. To change settings at this level, you can use either the Set-ActiveSyncOrganizationSettings cmdlet or the Mobile Device Access page in EAC. The Edit button on that page displays the dialog box shown in Figure 4-4; next to it you see a summary of the current settings.

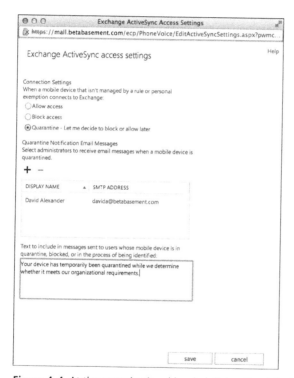

Figure 4-4 At the organizational level, defining the default behavior for unmanaged devices, who should receive quarantine notifications, and what text you want added to user quarantine notifications

Completely disabling Exchange ActiveSync

Notice that there's no global Off switch for EAS. If you want to disable EAS for all users, you have a couple of methods at your disposal:

- You can use Get-CASMailbox | Set-CASMailbox –ActiveSyncEnabled:false to turn off EAS for all existing mailboxes. However, as soon as you create a new mailbox, it will be enabled for EAS by default unless you use a cmdlet extension agent to run a script to disable it1 (or you do so manually). See *http://eightwone.com/2012/06/19 /postconfiguring-mailboxes-cmdlet-extension-agents-part-2/* for a primer on how to work with cmdlet extension agents.

- You can use a firewall product such as Kemp Technology ESP or various products from F5 (or even the venerable ISA/TMG product line) to block or allow access to the EAS virtual directory based on user ID or group membership. This approach enables you to let users on the corporate network sync while preventing sync from the Internet except for permitted users.

There are three other methods of disabling EAS that were useful in Exchange 2010 but that are not suited for use in Exchange 2013 because the new Managed Availability components of Exchange 2013 interpret any of these actions as an application failure. It will try to resolve them through the standard set of actions—which can include restarting or bug checking your servers. I've included them here for completeness, but I advise against using them:

- You can remove the EAS virtual directory on all your Internet-facing CAS servers with the Remove-ActiveSyncVirtualDirectory cmdlet. This is easy to do but requires you to re-create the virtual directory later if you ever want to use EAS again. You can do this with the New-ActiveSyncVirtualDirectory cmdlet.

- You can disable all authentication methods on the EAS virtual directory of all Internet-facing CAS servers. This effectively prevents any client from connecting through EAS, and it's easy to change back if you want to enable it in the future.

- You can use the Internet Information Services (IIS) management tools to stop the MSExchangeSyncAppPool application pool, which prevents the EAS server component from running; you must do this on all servers, and it might restart when the server restarts.

---

1 One such script is available from *http://www.flobee.net/automatically-disable-activesync-for-new-mailboxes -in-exchange-2010/*.

CAS-level settings

Although EAC doesn't expose them, a few useful EAS settings are available at the CAS level. You can manipulate these settings with the Get-/Set-ActiveSyncVirtualDirectory cmdlets. The most interesting setting is probably BadItemReportingEnabled, which controls whether the user is told when an item (usually a calendar item) can't be synchronized for some reason. It's set to false by default; accepting the default is recommended unless you have a significant number of sync problems to troubleshoot. Users can become upset when they get a notification that sync is not working, even when the problem is related to a single item; without that notification, users might never notice the bad item.

Set-ActiveSyncVirtualDirectory also has a group of settings for managing client certificate authentication and settings for changing the URLs the virtual directory uses. None of these settings is required for normal use.

Mobile device mailbox policies

Unless you specify a different policy, Exchange applies the default mobile device mailbox policy to mailboxes when they are enabled for EAS. You can change the policy that is applied to a mailbox at any time. For example:

```
Set-CASMailbox -Identity 'Ray, Mike' -ActiveSyncMailboxPolicy "Field Sales"
```

Most of the settings included in mobile device mailbox policies are self-explanatory, and many of them are similar to policies you might have seen in other contexts such as Active Directory. Figure 4-5 shows the window that appears when you create a new policy; the same settings are available when editing a policy through EAC, but they're separated into two tabs (General and Security). Selecting the This Is The Default Policy check box tells Exchange to apply this policy to all mailboxes that are EAS-enabled going forward, and it applies that policy to any device that does not currently have an explicitly assigned policy on its owning mailbox.

The Allow Mobile Devices That Don't Fully Support These Policies To Synchronize check box requires a bit of explanation too. A device that recognizes and applies 100 percent of the settings in a policy is said to be fully compliant. Devices that can't apply policy settings are partially compliant; they accept the policy, but at least one policy setting can't be applied, either because it doesn't apply (for instance, a policy that turns off the camera applied to a device with no camera) or because the device doesn't honor that particular policy setting (for instance, a policy that turns off Wi-Fi on Apple iOS devices, whose EAS client doesn't honor that setting). Devices that refuse the policy (usually because the user cancels policy application) or that can't apply the policy are said to be noncompliant. In Exchange 2007 and Exchange 2010, these devices were called nonprovisionable devices, which is perhaps a better name because it indicates where the problem lies—the device can't or won't accept the policy through the normal provisioning mechanism. When this check box is selected, Exchange allows any device with proper credentials to authenticate, and it is set by default, meaning that customizing the default policy to apply the security settings you want still won't prevent noncompliant devices from syncing.

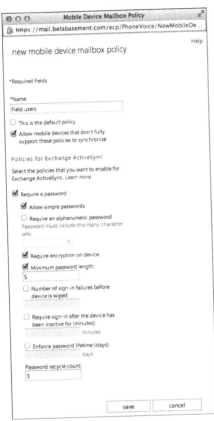

Figure 4-5 Creating a new mobile device mailbox policy so you can choose the password policy that will apply to the device

Many more policy settings are available when you use the Get/Set-MobileDeviceMailboxPolicy cmdlets. However, it is important to note that virtually no modern devices actually support the majority of these settings. For example, some policy settings enable you to restrict the use of Bluetooth, the on-device camera, removable storage cards, POP/IMAP, and Internet-access tethering. Of these, only the camera policy is supported on modern devices—and then only by iOS 5+ and Android Ice Cream Sandwich and later. Even Windows Phone 8 doesn't support the majority of existing EAS policies. This is unlikely to change in the future; if you need to control mobile device behavior beyond the basics of password policy control, you'll probably need a third-party solution.

To get more information about the specific policies a given device or operating system supports, the best source is the device or operating system manufacturer:

- Apple's support documents for Exchange ActiveSync (*http://help.apple.com /iosdeployment-exchange/mac/1.1/#exchange791e4e38*) don't mention Exchange 2013 as of this writing, but given how few EAS changes shipped in Exchange 2013, the document might still be useful.

- Microsoft has a brief reference paper available from *http://www.windowsphone.com /en-us/business/phone-management* that describes the (limited) set of policies Windows Phone 8 supports.

- A post on the Exchange team blog outlines the currently supported policy settings for Windows 8 and Windows RT Mail clients: *http://blogs.technet.com/b/exchange /archive/2012/11/26/supporting-windows-8-mail-in-your-organization.aspx*.

- Google has a list of policy support settings for Android 4.0.4 on the Galaxy Nexus, Nexus S, and Motorola Xoom. Although this is rather out of date, it still gives a decent snapshot of what pure Google devices (that is, those with a Google-provided EAS client) support: *http://static.googleusercontent.com/external_content/untrusted_ dlcp/www.google.com/en/us/help/hc/pdfs/mobile/ExchangeAndAndroid4.0.4.pdf.*

Certificate management

Dealing with SSL certificates on mobile devices can be a real adventure. Usually, mobile devices don't have a user interface to their on-device certificate stores, so discovering how to manage certificates on the devices can be difficult. If you are only using certificates issued by well-known public certification authorities (CAs), you might never encounter these difficulties. However, if you have an internal enterprise CA, or if you want to synchronize a mobile device to a CAS that uses self-signed certificates, the fun begins.

iOS 6 and Windows Phone 8 devices work smoothly; when the device owner puts in credentials, and the device detects an untrusted certificate, the user sees a prompt asking her whether she wants to continue with the sync operation, with an option to trust the certificate for future operations. This is similar to what happens in desktop web browsers, so it's fairly familiar to users (although it's a bad idea to encourage users to click OK or Accept blindly in security-related dialog boxes). Android EAS clients vary widely in how they handle self-signed certificates; some allow you to accept an untrusted certificate, but others flatly refuse.

It's necessary to point out here the difference between accepting an untrusted certificate for communication and trusting it. Accepting the certificate just tells the EAS client not to be concerned that the certificate doesn't appear to be valid. The certificate is neither added to the device trust list nor permanently stored. Trusting the certificate implies that the device user believes that the certificate is trustworthy and good and that it should be added to the device trust list and automatically trusted in the future.

If you need to load an Exchange server or CA certificate onto a mobile device, your options vary because the specifics of dealing with certificates on the device vary from platform to platform. As of this writing, here's how things stand with the most commonly used mobile operating systems:

- iOS (5.x and later) devices can load certificates by using Apple's iOS Configuration Utility; they can also open .cer files attached to email messages or in other repositories (such as SkyDrive or Dropbox folders) that are accessible from the device. You can also navigate to an HTTPS URL and, when the standard iOS untrusted certificate alert applies, click the Details button to get the alert shown in Figure 4-6, from which you can add the certificate to the on-device store. Note that after you've accepted a certificate on the device, you cannot remove it.

- Windows Phone 7, 7.5, and 8 devices can all open certificate files if you can get them onto the device somehow (including as an attachment to a Windows Live/Outlook. com email message). However, the prompt that Microsoft Internet Explorer shows when navigating to a website secured with an untrusted certificate allows you to continue the connection but doesn't give you a way to save that certificate for later or to make the trust permanent unless you've already installed the root and intermediate certificates. As with iOS devices, when the certificate is on the device, the only way to get rid of it is to reset it to factory settings.

- Android devices might or might not be able to open certificates directly on the device; it depends entirely on the version of Android and on any device-specific or vendor-specific customizations applied to the operating system. You need to search the Internet for advice on how to do this for your specific devices.

- Windows 8 and Windows RT devices can open the certificate file from a mail message or a file; Windows asks whether you want to install the certificate. If you agree, the Certificate Import Wizard launches

One simple way to publish certificates for all manner of devices is to make them available as downloadable .crt files from a webpage. Device users can visit the page and click the link for the appropriate root or intermediate certificates, at which point the device should offer to install them in its local store.

Figure 4-6 On iOS devices, you can add a certificate to the local store by using Safari

Handling users who leave the company

Disabling an Active Directory account doesn't necessarily prevent that user from synchronizing his device with EAS! For up to 24 hours after you disable the account, a device with
an existing sync partnership on the disabled account's mailbox might still be able to sync
messages. This long-lived and often unexpected connection is because the hanging sync
interval can combine with token caching performed by both Exchange and IIS to cache
a user's authentication cookie. As long as the cookie doesn't expire, IIS does not try to
authenticate the user again, so the disabled account doesn't cause synchronization to fail.
The length of time varies, but the exposure remains the same.

If it's critical to prevent a user from synchronizing mail after her account has been disabled,
you need to do several things to minimize her ability to continue synching. Suppose you

wanted to do your best to make sure a user named Marie couldn't sync her EAS devices after leaving the company.

1. If you intend to erase Marie's devices, trigger the remote wipe and make sure that it completes before disabling the account. Remember, the wipe request is passed to the device when the device attempts a sync after authenticating. If the device cannot authenticate because the account has been disabled, it won't receive the wipe request.

2. If you can't or don't want to erase the device, get Marie's list of device IDs and then block them by setting the ActiveSyncBlockedDeviceIDs parameter on her mailbox accordingly; something such as this will work:

```
Get-CASMailbox marie | Select ActiveSyncAllowedDeviceIDs,
ActiveSyncBlockedDeviceIDs
Get-ActiveSyncDeviceStatistics –mailbox marie | fl DeviceID
Set-CASMailbox marie –ActiveSyncBlockedDeviceIDs "id1, id2…idN"
```

The call to Get-CASMailbox provides an array of device IDs that currently appear on the allowed and blocked device list for her mailbox. However, because some of these devices might not currently be synchronizing with the mailbox, you must also call Get-ActiveSyncDeviceStatistics to get the list of devices that have current sync partnerships with the server. Then you should manually merge the list of device IDs to make sure that you cover them all in the blocking step.

3. Disable EAS for the user with EAC or by using Set-CASMailbox marie –ActiveSyncEnabled $false. This is necessary because the ActiveSyncEnabled flag can be cached for up to 20 minutes, and it might remain in the cache longer, depending on whether IIS token caching is enabled—so this setting might persist for quite a while, making it unsuitable as the only enforcement mechanism. However, you can recycle the EAS application pool on all Mailbox servers if you want to clear the token cache, although this will remove all other synchronizing users and force them to reconnect. This would be a terrible idea in a large environment unless the need to prevent the user from synchronizing was absolutely critical.

4. If possible, disable the mailbox for half a day or even a full day to allow for Active Directory replication delays. Disabling the mailbox prevents it from sending out of office (OOF) messages, triggering call answering rules, or triggering server-side mailbox rules, but it also reduces the chance that a sync operation will slip through. You want the mailbox to remain disabled until the account disablement (the next step) has had time to propagate.

5. Disable the Active Directory account.

All these changes take time to propagate. For example, changing the list of allowed device IDs on the mailbox causes an attribute change that must be replicated to all global catalog servers in your organization (or at least the ones CAS servers talk to). In general, you should assume that users can sync their devices for a period of time even after taking these steps, so plan accordingly.

Reporting on EAS sync and device activity

All the transactional information about communications between EAS clients and Exchange is recorded in IIS logs. You'll find information such as the protocol version of the devices that communicate with Exchange, the type of synchronization performed (mail, calendar, contacts, everything), statistics in terms of the number of operations performed (adds, changes, deletes), and specific operations such as OOF message creation. Although all this is available, it is buried in the mass of other data recorded in the IIS logs, and some help is therefore required to retrieve the correct data and interpret it in a human-friendly manner. The Export-ActiveSyncLog cmdlet is designed for just this purpose.

Export-ActiveSyncLog is run on a CAS. The cmdlet scans the IIS log file whose name you specify with the –Filename parameter, filters it for data relating to EAS operations, and uses these data to generate a set of reports. These are as follows:

- **Usage report (Users.csv)**   A summary of the total items sent and received (number of items and bytes) broken down by item type (email, calendar, and so on).

- **Servers report (Servers.csv)**   A summary of the servers hosting the mailboxes that are associated with ActiveSync requests.

- **Hits report (Hourly.csv)**   The total number of synchronization requests processed per hour plus the total number of unique devices that initiate synchronization requests each hour.

- **HTTP status report (StatusCodes.csv)**   A summary of the different HTTP error response codes and the percentage of the time that each code was encountered. The intention of the report is to give an indication of the overall performance of the server.

- **Policy compliance report (PolicyCompliance.csv)**   A summary of the number of devices that are compliant, partially compliant, and noncompliant.

- **User agent list (UserAgents.csv)**   A summary of the total number of unique users who have connected to ActiveSync during the report period organized by mobile device operating system (different versions of Windows Mobile, iPhone, Android, and so on).

Because the output files are in comma-separated value (CSV) format, you can open and interpret them to meet your own needs. You can open the files with Microsoft Excel or Microsoft Access or import them into a database to allow more sophisticated analysis and reporting based on data collated over an extended period. This is a useful cmdlet, but it has some limitations; it can't process logs from multiple servers at the same time, and the output is what it is—there's no way to customize the results of the reporting.

However, because the cmdlet just pulls data from the IIS logs, you can use other tools such as LogParser Studio to get whatever level of detail you want. In fact, in January 2012, Microsoft published the ActiveSyncReport.ps1 script on the Exchange team blog (*http://blogs.technet.com/b/exchange/archive/2012/01/31/a-script-to-troubleshoot-issues-with-exchange-activesync.aspx*). This script uses LogParser to collect usage data across multiple servers and give you more useful raw data to analyze, including information about the number of commands sent by devices and the hourly usage for each synchronized device.

Reporting on synchronized devices

The Get-MobileDevice cmdlet, new in Exchange 2013, gives you a set of data items for every synchronized mobile device, as you've seen. This is necessary but not sufficient for reporting. The Get-MobileDeviceStatistics cmdlet provides information about the synchronization status for a given mailbox. For example, here's an edited version of the information reported for a mailbox:

```
Get- MobileDeviceStatistics -mailbox "Paul Robichaux"


DeviceActiveSyncVersion       : 14.1
FirstSyncTime                 : 2/2/2013 5:10:18 AM
LastPolicyUpdateTime          : 2/2/2013 5:10:23 AM
LastSyncAttemptTime           : 2/3/2013 7:26:41 PM
LastSuccessSync               : 2/3/2013 7:26:41 PM
DeviceType                    : WP8
DeviceID                      : 00AB609A9828ACF8855AD26AC759F681
DeviceUserAgent               :
DeviceWipeSentTime            :
DeviceWipeRequestTime         :
DeviceWipeAckTime             :
LastPingHeartbeat             :
RecoveryPassword              : ********
DeviceModel                   : RM-820_nam_att_100
DeviceImei                    : 353680050361841
DeviceFriendlyName            : Lumia 920
DeviceOS                      : Windows Phone 8.0.10211
DeviceOSLanguage              : English
DevicePhoneNumber             : ********8120
MailboxLogReport              :
DeviceEnableOutboundSMS       : False
```

```
DeviceMobileOperator              : AT&T
Identity                          : betabasement.com/Users/Paul
Robichaux/ExchangeActiveSyncDevices/WP8§00AB609A9828ACF8855AD26AC759F681
Guid                              : f1ba1c68-77a4-4f04-8ed3-7dfa26c23334
IsRemoteWipeSupported             : True
Status                            : DeviceOk
StatusNote                        :
DeviceAccessState                 : Allowed
DeviceAccessStateReason           : DeviceRule
DeviceAccessControlRule           : WP8 (DeviceType)
DevicePolicyApplied               : Default
DevicePolicyApplicationStatus     : AppliedInFull
LastDeviceWipeRequestor           :
NumberOfFoldersSynced             : 6
SyncStateUpgradeTime              :
ClientType                        : EAS
```

INSIDE OUT It's actually useful data

Some interesting data are revealed here because you can see the devices that have synchronized with the mailbox, when they synchronized, and even the mobile operator. These data can provide the basis of some management reports such as the number of mailboxes that use mobile devices, an analysis of the devices being used, and the distribution of users across mobile operators. You could use these data for multiple purposes such as negotiating a better corporate deal with a mobile operator or planning a replacement strategy for old devices.

The problem with the Get-MobileDeviceStatistics cmdlet is that it functions on the level of a mailbox, and no cmdlet is available to provide aggregate data of the type that is useful for analysis. You don't want to review synchronization data for thousands of mailboxes to gain some understanding of what's happening on a server, so some code is required to fetch the necessary data and store it in a format that permits analysis.

This code uses the Get-CASMailbox cmdlet to fetch information about any mailbox with an ActiveSync partnership that's connected to an Exchange 2010 Mailbox server. The Get-MobileDeviceStatistics cmdlet then extracts statistics for each device (remember, someone can create partnerships with several mobile devices) and writes out these data to a variable. Eventually, after data have been fetched from all the mailboxes, the aggregated data are written into a CSV format file that can be used for later analysis.

```
$Devices = $Null
$Mbx = Get-CASMailbox -ResultSize Unlimited |
Where {$_.HasActiveSyncDevicePartnership -eq $True -and
$_.ExchangeVersion.ExchangeBuild.Major -eq"15"}

ForEach ($m in $Mbx)
{
$Devices += Get-MobileDeviceStatistics -Mailbox $m.Identity
}

$Devices | Export-CSV ExServer1ActiveSync.csv
```

The code works, but it's only appropriate for use in small deployments of fewer than 1,000 mailboxes, in which you won't run into problems processing a lot of data in memory after it's fetched from mailboxes. Another way of doing much the same thing is to use two loops. The first processes the list of mailboxes that have ActiveSync partnerships, and the second fetches information for each device that has synchronized with the mailbox. The resulting data are written out in a less verbose manner in a simple text file. The code has been used to generate monthly management reports in organizations supporting more than 30,000 mobile devices:

```
$Date = Get-Date -uformat "%Y%m%d"
$Logfile = "C:\Logs\ActiveSync-all-$date.txt"

$Lst = Get-CASMailbox -ResultSize Unlimited -Filter
{HasActiveSyncDevicePartnership -eq $True} | where {$_.ExchangeVersion.
ExchangeBuild.Major -ge 15}

ForEach ($CASMbx in $lst) {
        $Devices=(Get-MobileDeviceStatistics -Mailbox $CASMbx.name)
        if ($Devices) {
                foreach ($Device in $Devices) {
                        $ReturnObject=($Device | select DeviceModel,DeviceType,
LastSuccessSync,DevicePhonenumber,DeviceUserAgent)
                        Add-Content -path $Logfile ((ConvertTo-CSV
 -NoTypeInformation -InputObject $ReturnObject) | select -skip 1)
                }
        }
}
```

Whichever approach to reporting you take, the important point is to capture data that make sense for your organization and use them to build a solid and practical ActiveSync policy for your company.

Building device access rules

New mobile devices appear all the time, and users are tempted to buy these devices and then attempt to connect the devices to their mailboxes. Often, these connections occur without the knowledge or the intervention of an administrator. This isn't a problem if everything works and the device connects the first time and continues to synchronize mailbox contents perfectly, but it can become a problem when a user attempts to introduce a new device that doesn't comply with corporate security guidelines or runs an operating system the help desk can't support. For example, the original EAS implementation on the Palm Pre did not enforce the PIN locking feature, which is a crucial security issue for many companies, so users were told not to use these devices until Palm fixed the problem. The original Apple iPhone also caused concern for some companies because its implementation of all EAS security features was not as complete as its peers'. If you enable support for non-provisionable devices by allowing an open connect policy, essentially you allow any device that supports EAS to connect to Exchange and run the risk that the policies to enforce desired security behavior will never reach the device (or that the device will ignore them altogether).

Earlier in the chapter, the default allow/block/quarantine (ABQ) behavior that you can set using EAC or the Set-ActiveSyncOrganizationSettings cmdlet was discussed. After you configure that behavior, you see a list of quarantined devices when you open the Mobile Device Access page in EAC (see Figure 4-7). The icons above the list of devices display device statistics (the pencil icon), allow the device to connect, block it permanently, or create a device access rule.

Assume that the help desk receives notification that a user has attempted to synchronize with a new device called Whiz-Bang01. The administrators should now make the decision about how to deal with these devices. They can allow, block, or continue to quarantine. Because users are already attempting to connect, the decision is really between block and allow. After the decision is made, it is implemented with a new ActiveSync device access rule. These rules enable Exchange to block devices selectively by device type or model.

Chapter 4

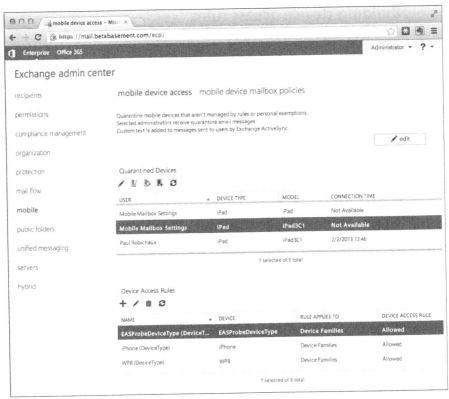

Figure 4-7 Quarantined devices show up in EAC and can be individually blocked or freed

The key to creating device access rules lies in the Characteristic and QueryString parameters. The values you can specify for Characteristic are UserAgent, DeviceModel, DeviceType, and DeviceOS. The QueryString parameter specifies what value you want to match against the characteristic. Thus, if you want to allow the Whiz-Bang01 device access, you can click the icon in EAC to free the device from quarantine or create an access rule from the shell like this:

```
New-ActiveSyncDeviceAccessRule -QueryString 'Whiz-Bang01'
-Characteristic DeviceModel -AccessLevel Allow
```

The question now arises about determining the correct values to use to identify a new mobile device when you create a new ActiveSync access rule. One simple way is to examine the characteristics reported in EAC for an ActiveSync partnership established with a mailbox. Open the Phone section of the Outlook Web App options page, select Mobile Devices, and then select the device you want to check from the list of known devices that have synchronized with the mailbox. Click the Details icon to see the kind of information shown in Figure 4-8.

Figure 4-8 Viewing mobile device characteristics reported by EAC

You can create access rules based on the device type, model, user agent, or operating system. In this example, the characteristics of the device are as follows:

- **Device name**   Black iPad

- **Device model**   iPad3C1

- **Device type**   iPad

- **Device operating system**   iOS 6.1.3 10B329

Clearly, some of these characteristics are broader than others. For example, if you create an access rule that allows any device of type iPad (with –Characteristic DeviceType –QueryString 'iPad'), you allow all generations of iPad from the original through the iPad mini.

You can also find these entries in the IIS logs on the CAS, but probably the simplest way to retrieve the most useful subset of this information is to use the Get-ActiveSyncDeviceClass cmdlet, which returns several interesting properties for each synchronized device (including

Chapter 4

the device model and device type). For example, by running Get-ActiveSyncDeviceClass | ft DeviceType, DeviceModel produces output like the following:

```
DeviceType                          DeviceModel
----------                          -----------
EASProbeDeviceType                  EASProbeDeviceType
iPhone                              iPhone
iPhone                              iPhone3C1
WP8                                WP8
WP8                                RM-820_nam_att_100
iPad                               iPad
iPad                               iPad3C1
```

Microsoft has provided another easy route to create device access rules. When you click the + icon in the Device Access Rules section of the Mobile Device Access page shown in Figure 4-7, the resulting New Device Access Rule dialog box includes buttons that enable you to browse through the list of device families and models that Exchange already knows about (based on devices that have been synchronized successfully). If you want to create a device access rule based on one of these characteristics quickly, you can easily do so from EAC; you still need to use New-ActiveSyncDeviceAccessRule if you want to key the rule on operating system version or user agent.

After creating the necessary ActiveSync device access rules, you can check them with the Get-ActiveSyncDeviceAccessRule cmdlet. For example, this output shows that the organization has three device access rules in place. All iPhones and Windows Phone 8 devices are allowed to connect, but smart phones are blocked.

```
Get-ActiveSyncDeviceAccessRule | Format-Table Name, Characteristic, QueryString,
AccessLevel -AutoSize
```

Name	Characteristic	QueryString	AccessLevel
iPhone (DeviceType)	DeviceType	iPhone	Allow
WP8 (DeviceType)	DeviceType	WP8	Allow
EASProbeDeviceType (DeviceType)	DeviceType	EASProbeDeviceType	Allow

When a user's device is blocked by a device access rule, the device is not allowed to synchronize. A new device access rule might also cause a device to be temporarily quarantined while Exchange awaits a human's decision on whether to permit the device to synchronize. In either case, the user receives an email to tell her what the problem is and what she should do. The information contained in the message helps an administrator understand what the issue is if the user seeks help. Of course, the user must read the message by using another client and might decide not to contact the administrator if she realizes that she's using an unapproved device.

Blocking devices on a per-user basis

In addition to creating device access rules to control the types of devices that can be connected to ActiveSync, you can allow or block individual devices for a user's mailbox. By
selecting the target mailbox in EAC and clicking the View Details link under Mobile Devices
in the right sidebar, you see the Mobile Device Details dialog box (Figure 4-9).

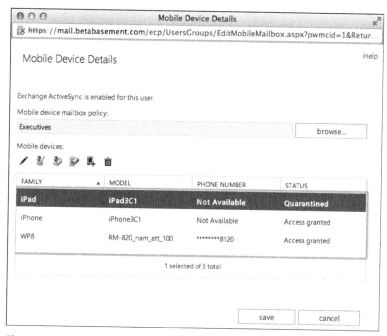

Figure 4-9 The Mobile Device Details dialog box through which to change the assigned mobile
device mailbox policy and manage devices associated with the mailbox

The icons above the device list provide a way to see the device details, allow or block the
selected device for this mailbox only, remotely wipe the device, or create a new device
access rule based on the selected device.

If you prefer, you can use the Set-CASMailbox cmdlet to set the
ActiveSyncAllowedDeviceIDs and ActiveSyncBlockedDeviceIDs parameters with a list of
device identifiers that should be allowed or blocked for a mailbox. The default value for
these parameters is $Null, meaning that any device can synchronize with a mailbox.

The first step in blocking devices on a per-user basis is to determine the device identifier.
The easiest way to discover a device's identifier is to connect it to Exchange. Afterward,
you can use the Get-ActiveSyncDeviceStatistics cmdlet to retrieve details about users'

ActiveSync activity, including the identifiers for each mobile device they have connected to Exchange. For example:

```
Get-ActiveSyncDeviceStatistics -Mailbox 'Orton, Jon'
```

You can add multiple device identifiers to the list, separating the identifiers with semicolons. For example, this command allows just one specific device to synchronize with Jon Orton's mailbox.

```
Set-CASMailbox -Identity 'Orton, Jon' -ActiveSyncAllowedDeviceIDs
'4B9207650054671AD0AEE83A424BCD7F'
```

To clear the device identifier to allow any device to connect to the mailbox:

```
Set-CASMailbox -Identity 'Orton, Jon' -ActiveSyncAllowedDeviceIDs $Null
```

If you have a list of devices and want to remove only a single device from the list, export the list to a variable, update the list in the variable, and then write it back with Set-CASMailbox:

```
$Devices = Get-CASMailbox -Identity 'Orton, Jon'
$Devices.ActiveSyncAllowedDeviceIDs -= '4B9207650054671AD0AEE83A424BCD7F'
Set-CASMailbox -Identity 'Orton, Jon' -ActiveSyncAllowedDeviceIDs
$Devices.ActiveSyncAllowedDeviceIDs
```

The same techniques can be used to block devices. For instance, update the ActiveSyncBlockedDeviceIds parameter with Set-CASMailbox. You might make a corporate decision to block Android-powered devices and then discover that someone is using one of these devices to access Exchange. A quick retrieval of the device identifier followed by input to Set-CASMailbox blocks further synchronization. (Creating a device access rule that blocks Android devices would have prevented this problem in the first place!)

Another device blocking–related trick you might need is to adjust the number of devices that an individual user is allowed to synchronize with his mailbox. By default, Exchange allows 10 device partnerships per mailbox. Depending on your user population, you might want to raise or lower this number; for example, the average user probably doesn't have more than three or four devices. To do this, you must update the EasMaxDevices setting on the policy by using Set-ThrottlingPolicy. If you have users who need more than 10 devices, you should create a separate throttling policy for them and apply it as needed rather than modifying the default policy.

Wiping lost devices

It is the nature of mobile devices that some are lost in airports, taxis, shops, and other places. In the same way, it's almost inevitable that some devices will never be recovered. Being able to wipe the device through a virtual command is therefore a necessity to protect the data held on the device. Administrators can wipe a mobile device by selecting the mailbox in EAC and then selecting the Manage Mobile Device option or by running the Clear-ActiveSyncDevice cmdlet. Users can erase their own devices through Outlook Web App, too; the Outlook Web App phone options page shows users which devices are currently synchronized with their mailboxes (Figure 4-10), and they can remove or wipe any of them. These options are available only if a user has first synchronized a device with her mailbox to make the device known to Exchange.

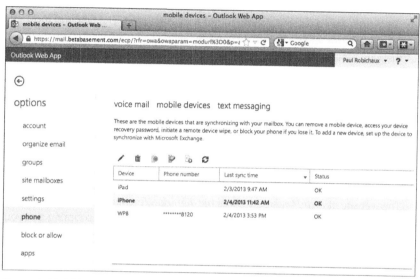

Figure 4-10 ECP option to wipe a mobile device

Debugging ActiveSync

Understanding what's happening as a mobile device synchronizes with an Exchange mailbox is simple in concept and complex in execution. Much can go wrong between when a message is created in a mobile client and when it is submitted for sending on the server. When problems arise and the user calls the help desk, an administrator can work through the basic problem-solving steps with the user to ensure that the connection is working and nothing else obvious is awry. After that, it can be a challenge to understand what might be going wrong.

To address the problem, Exchange maintains EAS logs to capture details of the interaction between mobile device and Exchange. The contents of these logs describe the events that occur as the device connects and retrieves information. Logging is off by default, so if a problem occurs with a device, the user must click Start Logging on the Mobile Devices option page to instruct Exchange to begin capturing the events. After he has worked

Chapter 4

through the steps to re-create the problem, the user can stop logging, and Exchange sends him the EAS log as an attachment to a message.

EAS logs are in XML format, and their contents take some time to interpret. However, these logs not really designed to be used by administrators. Instead, they are a diagnostic tool for Microsoft support personnel who have access to all the coded information that might appear in a log and can therefore diagnose what happened between a device and Exchange during a connection.

There are other data sources you might find useful, too. The first and most important is knowledge of the data path between the device and the Mailbox server. What path does the sync request take? Which devices, firewalls, and filters lie along that path? You might also get useful information from:

- Firewall logging tools that enable you to examine firewall rules that might be blocking traffic, timeout settings, and so on.

- Reverse proxy logs.

- Exchange event logs, provided you've set diagnostic logging to an appropriate level.

The website at *http://www.slideshare.net/himickey/exchange-active-sync-troubleshooting* has a useful presentation containing some additional troubleshooting tips you might find helpful.

Identifying and blocking badly behaved devices

Sometimes bugs in device firmware or client software results in side effects on the server. Perhaps the best-known case of this was the bug in iOS 6.1 that generated huge volumes of transaction logs. A bug in the client resulted in attempts to resynchronize calendar items endlessly, which in turn resulted in Exchange generating large numbers of transaction logs that filled up the log volumes. This bug was insidious because it occurred only when the device user created or modified a calendar appointment, so it didn't affect all users all the time.

Exchange 2003, Exchange 2007, Exchange 2010, and Exchange 2013 were all vulnerable to the bug, but only Exchange 2013 had an effective way to mitigate it. Until Apple fixed it, the workarounds for earlier versions were limited; you could block all iOS 6.1 devices, or you could watch the rate at which log files were created and hope that you could identify the bug's emergence to find and fix the bad item on each device that experienced the problem. The Exchange 2010 throttling features didn't help because throttling for EAS clients is limited to controlling the amount of CPU or clock time the client can consume. However, Exchange 2013 has a new feature that effectively and quickly blocks problem clients: Set-ActiveSyncDeviceAutoblockThreshold. This clumsily named cmdlet is quite powerful; with it, you can set thresholds for behavior that is considered offensive to the server and automatically block devices that exceed those thresholds. The cmdlet syntax is a bit confusing until you understand that there are already seven defined sets of thresholds (as you see if you run Get-ActiveSyncDeviceAutoblockThreshold | ft name). Here's what they do:

- UserAgentsChanges triggers when a device changes its user agent string.

- RecentCommands triggers when a device sends an excessive number of commands within the budgeting time period.

- Watsons triggers when something the device does causes a crash dump of one of the mobility-related services.

- OutOfBudgets triggers when the device exceeds, and stays above, its budget threshold.

- SyncCommands triggers when a device sends too many sync-related commands (for example, if it sends an excessive number of commands to sync the same item).

- EnableNotificationEmail controls whether you get a notification email when a device is auto-blocked.

- CommandFrequency triggers when the rate of arrival for commands exceeds the built-in threshold.

For each of these threshold sets, you can control four parameters with Set-ActiveSyncDeviceAutoblockThreshold:

- BehaviorTypeIncidenceLimit specifies how many times the client can do whatever the threshold specifies before it's triggered. For example, a BehaviorTypeIncidenceLimit of 2 for UserAgentChanges means the device can change its user agent twice without penalty, but a third change triggers a block.

- BehaviorTypeIncidenceDuration sets the time period during which the incidence limit is enforced. For example, setting –BehaviorTypeIncidenceLimit 2 and –BehaviorTypeIncidenceDuration 1440 indicates that the device is allowed two incidences of the specified behavior within 24 hours (or 1,440 minutes) before the block is triggered.

- DeviceBlockDuration controls how long the offending device is blocked.

- AdminEmailInsert contains custom HTML that is enclosed in the message the device's mailbox receives notifying its owner of the bad behavior.

Chapter 4

At present, you can't adjust any of the specific behaviors that trigger each threshold. For example, you can't specify individual commands that you want to exempt from triggering RecentCommands. Because Microsoft depends on this blocking mechanism to isolate poorly behaving devices automatically that sync to Office 365 mailboxes, it's fair to expect that it will expand and improve in future releases of Exchange.

Other mobile device management alternatives

Over time, Microsoft has introduced and then dropped mobile device management capabilities such as the ill-fated System Center Mobile Device Manager and the list of allowed and restricted applications introduced as an EAS policy setting in Exchange 2010. Exchange isn't intended to be a complete mobile device management solution, and that shows; EAS provides a convenient way to deliver security policies to a device, but it doesn't have much in the way of enforcement capabilities, and its utility is limited by how many policies the EAS client supports.

Microsoft has its own full-fledged device management solution, Windows Intune. Other vendors, such as BoxTone, Citrix Zenprise, and MobileIron, have their own solutions that provide more comprehensive device management, reporting, control, and auditing capabilities, including the ability to push (or block) specific applications to devices. If you need these more advanced capabilities, you won't be able to get them from EAS alone. However, EAS remains a robust and proven solution for delivering security policies and messaging data to a broad range of devices, and it will be with us for a long time to come.

Message hygiene and security

ere's a bit of a paradox: no one likes spam, and no one likes malware, and yet users and administrators have to wade through more and more of it every year. That is due to two reasons. First, for many companies, email has become the dominant means of communication with customers, but what a company sees as a marketing communication can appear as spam to the user. Second, spam and malware have both become major businesses in their own right; estimates of the impact of spam and malware vary so widely as to be meaningless, but it is fair to say that they have an impact in several ways. First, there are the direct resource costs; spam and malware messages cost you money to receive because they consume bandwidth, processing power, storage space, and user attention. Dealing with spam and malware by training users, cleaning up infected machines, and taking other remedial measures also imposes administrative and management overhead. Malware has a second tier of costs related to the damage it can cause and the value of the information that can be lost or compromised because of it; a malware infection that requires cleaning individual PCs can cost hundreds of thousands of dollars (or more) to remedy. For some organizations, there are additional threats. For example, defense contractors and government agencies around the world have been targeted frequently by extremely sophisticated malware widely believed to originate from attackers sponsored by or affiliated with various national intelligence and security agencies. Unlike run-of-the-mill crimeware, this malware attempts to steal and extract data from protected corporate networks, so blocking it is particularly important.

To help counteract these threats, you need a message hygiene system that can identify and block "bad" messages while leaving "good" ones untouched. The exact value of good and bad varies according to a number of factors, users' and administrators' tolerance for filtering mistakes, the risks involved in failing to catch a bad message or mistakenly filtering out a good one, and a whole host of associated political and technical issues. Leave aside the definitions of "good" and "bad" and focus on the other components; a good message hygiene system offers the ability to discern between good and bad content, filtering the unambiguously bad and providing a quarantine method so that suspicious messages can be manually inspected by humans (although quarantine systems must account for the fact that many messages will never be manually examined because there are so many of them). It will do this by systematically examining inbound messages, using a variety of methods, including checking the message origin and destination, its content (including any attachments and particularly any URLs in the message), and any metadata associated with the message.

To obtain this capability, administrators have two basic options. They can do either of the following:

- Outsource the cleansing of inbound mail to a specialized service provider such as Symantec MessageLabs or Microsoft and accept a cleansed stream of email from the service provider. The advantage of outsourcing message hygiene to a specialized third party is that you take advantage of its expertise in combating malware and spam. Specialized providers have deep probes into the dark side of email and can always react the most quickly to new attacks when they develop across the Internet. Larger services can have millions of users, increasing the odds that they can quickly identify and react to emerging threats. In addition, you don't waste valuable administrator, network, and computing resources to deal with the vast amount of unwanted email that appears on your company's doorstep because it's filtered out before you get it. However, the potentially significant disadvantage is that whatever filtering service you use is processing all your mail. Depending on the nature of your business, where the filtering service is, where your organization has offices, and the applicable data privacy laws in each of those jurisdictions, you might find that this poses an unacceptable degree of risk. Another drawback is that a badly behaving customer of the filtering service might cause the service's IP address range to be listed as a spam source, so your mail originating from the same IPs will be labeled as potential spam.

- Deploy your own systems to cleanse inbound mail as it arrives at your network. The usual approach is to remove as many obvious problem items as early as possible by dropping any message that is not addressed to a recipient that can be found in Active Directory and then apply a series of tests to determine whether items are spam, contain malware, or have attachments with unwanted content. Suspicious items can be dropped or stripped of problematic content, and then the cleansed stream can pass through to hub transport servers for delivery. The Exchange Server 2010 Edge Transport server is designed to perform email cleansing, but there is currently no equivalent role for Exchange 2013. If you decide you want to use an Exchange edge server, you can still deploy Exchange 2010 edge servers, which will work fine with Exchange 2013. Most administrators who want their own on-premises filtering choose from a number of other solutions from vendors such as Barracuda Networks and Cisco, which make dedicated physical and virtual appliances that provide message filtering. Open-source software solutions based on tools such as Sendmail, ClamAV, and qmail are another alternative.

INSIDE OUT   What does "received" mean?

At what point do you have to archive a received message when you're using archiving? The answer is that it depends. If your organization accepts a message from an outside source, and it is delivered to a user, it seems logical that the message would have to be archived. What about spam messages? It's hard to say whether those must be considered messages that must be archived because the laws and regulations that govern message archiving vary among jurisdictions. One way to finesse this issue is to use external filtering services to screen unwanted messages before they arrive at your servers in the first place; if the message is never accepted for delivery by your organization, you don't have to archive it. There's an additional nuance to consider, though: depending on the rules where you are, a message that is rejected as part of the SMTP conversation before the SMTP server actually accepts it might not have to be archived, but a message the server accepts has to be archived, even if it's immediately deleted by a later stage!

It's important to keep in mind that the messages leaving your organization need to be scanned too. The business impact of accidentally sending malware to a customer or business partner can be significant. In addition, if your network appears to be originating malware or spam messages, other filtering services might start filtering or blocking your outbound mail in an attempt to protect their own customers. Outbound filtering also helps you ensure that you're not leaking any data. For example, one common feature of hosted filtering systems is the ability to quarantine outbound email containing selected phrases so that you can block messages that refer to sensitive projects or topics from reaching the outside world. (You can also use Exchange transport rules and the new Exchange 2013 data loss prevention feature, both described in Chapter 2, "The Exchange transport system," to provide an additional layer of defense.)

Of course, security is best attained through multiple lines of defense (also known as *defense in depth*). Client-side junk-mail features also make an important contribution to dealing with unwanted content in user inboxes. It's tremendously difficult to protect users so well that they never see spam or receive malware. Spammers and criminals expend enormous time and effort concocting new techniques to mask bad content so that it penetrates the defenses erected by companies to protect users. It therefore follows that user education must provide the final layer of defense; users must be informed about the danger spam and malware represent and the actions they should take if suspicious messages make it into their inbox. All these questions are discussed in this chapter.

Chapter 5

A quick message-hygiene primer

It's helpful to have a shared understanding of some basic concepts behind message hygiene, starting with the term itself. *Hygiene*, of course, connotes health or wellness; its use in this context means that the goal is to keep the message stream free of contaminants and infection and to take measures to limit the spread of unhygienic content. In common usage, the term *message hygiene* refers to the process of filtering both inbound and outbound messages to block harmful or unwanted content. This content can come in three primary forms: spam, phish, and malware.

Spam

Spam isn't actually named after Hormel's SPAM meat; it's named after a semi-famous comedy skit by the British troupe known as Monty Python, involving Vikings and a diner with a very limited menu. The more pedantic terms are unsolicited commercial email (UCE) or unsolicited bulk email (UBE); they indicate that spam is unwanted. The term came into common use in 1994 after a pair of American immigration lawyers, Laurence Canter and Martha Siegel, began flooding Usenet with messages advertising their services. The term stuck and was quickly applied to email-based message floods. Over time, spammers' tactics have evolved in step with improvements in message filtering. Rather than sending spam from a single IP address (or a small range), for example, spammers now use networks of compromised home computers, each of which sends a steady trickle of messages. This tactic makes it harder to block spam because the recipient can't block it based on the originating IP address. Other changes in tactics include adjusting the content and format of messages to evade filters or adding random junk words or phrases from books to confuse filters that work by analyzing the statistical properties of English text. The best tactic in the spammers' arsenal, however, is volume. By sending out mind-boggling numbers of messages, the odds of getting enough responses to make money are pretty good. If you doubt this, reflect on the fact that spammers send out their messages only because they are profitable; if tomorrow morning every human with an email address stopped buying fake pills and other paraphernalia from spammers, all spammers would have to find honest employment.

Phish

The term *phish* is a clever way of indicating the nature of the beast: phishing messages are supposed to look like legitimate messages (or fish), but they're not. Phishers send out large volumes of fake messages that attempt to trick recipients into doing things such as logging on to their online bank accounts or entering their eBay or PayPal credentials in the phishers' website. The credentials the attackers gather can be used to steal money or goods, apply for credit cards, or get up to all sorts of other mischief. The quality and fidelity of phishing messages vary widely; they often contain obvious grammatical or graphical errors, but some are very good and can be detected only by looking carefully at their HTML source or at the links embedded in the message.

A subtype of phishing messages is known as *spear phish*; these are messages with malware attached that are targeted narrowly at a particular individual or group. For example, the 2011–2012 compromise of RSA Data Security began when an attacker sent spear-phishing messages containing a Microsoft Excel spreadsheet that exploited a previously unknown (or *zero-day*) vulnerability to install malware on the target machine. The RSA spear phish was sent to a small group of employees in the human resources department; it only took one employee opening the attachment out of curiosity to compromise that employee's machine, which in turn led to a broad compromise of RSA's network. (RSA's own account of the attack is at *http://blogs.rsa.com/anatomy-of-an-attack/* and makes for interesting reading—even large, well-funded security companies are not immune to attack!)

Malware

Malware is a generic term that refers to any kind of "bad" software. The term encompasses viruses, worms, Trojan horse software (including remote-access Trojans, or RATs), rootkits, and other assorted types of dangerous executable software. Although the exact taxonomy and history of malware is a fascinating topic, to Exchange administrators, it's largely irrelevant; we want to keep all such items out of user mailboxes, no matter the precise nature of the threat they pose. Malware is usually named by the agency or company that first identifies it; the industry standard is Computer Antivirus Research Organization (CARO) (see *http://caro.org/naming/scheme.html*), although Microsoft has its own variant, described at *http://www.microsoft.com/security/portal/shared/malwarenaming.aspx*. No matter the naming standard used, most of the time you'll see malware names consisting of a type, platform, family name, and variant, such as Trojan:Win32/Nacho.T. Naming standards are useful because different vendors and security practitioners can ensure that they're talking about the same actual executable.

Effective malware protection requires protection on any device on which a user can read messages. No malware filter can provide perfectly effective protection against all threats because attackers write malware to exploit previously undisclosed vulnerabilities in operating systems, applications, and utilities. No matter how quick vendors are to update their software, and scanner or filter vendors are to update the signatures they use for detecting malware, scanners can't detect a threat they don't yet know about. The nature of targeted malware attacks means that the attacker has powerful incentives to identify and exploit a previously undisclosed vulnerability so that its attack can continue for as long as possible before malware scanners are updated to recognize the particular attack vector it's using.

INSIDE OUT   Zero value for zero-day mitigation?

The brutal truth is that malware filtering systems are largely ineffective against zero-day exploits. That's because the exploits themselves are, by definition, previously unknown. Savvy attackers gather zero-day exploits and husband them, using them only against their most important targets; when a zero-day makes it out into the wild, it will be spotted at some point, at which time its signature will be added to anti-malware programs. Until that happens, though, the zero-day remains a threat that can't be easily detected.

If conventional malware filtering can't protect you against zero-day exploits, what can you do? There are several additional defensive layers you might find valuable. First is reducing the potential number of entry points for such an exploit. For example, consider whether your users should have Oracle Java and Adobe Flash—both of which have proved very attractive to zero-day authors—on their systems and, if so, in what configuration. Second, monitoring outbound data traffic can often provide an indication that a piece of malware is at work by highlighting unusual amounts of or destinations for traffic. For egress monitoring to be valuable, you must have a good idea of what your normal baseline traffic looks like, though, and this can be difficult to ascertain in some environments. Third, you need an aggressive campaign of user education, something easier said than done because users are primarily focused on doing their jobs and might not always be attentive to security concerns when opening attachments or visiting websites. For high-value targets such as your organization's key executives or researchers, you might want to set up special-purpose virtual machines (VMs) with limited network access for reading email and browsing the web; that way, if they are exposed to malware, only the VM is compromised.

Are you positive?

No discussion of message hygiene would be complete without mentioning the different types of potential matches a scanner might uncover. A true positive is what its name implies: a bad message that is correctly identified as bad. A false positive, however, is an innocuous message the scanner mistakenly identifies as bad. Likewise, a false negative is a bad message that is not recognized as such.

The problem with false positives is obvious. If the scanner is catching good messages and labeling them as bad, users won't get those messages when they should. If you've ever told a user to check her junk mail filter for a message she was expecting but didn't receive, you have firsthand experience with this problem. There are two ways to attack this problem.

One is to improve the accuracy of the scanner; the other is to provide a fine-grained mechanism for classifying messages. Instead of a binary spam versus legitimate message scale, for example, Microsoft uses a 10-point scale it calls the *spam confidence level* (SCL). An SCL of 10 represents a message that is positively known to be spam; a value of 1 indicates a message that is extremely unlikely to be spam; and the numbers in between indicate how likely the Exchange filtering system thinks it is to be a bad message. An SCL value of −1 indicates that the message is known to be good because it matched a specific rule or exception, such as coming from a trusted sender. You can set thresholds that remove messages, quarantine them, or deliver them directly to users' individual junk mail folders based on the message SCL.

Apropos of quarantine, many filtering systems include a mechanism that quarantines messages so that users or administrators can inspect them and decide whether they are bad or good. Good messages can be released to the original recipient; bad messages may be abandoned in the quarantine mailbox (where they eventually expire) or deleted. In Exchange, the anti-spam system has a quarantine mechanism, but the anti-malware version does not; if the scanner decides that a message contains malicious code, it's deleted, and it cannot be recovered.

Message security and protection in Exchange

Microsoft succinctly describes the goal of its anti-malware feature set in Exchange: to identify, block, and remove malicious content from the stream of incoming email. In a similar vein, the goal of the anti-spam features in Exchange is to identify and remove or quarantine spam messages. The difference is that quarantining malware is too risky—a careless or inexperienced user or administrator might accidentally release a piece of malware from quarantine. The risk is much lower for accidentally releasing a spam message.

To accomplish these goals, Microsoft has done two things. First, it has built an online service (formerly known as Forefront Online Protection for Exchange, or FOPE, and now called Exchange Online Protection, or EOP) that provides comprehensive malware and spam filtering as a hosted service. EOP is a key part of Office 365; licenses to use it are included with all Office 365 packages that include Exchange Online and with the Exchange Enterprise + Services client access license.

Second, Microsoft has built anti-spam and anti-malware filtering into the Exchange transport pipeline. This filtering is intended to supplement filtering done at or before the network perimeter, perhaps by an Exchange edge server or by a hosted service such as EOP or an on-premises appliance. You can use the Exchange native anti-spam and anti-malware filtering by itself, but keep in mind the earlier mention of defense in depth. It's better to have too many layers of protection than too few.

Chapter 5

Built-in security features

Although Exchange includes its own filtering that you can use, it's not quite accurate to say that it's unique to Exchange. Malware filtering is provided by the Microsoft anti-malware engine, which is shared with Microsoft Security Essentials, System Center 2012 Endpoint Protection, and the Windows Defender subsystem in Windows 8. The purpose of this engine is to scan content, using a set of predefined signatures and heuristics, to see whether it might be bad. The job of Exchange is to recognize sections of content, such as attachments, and then pass them off to the scan engine for checking. It also provides tools for adjusting a few of the scan engine settings. The anti-malware engine recognizes many common types of attachments, although you cannot control which attachment types are checked. Microsoft has not published a list of exactly which file types the built-in scanner checks.

Malware filtering happens as part of the transport pipeline on the mailbox server—after the message is received but before it is categorized or queued for delivery. The Front End Transport service on the Client Access Server (CAS) isn't involved with filtering in any way. Keep in mind that this layer of filtering only covers messages in transit—Exchange doesn't filter messages in the store, including messages submitted by users as drafts. It is a bit unusual that malware filtering is done on the mailbox server because the whole point of that filtering is to keep malware away from the mailbox server. However, now that there is no longer a dedicated hub transport role, that's what we're stuck with. As the engine scans each message, it adds a custom header: X-MS-Exchange-Organization-AVStamp-Enterprise: 1.0.

Junk mail filtering is a bit different. Earlier versions of Exchange (beginning with the Intelligent Message Filter for Exchange 2003) incorporated a scan engine based on the Microsoft SmartScreen engine. In Exchange 2010, Microsoft moved most of the filtering to agents that run as part of the transport pipeline on the edge and hub transport roles. Exchange 2013 essentially does the same thing; the Microsoft documentation says that "the built-in anti-spam agents that are available in Exchange 2013 are relatively unchanged from Microsoft Exchange Server 2010." That's in large measure because the basics of filtering spam haven't changed much since then; spammers are always trying to evolve the specifics of their messages to slip past filters, but the structure of how and when the filtering mechanism works hasn't really changed.

Client-side features

As discussed earlier in this chapter, anti-spam software relies on a variety of techniques to detect unsolicited commercial email. Even with the best possible array of bastion and anti-spam edge servers arranged to suppress incoming spam before it penetrates your network, it is inevitable that some percentage of spam will get through to user mailboxes. To provide defense in depth, Microsoft Outlook includes a spam filter; this client-side filter is based on the SmartScreen technology Microsoft originally developed to protect the consumer Hotmail servers. SmartScreen depends on exposure to a vast collection of spam to learn and recognize the characteristic signs that indicate potential spam. You can also use rules to block messages from specific senders, but general-purpose rules are slow to execute and are therefore unsuited to handle the rate of incoming email that busy mailboxes receive. The Outlook junk mail filter (JMF) runs as compiled code and executes quickly enough to avoid any perceivable delay in the delivery of new mail.

The Outlook JMF includes the ability to feed information back to the server filter agents. For example, when an Outlook user marks a message as coming from a trusted sender, that sender is added to the user's list of trusted senders Exchange uses to filter incoming messages. Any message originating from a sender or IP address that is explicitly marked as trusted is accepted without further filtering. Over time, these user-specific exemptions are aggregated and used to make filtering decisions for the entire organization.

Both Outlook and Microsoft Internet Explorer also include anti-phishing features; these features typically are configured to check URLs against a list of known-bad phishing sites in real time, so that when you attempt to load a URL that's known to be bad, you get a warning. Note that the Outlook filter works for mailboxes in cached Exchange mode only because it filters messages on arrival to the OST file.

The raw data that enable Outlook to filter messages are contained in a file called Outfldr .dat, which holds a large dictionary of keywords and phrases that the junk mail filter uses. You cannot add to the filter file, so you cannot train Outlook to respect your preferences. Instead, Microsoft issues regular updates for the filter file as part of its update service for Office (*http://www.microsoft.com/officeupdate*), so as long as you download and install the updates, you benefit from the latest ways to detect spam.

Assuming that you opt to use the JMF, Outlook checks new messages as they arrive. The default protect level is Low, but I prefer to run at High because experience with the filter has shown me that it does a pretty good job. The difference between Low and High is that the first setting filters only the really obvious spam, whereas the second does a much more thorough filtering job. You have the option to delete any mail immediately that the filter catches or have Outlook put these messages in your Junk E-Mail folder. I usually opt to delete messages immediately, but from time to time, I capture messages just to see what kind of spam is arriving. Outlook Web App doesn't offer quite the same control over junk mail filtering as Outlook does, but you can still input lists of safe senders and recipients (Figure 5-1) and always opt to accept email from your contacts. Outlook and Outlook Web App share the same junk email settings because these are stored in the root folder of the user's mailbox.

Chapter 5

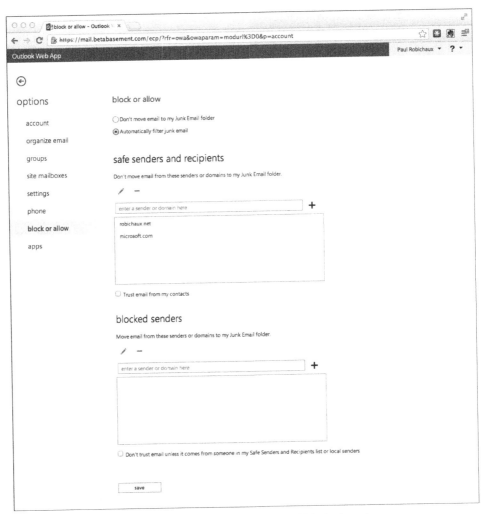

Figure 5-1 Outlook Web App settings page for allowed and blocked senders

Users have a degree of control over the client-side filters; they can disable junk mail filtering altogether in Outlook, of course, a step they often take from fear that they'll suffer false positives. They can also add senders to their individual trusted sender lists so that messages from those senders are exempted from server-side filtering. These lists are used as part of the Outlook overall filtering process; assuming that a message makes it to the Inbox, here's how Outlook processes it:

1.   Outlook checks the sender against your contacts. Any message from a contact is assumed to be safe because you have taken an explicit action to mark someone as a

contact, and you would not do this if you didn't want to receive email from her. Note that Outlook doesn't use the Suggested Contacts folder for this purpose.

2. Outlook checks the sender against the Global Address List. Outlook assumes that you are willing to read a message sent by another user who appears in your GAL. Your GAL can include users who are in other organizations or in hybrid Office 365/ on-premises configurations. (Note that you cannot use the filter to block messages from another user in the organization; to do this, you have to create a rule.)

3. Outlook checks the sender against your Safe Senders list. If you add someone to this list, you tell Outlook that you always want to receive email from him; Exchange publishes through the safelist aggregation process (described later in this chapter) so that it can be used in anti-spam processing.

4. Outlook checks the sender against your Safe Recipients list. If you add an address to this list, you tell Outlook that it's okay to accept any message that contains the address.

5. Outlook checks the sender against your Blocked Senders list. Outlook blocks any message from anyone on this list. The JMF also checks for incoming messages that are from any blocked domains or contain specific character sets. For example, because anyone I know in Russia sends me email in English, I block any other message that arrives in the Russian Cyrillic character set.

6. Run the JMF to examine the content of messages that have gotten this far but might still be spam.

The result of the filter is a ranking (think of a number between 1 and 100 in which 100 means that the message is absolutely spam) Outlook uses to determine whether a message is spam. If you opt for a Low level of protection, Outlook is cautious, and the ranking has to be very high before Outlook regards a message as spam. If you opt for a High level of protection, Outlook is more aggressive and moves the ranking bar downward.

When the Outlook JMF catches a message, the message displays an infobar indicating the actions Outlook took to remove potentially dangerous content from messages that end up in the Junk E-Mail folder. Messages are converted to plaintext, and all links to websites are disabled. This prevents users from accidentally clicking live links in messages when they review messages in the Junk E-Mail folder and being taken to sites they probably don't want to visit. Removing links also prevents web beacons from working. These are invisible links that spammers use as a form of phone-home signal to let them know when messages have been received by a live address. Because they know that a live address is in use, these addresses are much more valuable to spammers than addresses made up in an attempt to batter their way into a company.

Chapter 5

The Outlook JMF is pretty effective at blocking spam that gets through the Exchange anti-spam agents and gets better with each version. It even works when you attempt to recover a message from the deleted items cache; if Outlook thinks that the message is spam, it will not recover the message.

Although the Outlook JMF works well most of the time, occasionally you will find that Outlook moves a message into the Junk E-Mail folder when you think the message is perfectly legitimate. The opposite situation also occurs, and spam ends up in the Inbox, despite being totally obvious spam to the human eye. Either situation might cause you to question the effectiveness of the JMF. Here are some reasons these situations occur:

- Messages generated by applications are regarded as spam, for example, expense reports, notifications from Microsoft SharePoint Portal Server, subscription updates, distributions from newsgroups, and so on. Messages like this are often generated when an application makes an unauthenticated SMTP connection to a server to submit email, and because the connection is unauthenticated, the messages are suspicious because spammers might have attempted to hijack what seems to be a perfectly valid internal email address and use it for their purposes. In addition, the content of automatically generated messages might contain little text context, have URLs for pointers to application data, and lack a From field in their header, all of which are indications that a message might be spam. The solution is to add the sending address to the Safe Senders list or have the administrator of the application change it to use an authenticated SMTP connection.

- Obvious spam the filter doesn't catch might simply be due to a new tactic created by a spammer to outwit filters; unfortunately, spammers succeed in this respect all the time. In a company that operates a comprehensive anti-spam defense, you can expect to see one or two messages a week sneak through. Anything more is an indication that the defenses need to be updated. For example, you might need to download and install the latest version of the Outlook JMF data file.

- An illogical message moves between folders. If you still use mailbox rules to process incoming messages, Outlook might download message headers (to provide sufficient data for rules to process messages) and then download the full content (required for the JMF to process messages), only to find that rules move some messages to specific folders followed by a subsequent move to the Junk E-Mail folder after Outlook has run the JMF. The behavior is logical in computer terms, but the result can baffle users.

Given that spammers invent new techniques to get past filters all the time, even the best anti-spam defenses let some messages through. You can capture addresses from messages you know to be spam and add these addresses or complete domains to the Blocked Senders list to build up your own list of spammers gradually. You can export any of the Safe Senders, Blocked Senders, and Safe Recipients lists to a text file that can then be imported by another user.

The use of the Blocked Senders and Safe Senders lists is apparent, but the purpose of the Safe Recipients list is less so. Essentially, a safe recipient is a way to identify messages sent to a particular destination, often a distribution list or newsgroup of which you are part and from which you want to receive messages. You do not control the membership of the list or group, but you assume that whoever administers the list will make sure that it is not used for spam and that therefore any message addressed to the list is safe. If you couldn't mark the list as being safe, Outlook might assume that its messages are spam and suppress them. By marking the address of the list or any similar address as a Safe Recipient, you tell Outlook that it can ignore messages from this address when it applies its filters.

Exchange Online Protection

Cloud-based security services have some major advantages over self-hosted security. The biggest has to do with message volume; a cloud service with many customers will see a huge number of messages that can be analyzed to assess how much spam they contain or whether they contain malware. As soon as a URL is identified as malicious, for example, every other customer of the service will notice that messages containing that URL are fil-tered. The more messages that pass through the service, the better the odds that bad mes-sages will be identified and caught quickly, both because the service has more examples of messages to see and because users of the service can report messages to get them into the filtering pool.

Another major benefit is that the service screens out bad mail before it gets to you, so you don't spend bandwidth downloading it, CPU time filtering it, or disk space storing it. For large organizations, the savings in resource consumption and administrative time can be considerable.

There are two other related benefits to using a hosted security service. By their nature, you must adjust your Domain Name System (DNS) MX records to point to the service so it can pre-filter your mail. In case of an outage on your network, the service can still receive and queue your mail for later use, providing an additional bit of redundancy. In addition, you can configure your Exchange systems or perimeter firewalls to accept only inbound SMTP traffic from the IP address ranges your service uses. You can also designate those IP addresses as trusted, which means that messages from those IPs will be exempted from fur-ther filtering.

Exchange Online Protection (EOP) also offers a number of features that aren't available in Exchange itself (as do most other hosted filtering services), including the ability to filter based on the language of the message and the ability to customize filtering based on key-words in the message body or headers (or based on the presence or absence of specific headers). The most compelling feature EOP includes, however, is that it uses multiple anti-malware scan engines (currently, Kaspersky, Symantec, Authentium, and Microsoft engines are used), whereas the built-in scanner in Exchange 2013 only uses the Microsoft engine.

Chapter 5

Scanning messages with multiple engines is resource-intensive, but it adds protection by increasing the odds that the scan will catch a malicious message. Any time EOP scans a message, it stamps it with the X-MS-Exchange-Organization-AVStamp-Service: 1.0 header. This header prevents redundant scanning.

Another advantage of filtering services is that they are typically updated with new malware signatures and spam filtering criteria at least hourly and, sometimes, more often. The built-in Exchange content filtering mechanism downloads new malware signatures hourly and new anti-spam filtering criteria every two weeks, although you can download updates manually at any time by running an Exchange Management Shell (EMS) script.

INSIDE OUT Balancing the pros and cons of hosted filtering

New technologies often bring new laws and regulations, or at least highlight areas where existing ones might not apply. This is certainly true of the hosted services world. For example, consider what happens if you're a company based in the European Union (EU) and you use a U.S.-based filtering service. Does routing email through that service comply with the EU Data Protection Directive? Or what about when an employee of the filtering service, performing normal monitoring, becomes aware that one of your employees is doing something illegal in email? Case law for many aspects of on-premises email management is settled in most jurisdictions, but the same cannot be said when hosted services are involved.

Another aspect of hosted filtering you must take into account is control. Any time you use a hosted service, you are essentially making a bet that the service provider will do a better job than you can do yourself (where "better" might equate to "less expensive," "more available," "faster," or other criteria). However, you might also have to give up a significant degree of control. In the case of malware and spam filtering, the hosted service you choose might not give you any way to adjust filtering settings. For example, Symantec's well-regarded MessageLabs filtering service doesn't allow you to specify key phrases or senders to block, and it does not provide a way for you to change the set of file types that it scans and filters. Deciding on a hosted filtering service requires you to evaluate carefully the legal and practical aspects of outsourcing your filtering to a particular service, taking into account the cost, reliability, geography, and capabilities of the particular service. The cost aspect is especially important; when you pay for a hosted service, you might just be shifting the cost of message hygiene from an indirect cost the IT department bears to an explicit operating expense that appears as a direct cost. It might not be any cheaper, but it might appear to be cheaper because the cost goes to another part of the budget—and perhaps that can work to your advantage.

Major changes from previous versions

There are a number of significant changes from earlier versions of Exchange besides the obvious addition of an Exchange-integrated malware scanner. Probably the biggest is the fact that the Edge Transport role is no longer explicitly supported. You can still run Exchange 2007 or 2010 Edge Transport servers in your perimeter network, and they can synchronize and communicate with Exchange 2013 mailbox and client access servers perfectly well. (As of this writing, Microsoft hasn't announced any plans to release an Exchange 2013 Edge Transport role.)

Another important change is that Microsoft has dropped support for the Virus Scanning application program interface (VSAPI). Back in the time of Exchange 5.5, the smart engineers at Sybari figured out how to intercept calls to the Extensible Storage Engine (ESE) dynamic link libraries (DLLs) so that they could scan attachments and messages for viruses in real time on mailbox servers. Microsoft hated this idea, so it soon thereafter shipped a vendor-neutral application programming interface (API) for doing the same kind of scanning. This API matured over time, evolving into the VSAPI that was delivered in Exchange 2010. VSAPI enabled anti-malware scanners to scan messages and attachments stored in mailboxes and public folders in two ways. Background scans could run at any time; on-demand scans checked individual items when a client first requested them. This store-level scanning was valuable because it provided an additional layer of defense. Even if perimeter scanning failed to catch a new virus, the idea was that regular background scans, coupled with on-demand scanning, would catch any infected items that made it into user mailboxes. As of this writing, Symantec and McAfee have released Exchange 2013–aware versions of their tools; other major anti-malware companies will likely follow suit as the Exchange 2013 market matures.

Another significant change, which doesn't have any technical relationship to Exchange 2013, is nonetheless important. In September 2012, Microsoft announced that it was discontinuing several security products, including the Forefront line of application-specific anti-malware tools. Forefront Protection for Exchange (and the corresponding products for OCS/Lync and SharePoint) was removed from the product lineup in favor of EOP, leaving customers who want server-level anti-malware protection to find solutions from third-party vendors. Microsoft is clearly all in on the idea that cloud-based anti-malware and anti-spam filtering will be better for customers and for Microsoft.

Managing anti-malware scanning

The anti-malware scanner in Exchange is conceptually pretty simple to manage. Currently, a single anti-malware policy controls the settings available for malware scanning. The scanner uses only a single engine, and you can't manipulate its scanning settings or signatures directly. You cannot disable or remove the default policy, although you can turn off scanning as described later in this section. You can create or remove your own policies by using EMS; the policies you create will appear in EAC, and you can change settings for the default policy or your own policies through either EAC or EMS.

The settings for the policy are minimal. You can control what happens when malware is detected in a message. Your choices are to delete the entire message (the default behavior) or delete all the message attachments. Note that you don't have the option of deleting just the infected attachment; the scanner assumes, not unreasonably, that a message with multiple attachments might contain more than one piece of malware. For messages from which the attachments are deleted, you can choose whether to use the standard system alert text or your own. In either case, the purpose of this text is to indicate that the attachments appeared to be malware and were therefore deleted. When the entire message is deleted, the recipient doesn't receive any notification.

You can, however, set up notifications to the sender or your own administrators when the scanner catches a message. Sender notifications are further broken down by whether the sender or recipient is within or outside your organization. That means that you can use a more detailed message for internal senders, perhaps including instructions to contact the help desk. None of these notifications is very specific, though. For example, they don't tell you what specific malware item the scanner identified. There's also no reporting of the filter's catches other than the notification messages themselves. Improved reporting is one of the key selling points of EOP, so it seems unlikely that there will be better reporting in future updates to Exchange 2013 itself.

Apart from the notification options, which are self-explanatory when viewed in EAC, you can change only a couple of policy settings in EMS. You can use the BypassInternalFiltering and BypassExternalFiltering switches to skip the respective filtering passes. (See the "Disabling anti-malware scanning" section later in this chapter if you're wondering why you might want to do this.) The only other cmdlet switch of real interest is Set-MalwareFilterPolicy -MakeDefault, which enables you to create your own custom policy and apply it as the default for your organization. Because there are so few actual configuration options in the policy, it's probably simplest to customize the notification settings you want in the default policy rather than creating a new one of your own.

Managing server-level settings

The Get/Set-MalwareFilteringServer cmdlets give you a bit of control over the behavior of the filtering agent on an individual server. Although you can't directly change the way filtering works, you can use the parameters for Set-MalwareFilteringServer to control the following:

- How many times to retry a message that can't be scanned for some reason. The DeferAttempts parameter controls this; acceptable values are from 1 to 5, with a default of 3. After the set number of deferrals has been reached, the action varies according to why the message was deferred. If the scan engine failed or timed out, the message is returned with a non-delivery receipt (NDR). For all other errors, the message is retried for up to 48 hours. The first deferral retry will be after one hour, the next two hours after that, then three hours after that, and so on.

- How long to wait between scan attempts for a deferred item. Set the DeferWaitTime parameter to a number of minutes between 0 (meaning that items are immediately resubmitted) and 15. On the first deferral, the filter waits for the specified interval before retrying. On the second deferral, it waits for double the specified interval, and so on. When the item has run out of deferral attempts (as set by the DeferAttempts parameter), the timing described in the preceding bullet kicks in.

- How long to wait before deciding that a scan attempt has failed. Set the ScanTimeout parameter to the number of seconds (between 10 and 900; the default is 300) that must elapse before the engine decides that the scan attempt has failed.

- What to do if a message fails all its deferred scan attempts. The default is to block the message. You can use the ScanErrorAction switch to allow those messages through instead, although that probably isn't a great idea from a security perspective.

- Whether you want to rescan messages that have already been scanned by FPE/FOPE/EOP. If ForceRescan is set to $True, every incoming message is scanned, even if it's stamped with the X-MS-Exchange-Organization-AVStamp-Enterprise or X-MS-Exchange-Organization-AVStamp-Service scan headers mentioned earlier in this chapter.

- How often to fetch signature updates. The default is to do so once per hour. By changing the value of the UpdateFrequency parameter to the number of minutes you want to pass between updates, you can vary the interval up to 27 days or down to 1 minute. An hour is a reasonable default.

- Where to get signature updates. The PrimaryUpdatePath and SecondaryUpdatePath parameters control this behavior; you would typically use them when Exchange servers don't have direct access to the Internet to fetch signature updates from an internal staging server. To get the updates on the server in the first place, you can examine the contents of the Update-MalwareFilteringServer.ps1 script included in the Exchange scripts directory. The UpdateTimeout parameter specifies the interval, in seconds, that you want the server to wait before switching from the primary to the secondary update path.

Chapter 5

> **Note**
>
> Exchange 2013 release to manufacturing (RTM) includes some cmdlets that appear to provide functionality for releasing messages that contain malware from quarantine: Get/Remove/Resume-MalwareFilterRecoveryItem. However, these cmdlets aren't supposed to be visible because they are intended for use only by the Microsoft Office 365 operations team. They will eventually disappear. More important, they don't have anything to do with quarantine; they are used to control processing of items in the malware scanning queue that have caused problems such as hangs or freezes in the scanner.

Disabling anti-malware scanning

If you want to disable anti-malware scanning, you have three choices. You can disable scanning altogether at the server level, you can bypass it at the server level, or you can bypass it as part of a malware scanning policy.

The difference between disabling and bypassing is subtle. When you disable scanning, you turn it completely off. The transport agent that performs the scans is removed from the transport pipeline, and the scheduled task that downloads signature updates is disabled. When you bypass scanning, signature updates still occur, and the malware scanner remains in the transport pipeline, but it doesn't actually scan any messages.

The use cases for bypassing and disabling scanning are quite different. You'd typically disable scanning only if another malware scanner is active; even then, the extra protection you get from Exchange scanning messages is probably worth the minor performance cost of leaving scanning enabled. Bypassing scanning is normally done for maintenance and troubleshooting purposes, and it's intended to be temporary.

Both these actions can be performed only from EMS. To disable scanning, you run the Disable-Antimalwarescanning.ps1 script from the Exchange install directory's Scripts subdirectory (pointed to by the $ExScripts built-in variable). There's also a corresponding script, Enable-Antimalwarescanning.ps1, to turn it back on. When the script finishes, the filter is immediately disabled on that server. You can check the state of filtering by using the Get-TransportAgent cmdlet to look at the state of the Malware Filter agent; if it is set to $True, the filtering agent is enabled. If you want to bypass (or not bypass) filtering, you must use the Set-MalwareFilteringServer cmdlet with the -BypassFiltering switch on the target server.

Configuring server-based third-party anti-malware scanners

Two major classes of anti-malware scanners are available for Microsoft Windows servers: those that are aware of specific applications (such as Exchange) and those that are not. (There are also protocol-based scanners that inspect the SMTP conversation between server and client, inspecting the message headers, bodies, and attachments; these are often found in hosted scanning services or appliances.) Most vendors refer to their non-Exchange-aware scanners as file-based or file-level scanners because they check the contents of files on disk, looking for malware signatures. Many such products also hook into the Windows I/O manager so that when applications try to open a file, the scanner gets a chance to check it first.

File-level scanners typically scan files on disk as a background task and provide on-demand scans for programs and files as they are loaded into memory. Items that appear to contain malware are quarantined or removed. The problem, of course, is that Exchange databases and transaction logs can contain data that triggers a false positive, leading the scanner to try to fix a file that contains critical Exchange data.

Many organizations have policies that require the use of anti-malware scanners on every server. Others have policies that require the use of a particular vendor's scanners, even if that vendor doesn't make an Exchange-aware scanner. If you're subject to these policies, what can you do? Do these problems mean that you shouldn't run file-level scanners on Exchange servers? Not necessarily, although if you have the option of using only Exchange-aware products, that would probably be a better choice. Microsoft recognized some years ago the risks of using non-Exchange-aware scanners on Exchange servers, and it's released guidelines for doing so without putting Exchange at risk. Microsoft has a complete list of guidelines for Exchange at *http://technet.microsoft.com/EN-US/LIBRARY/BB332342(V =EXCH.80).ASPX*, but they can be summarized as follows:

- Don't let the scanner scan any data file Exchange owns, including transport queues, databases, transaction logs, Offline Address Book (OAB) files, Group Metrics files, log files for the CAS or mailbox server processes,and diagnostic files Managed Availability uses. Most scanners allow you to exclude specific directories, which is important to ensure that you don't fail to exclude any of the important files.

- Turn off process-level scanning on the Exchange processes themselves and on critical Windows processes such as the Windows failover clustering service and the Microsoft Windows PowerShell interpreter.

- Tell the scanner to ignore any file with an extension that indicates it belongs to Exchange, including .edb, .chk, .que, and the variety of content indexes that Search Foundation in Exchange 2013 generates.

With these settings in place, you greatly reduce the chance that your scanner will cause problems for Exchange by blocking a file when Exchange needs it or by cleaning a file that

Chapter 5

isn't infected. However, keep in mind that even with these restrictions in place, Microsoft support will probably ask you to disable (or even remove) file-level scanners completely from your Exchange server if you ask for support. You should also be aware that a misbehaving, misconfigured, or poorly written scanner can impose a significant load on your Exchange server; your existing performance monitoring system should alert you if this happens.

INSIDE OUT Reporting suspected malware

Microsoft has an extremely active (and quite talented) team that analyzes malware and contributes that analysis to the malware-fighting community. Its regularly updated Security Intelligence Report (*http://www.microsoft.com/security/sir*) is fascinating reading if you're at all interested in the nuts and bolts of the global computer-crime market. If you run across a file you think might be malware, the Microsoft Malware Protection Center portal includes a submission page at *https://www.microsoft.com/security/portal /submission/submit.aspx*, where you can submit the file for analysis.

Managing anti-spam filtering

The nature and behavior of Exchange anti-spam filtering is quite different from the anti-malware scanner. Spam is annoying but rarely dangerous; however, malware is much more easily identified than spam, so the spam filtering process itself is actually more complex than you might expect.

There are essentially two rather different spam filtering systems that you might encounter in Exchange 2013 deployments: the built-in system, which uses a series of transport agents that aren't configurable; and the filtering system implemented in EOP, which is much more flexible. Each system requires you to take some action before you can use it:

- The built-in filtering system must be enabled on each mailbox server on which you want filtering to occur, as described in the "Enabling anti-spam filtering on mailbox servers" section later in this chapter.

- FOPE/EOP requires you to have an active subscription for it and requires the DNS MX records for your domain to point to it so it can receive and filter your mail. For details on how to do this, see the EOP setup guide available from *http://technet.microsoft .com/en-us/library/fope-setup-and-provisioning-instructions.aspx*.

Methods of spam filtering

Exchange uses six distinct methods for filtering spam. Each method focuses on some characteristic of the message, such as its origin or its content; the method has to make a decision about the likelihood that the message is spam based on both its evaluation of the message and its knowledge, if any, of what any other method might have thought of the message.

Because Exchange 2013 divides the responsibility for email transport between the CAS and mailbox roles, some types of spam filtering happen on the CAS, but others happen only on the mailbox role. It's probably most helpful to divide filtering methods into two categories: those that operate on information that's provided as part of the SMTP protocol conversation and those that rely on information provided in the message content itself. Protocol filtering can happen at any time during the SMTP exchange, whereas content filtering can't take place until the message has been accepted by the receiving server; until that happens, there's not enough data for the server to use to make a correct decision about the message disposition.

Protocol filtering methods include connection filtering, sender filtering, recipient filtering, and the use of Sender ID. Content filtering methods include content filtering itself and the use of sender reputation data. These filtering steps take place as part of the transport pipeline described in Chapter 2. As you might remember, the pipeline mechanism gives Exchange a way to manage transport operations in a predictable sequence.

Connection filtering

Connection filtering means simply that the receiving SMTP server decides whether to accept an incoming SMTP request based solely on the IP address of the sending server. Although the Front End Transport service on the CAS is in charge of initially accepting SMTP connections, it doesn't do connection filtering.

Exchange connection filtering enables you to specify two lists of IP addresses: an allow list, which contains IP addresses of servers whose messages should be uncritically accepted, and a block list, messages from which will be automatically blocked. You can specify the contents of these lists yourself, or you can outsource the maintenance of your lists by configuring Exchange to use a third-party service that provides preconfigured block and allow lists. These providers work by maintaining DNS servers that return a specific result when queried with an IP address—if the result is NXDOMAIN (the error code for a nonexistent domain), the address is not on the list.

> **Note**
> You can easily find third-party list providers by searching for DNSBL or DNS RBL. That might tempt you to add as many providers as you can find to your Exchange server—but keep in mind that every incoming SMTP connection will generate DNS queries. Although these should be cached by the DNS client on the Exchange server, large numbers of queries can cause a delay that can add up on busy servers. It's a better idea to stick to a small number of providers to prevent unnecessary delays.

Sender filtering

Sender filtering operates by examining the address the sender claims during the SMTP conversation. The Sender Filter agent examines the contents of the MAIL FROM: SMTP header, compares it against the list of blocked and allowed senders and domains that you have configured, and then either rejects the message or accepts it and marks it as coming from a blocked sender. This mark is used later when calculating the sender reputation and spam confidence scores for the message. (The sender's reputation is also used as input in this decision, as described in the "Sender reputation" section later in this chapter.)

Microsoft documentation points out two interesting things about the Sender Filter agent. First, it only works on messages that come from unauthenticated senders. Messages that come over trusted receive connectors or from users who authenticate to the server (for instance, POP or IMAP users) are not filtered. Spam filtering is actually a permission on the connector, and authenticated connections get the Bypass Spam Filtering permission. Second, because a sender is free to omit or forge the address in the MAIL FROM header, Microsoft warns that you should use multiple filtering methods, not just the Sender Filter agent.

Recipient filtering

In a normal SMTP conversation, the next command sent by the sender after MAIL FROM will be one or more RCPT TO commands listing the intended message recipients. The Exchange Recipient Filter agent can filter these recipients by checking them against a block list of recipients who should never receive mail from unauthenticated senders or by verifying that the target recipient exists in the Exchange organization. Messages that are sent to blocked or unknown recipients are rejected; messages sent to legitimate recipients are accepted and sent to the next stage in the transport pipeline.

The Recipient Filter agent also performs *tarpitting,* which is the process of intentionally slowing down a connection to discourage misuse. The default configuration of the Recipient Filter agent makes it possible for an attacker to try every possible address to see whether it's accepted, building a list of known-good addresses from the response. For example, the attacker can start with aaron@contoso.com, then try alice@contoso.com, then arabella@contoso.com, and so on. This so-called harvesting attack can easily be automated, so attackers can work through very large dictionaries of potential email addresses with little effort. Tarpitting discourages this by adding a delay between the time the server receives the RCPT TO command and the time it returns a response. The idea is that this added delay makes harvesting attacks too slow to be worthwhile for an attacker, who will go bother some other company that doesn't have tarpitting. In addition, tarpitting raises the cost for spammers to send large volumes of messages by increasing the intra-message delay, again with the idea that they'll take their business elsewhere. You can adjust the tarpit interval with the Set-ReceiveConnector –TarpitInterval cmdlet.

> **Note**
>
> The Recipient Filter agent performs directory lookups for recipients only for authoritative domains. If your servers are configured to relay mail for other domains, mail sent to addresses in those domains can still be matched against the blocked recipients list but won't be checked to verify that the recipient is valid.

Sender ID

Sender ID is a vendor-neutral industry standard that was intended to address a vexing problem: How do you know that a message came from a particular sender? Consider the case of a postal letter. If you receive a letter with a return address of 1600 Pennsylvania Avenue, Washington, DC, you might believe that it originated at the White House. However, if the address is written in crayon, or if the postmark indicates that the letter was mailed from Albuquerque instead of Washington, you might (rightly) doubt the accuracy of the address. SMTP itself doesn't provide a way for a recipient to crosscheck any aspects of the sender's identity, so Sender ID was born in 2006.

Sender ID works by checking the IP address that originated the message against Sender Policy Framework (SPF) records registered in DNS. The SPF record for an organization is supposed to contain the IP addresses of all the SMTP servers that are authorized to send mail on behalf of that organization. For example, say that all of Contoso's email originates from 172.16.250.25 and 172.16.250.27. To create an SPF record, Contoso's administrator uses the handy wizard that Microsoft maintains at *http://www.microsoft.com/mscorp/safety /content/technologies/senderid/wizard/*, plugs in those IP addresses, and tells the wizard that no Contoso email will ever originate from any other server. She gets the following result:

```
v=spf1 ip4:172.16.250.25 ip4:172.16.250.27
```

Chapter 5

The result indicates that the only IP addresses that should be considered valid origins for Contoso mail are the two listed. By adding that SPF statement as a text resource record on Contoso's public DNS server, any server that uses SPF can check mail that appears with contoso.com in a MAIL FROM header. The receiving server might query DNS for the SPF record, parse it to see the addresses from which Contoso says it will send mail, check those addresses against the sending server's actual address, and then decide to accept the message, reject it completely, delete it silently, or mark it as having failed the Sender ID filter so that other filters (including the Outlook JMF) can decide what to do. As an alternative, the receiving server could do a DNS reverse lookup of the sending IP to see whether it corresponds to a registered A or MX record for the originating domain. Some large ISPs, such as freenet.de in Germany, do this instead of using Sender ID checks, but Exchange doesn't.

A given message can have one of seven Sender ID statuses, as shown in Table 5-1. The Sender ID status is actually stored with each individual message as a MAPI property; the client-side Outlook JMF uses it in addition to the Sender ID agent.

TABLE 5-1 SPF check statuses

Status	What it means
Pass	The IP address and sender address match the SPF record.
Neutral	The SPF record didn't explicitly specify that the sender IP is or is not acceptable.
Soft fail	The sender's IP address isn't in the SPF record, but the SPF record contains "~all" so the IP address is still acceptable.
Fail	The sending domain has an SPF record, and the sender's IP isn't listed in it.
None	The sending domain doesn't have a matching SPF record.
TempError	The DNS SPF record couldn't be retrieved because of a temporary problem.
PermError	The DNS SPF record was found, but it's malformed and can't be used.

The soft fail result deserves an additional explanation. You can add "~all" at the end of your SPF record to specify that any other IP address should be treated as a possible match but not a definite one. That essentially means that a spammer who fakes your domain will have its messages tagged as soft fail because their IP addresses don't match the contents of your SPF record. It is a better idea to omit "~all" in your SPF records to force failure of any messages sent from IP addresses not included in your SPF record, although if you change the IP addresses that can originate messages, you must first add them to the SPF record and wait for the record to propagate through DNS.

Microsoft has a fairly extensive discussion of Sender ID available at *http://www.microsoft .com/mscorp/safety/technologies/senderid/default.mspx*. It's well worth a read if you want a better understanding of how the protocol works and what to use it for, although that site's information on Exchange is far out of date.

Content filtering

Content filtering is what most users (and administrators) think of when they think of spam filtering. The Exchange Content Filter agent filters messages based on the contents of the message. You can specify individual words or phrases that should cause the filter to block the message (by setting its SCL to 9) or allow the message (by setting its SCL to –1). These magic words are known as *block* and *allow* phrases, respectively. These phrases are evaluated in addition to the phrase library Microsoft makes available, which Microsoft updates every two weeks and which is downloadable through Microsoft Update.

Except for adding or removing allow or block phrases, you can't do anything to customize the behavior of the Content Filter agent.

Sender reputation

"Sender reputation" sounds like an odd way to evaluate messages, but we all continuously make business and personal judgments based on the reputation of the entity with which we're dealing. The Exchange sender reputation engine uses several factors to calculate a sender reputation level (SRL). This calculation persists over time, so a sender's SRL can change according to the sender's behavior—the sender reputation process learns whether a particular sender is likely to be sending good or bad messages. A good sender can turn bad over time, and a bad sender can likewise reform.

The SRL calculation involves four distinct factors; in this list, remember that "sender" refers to the IP address that's originating the connection request:

- Whether the sender's traffic is being routed through an open proxy server. The sender reputation process determines this by trying to make an outbound proxy connection of its own through the sender's IP address, targeted at the Exchange server itself. If this loopback connection works, the sender is obviously using a proxy, and that's factored into the SRL calculation.

- Whether the sender's initial EHLO/HELO request is legitimate. Does the name provided with the EHLO match a DNS name associated with the IP address? Does this name match the name provided on previous connection attempts? Is the provided name a DNS name or just a local host name or IP address? All these factors are used to evaluate the likelihood that the request is legitimate.

- Whether the sender has correct reverse DNS data for the IP address that contacted the Exchange server. In other words, does a reverse lookup on the IP address return the same name as was presented in the EHLO exchange?

- What the SCL ratings for previous messages from the same sender look like. The ratio of messages with high SCLs to those with low SCLs is included as part of this calculation, as is the number of high-SCL messages originating from the sender in the previous 24 hours.

The SRL value for each sender is an integer from 0 through 9; 0 indicates that the sender is very unlikely to be a spammer, and 9 indicates that he very likely is. The SRL is fed to other parts of the anti-spam filtering pipeline. In particular, you can configure an SRL threshold value that is passed to the Sender Filter agent; that agent will block messages from senders whose SRL exceeds the threshold.

Safe lists and aggregation

Individual users can add senders to their own, mailbox-specific lists of blocked and trusted senders. Through a process known *as safelist aggregation*, Exchange mailbox servers can read individual users' lists and combine their contents into an organization-wide block or allow list the Content Filter and Sender Filtering agents evaluate. Each Outlook user generates what Microsoft calls a safelist collection that contains a list of up to 1,024 items drawn from the following categories:

- Senders and recipients the user has explicitly marked as safe. The set of these senders and recipients is referred to as the Safe Senders list.

- Senders the user has explicitly marked as blocked. The set of these items is known as the Blocked Senders list.

- Domains the user has explicitly decided to trust. These domains aren't normally included in aggregation because a single clueless user who adds a large ISP domain (such as *@comcast.com or *@freemail.fr) might accidentally expose the entire organization to spam originating from those domains.

- Contacts from the user's Contacts folder. Aggregated contacts from sources such as LinkedIn and Facebook aren't included.

- Addresses to which the user has sent mail. The assumption is that replies from those addresses should be treated as legitimate mail.

Exchange uses the SHA-256 hash algorithm to store hashes of these items rather than the full text of the items. The Junk Email Options mailbox assistant gathers these hashes and writes them to three attributes on users' Active Directory accounts: msExchSafeSenderHash, msExchSafeRecipientHash, and msExchBlockedSendersHash. The values of these attributes are aggregated on each mailbox server then used during filtering; the email address of the sender is hashed and compared against the hashed values stored in the aggregated Safe Senders and Blocked Senders lists. If a match is found, Exchange can immediately handle the message without further filtering, either exempting it from further filtering or blocking it. If you're using the Exchange edge role or the EOP service, those hashes are transferred as part of the synchronization process. Because only the hashes and not the addresses themselves are transferred, an attacker who compromises the external edge or EOP server doesn't get any useful address data.

Enabling anti-spam filtering on mailbox servers

Now that you understand how the anti-spam agents do their work, it's time to point out that they are disabled by default on all mailbox servers. This is fine if you have external services or devices filtering your email stream; if not, or if you want an additional layer of filtering, you'll need to enable the anti-spam agents on the mailbox servers. Microsoft provides a script to do this—Install-AntiSpamAgents.ps1 is installed in the Exchange scripts directory and can be run at any time to add the anti-spam transport agents to the transport agent pipeline on a mailbox server. After running the script, you need to restart the Exchange transport service before the agents start doing their work.

After installing the agents, you must use Set-TransportConfig –InternalSMTPServers to specify the IP addresses of any internal SMTP servers in your organization that will be sending mail to Exchange. The IP addresses you specify are exempted from Sender ID checks—a good thing, given that they would probably fail such checks if they were done, thus needlessly marking messages from your internal servers as possible spam.

The spam filtering pipeline

The Exchange filtering mechanism is implemented as a set of transport agents. As you learned in the "Transport architecture" section of Chapter 2, transport agents are chunks of code that run in a preset order when fired by particular kinds of SMTP events. Rather than worry about the specific priority and event associated with each of the anti-spam agents, it's simpler just to consider them in order. Running the Get-TransportAgent cmdlet on a mailbox server that has the anti-spam agents installed reveals the order:

```
[PS] C:\Windows\system32>Get-TransportAgent
```

Identity	Enabled	Priority
Transport Rule Agent	True	1
Malware Agent	True	2
Text Messaging Routing Agent	True	3
Text Messaging Delivery Agent	True	4
Content Filter Agent	True	5
Sender Id Agent	True	6
Sender Filter Agent	True	7
Recipient Filter Agent	True	8
Protocol Analysis Agent	True	9

Chapter 5

The Transport Rule agent has to run first to ensure that messages are journaled (or other-wise processed by transport rules as appropriate), and then the Malware Filter agent runs. Then the Content Filter, Sender ID, Sender Filter, and Recipient Filter agents run, followed by the Protocol Analysis agent. This last step is when the SRL is computed, although earlier stages in the pipeline can use the previously computed SRL values for a sender.

Controlling protocol filtering

Each of the protocol filtering steps has its own set of cmdlets for managing its settings. None of these settings is exposed in EAC. Luckily, though, most spam filtering settings are infrequently changed because the Content Filter does most of the heavy lifting, and its set-tings are automatically updated through Microsoft Update.

Controlling connection filtering

The only real control you have over connection filtering is by manipulating the allow and block lists. (The edge role has some additional controls, but these didn't make it into the consolidated Exchange 2013 roles.) You can apply this control in one of four ways:

- You can manage individual entries on the lists with the Add-, Get-, and Remove-IPAllowListEntry and –IPBlockListEntry cmdlets. For example, running Add-IPAllowListEntry –IPRange 216.82.250.0/24 cmdlet results in the following output:

```
Identity        IPRange              ExpirationTime            HasExpired
--------        -------              --------------            ----------
   2            216.82.250.0/24      12/31/9999 3:59:59 PM     False
```

To create an entry, you may specify a single IP address or a range (either by using CIDR notation, as in this example, or by specifying start and end addresses). When you create the entry, you can also provide a comment and an expiration time after which the entry is automatically removed. You can't modify allow or block list entries individually after you've added them; if you get something wrong, you have to delete the individual entry and re-add it.

- You can specify list providers that Exchange will query. Examples of well-known list provider services include Spamhaus (*http://www.spamhaus.org/sbl*) and DNSBL (*http://www.dnsbl.info*). To use a provider, first you have to create a provider by using the Add-IPAllowListProvider or Add-IPBlockListProvider cmdlet. This requires you to specify the name of the list provider, the DNS server the provider requires you to use, and whether the provider will return explicit status codes or a bitmask indicating why the target server is on the list. Normally, you'll use the –AnyMatch:$true parameter for block list providers to indicate that you want to treat any answer from the server as an indication that you shouldn't be accepting mail from that particular IP address. You can also use Add-IPBlockListProvider –RejectionResponse to specify a custom string that will be delivered as part of the "now go away" message that Exchange returns as part of the SMTP conversation when a sender's IP appears on the block list. Many sites set the custom message to a short phrase including the URL of the RBL provider so that senders whose messages are inadvertently blocked know what to do about it. There are corresponding Get-, Set-, Remove-, and Test- cmdlets for both allow and block lists, too.

- You can change the configuration that applies to the allow or block lists themselves with the Set-IPAllowListConfig and Set-IPBlockListConfig cmdlets. You can enable or disable the use of the server-specific block list by using the –Enable switch; when filtering is enabled, you can further control whether the allow or block list is used for external or internal email with the ExternalMailEnabled and InternalMailEnabled switches.

  The Set-IPBlockListConfig cmdlet adds two parameters specific to block lists. You can configure separate text responses that are returned when the message is rejected. The –MachineEntryRejectionResponse text is included in the NDR generated when a block list entry based on SRL scoring rejects a message, whereas the text specified in –StaticEntryRejectionResponse is sent back as an SMTP response when the connection is blocked because of an entry on the block list.

- You can change the settings that configure how Exchange uses allow or block list providers by using the Set-IPBlockListProvidersConfig and Set-IPAllowListProvidersConfig cmdlets. With either type of list, you can turn the use of providers on or off with the –Enabled switch; you can also set whether the block or allow list providers you've specified should be used for internal mail, external mail, both, or neither. To accomplish this, use the –ExternalMailEnabled ($true by default) and –InternalMailEnabled ($false by default) switches. The Set-IPBlockListProvidersConfig also has an additional switch; -BypassedRecipients accepts a multivalued list containing the SMTP addresses of senders whose mail should never be filtered, even if the originating address fails a provider list check.

Controlling recipient filtering

Exchange can perform two types of recipient filtering. First, it can use an administrator-defined, site-specific list of recipients that should never receive external email. Microsoft often cites the example of an internal help desk address, which outside senders can't use and which therefore shouldn't receive Internet email. Second, it can look up recipients in the Global Address List (GAL) to verify that they exist, rejecting or ignoring any message sent to a nonexistent recipient. Unlike connection filtering, which can take place without any reference to the organization's Active Directory, recipient filtering benefits greatly from being able to look up recipients in Active Directory; this is a key part of the value offered by the Edge Server role in Exchange 2007 and Exchange 2010.

You use the Get- and Set-RecipientFilterConfig cmdlets to manage recipient filter behavior. Start with something simple: disabling the recipient filter altogether. It's enabled by default, but you can disable it using the –Enabled:$false switch, although this leaves the Recipient Filter agent in the transport pipeline.

After recipient filtering is enabled, you can choose whether it applies to internal or external email by using the InternalMailEnabled and ExternalMailEnabled switches, the same as connection filtering. You can also specify blocked recipients by specifying a comma-separated list to the –BlockedRecipient switch (for instance, Set-RecipientFilterConfig –BlockedRecipient helpdesk@contoso.com,CEO@contoso.com) and setting the –BlockListEnabled flag to $True. By default, recipient blocking is turned off, which is okay because it's not a terribly useful feature for most organizations.

The most useful setting for Set-RecipientFilterConfig is probably –RecipientValidationEnabled; when it's set to $True, the Recipient Filter agent performs directory lookups for each recipient specified in an RCPT TO command, rejecting or blocking messages to nonexistent senders.

Controlling sender filtering

Sender filtering is enabled by default on servers that have the anti-spam agents installed; you manage its enablement and its other settings by using the Set-SenderFilterConfig command. The –Enabled, –ExternalMailEnabled, and –InternalMailEnabled switches work the same as they do for connection and recipient filtering.

Set-SenderFilterConfig has three groups of options you can use to do the following:

- You can control which domains, subdomains, and senders are blocked using (respectively) the –BlockedDomains, –BlockedDomainsAndSubdomains, and –BlockedSenders parameters. Each of these can accept up to 800 domains or sender names; you probably won't need that many because you can use the * wildcard for senders. (For instance, *@contoso.com will block all senders originating at the Contoso domain.)

- You can control what happens when a message triggers the filter. It can be rejected, or the sender filter can stamp the message status on the message. The –Action switch sets this behavior.

- You can block messages based on the sender. To block messages in which the sender name is blank, use the –BlankSenderBlockingEnabled flag. To block messages sent by senders who appear on the aggregated Blocked Senders list, set

–BlankSenderBlockingEnabled to either Delete or Reject, depending on whether you want the message to generate an NDR or silently disappear.

Controlling the use of Sender ID

Sender ID was designed to be flexible because Microsoft realized that the usefulness of having a protocol to help verify senders' information had to be weighed against the fact that many senders wouldn't or couldn't adopt it, so that automatically blocking mail from sending systems that don't use Sender ID would result in high numbers of false positives. The key aspect of this flexibility is that the Sender ID agent persists information about the nature of the failure when a message fails a Sender ID check so that later stages in the pipeline can use that information to decide what to do.

These failures come in two flavors. First, the Sender ID agent might think that the message comes from a sender who's spoofing its domain information; this can happen when the sender has a misconfigured Sender ID record. It might otherwise be because she is actually a spammer. Second, the Sender ID agent might be temporarily unable to fetch the Sender ID SPF record for a domain, usually because of a DNS failure.

You configure the Sender ID agent's behavior with the Set-SenderIdConfig cmdlet.

The Sender ID agent understands three actions: it can stamp the Sender ID status of the message on the message (the default behavior), it can reject the message with a 5xx SMTP error, or it can silently delete the message. You can specify separate actions for outright failures (corresponding to a status of Fail in Table 5-1) and temporary failures (corresponding to TempError in Table 5-1) with the SpoofedDomainAction and TempErrorAction parameters to Set-SenderIdConfig.

As with most of the other filtering agents, you can specify senders or recipients whose mail should be exempted from Sender ID filtering, in this case by using the BypassedRecipients and BypassedSenderDomains parameters to Set-SenderIdConfig.

Microsoft has also provided the Test-SenderId cmdlet, which provides a simple way of testing to see what Exchange would do when given a particular combination of IP address and domain. To see how this works, examine the Microsoft SPF configuration:

```
[PS] C:\Windows\system32>nslookup
 Default Server:  pao-dc01.betabasement.com

   Address:  10.0.0.100

> set query=txt
> microsoft.com
```

```
Server:  pao-dc01.betabasement.com
Address: 10.0.0.100
Non-authoritative answer:
microsoft.com   text =

        "v=spf1 include:_spf-a.microsoft.com include:_spf-b.microsoft.com
include:_spf-c.microsoft.com include:_spf-ssg-
 a.microsoft.com ip4:131.107.115.215 ip4:131.107.115.214 ip4:205.248.106.64
ip4:205.248.106.30 ip4:205.248.106.32 ~all"
```

The SPF record lists five explicit IP addresses plus "~all" as possible origins for messages. If
you use Test-SenderId with one of those IP addresses, you should get a pass:

```
[PS] C:\Windows\system32>Test-SenderID -IPAddress 131.107.115.215
-PurportedResponsibleDomain microsoft.com


    RunspaceId    : 520d4a86-610f-4f22-b14d-97655e1840ca
    Status        : Pass
    FailReason    : None
    Explanation   :
```

Sure enough, that IP address passes. Try another IP address. 65.55.57.27 is one of the IP
addresses associated with *http://www.microsoft.com*.

```
[PS] C:\Windows\system32>Test-SenderID -IPAddress 65.55.57.27
-PurportedResponsibleDomain apple.com


    RunspaceId    : 520d4a86-610f-4f22-b14d-97655e1840ca
    Status        : SoftFail
    FailReaso     : None
    Explanation   :
```

Not surprisingly, doing a Sender ID check of a Microsoft IP address against the apple.com
domain generates a failure—in this case, it's a soft fail because Apple's SPF record includes
"~all". However, IBM's SPF record only contains "-all", meaning that no IP address that is not
specifically listed is authorized to send mail for the ibm.com domain. Testing the Sender ID
agent against it, then, should produce a failure:

```
[PS] C:\Windows\system32>test-senderid -ipaddress 65.55.57.27
-PurportedResponsibleDomain ibm.com


    RunspaceId    : 520d4a86-610f-4f22-b14d-97655e1840ca
    Status        : Fail
    FailReason    : NotPermitted
    Explanation   :
```

Controlling content filtering

Content filtering is the area of Exchange anti-spam filtering in which administrators have the most direct control over what the filter agent is looking for. You can change the way the filter operates by setting trigger phrases that bias the filter for or against certain messages or by setting SCL thresholds that force the filter to take certain actions based on the message SCL. You can also enable or disable the filter altogether or control whether it's applied to internal or external messages by using the familiar –Enabled, –InternalMailEnabled, and –ExternalMailEnabled arguments to Set-ContentFilterConfig.

Use Set-ContentFilterConfig to exempt recipients, senders, or domains from filtering using the –BypassedRecipients, –BypassedSenderDomains, and –BypassedSenders parameters. A message originating from a bypassed sender or domain or sent to a bypassed recipient will automatically be exempted from further content filtering.

Adding trigger phrases to the content filter

By using the Add- and Remove-ContentFilterPhrase cmdlets, you can manage the list of phrases or terms the filter looks for. When you add a content filter phrase, you must specify the phrase and whether you want to treat it as a good or bad influence. This isn't metaphorical; you actually use the –Influence GoodWord or –Influence BadWord parameters to Add-ContentFilterPhrase. Setting a phrase as good automatically marks any messages containing it with an SCL of 0 (guaranteed nonspam), whereas a message containing a phrase marked as a bad influence receives an SCL of 9.

Setting SCL-based behavior

The Content Filter agent can take action based on the SCL of a message. To be more specific, there are three possible actions for messages: the message can be quarantined, it can be rejected with an NDR, or it can be deleted without an NDR. Each of these actions is independently controlled and has its own SCL level. For example, you can specify that messages with an SCL of 6 should be quarantined, and messages with an SCL of 7 or above should be rejected with this command:

```
Set-ContentFilterConfig –SCLQuarantineEnabled $true –SCLQuarantineThreshold 6
  –SCLRejectEnabled $true –SCLRejectThreshold 7 –QuarantineMailbox junk@contoso.com
  –RejectionResponse "Contoso does not accept spam messages"
```

Note that this command enables the SCL quarantine and rejection behaviors, sets thresholds for them both, and adds an optional message that's included in the NDR returned to the sender. Because you've enabled quarantine, you must also include the SMTP address of the quarantine mailbox you want to use.

Chapter 5

Controlling sender reputation filtering

The Set-SenderReputationConfig cmdlet is the only means of controlling how sender reputation filtering actually works. It has a lot in common with Set-ContentFilterConfig; both cmdlets enable or disable filtering for internal or external mail, and both cmdlets provide a way to block or reject messages based on a computed score indicating their likelihood of being spam. Because the sender reputation filter uses SRLs as its metric for whether a message is good or bad, there are some terminology differences, but the intent is basically the same.

Blocking messages from disreputable senders

Probably the most common use for Set-SenderReputationConfig is enabling the blocking of messages from senders with poor reputation scores. To be more specific, you can block messages from senders whose systems are open proxies. Separately, you can adjust the SRL threshold at which the sender reputation is considered bad, but this doesn't actually block anything—it just biases the SRL input that is used when filtering messages.

This command enables SRL-based blocking, sets the SRL blocking threshold to 7, and specifies that any sender whose messages are blocked should be banned for 24 hours:

```
Set-SenderReputationConfig –SenderBlockingEnabled $true –SrlBlockThreshold 7
–SenderBlockingPeriod 24 -OpenProxyDetectionEnabled
```

Checking for proxies

It might seem odd that the preceding sample command includes OpenProxyDetectionEnabled; it is only there because the SenderBlockingEnabled option blocks senders based only on their proxy status. To enable sender blocking, you must also enable open proxy detection. Proxy detection works by trying to get the sender's system to create a proxied connection back to your Exchange server, meaning that your Exchange server is initiating an outbound connection itself. Because this might require the Exchange server to traverse a proxy server itself, Set-SenderReputationConfig includes parameters for setting the outbound proxy server name, port, and type—ProxyServerName, ProxyServerPort, and ProxyServerType, respectively.

Controlling how Exchange interacts with client-side junk mail filtering

As you learned earlier in this chapter, Outlook has its own built-in junk mail filtering system. It can operate by itself, but it can also work in conjunction with the sender-side and organization-side filtering built into Exchange. For example, an individual Outlook user's list of blocked and safe senders can be consumed through the safelist aggregation process described earlier so that her filtering settings are applied globally. The user's specific settings are shared and used by Outlook 2007, Outlook 2010, Outlook 2013, Outlook Web App 2010, and Outlook Web App 2013.

The Outlook junk mail filter (JMF) is actually implemented as a hidden server-side rule; when users change their Blocked Senders or Safe Senders lists, the addresses they specify are modified on the rule itself. Because the size of individual server-side rules is limited to 512 KB, the number of items users can add to their Blocked Senders and Safe Senders lists varies; they get a total of 512 KB of space for both those categories. Although this gives users a great deal of flexibility and individual control, it is often useful for administrators to be able to see and change user-level junk filtering settings. For that reason, Microsoft has provided the Get/Set-MailboxJunkEmailConfiguration cmdlets, which enable administrators to make changes to an individual user's blocked and trusted domains and senders and to a few additional related settings.

> ## Note
>
> In the rare case that a user's junk mail rule becomes corrupted, you might notice that messages are being mishandled. The notable symptom of such corruption is that previously trusted senders or domains are suddenly being treated as spam. To fix this, the simplest solution is to use MFCMAPI to remove the user's junk mail rule altogether; the next time he launches Outlook or opens Outlook Web App, the rule is re-created, although without the Blocked Senders and Safe Senders list items. You can also use the Update-Safelist –EnsureJunkEmailRule switch to enable the junk mail rule forcibly if it is somehow turned off.

The TrustedSendersAndDomains and BlockedSendersAndDomains properties are multi-valued and contain the corresponding list of senders and domains you want to manage. Because they're multivalued, you can most easily manipulate them by storing their value in a temporary variable, making the changes you want, and then putting them back, like this:

```
$Temp = Get-MailboxJunkEmailConfiguration "David Alexander"
$Temp.TrustedSendersAndDomains += "microsoft.com"
$Temp.BlockedSendersAndDomains += "thephone-company.com"
Set-MailboxJunkEmailConfiguration -Identity "davida" -TrustedSendersAndDomains
$Temp.TrustedSendersAndDomains -BlockedSendersAndDomains
$Temp.BlockedSendersAndDomains
```

Besides modifying the trusted and blocked lists the rule uses, you can control the use of the junk mail rule in these ways:

- The –Enabled switch controls whether the rule is evaluated at all; set it to $False to turn off the Outlook junk mail rule altogether. Note that this doesn't turn off the Outlook JMF completely—content-based filtering will still occur.

Chapter 5

- If you set –TrustedListsOnly to $True, the junk mail rule will reject mail from any sender or domain that isn't on the TrustedSendersAndDomains list. This is a quick way to filter mail to mailboxes that random senders shouldn't be able to reach.

- The ContactsTrusted switch controls whether the contents of users' Contacts folders are to be treated as trusted. This is set to $True by default.

It's also worth mentioning the Update-SafeList cmdlet in this context. Normally, safelist aggregation happens automatically. However, if you need to force an aggregation update immediately, Update-SafeList is the way to make it happen. The cmdlet pulls the Safe Senders and Blocked Senders lists from the specified mailbox, hashes the addresses as previously described, and updates the aggregated lists used throughout the Exchange organization. You can specify the Universal Principal Name (UPN) or primary SMTP address of the mailbox you want to update as the first parameter to Update-SafeList, or you can use Get-Mailbox (with appropriate selection and filtering) to pick a set of mailboxes whose safelist data you want to update.

Working with quarantined messages

If you choose to allow incoming spam to be quarantined, you are essentially assuming the responsibility of reviewing tons of spam messages and forwarding those that are actually acceptable to the intended sender by using the Send Again feature in Outlook, which redirects mail instead of forwarding it. When you enable quarantining of spam messages in Exchange, messages whose SCL is at or above the quarantine threshold you set with Set-ContentFilterConfig –SCLQuarantineThreshold are redirected to the quarantine mailbox. Quarantined messages are attached to NDRs that Exchange sends, so when you view them in the quarantine mailbox, all quarantined messages have the same sender—your organization's postmaster address.

Microsoft recommends that you create a dedicated Exchange mailbox database for the quarantine mailbox. Given that Exchange 2013 is designed to accommodate mailboxes of 100 GB or larger, this strikes me as overkill unless you expect very high volumes of spam. Whether or not you create a separate database for it, you need to create a quarantine mailbox and associated user account. You can set mailbox quotas, retention limits, and so on for the quarantine mailbox just as you would for any other mailbox type.

After the mailbox is created, you can instruct Exchange to start using it with Set-ContentFilterConfig, which you must use to enable quarantine and to specify the SMTP address of the quarantine mailbox. The following command performs both of these steps and sets the quarantine SCL to 6:

```
Set-ContentFilterConfig –SCLQuarantineEnabled $true –QuarantineMailbox
spam@betabasement.com –SCLQuarantineThreshold 6
```

After you have run Set-ContentFilterConfig to enable the use of the quarantine mailbox, the spam will start to pile up. The quarantined messages will all have the same sender unless you follow the steps at *http://technet.microsoft.com/en-us/library/ee861109(v=exchg.150) .aspx* to create a new Outlook form that shows the original sender, which is stored as a property in the message. (Note that this procedure works only for Outlook 2007, Outlook 2010, and Outlook 2013, not for Outlook for Mac OS X or Outlook Web App.)

You can log on to the quarantine mailbox by creating a dedicated Outlook profile, adding the quarantine mailbox as an additional mailbox to your existing profile, or granting yourself delegate access to the mailbox; of course, you can also open the mailbox in Outlook Web App, but then you won't be able to view the original message sender.

You might find that you need to adjust the SCL quarantine threshold, too, if your filter is catching too many or too few messages. Keep in mind that as you change the quarantine threshold, you might also need to change other filtering thresholds to keep the various categories of mail going where you want them to go.

Unified messaging

U nified messaging (UM) is a topic that deserves a complete book in its own right; designing, implementing, and maintaining a complete unified communications system often requires the wisdom of Solomon, the patience of Job, and the technical acumen and troubleshooting skills of a master administrator. A great deal of negotiation and coordination must normally occur between the teams responsible for telecommunications and messaging within the company to ensure a smooth integration between the existing private branch exchange (PBX) system and the Exchange Server server and client components that deliver UM functionality.

The Microsoft vision for Exchange UM covers two related but separate aspects of information access. First, Exchange makes voice mail data equal to all the other data types Exchange can store, such as email, calendar items, and contacts. Voice mail messages are stored in the same way, processed and viewed using the same tools, and administered in exactly the same manner as every other mailbox-based item. In any client that can show you email, whether on a smart phone, tablet, or computer, you should be as able to see and work with voice mail messages as with another data type. Second, Exchange provides telephone-based access to your Inbox, calendar, and contact data. You can use the Outlook Voice Access (OVA) application to call your Exchange server, read and send email, interact with your calendar, and do a fair amount of productive work by using either speech recognition or dual-tone multifrequency (DTMF, also known as Touch-Tone) tones from your phone's keypad.

Both these aspects depend on being able to connect an Exchange UM server to a telephone system in some way, and that's where the majority of the complexity in UM deployment and management arises. The UM service itself is largely a self-tuning black box with relatively few adjustments or settings for you to manage after it has been deployed.

If you've already deployed UM with Exchange 2007 or Exchange 2010, the Exchange 2013 UM feature set will look very familiar. The Microsoft documentation coyly says, "The Unified Messaging feature set in Exchange 2013 is similar to previous versions of Exchange." That is a completely true statement; all the features listed in the "Major Exchange UM features" section later in this chapter existed in Exchange 2010. The primary change in Exchange 2013 is that the UM feature is no longer a separate role; its features have been divided between the Client Access Server (CAS) and Mailbox roles. Luckily, this architectural change is invisible to end users, and, in fact, is mostly invisible to administrators. UM now supports the use of Internet Protocol version 6 (IPv6). Apart from these changes, Exchange 2013 UM features are mostly just improvements on their Exchange 2010 counterparts.

A quick introduction to Exchange UM

The simplest way to think of Exchange 2013 UM functionality is this—it answers the phone. Everything else Exchange UM does derives from this simple functional statement. As you read this chapter, keep in mind that Exchange doesn't route phone calls, provide enterprise voice (EV) services, or perform any of the other tasks associated with PBX systems. Lync and Skype are the Microsoft solutions for providing voice calling, call routing, and interfaces to the worldwide phone network. All Exchange UM does is answer the phone and, optionally, enable the caller to leave a message; however, it does so with a wide array of customizable options and features.

Major Exchange UM features

Any discussion of Exchange UM must necessarily start with a discussion of what it does after it answers the phone; this prepares the ground for a deeper exploration of how the magic happens. Exchange UM has several major features that are worth exploring in more detail:

- Call answering is the core of Exchange UM. Exchange can answer calls in two basic ways. When someone calls a specific UM-enabled mailbox, Exchange can answer the call and enable the caller leave a message, or Exchange can answer all calls, play an audio menu to the caller, and let him choose a destination for the call by voice or DTMF input.

- Voice mail messages, after they are collected, are delivered to the recipient's mailbox server, whereupon they are treated like any other email message, with a few exceptions. Microsoft Outlook 2007, Outlook 2010, and Outlook 2013 have a custom add-in that provides some extra functionality, including the ability to play a voice mail message on the local computer's audio or to have the UM server call a user-specified phone number and play the message (a capability known as Play on Phone).

- Automated attendants provide a system for customizing call handling by giving callers a menu of options accessible through speech or DTMF input. Each menu option can route the call to a specific target or chain to another menu. By using this feature, you can build reasonably complex phone menus to answer incoming calls.

- Outlook Voice Access (OVA) is the voice equivalent of Outlook Web App or Outlook; it provides a telephone user interface (TUI) that enables UM-enabled users to interact with the contents of their mailboxes through the phone. You can have OVA read your email to you, after which you can reply to, delete, or move messages; you can also have OVA place outbound calls for you to other UM users (or, indeed, any number associated with a personal contact or a user in the Global Address List [GAL]). This makes it possible to call OVA and have it connect you to any user in the GAL, even if you don't have that phone number in your Contacts folder.

- Directory access and dial by name offer speech recognition of user and distribution group names. When combined with OVA and automated attendants, callers can tell Exchange whom they wish to speak to, using only the recipient's name instead of laboriously spelling out a name by using DTMF.

- Voice Mail Preview provides a quick text rendition of a voice mail message. It's intended to enable you to evaluate the importance and content of a voice mail quickly without having to listen to it; it is not intended to provide perfect accuracy.

- Exchange can light up or extinguish a message-waiting indicator (MWI), the little visible (or audible) indicator on some phones that signals the presence of an unheard voice mail message. MWI support is cleverly implemented using the familiar search folder mechanism, and it doesn't require (or allow) much configuration.

- Protected voice mail duplicates the earlier functionality of allowing callers to press a key (usually the asterisk [*]) to mark a message as private; private voice mail messages cannot be forwarded, and administrators can optionally limit the ability of users to play their own messages on arbitrary phones by using Play on Phone. Protected voice mail depends on having a functioning Active Directory Rights Management Services (AD RMS) infrastructure, which might limit its usefulness in the large segment of the Exchange market that doesn't have or want AD RMS.

- Fax support enables Exchange UM to recognize the distinctive sounds (known as calling number–generated tones, or CNG tones) produced by a call from a fax machine. Exchange 2013 doesn't support direct fax reception, but you can specify the URL of an external service to which fax calls can be redirected.

- Multiple language support comes in the form of installable language packs. Each language pack contains pre-recorded audio prompts (such as "After the tone, please record your message"), speech grammar files, automatic speech recognition (ASR) vocabulary files for commands and menu responses, and the necessary data for

transcribing voice mail preview messages. Not every language pack language is supported for voice mail preview.

- Call answering rules use an architecture similar to that of Outlook server-side rules
  to enable users to create rules for handling calls. For example, you can define a rule
  that forwards calls from your child's school automatically to your cell phone if you
  don't answer your office extension. These rules are quite limited in comparison with
  Outlook rules, but with the basic mechanism in place, there's great potential for
  expanding these rules to make them more capable and the tantalizing possibility of
  tying them into the Lync client and server.

Unified messaging concepts

You're probably familiar with most of the vocabulary used in this book to talk about various aspects of Exchange. Even if you're new to the Exchange world, you've used email as a
consumer before, so you know what words such as "message" or "header" refer to. Unified
messaging is intimately related to the often-mysterious world of telephony, though, so
understanding UM requires you to absorb some concepts and vocabulary that might strike
you as foreign.

The unified communications market

Microsoft uses the terms "unified communications" (UC) and "unified messaging" (UM) to
mean very specific things, not always the same things as other vendors who use the same
terms. In the Microsoft world, UC refers to systems that offer Voice over IP (VoIP)–based
voice, video, conferencing, instant messaging, and presence capabilities, often coupled with
email. UM refers specifically to systems that tie together email, calendaring, and voice mail.
In this frame of reference, the various generations of Lync Server are UC products, whereas
Exchange is a UM product.

When Microsoft first introduced Exchange UM in Exchange 2007, its primary competitors
in the UM market were companies that sold PBX systems, such as Avaya, Nortel, and Mitel.
These companies were interested in retaining the market share and revenue derived from
selling dedicated voice mail systems that plugged in to older PBXs. The Microsoft argument
was that, because Exchange 2007 UM integrated voice mail with companies' existing investments in Exchange servers, tools, and infrastructure, it provided both superior functionality
and lower capital and operating costs than older voice mail systems, an argument it won
handily. The Microsoft argument was especially effective for companies that were already in
the process of moving to VoIP-based systems and away from older PBX systems. However,
the market has shifted so that many former, older PBX vendors have moved into offering
more broadly integrated UC systems; for example, Cisco offers a broad portfolio of conferencing, voice, video, and messaging services under its Cisco UC umbrella. At the same time,
the market for PBX systems has largely shifted away from proprietary, hardware-based

systems such as those formerly sold by Nortel, Lucent, and Siemens to software-based PBXs from vendors such as Digium, 3CX, and Microsoft.

Microsoft makes much of the fact that Exchange UM is PBX-agnostic. It requires a PBX that speaks a few common protocols over Transmission Control Protocol (TCP); a broad variety of gateways and adapters can connect most PBXs built within the past 15 years or so to Exchange. However, one common reason customers give for not adopting Exchange UM is that they don't want to lose the value of their existing PBX or voice mail system—an objection that ignores both the cost savings and productivity upside of Exchange UM.

The exciting world of telephony

When you think about it, the worldwide public switched telephone network (PSTN) is somewhat of an engineering miracle. It provided robust, reliable, widely available inter-networked voice and data communications long before the Internet existed, and it still provides an effective communication method even where Internet service is unreliable or unavailable. Trying to compress every nuance of how the PSTN works, or even the vocabulary needed to describe it fully, into a single chapter of this book would be a losing effort. There are a few key concepts that can help you understand enough about the PSTN and plain old telephone service (POTS, the jokey name for analog service used worldwide by telephony experts) to carry on an intelligent conversation.

First is the notion that voice data is inherently circuit-switched; when Alice calls Bob, the PSTN establishes an end-to-end audio circuit between them through signaling systems that set up the call and provide clocking, billing, and other services to various devices along the call path. This circuit can be established equally well as an analog circuit over ancient copper wiring or as a series of audio packets traveling over fiber, using VoIP.

Second is that voice circuits, often referred to as trunks, can be aggregated. The T-1 line standard with which you might be familiar is actually 24 individual channels, each capable of carrying 64 Kbps of data—but 8 Kbps of each channel may be used for signaling, making 56 Kbps of each channel available for data. A wide variety of devices are used to convert between T-1-style channelized lines (and the equivalent E-1 and J-1 standards used outside North America) and digital systems, including both older and VoIP phone systems.

Third is the notion of a PBX: a private branch exchange or phone switch. The simplest way to think of a PBX is as a dedicated phone server. Modern software PBXs such as Microsoft Lync have largely replaced the proprietary dedicated PBX systems formerly sold by companies including Lucent, Avaya, and Nortel. However, the concept of the PBX remains relevant because the PBX is responsible for receiving incoming calls, routing them, and enabling users (or Exchange UM) to place outbound calls. Older PBX systems use a variety of signaling and modulation protocols to communicate with one another and with vendor-specific analog or digital telephones; chief among them is the QSIG protocol. Most of these protocols rely on time-division multiplexing (TDM), which is why older PBX systems are often referred to as TDM PBXs.

An individual PBX might use older protocols such as QSIG, or it might implement VoIP. In the latter case, it's an IP PBX. AudioCodes, Dialogic, Quintum, and NET make gateways that convert between older PBX systems and VoIP. To connect a PBX to Exchange 2013 UM, the PBX must either speak VoIP protocols natively over TCP (not UDP) or have a gateway that can do so on its behalf.

Microsoft maintains a list of gateways on TechNet at *http://technet.microsoft.com/en-us /library/ee364753(v=exchg.141).aspx*. The current version lists nine gateways that are supported for use with Exchange 2010; as of this writing, there is no separate list for gateways supported with Exchange 2013.

Another interesting concept is the idea of the extension. This is just a phone number. In the POTS world, an individual number is assigned to an individual device. Your cell phone and home phone, for instance, have two distinct numbers. An extension is a distinct identifier assigned to a particular device on a PBX. If Alice and Bob both work for the same company and are on the same PBX, they must have different extension numbers. However, if Alice works in Austin and Bob works in Birmingham, and each office has its own PBX, both may have the same extension—calls for each user must be routed to the appropriate PBX by some other means. Every UM object that can receive a call, including users, automated attendants, OVA, and UM servers themselves, has a unique extension the PBX must be able to reach. Notice that I didn't describe extensions as being numbers—they might be numeric, but they do not have to be.

The PBX needs a list of extensions that are attached to it and instructions on what to do if an extension is busy or remains unanswered when the PBX sends a call to it. This is often known as a call coverage map; think of it as a table with three columns: the extension number, where to transfer the call if the extension is busy, and where to transfer the call if the extension isn't answered. Some PBX systems have additional call routing features that work in the same general fashion, but this chapter is most interested in the no-answer and busy features.

Finally, it's important to understand number normalization or at least a little of it. The International Telecommunications Union (ITU) has published a standard known as E.164 that specifies how PSTN numbers should be formatted to enable seamless international dialing. E.164 numbers start with the optional string, Tel:, and are formatted to contain a plus sign, a country code, and whatever digits are required to identify that particular endpoint uniquely within the specified country. For example, the Microsoft main telephone number in the United States is Tel: +14258828080; the UK equivalent is +448448002400. Exchange doesn't normalize any numbers itself (although Lync can), but many UM features, such as calling line ID resolution, benefit from having numbers that are consistently formatted.

The Session Initiation Protocol (SIP)

The Session Initiation Protocol (SIP) is described in RFC 3261. If you take the time to read that RFC, you see that SIP is a protocol intended for use in signaling—the process of allowing two endpoints to establish a communications channel, negotiate settings, and exchange information about the communications—but not necessarily to communicate! The gateway devices mentioned in the preceding section convert between earlier protocols and SIP for call setup and teardown.

SIP has three primary functions:

- **Name translation and user location**   To provide a way for an endpoint to resolve a SIP address such as sip:paul@blackdotpub.com to a device or endpoint and to make sure sessions get to the right place.

- **Feature negotiation**   To provide a way for all participating devices in a given session to find the greatest common feature set. In the SIP world, this often involves negotiating which media types (voice, IM, video, and so on) an endpoint can provide and consume and the encoding and decoding methods (or codecs) it can use for any specific media type.

- **Participant management**   To allow endpoints to establish and terminate sessions and add, drop, transfer, or hold participants after a session is established.

As a protocol, SIP is straightforward; it looks a lot like SMTP and uses error codes and verbs in much the same way SMTP and HTTP do. The primary verbs of interest in Exchange UM conversations are:

- INVITE, which is used to initiate a session. When the PBX sends a call to Exchange to be answered, it does so by sending the INVITE verb.

- OPTIONS, which any endpoint in a session can use to express a preference or make a request to other endpoints in the session.

- NOTIFY, which an endpoint uses to tell another device that some interesting event has taken place. Endpoints can subscribe to notifications or send unsolicited notifications to any other endpoint they can reach.

Chapter 6

SIP conversations can also include headers. Here's an example showing a SIP invite from an IP PBX to an Exchange server:

```
INVITE sip:1001@10.0.0.101;user=phone SIP/2.0
Via: SIP/2.0/TCP 10.0.0.10:49629;branch=z9hG4bK
-13638de067f3d256802514fc072117b8;rport
From: "Alice" <sip:1002@pbx.contoso.com;user=phone>;tag=968
To: "Bob" <sip:1001@pbx.contoso.com;user=phone>
Call-ID: 235bc386@pbx
CSeq: 7107 INVITE
Max-Forwards: 70
Contact: <sip:1002@10.0.0.10:49629;transport=tcp>
Supported: 100rel, replaces, norefersub
Allow-Events: refer
Allow: INVITE, ACK, CANCEL, BYE, REFER, PRACK, INFO, UPDATE
Accept: application/sdp
User-Agent: snomONE/5.0.3
Diversion: <tel:1001>;reason=unavailable;screen=no;privacy=off
P-Asserted-Identity: "Exchange" <sip:10.0.0.101>
Content-Type: application/sdp
Content-Length: 321
```

The From and To headers are self-explanatory, although their format is a bit different from what you might be used to. Instead of an SMTP address, these headers contain an address in the form of a SIP uniform resource identifier, or URI. The URI has two parts, as does an SMTP address. The left side of the URI identifies a unique endpoint such as a user or a phone. This can be expressed as a phone number or a SIP address (such as paul or conf-room-102). The right side identifies the host or domain that services the endpoint. This can be an IP address or Domain Name System (DNS) name for a specific device, such as a PBX, or it can be a domain (such as contoso.com) that can be further resolved. SIP URIs can also contain other parameters such as a specific port number. In the current case, the SIP URIs that Exchange is receiving also contain a context indicating that the user's calling from a phone; PBX adds this context, and Exchange is free to ignore it, which it does.

Perhaps the most important header shown in the preceding block is the Diversion header. It signals who the call is actually directed to. Say that Alice, at extension 1001, called Bob, at extension 2002. Bob didn't answer, so the PBX sent a SIP INVITE to Exchange UM (which is the invite that's shown here). The PBX must use the Diversion header to indicate that the call is really for Bob. You'll see more about how this works when call flow is discussed in the "What happens when the phone rings" section later in this chapter. The Diversion header can also indicate a reason Exchange is getting the call. In this case, the reason field has a value of *unavailable*, indicating that there are no devices on which Bob is signed in—as will be the case for a softphone user who isn't signed in anywhere. Other values here could include *no-answer* or *busy*.

The SIP structure permits many other headers that look familiar such as the Content-Type and Call-ID headers. Call-ID is of particular interest because it contains a unique ID for this specific call. Just as you can trace the path of a message through your Exchange system by looking at the Message-ID header on various servers, the Call-ID header enables you to trace calls as they traverse PBXs and Exchange UM servers. In this case, the Content-Type header at the end indicates an SDP payload, so that should probably be the next topic!

Audio and the Real-Time Protocol (RTP)

The preceding description of SIP focused on its role as a signaling protocol. SIP itself doesn't carry audio data. Instead, SIP endpoints use the Session Description Protocol (SDP) to encode a description of which audio codecs they support. SDP, a text-based protocol defined in RFC 4566, isn't especially interesting to Exchange UM administrators except insofar as they can use it to see which audio codecs the remote PBX supports. The SDP data sent back and forth during the SIP conversation includes information about the IP addresses and ports used for the specified codec and the identity of the codec itself.

In the Alice–Bob conversation example listed earlier, the SDP payload included in the initial INVITE to the Exchange server indicates the codecs the PBX can use:

```
v=0
o=- 41051 41051 IN IP4 10.0.0.10
s=-
c=IN IP4 10.0.0.10
t=0 0
m=audio 60994 RTP/AVP 0 8 9 2 3 101
a=rtpmap:0 pcmu/8000
a=rtpmap:8 pcma/8000
a=rtpmap:9 g722/8000
a=rtpmap:2 g726-32/8000
a=rtpmap:3 gsm/8000
a=rtpmap:101 telephone-event/8000
a=fmtp:101 0-16
a=rtcp-xr:rcvr-rtt=all voip-metrics
a=sendrecv
```

This SDP offer shows that PBX is offering two flavors of G.711 PCM (shown as pcmu and pcma), G.722, GSM, and G.726 as codecs, all at 8 Kbps. Exchange supports only the G.711 audio codec for use with PBXs. (Note that a different set of supported codecs actually records voice mail messages.) There is no way to configure which codec Exchange advertises or accepts in the SDP portion of the SIP conversation; if you have a PBX that doesn't support G.711, you need a router or other device that can transcode from G.711 to whatever your PBX speaks. This is often an issue when Exchange UM is used with Cisco Call Manager (CCM) as the PBX; Exchange doesn't support the G.729 codec that CCM uses by default.

When SDP negotiation is complete, the Real-Time Protocol (RTP) is used to pass audio data back and forth between the UM server and the PBX. RTP is merely a format for carrying audio and video data between compliant endpoints, using a dynamically assigned set of TCP and UDP ports.

Unified messaging objects and attributes

Exchange UM depends on several Active Directory object classes, some of which represent objects in the phone system. Deploying Exchange UM requires you to configure these objects so that they accurately reflect the way your phone system is set up.

UM dial plans

The UM dial plan is analogous to an Active Directory site object. Just as the Active Directory site identifies a collection of subnets that are "near" one another, the UM dial plan identifies a set of PBXs that enable users to dial each other directly by extension number alone. The Exchange 2013 documentation says that "a UM dial plan represents a set of PBXs or IP PBXs that share common user extension numbers." Therefore, all PBXs in a dial plan must have the same number of digits in their extension, and, within a dial plan, all extensions must be unique. You can define one or many dial plans, with each dial plan containing one or more PBX systems.

To create a dial plan from either EAC or the shell, you only need a few things. The first two are very straightforward:

- A name, which may be up to 49 characters long and can't contain punctuation characters. When you create a dial plan, Exchange creates a companion UM mailbox policy named after the dial plan name with Default Policy added.

- The number of digits in the extensions used by the dial plan. You don't specify a range of extensions as part of the dial plan, just the number of digits those extensions use.

The next choice you must make is which type of dial plan to create. The type refers to how extensions are specified; more precisely, the dial plan type indicates how the URIs of callers and recipients are formatted. Which type you choose depends on how the PBXs in the dial plan format extensions; although we normally think of telephone extensions as being simple runs of digits, there actually are three methods of specifying extensions with which to contend:

- Dial plans that use unmodified extensions for dialing should have a type of telephone extension (often abbreviated as just telextn). This dial plan type covers the most common case: users dial three to five digits to reach internal phone numbers, with a prefix digit such as 8 or 9 required to dial numbers out on the PSTN. Extensions formatted using this URI type take the form of Tel:7285 or 7285@*PBX*, in which *PBX* can be either the IP address or FQDN of the PBX. (Of course, any time you specify the FQDN of a PBX, your Exchange servers must be able to resolve it to the correct IP address!)

- SIP URI dial plans are used for interoperability with PBXs that use SIP identifiers in lieu of numeric extensions. The most prominent examples of this type of PBX are the Microsoft Office Communications Server and Lync products; with these and similar systems, calls are placed directly to a user's SIP URI instead of to an actual phone number. As you might guess, this dial plan type is required if you want to integrate Exchange UM with Lync 2010 or Lync 2013. SIP URIs start with the string sip: and contain the user's SIP address plus an optional port such as sip:paulr@blackdotpub.com:5060.

- E.164 dial plans are used with PBXs that require, or at least guarantee, that all numbers passed by the PBX to Exchange UM are properly formatted according to the E.164 standard. These URIs are easy to recognize because they look like normal phone numbers, for instance, Tel:+14258828080.

The next decision you face is the level of security to use for the dial plan. The default level, Unsecured, does not encrypt either the SIP signaling data or the RTP audio stream. This is equivalent to the default behavior of SMTP; anyone who can sniff network traffic can see all the SIP headers and can reconstruct the RTP audio stream to recover the contents of voice mail messages. Choosing a security level of SIP Secured tells Exchange to encrypt the SIP signaling but leaves the RTP streams clear. The most secure level is Secured, in which both the SIP and RTP traffic is encrypted. Not every PBX supports all these levels; in particular, Lync refuses to communicate with Exchange UM servers that are in dial plans whose security level is set to Unsecured.

Your choice of dial plan type and security is dictated by the type of PBXs with which the dial plan will be used to communicate. However, bear in mind that secured and unsecured SIP traffic uses two TCP ports; unsecured traffic uses TCP 5060, and secure SIP uses TCP 5061. An Exchange 2013 CAS accepts both secured and unsecured traffic from any type of dial plan; this is known as dual mode. If you want to change this behavior, you may do so with Set-UMCallRouterSettings –UMStartupMode to set the startup mode to either TCP (for unsecured only) or TLS (for secured only) communications.

Each dial plan has a language associated with it. This language controls three things:

- What the pre-recorded system prompts say (such as, "Welcome to Microsoft Exchange Outlook Voice Access," or "Transferring you to the operator"). These prompts are played by the system to the caller in various circumstances and are professionally recorded by voice talent and packaged in UM language packs (more on which in the "Multilingual support in UM" section later in this chapter). The prompt files are located in the V15\Unified Messaging subfolder of the Exchange installation directory; each language has its own subfolder. It is possible to replace these prompt files with your own audio, but Microsoft doesn't support doing so.

- What language the system uses when recognizing spoken audio (known as auto-mated speech recognition, or ASR) and transcribing messages by using voice mail preview. This is important because Exchange doesn't attempt to discover what language the caller is speaking—it merely transcribes the caller's audio according to whatever language the dial plan is set to use. The results of transcribing audio in one language by using rules for a different language range from laughable to incomprehensible.

- What pronunciation and grammar rules are used for performing text to speech (TTS) and name recognition.

When you create a dial plan, you select the language you want the dial plan to use. However, you can pick only from the set of installed language packs—see the "Multilingual support in UM" section later in the chapter for more information on choosing and installing languages.

The final setting required to create a dial plan is the country code PBXs use in that dial plan. The presence of this setting more or less requires your dial plans not to cross international boundaries, which luckily isn't a problematic restriction for most organizations.

After you create a dial plan, you cannot change its extension length or type, its name, or the language it uses. However, you can rename it, change its country code, or change the security level by using the Set-UMDialPlan cmdlet or EAC.

UM dial plans aren't linked to servers—usually

In Exchange 2007 and Exchange 2010, you had to associate each UM server with a dial plan manually. Exchange 2013 removes that requirement because any Exchange 2013 UM server can accept calls from any defined UM IP gateway anywhere on your network. However, if you're using Office Communications Server (OCS) 2007 R2 or Lync as your IP PBX, you need to add your Exchange 2013 CAS and mailbox servers to the SIP dial plan on the Lync side for Lync to communicate with Exchange UM.

After creating a dial plan, you must configure it before you can use it. The "Dial plan settings" section later in the chapter describes the options you can set on the dial plan.

UM IP gateways

The UM IP gateway object represents the actual PBX systems that originate and receive calls on your network. Each PBX, gateway, or session border controller (SBC; think of SBCs as firewalls optimized for VoIP traffic that sit between your network and the public Internet) that you want to use with Exchange UM must have a corresponding UM IP gateway object because Exchange accepts only incoming calls from, or sends outgoing calls to, known gateway objects. This includes Lync servers; you create a UM IP gateway object for each Lync Standard edition server or Enterprise edition pool that you want to communicate with Exchange. Older PBXs require IP gateways to convert the circuit-switched telephony protocols they use to SIP and RTP and vice versa; IP PBXs can perform this conversion natively.

To create a UM IP gateway, the only two data items you need are the name you want the gateway object to have and its network address, either in the form of an FQDN that can be resolved in DNS or an IP address.

One interesting change in UM IP gateway behavior compared to Exchange 2010 is that Exchange 2013 fully supports the use of IPv6. Exchange 2010 allowed IPv6 only on networks on which IPv4 was also present, but Exchange 2013 is fully IPv6-native. You may use IPv6 only, IPv4 only, or a mixture of the two, depending on what your PBX systems require. However, if you are using IPv6, you must ensure that you specify either an IPv6 address or an FQDN when you define the gateway object—don't use an IPv4 address. If you use an FQDN, be sure that it resolves to the right IPv6 address, too. Microsoft also requires you to set the IPAddressFamily parameter on the gateway object to indicate that you permit it to use IPv6. By default, the IPAddressFamily value is set to IPv4Only; you must set it to Any or IPv6Only to enable IPv6 use.

UM hunt groups

The term "hunt group" is a telephone-related archaism; it refers to the days when electromechanical phone switches would hunt for the correct connection point by mechanically seeking across an array of contact points. In (slightly) more modern usage, the term now means a single phone number (known as the pilot number) that can accept calls that are then routed to any of a set of extensions. Suppose that you call a major airline; you dial a single number, but your actual call can be routed to any one of a large number of phone agents. That's a hunt group.

Exchange has hunt group objects, too, but they are used differently. Exchange uses UM hunt group objects to tie together a set of UM servers with a specific UM IP gateway object and dial plan. When the PBX or IP gateway sends an incoming call to the UM server, the SIP INVITE includes the pilot number. The UM server that receives the call checks the pilot number to decide whether it matches the hunt group to which the server belongs; if so, it answers the call. (Lync does something similar, except that it routes calls to the SIP URI of the automated attendant it's calling instead of using a numeric pilot number.)

To define a hunt group object, you need four things: a name, the name of the UM dial plan with which the hunt group should be associated, one or more pilot numbers that are attached to the hunt group, and the name of the UM IP gateway object to associate with the hunt group. Calls for a specific hunt group are sent to the pilot number for that hunt group.

Exchange 2007 and Exchange 2010 required hunt groups with individual pilot numbers. However, Exchange 2013 automatically routes calls to all Exchange UM servers in an organization; you need to define pilot numbers on the hunt groups only if you want specific servers associated with specific UM dial plans or gateways. Most Exchange 2013 UM deployments just create a single hunt group and leave the pilot number blank so that any UM server can answer any call.

UM mailbox policies

UM mailbox policies are perhaps the most familiar of the UM-related object types; that's because they are spiritually related to "regular" mailbox policies. Just as with mailbox policies, you define one or more UM mailbox policies and then change the settings on the policies to reflect what you want users to be able to do. After the policies are defined, you can assign them to users so that each user can have a maximum of one policy applied to his mailbox.

Each UM mailbox policy defines the following settings for users assigned to it:

- The length, complexity, and expiration policy for user PINs.

- Which specific UM features users may use; for example, you can disallow the use of OVA or voice mail preview.

- The text included in messages sent to users when they are enabled for UM, when their PIN is reset, or when they receive voice mail or fax messages.

- Whether users subject to the policy can place outbound calls and, if so, to what extensions or number patterns.

- Whether protected voice mail is allowed, mandatory, or unavailable. Two settings are available. The first is for calls originating from authenticated users, such as those using Lync or dialing in through OVA, in which Exchange knows the identity of the caller; the second is for anonymous calls such as those originating from the PSTN. Just as with SMTP mail, anonymous calls may include purported caller information (in the form of calling line ID data), but because it can't be verified, Exchange won't trust it.

You can define multiple UM mailbox policies, each of which is associated with a single dial plan. Remember that the UM mailbox policy objects exist so you can apply consistent settings to groups of users; you can always adjust individual settings on users as necessary. Assigning settings through policies, however, is the simplest way to ensure consistency because you can gather a set of mailboxes with Get-UMMailbox, filter or select the ones you want to modify, and then assign the policy with the UMMailboxPolicy switch for the Set-UMMailbox cmdlet.

Unified messaging architecture

The simplest way to summarize the Exchange 2013 UM architecture is to say that the mailbox server inherits all the services formerly hosted on the UM server role, whereas the CAS has some new services. (See Figure 6-1. The Unified Communications Managed API (UCMA) layer shown in the figure is a portable runtime used by Lync, Exchange, and other UC applications.) If you're not familiar with the prior implementation, this might not be a helpful description, so a bit more explanation might be useful.

The CAS runs a new service known as the Microsoft Exchange Unified Messaging Call Router service (Microsoft.Exchange.UM.CallRouter.exe). This service accepts calls from IP PBXs or gateways and then determines which UM server each incoming call should be routed to and sends it there using a SIP REDIRECT message. This is in keeping with the 2013 CAS design principle of being a proxy and router for data access, not the source of any data. The CAS doesn't accept or generate any media streams; all it does is initially accept the call and then hand it off to the mailbox server. For that reason, you must configure your IP PBXs and similar devices to pass calls to Exchange CAS servers only—mailbox servers won't accept calls directly. (The UM Call Router service is also responsible for updating the speech grammar files that Exchange uses for TTS and automated speech recognition; more on those in the "Multilingual support in UM" section later in this chapter.)

The mailbox server runs the Microsoft Exchange Unified Messaging service (UMService. exe) and a single worker process (UMWorkerProcess.exe). Incoming SIP INVITE messages are accepted by the UM service and passed to the worker process by using a SIP REDIRECT message. The worker process then uses RTP or secure RTP (SRTP) to establish a media channel with the IP PBX, which it then uses to answer the call, play a greeting, and so on.

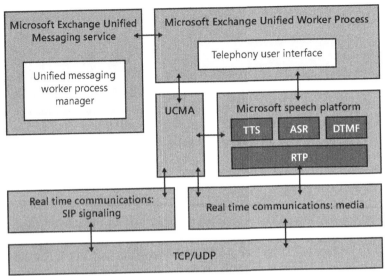

Figure 6-1 The UM architecture has components on both the CAS and Mailbox roles

Whether the CAS and Mailbox roles are on the same multirole server or not, all communication between the UM call router and the UM service itself takes place using TCP on a variety of ports. Table 6-1 shows the TCP ports used for communications from the outside world to the CAS UM call router, from the call router service to the mailbox UM service, and from the UM service to the UM worker process.

TABLE 6-1 **TCP ports Exchange UM uses**

Communication type	TCP port	Notes
SIP to CAS UMCallRouterService.exe	5060 (unsecured) 5061 (secured)	The CAS listens for inbound SIP traffic on these ports; you can change them with Set-UMCallRouterSettings.
SIP to mailbox UMService .exe	5062 (unsecured) 5063 (secured)	The Mailbox role listens for inbound SIP from the CAS on these ports; they cannot be changed.
SIP to UM worker process	5065 & 5067 (unsecured) 5066 & 5068 (secured)	All four ports are used when UMStartupMode is set to Dual. If it's set to TCP or TLS, only 5065 and 5066 are used. These ports cannot be changed.

RTP traffic sent to the mailbox server uses randomly chosen UDP ports between port 1024 and port 65535. Microsoft documentation mentions that you can change the range of ports the Mailbox role uses by setting the *AudioConnectionMinPort* and

AudioConnectionMaxPort values under the HKEY_LOCAL_MACHINE\SOFTWARE\Microsoft\ Microsoft Speech Server\2.0\ key but also mentions that this change isn't supported. In practice, you can change the ports and doing so is unlikely to break anything, but Microsoft doesn't recommend it or promise to help you if something does break unless you go back to using the default ports.

What happens when the phone rings

Now would be a good time to examine what actually happens when Exchange is asked to answer a phone call. Assume that Alice wants to call Bob. This can happen in several ways. In order of increasing complexity:

- Alice and Bob have extensions on the same IP PBX.

- Alice and Bob are on different PBXs within the same UM dial plan.

- Alice and Bob are on different PBXs in different UM dial plans.

- Alice's call is arriving from the PSTN.

Interestingly, we can substitute "an automated attendant" or "Outlook Voice Access" for Bob in the preceding list, and not much changes; the steps Exchange carries out after answering the call will be different, but the basics of call routing and answering remain the same.

Here's what the basic flow looks like:

1. Alice's call arrives at the PBX. The PBX rings the target extension. If the target extension is an automated attendant or OVA, the call goes straight to an Exchange 2013 CAS; if it's not, Bob's phone or softphone might ring. (In the PBX world, this condition is usually called *ring no answer*, indicating that the extension was rung, but no one picked it up.)

2. The PBX decides that Bob cannot answer the call. This might be because the extension is busy or because Bob didn't answer it. The PBX uses its call coverage map to decide where the call should go next; if it has been properly configured, the map tells the PBX to send the call to the pilot number of a UM server or UM hunt group.

3. The PBX sends a SIP INVITE to the Exchange 2013 CAS on TCP port 5060 (for unsecured dial plans) or TCP port 5061 (for secured or SIP secured dial plans).

4. The Exchange UM Call Router service accepts the INVITE and examines the Diversion header. This header indicates three things: who the call is originally from (Alice, in this case); who's sending it to Exchange (the IP PBX that accepted the call); and the

extension to which it is sent. This last value would be Bob's extension if the call is for him; if the call is intended for OVA or an automated attendant, the appropriate extension is included here.

5. The Exchange CAS redirects the call to an appropriate target server, using a SIP redirect. If the user mailbox is homed on an Exchange 2013 server, that server receives the call. If the user mailbox is on an earlier version of Exchange, Exchange attempts to redirect the call to a down-level Exchange UM server.

6. After the mailbox server receives the SIP request, it answers with a "302 Moved Temporarily" response, which tells the calling PBX to redirect the call to the UM worker process on the Mailbox server.

7. The UM worker process answers the call, performs an SDP exchange to agree on a set of audio parameters with the IP PBX, and opens an RTP or SRTP session to the originating IP PBX for audio playback.

8. The UM worker process plays the greeting, and then things proceed as outlined in the following section.

Call answering for a user mailbox

Let's deal first with Alice's call's arrival at the Exchange UM server with diversion information indicating that the call is intended for Bob. You know that the UM server needs to fetch Bob's greeting and play it, but how it figures out where to get the greeting is worth discussing.

Recall that the Diversion header information includes Bob's extension; it can also include the FQDN of the dial plan or PBX (depending on the PBX), for instance, 7285@mtvdp01 .contoso.com. The extension number is arguably the most important component. It constructs an Exchange UM (EUM) proxy address. You're no doubt familiar with how Exchange uses proxy addresses for SMTP and other protocols; EUM proxy addresses are identical in function to these more familiar address types except that they are formatted slightly differently. EUM proxy addresses follow this form:

```
eum:extensionNum;phone-context=dialPlanName.smtpDomain
```

The extensionNum portion of the EUM proxy address is the user's extension. Users might have multiple extensions; if so, they have multiple EUM proxy addresses. This is equivalent to creating multiple SMTP addresses for a mailbox. The dial plan name is taken directly from the name you supplied when you created the dial plan, and the smtpDomain portion is the primary SMTP domain for your Exchange organization. Whenever you assign or remove a UM extension for a user mailbox, the corresponding EUM address is immediately updated.

The trick that makes it easy for the UM server to find the mailbox that corresponds to a given extension number is that the EUM proxy address is stored as an indexed attribute on global catalog servers in the forest. When the Exchange 2013 Mailbox server answers the call, it can find the mailbox efficiently with a simple Active Directory query against the Global Catalog (GC) server; querying for an EUM proxy address based on the information in the Diversion header returns a mailbox globally unique identifier (GUID) (or a search failure if there's no such extension). If a mailbox exists with a matching extension, the mailbox server attempts to retrieve the user's greeting from the mailbox.

The greeting is stored as a folder-associated item (FAI) in the root of the user's Inbox folder. Because it's an FAI, it isn't visible to the user; although you can see the greeting and other FAIs by using a tool such as ExFolders or MFCMAPI, Microsoft doesn't support directly manipulating the greeting objects. The greeting the caller hears can take three forms:

- The user can record a full greeting by using the telephone user interface; this greeting (the maximum length of which is specified by the UM mailbox policy applicable to that user) can contain whatever the user wants.

- The user can record only a name; the system plays the name back as part of a system-generated greeting ("You have reached the mailbox of *name* . . .").

- If the user doesn't record a full greeting or a name, no audio greeting is stored, so Exchange instead uses its text-to-speech engine to produce a greeting based on the user's display name.

If the user's mailbox is on a different server, the Mailbox server that answers the call has to fetch it. If this fetch takes longer than a second or two, Exchange plays what's known as a comfort tone, a friendly sounding sort of beep-boop tone that tells the caller the UM server is still working on the call; you've probably heard similar tones when calling airlines, cellular carriers, or other companies with interactive voice response systems.

After fetching the greeting, Exchange plays it. At that point, two things can happen. If call answering rules are defined on the mailbox, Exchange executes them; if not, the caller is prompted to leave a message. Figure 6-2 illustrates the overall flow of operations that takes place at this point; you might find it useful as a reference.

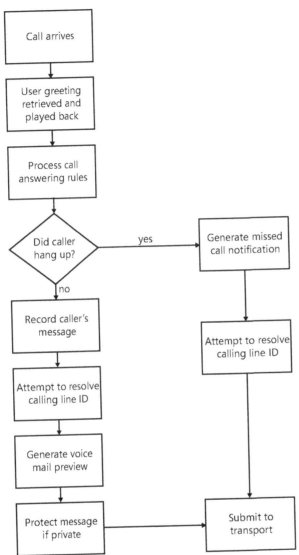

Figure 6-2 Flowchart showing the basic steps involved in answering a call for a user mailbox

Call answering rules

The simplest way to explain Exchange UM call answering rules is by analogy: they're like Outlook Inbox rules but for voice mail. You define rules on a mailbox that take effect when an incoming call arrives. If call answering rules are defined for a mailbox, the Mailbox server evaluates them in order from first to last; the first rule whose conditions match fires, and later rules will not be evaluated.

Much like Outlook rules or Exchange transport rules, UM call answering rules have conditions, which identify what should trigger the rule, and actions, which specify what should happen when the rule is triggered. You can specify five types of conditions:

- **Out-of-office enabled**   This condition matches any time your mailbox out-of-office (OOF) reply feature is enabled.

- **Calendar status**   When your calendar status at the time of the call is the specified combination of free, tentative, busy, or out of office, the condition will match. For example, you can create a condition that matches calls that arrive when your calendar says you're busy or away.

- **At what extension the caller calls you**   You can specify different rules for different extensions; this is useful for users such as executives who might have more than one extension because you can set call answering behaviors for a widely known extension and different behaviors for the boss's private number.

- **Time of day**   You can specify an explicit time period (with a start and end time, applied to any or all days of the week), or you can specify that the condition should match during working hours or outside working hours. The definition of working hours is taken from the setting associated with the individual mailbox, which you set using Outlook or Outlook Web App calendar options.

- **Who's calling you**   You can specify full PSTN phone numbers or extensions (though you cannot specify SIP URIs). Use the check box to specify that all contacts in your personal contacts folder should match; this provides a simple way to implement a rule that gives unknown callers one message and known callers another.

A catch-all Apply To All Calls condition enables you to set a rule that carries out the specified action in all cases.

On the actions front, you can set actions that transfer all calls to a specified number or extension; by default, callers can always press # to leave a voice message, although you can remove this action to prevent them from leaving a message. You can also give callers up to nine options in an automated attendant-style menu; each option represents an extension to which to transfer the call. Exchange UM uses TTS to turn the options you specify here into a spoken menu for callers. It's worth mentioning the find-me option, by which you can tell Exchange UM to ring two alternate numbers to find you without giving those numbers to the caller. For example, you could set up a find-me rule that would ring your home phone

Chapter 6

for 30 seconds and then ring your spouse's cell phone for 30 seconds, firing the find-me action only for users in your personal Contacts folder and only outside working hours.

One major difference between the more familiar Exchange transport rules and Outlook rules versus call answering rules is that call answering rules don't have exceptions. If a rule matches, its action is executed. This leads to two interesting possibilities. The first is that of a default call answering rule: if you want a rule always to apply to every caller, you can specify the Apply To All Calls condition. In Exchange 2010, you could simulate this behavior by creating a rule with no conditions, but Exchange 2013 makes this choice explicit. The second is when you create a rule with a condition but no action. To do this, you must remove the default action, which allows the caller to leave a voice message. A rule with no action causes UM to play the greeting and then immediately disconnect. This is a useful configuration when you want to make an announcement only. For example, you can create a call answering rule that plays a greeting that says, "This employee doesn't work for us anymore," or something similar, and then apply it to mailboxes of former employees.

If the action for a rule specifies that the call should be transferred to another extension or an outside number, Exchange UM on the Mailbox server transfers the call by using a SIP REDIRECT. If the transfer target is another Exchange UM mailbox, the cycle begins again when the UM server that serves the destination mailbox answers the call.

Recording a message or not

At some point during this process, the caller should reach a point when she can leave a message. She can then do one of two things: she can hang up, or she can leave a message. The latter case is more interesting because Exchange has to record audio, produce a voice mail preview (if it can, and if that feature is enabled), and then submit the message for transport. However, the former case is simpler; if the caller hangs up, Exchange creates a missed call notification, or MCN. The MCN contains much of the same information a voice mail message would, including the caller's number, the caller's name if the number could be matched, and the date and time of the call. Figure 6-3 shows an example MCN. The phone number and email are both hyperlinks; clicking the link for a phone number causes the client to use whatever handler is registered for the tel: URL type to call the caller back. In this case, only the caller's extension is shown because Exchange couldn't find any other phone numbers for the caller. (The full resolution process is described in the "Resolving calling line ID information" section later in this chapter.)

Figure 6-3 The missed call notification (MCN) showing who called and when but not what the caller wanted

Say that Alice elects to leave a message. In that case, Exchange records her audio message in a buffer until she stops speaking, presses the * key, or exceeds the maximum message length configured in whatever UM mailbox policy applies to Bob. The interesting question here has to do with the manner in which the message is recorded. First, the audio for the message is captured in RAM, not in a disk file; this becomes important in the discussion about how protected voice mail messages are processed. Second, one common objection to early Exchange UM deployments was the fear that including voice mail in users' Inbox folders would bloat the size and slow the performance of the Information Store. This fear turned out to be unfounded for two reasons:

- Voice mail messages tend to be much smaller than most other attachment types—a 30-second voice mail message takes up less than 100 Kb with most compression methods, a fraction of the size of the average Microsoft Word or PowerPoint document.

- Most users receive relatively few voice mails; for users who do receive voice mails, relatively few keep those messages for any length of time.

However, the codec used can make a significant difference in both the size of the message and how easy it is to listen to. Exchange 2007 supported three audio codecs: Windows Media Audio (WMA), G.711 PCM, and GSM 06.10. WMA offered better voice quality (in part because it uses 16-bit samples and in part because it has a better compression algo-rithm), but playback required a WMA codec too, meaning that users who wanted to listen to messages on Linux machines, handheld devices not running Windows Mobile, and so on were out of luck.

For that reason, Microsoft added MP3 as a supported codec in Exchange 2010; MP3 is the default codec because it offers a good blend of compression ability, voice quality, and por-tability. The G.711 codec doesn't compress audio at all, making it a poor choice unless you have users and devices that cannot use any other codec; the GSM codec has decent com-pression but worse audio quality than does MP3.

Deploy Lync, get a prize: better sound quality!

Office Communications Server and Lync use the Microsoft RTAudio codec to provide what's known as wideband audio, which greatly improves sound quality. However, you can't select RTAudio as a codec for voice mail messages unless you deploy OCS 2007 R2 or Lync and configure Exchange UM with a SIP URI dial plan. You must set the dial plan codec type to WMA, after which the UM server offers RTAudio as one of its supported codecs during SDP negotiation with the Lync/OCS server.

After the message audio has been recorded, the caller normally hangs up. It's also possible that he'll tag the message as private by pressing * if protected voice mail is enabled. Either way, after the call terminates, the RTP/SRTP connection to the PBX is terminated and so is the SIP conversation.

Voice Mail Preview

For a long time, computer speech recognition was considered to be one of the great problems in computer science, one that would require extremely sophisticated artificial intelligence to solve. It turns out that statistical modeling and brute force were more easily achieved ways to solve it, so that's what the industry has done. The Exchange 2013 Voice Mail Preview (VMP) feature is a triumph of speech recognition engineering, but the results might sometimes remind you of the tee shirt Apple gave to prospective employees that read "Help Apple wreck a nice beach"[1]; the results are often close but sometimes, well, not so much.

Voice mail preview is what Microsoft calls the ability to transcribe voice messages to text so that the messages can be read on a screen. It is speaker-independent, meaning that transcription works without requiring the system to be trained with audio of a particular

---

1 Read this phrase out loud, in English, if you don't get the joke at first.

caller's voice. It's continuous, so the caller doesn't have to pause between words or phrases. Therefore, it can be properly described as a speaker-independent continuous voice recognition system, a class of tool that includes the dictation functions in Windows 7, Windows 8, iOS, and Windows RT. Programs such as Dragon Naturally Speaking that must be trained for a particular user are known as speaker-dependent; the tradeoff is that speaker-independent systems are more convenient to use, but their recognition is less accurate.

The goal of voice mail preview is to give you a quick way to triage messages. The header information in the voice mail already tells you when the call was made and who made it; the voice mail preview is intended to tell you, with reasonable accuracy, what the call is about. It's useful when you can't easily listen to voice mail, such as on an airplane in flight or in a meeting when you're supposed to be paying attention. Note that the goal of this feature is not to provide word-for-word transcription with perfect accuracy.

That's because the transcription algorithms sometimes generate text that doesn't quite convey the meaning or intent of the message. All systems that integrate voice face the challenge of comprehending the meaning of voices that share a common language but use different tones, accents, and word patterns and even mix in words or phrases from other languages. Names can often be a particular challenge, especially if they are foreign to the expected language.

The Exchange VMP system deals with these challenges by making some assumptions. The biggest is that the preview is assumed to be a preview; perfect accuracy is not demanded. In addition, VMP only attempts to transcribe messages using whatever language is set for the dial plan, so if your dial plan language is set to French and a caller leaves a message in Russian, the transcription probably won't be usable. Messages longer than 75 seconds are skipped, too, because the longer a message is, the more likely it is to diverge from the language model specified in the language pack (see more discussion on this in the "Multilingual support in UM" section later in this chapter) and the less likely it is that VMP can correctly transcribe the message.

Human-powered transcription

Exchange 2010 included a feature by which you could send voice mail audio to an outside partner; humans would transcribe it and return it by SMTP to the recipient's mailbox. The UM mailbox policy settings that control this (VoiceMailPreviewPartnerAddress and VoiceMailPreviewPartnerID chief among them) still exist and can be set from Exchange Management Shell (EMS), but they're not present in Exchange Administration Center (EAC) or mentioned in the Exchange 2013 documentation, so this feature might have been dropped from Exchange 2013.

Chapter 6

For performance reasons, only the first 30 seconds of incoming messages are transcribed. Each UM server maintains a single queue for messages awaiting transcription; if more than five messages are in the queue, additional messages arriving in the queue are not transcribed. Messages that aren't transcribed instead include text, indicating that transcription wasn't available for the message; there's no way to recycle an untranscribed message to have it transcribed after being skipped.

Voice mail preview supports seven languages in Exchange 2013: U.S. and Canadian English, French, Italian, Polish, Portuguese (Portugal), and Spanish (Spain). One common question is why Microsoft chose this particular set of languages; for example, Italian and Polish are not spoken as widely as, say, Chinese or Japanese, and the UK market is the largest Microsoft market outside the United States. The decision to include languages for voice mail preview is not purely based on transcription accuracy; Microsoft performed user testing that combined measurement of transcription accuracy and measurement of users' satisfaction with the transcription. The languages included in voice mail preview all scored a 3.5 or better on the satisfaction scale (1 being the worst, 5 being the best) and have transcription accuracy of 60+ percent. The accuracy of the transcription is driven directly by the amount of voice mail data that Microsoft had available to test; it shouldn't be surprising that U.S. English had the most test data and thus has the best transcription accuracy. Canadian English scored about 20 percent lower on the user rating scale despite only around a 5 percent difference in transcription accuracy—demonstrating that cultural acceptance of speech processing systems is an important variable. To cite another example, the number of strong regional accents in the UK (including Irish, Scottish, Indian, Pakistani, and West Indian accent influences, to name only a few) has made it tough to develop a speech model with acceptable accuracy.

You might well wonder what Microsoft can do to improve the accuracy of existing languages or get enough data to include additional languages. It takes roughly 100 hours of voice mail messages to bring up a new language, and if you accept the common estimate that the average length of voice mail messages is about 30 seconds, you can start to see the outlines of the problem. Worse, accuracy improvement is driven by a roughly logarithmic relationship between the amount of input audio and the resulting accuracy. Doubling the amount of input audio doesn't produce a doubling of accuracy; Microsoft hasn't released the exact numbers, but one Microsoft product manager said that the requirement was for a "depressingly large" number of voice mail hours to improve accuracy for new languages.

To help address this, Exchange UM includes a feature by which you can send collected voice mail messages to Microsoft. When this feature is enabled, every voice mail a caller leaves is sent to Microsoft for analysis except for messages marked as private by the caller. (Messages so marked are exempted from collection even if you haven't implemented the information rights management infrastructure required for protected voice mail.) Messages sent to Microsoft are processed through the speech and machine learning algorithms that generate language pack data and are then reviewed by humans for accuracy. All the data collection and analysis are done in accordance with Microsoft privacy policies, meaning that there might be differences in what it does with the data, depending on where it's gathered.

Another way UM attempts to increase transcription accuracy is by learning new words. The UM Mailbox Assistant periodically gathers word lists, sorted by frequency of appearance, from Exchange content indexes. These lists provide UM with a list of the most frequently used words for each user's mailbox—and that list includes content from attachments. The UM Mailbox Assistant looks for unique words in that list that aren't currently in the voice mail preview lexicon; if it finds new words, it adds them to the user-specific transcription list kept in a folder-associated item within the user's mailbox. That list is then used during transcription. However, Exchange has to use the built-in phonetic rules for the selected language to figure out how the word is pronounced; words from other languages, or those with unusual pronunciations, still might not be recognized consistently. (See the "Scheduling UM work on the Mailbox server" section later in this chapter for more on how this task is scheduled.) The content indexing engine does all the hard work of gathering the words in the first place, so this process has little impact on the performance of the Mailbox role.

When the UM service generates a preview, its output is a block of XML data that contains timing information and transcribed text. This data is eventually stored in the PidNameAutomaticSpeechRecognitionData property of the message, but it instead appears as a separate attachment if the message is protected. Outlook uses this XML to synchronize the preview text and the corresponding audio; users can click individual words or phrases to hear the associated audio, which makes it easier to understand the correct meaning of phrases when transcription has gone awry. In addition, the voice mail preview engine tags contacts, phone numbers, dates, and email addresses to make them hyperlinks. After the preview data has been captured, the message moves to the next stage in the pipeline, protecting the message if it's been marked as private or submitting it to the transport pipeline if not.

Resolving calling line ID information

If you're of a certain age, you might remember that, once upon a time, you actually had to answer the phone to find out who was calling you. Since the mid-1980s, services that display the number of the caller on the recipient's phone have become ubiquitous. Caller ID was the trademarked name the Bell System companies in North America used for this feature; like Xerox and Kleenex, that trademark entered common use as a noun some years ago. Calling line ID (CLID) is the telephony term for systems that provide the caller's number to the recipient, so that's the term this book uses.

Exchange UM attempts to resolve the caller's number and display it in the voice mail message, as shown in Figure 6-4. The process it uses to do this is perhaps the most complex

Chapter 6

part of the UM role, at least in terms of explaining how it works. Exchange can use several potential data sources to turn the number into a name, including various Active Directory attributes for user objects and information stored in the user's personal Contacts folder. Knowing the order in which these data sources are evaluated is critical to understanding why Exchange came up with a particular name for a given number.

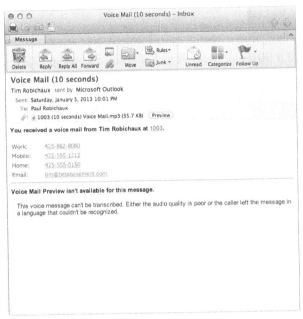

Figure 6-4 Exchange tries to resolve the caller's number into a name and then display the name and any associated numbers in the message

All number resolution depends on the number passed in from the IP PBX. If this number is wrong or malformed in a way that prevents Exchange from matching it, you shouldn't expect the number to be correctly resolved. In some circumstances, external calls from the PSTN might pass an incorrect or invalid number to the IP PBX; Exchange can only use the number it gets.

Say that Adam calls Barbara. The call arrives at the UM Call Router service, which extracts Adam's phone number (whatever it is) from the incoming Diversion header. Then the fun begins. (Bear in mind that at each step of the resolution process, if Exchange finds a match for the number, no further matching is done.)

The simplest possible case is when both users are UM-enabled users in the same Exchange organization and in the same dial plan. To test for this, Exchange creates an EUM proxy address from Adam's number, using the name of Barbara's dial plan. If the resulting EUM proxy matches an entry in Active Directory, that match is used. If no match is found, it might be because the users are in different dial plans within the same organization. Note that I didn't say "Exchange organization" because the two users might be in separate forests (and thus Exchange organizations) but still be within the same company, university, or other type of organization.

To test for this case, Exchange evaluates the set of equivalent dial plans on Barbara's dial plan. Equivalent dial plans are set using the –EquivalentDialPlanPhoneContexts parameter on each dial plan. For example, suppose that Adam is in the dial plan named REDDP02. contoso.com, and Barbara is in SYDDP03.pacific.contoso.com. If their administrator has designated SYDDP03.pacific.contoso.com as an equivalent dial plan on Adam's dial plan by running Set-UMDialPlan –id REDDP02.contoso.com –EquivalentDialPlanPhoneContexts "syddp03.pacific.contoso.com,syddp02.pacific.contoso.com,syddp01.pacific.contoso.com", Exchange constructs the right side of an EUM proxy address, using each of the equivalent plans in sequence, and attempts to find a match by using each of them.

If no match has been found, the next step is to determine whether the calling line ID is a SIP URI such as sip:paulr@blackdotpub.com. The test Exchange uses is simple: if the calling line ID contains an at sign, @, it's assumed to be a SIP URI, and that URI queries Active Directory for a match.

If the number starts with +, it's assumed to be an E.164 number. At this point, Exchange will attempt to query a relatively new Active Directory attribute that was added in Exchange 2010, msExchUMCallingLineIDs. This multivalued attribute is intended to hold additional numbers you want to match against a specific user. For example, Diane Prescott, a user at extension 0140, has a direct-dial line of 650-555-0140. You can add 6505550140, 16505550140, and +16505550140 to the msExchUMCallingLineIDs attribute on that account so Exchange can consider those numbers when it's evaluating a match. You can set the value of this attributes only with the Set-User cmdlet.

At this point, you might be wondering why it's necessary to add three very similar numbers to msExchUMCallingLineIDs instead of just adding the number once. The answer has to do with how Exchange actually resolves numbers. The PBX or gateway might provide a calling line ID with any number of digits. Diane's number might appear as 0140, 50140, 5550140, 6505550140, 16505550140, or +16505550140, depending on where she placed the call from, how the recipient's PBX is configured to pass numbers, and how any other PBXs (or the PSTN) involved in the call might have modified the number. You have to add multiple values to msExchUMCallingLineIDs to cover the possible mutations of the number that might be delivered by the various PBXs in the call chain. Along with setting msExchUM-CallingLineIDs, however, you also need to set numbering plan formats on the dial plan that tell Exchange how to expand partial numbers. As shown in Figure 6-5, the numbering plan formats defined on a dial plan represent masks (specified by the x characters) that supply a prefix for a number. Suppose that Diane places a call, which arrives at Exchange with a calling line ID of 50140. In this example, the mask of +165055xxxx matches, so Exchange uses +16505550140 as the basis for comparison.

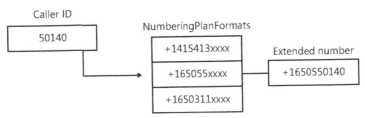

Figure 6-5 Numbering plan formats turning the number provided by the PBX into a fully expanded number that can be used to match

Numbering plan formats and the msExchUMCallingLineIDs attribute work together to make equivalent dial plan searches work properly. The incoming number from the PBX is expanded using the numbering plan formats, with the most specific match between the mask and the incoming number being used. Then the expanded number is used to search the indexed msExchUMCallingLineIDs values to (it's hoped) find a match.

If no match is found with msExchUMCallingLineIDs, the next step is to query the similar single-valued attribute named msRTCSIP-Line. This attribute is present in the schema only if OCS or Lync has been deployed; the attribute serves the same purpose as msExchUMCallingLineIDs, but OCS/Lync uses it instead. Because it's single-valued, it's not as useful for Exchange purposes, but because it might already have been populated, Exchange will use it.

INSIDE OUT Resolving a number without revealing it

Another very useful trick you can perform with msExchUMCallingLineIDs is to use it to resolve an inbound number to a name without revealing the number. For example, adding your CEO's cell phone number to his account's msExchUMCallingLineIDs value enables Exchange to match incoming calls from that number to the corresponding name without that number being visible in the GAL, missed call notifications, or voice mail messages. It will still be visible to users who have the requisite Active Directory permissions, however.

If the caller's number still has not been matched, the next step Exchange takes is to search the recipient's personal Contacts folder to find a match. This is a bit of a gamble; the search might take multiple seconds, depending on the size of the user's Contacts folder and the location of the recipient's mailbox relative to the UM server. In addition, it's likely that the numbers associated with contacts aren't in E.164 or any other standardized format. However, searching Active Directory at this point could generate more aggregate load in environments with large directories, so searching per-user data is defensible.

Searches against user-specific contact data only use items in the user's default Contacts folder; if the user has multiple or nested folders, her contents aren't included. In addition, the Suggested Contacts folder isn't used, and neither are associated folders such as the LinkedIn Contacts folder that appears when you use the Outlook social media integration. For each contact, Exchange looks at the Business, Home, and Mobile number fields, along with Business 2, Home 2, and Mobile 2. These attributes' values are reversed for the search so that if a contact's Home attribute contains the phone number +14195559199, it will be reversed to 99195559141+ when the search is done. Reversing the number in this way allows more efficient matching when there are many similar numbers (as there might be for large numbers of contacts that share the same country code, area code, or telephone exchange).

It's possible that the contacts search will turn up multiple matches because, unlike every other kind of CLID matching, searches of the Contacts folder can return multiple results. For example, consider when Adam receives a phone call from Barbara, a contact at Microsoft. If the Microsoft PBX emits its main number (+14258828080) as the caller's number, Exchange can't tell whether the call is actually from Barbara, Charlie, or Dina, so it will list all three numbers as possibilities. In this case, the number is actually treated as unresolved—the MCN or voice mail will say that the call is from +14258828080, and the first two matching names with that number will be displayed as the name.

INSIDE OUT No resolution against public folder contacts

One common misconception about matching calling line ID data against contact folders is that Exchange can use contacts stored in public folders. As much as organizations that use public folders heavily might wish this to be true, it's not, and never has been. Exchange will not resolve contacts against older or modern public folders, and Microsoft has shown no inclination to add this feature. CLID resolution also doesn't use Microsoft SharePoint contact lists, which seems slightly more likely to be included in a future release.

If no match can be found in the personal Contacts folder, it's back to Active Directory. Up to this point in the search process, Exchange has only used indexed Active Directory attributes. If the number remains unmatched, it can turn to a search process known as

Active Directory heuristic searching. "Heuristic" is a fancy synonym for guessing in this case because there's no guarantee that any given user will have any phone numbers defined in Active Directory, much less that the numbers will be in any sort of consistent format. The speed of the process depends on how long it takes to search the Contacts folder, but it's typically only a few dozen milliseconds.

When you enable heuristic searching on the dial plan, Exchange tries to find a match by using a subset of the telephone-related attributes in Active Directory. To be specific, the telephoneNumber, homePhone, mobile, facsimileTelephoneNumber, otherTelephone, otherHomePhone, otherMobile, and otherFacsimileTelephoneNumber attributes can be searched, in that order. It's a bit of a misnomer to say that Exchange searches these attributes; instead, when you edit these attributes, their values are copied to a UM-specific attribute, UMDtmfMap, when you run the Set-User, Set-Contact, or Set-MailUser cmdlets. Any tool, such as EAC, that runs these cmdlets thus updates the attributes, or it will happen automatically when the GAL grammar is updated by the UM Mailbox Assistant. As with searches against the personal Contacts folder, searches on UMDtmfMap take advantage of the fact that numbers in the attribute are stored in reverse order so that the most specific match will be the one used. However, the drawback to this increased efficiency is that you won't get accurate results unless UMDtmfMap is updated.

If Active Directory heuristic matching fails, Exchange can use the caller name, if the PBX provides it, as a last-ditch effort to display something instead of just a phone number. Many PSTN systems can provide the subscriber name, although it's usually all uppercase and truncated to 16 total characters (and often with the surname first, so that callers see something like ROBICHAUX PAUL). If the SIP INVITE includes a caller name in the From header, and if Exchange can't match the number by using any of the preceding methods, it uses this name.

Protected voice mail

Older voice mail systems have many good qualities, one of which is that their proprietary nature makes them well able to enforce privacy settings. A private voice mail message on these systems cannot be forwarded or distributed, and there are no alternate clients or entry points to the system, so a message so marked will probably remain private unless a recipient records and redistributes the audio. Exchange 2007 didn't have an equivalent of this feature, so voice mail messages could be forwarded just like any other unrestricted email message, leading to a risk of information disclosure.

To solve this problem, and not incidentally to reach feature parity with older systems, the Exchange product group added protected voice mail in Exchange 2010. When the feature is enabled, a voice mail message that is marked as private is wrapped by Active Directory Rights Management Services (AD RMS) so that the message can be read by the intended recipient only. The message and the audio attachment are both protected, so the recipient can listen to the message and read the transcription but can't save a copy of the message or audio, copy the audio, or forward the message to other users.

Protected voice mail requires three things. The feature must be enabled, AD RMS must be properly installed and configured, and the message recipient must have a suitable client. For example, the email client built into iOS devices cannot play back protected voice mail messages. Playback is normally allowed through OVA, Outlook, and Outlook Web App; however, Outlook 2007 and Outlook 2011 for Mac OS X do not support protected voice mail messages. Because Outlook Web App 2013 fully supports email messages that have been protected with AD RMS, it also provides direct access to the protected audio in protected voice mail messages. You can optionally configure the RequireProtectedPlayOnPhone property of the UM mailbox policy if you want to prevent users from listening to the message by using the standard media player in Outlook and Outlook Web App. When this setting is enabled, users have to use either OVA or the Play on Phone feature to play protected voice mail messages. Because you can restrict which numbers users can dial with Play on Phone, you can make it more difficult for users to, say, send their protected voice mail messages directly to *The New York Times*.

The AD RMS protection used by the protected voice mail feature cannot prevent every type of information disclosure. A recipient who's determined to release information has any number of alternatives, including manually transcribing the audio on paper or using a smart phone or other device to record the audio. The famous proverb that sayslocks help keep honest people honest definitely applies here.

Guidance on how to install and configure AD RMS is outside the scope of this book. However, a brief discussion of how it works and how Exchange interacts with it will illustrate how protected voice mail works.

The basic idea behind AD RMS is that clients can use a centralized RMS server to protect messages by encrypting them. Unlike S/MIME, in which messages are encrypted using the recipient's public key so that only the recipient can decrypt them, RMS messages are encrypted so that they include permissions information (known as usage rights) that specify what an authorized recipient can do with the message. For example, the recipient might be able to open and read a document or message but not print or forward it. The block of data that specifies the usage rights is known as a license.

AD RMS differs from S/MIME in another important way. The AD RMS server includes the ability for an authorized set of users (known as super users) to decrypt any content. This enables organizations to gain access to protected content even if all the authorized recipients have left the organization. It also makes various kinds of compliance scenarios easier to handle. Exchange uses this functionality to enable searching and archiving of AD RMS–protected messages and application of transport protection rules as described in Chapter 2, "The Exchange transport system."

Chapter 6

Because the RMS-protected message is encrypted, users have to have a compatible client to decrypt it; the client is responsible for enforcing whatever usage rights are embedded in the message. Office 2007, Office 2010, Office 2011 for Mac OS X, and Office 2013 all act as AD RMS clients, as does the Exchange CAS role—it can decrypt RMS messages on behalf of users using Outlook Web App if you've enabled that feature.

Figure 6-6 shows the contents of a protected voice mail message. The message is in Multipurpose Internet Mail Extensions (MIME) format, so it can be interpreted by any MIME-compatible client. However, not every part of the message is directly visible to the client. The outer message contains text that is visible to clients that don't support AD RMS. By default, it contains text telling the recipient that the message is RMS-protected and to open it in a compatible client to see the real contents. However, you can change the text that appears here by modifying the default text in the UM dial plan. The AD RMS–protected content is encapsulated in a single attachment named message.rpmsg. That attachment contains the RMS-granted license, encrypted versions of the message body, the audio file containing the caller's message, and the voice mail preview transcription if the message was transcribed. This is the same structure used for other types of AD RMS–protected messages; the difference is that the contents of the inner message are generated by the UM server.

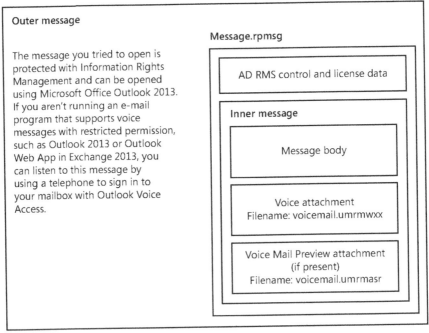

Outer message

The message you tried to open is protected with Information Rights Management and can be opened using Microsoft Office Outlook 2013. If you aren't running an e-mail program that supports voice messages with restricted permission, such as Outlook 2013 or Outlook Web App in Exchange 2013, you can listen to this message by using a telephone to sign in to your mailbox with Outlook Voice Access.

Message.rpmsg

AD RMS control and license data

Inner message

Message body

Voice attachment
Filename: voicemail.umrmwxx

Voice Mail Preview attachment
(if present)
Filename: voicemail.umrmasr

Figure 6-6 A protected voice mail message, which contains multiple parts

After the message has been protected with information rights management (IRM), it's ready to be sent to the actual recipient.

Submitting the message

At this stage of the UM message-recording process, the UM server has everything it needs to construct a complete message; it has recorded an audio response from the caller, identified the caller's phone number, and, it's hoped, resolved the number to its matching human-friendly name. The next step is to assemble a message header to go along with the body. This header contains an indicator of whether the message is an MCN or a voice mail, the resolved name and phone numbers of the caller, the recipient's name and SMTP address, and a call ID generated by the first UM server to receive the call. The call ID is similar to the message ID for SMTP messages; it's a unique identifier that you can use to trace the progress of a single call across multiple UM servers. The header file also identifies the name and extension of the audio attachment (or the protected voice mail attachment if the message is private). The Exchange Information Store translates some of these headers into MAPI properties on the message when the message is delivered to the recipient; for example, the PidTagMessageClass property of the message is set to IPM.Note.Microsoft .Voicemail.UM.CA for messages UM records when the called party doesn't answer his phone or IPM.Note.Microsoft.Missed.Voice for MCNs.

After the UM server submits the message to the transport system, UM is finished with the message. The only real exception is when transport submission isn't working. In Exchange 2013, the onus is on the sending server to queue messages that aren't accepted by the remote server until they can be delivered. The UM server queues up to 500 messages for eventual delivery; if the queue reaches that length, the server will stop accepting calls and will play a message that asks the caller to call back later. This is disconcerting, but it's easy to track by using a monitoring system (such as System Center Operations Manager) to watch the length of the outbound queue on the UM server.

Lighting the message-waiting indicator

One of the problems Microsoft faced when selling unified messaging as part of Exchange 2007 was seemingly simple: many customers, particularly those in markets such as the financial services and legal sectors, wanted a blinking light that would indicate when new voice mail messages were available. This was no more than parity with its earlier voice mail systems, but the Microsoft defense was that the message-waiting indicator (MWI) was an antiquated technology. "Why would you need an MWI when your voice mail appears in the same place as all your other email?" seems like a reasonable question, and yet customers balked at its absence. Responding to this demand, in Exchange 2010, Microsoft gave Exchange UM the ability to signal the presence of unread voice mail messages in a mailbox. The way it implemented this is rather clever.

You're probably familiar with the notion of search folders, and you'll notice that Exchange 2010 and Exchange 2013 automatically create a new search folder named Voice Mail in the mailbox of each UM-enabled user at the time that user is UM enabled. Because search folders are automatically updated by the Store, any client that accesses the Voice Mail search folder receives a list of all the voice mail messages currently in the user's mailbox. The UM Mailbox Assistant process subscribes to the Voice Mail search folder of each UM-enabled user on the mailbox server. Any time the number of unread items changes in any of those folders, the UM Mailbox Assistant receives a subscription notification, so it knows that either a new voice mail has arrived (thus causing the unread message count to increase by 1 in the target folder) or an existing voice mail message has been listened to, marked as read, or deleted (thus causing the unread message count to decrease by 1).

When the UM Mailbox Assistant notices a change to a subscribed Voice Mail search folder, it sends a notification by remote procedure call (RPC) to the UM server itself. The UM server then sends a SIP NOTIFY message to the gateway or PBX, which is responsible for actually notifying the user. This type of notification is known as an unsolicited notification; the PBX hasn't registered or asked for the notification. Some PBX systems, notably Cisco Call Manager, block unsolicited notifications by default, so you might have to ensure that unsolicited NOTIFY messages are allowed if you want to enable MWI.

The genius of this approach should now be clear. When Exchange sends the notification, making sure the user gets the notification is no longer an Exchange problem. The PBX is responsible for blinking the light, changing the dial tone, updating a visible counter on the phone, or doing whatever else it's supposed to do. One potential problem with this approach is that it depends on the presence of the Voice Mail search folder. If the folder is removed, it won't be re-created unless the user dials in to OVA to check her voice messages. There's currently no other way to re-create it.

The actual SIP NOTIFY message is straightforward; it's shown as being from and to the same extension, but the VIA header indicates that the actual notification is coming from the IP of an Exchange UM server (and the User-Agent header makes that explicit). The last three lines of the listing are the most interesting because they clearly indicate that there are messages waiting, which extension the messages are for, and how many messages there are. The first number in the Voice-Message line indicates the number of total messages; the second indicates the number of new messages.

```
NOTIFY sip:1001@10.0.0.10:5060;user=phone SIP/2.0
FROM: <sip:1001@10.0.0.10:5060;user=phone>;epid=C5B0E0C553;tag=cd4d465d19
TO: <sip:1001@10.0.0.10:5060;user=phone>
CSEQ: 8 NOTIFY
CALL-ID: 2685f10aa8f94fa883023d7598ad4094
MAX-FORWARDS: 70
VIA: SIP/2.0/TCP 10.0.0.102:63354;branch=z9hG4bK2fb9d47
CONTACT: <sip:1001@10.0.0.10:5060;user=phone>
CONTENT-LENGTH: 96
```

```
EVENT: message-summary
SUBSCRIPTION-STATE: terminated
USER-AGENT: RTCC/5.0.0.0 MSExchangeUM/15.00.0516.029
CONTENT-TYPE: application/simple-message-summary

Messages-Waiting: yes
Message-Account: sip:1001@10.0.0.10:5060;user=phone
Voice-Message: 2/2
```

In addition to this notification, you see event ID 1343 logged on the UM server (with a source of MSExchange Unified Messaging) if you have diagnostic logging turned up to Expert in the Unified Messaging\MWI General category. If the notification cannot be sent, that is also logged. Separate events indicate that the MWI couldn't be sent because the UM Mailbox Assistant couldn't access the user's mailbox database (event ID 1346) or mailbox (event ID 1345) or that the UM Mailbox Assistant couldn't make an RPC connection to the UM server (event ID 1360).

By default, Exchange sends MWIs to all users; the default UM mailbox policy created when you create a new dial plan allows MWI notifications, as do the default settings for the UM IP gateway objects you create. If you have a gateway that cannot process MWI notifications, or one that you don't want to receive them, disable MWI notifications on that gateway only with Set-UMIPGateway –MessageWaitingIndicatorAllowed:$false or by modifying the setting directly in EAC. If you don't want specific users to receive MWI notifications, disable MWI on the UM mailbox policy that applies to those users.

Speaking of specific, the UM Mailbox Assistant round-robins notifications against all the UM servers associated with the user's dial plan. The UM server in turn round-robins SIP NOTIFY messages to all gateways in the dial plan that are enabled for MWI. If the NOTIFY message fails, the UM server retries against a different gateway if any are available. This leads to a situation in which multiple MWI state changes that happen in rapid succession can cause the MWI on the user's device to be wrong, either indicating a message when there are none or failing to signal the presence of an unheard message. To fix this problem, Exchange UM implements a 40-second timer; when an MWI notification has been sent, no further notifications are sent for 40 seconds. This prevents rapid state changes from leaving the light in an incorrect state, although it does impose a delay that might cause a bit of user confusion. The UM Mailbox Assistant refreshes the state of every MWI at least every 12 hours; the process is staggered for all mailboxes in the database so that refresh messages are sent out gradually. This behavior protects against when a PBX restart or power loss leaves users' MWI notifications in an incorrect state, although there's no way to control the timing or frequency.

INSIDE OUT The do-it-yourself approach

The Office Communicator and Lync client applications have their own message-waiting indicators, and they offer single-click access to voice mail messages. However, they don't exactly use the MWI mechanism described earlier. Instead, when Lync receives the MWI NOTIFY message from the server, it publishes a special MWI flag inside the presence container for the user, so that all endpoints on which that user is signed in will get the MWI notification. If you point a Lync or Communicator client at a user whose UM mailbox is on Exchange 2007, the client will use Exchange Web Services (EWS) to check for voice mail messages and set the MWI state accordingly.

Call answering for an automated attendant

So far, this section has discussed the flow that occurs when an incoming call arrives for a user, not for an automated attendant (AA). The first several steps of the call answering process are the same: the PBX must determine that the call is for an extension that should be answered by Exchange UM, and then it must route the call to Exchange. However, if the call is directed to an extension associated with an automated attendant, you want Exchange to answer the call and play the series of prompts associated with the attendant instead of fetching a user's UM greeting. It's easy for Exchange to determine that a call is for a specific AA because each AA has one or more access numbers—think of these as extensions for the AA itself.

INSIDE OUT Languages and automated attendants

You can create an automated attendant by using any language you have installed on the UM server. By default, a newly created AA uses the language of the version of Exchange you have installed, even if the dial plan language is set to something else. Therefore, unless you install a localized version of Exchange, your AAs will default to U.S. English. Any time I discuss AA prompts in U.S. English, you can mentally edit the reference to your preferred language if you like. See the "Multilingual support in UM" section later in this chapter for more on how UM uses language packs.

An AA consists of several parts: one or more greetings, one or more menu navigation entries, and some settings that link the two. The basic idea behind the AA is that it plays a greeting that tells the caller what choices she has; depending on how the AA is configured (and what the greeting says!), users can choose an extension or person by saying a name, speaking a number, or dialing a digit. Because each AA has one or more access numbers, one AA can transfer a call to another AA. This makes it possible to build complex structures, such as a primary AA that tells the caller to press 1 for English, 2 for French, 3 for Spanish, and so on; each of those choices can transfer the caller to a language-specific AA that contains more choices.

Each AA can respond to either speech or DTMF digits, but not both. A speech-enabled AA can have a separate DTMF AA connected as a fallback; if Exchange can't understand the caller, it will offer to let the caller switch to the fallback DTMF AA.

When a call arrives at an access number that belongs to an AA, what happens next depends on whether the AA is enabled or disabled. If it's disabled, Exchange treats the call as if it were intended for the OVA subscriber access number; the caller hears the same prompts she would hear if she had dialed the subscriber access number directly. If the AA is enabled, Exchange determines which greeting to play. This is not as straightforward as it might seem because a single AA can have several possible greetings. Here's the process Exchange uses to decide which greeting the caller hears:

- If you don't change any of the default settings on the AA, callers hear, "Thank you for calling the Microsoft Exchange Automated Attendant," and then the default prompt for dial by name. Which prompt they get depends on whether the AA is speech enabled. If it is, callers hear, "To reach a specific person, just tell me their name." If not, they hear, "Use the keypad to spell the name of the person you're calling, last name first."

- If you specify a company name in the AA settings, and you don't record a custom audio greeting, Exchange uses TTS to read the company name instead of saying "Microsoft Exchange Automated Attendant" during the greeting.

- If you have recorded a custom greeting, without also creating separate greetings for business hours and nonbusiness hours, the caller hears it.

- If you've recorded business and nonbusiness hour greetings, the caller hears the appropriate greeting according to the local time on the UM server and the schedule you've set to define when business hours are. The nonbusiness hour greeting is also played during any date range that you've defined as a holiday.

- If you've recorded an informational announcement, it is played immediately after the greeting. If you've provided a business or nonbusiness hours greeting, the informational announcement comes between the greeting and any prompts. If you're using the system greeting, the announcement comes after the "Thank you for calling . . ." phrase but before the caller is prompted to choose a target extension.

Chapter 6

After the greeting has been played, menu navigation starts. You can specify separate navigation trees for business hours and nonbusiness hours, and the UM server chooses the appropriate one based on the local time when it receives a call. Whichever tree the UM server uses, the caller's experience is the same. If you have recorded a custom audio prompt, the caller hears it. This prompt is your chance to explain to the caller what you want him to do; for example, you could record a prompt that says, "Press or say 1 to reach the sales department. Press or say 2 to reach the customer service department. Press or say 0 to reach the operator." If you don't provide such a prompt, the UM service synthesizes one, using TTS based on the navigation choices you provide.

Each navigation entry contains a label (such as Sales or Support); this label is used for ASR (so the caller can say "sales" or "support") and TTS (so Exchange can read the label aloud if you don't record a navigation prompt). Each entry is associated with a single number (1–9); you can also specify a navigation entry that applies when the user doesn't provide any input. You can specify an optional audio file that's played when the entry is chosen ("Please hold for the sales department," for example). The entry also has an action. An entry can transfer the call to a specific extension, another AA, or even back to itself ("Press 9 to repeat this menu"). It can allow the user to leave a voice mail for a specific user, or it can announce the business location (which you must specify separately, using a text field in the AA settings) or hours (which are derived from the business hours you set on the AA itself).

Each AA is associated with a single dial plan. Exchange doesn't provide any AAs by default; you have to create any that you want. To create a new AA, use the simple form shown in Figure 6-7 to name the AA, indicate whether you want it enabled by default and whether it should be speech enabled, and specify its access numbers.

Custom prompt formats

All the custom prompts you use with an AA must be in a very specific format: a mono WAV file using PCM audio, with a 16-bit sample size and an 8 KHz sample rate. The UM server won't accept any other encoding; when you try to upload prompts through EAC, they'll be rejected with a helpful error message if they're in the wrong format. If you record the prompts yourself using the telephone user interface (TUI), they'll automatically be recorded in the correct format. The file names for the prompts must be unique, too.

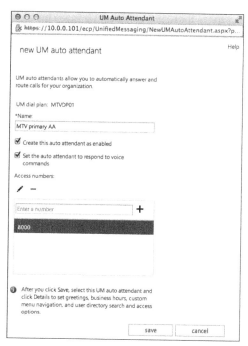

Figure 6-7   Creating a basic automated attendant (simple) and deciding the details (requires some thought)

Automated attendants and the GAL

One of the most useful aspects of AAs is that they can provide dial-by-name services; if you choose to enable it, callers can reach anyone directly who appears in the GAL just by saying the name (or spelling it with the phone keypad). There are a few nuances of this feature that you should be aware of, starting with the fairly obvious fact that a user whose mailbox is hidden from the GAL can't be reached through dial by name.

Each AA has independent settings for dial by name. You can control:

- Whether callers can transfer to users' extensions by saying or spelling their name.

- Whether callers can leave voice mail messages for users directly from the AA without transferring to their extension first.

- Whether callers are able to search the GAL by spelling a name or SMTP alias. If you enable this feature, you can scope the search to the dial plan associated with the AA or the entire GAL.

- How to handle the case when more than one user has the same name. You can have the AA include the user's title, department, or location; prompt the user for the target's alias; or inherit the specified behavior in the dial plan.

This last option requires a bit more explanation. Suppose that your company has three employees named John Smith—one in sales, one in support, and one in the legal department. When the AA prompts the caller to choose the target extension, and the caller says "John Smith," she'll hear a prompt that says, "There are multiple people with this name. Please select from the following options. For John Smith . . ." The selected item you chose in the AA settings follows, along with a digit, and then this is repeated for each of the other choices. If you told the AA to use the user's department, for example, the prompt says, "For John Smith, legal, press 1. For John Smith, sales, press 2. For John Smith, support, press 3." If you instead set the AA to use the user's location or title, the UM service reads out those items instead of the departments.

You can also specify whether you want the AA to allow transfers to the operator extension. This requires you to define an operator extension; you can separately give callers permission to transfer to that extension during business and nonbusiness hours.

Automated attendants and call transfers

By default, a newly created AA allows callers to transfer to users inside the organization. However, you can allow callers to transfer to any number. You do this by controlling which dialing rule groups the AA can use. Dialing rule groups, discussed in the "Placing outbound calls" section later in this chapter, provide a simple way for you to control what destinations outbound calls can reach.

AA transfers are known as unsupervised transfers because the UM service sends a SIP REFER message to the gateway or PBX, including a header (REFER-TO) that specifies the transfer target. After sending the REFER request, the UM server doesn't monitor the transfer to make sure that it works. One common problem encountered when initially deploying UM is that outbound transfers through AAs (or through the Play on Phone feature) result in the caller hearing dead air or a fast busy signal; this is almost always because the REFER operation was refused or mishandled by the gateway, but the gateway can't transfer the call back to the AA (and Exchange wouldn't accept it if it did), so the transfer fails.

Call answering for Outlook Voice Access

Call answering for OVA is similar in most respects to call answering for AAs; the call is answered directly by the UM server, which knows the call is for an object it owns and not for a user mailbox because it's directed to a subscriber access number. OVA can be configured to play a customized welcome greeting ("Welcome to Contoso Voice Access") or informational announcement ("Because of the recent hurricane, our IT support hours have changed"), and you can specify that callers can interrupt these announcements.

There are some significant differences between the two, however. First is that AAs are associated with a dial plan; only servers in a given dial plan can answer that AA. If you have multiple dial plans, you have to create matching AAs on each dial plan manually if you want consistent AA behavior across dial plans. However, any UM server can accept OVA calls, although the specific number users call is a property of the dial plan.

A perhaps larger difference is that callers to OVA may be (but do not have to be) authenticated. The default behavior is for OVA to use the extension passed in by the PBX to determine who's calling; OVA assumes that any call from a known extension is being placed by the owner of that extension, so when it answers, it plays the name associated with the mailbox and asks for the corresponding PIN. For example, if Alice Ciccu has extension 1001 and dials OVA from it, OVA plays its distinctive four-note tone, then says, "Alice Ciccu, please enter your PIN and then the pound key." If Alice instead dials OVA from extension 1002, which belongs to Bob Kelly, she'll hear Bob's name, but she can press the * key, and OVA will prompt her for her extension and then the corresponding PIN. Of course, there's no guarantee that an inbound call to OVA is coming from a UM-enabled user's extension. It could just as easily be coming from a user's cell phone, a bus station pay phone, or a VoIP softphone that emits 000-00-0000 as its calling line ID. For that reason, if the CLID OVA sees doesn't match a known extension, it assumes that it shouldn't assume anything about the caller's identity and asks for the mailbox extension.

After the call has been answered and the user has authenticated, the best way to think of what happens is like Outlook Web App: the user is interacting with an application that retrieves data from his mailbox and renders it appropriately. A detailed discussion of how to use OVA is outside the scope of this book; it's self-explanatory when you call it on the phone and in the Microsoft end-user documentation (which includes a large chart showing which key presses do what in DTMF mode).

Call answering for faxes

Call answering for faxes is something of a historical artifact. When Microsoft designed Exchange 2007, it wanted Exchange to receive, decode, and deliver incoming faxes. Although it shipped this feature, customer adoption of it was very low, primarily because it was only half useful. Exchange didn't include a way to send outbound faxes, so customers who wanted Exchange-based faxing still had to buy a third-party solution to send faxes. However, faxes are important in many areas of the world, particularly in the Middle East and Pacific Rim where non-Roman alphabets are the norm.

Rather than abandon faxing altogether, Microsoft made a change in Exchange 2010 to enable Exchange to recognize incoming fax calls and then redirect them to a third-party fax over IP (FoIP) service. The FoIP service would be responsible for receiving and decoding the fax and then returning it through SMTP. I say "decoding" because faxes sent over IP use the ITU T.38 protocol, which Exchange doesn't understand. However, the UM call router can recognize T.38 calls; they're set up using SIP just like voice calls, but instead of SDP leading to an RTP/SRTP payload, the payload contains T.38. (More precisely, the sending fax machine or server might be using native T.38, but more likely it's using the T.30 or T.4 fax protocols over the PSTN; in that case, the gateway or PBX is responsible for turning that data into T.38.)

The flow that actually takes place looks like this:

1. The fax call reaches the PBX or IP gateway, which routes it to the target extension.

2. If the user answers the call, she hears CNG tones; at that point, she can hang up (the sending fax machine will call back) or transfer the call to her own extension to let UM answer it again. If the user doesn't answer the call, the PBX eventually transfers it to the UM server by sending a SIP INVITE with SDP data, indicating that it's a voice call. The PBX hasn't heard CNG tones yet, so it doesn't know that the call is a fax at this point.

3. At some point after the UM server answers the SIP INVITE, the PBX hears the CNG tones, so it sends a new SIP INVITE to the UM server, this time indicating that the call contains T.38 data.

4. The UM server sends back a SIP status of 200 OK, which essentially puts the call from the PBX on hold.

5. The UM server queries Active Directory to find out whether the specified extension is allowed to receive faxes, and, if so, which FoIP partner should be used.

    If step 5 succeeds, the UM server sends a SIP REFER to the PBX containing the FoIP path.

6. The PBX sends a new SIP INVITE to the FoIP partner service.

7. The FoIP partner accepts the call, decodes the T.38 payload, and generates an SMTP message containing the fax data.

8. The FoIP partner service returns the fax to the Exchange user's mailbox through SMTP.

How does the partner service know who to send the fax to? Remember that the incoming fax call had to be sent to a particular extension, so the outbound request includes the SMTP address of the mailbox that owns that extension. Therefore, you can, if you wish, define a separate fax-only extension for a mailbox and then instruct the PBX always to forward calls on that extension directly to UM without ringing an endpoint. With that setup, the user essentially has a dedicated fax number; to do this, you must have enough spare extension numbers to give one to everyone who needs fax service.

After the incoming fax message arrives at the recipient's mailbox server, the mailbox server's UM Mailbox Assistant process passes the message back to the UM server, which stamps additional properties on the message and resubmits it to transport. After the message is delivered to the user's mailbox, it's ready for the user.

Placing outbound calls

One often overlooked feature of Exchange UM is that it can place outbound calls in three ways:

- **A blind transfer**   In this case, UM asks the PBX to transfer the call by using a SIP REFER, and then UM bows out of the conversation altogether. This method is used when a user call answering rule contains an action that specifies a call transfer, when an OVA user uses dial by name to dial a user from the GAL or a number from his personal Contacts folder, and when AAs transfer a call to a number (whether it's an internal extension or an external number).

- **A supervised transfer**   This takes place when UM remains in the call path until the call is answered and it knows the call's disposition. Call answering rules that use the find-me action use supervised transfers.

- **A plain outbound call**   This is the method used when an Outlook 2007, Outlook 2010, Outlook 2013, or Outlook Web App user uses the Play on Phone feature to tell the UM server to call her at a specified number.

The parts of a phone number

Most of the time, we think of phone numbers as just strings of digits with no special meaning attached to any part of the number. However, in the telephony world, a number of pieces of meta-information are attached to different parts of a telephone number. The role of the initial + sign in indicating that a number is formatted according to E.164 rules has already been discussed, and you're probably used to seeing phone numbers that contain a country code at the beginning. For example, the country code for the United States and Canada is 1, so any time you see a phone number that begins with 1 (for example, 1-318-555-1659), you can tell it's a U.S. number. However, the international standard for phone number structures specifies a number of other phone number parts, and you can define the dial codes you want to associate with each individual UM dial plan as follows (see Figure 6-8):

- The country code is one or two digits that indicate the country in which the target phone number is. It was originally added to allow direct-dial international calls in the 1960s. Examples include 49 (Germany), 44 (the UK), 598 (Uruguay), and 27 (South Africa).

- The outside line access code (which earlier versions of Exchange called the trunk access code) is the number you dial to get an outside line. For most PBX systems in North America, 9 is the single-digit code.

- The international access code is the number you dial to place an international call. In the United States and Canada, it's 011; in France (and many other countries), it's 00.

- The national number prefix is the number used to prefix all calls within a country. This is a little confusing because many countries have the same national number prefix and country code.

- The country or region code field is intended for countries such as France and Russia, where phone numbers are assigned by geographic region. For example, 401 is the region code for the Kaliningrad region; 471 is the region code for the Kursk region. Many countries, including the United States, refer to these codes as area codes; they are often mandatory when dialing any number, even within the same region.

In addition to these numbers, the dial plan provides a way for you to specify how another dial plan in your organization whose dial codes are different should be dialed. For example, if you had one dial plan in Canada and another in South Korea, you'd set the appropriate values in the controls in these two fields:

- Set the Country/Region Number Format field to tell Exchange how to dial the number of a user in another dial plan that has the same country code.

- Set the International Number Format field to specify how Exchange should dial the number of a user in another dial plan that has a different country code.

You can also use the Number Formats For Incoming Calls Within The Same Dial Plan controls to add formats to use when formatting numbers for calls between users in the same dial plan. For example, your dial plan specifies 5-digit extensions of the form 5xxxx, with direct inward dial numbers (DIDs) of 405-55x-xxxx. You'd use the + icon to add a new entry for 140555xxxxx, meaning that Exchange should prepend the 140555 to whatever number was actually dialed.

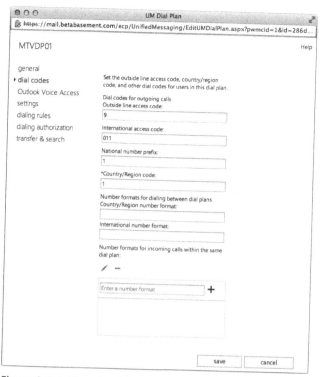

Figure 6-8 Setting the dial codes used for local and international access on the Dial Codes tab of the dial plan settings

The role of dialing rules

The three outbound-dialing situations mentioned earlier seem superficially similar, but the way Exchange actually handles them internally is quite different. However, all three types of outcalls are governed by dialing rules you can set. Dialing rules contain patterns of digits that you want to allow for outbound calls of all types. Because there are three types of possible outbound calls, you can apply dialing rules to three places: on a UM dial plan object, on a UM mailbox policy, or on an AA. You define rules on the UM dial plan and then authorize them on the dial plan, mailbox policy, or AA objects as needed.

Dialing rules are evaluated according to a two-step process. In the first step, known as canonicalization, Exchange converts the phone number to be dialed into a standardized format. This is required because until the number is canonicalized, Exchange has no idea whether it's a simple extension, a local number, a long distance number, or an international call, so it can't tell which dialing rules might apply. The second step, authorization, takes place when Exchange evaluates each dialing rule that might apply to the call (starting with the first rule defined and working down) until it either finds a matching rule, and the call is allowed to proceed, or it runs out of rules, and the call is denied. Rules are evaluated from most specific to least specific. For calls the AA places, its rules are evaluated first, whereas calls a user requests are checked against the applicable UM mailbox policy's rules first. If no match is found, the UM dial plan's rules are evaluated.

The PBX has rules, too

Dialing rules you create in Exchange aren't the only rules that might block a call. Your PBX might (and almost certainly will) have dialing rules of its own. It is common for Play on Phone calls, for example, to fail when the user requests an international call, not because the default Exchange rules block the call (they don't) but because the PBX has an international outdialing restriction. Any time you have problems placing outbound calls to numbers outside your phone system, a quick test is to try dialing the same number from a phone connected to the PBX to see what happens. If the PBX blocks the phone-initiated call, then a dialing rule is present on the PBX that you'll need to modify if you want to reach the number.

Canonicalization is a classic example of the computer science problem of string processing; Exchange provides a number and the canonicalization process must convert it into a common format. This process involves removing any whitespace or nonnumeric characters such as parentheses or dashes and truncating the number to remove any characters after an alphabetic character. Thus, (650) 555-1717 ext 204 is turned into just 6505551717. After any extra characters are removed, the number processor compares the length of the resulting number against the extension length of the dial plan. If they match—for example, if the passed-in number and the dial plan extension length are both five digits—Exchange assumes that the call is to an internal extension. If not, the number is evaluated to see whether it begins with +. If not, Exchange assumes that it's a local number and that it might need additional items, such as an area code. If the + is present, the number is treated as a properly formed E.164 number and evaluated to see whether it's an international call.

After the number's been stripped down, the dial codes defined on the dial plan, if any, are applied to the number. The outside line access code, if defined, is added to the beginning of the number, and the national number prefix is added next. If you specified a country code, it comes next, and then the number itself follows.

An example might help clarify how this all works. Suppose that David Alexander, a user in Sydney (country code 61, region code 3), is calling Antonio Bermejo in Barcelona (country code 34, region code 93). The two users are in different dial plans. Antonio's number is listed in David's contacts folder as +3493 800 702 444. David's UM server sees the + sign, looks at the country code, and detects that Australia and Spain are not, in fact, the same country. It adds the international dialing code (011 in Australia) and the outside line access code (generally 0 in Australia) to the beginning of the number, resulting in 0 011 34 93 800 702 444.

With that number in hand, the Exchange UM worker process can decide whether the user is permitted to place outbound calls to that number. At this point, the UM worker process knows what number it is being asked to dial; whether that number is an extension, local call, or international call; and whether the user is authenticated (more on authentication in following sections of this chapter).

What's in a dialing rule

Each dialing rule consists of four parts. First is the group name. Exchange has a fairly loose standard here; all rules that share the same name are considered to be part of the same group, although they are evaluated in top-to-bottom order. Next is the number mask. This is the pattern used to decide whether the number to dial matches the rule. You use "x" characters as wildcards to determine the pattern to match. For example, 9165055xxxxx matches 916505551212 and 916505573505 but not 916505503101. The number of exes you include is the number of digits matched by the pattern.

The next component of the dialing rule (see Figure 6-9) is the dialed number. This is the pattern Exchange uses to turn a number that matches the dialing rule into a dialable number. In Figure 6-9, the number mask and dialed number patterns are the same; this is often the case because setting them to the same value just specifies that the input number should be allowed and dialed without modification. You can also specify changes, such as turning an initial 8 (used in some systems to indicate a local external call) into a 9, representing an external long-distance call.

Figure 6-9 The dialing rule has a name, a number mask, and an output that indicates how to transform the outbound number

Dialing rule authorization

The authorization step involves examining each of the defined dialing rules to look for a match. Dialing rules don't apply to calls sent to extensions, so if the call is to an extension, no dialing rules are checked. Presuming the call is to a nonextension target, the next step is for Exchange to choose the correct set of rules; the dial plan has separate rule sets for local and international calls.

The rule group that should apply depends on whether the caller is authenticated. Authentication, in turn, depends on who's calling and where he's calling from:

- A call from a user who logs on, as with Play on Phone (which can only be requested from Outlook and Outlook Web App) or OVA, is always treated as authenticated.

- A transfer from an AA is always treated as unauthenticated.

- A transfer from a caller who triggers a call answering rule's find-me or call transfer actions is treated as authenticated. This might seem odd until you consider that UM knows that the call is really being originated by the call answering rule, which is associated with a known mailbox.

Dialing rule groups on the dial plan are used for unauthenticated callers. Dialing rule groups added to the UM mailbox policy are used for calls related to authenticated users. Dialing rule groups attached to a UM automated attendant are used only for calls generated by that AA.

In any case, Exchange evaluates all the rules by gathering them in each dialing rule group (the names of which are sorted alphabetically) and then sorting them from most specific to least specific and evaluating them. Each rule is tested to see whether the dialing mask matches the number. If so, the rule is considered a match, but evaluation continues—the most specific match of all available rules is used, not necessarily the first match.

If no matching rule is found, the call is not authorized, and the call attempt fails. If at least one rule matches, the call is allowed.

Blind transfers

Blind transfers are used for most types of outbound calls that Exchange UM can generate (find-me actions in call answering rules being the exception). In a blind transfer, the UM worker process just sends a SIP REFER back to the IP PBX. The PBX is supposed to use this REFER to redirect the call and create a new conversation path between the original caller and the target specified by the REFER headers. The UM server doesn't perform any kind of check to see whether the transfer succeeded, which can sometimes lead to unwelcome behavior. For example, suppose that an external caller dials in to an automated attendant and presses the key associated with a transfer to extension 30268. Suppose further that due to a PBX setup error, that extension isn't configured in the PBX. Exchange sends the SIP REFER to the PBX, and the PBX consults its call coverage map and then decides that it can't complete the call because the target extension doesn't exist. If someone dialed the nonexistent extension from a PBX-attached phone, she'd get a fast busy signal, and that's exactly what the external caller hears—forcing her to call back and try the automated attendant again.

Supervised transfers

The supervised transfer process is much more interesting because Exchange has to hold the original call open while it performs the transfer. Consider when Chase Carpenter, an outsider caller, dials the extension belonging to Samantha Smith, whose mailbox is configured with a call answering rule that offers Find Me as an option. Chase hears the mailbox greeting and call answering rule menu (based on the process already discussed); when prompted, he dials the digit associated with Find Me. Here's what happens next:

1. UM records Chase's name (or whatever else he says after the prompt) and then plays the comfort tone for him. That's all he hears during the remaining steps of the process.

2. The UM worker process initiates an outbound call to the number Samantha set as the target of her call answering rule. UM places this call by sending a SIP INVITE to the IP PBX.

3. Samantha answers the call or not. When, or if, the call is answered, the UM worker process plays Chase's name and asks Samantha to press 1 to accept the call. If the call is unanswered or answered by Samantha's voice mail, no one presses 1, and that tells the UM server that Samantha isn't there. However, if Samantha presses 1, the UM server knows that she's present.

4. If Samantha accepts the call, the UM worker process starts a supervised transfer by sending a SIP REFER with Replaces: and Referred-By: headers to the PBX. This is a special type of SIP REFER that tells the IP PBX to substitute one SIP conversation with another. In this case, you want the PBX to bridge the call logically from Chase to the UM server with the call from the UM server to Samantha, so that the result is a call from Chase, through the IP PBX, to Samantha's cell phone.

Multilingual support in UM

Exchange 2013 RTM includes language support for 26 languages, the same number as included in Exchange 2010. These languages are fully supported in Exchange; the language packs include ASR, TTS, and spoken prompts so that any of the supported languages can be used with Outlook Voice Access. Supported languages are as follows:

- Australian English (en-AU)

- Brazilian Portuguese (pt-BR)

- British English (en-GB)

- Canadian English (en-CA)

- Canadian French/Quebecois (fr-CA)

- Castilian Spanish (es-ES)

- Catalan (ca-ES)

- Chinese (Simplified Han, China) (zh-CN)

- Chinese (Traditional Han, Hong Kong) (zh-HK)

- Chinese (Traditional Han, Taiwan) (zh-TW)

- Danish (da-DK)

- Dutch (nl-NL)

- Finnish (fi-FI)

- French (fr-FR)

- German (de-DE)

- Indian English (en-IN)

- Italian (it-IT)

- Japanese (jp-JP)

- Korean (ko-KR)

- Mexican/Central American Spanish (es-MX)

- Norwegian Bokmål (nb-NO)

- Polish (pl-PL)

- Portuguese (pt-PT)

- Russian (ru-RU)

- Swedish (sv-SE)

- U.S. English (en-US)

Of these languages, only seven are supported for voice mail preview: U.S. and Canadian English, French, Italian, Polish, Portuguese (Portugal), and Spanish (Spain). If you have other language packs installed, the system will use them for ASR, TTS, and prompts but not for voice mail preview.

Each language pack includes a variety of components necessary to add support for the selected language. These components include:

- Pre-recorded system prompts. For example, the prompt users hear telling them to record a message and then hang up when finished has to be localized and recorded

Chapter 6

by a native speaker for each language pack. When the language pack is installed, these prompts are stored in a subdirectory of <Program Files>\Microsoft\Exchange Server\V15\UnifiedMessaging\Prompts\.

- Grammar files the mailbox server uses to look up the names of given users and groups in the directory.

- Grammar files for vocabulary used when talking to OVA. Phrases such as "clear my calendar" or "delete message" are localized and then stored in .grxml files specific to each language pack.

- TTS pronunciation rules and vocabulary so that email, calendar, and contact information can be read to callers by using appropriate pronunciation and vocabulary.

- Grammar and pronunciation rules ASR uses to enable callers to interact with UM using the voice user interface (VUI) in the language of the UM language pack.

Languages that are supported for voice mail preview include additional data, including statistical models of the language that the transcription engine uses to recognize the structure of text.

Installing and removing language packs

You may install as many of these language packs as you want; they can be downloaded from the Microsoft website and installed or removed at any time. The Get-UMService cmdlet shows you which language packs are installed on a server, and the list is visible on the settings page for dial plans and the General page for UM automated attendants.

You can install new language packs in either of two ways: using the installation utility bundled with each language pack or using Exchange's setup.com utility with the /AddUmLanguagePack switch. To remove a language pack, however, you must use setup.com with the /RemoveUmLanguagePack switch.

The U.S. English language pack is always installed, and you cannot remove it. For consistency's sake, Microsoft recommends installing the same language packs on all your UM servers.

Choosing the right language

Figuring out which language a caller hears can be a bit tricky. The actual language that's used depends on both who's calling and who's answering.

For calls to a user extension that are answered by a UM server, the dial plan language is used. Any system prompts the caller hears come from the language pack, and if she leaves a message, it will be transcribed using either the dial plan language pack (if that language supports voice mail preview) or U.S. English.

Calls to an automated attendant use the language set for that individual AA. The caller hears system prompts in the language pack language, and menu navigation labels, company locations, and other text items defined in the automated attendant are pronounced using the language pack's pronunciation rules. (I like this because it's a pleasure to hear the French and Canadian French language packs pronounce my last name properly!) Keep in mind that any custom prompts you record should match the language set for the automated attendant; if you change the AA language, be prepared to replace the prompts too.

Calls to OVA are answered using the language set on the user's mailbox if that language has an installed language pack. If the matching language pack isn't installed, OVA uses the default dial plan language. Users set their mailbox language when they first log on to the mailbox by using Outlook Web App (in which case, they can set it explicitly) or Outlook (in which case, it's set according to the active language in Windows). They or you can change it using the Set-MailboxRegionalConfiguration cmdlet or the regional settings page on the user's mailbox settings in Outlook Web App. However, the mailbox language setting is ignored when voice mail preview transcription takes place, which is a limitation that it's hoped will be revisited in a future version.

A few languages allow an alternate language to be used if the desired one isn't available. For example, if the user's mailbox settings specify Chinese (Hong Kong; zh-HK) as the language, but it's not installed, UM will use Chinese (Simplified; zh-CN) and Chinese (Traditional; zh-TW), in that order. Other languages that follow a similar progression include French, Spanish, and Portuguese. In those cases, alternate versions of the base language are used if possible. If not, or in the case of a language such as Russian or Korean that doesn't have a variant, Exchange will fall back to U.S. English. You can't change this ordering or add new substitute languages because these are hard-coded in the UM engine.

Deploying UM

For basic deployments, UM is surprisingly easy to deploy. In most environments, you need only a few basic objects, and a single server is sufficient. More complex environments might require a bit more work. This presumes that you have a functioning telephony environment set up so that PBX users can call one another, incoming calls from the PSTN are handled properly, and so on. A word of advice: if you have problems or shortcomings in your telephony system, it's a good idea to stabilize (and, if possible, fix) them before beginning your Exchange UM deployment. You should also plan to deploy any IP PBXs or gateways you might need.

Sizing and scaling UM

Microsoft has not yet released any sizing or scaling guidance for Exchange 2013 UM. Now that UM is a collateral feature on the Mailbox server role, though, the sizing and scaling guidelines Microsoft provides for Mailbox servers can be used. The UM role can accommodate up to 100 concurrent calls, and as you've seen, a maximum of five messages can be queued for voice mail preview transcription. If you anticipate having more concurrent calls or find that you frequently have more than five messages awaiting transcription, you can easily scale out by enabling UM on another Mailbox server (or by adding another mailbox server).

Microsoft fully supported virtualization of the UM role for Exchange 2010 SP1, and the same is true for Exchange 2013; you can virtualize both the CAS and Mailbox server roles, which means that the UM feature set is effectively virtualized along with them.

Preparing your network

Before your UM servers can answer any calls, they must be able to communicate with all the other devices involved in the call flow. That begins with the gateways or IP PBXs you're using; they need to be able to pass SIP and RTP traffic back and forth with the UM servers, so if you have any firewalls between the PBX and the UM servers, you must open not only the fixed ports SIP uses (5060 and 5061 at a minimum) but also the dynamic ports RTP/SRTP uses. This is true whether your IP PBX is a physical device or an application (such as the 3CX or snom ONE products).

If you're using an IP gateway to intermediate between an older PBX and Exchange, you have to verify that the IP gateway can communicate with both the PBX and your UM servers.

Microsoft used to have recommendations about locating the UM server and mailbox so that latency between them was minimized. Now that the UM role is part of the Mailbox server feature set, a bigger concern is probably latency between the Mailbox server and the IP PBX. There's no hard and fast guideline, but excessive latency can result in audio drops, stuttering, or excessive appearance of the UM comfort tone during calls. In the past, guidance from Microsoft has been to keep latency below 250 ms; Microsoft has not yet released updated guidance for Exchange 2013. Many VoIP products make extensive use of quality of service (QoS) or quality of experience (QoE) monitoring to help identify and drive resolution of these problems, so you might want to familiarize yourself with whatever similar tools your IP PBX vendor offers.

Installing UM

Because UM no longer exists as a separate server role, "installing the UM role" is a bit of a misnomer. It's more accurate to talk about installing the Mailbox and CAS roles. If you want details about these tasks, they are covered in *Microsoft Exchange Server 2013 Inside Out: Mailbox and High Availability* by Tony Redmond (Microsoft Press, 2013). After you've installed the appropriate number of Mailbox and CAS servers, the only remaining installation-related task is to add the desired UM language packs. It's better to do this as part of the server installation process because doing so enables you to set up dial plan and automated attendant objects initially with the right languages instead of having to go back and add them later. This greatly eases testing because you can immediately verify that you're hearing the expected language in OVA, call answering, and AA scenarios.

Creating core UM objects

After you've installed (at least one of) the Mailbox and CAS servers you want to use with UM, essentially five steps are required to complete your initial deployment: creating the UM dial plan objects, creating UM IP gateway objects, creating UM hunt groups, creating at least one UM mailbox policy, and (optionally) creating any UM automated attendants you plan to use. After you've created these objects, you can start configuring them as appropriate, and then you can enable users so that they start benefiting from UM features.

Creating UM dial plans

The dial plans you create must correspond to the dial plans you have defined on your existing phone system. (There are special considerations for creating dial plans if you're using Lync, which is discussed further in Chapter 7, "Integrating Exchange 2013 with Lync Server.") The primary items you need to create dial plans are the extension length, dial plan type, and VoIP security mode—all of which will be dictated by the PBX or Lync system with which you're connecting.

If you've installed multiple language packs as recommended previously, you can also specify the language you want your new dial plan to use. You can always install language packs and change the dial plan language later if you forget to do so up front.

When you create the dial plan, you also get a default UM mailbox policy for the dial plan. Many deployments find that a single UM mailbox policy is sufficient, either because they want all users in each dial plan to have the same settings or because the number of UM-enabled users is small enough that a single UM mailbox policy can cover all necessary settings.

Creating UM IP gateway objects

Creating UM IP gateway objects is quite simple; all you need is the name and IP address or FQDN of each UM IP gateway you want your Exchange UM servers to talk to. Remember that Exchange won't accept any inbound SIP requests from any IP address that isn't associated with a defined gateway object. This includes SIP softphones, if you're using them for testing, and conventional IP PBXs, gateways, and Lync servers. Whenever possible, you should use the FQDN of the IP PBX for two reasons: it insulates you from having to make changes if the IP address of a defined gateway changes, and it preserves your option to use secured or SIP secured communications with mutual Transport Layer Security (TLS). Both those dial plan types require the gateway object to be defined with an FQDN.

You have to create UM IP gateway objects after you define UM dial plans because part of the UM IP gateway creation process involves selecting the dial plan to which you want to bind the gateway object. You can't change this after you've created the UM IP gateway; if you need to do so, you'll have to remove and replace the UM IP gateway object, which is very simple to do from within either EAC or EMS.

Creating UM hunt groups

When you create a UM IP gateway object and bind it to a dial plan, Exchange creates a default hunt group for that combination named Default Hunt Group. This default object won't have a pilot identifier associated with it, meaning that it will answer all calls sent to it. If your PBX is configured to use a specific extension for the hunt group, you can set that extension as the pilot number for the hunt group, but this is optional.

Creating UM mailbox policies

UM mailbox policies are easy to create; their power comes when you start customizing them and applying the resulting customization to groups of users. The best way to get started with UM mailbox policies is to leave the default policy Exchange creates on the dial plan completely untouched. Create one or more additional UM mailbox policies if you like and customize them freely; you can then apply the new policies to test users and verify that they do what you want before rolling them out more broadly. This is the same process that you'd normally use for deploying other kinds of user-targeted policies such as Group Policy objects or Exchange mailbox policies, and that similarity of process is no accident.

Designing automated attendants

Nearly everyone living in the industrialized world has a horror story to tell about an unresponsive, poorly designed, or difficult-to-use interactive voice response (IVR) system. Although it's true that the IVR technology banks, airlines, universities, and other large organizations use has greatly improved over the 30 or so years since it was first deployed, it's also true that IVR can generate much more aggravation than it saves. By using Exchange, you can lay out automated attendants for your callers, which gives you great flexibility coupled with the power to provide lots of functionality to the caller at no additional cost to you. The other side of this ability is that you can also infuriate your callers (and potentially drive away customers or aggravate employees) if you do a poor job. Although this book doesn't have space to provide a comprehensive guide to IVR design, a few general design principles can make things easier for you as an administrator and for your callers:

- Keep IVR trees shallow and broad. Don't make users listen to long menus and then drill down into them; instead, offer a small number of choices that branch to other AAs as necessary. If you're tempted to include more than four or five choices in a single AA, consider whether it might be more effective to use two smaller AAs.

- Callers love dial by name. It's by far the easiest and fastest way to find individual people, so use it whenever you can.

- ASR in Exchange 2013 is quite good, but it's not perfect; very noisy environments can render it unable to understand users (or make it difficult for users to hear what the AA prompts say). As a best practice, plan on having a backup AA that understands DTMF to provide a telephone user interface for users who cannot, or don't want to, use a speech-enabled AA.

- Not every user will be comfortable with ASR. If you can, providing a quick, easily understood prompt (such as "Press zero for the operator or say the name of the person you want to dial") makes life much easier for these folks.

Help with automated attendant scripts

A quick Internet search, using phrases such as "automated attendant script samples," will turn up a wealth of suggestions for writing effective and useful automated attendant scripts. The best part is that the advice found at sites such as *http://operationstech .about.com/od/informationtechnology/a/PhoneAutoAttnd.htm* is useful even though it's not directly targeted at Exchange UM deployments.

The fastest way to design a set of automated attendants is to use your favorite drawing tool—Visio, a white board, or a piece of paper all work well—to diagram the structure of all the AAs you want to use. In most deployments, neither the telephony team nor the Exchange administrators are in charge of the contents of the AA, anyway, for one of two reasons. Either they've gotten a mandate to make the Exchange AAs sound just like those of the older system Exchange is replacing, or the powers that be want to design the AAs to present a particular marketing impression. In either case, your contribution might be limited to providing information on how Exchange AAs work and what can and cannot be done with AAs to meet the desired objectives.

Chapter 6

INSIDE OUT No, you can't customize the key bindings

One very common request from administrators in the planning stages of Exchange UM deployments is to customize the key bindings used in either AAs or OVA. Although you can choose which digits between 1 and 9 are used for menu navigation entries, you cannot remap the 0, *, or # keys (and you cannot change the spoken vocabulary to, for example, allow callers to say "agent" instead of "operator").

Enabling users for UM

After you've created all the necessary objects, you can start UM-enabling individual users. This is quite simple. After you have one or more users to enable, you can do so either in EAC or with the Enable-UMMailbox cmdlet. Which of these you choose is up to you, bearing in mind that EAC can be used only to assign extension numbers to telephone dial plans. Even if the user in question is part of a SIP URI or E.164 dial plan, you must still assign a numeric extension to him for use when logging on to OVA. You must use Enable-UMMailbox if you actually want to set a SIP or E.164 extension on the mailbox.

In addition to a numeric extension (whose length, remember, must match that specified in the dial plan), you must also specify a PIN for the newly enabled users. Exchange happily generates a random PIN for you, or you can specify one. The PIN itself is stored as a property of the mailbox object in the Exchange Store, but a hash of the PIN is stored as an Active Directory attribute to make logon authentication through OVA more efficient. The length and complexity of all mailbox PINs, including any initial PIN you specify, is controlled by the UM mailbox policy to which you've assigned the user.

When the mailbox has been UM enabled, the user gets a message with the (localized) subject line, "Welcome to Microsoft Exchange Unified Messaging." This message contains the user's initial PIN along with the message text you specified in the UM mailbox policy. The newly enabled user can start receiving voice mail messages and MCNs as soon as you enable him, although for best results he should log on to OVA to record his personal greeting (or at least his name).

Managing UM

After you have deployed UM, you might find that it requires relatively little day-to-day management. The most frequent UM-related task you'll perform might be changing user extensions to reflect changes on the physical phone system; in most organizations, the rate of change for IP PBXs and their configuration is very slow, which will limit how often you have to modify the corresponding objects in Exchange.

A quick note about permissions

The Exchange 2013 role-based access control (RBAC) implementation includes a management role group specifically for UM management; it's called, oddly enough, the UM Management management role group. The role group contains three roles: UM Mailboxes, UM Prompts, and Unified Messaging. Here's what they do:

- The UM Mailboxes role is used to configure UM-related settings on mailboxes; holders can run the Get/Set-UMMailbox cmdlets and make other adjustments on UM-related properties.

- The UM Prompts role enables holders to record new prompts for automated attendants or the limited set of system prompts that may be customized.

- The Unified Messaging role gives holders the power to manage services but not to customize prompts or modify UM-related mailbox properties. Holders of this role can also manage dial plans, hunt groups, and so on.

All these roles are scoped to the organization level; there's no way to limit them to smaller scopes.

It's worth noting that the Organization Management management role group confers all the same powers as the UM Management role group and then some; Org Management holders have full access to all UM configuration objects and settings. In addition, the UM service on the Mailbox role can also be started, stopped, or modified by users in the Server Management role group. The Unified Messaging role is intended primarily to enable the telephony team to manage Exchange UM objects that map to items in the real phone system. The UM Prompts role can be assigned to whomever is in charge of recording prompts (often the best-sounding employee on a particular team, regardless of whether that employee knows anything about telephony or UM), and the UM Mailboxes role can be assigned to the team that normally handles mailbox and user account management.

Managing UM server-level settings

Because there are two aspects to the UM server role—the UM call router, which runs on the CAS, and the UM server itself, on the Mailbox role—you need to know which behaviors are controlled on which part of the UM system. Even when the Mailbox and CAS roles are collocated, you still have to know which of the two cmdlet families to use. I say "cmdlet families" because many of the most interesting settings are not currently exposed in EAC; you have to use EMS with Get/Set-UMCallRouterSettings to manage settings on the call router and Get/Set-UMService to control settings on the UM service and worker process.

The Get/Set/Disable/Enable-UMServer cmdlets from Exchange 2007 and Exchange 2010 still work for those versions but aren't present (or usable) against Exchange 2013.

Chapter 6

Managing UM call router settings

There are relatively few settings that you can directly manage for the UM call router service. The call router is intended essentially as an opaque black box that just does its job with limited intervention (or control) possible from administrators. This approach has the advantage of requiring less work on the administrators' part, at least as long as the call router is working properly!

Of the parameters available with Get/Set-UMCallRouterSettings, the most interesting are the following:

- DialPlans is what you use to tie an Exchange 2013 CAS to a particular SIP dial plan for use with OCS 2007 R2, Lync 2010, or Lync 2013. It isn't necessary for you to set the value of DialPlans for ordinary operations, and in fact, you can't associate an Exchange 2013 UM call router or UM server with a telephone extension or E.164 dial plan. This attribute is blank by default. However, if you don't add the machines running the UM call router and UM services to the appropriate dial plans, you will find that Lync interoperability doesn't work, as detailed in Chapter 7, "Integrating Exchange 2013 with Lync Server." If you want to remove a server from all dial plans, set the value of DialPlans for that server to *$Null*.

- Use ExternalHostFqdn to set the FQDN the server advertises.

- ExternalServiceFqdn specifies the FQDN or host name of a load balancer that is handling mailbox servers.

- By default, a newly installed CAS allows UM traffic by using both IPv4 and IPv6. The permitted addressing schemes are reflected in the value of the IPAddressFamily parameter. When it is set to Any, both IPv4 and IPv6 are supported, but you may also restrict traffic to one family or the other. Whether you can change the assigned addressing method is controlled by the value of IPAddressFamilyConfigurable, which is true by default.

- The SipTcpListeningPort and SipTlsListeningPort parameters control the ports the UM call router process uses. Remember, these ports are where the IP PBX or gateway sends traffic, so changing the value of these parameters without making corresponding changes on the IP PBX will result in SIP setup failures.

- The UMStartupMode parameter controls whether this call router listens for secure, unsecure, or both types of SIP communications. When the startup mode is set to TCP, the call router participates in unsecured SIP communications only, listening on the port specified by SipTcpListeningPort. If the startup mode is set to TLS, it accepts TLS-protected SIP only and only on SipTlsListeningPort. If you set UMStartupMode to Dual, the call router simultaneously accepts requests on both ports. Note that if you change the value of UMStartupMode, you must restart the UM call router service before the change takes effect.

The online help for Set-UMCallRouterSettings lists a couple of deprecated parameters (including Status and MaxCallsAllowed) that no longer make sense in the context of a UM call router and two parameters (UMForwardingAddressTemplate and UMPodRedirectTemplate) that are available only to Microsoft for use in Office 365. The documentation just says these parameters are "reserved for internal Microsoft use." Even I don't know what they do!

Managing UM server settings

The settings available to the UM service (and, by extension, the worker processes) are slightly more complex. You view and change them with the Get/Set-UMService cmdlets.

Some of the settings available on the UM service are the same as settings on the UM call router; this makes perfect sense when you consider that in Exchange 2010 the call router and UM service were part of the same code base. In Exchange 2013 RTM, the DialPlans, ExternalHostFqdn, ExternalServiceFqdn, IPAddressFamily, IPAddressFamilyConfigurable, UMForwardingAddressTemplate, UMPodRedirectTemplate, and UMStartupMode parameters to Get/Set-UMService have the same semantics and behavior as their counterparts on Get/Set-UMCallRouterSettings.

> ### Like the default ports? Good; that's all you get
> Microsoft doesn't support changing the port numbers the UM service itself uses, so even though Set-UMService recognizes the SipTcpListeningPort and SipTlsListeningPort parameters, they don't actually do anything.

That still leaves a number of unique parameters that pertain to operations on mailbox servers:

- GrammarGenerationSchedule regulates when the grammar generation process starts. This parameter can contain only a single time per day, but you may set a separate time for each weekday if you wish. The default of 2 A.M. is probably fine for most sites, though. (For more on what happens during GAL grammar generation, read on!)

- IrmLogEnabled (which defaults to true) controls whether the server keeps a log of IRM operations. The related IrmLogMaxAge, IrmLogMaxDirectorySize, IrmLogMaxFileSize, and IrmLogPath properties control various aspects of log housekeeping.

Chapter 6

- MaxCallsAllowed specifies the number of concurrent voice calls the target UM server is allowed to process. This value defaults to 100, which was always described as the limit for Exchange 2007 and Exchange 2010 UM servers.

- SIPAccessService is only used in conjunction with Lync. Normally, the UM server uses any Lync pool or edge server it can reach, which can lead to unwanted cross–wide area network (WAN) traffic. By specifying the FQDN of the Lync pool or edge server you want a particular Exchange server to use, you can restrict that Exchange server to communicating only with the target Lync server. You must use the internal FQDN of the Lync server here, not the external or load-balanced names.

Get-UMService also returns a multivalued property named Languages that shows you which UM language packs are installed on the server. This is a read-only property because you can modify the installed languages only by adding or removing language packs as described earlier in this chapter.

One thing you can do with the UM service that's not possible with the UM call router is tell the service to stop answering calls with the Disable-UMService cmdlet or tell it to start answering calls again with Enable-UMService. Any calls currently in progress when you disable the service are handled normally, but as soon as you disable the service, it stops accepting new calls until you enable it again.

Using certificates with UM

The mechanics of requesting and assigning certificates for Exchange roles have already been discussed. After you have obtained suitable certificates for the CAS and mailbox servers that act as UM servers, you install them using Enable-ExchangeCertificate as you would for any of the other roles—just make sure that you remember to specify the appropriate role. The Exchange 2013 version of the Enable-ExchangeCertificate cmdlet has separate roles for the UM call router and UM server components. In Exchange 2007 and Exchange 2010, you'd use Enable-ExchangeCertificate –Services UM to assign a certificate to a UM server; now you can use "UM" to assign to the UM service and UMCallRouter to assign to the call router only. The distinction is important because the call router is the main component that interacts with IP PBXs and will thus benefit from TLS the most. However, the UM server can also use TLS when interacting with the PBX, so if you're planning to use secured or SIP secured dial plans, you must install certificates for both roles. It is perfectly okay to install the same certificate for both the UM and UM call router roles if you like.

After Get-ExchangeCertificate shows the correct certificates for the roles you want them to have, you still must tell the UM call router and/or UM services that they should make and accept secured connections. To do this, you use the –UMStartupMode dual parameter with Set-UMCallRouter or Set-UMService, respectively. Keep in mind that you must restart the respective services after making this change.

It is worth pointing out that many IP PBX and gateway products are picky about what certificates they will accept. Different vendors have very different approaches toward certificate management. Some provide a web interface with which you can request certificates from an arbitrary certificate authority (CA) and load your own trusted roots, whereas others are much less configurable. To avoid trouble, you are probably best off ensuring that your gateways and PBXs, Exchange servers, and Lync servers (if any) are using certificates from the same CA if possible or, at least, from CAs that are cross-certified. Lync in particular is likely to refuse to communicate with an Exchange server at all when it believes its certificates are invalid or untrustworthy. Although it is technically possible in many cases to provide VoIP security by using the self-signed certificates Exchange generates, this is likely to cause you more trouble than it is worth as you try to get the other telephony devices with which you want to talk to accept the self-signed certificates.

GAL grammar generation

One often-ignored aspect of Exchange automated speech recognition capability is that it depends on having a speech grammar to use when interpreting what the caller says. Much of the necessary grammar data is included in the UM language pack for a specific language; that's how Exchange UM knows, for instance, that the verb order in German is very different from the order used in English or Italian, so it can recognize commands such as "clear my calendar" (meinen Kalender löschen in German) in various languages. However, the prepackaged grammar necessarily has gaps. It doesn't contain information about the names of distribution groups or users in the organization, and it doesn't necessarily have all the data required to provide ASR for the automated attendants you build in a particular environment. The UM server needs this information to be able to recognize speech input from the caller, so Exchange includes a mechanism to generate an organization-specific speech grammar based on the unique aspects of that organization. This grammar is usually called as a GAL grammar, and the process by which it is created is known as GAL grammar generation.

Grammar files for the languages installed on a UM server are stored in \Program Files \Microsoft\Exchange Server\V15\UnifiedMessaging\Grammars, with subdirectories for each installed language. There are grammar files for calendar, contact, and email manipulation and separate grammar files for the main OVA menu and common words used across scenarios. (There's also a mystery file, mowascenarios.grxml; I don't know what it's for.) If you open any of these files, all of which have a .grxml extension, you see that they look like normal XML with some JavaScript mixed in. These files aren't intended to be customized or modified by administrators, and doing so isn't supported.

However, the GAL grammar generation process also creates a separate set of grammar files that are specific to the dial plans and AAs your organization contains. The entire GAL generates a single grammar, Gal.grxml, that contains all mail-enabled users and contacts (except those that are hidden from the GAL by using the msExchHideFromAddressLists attribute). Each dial plan gets a grammar containing the names of the UM-enabled users in that dial plan, and each address list gets a similar file containing the names of the UM-enabled users in the address list. The dial plan and address list grammar files are named with their identifying GUIDs. There's also a single file, named DistributionList.grxml, that contains entries for each distribution list that is visible in address lists. These organization-specific grammar files are stored in the system arbitration mailbox.

When you first install UM, only the factory grammar files are present. Adding a server to any dial plan in the organization triggers an update for that dial plan only. These grammar files are generated daily at 2 A.M. on the mailbox server that hosts the system arbitration mailbox. You must ensure that address list or user changes are complete before that time and that address lists have been updated before the GAL grammar process runs. Because the resulting grammar files are in the arbitration mailbox, all Mailbox servers can download them, after which they're stored in the Cached folder in the same directory as the factory-provided language packs.

To find the mailbox that contains the UM grammar files, use the following command:

```
Get-Mailbox -arbitration | where {$_.PersistedCapabilities -like "*UM*"} | fl Name,
PersistedCapabilities
```

This shows you which of the arbitration mailboxes contain UM data; the *OrganizationCapabilityUMGrammar* value indicates that a particular mailbox might contain UM grammar data, whereas the *OrganizationCapabilityUMGrammarReady* value indicates that it does contain UM data. (The related OrganizationCapabilityUMData value indicates that the arbitration mailbox contains AA prompts.)

INSIDE OUT   Forcing grammar regeneration

In Exchange 2007 and Exchange 2010, you can run the GalGrammarGenerator.exe tool to update the organization-specific grammar files manually. Exchange 2013 doesn't have a separate executable because the grammar files are generated by the UM Mailbox Assistant process. If you need to regenerate the grammar files manually, you can stop the UM Mailbox Assistant service on the Mailbox server that has the arbitration mailbox, remove the grammar files, and restart the service.

The key thing to remember about grammar generation is that newly added users or DLs will not be addressable through ASR until after the grammar has been updated. Suppose that you add 10 new users at 5 A.M. (For clarity, say that it's 5 A.M. local time on whatever mailbox server is actually generating the grammar, not necessarily 5 A.M. local time where you are.) If grammar generation keeps its default schedule of 2 A.M., the users you add won't be addressable through OVA, through dial by name, or in automated attendants for nearly 24 hours. This argues in favor of either moving grammar generation to a more convenient time or accepting, and teaching users, that new users will not immediately be reachable through ASR.

Scheduling UM work on the Mailbox server

If you read *Microsoft Exchange Server 2013 Inside Out: Mailbox and High Availability*, you're familiar with how the workload of assistant processes running on Mailbox servers is controlled by the Exchange work cycle implementation. Some of the Mailbox server management tasks that run under the work cycle system have to do with UM, so it's worth mentioning what they are and refreshing your memory about how you control them.

You probably remember that the idea behind work cycles is to specify how often you want something to happen and then let Exchange decide how to reach that target. For example, a work cycle that says you want a task run on all mailboxes every seven days on a server with 2,000 mailboxes should result in Exchange processing about 300 mailboxes per day, scheduling the work during times of low demand (and using throttling when needed to ensure fair access to resources). At a specified interval known as the work cycle checkpoint, Exchange updates the list of objects that need to be processed, reprioritizing and rescheduling them as necessary to fit them all into the work cycle time period.

Set-MailboxServer has parameters by which you can control scheduling of three UM Mailbox Assistant tasks that run on the Mailbox server role:

- **Top N word collection for Voice Mail Preview**   This task crawls the Exchange content index for each mailbox, looking for unusual words that aren't already in the system or user voice mail preview lexicon; it then stack-ranks the words it finds and adds the most common ones to a user-specific dictionary. The TopNWorkCycle and TopNWorkCycleCheckpoint parameters control how this task runs; by default, the work cycle is seven days with daily checkpoints.

- **Gathering data for UM call reports**   This task, which is controlled by the UMReportingWorkCycle and UMReportingWorkCycleCheckpoint, involves crawling the UM call reports stored in the arbitration mailbox and using the found data to prepare UM call reports. By default, this happens daily.

- **Generating GAL grammar files**   You can't generate the GAL grammar in isolation, but you can adjust the DirectoryProcessorWorkCycle setting (which is marked as reserved for internal Microsoft use) if you want to control the schedule.

Dial plan settings

The UM dial plan has seven groups of settings (Figure 6-10). You can display the dial plan settings by opening a dial plan in EAC and clicking the Configure button. The General tab has only a single option, that of the security mode on the dial plan. The other tabs are somewhat more interesting.

You use the Dial Codes tab to set the outside line and international access codes, the country or region code, and the national number prefix. You typically set this once and then forget about it.

The Outlook Voice Access tab (Figure 6-11) enables you to specify the optional welcome greeting and informational announcement audio files. Although these are optional, the other setting on the OVA tab is critical—the Outlook Voice Access Numbers list contains the list of numbers users can dial to reach OVA. If you don't put any numbers in this list, users on that dial plan will not have a dial plan–specific extension number to call OVA. (However, they might still be able to reach OVA by dialing the OVA extension assigned to another dial plan.)

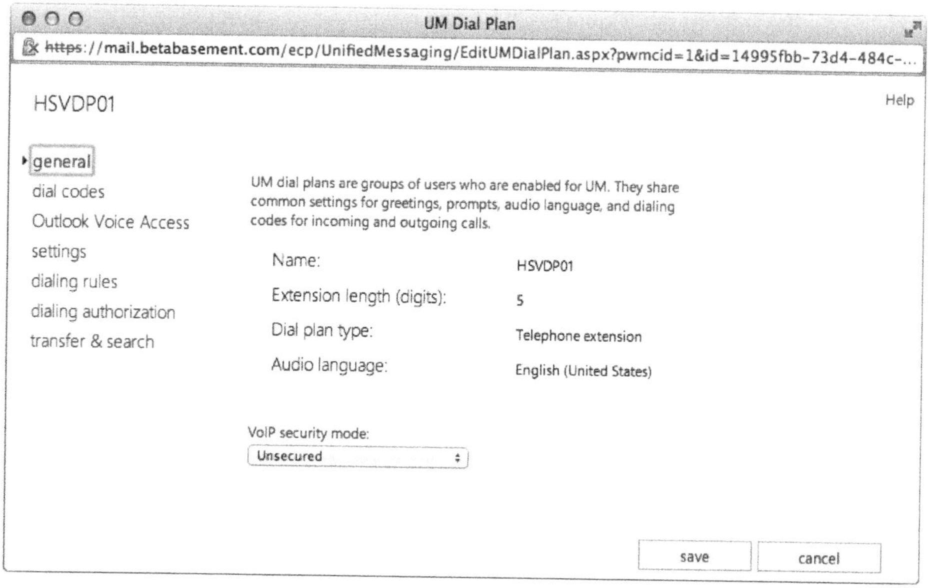

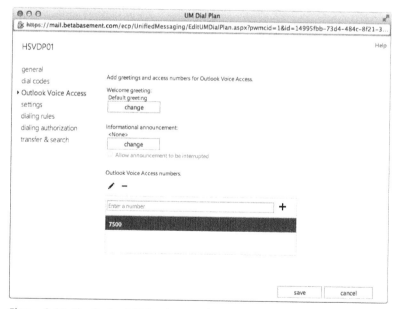

Figure 6-10 The General tab of the dial plan page that enables you to change the VoIP security mode, but that's all

Figure 6-11 The Outlook Voice Access tab, on which you set the OVA access number and any optional greetings you want to use

Chapter 6

The Settings tab (Figure 6-12) has the majority of the interesting settings for the dial plan object. Almost all the settings here are self-explanatory, with the possible exception of the Number Of Input Failures Before Disconnecting setting. That tells the UM server how many times the caller can fail to answer a prompt, or say or dial something UM doesn't recognize, before the server gives up and disconnects the call completely.

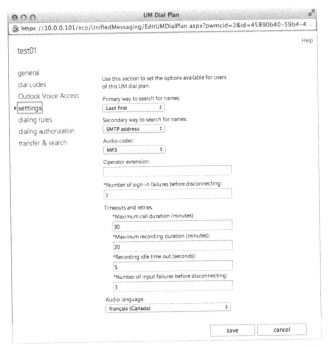

Figure 6-12 The dial plan Settings tab, on which you set the dial plan audio language

- The Primary Way To Search For Names and the Secondary Way . . . drop-down lists tell UM how to search for spoken names. When a caller speaks a name, Exchange first attempts to interpret it as whatever data type is specified in the Primary Way drop-down list. If it can't find a match, it tries the method specified in the Secondary Way drop-down list.

- The Operator Extension is the number to which to transfer calls when the caller requests an operator, either by dialing or by speech. This should ideally be an extension assigned to a live human, although you can make it any extension to which Exchange can transfer a call.

- The Audio Language drop-down list controls what language the dial plan uses when performing ASR.

The Dialing Rules and Dialing Authorization tabs give you a way to control what outbound numbers may be dialed by users whose servers are in this dial plan. As described earlier (in the "The role of dialing rules" section of this chapter), you create rules and assemble them into dialing rule groups that specify how to match and transform dialed numbers by using the Dialing Rule tab, and then you use the Dialing Authorization tab to specify which dialing rule groups you want to use for international and local or regional calls. You can also separately control whether users may transfer calls to internal extensions at two levels of granularity: you can allow calls to any extension or to extensions in the same dial plan.

Use the Transfer & Search tab (Figure 6-13) to control how or whether callers search for users in the GAL. The first check box at the top controls whether callers may use dial by name to reach UM-enabled users; the second check box governs whether callers have the option to leave a voice mail message for an extension without ringing it first.

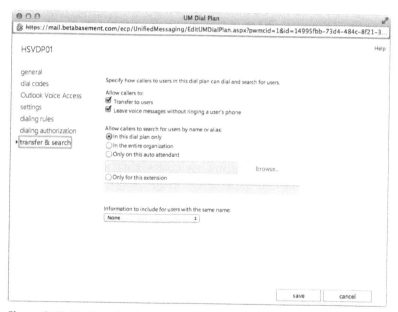

Figure 6-13 The Transfer & Search tab, by which you control how callers perform searches when they use dial by name

By default, dial by name is enabled, but it is scoped to the dial plan only, so callers can't search for users in other dial plans. You can scope the search to the entire organization or to choices in an automated attendant, if you wish, or even to a specific extension. In addition, by using Set-UMDialPlan to change the value of the ContactScope attribute on the dial plan object, you can control which specific address list or organizational unit (OU) the search uses when it's scoped to the entire organization. On this tab, you can also specify what additional information callers hear when they specify a name that has more than one match in the selected scope.

Additional dial plan settings with Set-UMDialPlan

Besides the settings exposed directly in EAC, many parts of Exchange have features that are only accessible through EMS, and UM is no exception. The settings in the following list are used with Set-UMDialPlan to control aspects of caller behavior that cannot be managed through EAC currently.

- AllowHeuristicADCallingLineIdResolution controls whether Active Directory heuristic resolution is used during CLID resolution.

- AutomaticSpeechRecognitionEnabled and CallAnsweringRulesEnabled control the availability of the named features for servers in the dial plan. If ASR or call answering rules are enabled at the dial plan level, they can still be disabled for an individual UM mailbox (or automated attendant in the case of ASR).

- DefaultOutboundCallingLineId contains the phone number you want to be emitted when UM servers in this dial plan place outbound calls. Normally, the extension number of the user requesting the outbound call is used, but if you specify a number here, it is used instead.

- Extension is the extension number the UM server uses as the sender when placing dial-by-name calls. Normally, this is left blank, but if you want dial-by-name calls to appear to come from a specific extension, you can set this value to the desired extension.

- FaxEnabled can prevent UM servers in this dial plan from answering fax calls. When this is set to $False, the UM server just ignores incoming T.38 calls from the gateway.

- InfoAnnouncementEnabled and InfoAnnouncementFilename enable you to set whether an informational announcement is played and, if so, what it says. When you set this on the dial plan, it applies to all AAs in the dial plan.

- TUIPromptEditingEnabled, when set, enables users with the correct permission to record prompts for automated attendants. Setting this value on the dial plan overrides the prompt editing setting on the automated attendants assigned to the dial plan.

- UMAutoAttendant is the one setting you can use to customize key-press behavior for the nondigit keys in automated attendants. Set it to the name of the AA you want executed when the caller presses *.

The following command enables heuristic calling line resolution, turns off fax reception, and sets the AA reachable by pressing the * key to the ContosoStandard AA:

```
Get-UMDialPlan   | Set-UMDialPlan -AllowHeuristicADCallingLineIDResolution $true
-FaxEnabled $false
-UMAutomatedAttendant "ContosoStandard"
```

UM IP gateway settings

The good news about UM IP gateway objects is that they require little to no management and have very few settings you can access. The bad news is that you can access very few settings. You can edit the name and FQDN or IP address of the gateway, set whether the gateway should receive MWI notifications, and select whether it should receive outbound calling requests. These parameters are all set in EAC and, when set, typically don't need to be changed. Only two parameters to Set-UMIPGateway are interesting enough to mention: DelayedSourcePartyInfoEnabled and Port. Port does what you'd expect: set it to the value of the TCP port on which the gateway is listening. The overwhelming majority of UM IP gateways use TCP 5060, but if they don't, this is your avenue for changing it.

Use DelayedSourcePartyInfoEnabled when you have an IP PBX or gateway that doesn't send diversion information in the initial SIP INVITE. You know you might need this if you never get caller ID resolution information on calls from certain gateways; setting DelayedSourcePartyInfoEnabled to true tells Exchange not to accept the initial INVITE, which should force the SIP peer to send another INVITE after it has diversion information available.

UM mailbox policy settings

The UM mailbox policy is your primary means of controlling which UM features users get. Although you can enable or disable many of these features at the dial plan or UM server level, it is usually more efficient to set them in a UM mailbox policy and apply that policy to users; that way, if you move users or servers around, the settings applied to their access stays consistent. Figure 6-14 shows the General tab of the UM mailbox policy settings; that should give you a good idea of the kinds of settings that can be managed at the policy level. (Note that a number of UM mailbox policy settings cannot be set from within EAC, too.)

Figure 6-14 The UM mailbox policy general settings, the most productive way to give users a consistent set of UM features

The Message Text tab adds a much-requested feature from prior versions of Exchange. You can create custom text messages for four cases: when a user is UM enabled, when her UM PIN is reset, when she receives a voice message, and when she receives a fax message. The custom messages, which can consist of up to 512 plaintext characters, are sent along with the system-generated content that normally appears. You can use these messages to give your users site-specific or company-specific information, such as the internal extension for the help desk.

The PIN Policies tab includes controls for setting the minimum PIN length, whether PINs expire (the default is that they do, after 60 days) and how many times the wrong PIN can be entered before forcing a PIN reset or account lockout. The PIN Recycle Count field is poorly named; it refers to the number of previous PINs that are kept on file to prevent users from changing back and forth between two or three PINs each time they change PINs.

You have already seen everything on the Dialing Authorization tab; the user interface is identical to the previous version. The only difference is that the authorizations you select here apply to all users in the policy, not to every user in the dial plan.

Use the Protected Voice Mail tab to disable the use of protected voice mail for authenticated and unauthenticated callers. Interestingly, if you try to enable protected voice mail, Exchange immediately checks whether you have at least one AD RMS server in the organization as soon as you click the Save button in the UM mailbox policy window. If it can't detect one, you won't be able to enable the use of protected voice mail. There are two other useful options here: Require Play On Phone and Allow Voice Responses To Email And Calendar Items. The first of these controls whether users are allowed to listen to protected voice mail messages directly on their computers. When this option is set, the only way for a user to hear a protected voice mail is to tell Outlook or Outlook Web App one phone number on which to play it. This helps security by making it more difficult for users to capture audio of a protected message. The other setting controls whether users may respond to items by leaving an audio message. EUM does not allow you to dictate responses to email or calendar items by using ASR, so when this option is set, users can use the reply command to attach an audio file to the reply so that recipients can hear what they said.

Additional UM mailbox policy settings with Set-UMMailboxPolicy

Besides the settings exposed directly in the EAC GUI, many parts of Exchange have features that are only accessible through EMS, and UM is no exception. The settings in the following list are used with Set-UMMailboxPolicy to control aspects of caller behavior that cannot be managed through EAC currently:

- When set to true, AllowPinlessVoiceMailAccess gives users access to their voice mail through OVA without requiring them to enter a PIN if they're calling from their own extension. This is a common feature of older voice mail systems. However, users must still enter a PIN to access other OVA features, including email.

- AllowSMSNotification controls whether users may opt to receive SMS (text message) notification when a new voice mail arrives. When SMS notification is enabled, the UMSMSNotificationOption parameter controls whether users get these notifications for voice mails only, voice mails and MCNs, or neither.

- AllowTUIAccessToCalendar, AllowTUIAccessToDirectory, AllowTUIAccessToEmail, and AllowTUIAccessToPersonalContacts control access to those specific features through OVA. When you disable a feature by setting the corresponding parameter to false, OVA doesn't include options for that feature in the spoken options callers hear, so they can't access them.

- AllowVoiceResponseToOtherMessageTypes regulates whether users may use OVA to send audio responses to mail messages or calendar invitations.

Several parameters are associated with outsourced Voice Mail Preview: VoiceMailPreviewPartnerAddress, VoiceMailPreviewPartnerAssignedID,

Chapter 6

VoiceMailPreviewPartnerMaxDeliveryDelay, and VoiceMailPreviewMaxMessageDuration. I have a query in to the PG to see whether these are still supported in 2013.

INSIDE OUT Restricting telephone user interface access

One of the most common requests in new deployments of Exchange UM is to give users access to a subset of OVA features. For example, some sites want to allow UM-enabled users to access their email with OVA but not to search the GAL with it. The preferred way to do this is use the AllowTUIAccess . . . parameters previously described on a UM mailbox policy and then apply the policy. For example, to set a UM mailbox policy to disallow the use of OVA for the calendar and GAL, you'd use Set-UMMailboxPolicy –AllowTUIAccessToCalendar:$false –AllowTUIAccessToDirectory: $false.

Mailbox settings

Not that many unique options apply to UM-enabled mailboxes, presupposing that you're talking about mailboxes that already have UM features. If you want to UM-enabl an existing mailbox, you may do so through EAC by selecting the target mailbox in the Recipients view and using the Enable link under Unified Messaging in the right-side navigation bar. That starts a two-step process. First, you specify which UM mailbox policy you want assigned to the mailbox, and then you assign an extension number and PIN. You can do the same thing with Enable-UMMailbox, with the bonus that you can also choose which SMTP address receives the "Welcome to Exchange UM" email by setting the NotifyEmail parameter. You can also use the AutomaticSpeechRecognitionEnabled parameter to turn off ASR preemptively when you create the mailbox.

After the mailbox is UM enabled, you can use EAC to reset its PIN, change the UM mailbox policy that applies to it, add extensions, or add a personal operator extension (see Figure 6-15). This last setting requires an explanation. The personal operator extension is where calls are transferred when a caller asks for an operator transfer when calling that particular mailbox. For example, a senior executive might have her assistant's extension set as the personal operator extension so that callers to her mailbox are transferred to the assistant rather than to the company operator. You can't change the user's assigned primary extension; to do so, you must UM-disable the mailbox and then re-enable it.

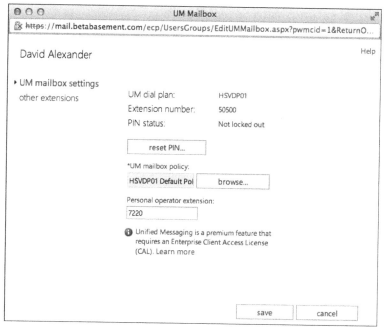

Figure 6-15 Relatively few mailbox-related UM settings exposed through EAC

Disabling a mailbox so that it can no longer use UM is simple; you can do it from EAC or with Disable-UMMailbox. Note that UM-disabling a mailbox doesn't affect the mailbox contents in any way, and it's easily reversible; just re-enable the mailbox, and users regain their previous functionality (although they lose their existing PIN assignment).

Two EMS cmdlets relate to PIN management. You can use Set-UMMailboxPIN to reset the PIN for a given user (which you can do in EAC also and users can do themselves through Outlook Web App). You can provide a PIN to use, or Exchange can generate one. Perhaps more useful, you can use Set-UMMailboxPIN with the –LockedOut parameter to block users from accessing UM features without affecting any other aspect of their mail experience.

You might think that Get-UMMailboxPIN would thus enable you to retrieve the user's PIN, but it doesn't. Instead, it tells you whether the targeted account has an expired PIN, whether it's locked out, and whether the mailbox has been through the first-run UM experience in OVA, during which users set their greetings and preferences. This is a handy way to find users who haven't set their greetings, for example—Get-UMMailboxPIN | where {$_.FirstTimeUser –eq $true} gives you a list.

Additional settings with Set-UMMailbox

Most of the parameters available to Set-UMMailbox are identical to the ones described earlier in the section on UM mailbox policies. However, three parameters are worth mentioning:

- AllowUMCallsFromNonUsers tells Exchange whether the mailbox should be included in dial-by-name results. When this parameter is set to true, the mailbox can still be reached by calling its extension directly or through transfers from another user's personal Contacts folder, but callers using OVA or an automated attendant cannot transfer to it by searching the GAL.

- AnonymousCallersCanLeaveMessages controls whether incoming calls without calling line ID information may leave messages.

- VoiceMailAnalysisEnabled controls whether voice mail messages left for this mailbox are sent to Microsoft for analysis. This setting can be changed independently of the value of the corresponding setting on the UM mailbox policy or dial plan. However, be aware that there's no equivalent of the InformCallerOfVoiceMailAnalysis setting at the mailbox level. Turning on VoiceMailAnalysisEnabled on an individual mailbox might therefore make it possible for voice mail messages to be sent to Microsoft without the caller knowing, which might run afoul of privacy laws in some jurisdictions.

Call answering rules

Call answering rules are normally managed directly by users, who create and change them using Outlook Web App or Outlook. However, Exchange 2013 introduced EMS cmdlets that enable you to work with rules in bulk. This is very useful if you want to do something such as create a default rule for departed employees that plays an informational announcement saying that they've left the company.

The cmdlets used for call answering rule management all have the UMCallAnsweringRule suffix; as you'd expect, there are cmdlets to create and remove rules (New- and Remove-), disable or enable individual rules, and see or change the properties of existing rules (Get- and Set-). These cmdlets are well explained in Microsoft documentation, but it's worth pointing out that New-UMCallAnsweringRule and Set-UMCallAnsweringRule give you some options that are not available in the current version of Outlook Web App. The most important is that instead of providing a phone number to match the "The caller is . . ." condition, you can specify a personal contact or an entry from the GAL as values for the CallerIDs parameter (although this requires you to provide the store ID of the contact or the legacyDN value for the GAL object). The syntax for setting conditions by using the EMS cmdlets is a bit torturous; the documentation is a good guide, but be prepared to do some experimentation.

Automated attendant settings

Measured by the number of available settings, the automated attendant object is probably the most complex piece of Exchange UM. The good news is that because most everyone in the industrialized world has had to interact with IVR systems before, the options you have available to administer AAs should be familiar. Because AAs are associated with a given dial plan, you access them from the dial plan properties. After you've selected an AA and opened it in EAC, you see the General tab of the AA properties, as shown in Figure 6-16. The properties on this page control the most basic aspects of the AA's operation, including which language it will use, which extensions it will answer, and whether it will accept voice commands. You can also specify a business name and location; the AA uses these text fields to tell callers the name of your business and where it is, upon request.

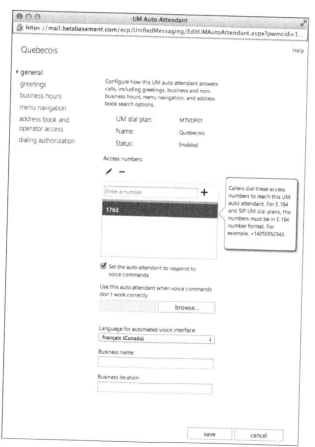

Figure 6-16 The basic settings that control the AA's behavior on the General tab

Most of the other tabs are extremely straightforward:

- Use the Greetings tab to specify separate audio files for business hours, nonbusiness hours, and informational greetings. You can specify whether you want the informational greeting to be interruptible, but that's it.

- The Business Hours tab shows a grid that visually indicates which hours are business hours (the ones in blue) versus nonbusiness hours. A button enables you to configure the included hours; a separate set of controls enables you to specify holidays. For each holiday you create, you may add an announcement that plays (presumably with seasonally appropriate music or sound effects).

- The Dialing Authorization tab does the same thing it does in the dial plan and UM mailbox policy objects: it gives you a scoped way to specify which calls may be placed from the AA.

That leaves two tabs of interest. The Address Book And Operator Access tab contains settings very similar to those found in the Transfer And Search tab of the dial plan object but with some baffling semantic differences. For example, the labeling of the settings that control whether callers can use dial by name or leave a voice message without ringing an extension are different between the two tabs. You can turn off GAL searching by name completely in the AA (by clearing the Allow Callers To Search For Users By Name Or Alias check box), which you can't do on the dial plan. The biggest difference between the two dialog boxes, however, is that on the AA, you can set an extension to be used when the caller wants to transfer to an operator, and you can control whether such transfers are allowed during business or nonbusiness hours.

The Menu Navigation tab (Figure 6-17) is the most complex part of the AA settings world. You use this tab to specify the greetings you want played when the AA answers calls during business and nonbusiness hours, and you specify independent menu navigation choices for those time periods. Each navigation choice specifies a digit or phrase the caller must provide to match that choice, plus an action (including transferring the call to an extension or another AA). You can also specify an audio file that should be played after the caller's navigation choice. Each AA may have up to nine of these menu navigation choices defined; the 0 key is reserved for transfers to the operator.

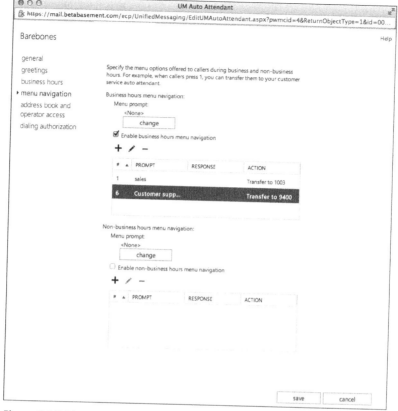

Figure 6-17 Menu navigation, at the heart of automated attendants

Additional settings with Set-UMAutoAttendant

A few other useful settings are available on AA objects, but they're not exposed in EAC. However, you can set them using Set-UMAutoAttendant. The relevant settings are as follows:

- Use ForwardCallsToDefaultMailbox to change an AA quickly so that all calls it receives are instead forwarded to a single UM mailbox (which you must set in the Default-Mailbox property on the AA). This can be useful if you want all calls to an office or department to be funneled to one place instead of processing them through the normal AA mechanism.

- Use StarOutToDialPlanEnabled to turn on a semi-hidden AA feature. When enabled, callers who dial * are transferred to OVA so they can log on and use OVA normally.

Chapter 6

- Use TimeZone and TimeZoneName to tell the AA to use a different time zone when calculating business and nonbusiness hours. If you don't set these, the server's time zone is used.

- Use WeekStartDay to adjust the starting day of the workweek, as might be required by regional custom.

INSIDE OUT   Creating a voice mail jail

Another common request in Exchange UM deployments is to provide an automated way for callers to leave voice mail messages—only. In this scenario, the goal is usually to give the outside world a one-way system for communicating with internal users. This is simple to do. Create an automated attendant and turn off ASR and then turn off all the other interesting features, including call transfer and dial by name. You can do that with a pair of EMS command lines similar to the following:

```
New-UMAutoAttendant -Name VoiceMailJail -SpeechEnabled $false -status enabled
-UMDialPlan <something> -PilotIdentifierList 7599
Set-UMAutoAttendant -id VoiceMailJail -allowExtensions:$false
-callSomeoneEnabled:$false
-nameLookupEnabled:$false -sendVoiceMsgEnabled:$true
```

After the automated attendant is set up, you can create a custom greeting for it, telling callers to say the name of the person for whom they want to leave a voice mail message, and then set up the PBX to transfer calls to it appropriately.

Unified messaging and the future

The ability to put all your voice mail messages and related data into the same store as all your other messaging data is undoubtedly powerful. With that basic functionality in place, Microsoft is free to add more intelligence to the process; voice mail preview is a good preview of the kinds of machine-assisted benefits you might reasonably expect in future iterations of the UM role. However, there's still the question of how to tie in Exchange UM with Microsoft Lync, an increasingly popular choice for PBX replacement. The next chapter explores Lync-UM integration.

Integrating Exchange 2013 with Lync Server

Microsoft has a long track record of building complementary products that are better together (to use its most common phrase), and Exchange Server and Lync Server are good examples of capable products that benefit from being deployed together. In Chapter 6, "Unified messaging," you learned about how Exchange unified messaging works, with the bottom line being that unified messaging (UM) answers the phone when it rings. Now it's time to discuss what happens and how to manage when Exchange is integrated with Lync 2013, the latest generation of the Microsoft real-time communications product.

A quick history of Lync

If you've been around Exchange long enough, you might remember that Exchange 2000 included its own instant messaging and conferencing server. As far back as the late 1990s, it was clear that real-time communications in the form of instant messaging (IM) and conferencing was a natural complement to the asynchronous world of email. The Exchange 2000 IM and conferencing products never gained any traction in the marketplace, and Live Communications Server (LCS), which made its debut in 2003, replaced them. LCS 2003 implemented presence using a protocol known as SIMPLE, a set of extensions to the Session Initiation Protocol (SIP) described in Chapter 6.

In 2005, LCS was upgraded to LCS 2005 and included more web conferencing features gained when Microsoft acquired the Live Meeting product as part of its 2003 purchase of PlaceWare. What we recognize today as Lync really started with the release of Office Communications Server (OCS) 2007, which added audio conferencing and voice over IP (VoIP) to the basic instant messaging and presence (IM/P) features present in LCS. Some 364 days after OCS 2007 was released, Microsoft released OCS 2007 R2, which greatly improved the call management and routing features of OCS 2007. OCS 2007 R2 also included dial-in audioconferencing, and it integrated the persistent group chat engine that Microsoft got when it acquired Parlano.

Lync 2010 and Lync 2013 both built on the OCS 2007 R2 technology core, although they were rewritten in managed code and sport a new browser-based management console that relies on Silverlight (see Figure 7-1). Like Exchange 2010 and Exchange 2013, the Lync Server products are managed with tools that are based on Microsoft Windows PowerShell; anything that you can do from the Lync management console, you can do from the Lync Management Shell (LMS). Lync also sports a much more robust distributed architecture that supports what the Lync team calls a survivable branch appliance, or SBA; you put an SBA in your remote or branch offices so that users there can continue to make and receive phone calls in the event of an outage that affects connectivity to your central Lync deployment.

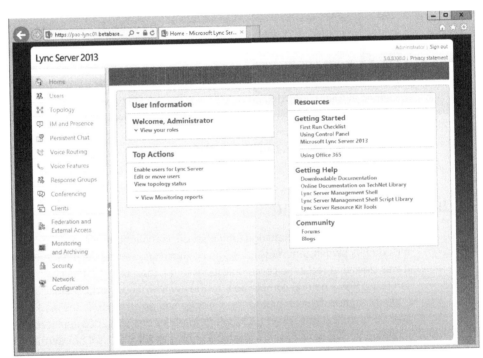

Figure 7-1 The Lync 2013 management interface, based on Silverlight

In addition to the on-premises version of Lync Server, Microsoft makes Lync available in many of its Office 365 service plans and in a multitenant version known as the Lync Hosting Pack (LHP). In general, for the purposes of this book, the hosted and on-premises services have identical capabilities; important differences will be noted where they exist.

INSIDE OUT   Hybrid voice

Among its many other capabilities, Lync 2013 is technically capable of combining local telephone service with hosted Lync services. In particular, the Office 365 version of Lync 2013 used to support a mode known as hybrid voice, by which Office 365-enabled users could associate ordinary dial-up numbers with their cloud accounts so that any user of the public switched telephone network (PSTN) could dial a number and cause the Office 365 user's Lync client to start. However, in August 2013, Jajah, the only service provider offering Office 365 hybrid voice connectivity, discontinued its service, and as of this writing, no other provider has stepped forward to offer a similar service—a real shame given how useful hybrid voice capabilities are.

Combining Lync and Exchange

It's natural to wonder what benefits you gain from combining Lync and Exchange. Although email is almost universally considered a core requirement for businesses of all sizes, the same cannot yet be said for IM/P, conferencing, and Enterprise Voice services.

What Lync provides

Lync 2013 is a pretty rich communications platform. In fact, about the only communications modality it doesn't support is email. A fully realized Lync deployment with all major features enabled delivers a variety of communications methods, which Microsoft often calls modalities:

- Instant messaging and presence for two or more parties. Microsoft refers to multi-party IM conversations as conferences.

- Enterprise Voice services that enable Lync to replace private branch exchange (PBX) systems. These services, although complex, are extremely powerful; they include the ability to set up response groups (think of them as distribution groups for incoming phone calls) and a variety of other tools for call management and control. Lync provides phone number normalization and call routing and supports Call Admission Control, or CAC, and quality of service, or QoS. Lync also provides routing of Lync voice calls to and from the PSTN, using a SIP trunk provider, IP PBX, or IP gateway. Those services enable a PSTN user with a phone to call a Lync user by running the Lync client on her laptop, tablet, mobile device, or web browser—and vice versa.

- Multiparty audio and video conferencing using Microsoft Lync clients running under Windows 7, Windows 8, Windows RT, and Mac OS X. The Lync 2013 implementation of these conferences is pretty slick; it shows a grid of attendees' video feeds so you can see who's talking, who's engaged and attentive, and who's not.

- Dial-in audio conferencing so that PSTN users can join meetings too; dial-in conferencing can be provided by Microsoft partner companies, external PBX systems, or Lync itself. Many Lync customers, including Microsoft itself, use this capability to allow outside participants to join Lync meetings; when set up properly, attendees can use the Lync client if they have Lync access or dial in through the PSTN if they don't.

- Archiving features to capture the contents of IM conversations, record conferences locally, and preserve details of who communicated with whom, when, and with what tools.

- Persistent chat rooms that enable users to check in, post and read conversations, and have them archived.

- Lync Web App, a web client that provides IM/P and conferencing access (including video and audio over IP) to users running Internet Explorer, Chrome, Safari, and Firefox on Microsoft Windows, Mac OS X, and some Linux variants.

- Mobile apps to provide access to IM/P, Enterprise Voice (EV), and conferencing on Windows Phone, iOS, and Android.

- Application programming interfaces (APIs) for building EV and IM/P-enabled line-of-business applications. Exchange uses one of these APIs, the Unified Communications Managed API (UCMA), to implement large parts of the Exchange UM role.

In summary, if you deployed Lync without Exchange, you could provide telephone service, desktop audio and video conferencing, and IM/P to your users, but you could not provide email, calendaring, or other Exchange functionality.

INSIDE OUT Lync client functionality varies

Some of Lync Server's functionality is server-based, such as its archiving functions and APIs for building communications-enabled business process (CEBP) applications. Other functionality depends on the client, and there are several Lync clients with differing levels of functionality. Because this isn't a Lync book I won't go over every detail, but in general you might find it useful to know about the following types of clients:

- The full Lync client, which offers all of the conferencing, video, audio, and IM/P features but requires Windows Vista or later and is licensed as part of Microsoft Office.

- The Lync Basic client, a version that includes basic IM/P compatibility and is intended for users running Windows XP and organizations that haven't licensed a version of Office that includes the full client.

- The Lync client for Mac OS X, which offers AV, conferencing, and IM/P functionality. Compared with the Windows versions, its device support is limited, and there are many features (such as desktop sharing and conferencing from a browser) that sometimes or almost work; clearly this client isn't receiving the level of attention that the Windows versions do.

- Mobile clients for Windows Phone, Windows 8 and RT, iOS (both iPhone and iPad), and Android devices. The features of these clients vary according to platform. In general, the Windows 8 and RT versions have the most features, with the iOS versions in second place and the Android version following.

There is no desktop client for Linux, although you can use the open-source Pidgin client with the open-source SIPE plugin to get IM/P functionality. In general, as long as the client works properly with Lync, users should be able to access the Lync–Exchange integration features discussed in this chapter, although some features (such as access to high-resolution contact photos) are only available in the full Windows client.

What Exchange adds to Lync

In Chapter 6, I highlighted the major features of Exchange unified messaging (UM): Exchange UM answers the phone, plays greetings as part of an automated attendant (AA) or from a user's mailbox, routes calls through the AA and Outlook Voice Access (OVA) mechanism, and enables callers and subscribers to send and receive voice messages. The feature set of Lync is almost perfectly complementary to that of Exchange: Lync provides telephony services that make the phone ring in the first place so that Exchange can answer it!

From an Exchange standpoint, Lync and Exchange work well together because Lync can replace traditional or IP PBX systems. When Alice picks up her PSTN phone to call Bob, Lync can receive the incoming call, ring Bob's extension (which might actually be the Lync client, a Lync-compatible hardware phone, or a traditional phone connected to an older PBX that Lync can talk to through a gateway), and then transfer the call to Exchange UM if Bob doesn't answer. If you go back and read Chapter 6, any place you see mention of an IP PBX, you can mentally substitute Lync, and you'll have the right idea.

When you deploy Exchange 2013 alongside Lync 2010 or Lync 2013, you get the following:

- Outlook Web App can display a user's list of Lync contacts, including his presence status. While logged on to Outlook Web App, a Lync-enabled user can start and respond to IM conversations and update his own presence status.

- The Lync client displays an icon to indicate when a user has unread voice mail messages in her Exchange mailbox. A single click of the icon plays the voice mail without requiring the user to dial in to OVA or authenticate to the Exchange server.

- If they are enabled, missed call notifications appear in the Lync client and in the user's Exchange mailbox. Users can configure the Lync client to send calls to voice mail after a set time interval, which causes Exchange to generate a missed-call notification (MCN) if the caller doesn't leave a message.

- Users can configure the Lync client to store conversation history entries (including the contents of IM conversation and entries logging when voice or phone calls were made or received) in the Conversation History folder in the Exchange Inbox. This setting can be configured in Group Policy.

- The Lync client can retrieve and display out of office (OOF) messages, free/busy information, and contact and Global Address List (GAL) information that it retrieves from Exchange using EWS and/or Messaging Application Programming Interface (MAPI). It's smart enough to take delegate relationships into account, too.

INSIDE OUT Conversation history versus archiving

Some users love the idea of keeping their own copy of IM communications in a convenient location—they're the target audience for Lync's ability to use the Conversation History folder in a user's Exchange mailbox. However, this is not the same as archiving IM traffic because users are free to opt out of storing their conversations in the Conversation History folder, and they are free to delete or modify individual items in the folder itself. Lync includes an archiving feature that reliably captures IM traffic, call detail records, and the audio and video content of web conferences. In versions of Lync Server prior to Lync Server 2013, the archiving feature required a separate archiving server; in Lync Server 2013, you can tell Lync to archive this data to Exchange mailboxes using the native Exchange single-item recovery mechanism, as described in the "Integrating Exchange archiving with Lync Server" section later in the chapter.

Some additional features in Lync 2013 are enabled when Exchange 2013 is present. Perhaps the most immediately noticeable one is that Lync can display higher-resolution contact photos, if they're present, by pulling them from users' mailboxes or aggregated contacts stored in a new repository called the Unified Contact Store (UCS). EWS provides APIs for fetching photos, and Exchange can automatically scale photos to provide the requested size to the client. Only the Lync 2013 and Lync Web App clients use the full-resolution photos, however.

What about UCS? It is a new Exchange 2013 feature designed explicitly to allow Lync to offload contact storage from its own SQL Server database to Exchange; to summarize, UCS provides a single repository for contact data across Office products. Instead of keeping some data in Exchange, some in the user-specific contact lists in the back end of the Lync server, and some in Microsoft SharePoint, all user contact data can be aggregated and stored in UCS, where it is made available to all the user's applications.

Lync 2013 uses UCS through a new framework known as the Lync Storage Server (LYSS) framework. LYSS uses EWS to store and retrieve the contact data that Lync users create and use. Exchange 2010 and Lync 2010 pull contact photos from the thumbnailPhoto attribute of user accounts in Active Directory; that attribute can only hold photos sized to 96 x 96 pixels, with a maximum size of 10 KB. This isn't enough to give a good view, so the Lync 2013 client scales up the thumbnails to 278 x 278 pixels—this makes the picture larger but uglier. When you deploy Exchange 2013, the storage mechanism changes; each user's photo is stored in his mailbox and has a maximum resolution of 648 x 648 pixels. The Microsoft Outlook 2013 client doesn't use the high-resolution pictures, but other clients can; Exchange automatically posts lower-resolution thumbnail images to Active Directory for clients that can't use the new resolution.

Exchange can archive Lync conversations, conferences, and call detail records so that they are discoverable using the new SharePoint eDiscovery console. This feature depends on the presence of the Purges subfolder of the Recoverable Items folder, from which Exchange eDiscovery searches can retrieve conversation data. This chapter covers how to integrate Lync with Exchange to enable Exchange archiving of Lync items.

For more information on how item recovery and eDiscovery work from the Exchange side, see Chapter 11, "Compliance management," in *Microsoft Exchange Server 2013 Inside Out: Mailbox and High Availability* (Microsoft Press, 2013).

Lync integration concepts and architecture

Lync architecture is not necessarily more complex than that of Exchange, but it's different; if you're used to the Exchange model, there might seem to be a bewildering array of services and components to know. There are a few basic things you need to know about

Lync, which comes in two editions; Standard edition servers are intended to stand alone, whereas Enterprise edition servers can be grouped into pools for redundancy and load balancing. (You can build redundant Lync configurations by using Standard edition servers and load balancers, too.) It is confusing, but the Lync world uses the word "pool" to refer to both types of server, so you will hear people say things like "a Standard edition pool." A real Enterprise edition pool consists of one or more front-end servers and a back-end server. Standard edition servers and pools are logically interchangeable for the purposes of this book; you can integrate Exchange with either or both. In most cases, a Standard edition server acts just like an Enterprise edition front end. If it helps, you can think of an Enterprise edition pool as akin to a Client Access Server (CAS) array, whereas a Standard edition server is like a single CAS.

The minimum Lync deployment required to work with Exchange is a single Standard edition server. You can add other Lync Server roles, such as mediation servers (which provide PSTN connectivity and integration and are usually integrated with the Front-End [FE] role), edge servers (which do pretty much what you'd expect), and so on, but none of these is required for Exchange integration, and I won't discuss them further.

For much more on Lync configuration, design, and deployment, see *Microsoft Lync 2013 Plain & Simple* (Microsoft Press, 2013).

Exchange administrators are accustomed to the idea that everything important about Exchange is stored in Active Directory. Lync departs from this model, depending instead on the Lync Central Management Service (CMS). The CMS stores topology and configuration data as a SQL database that all Lync 2010 or 2013 servers in an organization use to tell them about the Lync environment. Exchange doesn't interact directly with the CMS, but many of the configuration steps you need to take to configure Lync for interoperability with Exchange 2013 result in changing data in the CMS through either the Lync management web interface (the Lync Server Control Panel, or LSCP) or the LMS.

When you make a change to a Lync environment, it might not be visible to the existing Lync servers until you update the shared topology in CMS. You normally do that with the Lync Topology Builder, a tool that has no counterpart in Exchange (Figure 7-2). To add or remove servers in a Lync environment, or to add or remove server roles from an existing server, first you use the Topology Builder to specify the changes, and then you publish the topology to the CMS. Only then do you actually use the Lync Deployment Wizard or LMS to make the changes. This approach forces you to think carefully and deliberately about what you're going to do before you do it, but it can be a little disconcerting to Exchange administrators who aren't used to it.

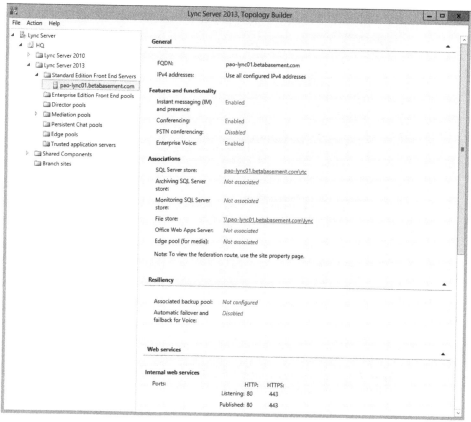

Figure 7-2 The Lync Topology Builder, used to add or remove servers or server roles or to create new Lync sites or topologies

Speaking of the Deployment Wizard, see Figure 7-3. This wizard is the tool you actually use to install Lync, request and update certificates, and so on. A complete discussion of the wizard's features is outside the scope of this book, but you should be familiar at least with the fact that it exists before proceeding with your Lync–Exchange integration process.

What about the clients? The Lync client family has grown quite a bit in the past few years. It now includes desktop clients (Lync 2010 and Lync 2013 for Windows and Lync 2011 for Mac OS X), a Windows 8 client (called Lync MX by most of the Lync world), and mobile clients for Windows Phone, Android, and iOS devices. These clients all use SIP and various related protocols to talk to Lync, but it's important to understand how they interact with Exchange.

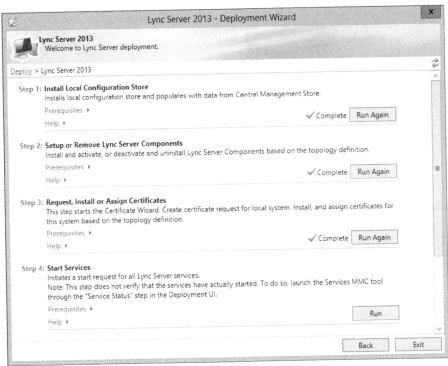

Figure 7-3 The Lync Deployment Wizard, the primary tool you use to make changes to the local configuration of a specific server

First and foremost, all these clients use EWS to retrieve voice mail and missed-call notifications, read and delete voice mail messages, and retrieve calendar data (including free/busy data, working hours, and OOF messages). When you have Exchange 2013, Lync 2013, Lync MX, and some Lync mobile clients can also use EWS, either directly or through LYSS, to retrieve user photos. How do these clients find the correct EWS endpoint? They use Exchange Autodiscover, of course, as any well-behaved client would. That means that for correct client behavior, you need to ensure that EWS and Autodiscover work properly and are accessible, internally or externally, from wherever your Lync clients connect. (Lync also has its own Autodiscover mechanism that clients can use to find a Lync server to talk to, but it's outside the scope of this chapter.)

The Lync clients for Windows can also connect directly with Outlook for Windows through the Outlook Object Model (OOM). For example, when you click the icon to send a mail message to one of your IM contacts, the Lync 2013 client makes an OOM call to Outlook to open a new message composition window. Outlook for Windows and Mac OS X both tie into client APIs provided by the Lync clients to enable presence icon indications next to user names and the right-click context menu commands for starting IM conversations or conferences.

Certificates, trust, and permissions

Jens Trier Rasmussen, a Microsoft consultant and frequent blogger, has written perhaps the most succinct description of the prerequisites for integrating Exchange and Lync in an article on his excellent blog (*http://blogs.technet.com/b/jenstr/*): you need both trust and permissions. Like many succinct descriptions, this one requires some explanation.

Trust, certificates, and OAuth

First, Lync and the servers it talks to must trust each other. Lync depends on mutual authentication for both servers and clients. That is, a Lync server will only talk to a server with whom it can establish a trust relationship. Lync 2013 does this through the OAuth protocol, which is described on its website (*http://www.oauth.net*) as an "open protocol to allow secure authorization in a simple and standard method from web, mobile, and desktop applications." OAuth represents authentication as a three-way process; if server A wants to communicate with server B, both A and B request authentication tokens from a central authentication server and then exchange them to establish trust. Exchange 2013 and SharePoint 2013 also use OAuth for mutual server authentication, so one of the required integration steps for linking Lync and Exchange is to establish an OAuth connection between the servers. This requires having a mutually trustable certificate. Exchange issues its own self-signed authentication certificate labeled Microsoft Exchange Server Auth Certificate, whereas Lync expects that, as part of the deployment process, you will request an OAuth certificate, using either your own internal certificate authority (CA) or a public CA. The Lync OAuth certificate is labeled OAuthTokenIssuer, and you must either request it as part of performing the certificate setup step in the Lync deployment wizard or manually request and install a certificate following the directions on TechNet at *http://technet .microsoft.com/en-us/library/jj205253.aspx*.

Partner applications and permissions

When the OAuth trust relationship is in place, you still need to define partner applications on each side. A partner application is an object that represents an application the server can talk to. For example, Exchange expects to see a partner application for Lync, so you must create one (using the process outlined in the "Creating partner applications" section later in the chapter); likewise, you must create a partner application representing Exchange for Lync. Partner applications publish a set of authentication metadata that specifies what authentication methods and credentials the partner application can consume and produce.

It's important to understand that the partner application object defines a system, not an individual server. You need one partner application object for Lync and one for SharePoint 2013, not one object for each server of that type.

OAuth enables you to assign permissions to partner applications; as part of the integration process, you need to assign role-based access control (RBAC) permissions to the partner applications to control what Exchange data and services they can use. Interestingly, the internal representation used for partner applications differs between Lync and Exchange; Exchange links each partner application to a disabled user account and assigns RBAC permissions to it, whereas Lync stores partner application objects and permissions in CMS.

Lync maintains an object known as the known servers table (KST) to track which servers it is allowed to talk to. The Lync services update the KST based on information they draw from the topology published in the CMS. However, the topology doesn't contain any information about Exchange servers, so Lync will not talk to Exchange servers unless these servers are added. This can happen in two ways. First, Lync automatically discovers any Exchange 2010 or Exchange 2013 servers that are running the Exchange Unified Messaging Call Router service and hosting a SIP dial plan, and it adds them to the KST. For Exchange servers that are running both the CAS and Mailbox role, no further action is necessary. However, if you have a server running Outlook Web App (either an Exchange 2013 Mailbox server or an Exchange 2010 CAS), regardless of whether you have configured that server as a UM server, and you want to integrate its instance of Outlook Web App with Lync, you must manually create a trusted application pool in Lync representing that server. Lync will not automatically discover it.

What if you create a trusted application pool for a multirole server? You'll immediately know that you've done something wrong because Outlook Web App integration with Lync will quit working, and you'll see event ID 14653 logged on the Lync server from the LS Protocol Stack component. The fix is simple; either restart the RTCSRV service on the Lync server or merely remove the application pool that you added. In either event, Outlook Web App on the affected server will start working again.

The rest of integration

After trust and permissions are assigned properly, you might have additional integration steps to perform. Which specific steps you take depend on what you want to do. You can enable presence and IM in Outlook Web App, allow Lync calls to be answered by Exchange Unified Messaging, enable the use of the Exchange Unified Contact Store, and manage high-resolution user photos. Each of these features can be integrated separately, so you can choose exactly what you want your integrated Exchange and Lync environment to look like.

Initial integration steps

Before you can begin integrating specific features in Exchange 2013 with Lync 2013, or vice versa, you have to take a few steps to prepare the Exchange servers.

Installing prerequisites on Exchange servers

The first step to integrating Lync and Exchange is to verify that you have all the required prerequisite software bits on your Exchange servers. Exchange 2013 already requires the UCMA 4.0 runtime on both CAS and Mailbox servers. If you aren't completely sure it is present, you can check whether HKLM\SYSTEM\CurrentControlSet\MSExchange OWA \InstantMessaging\ImplementationDLLPath contains a value that points to an installed copy of Microsoft.Rtc.Internal.Ucweb.dll. As long as that DLL is present and pointed to by the registry key, you're all set. (Note that if you want to integrate Exchange 2010 with Lync 2013, you can, but you will need to download and install the UCMA runtime; it is not a prerequisite for installation in that version.) Having said this, because UCMA 4.0 is a prerequisite for both the Mailbox and CAS roles in Exchange 2013, the odds that it will suddenly disappear after you have Exchange installed are very low.

Configuring server authentication

Exchange 2013 includes a set of cmdlets for managing OAuth. In normal operation, you will probably never see or use them because Exchange, along with Lync and SharePoint, attempts to make OAuth an invisible background process that just works. The one case in which you might need to manage OAuth manually on Exchange is when you want to change the certificate Exchange uses for server-to-server OAuth. The default Microsoft Exchange Server Auth Certificate will always be used by default for OAuth. It starts with a validity period of nearly five years (1,800 days), and Exchange automatically renews it when necessary. You can use the Set-AuthConfig cmdlet to specify a different certificate; one reason to do this is if you wanted to configure Exchange to perform OAuth exchanges with a system that doesn't accept self-signed certificates.

A second, perhaps more likely, reason to use Set-AuthConfig is if the Microsoft Exchange Server Auth Certificate is removed from the Exchange server's personal certificate store. If this certificate is missing, Exchange can't perform its part of the OAuth token exchange, and you will not be able to create partner applications on the Lync side. If you suspect that this is the problem, you can use EMS to check which certificate the OAuth provider thinks it should be using, like this:

```
get-authconfig | select *thumbprint | fl


    CurrentCertificateThumbprint  : F8DB6FE019548C945D01FAF7C0447DD172CA9899
    PreviousCertificateThumbprint :
    NextCertificateThumbprint     :
```

Armed with that thumbprint, you can run Get-ExchangeCertificate and verify that you have a matching entry in the list of available certificates. If you do not, you should do the following:

1. Generate a new 2,048-bit self-signed certificate with New-ExchangeCertificate.

   This cmdlet requires you to specify the services for which the certificate will be used and tell it to use SMTP, but don't allow it to overwrite the existing SMTP certificate assignment. You need the certificate thumbprint associated with this certificate.

   ```
   New-ExchangeCertificate -KeySize 2048 -PrivateKeyExportable $true
   -SubjectName "cn=Microsoft Exchange Server Auth Certificate"
   -FriendlyName "Microsoft Exchange Server Auth Certificate" -Services smtp
   ```

2. Use Set-AuthConfig to assign the newly generated certificate with an immediate effective date. The –Force parameter is required because otherwise Set-AuthConfig will complain that the certificate's NotValidBefore date isn't at least 48 hours in the future. This cmdlet automatically pushes out the certificate to all CAS servers in the Exchange organization.

   ```
   $today = get-date
   Set-AuthConfig -NewCertificateThumbprint thumbprint
   -NewCertificateEffectiveDate $today -Force
   ```

3. Publish the new certificate with Set-AuthConfig –PublishCertificate.

4. Remove any traces of the previous certificate, using Set-AuthConfig –ClearPreviousCertificate.

5. Use iisreset to recycle Internet Information Services (IIS) on all your CAS and Mailbox servers.

   Note that when you do this, any existing client connections to IIS on those machines will be lost.

Configuring Autodiscover

Exchange and Lync both offer Autodiscover services to their clients. Lync Autodiscover is outside the scope of this chapter because Lync clients such as the Windows Phone and iOS mobile clients use it. In contrast, desktop, mobile, and web Lync clients all use Exchange Autodiscover. You might think that Lync or the clients could perform Autodiscover the same way Outlook or a mobile Exchange client would . . . but no. You must manually configure Lync to specify the URI of the Exchange Autodiscover service. If you don't do this (and the need to do so is not clearly specified in the Microsoft documentation), your Lync clients might complain that they cannot reach Exchange for the services described earlier in the "Combining Lync and Exchange" section. Because Lync clients don't use service connection points (SCPs) as Outlook does, and they don't follow the same discovery process described in Chapter 3, "Client management," setting this URI properly is critical.

To tell Lync which Exchange Autodiscover URI to use, run the Set-CSOAuthConfiguration cmdlet and specify the ExchangeAutodiscoverUrl switch, like this:

```
Set-CSOAuthConfiguration –ExchangeAutodiscoverUrl
https://autodiscover.betabasement.com/autodiscover/autodiscover.svc
```

Keep in mind that this interface uses the Simple Object Access Protocol (SOAP) Autodiscover interface rather than the earlier version, which is retrieved with an HTTP POST.

Creating partner applications

The terminology Microsoft uses to refer to OAuth partner applications is a little confusing. When Microsoft refers to configuring Lync Server 2013 as a partner application for Exchange, what it really means is adding a partner application object to Exchange that represents Lync. Likewise, configuring Exchange as a partner application means telling Lync that Exchange exists and is a partner. I'll follow that usage here even though it's a bit confusing.

Configuring Lync as a partner application for Exchange

The only supported way to create the partner application objects on which Exchange 2013 depends for server-to-server OAuth is to run an EMS script, Configure-EnterprisePartnerApplication.ps1. When you run this script, stored in the Exchange scripts directory (available through the $ExScripts variable), to set up Lync integration, it creates the necessary partner application object, associates it with a disabled user account object named LyncEnterprise-ApplicationAccount, and saves the URL of the authentication metadata the partner is supposed to supply.

Before you run the Configure-EnterprisePartnerApplication.ps1 script, you should verify that your partner application (Lync, in this case) is properly provisioned. To do this, log on to one of your Exchange servers and use a browser to retrieve *https://yourLyncServer /metadata/json/1*. This is the default URL at which Lync servers publish the authentication metadata. If you get a certificate warning, fix it; that means Lync is using a certificate the Exchange server doesn't trust.

After that's done, running the script is a very simple task. The only thing you need to know is the FQDN of the Lync server whose authentication data you want to consume. You trigger the script like this:

```
.\Configure-EnterprisePartnerApplication.ps1 –AuthMetaDataUrl https://pao-lync01
.betabasement.com/metadata/json/1 –ApplicationType Lync
```

```
Creating User <LyncEnterprise-ApplicationAccount> for Partner Application.
Created User <betabasement.com/Users/LyncEnterprise-ApplicationAccount> for
Partner Application.

Assigning role <UserApplication> to Application User <betabasement.com/Users
/LyncEnterprise-ApplicationAccount>.
Assigning role <ArchiveApplication> to Application User <betabasement.com
/Users/LyncEnterprise-ApplicationAccount>.

 Creating Partner Application <LyncEnterprise-cae9e7dd1c0f461ab339c2a4bde0a65b>
using metadata <https://pao-lync01.betabasement.com> with linked account
<betabasement.com/Users/LyncEnterprise-ApplicationAccount>.

 Created Partner Application <LyncEnterprise-356c4f9649354c14964fabcc099b9d55>.

 THE CONFIGURATION HAS SUCCEEDED.
```

> **Note**
> If you have multiple domains in your forest, you might need to use the
> −DomainController switch with Configure-EnterprisePartnerApplication.ps1 to ensure
> that the application objects are created in a domain that your Exchange servers can
> easily reach.

In case you don't believe the The Configuration Has Succeeded message, you can use the Get-PartnerApplication cmdlet to verify that the partner application was created.

Configuring Exchange as a partner application for Lync

You must also create a partner application object that Lync can use to see Exchange. To accomplish this, use the Lync Management Shell (LMS) and its New-CsPartnerApplication cmdlet. You can do this in either of two ways. First, Microsoft provides a complete script at *http://technet.microsoft.com/en-us/library/jj204975.aspx* that you can copy, paste, and run; the script creates partner objects for both Exchange and SharePoint. As an alternative, you can just run the New-CsPartnerApplication cmdlet itself; this is simpler, so it's normally the course I recommend.

New-CsPartnerApplication expects to be given three parameters: an identifier specifying the partner application to which you're connecting, the trust level that partner should have, and the authentication metadata URL. Exchange 2013 servers publish their authentication metadata as part of the Autodiscover virtual directory; the Lync documentation recommends using the Autodiscover public FQDN in the metadata URL (for instance, *https://autodiscover.betabasement.com/Autodiscover/metadata/json/1* instead of *https://pao-ex03.betabasement.com/Autodiscover/metadata/json/1).*

Here's an example of creating a new application object for an Exchange server in the betabasement.com domain:

```
New-CsPartnerApplication -Id Exchange -ApplicationTrustLevel Full -MetadataUrl
https://autodiscover.betabasement.com/autodiscover/metadata/json/1
```

```
Identity                            : Exchange
AuthToken                           : Value=https://autodiscover.betabasement
.com/autodiscover/metadata/json/1
Name                                : Exchange
ApplicationIdentifier               : 00000002-0000-0ff1-ce00-000000000000
Realm                               : betabasement.com
ApplicationTrustLevel               : Full
AcceptSecurityIdentifierInformation : False
Enabled                             : True
```

If you try to run New-CsPartnerApplication and it fails with an error indicating that a Secure Socket Layer (SSL) trust could not be established, it is likely because you're still using the Microsoft Exchange Server Auth self-signed certificate. There's no reason not to use it, but you might need to add a DNS CNAME record for Autodiscover.yourdomain.com and ensure that it points to an Exchange 2013 CAS. You should also verify that you can load *https://autodiscover.yourdomain.com/Autodiscover/Autodiscover.xml* from a browser on the Lync server without getting any certificate errors; the default Exchange self-signed certificates don't include a subject alternative name (SAN) for Autodiscover, so you might need to issue a new certificate to cover this case. (For more details on certificates and Autodiscover, see the "Autodiscover" section in Chapter 1, "Client access servers.")

Testing the partner application objects

First, ensure that the basic browser-based checks work. On the Exchange server, verify that you can load the Lync partner authentication metadata and, on the Lync server, verify that you can load the Exchange partner authentication metadata. When those tests work properly, you have a few options. The most useful one is probably to run the Test-CsExStorageConnectivity cmdlet from the Lync server. This tests the OAuth connection by attempting to use LYSS to store a conversation item in a selected user's Conversation History folder. If the test doesn't pass, the most likely culprit is a problem with the OAuth certificate assigned on the Exchange server. Some users have reported that the default configuration, which uses the self-signed Microsoft Exchange Server Auth certificate, won't pass Test-CsExStorageConnectivity, so it might be necessary to replace that certificate with another one as described earlier in this chapter.

Enabling IM and presence integration in Outlook Web App

The process of enabling IM and presence in Outlook Web App has a few twists and turns, depending on what your Exchange configuration looks like. If your Exchange servers combine the CAS and Mailbox roles, setup is simplified because you don't need to set up trusted application pools in Lync. If you have single-purpose CAS or Mailbox servers, you need to perform the steps listed in the "Configuring IM/P with single-role servers" section first.

The overall architecture of IM/P integration in Outlook Web App 2013 is very similar to that of its predecessor; an application runs on the Exchange server and uses the Lync APIs to retrieve contacts and their presence status, start and answer IM conversations, and so on. This application has been upgraded, and the manner in which you configure it has changed from Exchange 2010, but the basic idea is the same. For that reason, if you've previously set up IM/P connectivity for Exchange 2010 and Lync 2010, review the steps in the rest of this section carefully.

Configuring IM/P with single-role servers

In addition to the OAuth and partner application configuration changes required to enable integration with Exchange, Lync requires you to create a topology entry that gives it permission to add Exchange to the known servers table. This is done automatically by the Lync KST processing code for multirole servers if those servers host SIP dial plans, but if you have single-role servers, or your multirole servers do not have any SIP dial plans, you have to do it yourself. To do this, perform these four steps:

1. Get the site name and site ID of the Lync site in which you're putting these objects. This is easily done with the Get-CsSite cmdlet:

   ```
   Get-CsSite | Select SiteId, DisplayName
   ```

2. Create a trusted application pool. This pool is a Lync container object that contains individual trusted application objects; the container is part of the Lync topology and is replicated through the CMS. To do this, feed the New-CsTrustedApplicationPool cmdlet to the FQDN of the Outlook Web App server, the FQDN of the Lync pool or Standard edition server you want to host the pool object, and the Lync site ID.

   ```
   New-CsTrustedApplicationPool -Id pao-ex01.betabasement.com -Registrar
   pao-lync01.betabasement.com -Site HQ -RequiresReplication $false
   ```

   The -RequiresReplication flag is important because it controls whether the Lync CMS attempts to replicate configuration information to the target application. In this case, the target is an Exchange server that can't handle CMS replication traffic, so you need to tell Lync not to replicate to it, or you'll see CMS replication errors.

3. Use New-CsTrustedApplication to create a trusted application representing Outlook Web App within the trusted application pool, like this:

    ```
    New-CsTrustedApplication -ApplicationId OutlookWebApp
    -TrustedApplicationPoolFqdn pao-ex01.betabasement.com-Port 4444
    ```

    Lync essentially ignores the ApplicationId, so you can put in whatever value you want. The value you specify for Port can be any unused TCP port.

4. Publish the trusted application pool and trusted application in the Lync topology so that the CMS propagates it throughout the Lync organization. This is a simple matter of running the Enable-CsTopology cmdlet, which doesn't require any arguments. After publishing the new topology, it might take some time before the topology has replicated to all servers in the pool.

After these steps are complete, you're ready to configure Exchange to talk to Lync.

Completing IM/P integration

One major difference between Exchange 2010 and Exchange 2013 is that you configure IM/P integration in Outlook Web App in different places. In Exchange 2013, you must edit the Outlook Web App web.config file on the Mailbox server, which is overwritten each time you install a cumulative update (CU) or service pack. You don't configure anything on the CAS, and you don't use the Set-OWAVirtualDirectory cmdlet to configure the certificate.

The first thing you need to do is decide which Mailbox servers will provide Lync integration. Most organizations enable this on either all their servers or none of them; if you want to allow or deny IM/presence for specific users, you can do so using Outlook Web App policies, as described in Chapter 3. After you've done that, you must use Set-OWAVirtualDirectory to enable IM connectivity by specifying both that IM is enabled and that you are connecting to Lync. Oddly, the default state of the virtual directory is to enable IM but to set the IM system type to None. To fix this, do the following:

```
Get-OWAVirtualDirectory | Set-OWAVirtualDirectory -InstantMessagingEnabled $true
-InstantMessagingType OCS
```

Of course, if you want to enable IM/P integration on a subset of your Mailbox servers, you can specify those servers or use various Windows PowerShell tricks to select only the set of servers you want.

You have to make the same change to any Outlook Web App policies you've created; even the default policy, which enables IM integration by default, doesn't have the IM interoperability type set. A quick command such as the following will get you fixed up:

```
Get-OWAMailboxPolicy | Set-OWAMailboxPolicy -InstantMessagingType OCS
```

The next step is to get the thumbprint of the certificate your Mailbox servers will be presenting to Lync. The Lync servers must trust the CA that issues this certificate; you can use an internal enterprise CA or a public CA, provided that its CA chain is available to Lync and marked as trusted. The simplest way to get this thumbprint is to run Get-ExchangeCertificate, which includes the thumbprint as one of its default output parameters. For Lync to accept the certificate, the certificate subject name (SN) must match the FQDN of the Mailbox server, and the FQDN of the Mailbox server must appear as a subject alternative name in the certificate.

To tell Exchange to use that particular certificate, you edit the Outlook Web App web.config file. This is not intrinsically difficult, but because web.config is an XML file, you must be careful not to misplace any punctuation. Two items need to be added to the file: the FQDN of the Lync pool or Standard edition server you want the Mailbox server to talk to and the thumbprint of the certificate you'll use. You add these two values to the <AppSettings> element of the web.config file, which is located in the V15\ClientAccess\Owa subdirectory of the Exchange installation directory. For example, to configure IM integration on my lab systems, I added the following lines to the web.config file on each of the Mailbox servers:

```
<add key="IMCertificateThumbprint" value="CD03022496057C69B75BDA18141C0F78A1F1FEA0"/>
<add key="IMServerName" value="pao-lync01.betabasement.com"/>
```

Exchange expert Maarten Piederiet suggests using a script such as the following (which he graciously provided) to update web.config; scripting the changes greatly simplifies updating Exchange with CUs or service packs because those updates are guaranteed to wipe out your localized changes.

```
#IM integration
$Server=$env:Computername
$PoolName='pao-lync01.betabasement.com'

# Get default certificate thumbprint; please note that this is looking for non
self-signed certificates

$CertThumbprint=(Get-ExchangeCertificate | Where {$_.Services -match "IIS"
-and !$_.IsSelfSigned -and $_.Status -eq "Valid"}).Thumbprint

Get-OWAVirtualDirectory "$Server\*" | Set-OWAVirtualDirectory
-InstantMessagingType OCS -InstantMessagingEnabled:$true

#Helper function to modify .config files
function Set-AppSetting {
   [cmdletBinding(SupportsShouldProcess = $true)]
   param(
           [parameter(Position = 0, ValueFromPipeline = $false,
ValueFromPipelineByPropertyName = $true, Mandatory = $true, HelpMessage = "No value
specified")]
           [string]$ConfigFile="",
           [parameter(Position = 0, ValueFromPipeline = $false,
```

```
    ValueFromPipelineByPropertyName = $true, Mandatory = $true, HelpMessage = "No key
    specified")]
            [string]$key,
            [parameter(Position = 0, ValueFromPipeline = $false,
    ValueFromPipelineByPropertyName = $true, Mandatory = $true, HelpMessage = "No value
    specified")]
            [string]$value
    )
    if (Test-Path $ConfigFile){
            [xml]$xml = Get-Content $ConfigFile
            [string]$currentDate = (get-date).tostring("MM_dd_yyyy-HH_mm_ss")
            [string]$backup = $configfile + "_$currentDate"
        Copy-Item $configfile $backup

Node=$xml.configuration.appsettings.SelectSingleNode("add[translate(@key,
  'ABCDEFGHIJKLMNOPQRSTUVWXYZ','abcdefghijklmnopqrstuvwxyz')='"+$key.ToLower()+"']")
            if (!$Node) {
                $Node = $xml.CreateElement('add')
                $Node.SetAttribute('key', $key)
                $Node.SetAttribute('value', $value)
                $xml.configuration.appSettings.AppendChild($Node) | Out-Null
            } else {
                $Node.SetAttribute('value', $value)
            }
                $xml.Save($ConfigFile)
    }
} # end function Set-AppSetting
# Path to OWA web.config file
$OWAconfigPath=Join-Path $ExInstall "ClientAccess\Owa\web.config"

#Change settings in web.config
If ($CertThumbPrint) {
    Set-AppSetting -ConfigFile $OWAConfigPath -Key "IMCertificateThumbprint"
-Value $CertThumbprint
    Set-AppSetting -ConfigFile $OWAConfigPath -Key "IMServerName" -Value $PoolName

    #Restart OWA app pool
    & $env:windir\system32\inetsrv\appcmd recycle apppool
/apppool.name:"MSExchangeOWAAppPool"
}
```

After configuring the web.config file, you have to restart the Outlook Web App application pool in IIS. You can do this from the IIS Manager application, but it's probably faster to do it from the command line with

```
C:\Windows\System32\Inetsrv\Appcmd.exe recycle apppool
/apppool.name:"MSExchangeOWAAppPool"
```

At this point, you should be able to observe two changes on the Mailbox server even before trying to log on to a Lync-enabled user account in Outlook Web App. First, you should see a new directory named InstantMessaging in the Logging subdirectory of the

Exchange server installation folder (normally c:\program files\Microsoft\Exchange Server \v15). If you don't see the InstantMessaging folder, the Mailbox server doesn't think it should be attempting to talk to Lync at all. One common cause of this is failure to set the InstantMessagingType flags on the Outlook Web App virtual directories and mailbox policies. You should also see event ID 112 from source MSExchange OWA (Figure 7-4) indicating that the integration application is up and running. After verifying those two items, you can launch Outlook Web App, sign in with a Lync-enabled user, and verify whether IM connectivity is working.

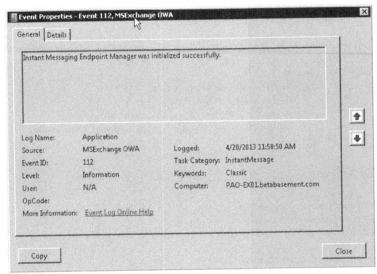

Figure 7-4 Event ID 112 indicating that the Outlook Web App IM endpoint manager has started; if you don't see it, something is wrong

Troubleshooting Outlook Web App IM integration

In my experience, very few deployments of IM integration with Outlook Web App work flawlessly the first time, so a good understanding of how to troubleshoot common issues is helpful.

The first troubleshooting step is to determine whether the integration code is even active. Outlook Web App will not attempt to enable integration on a server until you have the InstantMessagingType set to OCS for at least one Outlook Web App mailbox policy and on the server itself. If you don't see event ID 112 and the InstantMessaging logging directory, this is likely the reason.

If the integration code appears to be running, your next step should be to examine the logs in the InstantMessaging directory. Here's an example of a log file showing a common and easily fixed problem:

```
#Software: Microsoft Exchange Server
#Version: 15.0.0.0
#Log-type: Sync Logs
#Date: 2013-04-20T18:52:54.903Z
#Fields: date-time,thread-id,level,user,subscription-guid,
subscription-type,logentry-id,context,property-bag
 2013-04-20T18:52:54.903Z,23,5,,,,0,DEBUG:IM Certificate with thumbprint
48C035DA23BB3253E9A08A92F3C736124158E0A1 could not be found.,
 2013-04-20T18:52:55.103Z,23,5,,,,0,DEBUG:Globals.Initialize: Initialization
failed.,
```

The log makes it clear that the problem occurred because the certificate thumbprint specified in the web.config file points to a nonexistent certificate. The fix is simple—correct the thumbprint, save web.config, and recycle the application pool.

Error codes in Lync are fairly opaque; when you look at logs in the InstantMessaging directory, you might find that the errors Lync reports don't tell you much of anything. Although a complete discussion of Lync logging is beyond the scope of this book, you will probably find that the OCSLogger tool (part of the Lync 2013 Debug Tools, available for download from *http://www.microsoft.com/en-us/download/details.aspx?id=35453*) will give you information that is more useful. To use OCSLogger, you must start it and then select the components for which you want to log data and the individual flags for those components. This is somewhat similar to changing the diagnostic logging level for Exchange components, with the selected flags indicating the specific items you want logged. To see what's happening with Outlook Web App integration, select the SIPStack component and the All Flags item, as shown in Figure 7-5.

Then you can start logging by clicking the Start Logging button and signing in or sending an IM. After doing so, stop logging; click the Analyze Logs button, and OCSLogger will open the logs in the well-known (at least to Lync admins) Snooper tool (see Figure 7-6), which visually highlights errors and warnings. The Messages and Trace tabs in Snooper have similar information, but the organization and presentation on the Messages tab usually makes it easier to see what's happening in the selected logs. The selected item in Figure 7-6 is an error whose text indicates that the server communicating with the Lync Server computer isn't configured as a peer, so Lync won't talk to it. This is probably the result of failing to add the selected server as a trusted application endpoint as described earlier in the chapter.

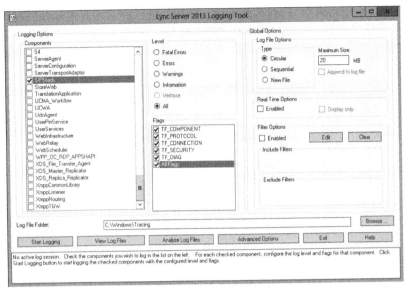

Figure 7-5 The Lync Server 2013 Logging Tool capturing error and tracing information you can analyze to isolate various types of problems

Figure 7-6 Snooper showing data from Lync log files, color-coding them to indicate errors and warnings

You can also use the Central Logging Service in Lync as a troubleshooting aid, but it is more complex; see the Lync documentation (*http://technet.microsoft.com/en-us/library/jj688101 .aspx*) for more details on how it works.

Integrating Exchange UM and Lync Server

Perhaps no area of integration between Lync and Exchange is more complex than UM integration. However, after you have a functioning Exchange UM set up (as detailed in Chapter 6) on the premises, tying it together with Lync is fairly simple because Exchange treats Lync as just another IP PBX. (Configuring integration between hosted Lync and on-premises Exchange, or vice versa, is significantly more complex and also rare, so these cases aren't covered here.)

For the remainder of this section, I'll assume that you have read and applied the material in Chapter 6. You don't have to have a completely functional Exchange UM environment, but you should understand the concepts covered therein to set up integration successfully between Exchange UM and Lync.

Exchange UM integration concepts

You need to keep a few simple facts about the relationship between Exchange UM and Lync in mind.

First, you can use Exchange UM with Lync even if you don't have telephony integration. Users who have Lync on their desktop can still make PC-to-PC voice and video calls, and when those calls are unanswered, Lync Server can route them to Exchange UM for voice mail handling. For this to work, your Lync users must be Enterprise Voice–enabled, though. Enterprise Voice is a fascinating and complex topic that is far outside the scope of this book.

Second, remember the unit of integration between the two is the dial plan. Exchange needs to be configured with a secure SIP dial plan that has the correct extension length to match your Lync dial plan. Part of the integration process involves running a script in Exchange that grants Lync access to read the UM Active Directory objects and essentially a list of trusted Exchange servers on each Lync pool so they can trust incoming connections from Exchange.

Exchange UM services can operate in three startup modes: unsecured, secured only, or dual mode. Lync talks only to secured dial plans, so the UM and UM Call Router services on servers in those dial plans must be configured to secured only or dual mode and must have appropriate certificates.

In this case, appropriate certificates means certificates Lync can verify to establish a trust chain. The FQDN of the server must appear in the subject name of the certificate. Microsoft recommends installing the same certificate on every server, which might require you to do some creative work to ensure that you have the right certificates and subject alternative names on those certificates.

Initial setup

Before you can connect Exchange UM to Lync for voice mail, you must first ensure that server-to-server authentication is working and that you can visit each server's default web-page from the other without receiving certificate errors.

Configuring Exchange for integration

If you've already set up Exchange UM, it is probably because you wanted to integrate it with an existing IP PBX. If this is the case, you probably want to add a new dial plan just for communicating with Lync. Because an Exchange server can be a member of multiple dial plans, this is straightforward. However, if you have not yet set up Exchange, you will certainly need a Lync-compatible dial plan. Fortunately, this is easy to accomplish with New-UMDialPlan or Exchange Administration Center (EAC). Here's an example showing how to use New-UMDialPlan to accomplish this:

```
New-UMDialPlan -Name "PaloAltoLync" -VoIPSecurity "Secured"
-NumberOfDigitsInExtension 4 -URIType "SipName" -AccessTelephoneNumbers 2100
```

You should plan to create one SIP dial plan for each Lync dial plan or location profile you want to enable for UM integration. In many deployments, that means you need only one dial plan, but larger, more distributed deployments might require multiple new dial plans. Whether you use an existing dial plan or create new ones, you must enable these dial plans to use Transport Layer Security (TLS). This requires you to have assigned a valid certificate for the UM service, but you can't assign a certificate with Enable-ExchangeCertificate until after you've enabled TLS on the dial plan. Start with a command like this:

```
Set-UmService -Identity "pao-ex01.betabasement.com" -DialPlans "PaloAltoLync"
-UMStartupMode "Dual"
Set-UmCallRouterSettings -DialPlans "PaloAltoLync" -UMStartupMode "Dual"
```

Each of these commands produces a warning message telling you that the corresponding service cannot be restarted until you actually assign a certificate, so that makes a logical next step. Use Enable-ExchangeCertificate to assign a (valid) certificate to the UM and UM Call Router services, like this:

```
Enable-ExchangeCertificate -Thumbprint 48C035DA23BB3253E9A08A92F3C736124158E0A1
-Services IIS, SMTP,UM,UMCallRouter
```

With the UM and call router services set to dual startup mode and a certificate assigned, it's safe to restart the services.

You have to add all CAS and Mailbox servers to the dial plan you just created. That's because any UM Call Router or UM server can receive and answer calls for any user, so if you have multiple servers and don't complete this step, you might notice some calls not being answered. If you have multiple SIP dial plans, you need to add each CAS and Mailbox server to each of the dial plans.

At this point, if you have not created a UM mailbox policy and automated attendant (AA) for your users, you should do so if you want to use these features.

The next step in the process is to run the script Microsoft provides for automatically creating the necessary Active Directory objects to tie Lync and Exchange together: ExchUcUtil. ps1, which lives in the Exchange scripts directory (\program files\Microsoft\Exchange\v15 \scripts). When you run this script, it does three things:

- It creates UM IP gateway objects for each of the Lync 2013 Standard edition servers or Enterprise edition pools.

- It creates hunt group objects for the new UM IP gateway objects it created.

- It grants permissions on the UM dial plan and UM auto-attendant objects to the RTCUniversalServerAdmins and RTCComponentUniversalServices universal security groups, which Lync creates at setup time.

Run the script from Exchange Management Shell (EMS), and it will produce a long block of output telling you, in essence, whether it did these three things. To verify that the script behaved as expected, you can use the Get-UMHuntGroup and Get-UMIPGateway cmdlets to check whether there are newly created objects that map to the Lync Standard edition or Enterprise edition servers in your topology.

After running the script, you must perform a couple of cleanup tasks. You need to restart the Lync Front-End service (RTCSRV) on all your servers so that it will detect the changes the Exchange script makes. If you have defined more than one UM IP gateway, disable outbound calling on all the UM IP gateway objects except one. It doesn't matter to Lync which one you choose, although Microsoft recommends picking one that can handle the volume of outbound calls you expect to traverse the gateway. Funneling all outbound calls through a single gateway makes the call routing process much more predictable because the calls all have to go to the designated gateway.

When you have made these changes, you must create an AA for each SIP dial plan. You can do this using the techniques described in Chapter 6; each AA should be associated with the dial plans you created earlier. Lync expects the access numbers for these AAs to be in complete E.164 format.

The final step is to use EAC or EMS to UM-enable each of the user accounts that will be accessing UM through Lync. This requires you to assign them to a SIP dial plan and give them a SIP address.

Configuring Lync for integration

Lync uses dial plans too; conceptually, they are very similar to Exchange dial plans except that they include a number of other settings that are required for normalizing phone numbers, controlling call routing, and other PBX-style features. Lync includes a global dial plan, but you can create your own dial plans by using LSCP or LMS. Exchange 2007 and OCS 2007 required dial plans used for integration to have matching counterparts on each side, but that requirement is no longer in place. If you're curious about the names Exchange is using for its dial plans, you can check the attribute of the dial plan object that stores its FQDN, known as the phone context, with a command like this:

```
(get-umdialplan).phonecontext
```

```
MTVDP01.betabasement.com
HSVDP01.betabasement.com
PaloAltoLync.betabasement.com
```

If you want to create new dial plans in Lync, you can (although, again, this is not required for Exchange UM integration). To do this, open the Lync web administration console, switch to the Voice Routing tab on the left, and use the New command from the toolbar to create a new User dial plan. (You can't change the name of Site or Pool dial plans, so they're not usable for UM integration.) Name the dial plan, specify the outside access code if there is one, and then click OK to add the dial plan to the list. Figure 7-7 shows the Lync management console with three new dial plans added. Note that the State column shows the new dial plans as Uncommitted. This is an important difference between the Lync management console and EAC; when you make changes in the Lync console, they are not persisted until you commit them. Clicking the Commit command in the toolbar displays a summary of the changes you've made so that you can review them before actually accepting them as part of the Lync configuration.

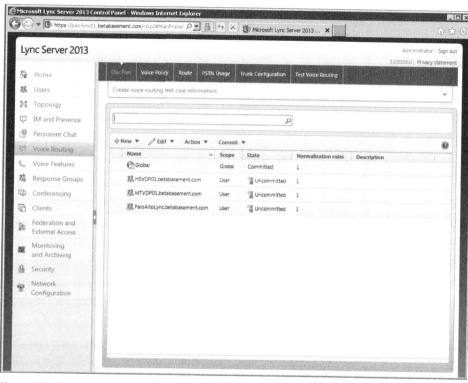

Figure 7-7 The Lync Server management interface showing three new dial plans that correspond to Exchange UM SIP dial plans; the dial plans haven't been committed yet

Like Exchange, Lync ships with a configuration tool that you must run as part of the Lync–Exchange UM integration process. This tool, OcsUmUtil.exe, is delivered in the c:\program files\common files\Microsoft Lync Server 2013\Support subdirectory, not an obvious place to look for it. OcsUmUtil creates contact objects for each of the Exchange AAs you created earlier in the integration process. The tool is a little nonintuitive; here's how you use it.

1. Launch the tool.

2. Click the Load Data button at the bottom of the tool's window. This queries Active Directory to look for dial plans that have matching names in both Lync and Exchange; these dial plans, if any, will be displayed in the SIP Dial Plans list. (See Figure 7-8.) If you have created any AAs for any of the dial plans shown in this list, the dial plan will have a red exclamation-mark icon indicating that it's not completely configured; this is normal.

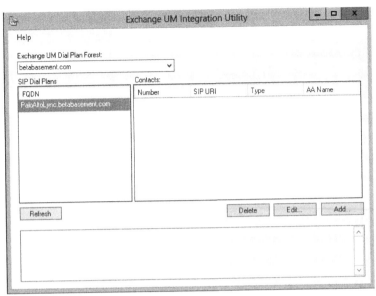

Figure 7-8 OcsUmUtil, showing one dial plan object that has been loaded but not yet configured

3. Select the dial plan you want to set up for UM integration and click Add. This will show the Contact window you see in Figure 7-9.

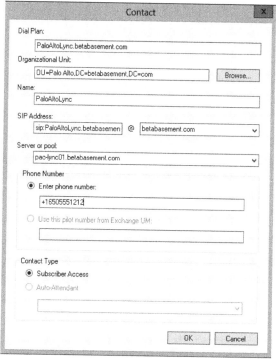

Figure 7-9 Creating a contact so Lync can find the OVA subscriber number

4. Specify the details for the contact, keeping in mind whether you're creating a contact for an AA associated with the dial plan or for subscriber (OVA) access:

● You can specify an organizational unit (OU) in which the contact will be created.

● The SIP address will be filled in by default, although you may change it if you like.

● The utility will fill in the Server Or Pool field with the FQDN of the Lync server from which you run the tool. You might want to change this to the Lync server or pool you expect to handle the highest volume of calls from your users.

● Specify the E.164 number for the AA in the Phone Number field. If you're creating a contact for an AA, the AA's pilot number should appear automatically; if there's no AA yet, or if you are creating a subscriber access contact, you need to provide an E.164 number.

● Specify whether this contact is for subscriber access (as shown here) or for an AA.

5. When you click OK, the contact will be created immediately. After you repeat this process to create the contacts needed for OVA and AA access, the information displayed in the tool's window will resemble Figure 7-10.

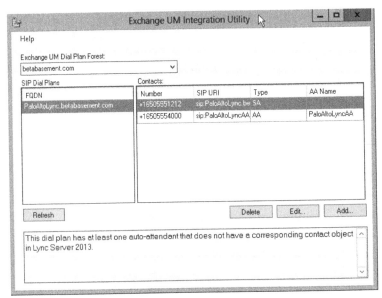

Figure 7-10 OcsUmUtil, showing one dial plan object that has been loaded and configured with OVA and AA contacts

If you have not already done so, enable users for Lync Enterprise Voice, too.

Testing your work

When you have completed the integration steps, you will need to verify that everything is working properly. There are several ways to do this, beginning with the obvious: fire up the Lync client and call another UM-enabled Lync user to see whether you can leave her a voice mail. You can also use the Test-CsExUMConnectivity and Test-CsExUMVoiceMail cmdlets; these are complementary but quite different. The former checks to verify that the specified Lync user can establish a connection to the Exchange UM services; the latter actually simulates a phone call and voice mail session. To provide a complete end-to-end test path between two users named KC and David, you could do the following:

```
Test-CsExUMConnectivity -TargetFqdn pao-lync01.betabasement.com -UserSipAddress
kc@betabasement.com
Test-CsExUMConnectivity -TargetFqdn pao-lync01.betabasement.com -UserSipAddress
david@betabasement.com
$cred=Get-Credential -UserName betabasement\kc -message "KC is sending a voice mail
to David"
Test-CsExUMVoiceMail -SenderSipAddress kc@betabasement.com -ReceiverSipAddress
```

```
david@betabasement.com -SenderCredential $cred -WaveFile voicemail.wma
$cred=Get-Credential -UserName betabasement\david -message "David is sending a voice
mail to KC"
Test-CsExUMVoiceMail -SenderSipAddress david@betabasement.com -ReceiverSipAddress
kc@betabasement.com -SenderCredential $cred -WaveFile voicemail.wma
```

The first two lines verify that basic connectivity between the Lync and Exchange UM servers
is functional. If David and KC had mailboxes on the same Exchange server, you could cheat
a bit and execute only one of these tests. The next line fetches credentials for KC's account
so that Test-CsExUMVoiceMail can log on to the test mailbox, followed by the actual call to
Test-CsExUMVoiceMail. The process is then reversed to send a test voice mail from David
to KC.

Enabling the Unified Contact Store for Lync users

The Unified Contact Store (UCS) is automatically enabled on Exchange, and Lync can immediately take advantage of it, but your users won't be able to access it until you enable it for
their use. To be more specific, the Lync policy that controls whether the UCS is available is
already set to $True; you can verify this by running the following cmdlet:

```
Get-CsUserServicesPolicy -id Global
```

This should show that the UcsAllowed parameter for the default policy is set to $True.
When you enable UCS, it becomes available immediately; however, if you later disable it,
clients will still use it until you use the Invoke-CsUcsRollback cmdlet, which moves users'
contacts from UCS back to the Lync server-side storage.

If you don't want to enable UCS for all users, you can create a new user services policy,
enable it for UCS, and then disable the default policy for UCS. Something like the following
will work to assign UCS access to two users named paulr and tonyr and disable it for other
users:

```
Set-CsUserServicesPolicy -id Global -UcsAllowed $false
New-CsUserServicesPolicy -id "UCSEnabledUsers" -UCSAllowed $true
Grant-CsUserServicesPolicy -id "paulr" -PolicyName "UCSEnabledUsers"
Grant-CsUserServicesPolicy -id "tonyr" -PolicyName "UCSEnabledUsers"
```

You can also enable or disable UCS at the Lync site level or by using user tags, both of
which are discussed in more depth in the Lync documentation. When you have defined the
users to whom UCS is available, individual users to whom a UCS-enabled policy applies will
gradually switch over to using UCS. Each time a Lync client logs on, it exchanges provisioning information with the server; the client sends headers indicating what its capabilities
are, and the server responds with provisioning instructions. In the case of UCS, the Lync
2013 client sends a header (Supported: ms-ucs-ready) to signal that it can use UCS. Then
it requests an EWS subscription for the contacts in UCS. (Older clients won't send these, of

course.) When the server sees the ms-ucs-ready header, if the user is enabled for UCS but his contacts have not yet been migrated, the server uses LYSS to migrate the contacts. The subscription request succeeds or fails, depending on whether the user is enabled for UCS and whether his contacts have already migrated. After the user's contacts have been moved to UCS, he will see a message similar to the one shown in Figure 7-11; after quitting and restarting Lync, his account will begin using UCS.

Figure 7-11 The Lync 2013 client showing this dialog box to force the user to quit and restart Lync

To verify the switch, you can check the Lync configuration settings window by Ctrl+right-clicking the Lync icon in the system notification area and choosing Configuration Settings. The resulting dialog box, shown in Figure 7-12, contains an entry named Contact List Provider; its value will say either "Lync Contact Provider" or "UCS."

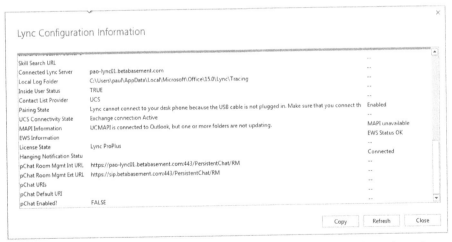

Figure 7-12 The Lync Configuration dialog box showing a number of configuration values, including whether the client is currently using UCS

Another way to verify that UCS is enabled for a user is to look for a folder named Lync Contacts as a subfolder of the default Contacts folder; if you see it in either Outlook 2013 or Outlook Web App 2013, you see details of the users in the Lync Contacts folder. Other clients that are not UCS-aware, such as Outlook 2011 for Mac, show the Lync Contacts folder, but only the SIP address for the contacts is shown. The Lync 2013 client itself shows both the contents of this folder and other contacts taken from the default Contacts folder.

After a user has been enabled for UCS, any change she makes to her contact list in Lync 2013 will be copied back to the Lync Contacts folder. However, the reverse is not true; you can't go into Outlook 2013 or Outlook Web App 2013 and add or modify contacts in the Lync Contacts folder. Hopefully, Microsoft will enable this functionality in the future.

INSIDE OUT Preventing users from opting out

Lync is designed to work with Outlook, and the default setting in Lync is to use Outlook and Exchange as the default personal information manager (PIM) for Lync. If you change the default PIM to None, the Lync client cannot do any of these things, and users might also be able to turn off the Save Instant Messaging Conversations In My Email Conversation History Folder and Save Call Logs In My Email Conversation History Folder. Microsoft recommends preventing users from changing the PIM setting by creating a DWORD value named PersonalContactStoreOverride beneath the HKEY_CURRENT_USER\Software\Policies\Microsoft\Communicator key and setting it to 0. If you decide to do this, you should probably use Windows Group Policy objects to apply this change uniformly to all your computers.

There are two special considerations for users who are being migrated: if you move a user who is on Exchange 2013 and Lync 2013 back to an earlier version of either product, UCS will break for that user. This can happen in two ways:

- **Lync migrations** These include moves for users hosted on Lync 2013 who migrate back to a Lync 2010 pool or server and for users who move cross-premises (either from on-premises to Lync Online or vice versa). In this case, the Move-CsUser cmdlet moves the user's contacts from UCS back to the Lync store as part of the migration.

- **Exchange migrations** A user whose mailbox is on Exchange 2013 and migrates back to Exchange 2010 must be manually switched from UCS back to Lync storage with the Invoke-CsUcsRollback cmdlet or moved back to a Lync 2010 pool. You must move the user off UCS before moving his Exchange mailbox back to Exchange 2010.

There's no way to force a user to move from Lync storage to UCS, though; when the user becomes subject to a policy that allows UCS, it can take up to seven days before that policy is applied.

TROUBLESHOOTING

Lync client reports that it can't communicate with Exchange
A default installation of Exchange 2013 leaves the ExternalUrl property of the EWS virtual directory blank. This makes the Lync 2013 client very unhappy; if you check its configuration settings (see Figure 7-12), it will show that EWS is not deployed. The truth is that EWS is deployed, and the Lync client might even be able to reach the internal URL. In fact, it might be able to reach the external URL if it knew what URL to use! To fix this, use Set-WebServicesVirtualDirectory to set the correct value for the ExternalUrl property (as described in Chapter 1). The Lync 2013 client should notice the change within a few minutes.

Working with high-resolution photos

Outlook 2010, Lync 2010, and SharePoint 2010 featured the ability to display user photos in some parts of their respective user interfaces. This added a friendly note to these applications in addition to making it possible to identify your correspondents better. However, there were several limitations to the photo implementation in these products: photos had to be stored in the Active Directory thumbnailPhoto attribute, which limited them to 10 KB in size (and, not incidentally, required a schema change to enable thumbnailPhoto to be stored on global catalog servers). The photos were limited to a measly 96 × 96 pixels, which looked terrible when the Lync client stretched them for its display.

To fix this, Microsoft enabled a new photo storage and processing system in Lync 2013, Exchange 2013, and SharePoint 2013. Exchange is now solely responsible for storing photos. Each user can add her own photo to her mailbox by using Outlook Web App; administrators can also assign photos to individuals, either allowing each user to approve his own photo or forcing it to be applied. The photo is stored as a folder-assisted item (FAI) in the root of the user's mailbox, with a message class of IPM.UserPhoto.

The Exchange 2013 mailbox role can provide photos in three sizes:

- **648 × 648 pixels**   This is the full-size version that only Lync 2013 and Lync Web App 2013 display. These clients use EWS to retrieve the photo directly. Users may upload photos with a higher resolution through Outlook Web App, but if they do, the photo will be downscaled to a maximum of 648 x 648 pixels.

- **96 × 96 pixels**   This is the size Outlook Web App 2013 and Outlook 2013 use, both of which use EWS to retrieve user photos.

- **64 × 64 pixels**   When you upload a higher-resolution picture using Exchange 2013, it downsamples the picture to 64 × 64 pixels and stores it in the thumbnailPhoto attribute of the user's account. However, if you edit the thumbnailPhoto attribute manually, its value is not propagated back to the same-size image stored in the user's mailbox.

Thanks to this architecture, earlier clients can still see photos; when a user uploads her high-resolution photo to her Exchange mailbox, Exchange publishes the thumbnail to Active Directory. The Lync address book service copies the thumbnail photo to the Lync address book so that Lync 2010 clients can see it too.

INSIDE OUT   The mystery PhotoGarbageCollection service

If you look at the log directory (which defaults to c:\program files\microsoft\exchange server\v15\logs) on an Exchange 2013 Mailbox server, you'll see a directory named PhotoGarbageCollectionService. This leads to the natural questions of what this service is, what it does, and why it doesn't seem to be documented anywhere. In this case, the answer is simple: the service removes "draft" photos, which have been uploaded by users but not assigned to their mailboxes. Remember that users can use OWA to upload a photo, but until the user or administrator assigns that photo to the mailbox, it remains as a JPG file in the upload directory. The PhotoGarbageCollectionService (which isn't a standalone service anyway) is responsible for cleaning up these orphaned files after their seven-day waiting period has expired.

Assigning photos to users

There are three ways to load high-resolution pictures into Exchange to make them available to users. The simplest way is to let users upload their own pictures through the options page of Outlook Web App, as shown in Figure 7-13, or through the Settings dialog box in the Lync 2013 client. Users can upload their own photos provided they have the MyBaseOptions or MyContactInformation user role assignments.

Figure 7-13 Users can upload their own photos through the Outlook Web App settings interface

Administrators can also upload photos for users with the Set-UserPhoto cmdlet. This requires you to read the photo data into an array of bytes and then pass that array to Set-UserPhoto—an odd requirement because it seems simple enough to have Set-UserPhoto take a file as input. Here's an example:

```
$photo = ([Byte[]] $(Get-Content -Path "\\PAO-FS01\UserPhotos\MichaelTucker.jpg"
-Encoding Byte -ReadCount 0))
Set-UserPhoto -Identity michaelt -PictureData $photo
```

At this point, the photo is stored in the user's mailbox as a preview item. The only difference between a photo and a preview is the message class; photos are of class IPM. UserPhoto, whereas previews are of class IPM.UserPhoto.Preview. It won't appear to the user until the administrator runs the Set-UserPhoto cmdlet again with the –Save flag:

```
Set-UserPhoto -Identity michaelt -Save
```

When users upload their profile pictures, the uploaded picture is stored as a preview item until the user clicks the Save button in the photo upload page. This preserves the upload while still giving the user a chance to change pictures if he doesn't like the selected one.

Newly uploaded photos should be immediately visible to clients that can display them. You can also check on an individual user's photo by requesting it directly in a browser. For example, this URL attempts to display the high-resolution photo associated with Michael Tucker's mailbox:

```
https://pao-ex01.betabasement.com/ews/Exchange.asmx/s/GetUserPhoto?email=michaelt@
betabasement.com&size=HR648x648
```

Because all the clients currently capable of displaying high-resolution photos retrieve them from Exchange through EWS, if you don't see a photo in a client, it is probably due to EWS connectivity problems between the client and the target Mailbox server.

Integrating Exchange archiving with Lync Server

Archiving is a feature that either inspires passionate interest or complete disregard. Some organizations have legal, regulatory, or operational requirements that mandate archiving communications data, so they tend to be very interested in finding the most efficient means possible of doing so. Organizations that do not have any of these requirements tend not to deploy archiving because they don't see the business value in doing so. The new archiving features in Lync 2013, Exchange 2013, and SharePoint 2013 are clearly aimed at the first group.

What archiving integration means

The basic motive behind integrating archiving across these three products is that courts treat all electronic records as discoverable unless you can convince them that producing records would be too difficult. Suppose Woodgrove Bank receives a subpoena to produce records pursuant to a bankruptcy proceeding; opposing counsel and the court will expect all records that might be relevant, no matter where they are stored. When you deploy the Office 2013 server products, SharePoint 2013 provides an interface for discovery and case management that can search across Exchange, SharePoint, and Lync data. However, Exchange retains its own search and eDiscovery features, as described in Chapter 11, "Compliance management," of *Exchange Server 2013 Inside Out: Mailbox and High Availability*.

Understanding Lync archiving

Lync Server archiving can be configured to work in a couple of ways. First, by default, Lync doesn't archive anything. Second, you can enable archiving of instant messages, call detail records, and web conferencing content by using the built-in archiving functionality. This archived data is stored in a SQL Server database, and there is an active ecosystem of third-party scripts, tools, and add-ons for searching, reporting, and otherwise processing it. Third, you can instruct Lync to archive IM and conference data by storing it in Exchange 2013. This third option actually uses the Exchange in-place hold mechanism, making a true archiving solution. Users can still choose to save their IM conversations to the Conversation History folder, but that is done on the client side, so it's not really suitable for meeting archiving requirements.

These controls are applied in two ways. You control the behavior of archiving using the Set-CsArchivingConfiguration cmdlet, which enables you to control whether archiving is possible at all, and, if so, what data are stored in what location. You can also define archive policies, which give you finer-grained control over archiving by letting you specify whether internal, external, or all communications are archived. Archive policies also let you define scopes at the Lync site (which are similar to, but separate from, Active Directory sites) level, the Lync pool level, the entire organization, or individual users or groups.

Lync starts with a single global archive configuration and a single global archive policy. The default configuration disables archiving, and the default policy specifies that neither internal nor external communications should be archived. This setup is equivalent to running Set-CsArchivingConfiguration –Identity Global –EnableArchiving $false. This default configuration is perfectly suitable for companies that don't want to use archiving.

Enabling Lync archiving to Exchange

If you want Lync data archived to Exchange, you must complete several related steps. First, you must decide on the details of your archiving policy. Many organizations use the default global scope, although you can create smaller scopes if that makes sense. You must decide which specific data items you want archived (either IM transcripts or both IM transcripts and web conferencing sessions). These questions are largely a matter for your compliance team, your legal department, and any business stakeholders who might be involved with records retention, compliance, or archiving; they are nontechnical decisions.

When you've answered these questions, you can actually enable archiving. The first step is to enable archiving on the configuration scopes where you want to use it. This will most often be the global configuration, so to enable global archiving of IM and web conference traffic to Exchange, you would do something like this:

```
Set-CsArchivingConfiguration -Id global -EnableExchangeArchiving $true
-EnableArchiving ImAndWebConf
```

When you execute that command, Lync can start archiving traffic, but it will not do so until you specify an archiving policy that enables archiving on the organization, specific sites, or specific users. There are two ways to do this: you can modify the global archiving policy, or you can create or modify additional archiving policies that only apply to the scopes you want. The first option is the simplest; this command enables archiving of internal and external IM and web conferences:

```
Set-CsArchivingPolicy -Id global -ArchiveInternal $true -ArchiveExternal $true
```

If you choose to use a custom policy, you create it with New-CsArchivingPolicy and then apply it to the correct scope with Grant-CsArchivingPolicy.

The exception to the foregoing description is when Lync and Exchange are in separate forests (as they might be in a hybrid deployment). In that case, you must use the ExchangeArchivingPolicy switch with Set-CsUser to specify how you want archiving to work. Suppose you have a user named Julia Ilyina whose Lync traffic you need to archive. Your Lync servers are in forest A, and Julia's Exchange mailbox is in forest B. You've already enabled archiving as previously described, and now you want to ensure that her traffic is archived. You can use Set-CsUser –ExchangeArchivingPolicy to do one of four things:

- The default is to leave this value uninitialized, in which case, archiving for Julia will be controlled by whether she has an Exchange in-place or litigation hold on her mailbox. If she does, Lync traffic will be archived to her Exchange mailbox according to the type of hold and the settings for it that are currently active; if not, her traffic will be archived in Lync.

- Set this flag to UseLyncArchivingPolicy to force Lync to archive her traffic in the Lync archiving server. In this case, you have to use whatever Lync archiving system you use to query for Julia's traffic; only conversation data from her Conversation History folder (if any) will be retrieved when you search through Exchange or SharePoint.

- Set this flag to ArchivingToExchange if you want to ensure that her traffic is archived to her Exchange mailbox irrespective of the in-place hold state of her mailbox. In this case, Julia's IM traffic will be archived no matter what type of hold (if any) is set on her mailbox.

- Set this value to NoArchiving if you don't want her traffic archived at all. This setting overrides any other archiving policies, so you would use it if you wanted to exempt Julia positively from archiving.

When you search for content that has been archived by Lync in Exchange, you can limit the item types returned by the search to Lync items only, which is useful when you have reason to believe that the responsive records were originally created in Lync.

You might wonder why there are so many different conditions that apply to Julia's mailbox; the reason is that Lync and Exchange archiving integration work whether both products are on-premises, one is on-premises and one is in the cloud, or both are in the cloud. That necessarily makes this more complex, but the price of this additional complexity is greater flexibility.

On to the cloud

Lync Server has been an extremely fast-growing business for Microsoft; like Exchange, it requires a distinct skillset and its adoption rate has been limited in part by how quickly people could learn to deploy and operate it. The Office 365 product line has been growing even faster than Lync, though, and in the next chapter we'll delve into the basics of Office 365 deployment and administration.

Office 365: A whirlwind tour

It seems pretty clear that Microsoft believes in its software + services model, in which it offers both software that you can install on your own premises (known, unsurprisingly, as on-premises software) and services that run the same software on an industrial scale in Microsoft data centers. The proof is in the launch of Microsoft online business services (as distinct from its consumer-focused services such as Bing and Xbox LIVE). Starting with the acquisition of PlaceWare in 2005, which gave Microsoft the Live Meeting service, it has steadily expanded its portfolio of business services while engineering its enterprise server software to support businesses better through improved monitoring, automation, and scalability.

Office 365 is the current pinnacle of the Microsoft online business portfolio. It is essentially a world unto itself; it combines almost all the features of Exchange Server 2013, Lync Server 2013, SharePoint 2013, Office web apps, and directory synchronization into a single package. A company that deploys Office 365 can have full Active Directory capability and use almost every feature of Exchange, Lync, and SharePoint without deploying any of its own servers. Customers can choose to buy individual services, such as Exchange Online, or they can subscribe to bundles known as plans that combine multiple components. (It is common to hear Microsoft engineers, developers, marketing staffers, and executives refer to Office 365 as the service, and I'll use that terminology here.)

Microsoft announced in July 2013 that Office 365 was its fastest-growing-ever server product, dethroning Lync Server, the previous champion. In addition, when Microsoft announced changes to the software servicing model for Exchange 2013 in February 2013, it announced that new features and updates will be delivered first to Office 365 and then to on-premises Exchange 2013 users—an inversion of the previous deployment scheme. Both of these facts testify to the importance of the service to Microsoft as a revenue engine and a technology platform and to the adjustment that administrators of all Microsoft server products will have to make in the next few years. The service is here, and it won't go away, so we have to learn to deal with it.

Having said that, this chapter is intended to give you a good beginning knowledge of the basic steps required to deploy and operate Office 365. The deployment process is complex enough that it can't be comprehensively covered in a single book chapter; it would take an entire book to give a complete treatment. Fortunately, Microsoft has provided good documentation that covers the detailed steps necessary to get up and running on the service, and I'll be referring to it often. A complete deployment of Office 365 that includes SharePoint, Lync, and Exchange is less complex than deploying those products on-premises but more complex than deploying hosted Exchange alone, and Exchange is all I'll be covering in this chapter.

> **Note**
> One of the difficulties inherent in writing about cloud services is that they can change rapidly and often. The screen shots of Office 365 in this chapter reflect its appearance and function as of late 2013, but it's likely that some of the underlying Office 365 code will change, so don't be surprised if what you see on screen doesn't exactly match what you read here.

What is Office 365?

Microsoft has dozens of pages of marketing materials on its main website and the *http:// www.office365.com* site, most of which is dedicated to explaining what Office 365 is and why you should buy it. Rather than repeat that information, it's more useful in the context of this book to talk about the technical aspects of the service and how to determine which components, if any, make sense for you to use.

The first thing you should know about Office 365 is that, at least for Exchange, the software that Microsoft runs and the software that we run on our own servers is identical, but there are functional differences. If you carefully read the Exchange 2013 documentation on TechNet, you'll see that many cmdlet parameters are marked as "Reserved for internal Microsoft use" and not otherwise documented. That's because they're used in the service and either have no effect or are not enabled in on-premises installations. However, some Exchange 2013 features are available on-premises but not yet offered as part of the service. Just because the underlying bits are identical doesn't mean that the software's capabilities as delivered are identical. One good way to keep track of the differences is to check the service description page that Microsoft maintains at *http://technet.microsoft.com/en-us /library/exchange-online-service-description.aspx*. It is not always perfectly in sync with the actual service because sometimes new features are added to the service before they show up in the document, but it's a good starting point.

The many faces of Office 365

Microsoft has muddied the waters a bit by using the Office 365 name for two completely different things. There's the Office 365 service, which businesses of all sizes use and which includes both clients (including the Office 2013 applications and the Lync 2013 client). Then there's the Office 365 Home Premium service, which is a subscription bundle consisting of the Office 2013 applications, bundled minutes for Skype calling, a larger storage allocation for the SkyDrive service, and a few other goodies.

> **Note**
>
> Somewhat confusingly, you can't use the Office 365 Home Premium applications with the Office 365 service itself. However, because most Office 365 service plans include usage rights for Office 2013, that shouldn't be a problem.

Microsoft describes the Office 365 service components as "customizable but not configurable." That's an important distinction. You cannot, for example, create new Database Availability Groups (DAGs) or mailbox databases with Office 365. The Microsoft data center operations team takes care of designing DAGs and database layouts to provide the desired degree of availability and resilience. However, you can still customize the environment with transport and data loss protection rules, various kinds of policy objects (including Outlook Web App, Mailbox, and Exchange ActiveSync policies), and so on.

Plans and licensing

Office 365 is licensed on a subscription basis. This is both easier to understand and more complicated than the way Exchange and Lync are licensed for on-premises use. Instead of the familiar client access licenses (CALs) that you have to buy for on-premises products (including Windows Server, of course), you buy per-user subscriptions for Office 365. If you have 100 users, you need 100 user licenses, no matter how many devices they use or where they are located. That's the easier to understand part.

The more complicated part comes from the way Microsoft aggregates features into different plans. Different plans include different features, and they have different prices. In a way, this is a welcome innovation; it means you don't have to pay for features, such as journaling or unified messaging, that you don't want to use. However, it complicates the process of planning for and operating Office 365 deployments because you have to be mindful not only of how many subscriptions you need but also of which plans you'll subscribe to.

As of this writing, Microsoft sells the Office 365 service in several plans. The current business plans are as follows:

- Office 365 Small Business offers hosted email, instant messaging and presence, SkyDrive Pro, and SharePoint access for up to 25 users. It doesn't include rights to run Office 2013 applications, so you either have to supply your own desktop Office software or have your users use the Office web apps suite, and it cannot be integrated with Active Directory.

- Office 365 Small Business Premium adds the ability to run Office 2013 (except for InfoPath) on your organization's PCs, plus support for site mailboxes and the iPhone version of Microsoft Office, to the services available in the Small Business plan.

- Office 365 Midsize Business is available for companies with 300 or fewer users. It adds InfoPath support and the ability to perform directory synchronization with your on-premises Active Directory to the Small Business Premium plan.

- Exchange Online Plan 1 provides basic email service. (There are corresponding plans for Lync and SharePoint.) Often referred to as kiosk mode or P1, this plan enables users to connect with IMAP/POP, Exchange ActiveSync, or Outlook Web App, but not with Outlook. It omits many Exchange features, including unified messaging, legal hold, integration with Lync, and eDiscovery. You can synchronize your Exchange Online service with your on-premises Active Directory.

- Office 365 Enterprise E1 is designed for larger organizations. It includes email, IM/presence, SharePoint, SkyDrive, and site mailbox support, along with Active Directory synchronization. However, E1 users don't have rights to run the desktop version of Office.

- Office 365 Enterprise E3 is the next step up from E1. It includes everything from E1 plus usage rights for desktop Office, the ability to use hosted unified messaging services, permission to run the iPhone version of Office, and support for eDiscovery, archiving, and legal hold.

- Office 365 Enterprise E4 is the top-of-the-line plan (at least for now). It includes everything from E3 plus support for information rights management (IRM) and license rights to use on-premises Enterprise Voice with Lync.

The plans that include license rights for the desktop version of Office have a very welcome add-on—each user for whom you purchase a subscription may install Office on up to five devices. That means that if you buy an E3 subscription for Jessica, she can install Office on her work desktop, her work laptop, and her home laptop, a major boon for companies that want to facilitate, if not encourage, remote and after-hours work.

INSIDE OUT   Switching plans and the speed of the cloud

When I first started writing this chapter, Microsoft had one set of rules for switching between plans. Midway through the writing process, it announced an expanded set of rules with more possible switching options—and the blog post in which it announced it promised a forthcoming expansion in switching options due by the end of 2013. This is a great example of how cloud-based services allow Microsoft to make changes quickly in response to customer demand, market shifts, or technical enhancements.

Which of these plans you choose depends on the size and composition of your organization, what you currently have deployed, and what you want your users to be able to do, a question I'll explore later, in the "Is Office 365 right for you?" section of this chapter.

INSIDE OUT   Which version of desktop Office are you getting?

The question of which Office 365 plan is right for you can be difficult to answer. However, Microsoft makes plain that one of the major benefits of Office 365 is that, as long as your subscription is active, you have the right to use the latest and greatest version of Office. This can be either a blessing or a curse, depending on your organization's requirements.

For instance, being able to deploy new versions of Office as soon as Microsoft makes them available, with no additional license costs, certainly sounds attractive. Many Microsoft customers purchased Software Assurance (SA) to give them discounted upgrade rights when new versions ship, but SA contracts have three-year terms, and Microsoft doesn't always ship new versions of its major products within three-year windows.

However, just because you're not paying a license fee doesn't mean that your Office upgrade is free. There are always costs associated with updating enterprise software. Before you can roll out a new version of Office, for example, you must consider whether your existing documents will be compatible, how you'll handle exchanging documents with outsiders who might not have the same software you do, and how you will train your users on the new version. All these considerations have an associated cost. For example, if you're using Outlook 2003 now, you'll need to upgrade to a newer version to use Office 365, but when you do, you might need to migrate your users' profiles, and you will certainly need to train users on the new version, both of which have an associated cost.

Office 365 plans that include desktop versions of Office currently offer Office 2013 for Windows or Office 2011 for Mac OS X. One nice feature of the subscription system is that these versions are licensed interchangeably; if you buy 5,000 seats of Office 365 Enterprise E3, for example, it doesn't matter to Microsoft how many of those users run Windows and how many run Mac OS X.

There are additional plans for educational institutions (Office 365 Education A2, Office 365 Education A3, and Office 365 Education A4) and government agencies (Office 365 Government G1, Office 365 Government G3, and Office 365 Government G4). The availability of these plans is further stratified by country and region; the only way to know whether your particular educational institution or government agency qualifies is to look at the local Office 365 pages for your country or region and see what Microsoft is offering.

> **Note**
> There's a large chart showing exactly which features are available in which plans on the Microsoft website at *http://technet.microsoft.com/en-us/library/office-365-platform -service-description.aspx*. This makes for interesting reading as you consider which plan might be right for your organization, or if you just want to see what's in the various plans.

Dedicated vs. shared

Microsoft offers a set of dedicated services, too; in this model, your organization actually gets its own set of dedicated resources running Office 365. These servers are managed and configured by Microsoft, just as the shared service is, but your organization's data are segregated from other clients' data. Microsoft details its dedicated Office 365 variants at *http://technet.microsoft.com/en-us/library/dn270088.aspx*; these are known as the D plans (as in Exchange Online Plan 2D), and there are some significant differences in cost and capability between the E-series and D-series plans.

As if that weren't confusing enough, there is yet another set of dedicated plans that Microsoft describes as being suitable for "security, privacy, and regulatory compliance requirements for U.S. federal government agencies requiring certification under the Federal Information Security Management Act (FISMA) of 2002 and for commercial entities subject to International Traffic in Arms Regulations (ITAR)." Microsoft refers to *these* plans as ITAR-support plans, and they have their own set of service descriptions, available at *http://www .microsoft.com/en-us/download/details.aspx?id=23910*.

A word about pricing

There's a one-word explanation of Office 365 pricing: variable. Enterprise software vendors have always been able to play all sorts of pricing games to attract and retain business. For example, IBM used to give steep discounts on otherwise expensive software to induce customers to buy bigger mainframes, and Microsoft offers an Enterprise Agreement (EA) framework that offers significant discounts to customers who commit to buying large volumes of server and desktop products together.

Although it might be packaged and sold differently from traditional on-premises products, Office 365 is no different when it comes to pricing. Although the Microsoft website lists base subscription prices, usually expressed as per-user, per-month costs, for most Office 365 plans, these prices vary by country, and they are always subject to discounts from Microsoft or partner salespeople who are eager to book new customers. The quoted prices are based on signing at least a one-year service agreement. You might be able to get discounts by signing a longer term, and it's a safe bet that if you want to migrate from Lotus Notes, Novell GroupWise, Google Apps Premier Edition, or another direct competitor to Office and Exchange, Microsoft will be willing to cut its prices to encourage the move.

Keep in mind that, unlike conventional enterprise software, the price you pay now might change later because you're buying a subscription, not making a one-time payment to acquire a license. One of the key advantages to cloud-based services is how predictable their costs are, but keep in mind that those costs can change after the initial term of your subscription is up.

Is Office 365 right for you?

This is really a philosophical and political question, not a technical one, but it includes a number of factors. Cloud services can offer great benefits, but they also offer unique challenges and potential failure modes. The decision to move some or all of your operations to the cloud is not one to take lightly. The factors that influence this decision are the same for any hosted service, not just for Microsoft offerings.

The big bet

Whenever you adopt a cloud service, you are essentially betting that the service provider will do something you cannot. You may be betting that the service provider will give you better uptime or security than your current environment, or that it will deliver similar performance and service quality at a lower cost, or that it will provide features and services not available in your existing environment.

Whether this is a smart bet hinges both on the quality of the service your potential cloud provider is offering and on the quality of your existing service, whatever it is. (After all, you can move to Office 365 or another hosted service from platforms other than Exchange!) When deciding whether a move to the cloud is right for you, you must be willing to take a hard, dispassionate look at your current environment to give it a fair assessment—and you must be realistic about the nature of the transition. You might not know the answers to all these questions yourself, but keep in mind that business decision makers in your organization might be asking them too, so being prepared to answer them is important. Questions you might ask, or *be* asked, include:

- What is the *actual, measured* uptime of your email service as a whole? If you don't know the answer, you can't accurately compare the service level a cloud provider promises against what you have now.

- How would you rate the skill level and experience of your messaging team? Does it have a good track record of resolving major problems quickly?

- What does it cost you, per user per year, to operate your unified communications systems (including Exchange and Lync)?

- What do your users think about the services they are getting now? Are they happy with the quality, reliability, and feature set of the current on-premises deployment?

- Where are your Exchange servers physically located, and where are your users? Do the sites where your users are have reliable Internet connectivity?

- Are there regulatory or business requirements that argue in favor of moving to the cloud? For example, perhaps you face new regulatory changes that require data loss prevention or eDiscovery capabilities that your current system doesn't have.

- Are there specific features in your current environment that are especially important to users or your business? Public folders or integration with on-premises customer relationship management (CRM) systems might be examples of such features. Another thing to watch out for is features that are favorites of key decision makers. More than one well-planned migration has been torpedoed by the sudden discovery by a C-level executive that the new system does something differently than the old one.

- What is the proposed timeline for moving to the new system? Can you do it in stages, or does it have to be done all at once? Does that timeline mesh with your staff's availability and capabilities? Are scheduling limits imposed by the business? (For example, a retail business probably won't want to migrate during the holiday season.)

There are literally hundreds of other questions you can and should ask as you consider whether to move to Office 365 or any other cloud-based service, but these will get you started. A large number of other questions will arise when you start using the Microsoft planning and assessment tools for Office 365, which the "Assessing your Office 365 readiness" section later in this chapter covers. In the meantime, you might find it helpful to review the "Exchange Deployment Options" white paper (*http://www.microsoft.com/en-us /download/details.aspx?id=18206*), which outlines the different deployment models that include Office 365. Although the current version only covers Exchange 2010, the basic concepts remain the same.

INSIDE OUT Office 365: It's all physical

Virtualization has been a hot topic in the enterprise IT world for several years now, and it shows no sign of cooling. Given the many claims we've all seen about the superior economics, manageability, and scalability of virtualized solutions, you might think that Internet-scale systems such as Office 365, Google Apps, or Apple's iCloud are heavily virtualized, but they aren't. In fact, 100 percent of Office 365 operations are run on physical servers; Google and Facebook have designed their own custom server hardware, but Microsoft uses servers from partners such as Dell and Hewlett-Packard.

Most of the servers that power Office 365 and other Microsoft cloud services are organized into large shipping containers, each containing about 1,400 servers. Somewhat surprisingly, each container has only three connections coming from it, known colloquially as ping, pipe, and power (network, water for cooling, and electricity). A single container's servers might be dedicated to many services; this helps provide redundancy as opposed to having dedicated containers for each service. The local data center operations team monitors the physical hardware and infrastructure, performing tasks such as making sure that no birds are stuck in the building air intake vents (yes, really), that cooling water is available where needed, and so on. Failure of an individual server in a container doesn't require any action—its workload is automatically shifted to another server. When a certain percentage of a container's servers are considered failed, the container itself can be taken offline for maintenance.

When you consider that Microsoft has a large number of data centers (somewhere between 10 and 100; it has not publicly said exactly how many), with a huge number of servers and more than 200 cloud services on offer, this building-block approach makes perfect sense. In this model, ruthless configuration specification and management processes help ensure as much consistency as possible in the design and operation of the hardware that runs the services, which lowers the operating costs for Microsoft. It will be interesting to see whether the many Hyper-V scalability and manageability improvements in Windows Server 2012 and Windows Server 2012 R2 will cause Microsoft to reconsider the use of virtualization for its cloud services.

Hybrid or hosted?

It is important early on to decide on the mode in which you will deploy Office 365. You have three basic choices:

- You can set up a greenfield Office 365 deployment, either with or without directory synchronization, and create new mailboxes on the service without connecting to your on-premises Exchange organization. This is generally pretty rare for existing Exchange customers, although it is not uncommon for organizations that are migrating from other systems.

- You can move all your users to Office 365. In this scenario, known as *hosted mode*, you are leaving on-premises Exchange completely and won't keep any servers of your own after the move is complete. This is often the choice of small to midsize organizations that want the predictable costs and (at least potentially) higher uptime and performance of Office 365 compared to their on-premises operations.

- You can keep at least one Exchange server on-premises and move some fraction (large or small) of your users to the service. Microsoft calls this *hybrid mode* (it was formerly known as rich coexistence), and it is, by far, the most common scenario for deploying Office 365 in enterprises. (Smaller deployments tend to perform cutover migrations.) Even if your goal is to end up in a fully hosted deployment, you will probably get there by deploying in hybrid mode, moving mailboxes to the service, and then decommissioning your on-premises servers.

When you deploy in hybrid mode, you get a lengthy list of features, all of which are driven by the fact that the Exchange organization you host on-premises and the one Microsoft hosts on your behalf are treated as a single unit by Exchange. These features include a shared Global Address List (GAL), shared access to calendar and free/busy data, seamless mail routing between your on-premises and hosted mailboxes using one namespace, and centralized mailbox management through Exchange Administration Center (EAC) and Exchange Management Shell (EMS). It would be very interesting to see trend data to indicate how many hybrid mode deployments end up converting to fully hosted deployments.

You can set up a hybrid mode deployment by using an on-premises Exchange 2003, Exchange 2007, Exchange 2010, or Exchange 2013 environment. If you use Exchange 2003 or Exchange 2007, you will probably need to set up an Exchange 2013 server that runs the CAS and Mailbox roles. This server is known as a *hybrid server* because its function is to enable hybrid operations by giving the Office 365 servers running Exchange 2013 a compatible endpoint to talk to. (This was also true for previous versions of Business Productivity Online Services [BPOS] and Office 365 when they were running Exchange 2010.) Here are the rules to keep in mind:

- Exchange 2003 needs an on-premises Exchange 2010 SP3 hybrid server.

- Exchange 2007 needs an on-premises hybrid server running Exchange 2010 SP3 or Exchange 2013 CU2 or later.

- Exchange 2010 SP3 doesn't require a hybrid server. However, you can deploy one if you want to take advantage of Exchange 2013–only features for integration.

- Exchange 2013 doesn't require a hybrid server at all.

You can think of the hybrid server as a gateway; it acts as the interface between Office 365 servers and your own. For example, when you move a mailbox from your on-premises servers to the cloud, the Mailbox Replication Service (MRS) on the Office 365 side contacts the MRS proxy on your premises to execute the move. Office 365 servers are responsible for coordinating and executing the move. The process of getting a license key to install the hybrid mode server has been confusing in the past; now you just request it from Office 365 support after you've set up your subscription. It will issue the license key, you plug it into EAC, and that's it. This key is only licensed for running the hybrid server. Its license agreement doesn't allow you to host mailboxes or public folders, run unified messaging, or do anything else.

Of course, there are many aspects of Exchange that you don't get to manage in hosted or hybrid mode. You cannot create or manage mailbox databases, DAGs, connectors, or most other types of non-mailbox objects on the service side, so if you were thinking of creating a DAG that has Microsoft servers as members, forget it. If you want complete control over all aspects of your messaging environment, Office 365 probably isn't the right choice for you.

Chapter 8

INSIDE OUT   Best practices for recipient management: Keep an on-premises server

Strictly speaking, it is not *required* to keep any on-premises servers when you move to a fully hosted Office 365 deployment. However, it is a really good idea to do so. Managing your recipients by using the native Exchange tools (whether you use EMS or EAC) ensures that as you change recipient attributes, add or remove users, and modify groups, the changes are properly stored in Active Directory Domain Services (AD DS) and replicated, where appropriate, to Office 365 through dirsync. Every object in a dirsync environment has an attribute that indicates its *source of authority*, or which side of the connection owns the object. The source of authority for an object can be either the service or your on-premises deployment. Objects that were originally created on-premises will show this in their source of authority.

The potential for problems begins with this fact because, if you have objects that belong to the on-premises environment, Office 365 will not let you modify their attributes using its tools; you must make those changes on the on-premises side. If you don't have any Exchange servers present on-premises, you can only modify Exchange-related objects using ADSIEdit, your own scripts, or other methods Microsoft doesn't support. Furthermore, installing the Exchange management tools alone to modify objects in a hybrid deployment, without including at least one CAS and Mailbox server, won't work either because the Exchange management tools depend on remote Windows PowerShell, which is only provided by the Mailbox server role.

In summary, if you have a hybrid-mode Office 365 deployment, you should plan to keep at least one on-premises Exchange CAS and Mailbox server around even if you move all your mailboxes to the cloud. The exception is if you're using Windows Azure Active Directory (WAAD), in which case, it (and not your on-premises AD DS implementation) will be considered the source of authority.

Connectivity

Of course, any attempt to use a cloud-based service will depend on having access to the cloud—more precisely, the Internet. It is surprising how many organizations overlook this fact until very late in the Office 365 planning and deployment process. A good heuristic is to consider whether users on a particular site have enough bandwidth *now* to connect by using their preferred client. An Office 365 deployment generally won't use any less bandwidth, although more of it may be directed to the Internet than to internal servers, depending on where your clients are and how much of your mail flow is to and from the Internet versus to internal users. One of the key portions of the recommended Office 365 readiness assessment is to evaluate carefully how much bandwidth is actually available between each site where users will be located and the Microsoft data center. This is especially important for deployments that involve multiple countries; when you sign up for Office 365, you must specify the country you're in, which drives the data center in which your data is stored. After you choose a country, you can't change it later. If you are planning to use Lync as part of your Office 365 deployment, separate tools are available on the Microsoft site for assessing the amount of bandwidth you'll need for site-to-site audioconferencing and videoconferencing.

Uptime and support

One of the most common reasons that organizations consider moving to the cloud is the notion that they'll be able to get better uptime for their messaging and collaboration environments. The thinking is generally that a major cloud service provider will have robust processes, reliable hardware, and the operational maturity to run Exchange and Lync at high scale and with very high uptime. This line of argument leads to two questions: what does "very high uptime" mean, and what happens when you need help of some kind?

Service level agreements

Part of the usual negotiation with a cloud services provider is the execution of a service level agreement (SLA) that describes the level of availability to which the provider is committing, how outages are handled, where the boundaries for support lie, and the financial compensation, if any, that might be due if a service does not meet the contracted uptime. SLAs from large companies tend to be very precisely specified because ambiguity in definitions doesn't sit well with their legal departments.

Of course, signing an SLA is easy, but monitoring end-to-end performance and availability to tell whether the vendor is meeting its commitments and understanding the impact of local and cloud support is more complicated. Because of this factor, many service providers will only guarantee an SLA for the portion of the service they control. If you can't reach the cloud service because of a problem with your Internet connection, for example, that outage doesn't count against the cloud provider's uptime targets.

The default SLAs for Office 365 are available from the Microsoft website at *http://www .microsoftvolumelicensing.com/DocumentSearch.aspx?Mode=3&DocumentTypeId=37.* Interestingly, the same SLA covers not only Office 365 but also services such as Bing Maps for Enterprise and Windows Intune. Each service has its own definition for what constitutes downtime, but downtime is calculated the same way for all the Office 365 services:

((User minutes – downtime) / user minutes) × 100

For each month, downtime is the sum of the length (in minutes) of each outage that occurs during that month multiplied by the number of users affected by that outage. For any month in which the uptime percentage is less than 99.9 percent, you get a credit, the amount of which increases as downtime increases. Microsoft says that Exchange Online, Exchange Online Archiving, and Exchange Online Protection (EOP) have zero planned downtime, although other Office 365 components have planned monthly maintenance windows that don't count against the monthly uptime percentage. Interestingly, the service-level commitment from Microsoft for EOP is 99.999 percent, and there are separate SLAs for the false positive and spam filtering effectiveness rates—an indication of the high confidence Microsoft puts in the quality of those services.

Support boundaries

Given how the Internet connects your network to the cloud, you can expect transient network hiccups that cause clients to lose connectivity from time to time. After all, no one is responsible for the Internet, and no one guarantees perfect connectivity across the Internet all the time. (That's why cached Exchange mode is such a valuable feature of Outlook, although organizations using desktop virtualization or thin client software might find that they can't make effective use of cached Exchange mode.) Problems happen inside networks, even those that are under the sole and exclusive control of a single company. You have to be able to understand where local problems are likely to occur and how to address them quickly before you escalate to the service provider to see whether the problem is at its end. For example, an outage might occur in your network provider that links you to the Internet, a firewall or router might become overloaded with outgoing or incoming connections and fail, or a mistake in systems administration might block traffic outside your network. The real point here is that if you move email to the cloud, you cede the ability to have a full end-to-end picture of connections from client to mail server and only have control over the parts that continue to reside inside your network. Users will hold the local help desk accountable when they can't get to their mailboxes, and that creates a difficult situation when you cannot trace the path of a message as it flows from client to server, you cannot verify that connections are authenticated correctly everywhere, and so on. In fact, because there are so many moving parts in an Office 365 deployment that could break, including the Internet link, it is very difficult to hold a service provider to an SLA unless there is unambiguous proof that the cloud service failed.

Some organizations that purchase Office 365 subscriptions buy them through a Microsoft partner. For example, you might choose to work with a systems integrator to modernize your entire infrastructure by updating desktop hardware, moving to the latest version of Windows, and moving to Office 365, all through one contract and vendor. Some partners provide their own tier of support for their customers, whereas others expect you to go directly to Microsoft for Office 365 support. It is well worth asking hard questions about who will help you in case of a problem *before* you start paying.

Experience will prove how easy it is to manage availability in the cloud. For now, the weakness in management and monitoring tools complicates administrators' ability to verify that an SLA is being met whenever an application relies on connectivity outside the network boundary that the organization controls. Indeed, problems exist in simply getting data from the different entities that run the corporate network, intermediate network providers, and the hosting providers in a form that can be collated to provide an end-to-end view of how a service operates. It might be possible to get data from one entity or another, but the data is likely to be inconsistent with data from other entities, be impossible to match up to provide the end-to-end view, or use different measurements that make it difficult to synchronize.

Service desk integration is another related but different issue. You probably need some method to route help desk tickets from the system currently in use to the service provider and maintain visibility to the final resolution of the problem. Given the wide variety of service desk systems deployed from major vendors, such as IBM, CA, and HP, and the lack of standards in this area, this isn't an easy problem to solve.

INSIDE OUT   What about backups?

One theoretical advantage of the cloud is that someone else does all the bothersome maintenance that you don't want to do, such as backups. It can be argued that with a solid DAG design, you don't need to do backups much anyway, but there are still cases in which this might not be true. For example, suppose that you have a regulatory requirement to keep archived data for five years or even longer—one customer I am familiar with has a requirement to keep its data for *16 years*. It's an open question whether any cloud service will still exist in the same form 16 years from now, but then again the difficulty of being able to restore an Exchange backup from 2013 in 2029 is certainly pretty high. The original backup media might not even be readable by then— think back to the early 1990s and ask yourself whether you could read a backup today that was stored on Zip disks or SyQuest cartridges from that time.

If you want backups for disaster recovery in the cloud, you don't really have many options. Microsoft maintains the mailbox databases, and it won't give you access to back them up directly; you could export all your mailboxes to PSTs or something, but that's probably not workable at any real scale. However, if you need backups to provide long-lived archiving or retention, you might find that existing features such as Exchange 2013 support for in-place hold enable you to preserve the data you need, at least as long as that feature's offered. Be aware, though, that some features of earlier versions of Exchange, such as the ability to restore individual folders from the deleted items store, are no more.

See Chapter 11, "Compliance management," in *Microsoft Exchange Server 2013 Inside Out: Mailbox and High Availability* (Microsoft Press, 2013) by Tony Redmond for more details on the differences between Exchange 2013 retention and recovery features and those of prior versions.

Privacy and security

Concerns about privacy, security, and information disclosure are probably the biggest deployment blockers for cloud-based business services such as Office 365. Some companies flatly refuse to consider use of these services, and many have chosen to block consumer-oriented services such as Microsoft SkyDrive, Google Drive, and Dropbox to help reduce what they see as a risk of loss or exposure of sensitive company data from employees who turn to these services to simplify their work patterns. Cloud-related privacy and security concerns can take many forms, including:

- Concern that service administrators will have access to your organization's data. This is a problem that is essentially solved by use of your local sheriff. If you have a malicious administrator who's reading things she shouldn't, you generally need a way to audit access (a topic covered in *Microsoft Exchange Server 2013 Inside Out: Mailbox and High Availability*) to catch the perpetrator, and then you engage local or national law enforcement when you have the proof.

- Concern that your data, or the service, will be subject to malicious attacks by individuals, groups, or nation-states. It is unlikely that most of us will ever have to worry about specific attacks targeted directly at us, although most cloud service companies are used to deflecting distributed denial of service (DDoS) and other attacks mounted by organized groups such as Anonymous or individual miscreants.

- Concern that your data or communications will be monitored by governments. The 2013 disclosure of widespread tapping by the U.S. National Security Agency (NSA) and other intelligence agencies spotlighted this risk. Under current U.S. law, Microsoft is legally obligated to comply with disclosure requests that it receives from U.S. intelligence, security, and law enforcement agencies. (Note that I am *not* arguing that these requests are legal or constitutional, merely that Microsoft is presently obligated to honor them.) However, the Microsoft general counsel said in mid-2013 that Microsoft had received only four requests for company data (as opposed to data from individuals using Microsoft services such as Outlook.com or Skype), so in general, I think the risk of lawful access to stored data is fairly low. Interception in transit, however, is a different story. Microsoft protects customer data from interception by using Transport Layer Security (TLS) and Secure Sockets Layer (SSL), but that's no help when the government comes calling. The public outrage, both in the United States and abroad, will quite likely fuel new restrictions on what government agencies can do, but that will probably require sustained public scrutiny and pressure. In the meantime, many companies outside the United States are eagerly looking around for cloud services providers who aren't based in the United States, and this might prove to be a problem for Microsoft and its primary competitors in the cloud applications market.

The Microsoft data center operations are certified to a standard known as SAS 70. This is essentially the gold standard for personnel, network, and operational security at data centers; although the SAS 70 standard might not be perfect, it is widely recognized and trusted. The fact that Microsoft has undertaken the effort to have its data centers certified, and that its major competitors have not (or have not announced such certification if they have it) speaks well for the efforts of Microsoft to meet the privacy and security needs of its service customers. In addition, the Office 365 service itself is certified to the ISO 27001 standard, and Microsoft is willing to sign agreements with individual customers certifying that the service accepts responsibility for data subject to the U.S. Healthcare Insurance Portability and Accountability Act (HIPAA) and EU Safe Harbor requirements—a significant responsibility.

The page at *http://www.microsoft.com/online/legal/v2/en-us/MOS_PTC_Security_Audit.htm*
summarizes the audits and certifications that Microsoft has performed on its hosted services;
it also contains a summary of what these audits indicate and a list of frequently asked questions about the security auditing process. In addition, Microsoft has produced a white paper
(*http://www.microsoft.com/en-us/download/details.aspx?id=26552*) that outlines the security
standards and practices applied to the Office 365 service. Both make interesting reading if
you're interested in security.

Cost

How much does Office 365 cost? That's like asking, "How long is a piece of string?" I've
already mentioned, briefly, the subscription cost; it's very tempting to multiply the number
of users you have times the per-month rate quoted on the Microsoft website and call that
the cost figure. However, license costs can vary (up *or* down), and many other costs are
associated with messaging infrastructure that might not go away just because you migrate
to Office 365. For example, if you keep on-premises servers for directory synchronization or
for maintaining hybrid operations, the cost to purchase, license, power, and maintain those
servers remains. Even if you move your Exchange services completely to the cloud, there
are training, operations, and maintenance costs—and let's not forget bandwidth, without
which most cloud services are useless.

Another factor to watch out for is that of hidden costs. If you've purchased an airline ticket
in the past few years, you've probably noticed that many airlines have added fees for services that were once included, such as checked baggage or in-flight meals. Microsoft isn't
doing much of this unbundling yet; to the contrary, the various Office E plans include a
number of services that have been separately billed in the past. For example, the Office E3
plan includes unlimited personal archive storage space, which used to be sold per gigabyte
under the old Exchange Hosted Archiving banner. As adoption of Office 365 grows, it is certainly possible that Microsoft will unbundle some features that are now included in the cost.

You should probably also factor in the possible cost to leave the cloud if you find that it's
no longer a good fit for your business requirements. Most cloud services, including the
one from Microsoft, ask customers to sign a contract for a minimum two-year or three-
year term, so leaving the contract early will cost you money. Even if you wait for its term to
expire before migrating back to on-premises operations, you can't wait until the contract
end date to start the migration process—instead, you need to get an early start on planning your reverse migration so that you can account for any associated costs (such as buying new Mailbox servers or other hardware).

Unique service features

Microsoft makes a point of emphasizing that the on-premises and service versions of
Exchange 2013 use the same code base. This is certainly true, although there are many differences in what that code does when run. A great example: as of Exchange 2013 RTM CU2,

there's a very useful service feature that isn't available on-premises. This feature, known as *inactive mailboxes*, enables you to mark a mailbox as inactive, indicating that the user who owned it is no longer using it (perhaps because he left the company). The idea is that you mark departed users' mailboxes as inactive; their data remains accessible for eDiscovery searches, but you don't have to pay for an Office 365 license for that mailbox. Another example is the Set/Get-MailboxSentItemsConfiguration cmdlets, which were introduced to on-premises Exchange 2010 SP2 but are not present (yet?) in either Exchange 2013 or Office 365.

Service-first features can be useful and desirable, but they mark a worrisome possibility: a future in which Microsoft ships desirable features *only* as part of the service, as was initially the case with the Outlook Web App for Devices app described in Chapter 3, "Client management." It remains to be seen whether inactive mailboxes will be backported to the on-premises code or other service-only features will emerge.

Hybrid operations, migration, and coexistence

Office 365 is like many other products in that it has its own vocabulary that you must master as part of the deployment process. In Microsoft parlance, a *hybrid* deployment is one in which you maintain your own on-premises servers and link them to Office 365. You can mix and match Office 365 products in a hybrid deployment; for example, you could have an on-premises Exchange deployment and a hybrid Lync deployment within the same organization. (This deployment mode used to be called rich coexistence, which is more descriptive but also clunky-sounding.) Most organizations will use hybrid deployments for at least part of their Office 365 life cycle because the easiest way to get onto Office 365 in the first place is to set up a hybrid deployment and then move your mailboxes from on-premises servers to the cloud.

Another deployment approach is to *migrate* from on-premises services to Office 365 services. In this context, "migration" means what it always has: moving data from one system to another. In an Office 365 migration, you set up a brand-new Office 365 tenant and then move your users from your on-premises operations to the cloud. This can be done all at once (a *cutover* migration, when all users switch to the new system at once) or in phases (a *staged* migration).

The role of directory synchronization

Whether you operate in hybrid mode or migrate your users, you have to choose how to link your existing user accounts in your on-premises Active Directory with Office 365 (although if you set up a brand-new Office 365 tenant and treat it as a separate forest, with separate user credentials, you don't need synchronization). The process of deploying Office 365 in hybrid mode is logically equivalent to operating a cross-forest deployment because that's exactly what you're doing.

Directory synchronization (or just *dirsync*) is the catchall term that refers to the process of synchronizing the contents of your on-premises Active Directory with Office 365. The goal of Office 365 dirsync is to get a subset of the attributes for a subset of the objects in your on-premises Active Directory into the cloud so that the Microsoft servers can authenticate your users, make mail routing decisions, and do all the other things for which Exchange depends on Active Directory. (Microsoft Knowledge Base article 2256198 describes the exact objects and attributes that are synchronized; it makes for interesting reading.) This synchronization is bi-directional, although most of the synchronized data flows from your organization to the cloud. To be more specific, the Office 365 dirsync tools sync your user account and group data to the Windows Azure Active Directory (WAAD) service, which is the directory service that Office 365 uses. A small number of attributes (including msExchArchiveStatus, which indicates whether an archive mailbox is associated with a user mailbox, and msExchUserHoldPolicies, which signals whether any legal hold policies are applied to the user) are synchronized from the service back to your on-premises AD DS installation.

Dirsync requires you to install the Windows Azure Active Directory Sync tool on a server in your organization (although it's perfectly okay to use a virtual machine for this role). As installed, the synchronization tool will synchronize only 50,000 objects. If you create a custom domain (see the "Domains" section later in this chapter), the limit on the total number of objects you can sync rises to 300,000 Active Directory objects. If you need to sync more than that, you have to ask Microsoft to raise the synchronization limit on your Office 365 environment by filing a support ticket. However, whether you hit the 300,000-object limit or not, if you have more than 50,000 objects, you need to provide a separate SQL Server instance for the tool to use.

Installing the tool creates a service account named MSOL_AD_SYNC and a universal security group named MSOL_AD_Sync_RichCoexistence that the tool uses to read the Active Directory objects it will synchronize. The needed permissions are assigned to the group, which has MSOL_AD_SYNC as its only member. If anything happens to this account or group—say, if its password is changed—synchronization will fail. The synchronization process logs events on the computer on which it's running, so you can check them to ensure that synchronization is working properly.

You will initially have to perform a full synchronization, but after that, changes are synchronized every three hours. You can also force a synchronization by using the Start-OnlineCoexistenceSync cmdlet, which requires you to load the set of cmdlets included with the directory synchronization tool first by running the DirSyncConfigShell.psc1 script included with the tool.

INSIDE OUT   Dirsync software versions: At cloud speed

If you're accustomed to the somewhat leisurely release cadences of most add-on tools for Exchange, it might surprise you to see the pace at which the Office 365 dirsync tools are updated. The dirsync team aims for a monthly update cadence, but it has the flexibility to release updates more or less frequently depending on the nature and scope of the updates and what the broader Office 365 team is doing. The team maintains a version history update log at *http://social.technet.microsoft.com/wiki/contents /articles/18429.windows-azure-active-directory-sync-tool-version-release-history.aspx* so you can keep track of what changes they're making and when if you're interested.

Single sign-on and federation

"Federation" is a common term in the Exchange world now, which is funny given that it didn't really exist a few years ago. In the sometimes-confusing world of identity management, *federation* is usually understood to mean linking organizations so that they share identity or user data. In Exchange, we're familiar with concepts such as calendar federation, which enables users in one organization to see another organization's user free/busy data, and then there's Lync federation, which enables users in one organization to exchange instant message and presence data with users from other organizations. In the context of Office 365, federation means that the Office 365 service can ask your organization's Active Directory to authenticate users through the Active Directory Federation Service (AD FS) tool (or other identity providers if you have them; to be precise, AD FS is only one of the *token providers* that Office 365 can use for federation. There are others, such as Shibboleth, but I won't discuss them further.).

Microsoft refers to the standard Office 365 identity objects as *cloud identities*. When you provision a new Office 365 user, he gets a cloud identity and can immediately start using the service even if you don't have dirsync, password sync, or federation set up.

AD FS enables you to set up a federated authentication relationship so that Office 365 servers can ask your on-premises Active Directory servers to authenticate users who try to access Office 365 resources. Microsoft refers to this as using *federated identities*, and when you do so, your users get *single sign-on*, or SSO; users sign in to their workstations as they normally do, using domain credentials you issue, and then Office 365 uses AD FS to verify those credentials and grant or deny access according to the result it gets. Think of this as a supersized version of the familiar Active Directory pass-through authentication process. It's not mandatory to do this, but it is considerably more convenient for users than requiring them to enter two sets of computers. In addition, because AD FS uses your on-premises

Active Directory to authenticate users, policy settings (such as password expiration times and logon hour restrictions) are honored; *your* domain controllers decide who gets access, whereas with password sync, the Microsoft domain controllers authenticate users who request service access using their policies.

INSIDE OUT Put your cloud services inside the cloud

So far, I've been talking about AD FS and directory synchronization as things you do on-premises, but there is no absolute requirement to do it that way. Microsoft supports running both AD FS and the Office 365 dirsync tool in Windows Azure virtual machines (VMs). Putting your dirsync components into the cloud offers some intriguing benefits, such as improved disaster recovery and flexibility. For example, you can use Azure to provide high availability even if you only have one physical location—just put additional VMs into the cloud. However, doing so also introduces some technical challenges. For example, AD FS in the cloud might impose excessive latency if your domain controllers are all on-premises, which is why Microsoft suggests that you consider putting at least some of your domain controllers in the Azure cloud, too. After you do that, it's a fairly short step to moving entirely to WAAD, which I assume is what Microsoft has in mind.

The "Deploying Office 365 Single Sign-On using Windows Azure" white paper (*http://www.microsoft.com/en-us/download/details.aspx?id=38845*) has a good explanation of how to set up Azure as the host platform for your directory synchronization and the pros and cons of doing so.

Chapter 8

Password synchronization

In addition to synchronizing the Active Directory objects that define which users exist in your organization, you can synchronize passwords with the service. It's important to understand a nuance in this process: the *passwords* are synchronized, but the *accounts* are not. For example, if you implement directory synchronization and password synchronization but not single sign-on, a user with the account carrie@contoso.com and a password of Alpine29 will use those credentials to log on to systems in the Contoso forest, but to log on to Office 365, she'd use carrie@contoso.onmicrosoft.com with the same password. In terms of convenience, this is midway between using completely separate sets of credentials and implementing SSO. You can make things easier by adding contoso.com as a custom domain (and doing so for any other UPNs you want to support), in which case, the combination of ordinary dirsync and password synchronization will enable her to log on using her Contoso account.

Password synchronization doesn't synchronize the passwords themselves; Active Directory doesn't store the unencrypted passwords anyway. Instead, it stores hashes of the password, and the password synchronization process synchronizes those hashes. The password synchronization process is identical to the process used to synchronize directory data, but it runs more frequently; Microsoft documentation says that password changes are synchronized "within minutes," by which it really means that the default synchronization interval is two minutes. Every object that is synchronized to the cloud will also have its password synchronized; if you don't want a particular object to have its password synchronized, your only choice is not to synchronize that object at all.

Remember that this synchronization goes only one way, from the on-premises account to the cloud. The password complexity policy you set on-premises will override any policy you have set in the cloud. More important, when you enable password synchronization, the cloud passwords will never expire, so users whose passwords expire on-premises can still log on to cloud services even though their passwords won't work for on-premises services.

Hybrid mode

Small organizations (say, fewer than 500 or so seats) seem to be most attracted to the idea of moving completely to the cloud. Larger companies are being more cautious for a variety of reasons, both political and technical. If you aren't ready to move all your Exchange mailboxes to the cloud and decommission your on-premises Exchange servers, that's all right; you can deploy Exchange 2013 in hybrid mode instead. In this mode, you keep on-premises directory and Exchange servers, with some users hosted on-premises and some on Office 365. Which users go where is entirely up to you.

In hybrid mode, you are really running two logically separate Exchange organizations in two Active Directory forests: your on-premises organization in your own forest and an Office 365–hosted Exchange organization in a WAAD forest that Microsoft controls and maintains. That's why you will often see Microsoft referring to an "Exchange Online organization" in its documentation; many of the features of hybrid mode are available any time you set up organizational trust and federation between two Exchange organizations.

Hybrid mode features

Microsoft touts a number of features and benefits that come from hybrid mode deployments, including the following:

- **A single shared SMTP namespace**   For example, Fabrikam users can receive mail at *@fabrikam.com* addresses whether their mailbox is hosted on-premises or on the service. Mail routed between the two services is automatically secured using TLS, as described in Chapter 2, "The Exchange transport system."

- **All users sharing a single unified GAL**   As you add and remove mailboxes on either the on-premises or hybrid side, those users appear in the GAL just as though your organization were entirely on-premises.

- **The ability to move user mailboxes seamlessly back and forth between the cloud and your own servers**   It's hard to overstate either how convenient this is or how much of a technical improvement it is compared to the mechanics of moving mailboxes in older versions. (For more about how the Mailbox Replication Service [MRS] enables this, see *Microsoft Exchange Server 2013 Inside Out: Mailbox and High Availability*.)

- **The ability to split user mailboxes and personal archives**   Because the Office 365 E3 plan offers unlimited storage for personal archive mailboxes, some companies are keeping some or all their mailboxes on-premises but giving their users archive mailboxes hosted in the cloud. This can be substantially less expensive than provisioning and managing on-premises archives if you can accept the feature constraints of the Exchange Personal Archiving feature, as discussed in *Microsoft Exchange Server 2013 Inside Out: Mailbox and High Availability*.

- **Free/busy and calendar sharing between on-premises and cloud users**   This requires you to configure a federation trust between your on-premises organization and Office 365; while you're at it, you can federate with other Exchange organizations (whether they're on Office 365 or not).

- **Centralized control of inbound and outbound mail flow**   You can configure all inbound and outbound messages to be routed through the on-premises Exchange organization first or through the cloud first. Because Office 365 subscriptions generally include licenses for the Exchange Online Protection (EOP) service, it's a good idea to plan on having your inbound mail travel through EOP and then to Office 365, which will send mail for your on-premises users back where it belongs.

- **A single URL for access to Outlook Web App for both on-premises and Office 365 users**   Thanks to the magic of the Client Access Server (CAS) role, users can connect to on-premises certificate authorities (CAs) and be automatically routed to the correct endpoint.

- **Centralized mailbox management** using the on-premises EAC plus the ability to manage both on-premises and Office 365 objects and settings through on-premises EMS.

Some hybrid features (such as the ability to search both on-premises and archive mailboxes simultaneously) require you to deploy AD FS.

Setting up hybrid mode

To enable hybrid mode, you run the Hybrid Configuration Wizard (HCW), an on-premises executable file that's installed when you install Exchange 2013. The wizard is normally something you run only once; it creates a new object known as the hybrid configuration object (*HybridConfiguration*) in Active Directory, fills it with settings appropriate to your organization, and makes the corresponding changes to objects in your Exchange Online organization. You can rerun the HCW at any time to change the settings for your organization; when you do, the HCW changes any settings you've specified and pushes the changes out to the Office 365 side. This process has five steps (see Figure 8-1):

1. Run the wizard and make your configuration choices. The wizard runs the Update-HybridConfiguration cmdlet, which starts the Hybrid Configuration engine.

2. The engine examines the content of the HybridConfiguration object in Active Directory, which was updated when you saved your changes in the wizard. Microsoft calls these settings the desired state because they represent the configuration you just asked the wizard to apply.

3. The engine performs several discovery tasks to find out how the current on-premises organization is configured: which servers exist, which accepted domains are in use, and so on.

4. The engine performs the same discovery tasks against the Office 365 organization.

5. The engine compares the desired state with the current state of both your on-premises and service organizations and then changes both configurations as needed to match the desired state.

Later in the chapter, you walk through the steps necessary to configure hybrid mode for an Exchange 2013 organization so you can see the wizard in action.

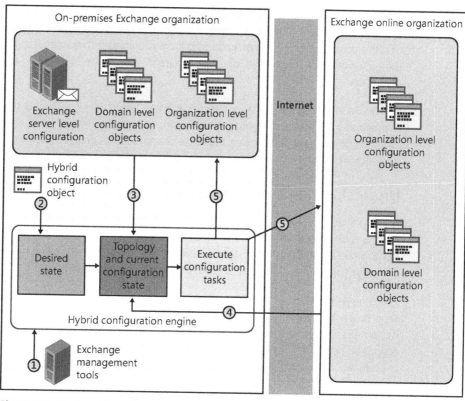

Figure 8-1 The hybrid configuration process

Managing hybrid mode

Microsoft has put a lot of effort into making hybrid mode work as much as possible like on-premises mode; you use EAC and EMS to manage the user and Exchange objects that belong to you, just as you would in an on-premises only deployment, even if some of those objects actually are hosted on Microsoft servers and not yours. As is typical of every other part of Exchange, some hybrid mode features can be configured using EAC and the HCW, whereas other tasks require you to use EMS. One of the claimed benefits of cloud-based services is the ease and speed at which they can be updated; I hope this is the case for EAC so that it quickly gains parity with EMS.

Keep in mind that there are many settings and features of Exchange that you cannot configure in Office 365. For example, tenant administrators aren't allowed to create or remove mailbox databases or DAGs, and many of the parameters for cmdlets you are allowed to run are inaccessible.

However, you still retain full control over the user and group objects that are on the service and the licenses allocated to them. Thanks to the magic of directory synchronization, changes you make on-premises are automatically replicated to the service; if you're not using dirsync, then you use EAC and EMS against Office 365 to manage cloud identities for your users.

For the most part, managing a hybrid-mode organization on a day-to-day basis is identical to managing an on-premises organization; you monitor the state of your servers and connections, fix anything that breaks, and make changes as needed to support your business's requirements.

Understanding types of migration

Although you can always create a brand-new Office 365 tenant and provision it from scratch, most organizations want to move users and data from their existing environment to the cloud instead. Microsoft documentation refers to four methods of migrating to Exchange Online; the differences among them can be somewhat subtle.

In a *cutover migration*, you move up to 1,000 of your organization's mailboxes over to the service. The idea is that you migrate the mailboxes and then decommission your on-premises servers, switching entirely to the cloud, although that isn't required. Cutover migrations cannot be performed if you have configured dirsync because it is intended to be used for hybrid operations; cutover migrations are typically a once-and-done process.

In a *staged migration*, you move your mailboxes in stages or phases. This name is really misleading because staged migrations can only be used when migrating from Exchange 2003 or 2007—if you're migrating from a newer version, you must perform either a cutover or hybrid migration. Staged migrations require you to set up coexistence between your existing organization and your Office 365 tenant; you configure mail flow and authentication so that users can talk to one another, and then you start migrating mailboxes in batches. Staged migrations also require directory synchronization so that the service will have access to the directory data necessary to move and link mailboxes.

Cutover and staged migrations don't give you access to most of the interesting integration features you might want. To name three quick examples, there's no free/busy integration, MailTips don't work, and you don't get access to cloud-based personal archives.

In a *hybrid-based migration*, you set up a hybrid-mode organization and then move mailboxes to it. You have a great deal of flexibility when deciding which mailboxes to move and when. The migration tools described in *Microsoft Exchange Server 2013 Inside Out: Mailbox and High Availability* enable you to create migration batches containing the users you want to migrate and then start the batches when it's convenient for you. Third-party migration tools from companies such as Dell/Quest and Binary Tree can also be used to give you more control over when and how the actual movement of mailboxes takes place. As with staged migrations, hybrid migrations require dirsync of some kind, but, unlike them, you get the full array of hybrid features: free/busy access, MailTips, and the ability to move mailboxes from the cloud back to your on-premises servers, for example.

Finally, the fourth type of Exchange Online migrations is IMAP-based migrations, either from Exchange or from non-Exchange systems such as GroupWise, Lotus Notes, or Google Gmail. If you're migrating from an earlier version of Exchange, IMAP migrations are really feature-poor. This migration type is very simple: you create user accounts in Office 365 for the mailboxes you want to import (of course, this can be scripted using EMS), and then you feed a comma-separated value (CSV) file containing the user credentials and IMAP endpoint data to the Exchange Migration dashboard in EAC. The Migration service (described in *Microsoft Exchange Server 2013 Inside Out: Mailbox and High Availability*) creates IMAP migration requests and then moves data from the endpoint to the specified user mailbox. After the initial synchronization, the contents of the migrated mailboxes are incrementally synchronized every 24 hours until you finalize the migration, at which point, no further synchronization is performed. At some point during this process, of course, you have to update your mail flow configuration so that mail for your organization goes to Office 365 instead of to the existing server.

Assessing your Office 365 readiness

One of the big advantages of cloud-based services such as Office 365 is that they can be updated at any time. Microsoft has certainly demonstrated this with the Office 365 assessment and readiness tools; the goal of these tools is to help you determine what you need to do to deploy Office 365 successfully in whatever configuration makes sense for your business.

The basic process of readiness assessment is simple: you sign up for a trial of the service, and then you run a set of web-based Microsoft tools that interview you about your business requirements, point out limitations and capabilities of the service, and coach you through the setup process. As Microsoft gets more experience with cloud deployments and customer feedback, it updates the tools, so the steps I present here (and the associated screen shots) will probably change over time.

Signing up for the service

The first step is to visit Office365.com and sign up for the service. New subscribers get 30 days free of whatever plan they select, with a number of licenses that varies by plan. For example, if you select the Office 365 Midsize Business plan, you get 25 user licenses during the trial. Signup requires you to provide a physical address and to choose a domain name, which is used as a subdomain of the *onmicrosoft.com* domain used for Office 365 services.

(Interestingly, Microsoft doesn't ask for any payment information such as credit card numbers when you first sign up.) For example, if you want to sign up Contoso Industries for the service, your Office 365 domain would be *contoso.onmicrosoft.com*, and the initial user ID you specify as part of the trial signup would be in that domain too. You can also use your own organization and domain for sign-in (for instance, paulr@contoso.com instead of paulr@contoso.onmicrosoft.com) as you saw in the "The role of directory synchronization" section earlier in this chapter.

As soon as you complete the sign-up form, you'll be taken to the Office 365 administration portal (Figure 8-2); it's always accessible if you log on to *https://portal.microsoftonline.com*. Congratulations! You're now on Office 365 and can stop reading because all the work is done. Actually, that's not even close to true!

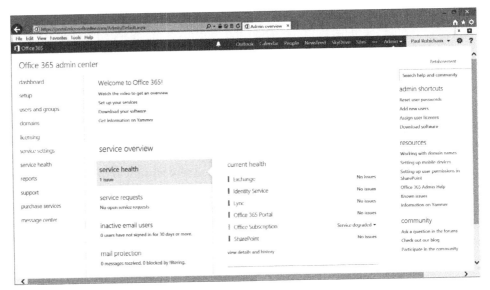

Figure 8-2 The Office 365 administration portal

The OnRamp process

Microsoft has given the assessment tool the catchy name of OnRamp (*http://onramp .office365.com*). You need a Microsoft account (formerly known as a Windows Live ID, or WLID) to use OnRamp, although you can sign up for one as part of the OnRamp process if you don't already have one.

The first question you'll be asked is which services (Exchange, Lync, SharePoint, and Office desktop software) you plan to use. Your choices here drive which other questions you'll see later in the process; for example, if you select SharePoint, you'll see questions about SharePoint.

Next, you'll be asked about how you want to provision user accounts. You can manage accounts directly from Office 365 only, use dirsync, or use AD FS. Depending on which option you choose, you'll notice that the Setup area on the right side of the window changes between one of three values: Easy, Advanced, and IT Professional (see Figure 8-3). This is intended to give you a quick gauge of how complex your deployment is likely to be, although I suspect it's also intended to warn tinkerers with little IT administration background that they're preparing to get in over their heads.

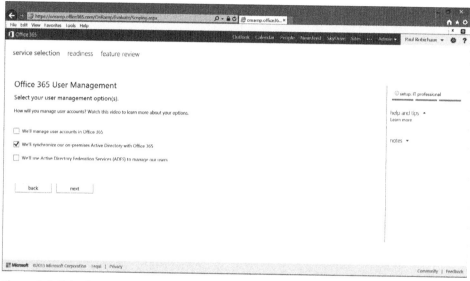

Figure 8-3 Selecting a user management option in the OnRamp tool

The third initial question is how, or whether, you're migrating mailboxes. You can specify whether you're migrating from Notes, GroupWise, an IMAP system, an earlier version of Exchange, or not at all. In the Exchange case, you also have to pick whether you're doing a cutover, staged, or hybrid migration.

At this point, if you've chosen any options that OnRamp thinks are too complicated for the average novice IT person (as evidenced by a setup rating of Advanced or IT Professional), the tool will ask you to confirm whether you know what you're doing well enough to proceed. If not, you can go back and change your answers, and you can use a link to find a partner to help you with your deployment.

OnRamp might offer to run a set of automated checks for you. This requires you to install a small piece of software named cmdletexecutioncontrolsetup.cab, and it might require other prerequisites, depending on where you run it from. For example, the automated checking tools require version 4 or later of the .NET Framework, and you will probably have to install the Windows Azure Active Directory sign-in assistant and Windows PowerShell extensions unless you've previously installed them. For best results, you should run it from the domain-joined computer on which you intend to run the dirsync tool or AD FS, whichever you're using.

The automated tools begin by asking you for credentials for an administrative account on the Office 365 tenant; without this, of course, you can't proceed. For each category of checks, you'll see a simple icon indicating whether the checks passed or failed, along with a link to see more details of the test and the test results (see Figure 8-4). If you run the environmental check at this point in the setup process, it will probably fail because you haven't set up everything yet. For example, the test shown in Figure 8-4 is on a system on which dirsync hasn't been set up, so naturally the "Has dirsync happened in the last three hours?" test fails, and that in turn causes a failure of the overall check.

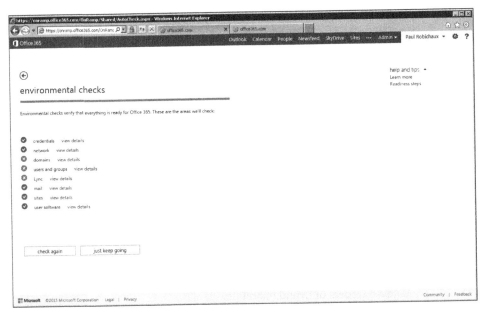

Figure 8-4 Results from an environmental check

For that reason, you must plan to use the readiness checker as part of an iterative process; you'll run the tool, see whether it reports any errors, fix anything that's broken, and then run it again.

Whether or not you perform the automated checks, OnRamp will give you a set of steps to perform to set up the configuration you indicated. The exact readiness steps you see will depend on the answers you gave to the preceding three questions. For example, when I chose to set up dirsync for a hybrid Exchange 2013 organization, without using AD FS, OnRamp produced a list of seven steps, as shown in Figure 8-5. It's interesting that these steps primarily revolve around setting up and configuring dirsync; the last step is to run the

HCW in Exchange, which seems like it would be the most important step—but you can't complete the HCW successfully until all the other steps have been completed.

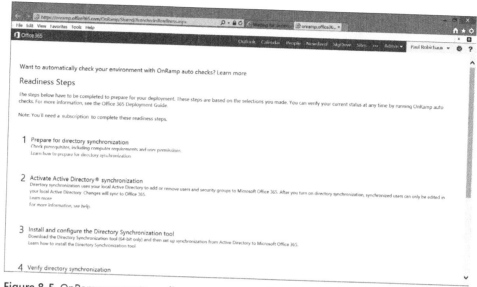

Figure 8-5 OnRamp suggests readiness steps

Setting up a hybrid organization

Directory synchronization is a key part of the integration between on-premises and hosted Exchange because it gives both sides a common frame of reference for user and group information. The initial setup of the Microsoft dirsync tool is pretty painless, but you can make a number of adjustments during the initial setup or later, and it pays to know what those are and to choose your options carefully.

Enabling directory synchronization

Before you can sync your Active Directory domain information with WAAD, you have to tell the Office 365 back end that you want to enable directory synchronization. You do this from the Office 365 portal. Select the Users and Groups tab; an Active Directory Synchronization: Set Up link appears above the user list. Click it to see a page listing several configuration steps. The one in which you're interested now is labeled Activate Active Directory Synchronization. Click the Activate button, and a confirmation dialog box appears; if you confirm your choice, the necessary back-end changes will be made to allow WAAD to sync with your environment. These changes can take up to 24 hours to become effective; until they do, you cannot actually synchronize your directory, although you can proceed to installing the dirsync tool.

Running the IDFix tool

One way you can help prepare for dirsync, even a long time in advance of your actual synchronization, is to check your on-premises Active Directory data for problems that will prevent synchronization. Potential problems include bad or missing values for mandatory attributes on objects, bad access control lists (ACLs) on key objects, and so on. It's much easier to fix those problems before you start synchronizing with WAAD, and to that end, Microsoft has shipped a repair tool known as IDFix. When you download it from the Microsoft website anxd install it (it goes into c:\Deployment Tools\IDFix\ by default), you can run it to check your entire on-premises Active Directory for items that would cause errors if you tried to synchronize them, and the tool enables you to repair most of those errors quickly. After you get a clean bill of health from IDFix, you can proceed with your dirsync implementation.

To run IDFix, download and install it, including the odd but required step of renaming its executable file from IDFix.exe.rename to just IDFix.exe. When you run the tool, a privacy warning tells you that because IDFix can download personally identifiable information and save it as a CSV file, only administrators should run it, and they should be mindful of the risk of a data breach if the resulting data are exposed. When you've read and dismissed that warning, the tool itself will open. If you want to check every object in your on-premises directory, click the Query button in the menu bar; if you want to limit your query to a subset of the directory, use the filter icon to define a base for the search. Figure 8-6 shows the results of running IDFix against a test directory where most of the users were created with a poorly written Windows PowerShell script that turned out not to handle escaping special characters properly. The status line at the bottom of the window shows that 1,094 user objects are in the directory and that 19 of them will cause errors when synchronization starts.

The Value column shows the current value of the suspect attribute, and the Update column shows the revised value the tool suggests for repairing the problem. The Error column indicates what the tool thinks the problem is; in this case, most of the reported entries have illegal characters, but there are a couple of duplicates and one name that has a format problem. (It contains a space, and it shouldn't.)

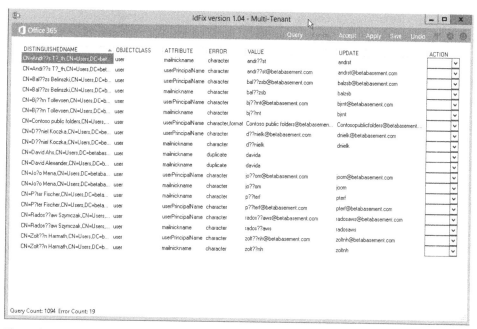

Figure 8-6 Results of running the IDFix tool against a directory with several bad attribute values on user objects

The Action column is a little tricky to understand because it can take on one of several values:

- EDIT means that you want the tool to apply the value in the Update column to fix the problem. This is normally what you'll use for character and format errors.

- COMPLETE means that you don't want the tool to fix the reported problem.

- REMOVE is used to specify that you want the tool to strip the suspect attribute. You'll normally use this if you just want to jettison the bad value and fix it yourself. You can combine this with COMPLETE to fix duplicates, too; select COMPLETE for the object that should have the selected value and then select REMOVE for any other object that has a duplicate value.

- FAIL means that the tool has no idea how to suggest a fix for the problem.

You don't have to apply the changes immediately that the tool suggests; that's why you have to select an action by using the Action column or use the Accept button in the menu bar to tell the tool to set the actions for you (except for format errors, which must be manually repaired). "Measure twice, cut once" is definitely a great rule to follow when dealing with Active Directory changes. To that end, you can export the suggested changes as a CSV file or in LDAP Data Interchange Format (LDIF); this greatly eases the process of reviewing changes to ensure that you don't break anything important.

When you're happy with the changes on which you and the tool have decided, click the Apply button, and IDFix will write them back to your on-premises directory. I suggest waiting 30 minutes or so to allow for Active Directory replication latency; then rerun the tool as a double-check before enabling directory synchronization.

Installing and configuring the dirsync tool

Before proceeding, you need to decide where you'll install the dirsync tool. Although it might seem perfectly logical to put it on a domain controller, that's not supported, so you'll need to find another home for it. Many organizations use dedicated VMs for dirsync because the ongoing synchronization workload is generally pretty low.

On that machine, you'll need to download the tool itself, which is currently available from the Microsoft website at *http://technet.microsoft.com/en-us/library/jj151800.asp*, and then install it. While it's installing, you should gather the credentials you'll use both for on-premises administrator access and administrator access for Office 365; the tool will ask for them as part of the sync process.

After the tool is completely installed, it will start its configuration wizard, as shown in Figure 8-7. The initial summary screen reminds you that you'll need the credentials I mentioned earlier; the list of items on the left side of the wizard window gives you a good idea of what the wizard will ask you during the process. Click Next to dismiss the first page, and you'll be prompted to enter the Office 365 tenant administrator credentials you want to use. Enter them and click Next again. The tool will cache the password you enter here, so if you change the password later, you will need to update the cached copy by rerunning the wizard, or dirsync will come to an abrupt halt.

Next, enter administrator credentials for your on-premises organization. These credentials are not saved; instead, they are used to assign permissions to the MSOL_AD_SYNC account, which actually performs the synchronization. Click Next.

The wizard next wants to know whether you'll enable hybrid mode. This might seem like an odd question to ask at this point, but its intent is to determine whether the dirsync tool will be retrieving data from WAAD and writing it back to your organization's local Active Directory. If you're planning to use Exchange, Lync, or SharePoint in hybrid mode, make sure the Enable Hybrid Deployment check box is selected and then click Next.

If you want to enable password synchronization, the next wizard page gives you the means to do so by selecting the Enable Password Sync check box. If you don't want password sync now but decide to add it later, you can do so by rerunning the wizard. When you click Next from this page, the wizard configures the local directory synchronization instance with the settings you chose. However, the directory is *not* synchronized until you encounter the final page of the wizard (Figure 8-8), select the Synchronize Your Directories Now check box, and then click the Finish button.

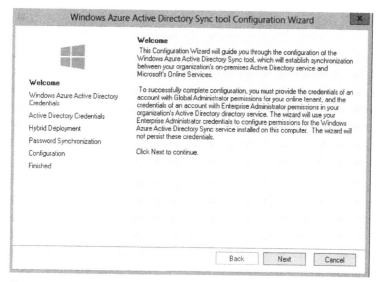

Figure 8-7 The Welcome page of the Windows Azure Active Directory Sync tool

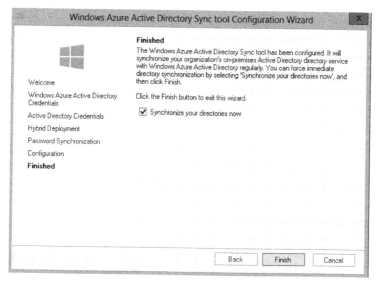

Figure 8-8 The final page of the Windows Azure Active Directory Sync tool

At this point, you'll need to wait for the sync process to begin so you can see whether it worked.

Filtering dirsync

You might not want to synchronize every object in your on-premises directory. If that's the case, you can use dirsync filtering to select a subset of on-premises objects for synchronization to the cloud. Luckily, filtering can be added at any time; if you start or stop filtering, the next sync cycle will add or remove objects as needed to ensure that the cloud has only the objects that match the filter. You can apply synchronization filters with three scopes: organizational unit (OU), user attribute–based, or Active Directory domain. The first two are very straightforward: filter by OU, for example, and you get only the user objects contained in that OU. Attribute-based filtering is simple to understand, too—specify a rule and only objects with attribute values that match the rule are synchronized.

The process for configuring filtering requires you to modify the dirsync configuration manually, using the miisclient.exe tool, as described at *http://technet.microsoft.com/en-us/library/jj710171.aspx*. Rather than include step-by-step directions here, I've chosen to point you to that article because as the dirsync tools evolve and improve, the required steps are likely to change—one of the perils of cloud services is that they can change faster than books can!

Verifying that dirsync is working

There might not be any immediate signs that dirsync is working during your initial synchronization (although if there are errors, you might see error report emails turning up in your administrator's Inbox; more on that in the next section). How can you tell whether dirsync is running properly or whether it has completed already? The solution Microsoft suggests is, in my opinion, a poor one—log on to the Office 365 portal and see whether your on-premises objects show up there and then make a change to an on-premises object and verify that the change shows up too. This certainly works, but it's an awfully blunt instrument. It's probably easier to check the event log to verify that the scheduler is working and that synchronization operations are proceeding as they should. You can also run the tool itself in graphical user interface (GUI) mode by launching Program Files\Microsoft Online Directory Sync\SYNCBUS\Synchronization Service\UIShell\miisclient.exe.

Password synchronization

Password synchronization is refreshingly straightforward: either it works, or it doesn't. The password, after all, is essentially just an object associated with a user account, which is why the dirsync tool copies every synchronized account's password when you have password synchronization enabled.

Password synchronization happens on its own schedule, one that you can't control. If you want to monitor the progress of password synchronization to verify that it's working normally, you can look for a few events in the Application event log:

- Event ID 656 indicates the start of a sync request; the event description contains a list of all the user accounts for which synchronization has been requested, with up to 50 accounts included in each request.

- Event ID 657 logs a set of users for which password synchronization succeeded. Ideally, you'll see event ID 656 and event ID 657 right next to each other with a 1:1 match between the names of accounts for which sync was requested and those for which it succeeded.

- Event ID 605 is logged when a password sync operation fails. The event description lists all the objects that failed to synchronize, but it doesn't tell you why the synchronization failed; you're on your own for that.

- Event ID 611 indicates that a password sync was running when a dirsync started, either on its schedule or because you started one manually. Password syncs are always paused when a dirsync starts, and that's what this event is telling you.

Troubleshooting dirsync

One clear sign that you're using a cloud-based service that behaves differently from Exchange is that the service might send you email messages such as the one shown in Figure 8-9. These messages are sent to the alternate contact email address you specified when signing up for the service, so keep an eye open for messages indicating problems with dirsync. You won't receive a message when dirsyc succeeds, so no news is good news.

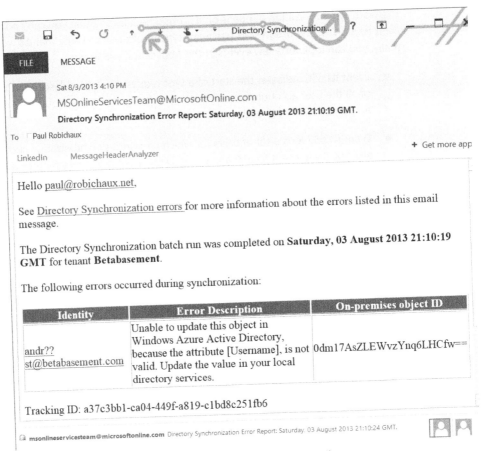

Figure 8-9 A dirsync error message sent from Office 365 by email

In general, the error messages the dirsync process produces are very straightforward. As long as the sync service itself is running, errors during synchronization generally fall into one of a small number of categories. First, the problem might be that the local dirsync process can't connect with Windows Azure, either because it's having network problems or because the network credentials it's using are incorrect. This is simple to identify and fix.

You might also encounter an individual object that can't be synchronized because one of its attributes is malformed in some way. For example, a multivalued attribute might have a bad value that prevents the sync engine from synchronizing it, or an ordinary, single-valued attribute might have a value that's too long for the sync tool. You'll be able to tell when something like this happens because the updated object won't appear in the cloud *and* because the sync tool will notify you (generally by email like the message shown in Figure 8-9) which specific object had the problem and what's wrong with it.

Using AD FS

AD FS is fairly complex to install and deploy; it's easier to deploy than Exchange but more challenging than a typical Windows installation. For that reason, rather than discuss it in depth here, I recommend that you begin your AD FS deployment plans with a careful review of the AD FS deployment checklist at *http://technet.microsoft.com/en-us/library /jj205462.aspx*. The checklist covers such topics as planning your deployment (including the number and location of servers needed to handle your expected user base), the role of AD FS proxies and where (and how) to deploy them, and establishing connectivity between AD FS and WAAD.

Throughout this process, if your organization doesn't already have experience with using AD FS, it might be well worth hiring help to plan and, possibly, to execute your AD FS implementation to smooth the process—given how important AD FS is, anything you can do to reduce the likelihood of problems is worth considering.

Mail flow

The purpose of an email system is to send and receive email, so naturally configuring mail flow as part of your Office 365 deployment is critically important. If you're using Office 365 as a standalone solution, you don't have much work to do other than setting up Domain Name System (DNS). However, if you plan to use Office 365 in hybrid mode or as part of a staged migration, you have to make some decisions about how you want incoming and outbound mail to be processed and then change your environment to implement those decisions.

Your mail flow options

When you combine Office 365 with on-premises Exchange, there are two potential destinations for incoming email: it can be delivered directly to you, or it can be delivered to the service. Either way, the receiving server can examine the recipient addresses, decide which Mailbox server should receive the message, and route it accordingly. From that perspective, you could argue that it doesn't matter how you configure inbound mail flow, and you'd be correct. The reasons for preferring one side or the other for initial mail delivery are usually organizational or political, not technical. For example, organizations that are required to journal all incoming mail often prefer to have the mail journaled on arrival at their organization, with further routing to Office 365 mailboxes taking place later. (Having said that, it is worth noting that Microsoft documentation says that the "[Office 365] tools [mainly the Directory Synchronization tool] are optimized for pointing your MX record to your on-premises Exchange system as the authoritative domain.")

Some organizations that use Exchange have mail flowing directly to their own networks, where it's filtered through an Exchange edge server computer, an appliance, or some other mechanism before the filtered mail is passed on to internal servers for routing and delivery. However, a large (and growing) percentage of the Exchange world instead uses hosted filtering services. Many Office 365 plans include CALs for the EOP service, which is also available separately for customers who want that service alone. (The pros and cons of each of these approaches are discussed in more detail in Chapter 5, "Message hygiene and security.")

Generally, I lean toward having all incoming mail delivered to the service for two reasons. First, the filtering EOP offers is excellent, and it's backed by an SLA that refunds your money if its protection falls below the agreed level. Perhaps more important, Office 365 and EOP can accept and queue mail for your on-premises servers even if you have an outage that knocks them offline; provided your servers come back up and begin accepting mail within the 72-hour default timeout period, you won't lose any inbound mail.

Setting up connectors

No matter which endpoint you choose to receive mail, you need connectors to link your on-premises and Office 365 organizations. As you learned in Chapter 2, the Exchange transport system trusts messages that originate from trusted connectors, which is exactly what you want for mail transport between the on-premises and service sides. Imagine how embarrassing it would be to have messages originating from an on-premises user marked as spam when they arrived at the service—a scenario that proper connector configuration can eliminate.

Figure 8-10 shows one possible arrangement of these connectors: a hybrid mail flow con-figuration by which mail received from and sent to the Internet passes through EOP, with TLS-protected connectors used to transfer mail between EOP and both the on-premises and hosted components of the network. Note that Microsoft creates and maintains the connectors between EOP and Office 365, so you don't have to (in fact, you *can't*) do any-thing to configure them.

Office 365 also supports the opposite of this configuration, by which all inbound and out-going mail is passed through your on-premises organization. Microsoft refers to this as *centralized mail transport*, and its primary use is for organizations that need all their mail to flow through an on-premises journaling or archiving system. Centralized mail transport is enabled through a check box in the Hybrid Configuration Wizard (HCW), but most sites won't use it.

The HCW sets up the connectors you need; when they are active, you shouldn't have to do anything to maintain them. Although there is no technical reason you couldn't create the necessary connectors yourself, it would be a waste of time—just use the HCW.

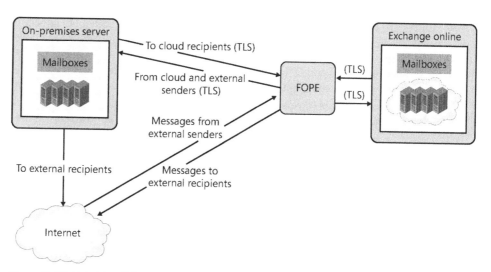

Figure 8-10 Hybrid mail flow

Domains

When you create a new Office 365 tenant, you get a domain in the *onmicrosoft.com* namespace. For example, if you create a tenant for Tailspin Toys, you get something like *tailspin.onmicrosoft.com*. This domain is perfectly usable as a Universal Principal Name (UPN) and a domain for SMTP email, Outlook Web App access, Lync Session Initiation Protocol (SIP) addresses, and so on, but it's ugly, and virtually every organization will want to use its own domain for both logon and addressing for email, SIP traffic, and so on. To do this, you configure Office 365 to tell it what custom domains you want to use. This is a simple process, but multiple steps and some waiting are required because Microsoft wants to verify that the actual owner of the domain is the one who's registering it for Office 365. Imagine the problems that might ensue if any random person could register any domain with Office 365.

To register a domain, you need to log on to the Office 365 administration center and switch to the Domains tab. You'll see the default *onmicrosoft.com* domain you already have there. Click the Add A Domain link, and a wizard will start. Three steps are required in the wizard, plus a fourth that's sort of submerged in the documentation but is nonetheless important:

1. Pick a domain name and confirm that you own it. This confirmation takes place by a simple process: Microsoft gives you a text string, and you add it as a DNS TXT record subordinate to the DNS domain. The thinking here is that if you control the DNS server for a domain, that's sufficient proof that you own the domain itself. The trick is that if you use a third-party DNS service, you might have to wait to make the change,

and the nature of DNS means that some replication and query latency will likely be involved whether the DNS server is yours or not.

2. Add users and Office 365 licenses to that domain. This is necessary because you might have multiple domains within a single Office 365 tenant; for example, if your organization divides resources according to geographical or functional boundaries, you might need separate domains for northamerica.contoso.com, emea.contoso.com, and so on.

3. Configure the appropriate DNS records for your use of Office 365. For example, you might need to create or change DNS MX records to get your mail flowing to Office 365. If you're using Lync Online as part of your Office 365 subscription, you'll have more work to do.

4. Go back to the Office 365 admin portal; in the upper-right corner (just below your username and the sprocket settings icon), you'll see your organization name. Click that link and then make sure the new custom domain you just added is set as the default domain.

Confirming ownership of your domain

Confirming your domain tells Microsoft that you are explicitly affirming that you own it. There are two ways to do this: you can add an MX record or a DNS TXT record, each of which will contain a unique ID that Microsoft assigns when you create a new Office 365 tenant. The tenant ID is an eight-digit decimal number, and you use it as the target. For example, if you choose to create a TXT DNS record, it will have a target of MS=msxxxxxxxx, and if you create an MX record, it will point to msxxxxxxxx.msv1.invalid.outlook.com. These records aren't used for anything other than proving that you control the DNS records associated with the domain.

The Office 365 setup tool contains links to step-by-step instructions for many common DNS providers, and it even includes a sample email message (with the correct tenant ID values filled in) that you can send to your provider if you want it to do the work instead.

After the DNS record has been added, you return to the Office 365 portal and click the Done, Verify Now button visible at the bottom of the window (Figure 8-11). Microsoft recommends waiting at least 15 minutes to allow DNS caching to take its normal course, but you might find that you have to wait a longer interval, depending on your DNS provider. After Office 365 has successfully verified the record you create, go back to the Add A Domain Wizard page to continue.

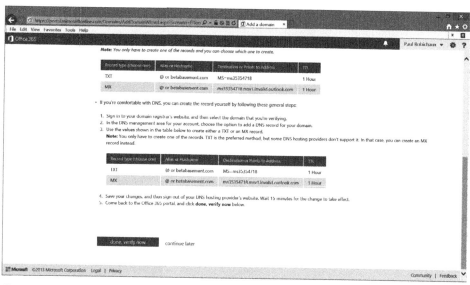

Figure 8-11 Setting up and confirming ownership of your domain

Adding users and assigning licenses

This step is how you add users and assign licenses for them if you're not using any form of dirsync. If you are using dirsync, the users are added for you as your directory synchronizes to the Windows Azure Active Directory (WAAD), but you still need to assign licenses from your subscription to the users you want to have access to Office 365.

If you are not using dirsync, you have to add users yourself, either by filling out a form for each user, which asks for first and last name, preferred email address, and so on or by uploading a CSV file containing the details necessary to provision the users. In both cases, the last step of the user creation process is granting licenses, which also has to be done for dirsync users. The process is covered later in the chapter in the "Licensing users" section.

Configuring DNS records for the new tenant

The nature and amount of DNS configuration you have to perform depends on which Office 365 services you're deploying. For Exchange Online, plan to set up records pointing your clients to the Office 365 Autodiscover service, and depending on how you chose to set up mail flow, you might also need to set up or change MX records. Deploying Lync Online or SharePoint Online requires you to make an additional set of DNS changes not covered here. The setup section of the Office 365 portal offers a link that enables you to set up DNS and to set the domain purpose of your domain (that is, which services you'll be using with it). Figure 8-12 shows this page, with four steps shown. Set the domain purpose, configure connectors to an on-premises organization, add the necessary DNS records, and finish the configuration by saving it.

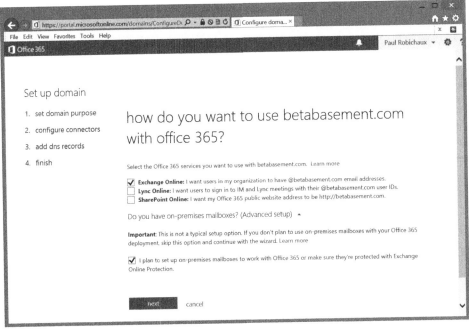

Figure 8-12 Specifying the domain purpose for a new domain

If you've selected a hybrid configuration on this page, the Setup Assistant requires you to verify that your inbound and outbound mail connectors are set up before proceeding.

Generally, you need four DNS records for Exchange Online:

- An MX record with priority 0 pointing to your-tenant-name.mail.protection.outlook .com. For example, Contoso's MX record should point to contoso-com.mail .protection.outlook.com.

- A DNS CNAME record for autodiscover.yourdomain.com pointing to autodiscover .outlook.com.

- A Sender Policy Framework (SPF) record (as described in Chapter 5) with contents v=spf1 include:spf.protection.outlook.com –all.

- A CNAME for msoid.yourdomain.com pointing to clientconfig.microsoftonline-p.net. The Microsoft Online Services Sign-in Assistant uses this record, a piece of desktop software you can install to ease the process of user sign-in if you don't have SSO configured. (See *http://community.office365.com/en-us/wikis/sso/534.aspx* for more on this tool and how to use it.) Unlike the other three record types, this record is optional.

After the DNS records you need have been updated, you need to wait long enough for them to propagate before continuing with the Office 365 setup process.

INSIDE OUT When should you create these records?

It is not mandatory to set up these records immediately. For a hybrid deployment, you probably won't set them up until you're ready to start routing Autodiscover and SMTP traffic to the service. Even when you do set them up, you might not need all of them. For example, if you will be using centralized transport, you will most likely not configure the MX or SPF records.

When should you create the needed records? In general, the time to do so is before you want to start routing mail through EOP, which uses the SPF record you create to help eliminate forged spam that appears to come from your domain. It's important to note that the Office 365 recommendation is to use the -all option. This means that senders other than those included in the spf.protection.outlook.com records should not be accepted. If you have other solutions in place (such as marketing tools) that send as your domain, using this option can break them. The solution (as described more fully in Chapter 5) is to modify the SPF record to contain the IP addresses of any server that should be authorized to send SMTP mail on behalf of your domain, as in this example:

```
v=spf1 include:spf.protection.outlook.com ip4:19.68.3.2 -all
```

INSIDE OUT What about the Exchange Deployment Assistant?

Microsoft first introduced the idea of a tool to help ease the process of Exchange deployment back in Exchange 2003. At that time, every deployment pretty much had to be treated as a unique process, so the introduction of a systematic process (and an automated tool) that could ask you questions about the desired end state and then provide customized guidance was rightly treated as a valuable development. Over time, Microsoft has made various changes, some major and some minor, to the Deployment Assistant. In its current form, the assistant is really two web-based applications, one for Exchange 2010 and one for Exchange 2013, both of which are available from the Microsoft website at *http://technet.microsoft.com/en-us/exchange/jj657516.aspx*.

The whole point of the Deployment Assistant is to give you customized guidance for your particular situation, so rather than walk through every available option, it makes more sense to examine the process of using the assistant. The obvious starting question is the deployment mode you prefer: on-premises only, cloud only, or hybrid. All the other choices you might make in the assistant stem from this choice. As an example, say you choose a hybrid deployment. You need to answer a few simple questions:

- What version, if any, of Exchange do you currently have deployed on-premises?

- Do you want to use single sign-on?

- Do you want all inbound mail to flow through EOP, or do you want centralized mail routing so that mail flows to your organization first?

- Will you be using an Exchange edge transport server?

In contrast, if you choose an on-premises deployment, the first question asks whether you're doing a greenfield deployment or upgrading, and (if upgrading) whether you're upgrading from Exchange 2007, Exchange 2010, or a mixed organization that contains both.

After you've answered the introductory questions, the assistant displays a page of answers to frequently asked questions such as, "What do I do when I finish a step?" and "Can I print this stuff?" These answers underscore the fact that the assistant produces a checklist of things that you need to do; it doesn't automate the actual process of deployment for you.

Checklist items are organized into sections such as Configure Hybrid Deployment Prerequisites. Within each section, you'll find one or more checklist items. Each checklist item consists of a brief description, an estimate of the time required to complete the step, and the individual actions required to complete the step, usually presented as a numbered list. The best part of these checklist items is the How Do I Know This Worked? section, which gives you an essentially foolproof way to verify that the item was accomplished properly before moving on to the next step. Some checklist items might also include links to other resources such as documentation for cmdlets or descriptions of Exchange architecture features.

The Deployment Assistant is useful even if you've done many Exchange deployments because it provides a systematic playbook you can follow to ensure that you don't miss any steps. Even if you're not planning an immediate deployment, it's still a worthwhile tool to use to familiarize yourself with your options, particularly as you consider how to move from your existing environment to a cloud-based or hybrid-based solution including Office 365.

Running the Hybrid Configuration Wizard

Hybrid configurations actually are important enough to Microsoft to appear at the top level of the EAC interface. The Hybrid tab is the last tab on the left side of the EAC window. Clicking it for the first time brings up a deceptively simple page containing one sentence describing what hybrid mode is and a single Enable button. Clicking it starts the HCW for the first time, which in turn prompts you to sign in to Office 365, using an account with adminis-trator privileges on your tenant organization. At this point, you might see a complaint from EAC if you haven't added EAC to the trusted Internet sites list in your browser; it depends on cross-site cookies for authorization and can't load if you have such cookies disabled.

After you have signed in to both your on-premises environment and the Office 365 man-agement portal, the first page of the Hybrid Configuration Wizard (HCW) asks you to confirm that you really do want to set up hybrid mode for your organization. Clicking Yes advances you to the next step, which is a check to verify that you have the necessary DNS TXT record to prove ownership of your domain for Exchange federation. This isn't the same as the ownership TXT record mentioned earlier, in the "Configuring DNS records for the new tenant" section. That record proves that you own the domain for purposes of setting up an Office 365 tenant that uses it, whereas a token such as the one shown in Figure 8-13 is intended to prove that you own a particular on-premises Exchange organization and are willing to enable federation on it.

Figure 8-13 Retrieving the federation token value

The next phase in the initial HCW setup is to tell Exchange how you want mail to flow. Your choices (as shown in Figure 8-14) are to configure either your edge servers (which you probably don't have) or your Client Access Server (CAS) and Mailbox servers for secure transport to and from Office 365. The Enable Centralized Mail Transport check box, if selected, tells the HCW that you want mail routing configured to pass all traffic through your on-premises servers first, as described earlier in the chapter.

Figure 8-14 Configuring mail flow

If you choose the Configure My Client Access And Mailbox Servers For Secure Mail Transport (Typical) button, the next step of the wizard enables you to specify which CAS servers in your organization you want to act as endpoints for the Office 365 connectors. If you're familiar with the concept of bridgehead routing servers from earlier versions of Exchange, this will seem familiar. The step after that will ask you to select which Mailbox servers should be used as endpoints for the send connectors the HCW adds.

The next step in the HCW asks you to pick a certificate to use for TLS traffic to and from Office 365. You cannot use self-signed certificates to talk to Office 365, and you cannot use certificates issued by an on-premises Windows certification authority unless it derives its authority from a trusted root certificate from a third-party CA. In addition, if the subject name of the certificate is longer than 256 characters, the HCW will balk and refuse to use it until you get a reissued certificate with a shorter name—not something you want to discover for the first time when actually running the HCW.

After the certificate is set, you must specify the FQDN of the server to which EOP will connect for delivering inbound mail. This FQDN must be externally resolvable from the Internet because EOP uses it as the target server name. (See Figure 8-15.)

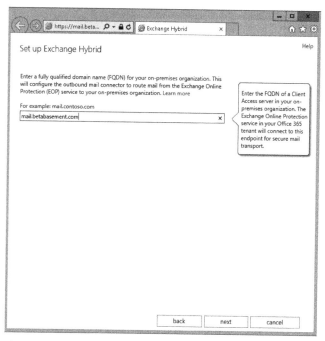

Figure 8-15 Setting the FQDN for inbound traffic from EOP

The HCW requires Organizational Management access to your Exchange organization object, so the next step in the configuration process is for you to enter the credentials you want it to use when modifying the organizational object and its children. It might seem odd that you have to reenter these credentials, given that you're running the HCW as an Exchange administrator already; however, entering them again enables you to specify a particular privileged or service account instead of using your normal user or administrator account. You'll also be asked to enter your Office 365 administrative credentials for the same reason.

After entering the credentials, the last HCW step is to click the Update button, at which point the HCW will apply the changes you requested. It's interesting that, unlike the standard behavior of Microsoft wizards, there's no summary page to show you what changes the wizard will make. After you click that button, you'll see a progress dialog box like the

one shown in Figure 8-16. Although you can click the Stop button at any time, that doesn't
undo any changes the HCW has already made.

Figure 8-16 The HCW progress dialog box

Remember that the HCW is actually making changes to the Exchange objects in your
forest and then using the Update-HybridConfiguration cmdlet to put the changes in
action. The actions the HCW and Update-HybridConfiguration take are logged by default
to the logging directory (usually c:\program files\Microsoft\Exchange\V15\logging
\Update-HybridConfiguration). Reviewing these logs gives a clear idea of which cmdlets
are run when. You need to be familiar with the contents of the logs when troubleshooting
setup problems. For example, this excerpt shows the results of an HCW attempt that failed
because the DNS TXT record that proves domain ownership wasn't properly configured.
As the log shows, the Set-FederatedOrganizationIdentifier cmdlet failed when it was run
on-premises. Each cmdlet indicates whether it was run on-premises (Session=OnPrem) or
against the online tenant (Session=Tenant), and the complete text of both the cmdlet and its
output are included, so it's fairly simple to identify the cause of the failure so you can fix it:

```
[08/10/2013 15:50:21]   INFO : --------------------------------------------------
-------------------------------------------------------------------------
----
[08/10/2013 15:50:21]    INFO : Task='Configure Organization Relationship'
```

```
  Step='NeedsConfiguration' START
  [08/10/2013 15:50:21]    INFO : Task='Configure Organization Relationship'
  Step='NeedsConfiguration' FINISH Result=True Time=0ms
  [08/10/2013 15:50:21]    INFO : ---------------------------------------------
---------------------------------------------------------------------------------
----
  [08/10/2013 15:50:21]    INFO : Task='Configure Organization Relationship'
  Step='Configure' START
  [08/10/2013 15:50:21]    INFO : Session=Tenant Cmdlet=Get-OrganizationConfig
START
  [08/10/2013 15:50:21]    INFO : Session=Tenant Cmdlet=Get-OrganizationConfig
FINISH Time=915.9514ms
  [08/10/2013 15:50:21]    INFO : Session=OnPrem Cmdlet=Get
-FederatedOrganizationIdentifier -IncludeExtendedDomainInfo: $false START
  [08/10/2013 15:50:22]    INFO : Session=OnPrem Cmdlet=Get
-FederatedOrganizationIdentifier FINISH Time=93.1476ms
  [08/10/2013 15:50:22]    INFO : Session=OnPrem Cmdlet=Set-Federationtrust
-Identity 'Microsoft Federation Gateway' -RefreshMetadata: $false START
  [08/10/2013 15:50:23]    INFO : Session=OnPrem Cmdlet=Set-Federationtrust
FINISH Time=1428.2632ms
  [08/10/2013 15:50:23]    INFO : Session=OnPrem Cmdlet=Set
-FederatedOrganizationIdentifier -AccountNamespace 'betabasement.com'
-DelegationFederationTrust 'Microsoft Federation Gateway' -Enabled: $true
-DefaultDomain $null START
  [08/10/2013 15:50:25]    ERROR : System.Management.Automation
.RemoteException: Proof of domain ownership has failed. Make sure that the TXT
record for the specified domain is available in DNS. The format of the TXT
record should be "example.com IN TXT hash-value" where "example.com" is the
domain you want to configure for Federation and "hash-value" is the proof value
generated with "Get-FederatedDomainProof -DomainName example.com".
  [08/10/2013 15:50:25]    INFO : Session=OnPrem Cmdlet=Set
-FederatedOrganizationIdentifier FINISH Time=1785.329ms
  [08/10/2013 15:50:25]    ERROR : Subtask Configure execution failed: Configure
Organization Relationship
                          Execution of the Set
-FederatedOrganizationIdentifier cmdlet has thrown an exception. This may
indicate invalid parameters in your hybrid configuration settings.
                          Proof of domain ownership has failed. Make
sure that the TXT record for the specified domain is available in DNS. The
format of the TXT record should be "example.com IN TXT hash-value" where
"example.com" is the domain you want to configure for Federation and "hash
-value" is the proof value generated with "Get-FederatedDomainProof
-DomainName example.com". at Microsoft.Exchange.Management.Hybrid
.RemotePowershellSession.RunCommand(String cmdlet, SessionParameters
parameters, Boolean ignoreNotFoundErrors)
  [08/10/2013 15:50:25]    INFO : Task='Configure Organization Relationship'
  Step='Configure' FINISH Result=False Time=4253.7404ms
  [08/10/2013 15:50:25]    INFO : ---------------------------------------------
---------------------------------------------------------------------------------
----
```

In this case, the problem was that the on-premises servers were configured to use an internal DNS server that did not have, and could not see, the required proof record. After the DNS configuration was fixed to make that TXT record visible to HCW, the configuration completed normally.

If you have to use the Back button in the HCW to retry a failed operation, keep in mind that it won't remember your password—if you just click the Update button after a failure, the wizard will appear to start but then immediately fail with a credential error. You'll have to use the Back button to go back and reenter both your on-premises and tenant credentials before proceeding.

Moving users to the cloud

As part of your messaging hybridization, you'll almost certainly want to put some, or perhaps all, your users' mailboxes in the cloud. When your hybrid environment is set up properly, this is as simple as moving a mailbox—because that's actually what happens. The on-premises Mailbox Replication Service (MRS) pushes the mailbox contents to the MRS running on an Office 365 server. The entire process, which is described in *Microsoft Exchange Server 2013 Inside Out: Mailbox and High Availability*, works the same between on-premises and cloud servers as it does between two on-premises servers.

The process of onboarding your users to Office 365 really has a few separate steps, though. You have to license the users so that they can log on to the service, and then you have to move their mailboxes. Before you do either of those, you might wish to set up and use a test mailbox to verify that your hybrid setup is fully functional.

Creating a test mailbox

Microsoft recommends that you create a test mailbox on the service to verify that coexistence and hybrid operations are working the way you want them to. This is a simple matter of creating a new user as you normally would in EAC but making sure that the Office 365 User user type is selected when you click the plus (+) button on the Mailboxes tab in EAC (see Figure 8-17). When you create a mailbox using this method, the user object for the new mailbox is created in your on-premises Active Directory, dirsync copies the object to the cloud, and the mailbox is created on the Microsoft servers. That means either that you'll have to wait for dirsync to complete or force a manual update before the test mailbox will be visible.

After the test mailbox is created and available, you should use it to verify that everything works the way you expect. At a minimum, you should check that:

- The testexchangeconnectivity.com website runs its Autodiscover checks without error. If you encounter problems here, it's critical to fix them because if Autodiscover doesn't work properly, you won't be able to move mailboxes to the cloud, and many client operations won't work.

- You can log on to the service version of Outlook Web App by using the newly created mailbox and that, if you go to your on-premises Outlook Web App URL and enter those credentials, it proxies properly.

- You see the expected data in the global address list (GAL) while logged on as the test user.

- Mail to and from the test user flows properly to both internal recipients and Internet recipients.

- Outlook Anywhere and Exchange ActiveSync function properly (if you're using them and if you have enabled them for the test user).

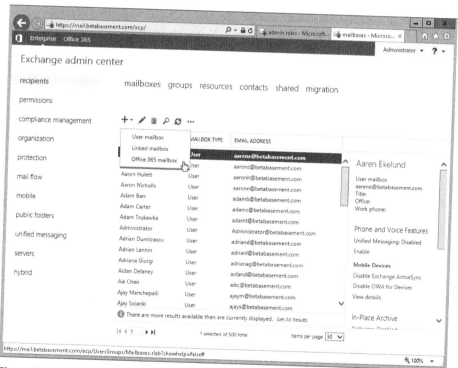

Figure 8-17 Adding an Office 365–hosted mailbox from on-premises EAC

Licensing users

Whether you create users directly on the service or use dirsync, you need to assign Office 365 licenses to any users whose mailboxes you want to move to the service. When you assign a license to a user, you're telling the service that the user in question should have permission to use Office 365–based services; in fact, unlicensed users can't connect to the service. Plan to assign licenses to every user whose mailbox you want to host in Office 365; depending on what other Office 365 services you use, you might need to assign licenses to other users, too.

The process of license assignment is simple, but if you don't know the trick, it can be frustrating. There's no way in EAC to assign licenses, even though you might expect that to be the logical place to do so. Instead, you use the Office 365 portal itself. Here's what to do:

1. Log on to the Office 365 portal (*https://portal.microsoftonline.com*) using an account that has tenant administrative privileges on your tenant.

2. Switch to the Users And Groups tab.

3. Identify the users to whom you want to assign licenses. If you have many users to license, you might want to create a custom view showing only users who are synchronized but not licensed. To do this, click the filter icon (the one that looks like a funnel) and then choose New View from the pop-up menu. When the New View window appears, scroll down toward the bottom and make sure the Synchronized Users Only check box is selected; fill in whatever other criteria you want to use for the view.

4. Select the users who are to be licensed by selecting the check box next to their names.

5. Click the Activate Synced Users link on the right side of the window. That brings up a separate page (Figure 8-18), on which you specify what country the users are in and the specific Office 365 features to which you want them to have access. The available features might vary by country, and Office 365 might not be available in some countries. (Microsoft has also been kind enough to add a link in this window to enable you to buy more licenses, a feature reminiscent of grocery stores that put snacks and candy in the checkout lines to encourage impulse buying.)

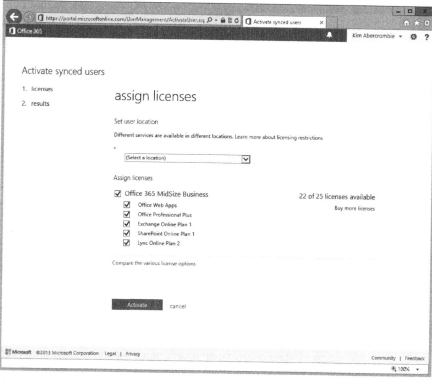

Figure 8-18 Assigning licenses to users

6.   Click the Confirm button, and the users will be granted licenses if you have enough unallocated licenses for the number of users you've selected. The summary page that appears after this step will indicate clearly which users have licenses assigned and which do not.

If you have lots of users to license, you might find it more productive to script this operation. Exchange consultant Brian Reid has some example scripts posted at *http://blog .c7solutions.com/2011/07/assign-specific-licences-in-office-365.html* that outline the process of using the Set-MsolUser and Set-MsolUserLicense cmdlets to assign users to the plans you want.

Moving user mailboxes

To move an on-premises user completely to the cloud, you need to move her mailbox from your on-premises servers to the cloud. This is a simple matter of selecting the user mailbox in EAC and clicking the Move Mailbox link or running EMS (against Exchange Online, not your on-premises environment) and using New-MoveRequest. If you're moving multiple mailboxes, you should probably consider creating a migration batch. Note that when you move a mailbox to Office 365 by using EMS, you must initiate the move from the Office 365 tenant domain. This requires you to have EMS set up to use the remote tenant (as described later in the chapter) and to initiate the move request by using the New-MoveRequest cmdlet from the cloud, like this:

```
New-MoveRequest -Identity KimAbercrombie -Remote -RemoteHostName mail.contoso.com
-TargetDeliveryDomain service.contoso.com
```

All the normal caveats and cautions applicable to moving mailboxes still apply here. In particular, remember that when you move a mailbox that has delegates, you need to move the delegates at the same time. If you cannot do this, you can use the Exchange federated sharing features to preserve access. In the same vein, if you have a user whose mailbox is enabled for unified messaging (UM), you'll need to re-enable it for UM after moving it to the service because moving the mailbox out of its original dial plan will automatically disable its UM access.

There's an additional issue to keep in mind: throttling. Office 365 servers might limit the rate at which you can move mailbox data to user or personal archive mailboxes. For more on this, see the "Dealing with throttling" section later in this chapter.

Managing a hybrid organization

Managing a hybrid organization is very much like managing an on-premises-only organization except that you have a few more things to manage; dirsync and password synchronization are prominent examples. The changes in EAC to support hybrid organizations are fairly subtle. You'll notice that the very top of the EAC window has changed. There are separate tabs, labeled Enterprise and Office 365, and clicking the appropriate tab takes you to the associated version of EAC. Thanks to the magic of role-based access control (RBAC), both the on-premises and cloud versions of EAC show only the commands and options to which you have access, which means that many more settings are available in your on-premises organization than on the Office 365 side. For example, on the Mailboxes slab of the Recipients tab in EAC, you'll see the plus (+) icon to add mailboxes when you look at your on-premises account, but you won't on Office 365 because, even as a tenant administrator, you don't have permission to create mailboxes there.

Connecting Windows PowerShell and EAC to the service

The good news first: you don't have to do anything for EAC to notice that you're using a hybrid tenant. After you successfully complete the HCW, and the hybrid configuration objects have been published, EAC automatically shows you the Office365 tab you use to configure hybrid objects. However, just as with pure on-premises deployments, there are tasks that require you to use EMS instead and require you to know how to connect an existing EMS session to the tenant domain.

This process is really simple, and you'll probably do it often enough that it's worth defining an alias or including the necessary script in your Windows PowerShell user profile. First, you need to capture a credential object for an account that has tenant administrative rights on your Office 365 tenant:

```
$cred = Get-Credential
```

Armed with that credential, you can create a new Windows PowerShell session to Office 365:

```
$session = New-PSSession -ConfigurationName Microsoft.Exchange
-ConnectionUri https://ps.outlook.com/powershell -Credential $cred -Authentication
Basic -AllowRedirection
```

After creating the session, just import it to make it available:

```
Import-PSSession $session
```

INSIDE OUT Set a specific prefix for cloud cmdlets

Exchange MVP Steve Goodman passed on this handy suggestion: you can use the –Prefix parameter to Import-PSSession to assign a specific prefix to cmdlets in that session. For example:

```
Import-PSSession $session -Prefix Cloud
```

This command will cause all the cmdlets loaded in that session to use the prefix Cloud as part of the object. Get-Mailbox therefore becomes Get-CloudMailbox, and so on.

This is especially useful if you want to be able to manage Exchange Online and Exchange On-Premises from a single Windows PowerShell session or write scripts that target both environments.

Enabling customization

When you create a new Office 365 tenant, Microsoft says that the tenant organization is *dehydrated*. This doesn't literally mean that you have to add water to it; it means that a number of settings are not set, and space for them is not allocated. For example, the Active Directory objects that hold transport rule settings don't exist; given that most tenants never set up transport rules, not creating their container by default saves a small amount of space. Multiply that small amount by a large number of tenant organizations, and the savings add up quickly.

Before you can create or customize transport rules, sharing policies, retention policies, Outlook Web App mailbox policies, or RBAC policies on a tenant, you must rehydrate the tenant, which you do with the Enable-OrganizationCustomization cmdlet. This cmdlet must be run from a remote Windows PowerShell session established with your Exchange Online organization. Both EMS and EAC will tell you to run this cmdlet if you try to change a setting or create an object that requires a hydrated tenant.

Even after rehydrating your tenant, you will find that some objects, such as Exchange ActiveSync device access policies, are not automatically copied from the on-premises environment to the service. Address book policies (ABPs) are a particular culprit here because they are often used to simulate the appearance of multiple tenant organizations. If you want to use ABPs seamlessly in a hybrid mode organization, give the necessary personnel the Address Lists RBAC permission on the tenant and then define one or more ABPs, using attributes that are synchronized as part of dirsync. Do the same on-premises, and your ABPs will have matching contents.

Changing hybrid settings after deployment

You can rerun the HCW at any time you like, or you can change your hybrid settings yourself, using the Set-HybridConfiguration cmdlet. In either case, you can adjust the same settings that you saw when originally running the HCW, including the set of transport servers that are permitted to send and receive mail through EOP and the set of SMTP domains that you want to use. Changes you make through either the HCW or Set-HybridConfiguration take effect immediately on-premises, although there might be a slight delay before all the changes you make are reflected on both sides of the connection.

Dealing with throttling

Back in ancient times, when mainframes ruled the earth, performance management dictated that users, and applications, were subject to budgets for the resources they could use. These budgets were sometimes implemented as limits on how much CPU or memory a given process could consume; another popular approach was to let clients use what they needed and then bill their departments for resources actually used. As enterprise computing moved toward decentralized systems that weren't widely shared (and didn't have good accounting or budgeting controls anyway), this idea fell out of favor in most contexts. However, this kind of accounting and resource control is a must for large-scale shared services; Microsoft and other cloud providers must have a way to prevent a single client (or tenant organization) from using so many resources that other clients and tenants can't use the service. The mechanism that Exchange Online uses is the standard Exchange throttling mechanism, as described in *Microsoft Exchange Server 2013 Inside Out: Mailbox and High Availability*, but there's a twist—Microsoft sets the throttling policy, not you. In normal operations, this won't be a problem because the limits are set to a reasonably generous level. Problems might arise when you're doing something unusual, though, such as importing a large volume of data from PST files into personal archives or moving lots of mailboxes. Of course, you might also experience throttling-related performance problems if badly behaved client applications trigger throttling limits, as was the case with the Apple iOS Mail app included with the iOS 6.0 and iOS 6.1 updates.

Three types of throttling are of interest to Office 365 administrators:

- User throttling applies to individual user accounts. Microsoft describes this as the "most restrictive type of throttling" in the Office 365 documentation, by which it means that user throttling has the lowest limits and is thus the most likely to be triggered. In ongoing operations, you're most likely to encounter these limits because of a misbehaving client application, but during migration, they can be triggered by migration applications that use Exchange Web Services (EWS) or Outlook Anywhere to move user mailbox data. The service can't tell the difference between normal mail traffic and migration traffic; it just sees a volume of traffic that exceeds the throttling limit, so it clamps down.

- Migration service throttling is specific to the Migration service, which is responsible for ingesting data to personal archives and mailboxes. These throttling limits come into play when you're doing staged, cutover, hybrid, or IMAP migrations (because all of these pass traffic through the MRS and Migration services, so standard MRS throttling mechanisms apply). Although you can't adjust the throttling policy that applies to the Migration service, when you create a migration batch, you can control how many mailboxes are moved at one time; the default is three, but you can choose any number up to 10 in EAC, or for extra fun, you can crank the number up to 50 using Set-MigrationBatch –MaxConcurrentMigrations (although you must do this after you create the migration batch but before you start it). By default, Office 365 currently throttles each tenant to a MaxConcurrentMigrations limit of 100, so you can have two concurrent batches of 50 each, 10 batches of 10, or 100 batches of 1.

- Resource health-based throttling refers to the throttling the service does when for some reason its health is subpar. The example Microsoft cites in its documentation is a mailbox move that's throttled because there are no healthy copies of the target mailbox database. Because these throttling settings are applied only when the service health is compromised, you will see them enforced infrequently.

Most of the discussion about Office 365 throttling revolves around ways to improve throughput when moving large volumes of data into the service. For example, I was recently involved with a migration of an 11,000-user organization that was moving from Lotus Notes to Office 365. It had about 10 TB of mail data to be imported, and, naturally, it wanted to do it in the minimum amount of time possible. In this situation, your first thought might be just to raise the throttling limits temporarily. Although you can always ask Microsoft to raise your throttling limits by filing a support ticket, the odds that it will actually do so are pretty low. The process of finding the right contact within Microsoft to approve such a request is opaque and filled with dead ends and twisty little passages. Instead, it is better to take advantage of the fact that you can schedule multiple concurrent migrations against multiple endpoints; remember that when you migrate data onto Office 365, the Microsoft servers contact *your* MRS proxy endpoint to pull data. If you can expose multiple MRS proxy endpoints, you can have multiple migrations in parallel, although depending on the targets, you might still run into concurrency limits on the number of moves to a particular target server or mailbox database. The current limit is 100 moves per tenant.

Field experience has shown that it's possible under normal conditions to get migration rates of up to 4 or 5 GB per hour for a single migration stream, assuming, of course, that your network supports that rate of throughput between your servers and Microsoft data centers. Performing multiple concurrent migrations can thus push that rate up considerably. It is worth noting, of course, that overall migration throughput is also throttled by how fast your servers can perform and whatever throttling policies you have in place on your side.

There is a workaround that might be useful, but it isn't guaranteed to be usable in the future. If you create your own move requests using New-MoveRequest instead of the Migration service, your moves aren't limited to the throttling policies applied to the Migration service. However, you lose all the Migration service features, including reporting and tracking through EAC, so this isn't necessarily a great trade.

All-in on the cloud

Microsoft has made much of its ongoing investment in the cloud; this has led to natural questions about what the future holds for on-premises versions of Lync, Exchange, and SharePoint. Given the size of the on-premises market, the foreseeable future will almost certainly continue to offer new versions of these products. However, as cloud services mature and evolve, you'll see both a growing adoption of enterprise services such as Office 365 and an oscillation between on-premises and cloud deployments as organizations seek the ideal mix of both deployment types for their needs.

Index

About the Author

Paul Robichaux has been working with Exchange since version 4.0 and still finds new things to learn about it each day. A long-time contributing editor for *Windows IT Pro*, he currently works as a global principal consultant at Dell, focusing on Exchange and Lync. He's a Microsoft Exchange MVP and teaches the unified messaging portion of the Microsoft Certified Master | Exchange program.

Paul is a licensed private pilot, a fitness enthusiast, and a budding cook. You can keep up with him on his blog (*http://paulrobichaux.wordpress.com*) or on Twitter @paulrobichaux.

Now that you've read the book...

Tell us what you think!

Was it useful?
Did it teach you what you wanted to learn?
Was there room for improvement?

Let us know at http://aka.ms/tellpress

Your feedback goes directly to the staff at Microsoft Press,
and we read every one of your responses. Thanks in advance!

 Microsoft